The Editor

DONALD R. DICKSON is Professor of English at Texas A&M University. He is the author of *Tessera of Antilia: Utopian Brotherhoods & Secret Societies in the Early Seventeenth Century* and *The Fountain of Living Waters: The Typology of the Waters of Life in Herbert, Vaughan, and Traherne.* He is co-editor of *Of Paradise and Light: Essays on Henry Vaughan and John Milton in Honor of Alan Rudrum,* and contributing editor to *The Variorum Edition of the Poetry of John Donne: The Anniversaries, Epicedes and Obsequies.* He is editor and translator of *Thomas and Rebecca Vaughan, Aqua Vitæ: Non Vitis: Or, The radical Humiditie of Nature: Mechanically, and Magically dissected By the Conduct of Fire, and Ferment (British Library MS, Sloane 1741).*

A NORTON CRITICAL EDITION

JOHN DONNE'S POETRY

AUTHORITATIVE TEXTS

CRITICISM

Edited by

DONALD R. DICKSON

TEXAS A&M UNIVERSITY

W • W • NORTON & COMPANY • *New York* • *London*

W. W. Norton & Company has been independent since its founding in 1923, when William Warder Norton and Mary D. Herter Norton first published lectures delivered at the People's Institute, the adult education division of New York City's Cooper Union. The Nortons soon expanded their program beyond the Institute, publishing books by celebrated academics from America and abroad. By mid-century, the two major pillars of Norton's publishing program—trade books and college texts—were firmly established. In the 1950s, the Norton family transferred control of the company to its employees, and today—with a staff of four hundred and a comparable number of trade, college, and professional titles published each year—W. W. Norton & Company stands as the largest and oldest publishing house owned wholly by its employees.

This title is printed on permanent paper containing
30 percent post-consumer waste recycled fiber.

Every effort has been made to contact the copyright holders of each of the selections. Rights holders of any selections not credited should contact W. W. Norton & Company, Inc. for a correction to be made in the next printing of our work.

The text of this book is composed in Fairfield Medium
with the display set in Bernhard Modern.
Composition by Binghamton Valley Composition.
Manufacturing by the Maple-Vail Book Group, Binghamton.
Production manager: Benjamin Reynolds.

Library of Congress Cataloging-in-Publication Data

Donne, John, 1572–1631.
[Selections. 2006]
John Donne's poetry: authoritative texts, criticism / edited by Donald R. Dickson.
p. cm. — (Norton critical edition)
Includes bibliographical references and indexes.
ISBN-13: 978-0-393-92648-4 (pbk.)
ISBN-10: 0-393-92648-6 (pbk.)

1. Donne, John, 1572–1631—Criticism and interpretation. I. Dickson,
Donald R. II. Title.

PR2246.D53 2006
821'.3—dc22

2006046829

W. W. Norton & Company, Inc., 500 Fifth Avenue,
New York, N.Y. 10110-0017
www.wwnorton.com

W. W. Norton & Company Ltd., Castle House,
75/76 Wells Street, London W1T 3QT

7 8 9 0

Contents

Criticism   177

Preface

John Donne (1572–1631) was born into a prominent Roman Catholic family at a time when religious allegiances mattered a great deal (as the essays by Dennis Flynn and John Carey included in this Norton Critical Edition discuss). He entered and left Oxford at an early age to avoid taking the oath acknowledging the queen's supremacy over the Church of England (which was required at age sixteen and which would have compromised his Catholic faith), then studied for a time at Cambridge before leaving for the Continent. When he returned to London in the early 1590s, he studied law in preparation for service as a courtier. Within a few years Donne was private secretary to one of the most influential men in England and well launched on a brilliant career, until he betrayed his employer's trust by secretly marrying a young woman under his supervision, thus placing in jeopardy his plans for service as a courtier. He had already begun entertaining his friends with manuscript copies of his satires, elegies, and lyrics. The literary scene at that time was dominated by sonnet writers who drew inspiration from the Italian poet Francis Petrarch (1304–1374). Like many young men seeking to make their mark, Donne found his own voice by overturning the conventional modes and attitudes of these Petrarchan sonneteers and by embracing those of the Roman poet Ovid (43 B.C.–17 A.D.), also an outsider who recorded the foibles of the court of Augustus Caesar in his irreverent love poems. Donne too was an astute observer of human nature in an exuberant city at an exciting moment in its history— when the threat of the Spanish Armada had been miraculously thwarted and when Shakespeare, Marlowe, and Jonson were writing for the theaters that were the glory of Elizabethan London. His early poems render the kinds of experience typical of young gallants on the prowl in striking detail. In time Donne turned to a career in the Anglican Church, though not without recording some of his own misgivings and fears in his verse. At the end of his life, he would be hailed as the "Monarch of Wit" for his dazzling and ingenious poetic comparisons and for establishing a powerful new style of his own (see Thomas Carew's "An Elegy upon the Death of the Dean of Paul's, Dr. John Donne," below). After a period of comparative neglect, Donne was restored in the early twentieth century to his

rightful place among our greatest poets, especially for his love poems
that, in some moments, celebrate the transcendent possibilities of
sacred and earthly love or the anguish over its impermanence; at
others, the enthrallment of desire or a repulsion from its sheer car-
nality. In short, the broad range of human experience is brought to
life vividly and with dramatic intensity in his verse.

With the exceptions of the long commendatory poems on the
deceased daughter of one of his patrons and a few shorter pieces,
Donne's poems were only "published" in his lifetime in manuscripts
that traveled within his circle of friends and prospective patrons.
While over 5,000 separate transcriptions of his poems survive in
some 240 manuscripts (a few in as many as fifty separate copies)
only a single 63-line verse epistle survives in Donne's own hand. The
problems of authenticating the reading of any single manuscript wit-
ness is, accordingly, formidable. As a result editors have relied heav-
ily on the early printed texts. Once *Poems, by J. D. with Elegies on
the Authors Death* appeared posthumously in 1633, it was accorded
a great deal of authority by subsequent editors, despite the fact, as
we now know, it was set from printers' copies of varying degrees of
authority, none of which was in Donne's own hand. A comparison
of the 1633 edition to the likely manuscripts sources reveals that the
printer had "modernized" spelling and punctuation, or regularized it
with some house style. Furthermore, this first edition was substan-
tially revised in 1635, indicating that someone had developed serious
reservations about the reliability of the manuscripts used in setting
the prior edition. Nonetheless, the editions of 1633 and 1635 essen-
tially determined what was accepted as Donne's text and canon up
to the twentieth century. Indeed, most editions of his poems have
been based on the 1633 *Poems*, and the manuscript sources, no mat-
ter how authoritative, were largely ignored until the twentieth cen-
tury.

One of the hallmarks of the modern editing of Donne has been
the recovery of the manuscript sources, with a number of editors
producing scholarly editions based on a partial census of these man-
uscripts: notably, Alexander Grosart (1872), Herbert Grierson
(1912), Helen Gardner (1952, 1965), John Shawcross (1967), and
Wesley Milgate (1967, 1978). Since the early 1980s an international
team of editors and scholars has been at work on an authoritative
text based on a comprehensive study of all the textual artifacts. Sev-
eral volumes of the *Variorum Edition of the Poetry of John Donne*
have already been published; these efforts, moreover, have clarified
the relationship of the various families of manuscripts. The rationale
for my methodology is discussed more fully in the Note on the Texts
of Donne's Poems below. I have used the Westmoreland manuscript
as copy text where possible, though I have collated it against the best

exemplars from the most important families of Donne manuscripts—the Cambridge Balam, the Dublin Trinity, the O'Flahertie—and compared them with all seven of the seventeenth-century printed editions of the poems as well as with the major twentieth-century editions. I believe this has given me a sufficiently authoritative range of materials to establish a scholarly text for this Norton Critical Edition.

The critical essays range in time from Donne's contemporaries to our own (one piece being newly commissioned for this edition) and represent a variety of viewpoints. They are grouped by kind into four sections. The first, "Donne and Metaphysical Poetry," offers seventeenth-century views of Donne and his distinctive style; sections from Izaak Walton's 1639 biography that present a view of his struggle over his religious vocation; followed by essays from Dennis Flynn and John Carey on the significance of Donne's Roman Catholic upbringing and his apostasy from it. The second section offers insights on Donne's frequently overlooked early poems and on the social and literary milieu from whence they emerged. Essays by Arthur Marotti, M. Thomas Hester, Alan Armstrong, Achsah Guibbory, Margaret Maurer, and Heather Dubrow situate Donne's satires, elegies, and verse epistles within the world of the Inns of Court and the coteries that Donne frequented. An essay by the general editor of the new *Variorum Edition of the Poetry of John Donne*, Gary Stringer, on evidence of authorial revisions of "Satire 3" and the Elegies rounds out this part. The third section, on the Songs and Sonnets, supplies insights on Donne the love poet. Both Donald Guss and Patrick Cruttwell give classic summations of Donne's imitation of Petrarchan conceits and metaphors, which complement Dubrow's portrait of him as an anti-Petrarchan poet. Hester and Theresa DiPasquale likewise offer differing perspectives on one of Donne's most discussed poems, "The Flea," while Camille Wells Slights discusses the presence of his wife in the lyrics. The final section on the Divine Poems contains several definitive essays on Donne's struggles as a Christian, notably R. V. Young on grace in the Holy Sonnets and Louis Martz on traditions of meditation. Also included are essays on "Good-Friday, 1613. Riding Westward" and "Hymn to God, My God, in My Sickness."

This edition concludes with a chronology of Donne's life to supplement the selections from Walton and the vignettes that emerge from the essays (Flynn, Carey, Marotti, and Slights) and with a selected bibliography to provide some guidance for students seeking further resources, though nothing can replace the three volumes of John R. Roberts's magisterial bibliographies with their annotations and meticulous cross-indexing. I am very much indebted to the collective efforts of the Donne Variorum, especially to Gary Stringer, J.

Syd Conner, M. Thomas Hester, John R. Roberts, Paul Parrish, Dennis Flynn, Achsah Guibbory, Raymond-Jean Frontain, and Ernest W. Sullivan, II. With more than four thousand books and articles on Donne in the twentieth century, the enthusiasm for this remarkable man and wondrous poet has not flagged in the past four hundred years. I hope that my edition of *John Donne's Poetry* keeps that flame alight for the next generation of students of his poetry.

College Station, Texas   Donald R. Dickson

The Texts of
JOHN DONNE'S POETRY

Satires

Satire 1.[1]

    Away thou changling motley humorist,[2]
Leave me, and in this standing wooden chest,[3]
Consorted with these few books, let me lie
In prison, and here be coffin'd, when I die.
5 Here are God's conduits, grave divines;[4] and here
Nature's secretary, the philosopher;
And jolly statesmen, which teach how to tie
The sinews of a city's mystic body;
Here gathering chroniclers,[5] and by them stand
10 Giddy fantastic poets of each land.
Shall I leave all this constant company,
And follow headlong, wild uncertain thee?
First, swear by thy best love in earnest
(If thou which lov'st all, canst love any best)
15 Thou wilt not leave me in the middle street,
Though some more spruce companion thou dost meet,
Not though a captain do come in thy way
Bright parcel gilt, with forty dead men's pay,[6]
Nor though a brisk perfum'd pert courtier
20 Deign with a nod, thy courtesy to answer.
Nor come a velvet justice with a long
Great train of blue coats,[7] twelve, or fourteen strong,
Wilt thou grin or fawn on him, or prepare
A speech to court his beauteous son and heir.
25 For better or worse take me, or leave me:

1. The poetic model for a walk through city streets with a foolish companion was established by Horace (*Satire* 1.9). It probably dates from the early Inns of Court period, c. 1593; in one ms. it is titled "Satire: On the Humorist."
2. One afflicted by a surplus of a bodily humor: black bile, which leads to melancholy or depression; phlegm, to indifference or sluggishness; blood, to foolish optimism; and yellow bile, to choler or anger.
3. His study, described much like the small cells in Lincoln's Inn that had room for only a stool, a table, and some bookshelves.
4. Ministers, the *conduits* of God's word.
5. Historians gathering information.
6. The names of the dead were kept on rosters to pad the income of unscrupulous captains.
7. The livery of servants.

3

To take, and leave me is adultery.
O monstrous, superstitious Puritan,
Of refin'd manners, yet ceremonial man,[8]
That when thou meet'st one, with inquiring eyes
30 Dost search, and like a needy broker prize[9]
The silk, and gold he wears, and to that rate
So high or low, dost raise thy formal hat:
That wilt consort none, until thou have known
What lands he hath in hope, or of his own.
35 As though all thy companions should make thee
Jointures,[1] and marry thy dear company.
Why should'st thou (that dost not only approve,
But in rank itchy lust, desire, and love
The nakedness and barrenness to enjoy,
40 Of thy plump muddy whore, or prostitute boy)
Hate virtue, though she be naked, and bare?
At birth, and death, our bodies naked are;
And till our souls be unappareled
Of bodies, they from bliss are banished.
45 Man's first blest state was naked, when by sin
He lost that, yet he'was cloth'd but in beast's skin,
And in this coarse attire, which I now wear,
With God, and with the Muses I confer.
    But since thou like a contrite penitent,
50 Charitably warn'd of thy sins, dost repent
These vanities, and giddinesses, lo
I shut my chamber door, and "Come, let's go."
But sooner may a cheap whore, that hath been
Worn by as many several men in sin,
55 As are black feathers, or musk-colored hose,
Name her child's right true father, 'mongst all those:
Sooner may one guess, who shall bear away
Th'Infant'of London,[2] heir to an India:
And sooner may a gulling weather-spy
60 By drawing forth heaven's scheme[3] tell certainly
What fashion'd hats, or ruffs, or suits next year
Our supple-witted antic youths will wear;
Then thou, when thou depart'st from hence, canst show
Whither, why, when, or with whom thou wouldst go.

8. "Precise in observance of forms of politeness" (OED 2).
9. Pawnbroker's appraisal.
1. Property held for the joint use of a husband and wife (OED 4).
2. A wealthy heiress who was still a ward. Donne may also intend the Infanta of Spain whose claim to the English throne had been advanced at the time of the Armada.
3. "A diagram showing the relative positions, either real or apparent, of the heavenly bodies" (OED 2), here used to make fraudulent forecasts.

65 But how shall I be pardon'd my offence
That thus have sinn'd against my conscience?
        Now we are in the street; He first of all
Improvidently proud, creeps to the wall,[4]
And so imprison'd, and hem'd in by me
70 Sells for a little state[5] his liberty;
Yet though he cannot skip forth now to greet
Every fine silken painted fool we meet,
He them to him with amorous smiles allures,
And grins, smacks, shrugs, and such an itch endures,
75 As prentices, or schoolboys which do know
Of some gay sport abroad, yet dare not go.
And as fiddlers stop lowest, at highest sound,
So to the most brave, stoops he nigh'st the ground.
But to a grave man, he doth move no more
80 Than the wise politic horse would heretofore,
Or thou O elephant or ape wilt do,[6]
When any names the king of Spain to you.
Now leaps he upright, jogs me,'and cries, "Do'you see
Yonder well favor'd youth?" "Which?" "Oh, 'tis he
85 That dances so divinely." "Oh," said I,
"Stand still, must you dance here for company?"
He droop'd, we went, till one (which did excel
Th'Indians, in drinking his tobacco[7] well)
Met us; they talk'd; I whisper'd, "Let us go;
90 Maybe you smell him not, truly I do."
He hears not me, but, on the other side
A many-color'd peacock having spied,
Leaves him and me; I for my lost sheep stay;
He follows, overtakes, goes on the way,
95 Saying, "Him whom I last left, all repute
For his device, in handsoming a suit,[8]
To judge of lace, pink, panes,[9] cut, print, or pleat,
Of all the court, to have the best conceit."[1]
"Our dull comedians want him, let him go;
100 But oh, God strengthen thee, why stoop'st thou so?"
"Why? he hath travail'd." "Long?" "No, but to me

---

4. The outside position on a city street was more hazardous due to the refuse thrown from
   above; thus, the inside position was given to a superior as a courtesy.
5. Dignity or status.
6. In the 1590s a performing horse named Morocco, who answered certain questions from
   the audience, was exhibited in London along with a trained elephant and ape.
7. Tobacco had been newly introduced; originally, it was consumed as a liquid.
8. Line 96: For his ingenuity in adorning himself fashionably.
9. Decorative slashes (OED 7.2); *pink*: a "hole or eyelet punched in a garment for decorative
   purposes" (OED 3).
1. To have the best judgment.

(Which understand none), he doth seem to be
Perfect French, and Italian." I replied,
"So is the pox."[2] He answer'd not, but spied
105 More men of sort, of parts, and qualities;
At last his love he in a window spies,
And like light dew exhal'd, he flings from me
Violently ravish'd to his lechery.
Many were there, he could command no more;
110 He quarrel'd, fought, bled; and turn'd out of door
Directly came to me hanging the head,
And constantly a while must keep his bed.

Satire 2.[3]

Sir, though (I thank God for it) I do hate
Perfectly all this town, yet there's one state[4]
In all ill things so excellently best,
That hate, toward them, breeds pity towards the rest.
5 Though poetry indeed be such a sin
As I think that brings dearths,[5] and Spaniards in;
Though like the pestilence or old fashion'd love,[6]
It riddlingly catch men, and doth remove
Never, till it be starv'd out; yet their state
10 Is poor, disarm'd, like Papists,[7] not worth hate:
One, (like a wretch, which at bar judg'd as dead,[8]
Yet prompts him which stands next, and could not read,
And saves his life) gives idiot actors means[9]
(Starving himself) to live by his labor'd scenes.
15 As in some organ, puppets dance above[1]
And bellows pant below, which them do move.
One would move love by rhymes; but witchcraft's charms
Bring not now their old fears, nor their old harms:[2]
Rams, and slings now are silly battery,

2. Syphilis was thought to originate in France or Italy.
3. In some mss. this is titled "Satire I: Against Poets and Lawyers" or "Law Satire."
4. Courts of law are preeminently bad.
5. Famines.
6. True or sincere love.
7. Roman Catholics suffered so much under the law that they weren't worth persecuting.
8. Sentenced to death.
9. Those who could translate a Latin "neck-verse" (usually Psalm 51) could plead benefit of clergy to escape the gallows (as Ben Jonson did); those who were ignorant could not.
1. Puppets activated by air from the bellows of the organ were common.
2. Lines 17–18: Charming someone with poetry is as ineffective as magic spells.

20 Pistolets³ are the best artillery.
And they who write to Lords, rewards to get,
Are they not like boys singing at doors for meat?
And they who write, because all write, have still
That excuse for writing, and for writing ill.
25 But he is worst, who (beggarly) doth chaw
Others' wits' fruits, and in his ravenous maw
Rankly digested, doth those things outspew,
As his own things; and they'are his own, 'tis true,
For if one eat my meat, though it be known
30 The meat was mine, th'excrement is his own.
But these do me no harm, nor they which use
To out-swive⁴ dildos, and out-usure Jews;
To'out-drink the sea, to'out-swear the Litany;
Who with sins all kinds as familiar be
35 As confessors;⁵ and for whose sinful sake
Schoolmen⁶ new tenements in hell must make:
Whose strange sins, canonists⁷ could hardly tell
In which commandment's large receipt they dwell.
But these punish themselves; the insolence
40 Of Coscus only breeds my great offense,
Whom time (which rots all, and makes botches pox,⁸
And plodding on, must make a calf an ox)
Hath made a lawyer, which was (alas) of late
But a scarce poet; jollier of this state,⁹
45 Than are new benefic'd ministers, he throws
Like nets, or lime-twigs,¹ wheresoe're he goes,
His title'of barrister, on every wench,
And woos in language of the pleas, and bench:²
"A motion, Lady." "Speak Coscus." "I'have been
50 In love, ever since *tricesimo* of the queen.³
Continual claims I'have made, injunctions got
To stay my rival's suit, that he should not
Proceed." "Spare me." "In Hillary term⁴ I went,

---

3. Spanish coins, which are far more effective than battering rams or slings.
4. Out-copulate.
5. Priests who hear confessions.
6. Scholastic philosophers believed sinners were grouped according to particular sins in hell (as in Dante's *Inferno*).
7. Canon lawyers (as opposed to those who practiced civil law).
8. Eruptive pustules on the skin, usually the result of syphilis.
9. His status as a lawyer.
1. Used to snare birds.
2. Language of the Court of Common Pleas and the Queen's Bench; here, language sprinkled with legal terms.
3. The thirtieth year of the queen's reign (1588).
4. The first court term, 23 January to 12 February.

You said, If I return'd next 'size[5] in Lent,
55 I should be in remitter[6] of your grace;
In th'interim my letters should take place
Of affidavits." Words, words, which would tear
The tender labyrinth of a soft maid's ear,
More, more, than ten Sclavonians' scolding,[7] more
60 Than when winds in our ruin'd abbeys roar.
When sick with poetry,'and posses'd with Muse
Thou wast, and mad, I hop'd; but men which choose
Law practice for mere gain, bold soul, repute
Worse than imbrothel'd strumpets prostitute.
65 Now like an owl-like watchman, he must walk
His hand still at a bill,[8] now he must talk
Idly, like prisoners, which whole months will swear
That only suretyship[9] hath brought them there,
And to'every suitor lie in every thing,
70 Like a king's favorite, yea like a king;
Like a wedge in a block, wring to the bar,
Bearing like asses, and more shameless far
Then carted whores,[1] lie, to the grave judge; for
Bastardy'abounds not in kings' titles, nor
75 Simony'[2]and sodomy in churchmen's lives,
As these things do in him; by these he thrives.
Shortly'(as the sea) he'will compass[3] all our land;
From Scots, to Wight; from Mount, to Dover strand.[4]
And spying heirs melting with luxury,
80 Satan will not joy at their sins, as he.
For as a thrifty wench scrapes kitchen stuff,
And barreling the droppings, and the snuff,
Of wasting candles, which in thirty year
(Relic-like kept) perchance buys wedding gear;
85 Piecemeal he gets lands, and spends as much time
Wringing each acre, as men pulling prime.[5]
In parchments then, large as his fields, he draws

---

5. Assize or session of the court.
6. Someone having two titles to an estate who is adjudged to hold it by the earlier or more valid one. Coscus here has claim on the lady by her promise to allow his "return," but he pleads his right of first possession over his rival.
7. Refers to the barbaric sounds (to English ears) of Slavic speech.
8. Looking for money.
9. Having become liable for the debt of someone who has defaulted.
1. Convicted prostitutes were taken through the streets in carts to Bridewell prison for public whipping.
2. Buying or selling ecclesiastical preferments or benefices.
3. Encompass.
4. From Scotland in the north, to the Isle of Wight in the south, and from St. Michael's Mount in the southwest to Dover in the southeast.
5. Drawing a winning card (from a popular game *primero*); here, acquiring the best.

Assurances, big, as gloss'd civil laws,[6]
So huge, that men (in our time's forwardness)
90 Are Fathers of the Church[7] for writing less.
These he writes not; nor for these written pays,
Therefore spares no length; as in those first days
When Luther was profess'd, he did desire
Short *Pater nosters*, saying as a friar
95 Each day his beads, but having left those laws,
Adds to Christ's prayer, the power and glory clause.[8]
But when he sells or changes land, he'impairs
His writings, and (unwatch'd) leaves out, *ses heires*,[9]
As slyly'as any commenter goes by
100 Hard words, or sense; or in Divinity
As controverters,[1] in vouch'd texts, leave out
Shrewd words, which might against them clear the doubt.
Where are those spread woods which cloth'd heretofore
These bought lands? not built, not burnt within door.
105 Where th'old landlord's troops, and alms? In great halls
Carthusian fasts, and fulsome Bacchanals[2]
Equally'I hate. Means bless. In rich men's homes
I bid kill some beasts, but no hecatombs,[3]
None starve, none surfeit so; but oh, we'allow
110 Good works as good, but out of fashion now,
Like old rich wardrobes. But my words none draws
Within the vast reach of th'huge statute laws.

Satire 3.[4]

laughter

Kind pity chokes my spleen;[5] brave scorn forbids
Those tears to issue which swell my eyelids;
I must not laugh, nor weep sins, and be wise;   wisdom —
                                                  stoicism

6. Deeds of conveyance as large as commentaries glossing the law.
7. The earliest Christian thinkers who wrote vast tomes.
8. Luther added the final phrase to the Lord's Prayer.
9. By omitting the phrase "his heirs" from a deed of conveyance, an unscrupulous lawyer could try to secure the land himself.
1. Disputants or controversialists (OED, citing this passage); this characterization of unscrupulous practices among churchmen is ambiguous in that it may apply to Protestants or Roman Catholics.
2. Fasts by Carthusians (monks noted for their austerity) or drunken orgies in honor of Bacchus.
3. Ritual sacrifice of a hundred animals.
4. In some mss. this satire is titled "Of Religion" or "Upon Religion." Donne revised this poem several times; the copy text chosen (DT1) is different from that used for the other satires (NY3).
5. His natural pity controls the scornful laughter of the satirist. The spleen was believed to be the seat of both melancholy and laughter.

[handwritten: satire can't cure]

Can railing, then, cure these worn maladies?
5 Is not our mistress fair Religion,   *[handwritten: is religion worthy of devotion]*
As worthy of all our souls' devotion
As virtue was in the first blinded age?
Are not heaven's joys as valiant to assuage
Lusts, as earth's honour was to them? Alas,
10 As we do them in means, shall they surpass
Us in the end? and shall thy father's spirit
Meet blind philosophers[6] in heaven, whose merit
Of strict life may be imputed faith,[7] and hear
Thee, whom he taught so easy ways and near
15 To follow, damn'd? Oh, if thou dar'st, fear this: *[handwritten: fear of god is valor]*
This fear great courage and high valor is.
Dar'st thou aid mutinous Dutch,[8] and dar'st thou lay
Thee in ships, wooden sepulchers, a prey
To leaders' rage, to storms, to shot, to dearth?
20 Dar'st thou dive seas, and dungeons of the earth?
Hast thou courageous fire to thaw the ice
Of frozen North discoveries, and thrice
Colder than salamanders,[9] like divine
Children in th'oven, fires of Spain, and the line,[1]
25 Whose countries limbecks to our bodies be,
Canst thou for gain bear? and must every he   *[handwritten: your religion = a call for tolerance]*
Which cries not, "Goddess," to thy mistress, draw[2]
Or eat thy poisonous words? Courage of straw!
O desperate coward, wilt thou seem bold, and
30 To thy foes and his (who made thee to stand
Sentinel in his world's garrison) thus yield,
[handwritten: religious wars] And for forbidden wars leave the appointed field?   *[handwritten: self (internally) war — your own soul]*
Know thy foe: the foul devil, whom thou
Strivest to please, for hate, not love, would allow
35 Thee fain, his whole realm to be quit; and as
The world's all parts wither away and pass,
So the world's self, thy other lov'd foe, is
In her decrepit wane,[3] and thou loving this,

6. Philosophers who lived before the light of revelation.
7. Luther emphasized that believers must rely on the attribution of Christ's righteousness by vicarious substitution; see Romans 4:6–8.
8. Dutch Protestants were in a near continuous state of revolt against their Spanish conquerors; this phrase may express Roman Catholic sympathies.
9. Thought to be so cold-natured that they could withstand fire.
1. The equatorial regions overheat the body like an alembic; *children in th'oven*: three children who refused to worship a golden idol and were thrown into a furnace by Nebuchadnezzar, but who miraculously survived (Daniel 3:20–30); *fires of Spain*: heretics burned by the Inquisition; this phrase may express Roman Catholic antipathies.
2. I.e., draw a sword to defend himself.
3. That the world itself was decaying is one of the themes of *The First Anniversary*.

Dost love a wither'd and worn strumpet; last,
40   Flesh (itself's death) and joys which flesh can taste,
Thou lovest, and thy fair goodly soul, which doth
Give this flesh power to taste joy, thou dost loathe.
Seek true religion. O where? Mirreus,[4]   —a catholic
Thinking her unhous'd here, and fled from us,
45   Seeks her at Rome; there, because he doth know   they worship
That she was there a thousand years ago,   the outer clothes
He loves the rags so, as we here obey
The statecloth[5] where the prince sat yesterday.
Crants to such brave loves will not be enthrall'd,   Calvinist
50   But loves her only, who at Geneva is call'd   the Puritan
Religion, plain, simple, sullen, young,
Contemptuous, yet unhandsome. As among
Lecherous humors, there is one that judges
No wenches wholesome, but coarse country drudges.
55   Graius stays still at home here, and because   basically
Some preachers, vile ambitious bawds,[6] and laws   called them
Still new like fashions, bid him think that she   pimps (to
Which dwells with us, is only perfect, he   their religion)
Embraceth her, whom his godfathers will
60   Tender to him, being tender, as wards still   anglican
Take such wives as their guardians offer, or
Pay values.[7] Careless Phrygius doth abhor   atheist
All, because all cannot be good, as one   —atheist
Knowing some women whores, dares marry none.
65   Graccus loves all as one, and thinks that so   pantheism
As women do in diverse countries go
In diverse habits, yet are still one kind;
So doth, so is Religion; and this blind-   * notable linebreak
ness too much light breeds. But unmoved,[8] thou   have to choose
70   Of force must one, and forc'd, but one allow;   1 religion, and
And the right; ask thy father which is she,   be right √+
Let him ask his; though truth and falsehood be
Near twins, yet truth a little elder is.
Be busy to seek her; believe me this,
75   He's not of none, nor worst, that seeks the best.
To adore, or scorn an image, or protest,
May all be bad; doubt wisely; in strange way
                              !!!

4. Mirreus turns to Roman Catholicism; Crants, a Calvinist, to Geneva; and Graius, to the
   Church of England.
5. The canopy over a throne.
6. These preachers are "pimps" because they try to make others think that their church alone
   is the true one.
7. Compensations for refusing an arranged marriage.
8. Unswayed by Phrygius (who hates all) or Graccus (who loves all).

doubt wisely – an attitude
toward truth – severity of
intellectual commitment to problems

To stand inquiring right, is not to stray;
To sleep, or run wrong, is. On a huge hill,[9]
80 Cragged and steep, Truth stands, and he that will
Reach her, about must, and about go:
And what the hill's suddenness resists, win so.
Yet strive, so that before age, death's twilight,
Thy soul rest, for none can work in that night.[1]
85 To will implies delay, therefore now do.
Hard deeds, the body's pains; hard knowledge too
The mind's endeavors reach; and mysteries
Are like the sun, dazzling, yet plain to all eyes.
Keep the truth which thou hast found. Men do not stand
90 In so ill case here that God hath with his hand
Sign'd kings blank charters, to kill whom they hate,
Nor are they vicars, but hangmen to fate.
Fool and wretch, wilt thou let thy soul be tied
To man's laws, by which she shall not be tried
95 At the last day? Will it then boot thee
To say a Philip, or a Gregory,
A Harry, or a Martin[2] taught thee this?
Is not this excuse for mere contraries
Equally strong? Cannot both sides say so?
100 That thou mayest rightly obey power, her bounds know;
Those past, her nature, and name is chang'd; to be
Then humble to her is idolatry.
As streams are, power is: Those blest flowers that dwell
At the rough stream's calm head, thrive and do well,
105 But having left their roots, and themselves given
To the stream's tyrannous rage, alas, are driven
Through mills, and rocks, and woods, and at last, almost
Consum'd in going, in the sea are lost.
So perish souls, which more choose men's unjust
Power, from God claim'd, than God himself to trust.

Satire 4.[3]

Well; I may now receive,[4] and die. My sin
Indeed is great, but I have been in

---

9. Perhaps the "holy hill of Zion" (Psalms 2:6), though sacred mountains abound in scripture.
1. John 9:4: "the night cometh, when no man can work."
2. Philip II of Spain, Pope Gregory XIV, Henry VIII of England, or Martin Luther.
3. In some mss. this is titled "A Satire Against the Court" or "Satire 4: Of the Court."
4. The last sacrament (anointing with oils and Holy Communion) before death.

A purgatory,[5] such as fear'd hell is
A recreation and scant map of this.
5 My mind, neither with pride's itch, nor yet hath been
Poison'd with love to see, or to be seen.
I had no suit there, nor new suit to show,
Yet went to court. But as Glare[6] which did go
To'a mass in jest, catch'd, was fain to disburse
10 The hundred marks, which is the Statute's curse,[7]
Before he 'scapt, so'it pleas'd my destiny
(Guilty'of my sin of going) to think me
As prone to'all ill, and of good as forget-
full, as proud, lustful, and as much in debt,
15 As vain, as witless, and as false as they
Which dwell at court, for once going that way.
Therefore I suffer'd this. Towards me did run
A thing more strange, than on Nile's slime, the sun
20 E'er bred,[8] or all which into Noah's Ark came,
A thing, which would have pos'd[9] Adam to name:
Stranger than seven antiquaries' studies,
Then Africk's monsters, Guiana's rarities.[1]
Stranger than strangers; one who for a Dane,
In the Danes' massacre[2] had sure been slain,
25 If he had liv'd then, and without help dies,
When next the prentices 'gainst strangers rise.[3]
One whom the watch at noon lets scarce go by,
One t'whom th'examining justice sure would cry,
"Sir, by your priesthood[4] tell me what you are!"
30 His cloths were strange, though coarse, and black, though bare;
Sleeveless his jerkin was, and it had been
Velvet, but 'twas now (so much ground was seen)
Become tuftaffeta;[5] and our children shall
See it plain rash[6] awhile, then nought at all.
35 This thing hath travel'd, and saith, speaks all tongues,
And only knows what to all states belongs.
Made of th'accents, and best phrase of all these,

---

5. I.e., in court.
6. A fictitious character.
7. Statutory fine for attending a Roman Catholic Mass.
8. According to Pliny, small creatures were generated spontaneously by the sun in the mud of the Nile.
9. Puzzled.
1. Exotic creatures described by Sir Walter Raleigh, *The Discoverie of Guiana* (1596).
2. A massacre in 1012 of Danes in England by King Ethelred the Unready.
3. Riots against foreigners led by London apprentices in 1517.
4. Roman Catholic priests were subject to arrest and the death penalty if discovered.
5. A silken fabric with a nap arranged in tufts (OED, citing this passage).
6. A smooth fabric.

He speaks one language. If strange meats displease,
Art[7] can deceive, or hunger force my taste,
40   But pedant's motley tongue, soldier's bombast,
Mountebank's drug-tongue,[8] nor the terms of law
Are strong enough preparatives[9] draw
Me to bear this: yet I must be content
With his tongue, in his tongue call'd complement,
45   In which he can win widows, and pay scores,
Make men speak treason, cozen[1] subtlest whores,
Outflatter favorites, and outlie either
Jovius, or Surius,[2] or both together.
He names me,'and comes to me. I whisper, "God!
50   How have I sinn'd that thy wrath's furious rod,
This fellow chooseth me?" He saith, "Sir,
I love your judgment. Whom do you prefer,
For the best linguist?" And I sillily
Said that I thought Calepine's *Dictionary*.[3]
55   "Nay, but of men, most sweet Sir?" Beza[4] then,
Some Jesuits, and two reverend men
Of our two academies[5] I nam'd. There
He stopp'd me,'and said, "Nay, your apostles[6] were
Good pretty linguists, and so Panurge[7] was
60   Yet a poor gentleman; all these may pass
By travail."[8] Then, as if he would have sold
His tongue, he prais'd it, and such wonders told
That I was fain to say, "If you'had liv'd, Sir,
Time enough to have been interpreter
65   To Babel's bricklayers, sure that tower had stood."[9]
He adds, "If of court life you knew the good,
You would leave loneness." I said, "Not alone
My loneness is. But Spartans' fashion.
To teach by painting drunkards doth not last
70   Now; Aretine's pictures[1] have made few chaste;

---

7. Culinary art.
8. A quack's sales pitch.
9. Medicinals.
1. Cheat.
2. Paulus Jovius, an Italian historian (1483–1552), and Laurentius Surius, a German chronicler of saints' lives (1522–1578), were condemned by Protestants for their inaccuracies.
3. A polyglot dictionary edited by Ambrogio Calepino in 1502.
4. Theodore Beza (1519–1605), a French Calvinist known especially for his Latin translation of the Greek New Testament.
5. Oxford and Cambridge.
6. Reference to the gift of tongues at Pentecost (Acts 2:1–4).
7. Character in Rabelais's *Gargantua and Pantagruel*, skilled in a dozen languages.
8. To weary or exert onself (OED 1.b.) but with a frequent sense of "to travel."
9. God prevented the tower of Babel from being finished by introducing many languages.
1. Erotic paintings and lascivious poetry by Pietro Aretino (1492–1556).

No more can princes' courts, though there be few
Better pictures of vice, teach me virtue."
He like to'a high stretch'd lute string squeak'd, "O Sir,
'Tis sweet to talk of kings." "At Westminster,"
75 Said I, "The man that keeps the Abbey tombs,
And for his price doth with whoever comes,
Of all our Harrys, and our Edwards talk,
From king to king and all their kin can walk:
Your ears shall hear nought, but 'kings'; your eyes meet
80 Kings only; the way to it, is King's Street."[2]
He smack'd, and cried, "He's base, mechanic, coarse,
So'are all your Englishmen in their discourse.
Are not your Frenchmen neat?" "Mine? as you see,
I'have but one Frenchman; look, he follows me."
85 "Certes they'are neatly cloth'd. I'of this mind am,
Your only wearing is your grogaram."[3]
"Not so, Sir, I have more." Under this pitch[4]
He would not fly; I chaf'd him. But as itch
Scratch'd into smart, and as blunt iron ground
90 Into an edge hurts worse, so I, fool, found,
Crossing[5] hurt me. To fit my sullenness,
He to another key his style doth address.
And asks, "What news?" I tell him of new plays.
He takes my hand, and as a still, which stays
95 A sem'breve,[6]'twixt each drop, he niggardly,
(As loath to'enrich me so) tells many'a lie.
More then ten Holinsheds, and Halls, and Stows,[7]
Of trivial household trash he knows; he knows
When the queen smil'd or frown'd, and he knows what
100 A subtle statesman may gather of that.
He knows who loves whom, and who by poison
Hastes to an office's reversion.[8]
He knows who'hath sold his land, and now doth beg
A licence, old iron, shoes, boots or egg-
105 shells to transport. Shortly boys shall not play
At span-counter or blow-point,[9] but they pay
Toll to some courtier; and wiser than all us,

2. Street then leading from Charing Cross to Westminster Palace (now covered over by Parliament Street).
3. A coarse fabric of silk, mohair and wool (OED).
4. The height to which a trained falcon would fly.
5. Disputing him.
6. For a long interval (in music, the longest note).
7. Chroniclers of English history.
8. Succession to an important position.
9. Children's games.

He knows what lady is not painted. Thus
He with home-meats[1] tries me. I belch, spew, spit,
110 Look pale and sickly, like a patient, yet
He thrusts on more; and as if he'd undertook
To say *Gallo-Belgicus*[2] without book,
Speaks of all states and deeds, which have been since
The Spaniards came, to the loss of Amiens.[3]
115 Like a big wife, at sight of loathed meat,
Ready to travail, so I sigh and sweat
To hear his Macaron[4] talk, in vain; for yet,
Either my humor or his own to fit,
He, like a priviledg'd spy, whom nothing can
120 Discredit, libels now 'gainst each great man.
He names a price for every office paid;
He says our wars thrive ill, because delay'd;
That offices are entail'd,[5] and that there are
Perpetuities of them, lasting as far
125 As the Last Day; and that great officers,
Do with the pirates share, and Dunkirkers.[6]
Who wastes in meat, in clothes, in horse, he notes;
Who loves whores, who boys, and who goats.
I more amaz'd than Circe's prisoners,[7] when
130 They felt themselves turn beasts, felt my self then
Becoming traitor; and methought I saw
One of our giant statutes ope his jaw
To suck me in for hearing him. I found
That as burnt venom'd lechers do grow sound
135 By giving others their sores,[8] I might grow
Guilty, and he free. Therefore I did show
All signs of loathing; but since I am in,
I must pay mine, and my forefathers' sin
To the last farthing. Therefore to my power
140 Toughly'and stubbornly'I bear this cross; but th'hour
Of mercy now was come. He tries to bring
Me to pay'a fine to 'scape his torturing,
And says, "Sir, can you spare me?" I said, "Willingly."
"Nay, Sir, can you spare me'a crown?" Thankfully I

1. Gossip.
2. *Mercurius Gallo-Belgicus* was a compilation of continental news and gossip begun in 1594.
3. From the Armada of 1588 to the fall of Amiens to the Spanish in March 1597; thus this satire must date from 1597 (or later).
4. A fop.
5. An entail settled the succession of a landed estate, so that it could not be bequeathed by another possessor (OED); here, it means rights to offices have been settled in perpetuity.
6. Dunkirk was a haven for pirates.
7. Odysseus's men were turned to swine by Circe.
8. Venereal disease was thought to be curable if passed along to another.

145 Gave it, as ransom; but as fiddlers still,
    Though they be paid to be gone, yet needs will
    Thrust one more jig upon you: so did he
    With his long complemental thanks vex me.
    But he is gone, thanks to his needy want,
150 And the prerogative of my crown. Scant
    His thanks were ended, when I, which did see
    All the court fill'd with more strange things then he,
    Ran from thence with such or more haste, than one
    Who fears more actions, doth make from prison.
155 At home in wholesome solitariness
    My piteous soul began the wretchedness
    Of suitors at court to mourn, and a trance
    Like his, who dreamt he saw hell,[9] did advance
    It self o'er me'and such men as he saw there,
160 I saw at court, and worse, and more. Low fear
    Becomes the guilty, not th'accuser. Then,
    Shall I, none's slave, of high born or rais'd[1] men
    Fear frowns? And, my mistress Truth, betray thee
    To th'huffing braggart, puff'd Nobility?
165 No, no, thou which since yesterday hast been
    Almost about the whole world, hast thou seen,
    O Sun, in all thy journey, vanity
    Such as swells the bladder of our court? I
    Think he which made yon waxen garden and
170 Transported it from Italy to stand
    With us at London, flouts our court here, for
    Just such gay painted things, which no sap nor
    Taste have in them, ours are; and natural
    Some of the stocks are, their fruits, bastard all.
175 'Tis ten a clock and past: All whom the mews,[2]
    Ballone, tennis, diet, or the stews,[3]
    Had all the morning held, now the second
    Time made ready that day, in flocks are found
    In the presence, and I, (God pardon me)
180 As fresh and sweet th'apparels be as be
    The fields they sold to buy them. "For a king
    Those hose are," cry the flatterers, and bring
    Them next week to the theater to sell.
    Wants reach all states; me seems they do as well

---

9. Dante.
1. Someone elevated to high rank.
2. Stables.
3. Brothels; *ballone*: A game played with a "large inflated ball of strong double leather" that
was struck with the arm encased in a wooden brace (OED).

185 At stage, as court. All are players; whoe'er looks
    (For themselves dare not go) o'er Cheapside books,[4]
    Shall find their wardrobe's inventory. Now,
    The ladies come. As pirates, which do know
    That there came weak ships fraught with cochineal,[5]
190 The men board them and praise, as they think, well,
    Their beauties; they the men's wits. Both are bought.
    Why good wits ne'er wear scarlet gowns,[6] I thought
    This cause: These men, men's wits for speeches buy,
    And women buy all reds which scarlet dye.
195 He call'd her beauty lime twigs, her hair net;[7]
    She fears her drugs ill laid, her hair loose set.
    Would not Heraclitus laugh to see Macrine,[8]
    From hat to shoe, himself at door refine,
    As if the presence were a moschite,[9] and lift
200 His skirts and hose, and call his clothes to shrift,
    Making them confess not only mortal
    Great stains and holes in them, but venial
    Feathers and dust, with which they fornicate.
    And then by Dürer's rules[1] surveys the state
205 Of his each limb, and with strings the odds tries
    Of his neck to his leg, and waist to thighs.
    So in immaculate clothes, and symmetry
    Perfect as circles, with such nicety
    As a young preacher at his first time goes
210 To preach, he enters, and a lady which owes
    Him not so much as good will, straight arrests,
    And unto her protests, protests, protests
    So much as at Rome would serve to have thrown
    Ten cardinals into th'Inquisition;
215 And whisper'd "By Jesu!" so'often, that a
    Pursuivant[2] would have ravish'd him away
    For saying of Our Lady's psalter;[3] but 'tis fit
    That they each other plague; they merit it.
    But here comes Glorius that will plague them both,

---

4. Account books of clothing shops in Cheapside; since these gentlemen owe money, they fear being dunned.
5. I.e., women made up in rouge. Cochineal was a dye used to make rouge.
6. Ceremonial robes worn at universities and by government ministers.
7. Used to trap birds.
8. Even Heraclitus, known as the "weeping philosopher," would laugh at Macrine.
9. Mosque. Macrine tidies himself before entering court, like a Muslim before entering a mosque removes his shoes.
1. Albrecht Dürer, *Four Books on Human Proportion*(1528).
2. Public officer employed for searches.
3. An early form of the rosary, Our Lady's Psalter (a hundred and fifty Hail Marys) was instituted by St. Dominic c. 1200.

220 Who, in the other extreme, only doth
     Call a rough carelessness, good fashion;
     Whose cloak his spurs tear, whom he spits on
     He cares not. His ill words do no harm
     To him; he rusheth in, as if "Arm, arm!"
225 He came to cry. And though his face be'as ill
     As theirs which in old hangings⁴ whip Christ, still
     He strives to look worse; he keeps all in awe;
     Jests like a licenc'd fool, commands like law.
     Tir'd, now I'll leave this place, and but pleas'd so
230 As men which from jails to'execution go,
     Go through the great chamber (why is it hung
     With the seven deadly sins?).⁵ Being among
     Those Askaparts,⁶ men big enough to throw
     Charing Cross⁷ for a bar, men which do know
235 No token of worth, but "Queen's man," and fine
     Living, barrels of beef, flagons of wine,
     I shook like a spied spy. Preachers, which are
     Seas of wit and arts, you can, then dare
     Drown the sins of this place, for, for me
240 Which am but a scant brook, it enough shall be
     To wash the stains away. Though I yet
     With Maccabees'⁸ modesty, the known merit
     Of my work lessen: yet some wise men shall,
     I hope, esteem my writs canonical.

Satire 5.⁹

     Thou shalt not laugh in this leaf, Muse, nor they
     Whom any pity warms. He which¹ did lay
     Rules to make courtiers, (he being understood
     May make good courtiers, but who courtiers good?)
5   Frees from the stings of jests all who'in extreme
     Are wretch'd or wicked. Of these two a theme

---

4. Tapestries depicting the sufferings of Christ.
5. Cardinal Wolsey bought tapestries depicting the seven deadly sins in 1522 and hung them in the reception chamber at Hampton Court Palace.
6. A legendary giant, thirty feet tall; here, the imposing guards before the palace.
7. A large Gothic cross set up as a memorial. Elizabethans tossed large objects for sport (as the Scots continue to do with the caber toss in the Highland Games).
8. This apocryphal Old Testament work ends with great modesty; see 2 Maccabees 15:37–38.
9. In one ms. this is titled "Satire 5: Of the Misery of the Poor Suitors at Court." Donne's employer Sir Thomas Egerton was attempting to reform some of the procedures in the law courts.
1. Baldassare Castiglione, *The Book of the Courtier* (1528), set standards of decorum.

Charity and liberty[2] give me. What is he
Who officer's rage and suitor's misery
Can write and jest? If all things be in all,
10 (As I think, since all, which were, are, and shall
Be, be made of the same elements:
Each thing, each thing implies or represents.)
Then man is a world, in which, officers
Are the vast ravishing seas, and suitors,
15 Springs, now full, now shallow, now dry; which to
That which drowns them run. These self reasons[3] do
Prove the world a man, in which officers
Are the devouring stomach, and suitors
Th'excrement which they void. All men are dust;
20 How much worse are suitors, who to men's lust
Are made preys? O worse then dust, or worm's meat,
For they do'eat you now, whose selves worms shall eat.
They are the mills which grind you, yet you are
The wind which drives them; and a wasteful war
25 Is fought against you, and you fight it. They
Adulterate law, and you prepare their way
Like wittols;[4] th'issue your own ruin is.
Greatest and fairest empress,[5] know you this?
Alas, no more then Thames' calm head doth know
30 Whose meads[6] her arms drown, or whose corn o'erflow.
You Sir,[7] whose righteousness she loves, whom I
By having leave to serve, am most richly
For service paid, authoriz'd now, begin
To know and weed out this enormous sin.
35 O age of rusty iron![8] Some better wit
Call it some worse name, if ought equal it.
Th'Iron Age that was, when justice was sold; now
Injustice is sold dearer far. Allow
All claim'd fees, and duties; gamesters, anon
40 The money which you swear and sweat for is gone
Into'other hands: So controverted lands
'Scape, like Angelica,[9] the striver's hands.

2. Charity to pity the wretched and liberty to censure the wicked.
3. Same reasons.
4. Husbands who are aware of and complaisant about the infidelity of their wives (OED).
5. Queen Elizabeth I.
6. Meadows.
7. Sir Thomas Egerton (1540–1617), Lord Keeper of England, with a reputation as a virtuous man; from 1597–1602, Donne's patron and employer.
8. The present falls far short of the Golden Age; see also *First Anniversary*, lines 425–26.
9. In Ariosto's *Orlando Furioso*, Angelica escapes from her rivals' clutches while they fight over her; similarly, disputed lands are forfeited during legal wrangling.

If Law be in the judge's heart, and he
Have no heart to resist letter or fee,[1]
45 Where wilt thou'appeal? Power of the courts below
Flow from the first main head:[2] and these can throw
Thee, if they suck thee in, to misery,
To fetters, halters; But if th'injury
Steel thee to dare complain, alas, thou go'st
50 Against the stream, when upwards: when thou'art most
Heavy' and most faint. And in those labors, they
'Gainst whom thou should'st complain, will in thy way
Become great seas, o'er which when thou shalt be
Forc'd to make golden bridges, thou shalt see
55 That all thy gold was drown'd in them before.
All things follow their likes; only who have, may'have more.
Judges are gods; he who made and said them so,
Meant not men should be forc'd to them to go,
By means of angels.[3] When supplications
60 We send to God, to Dominations,
Powers, Cherubins, and all heavens courts, if we
Should pay fees, as here, daily bread would be
Scarce to kings; so 'tis. Would it not anger
A Stoic, a coward, yea a martyr,
65 To see a pursuivant[4] come in, and call
All his clothes, copes, books, primers[5] and all
His plate, chalices; and mistake[6] them away,
And ask a fee for coming? Oh, ne'er may
Fair law's white reverend name be strumpeted,
70 To warrant thefts: she is established
Recorder to destiny on earth, and she
Speaks fate's words, and but tells us who must be
Rich, who poor, who in chairs, who in jails.
She is all fair, but yet hath foul long nails,
75 With which she scratcheth suitors. In bodies
Of men, so'in law, nails are th'extremities,
So'officers stretch to more than law can do,
As our nailes reach what no else part comes to.[7]

---

1. Bribe. Grierson (II, 126) believes this satire was occasioned by Egerton's campaign against the abuses of the Star Chamber.
2. The queen.
3. With a pun on the English gold coin, called the angel-noble, which had the archangel Michael standing upon and piercing the dragon (OED).
4. Public officer employed for searches.
5. A prayer book or devotional manual used by the laity (usually Roman Catholic); copes: capelike vestments used chiefly in church ceremonies.
6. Mis-take; wrongly appropriate.
7. Our nails can scratch our posteriors.

Why bar'st thou[8] to yon officer, fool? Hath he
80 Got those goods, for which erst men bar'd to thee?
Fool, twice, thrice, thou'hast bought wrong, 'and now hungerly
Beg'st right; but that dole comes not till these die.
Thou'had'st much, and law's Urim and Thummim[9] try
Thou wouldst for more; and for all hast paper
85 Enough to clothe all the great Carrick's pepper.[1]
Sell that, and by that thou much more shalt leese,[2]
Than Haman,[3] if he sold his antiquities.
O wretch, that thy fortunes should moralize
Aesop's fables, and make tales prophecies.
90 Thou art that swimming dog whom shadows cozened,
And div'dst, near drowning, for what vanished.[4]

---

8. Remove your hat out of respect.
9. Jewels in the breastplate of Aaron (Exodus 28:30); Hebrew for light and integrity.
1. A large merchant ship. In 1592 a seven-decked Spanish ship, known as the Great Carrack, loaded with a cargo of pepper, was taken and brought to England.
2. Lose.
3. A collector of riches, Haman tried to have someone hung but ended on the gallows himself (see Esther 5–7).
4. In Aesop's fable a greedy dog loses his morsel when he sees its reflection in the water and opens his mouth to get that morsel too.

Elegies

Elegy 1.

The Bracelet.[1]

Not that in color it was like thy hair,
For armlets of that thou mayst let me wear;
Nor that thy hand it oft embrac'd and kiss'd,
For so it had that good, which oft I miss'd;
5 Nor for that silly old morality,[2]
That as those links are tied, our love should be,
Mourn I that I thy sevenfold[3] chain have lost;
Nor for the luck's sake, but the bitter cost.
O shall twelve righteous angels,[4] which as yet
10 No leaven of vile solder[5] did admit;
Nor yet by any taint have stray'd or gone
From the first state of their creation;
Angels, which heaven commanded to provide
All things to me, and be my faithful guide;
15 To gain new friends, t'appease great enemies;
To comfort my soul, when I lie or rise.
Shall these twelve innocents, by thy severe
Sentence, dread Judge, my sin's great burden bear?
Shall they be damn'd and in the furnace thrown,[6]
20 And punish'd for offenses not their own?
They save not me, they do not ease my pains,
When in that hell they're burnt and tied in chains.
Were they but crowns of France,[7] I cared not,

---

1. Though many mss. simply numbered the elegies, some supplied titles, which are used here to help identify them. This one is called "Elegy. To a Lady Whose Chain Was Lost. The Bracelet. Armilla" in H6.
2. A moral saying.
3. With seven loops.
4. A pun on the English gold coin, called the angel-noble, which had the archangel Michael standing upon and piercing the dragon (OED).
5. Debased by being soldered with lesser elements.
6. Lines 17–19: She has demanded that the poet's gold angels be melted down for a replacement bracelet.
7. French coins with a punning reference to the baldness resulting from syphilis, *their natural country rot.*

For most of them their natural country rot,
25   I think, possesseth; they come here to us
So lean, so pale, so lame, so ruinous.
And howsoe'er French kings most Christian be,[8]
Their crowns are circumcis'd most Jewishly.
Or were they Spanish stamps,[9] still travailing,
30   That are become as catholic as their king;
Those unlick'd bear whelps, unfil'd pistolets,[1]
That more than cannon shot avails or lets;
Which negligently left unrounded look
Like many angled figures in the book
35   Of some great conjurer which would enforce
Nature, as these do justice, from her course;
Which, as the soul quickens head, feet and heart,
As streams, like veins, run through th'earth's every part,
Visit all countries, and have slyly made
40   Gorgeous France, ragged, ruin'd, and decay'd,
Scotland, which knew no state, proud in one day,
And mangled seventeen-headed Belgia.[2]
Or were it such gold as that wherewithal
Almighty chemics[3] from each mineral
45   Having by subtle fire a soul out pull'd,
Are dirtily and desperately gull'd.
I would not spit to quench the fire they'were in,
For they are guilty of much heinous sin.
But shall my harmless angels perish? Shall
50   I lose my guard, my ease, my food, my all?
Much hope which they should nourish will be dead.
Much of my able youth and lustihead
Will vanish; if thou love let them alone,
For thou wilt love me less when they are gone:
55   Oh be content that some loud squeaking crier
Well pleas'd with one lean threadbare groat[4] for hire,
May like a devil roar through every street
And gall the finder's conscience, if they meet.
Or let me creep to some dread conjurer,[5]
60   Which with fantastic schemes fulfills much paper,

8. One of the titles of the French king was *Rex Christianissimus,* yet French coins often had their edges *circumcised* or trimmed.
9. Design impressed on a coin, hence the coin itself (OED 12.b).
1. Silver coins with rough edges (i.e., unmilled); *unlicked bear whelps*: bears were believed to lick their unformed cubs, or whelps, into shape after birth.
2. Spanish money had an effect on France, Scotland, and the seventeen provinces in the Low Countries.
3. Alchemists.
4. A small coin of little value.
5. A conjurer who might find the bracelet with astrological charts.

Which hath divided heaven in tenements
And with whores, thieves, and murderers stuff'd his rents[6]
So full, that though he pass them all in sin,
He leaves himself no room to enter in.
65 And if, when all his art and time is spent
He say 'twill ne'er be found; O be content.
Receive the doom from him ungrudgingly,
Because he is the mouth of destiny.
Thou say'st, alas the gold doth still remain,
70 Though it be chang'd and put into a chain.
So in those first fall'n angels resteth still
Wisdom and knowledge; but 'tis turn'd to ill.
As these should do good works and should provide
Necessities, but now must nurse thy pride.
75 And they are still bad angels, mine are none
For form gives being, and their form is gone.
Pity these angels yet; their dignities
Pass Virtues, Powers, and Principalities.[7]
But thou art resolute; thy will be done.
80 Yet with such anguish, as her only son
The mother in the hungry grave doth lay,
Unto the fire these martyrs I betray.
Good souls, for you give life to everything,
Good angels, for good messages you bring,
85 Destin'd you might have been to such a one
As would have lov'd and worshipp'd you alone.
One which would suffer hunger, nakedness,
Yea death, ere he would make your number less.
But I am guilty of your sad decay:
90 May your few fellows longer with me stay.
But O thou wretched finder whom I hate
So much, as I almost pity thy state;
Gold being the heaviest metal amongst all
May my most heavy curse upon thee fall.
95 Here fetter'd, manacl'd, and hang'd in chains,
First mayst thou be; then chain'd to hellish pains.
Or be with foreign gold brib'd to betray
Thy country, and fail both of that and thy pay.
May the next thing thou stoop'st to reach, contain
100 Poison, whose nimble fume rot thy moist brain:

6. Lines 60–62: Gardner (165) explains that the heavens were divided into twelve houses;
and that a *scheme* was a figure of the heavens with the seven planets and the twelve
zodiacal signs divided into eighty-four rows of houses or *tenements*. This conjurer has
packed his divisions or "rents" with shady characters to make money.
7. Orders in the angelic hierarchy that surpass mere angels. The poet pleads, nonetheless,
for her to allow his angels the *dignity* of their continued existence.

Or libels, or some interdicted thing
Which negligently kept, thy ruin bring:
Lust bred diseases rot thee'and dwell with thee
Itchy desire, and no ability.
105   May all the hurt which ever gold hath wrought,
All mischiefs which all devils ever thought,
Want after plenty, poor and gouty age,
The plagues of travelers, love and marriage
Afflict thee, and at thy life's latest moment
110   May thy swoll'n sins themselves to thee present.
But I forgive; repent then honest man.
Gold is restorative;[8] restore it then.
Or if with it thou be'st loath to depart,
Because 'tis cordial, would 'twere at thy heart.

Elegy 2.

The Comparison.

As the sweet sweat of roses in a still,[9]
As that which from chaf'd musk cat's pores doth trill,[1]
As the almighty balm of th'early east,[2]
Such are the sweat drops on my mistress' breast.
5   And on her neck her skin such luster sets,
They seem no sweat drops, but pearl carcanets.[3]
Rank sweaty froth thy mistress' brow defiles,
Like spermatic issue of ripe menstruous boils.[4]
Or like the scum, which by need's lawless law
10   Enforc'd, Sanserra's[5] starved men did draw
From parboil'd shoes and boots, and all the rest
Which were with any sovereign fatness blest.
And like vile lying stones in saffron'd tin,[6]
Or warts, or wheals, they hang upon her skin.
15   Round as the world's her head, on every side,
Like to the fatal ball which fell on Ide,[7]
Or that[8] whereof God had such jealousy,

[handwritten marginal note: unconventional imagery]

8. Gold was often used as a medicine.
9. An apparatus for distilling perfume, here from the fragrant essence of roses.
1. Trickle. The musk cat secretes a substance from which perfumes are made.
2. I.e., morning drops of dew.
3. An ornamental necklace (OED).
4. An image designed to shock: the *boils* may be those of venereal disease.
5. Catholic troops besieged Sancerre for nine months in 1573; 500 people starved to death.
6. A cheap necklace made of tin colored to look like gold.
7. The golden apple inscribed "to the fairest" that provoked an argument at a wedding, lead-
ing to the Judgment of Paris and the Trojan War.
8. The fruit of the Tree of the Knowledge of Good and Evil.

As for the ravishing thereof we die.
Thy head is like a rough-hewn statue of jet,
20   Where marks for eyes, nose, mouth, are yet scarce set;
Like the first chaos, or flat seeming face
Of Cynthia,[9] when th'earth's shadows her embrace.
Like Proserpine's white beauty-keeping chest,[1]
Or Jove's best fortune's urn,[2] is her fair breast.
25   Thine's like worm-eaten trunks, cloth'd in seal's skin,
Or grave, that's dirt without, and stink within.
And like that slender stalk, at whose end stands
The woodbine quivering, are her arms and hands.
Like rough-bark'd elm boughs, or the russet skin
30   Of men late scourg'd for madness, or for sin,
Like sun-parch'd quarters on the city gate,
Such is thy tann'd skin's lamentable state.
And like a bunch of ragged carrots stand
The short swoll'n fingers of thy gouty hand.
35   Then like the chemic's masculine equal fire,
Which in the limbeck's warm womb doth inspire
Into th'earth's worthless dirt a soul of gold,[3]
Such cherishing heat her best loved part[4] doth hold.
Thine's like the dread mouth of a fired gun,
40   Or like hot liquid metals newly run
Into clay molds, or like to that Ætna,[5]
Where round about the grass is burnt away.
Are not your kisses then as filthy, and more,
As a worm sucking an envenom'd sore?
45   Doth not thy fearful hand in feeling quake,
As one which gath'ring flowers still fear'd a snake?
Is not your last act[6] harsh and violent,
As when a plough a stony ground doth rent?
So kiss good turtles,[7] so devoutly nice
50   Are priests in handling reverent sacrifice;
And such in searching wounds the surgeon is,
As we, when we embrace, or touch, or kiss.
Leave her, and I will leave comparing thus,
She and comparisons are odious.

---

9. The moon in its early phases.
1. The chest containing the ointment of beauty that Psyche took from Proserpina.
2. In *Iliad* 24, Zeus doles out good or bad fortune from different urns as he sees fit.
3. Lines 35–37: The alchemical basis for this conceit is the analogy between the woman's womb and an alembic that makes possible the transformation of something base into a *soul of gold*; here, sexual satisfaction.
4. Her genitals.
5. A volcano in Sicily.
6. The sexual act.
7. Turtle-doves.

Elegy 3.

The Perfume.

Once and but once found in thy company,
All thy suppos'd escapes[8] are laid on me.
And as a thief at bar is question'd there
By all the men, that have been robb'd that year,
5 So am I, (by this traiterous means surpriz'd)
By thy hydroptic[9] father catechiz'd.
Though he had wont to search with glazed[1] eyes,
As though he came to kill a cockatrice,[2]
Though he hath oft sworn that he would remove
10 Thy beauty's beauty, and food of our love,
Hope of his goods, if I with thee were seen,
Yet close and secret, as our souls, we've been.
Though thy immortal mother which doth lie
Still buried in her bed, yet will not die,
15 Take this advantage to sleep out daylight,
And watch thy entries and returns all night,
And, when she takes thy hand, and would seem kind,
Doth search what rings and armlets she can find,
And kissing notes the color of thy face,
20 And fearing lest thou'rt swoll'n,[3] doth thee embrace,
And to try if thou long, doth name strange meats;
And notes thy paleness, blushings, sighs, and sweats;
And politicly[4] will to thee confess
The sins of her own youth's rank lustiness,
25 Yet love these sorceries did remove, and move
Thee to gull thine own mother for my love.
Thy little brethren which like fairy sprites
Oft skipp'd into our chamber those sweet nights,
And kiss'd and ingled[5] on thy father's knee,
30 Were bribed next day to tell what they did see.
The grim-eight-foot-high-iron-bound serving-man,
That oft names God in oaths, and only then,
He that to bar the first gate doth as wide
As the great Rhodian Colossus[6] stride

inclined

8. All her past transgressions, especially breaches of chastity (OED 7).
9. Insatiably thirsty.
1. From excessive alcohol.
2. A legendary serpent that could kill with its glance.
3. With child.
4. Shrewdly.
5. Caressed (OED).
6. A colossal statue of Apollo, considered one of the seven wonders of the ancient world.

35   Which, if in hell no other pains there were,
      Makes me fear hell, because he must be there,
      Though by thy father he were hir'd for this,
      Could never witness any touch or kiss.
      But oh, too common ill, I brought with me
40   That, which betray'd me to mine enemy,
      A loud perfume, which at my entrance cried
      Even at thy father's nose, so were we spied.
      When, like a tyrant king, that in his bed
      Smelt gunpowder, the pale wretch shivered.
45   Had it been some bad smell, he would have thought
      That his own feet, or breath, that smell had wrought.
      But as we, in our isle[7] imprisoned,
      Where cattle only and diverse dogs are bred,
      The precious unicorns, strange monsters, call,
50   So thought he good strange that had none at all.
      I taught my silks their whistling to forbear,
      Even my oppress'd shoes dumb and speechless were;
      Only thou bitter sweet,[8] whom I had laid
      Next me, me traiterously hast betray'd,
55   And unsuspected hast invisibly
      At once fled unto him, and stay'd with me.
      Base excrement of earth, which dost confound
      Sense, from distinguishing the sick from sound;
      By thee the silly amorous[9] sucks his death
60   By drawing in a leprous harlot's breath;
      By thee the greatest stain to man's estate
      Falls on us, to be call'd effeminate.
      Though you be much lov'd in the prince's hall,
      There things that seem exceed substantial.
65   Gods, when ye fum'd on altars, were pleas'd well,
      Because you were burnt, not that they lik'd your smell;
      You're loathsome all, being taken simply alone;
      Shall we love ill things join'd, and hate each one?
      If you were good, your good doth soon decay;
70   And you are rare, that takes the good away.
      All my perfumes I give most willingly
      To embalm thy father's corpse; what? will he die?

7. Britain.
8. The poet addresses the perfume from lines 53–70.
9. Lover.

Elegy 4.[1]

Jealousy.

Fond[2] woman, which wouldst have thy husband die,
And yet complain'st of his great jealousy.
If swoll'n with poison, he lay in his last bed,
His body with a sere bark[3] covered,
5   Drawing his breath, as thick and short, as can
The nimblest crocheting musician,[4]
Ready with loathsome vomiting to spew
His soul out of one hell, into a new,
Made deaf with his poor kindred's howling cries,
10   Begging with few feign'd tears, great legacies,
Thou wouldst not weep, but jolly,'and frolic be,
As a slave, which tomorrow should be free.
Yet weep'st thou, when thou seest him hungerly
Swallow his own death, heart's-bane jealousy.[5]
15   O give him many thanks, he's courteous,
That in suspecting kindly warneth us.
We must not, as we us'd, flout openly,
In scoffing riddles, his deformity;
Nor at his board together being sat,
20   With words, nor touch, scarce looks adulterate.
Nor when he swoll'n, and pamper'd with great fare
Sits down and snorts, cag'd in his basket chair,
Must we usurp his own bed any more,
Nor kiss and play in his house as before.
25   Now I see many dangers; for that is
His realm, his castle, and his diocese.
But if, as envious men, which would revile
Their prince, or coin his gold, themselves exile
Into another country, and do it there,
30   We play'in another house, what should we fear?
There we will scorn his household policies,
His silly plots, and pensionary spies,[6]
As the inhabitants of Thames' right side[7]
Do London's mayor, or Germans, the'Pope's pride.[8]

1. With its frank eroticism and the conniving to deceive the woman's husband, this elegy recalls Ovid's *Amores* (especially 1.4).
2. Foolish.
3. Some poisons were known to desiccate the skin like a dried bark; perhaps, also an allusion to the cere-cloth (or waxed cloth used as a shroud).
4. Playing in quick time. A *crochet* was a quarter note.
5. Jealousy that poisons the heart.
6. Servants hired to spy.
7. Southwark, a notorious gaming district, outside the mayor's jurisdiction.
8. I.e., German Protestants, living beyond the pope's effective control.

Elegy 5.[9]

Oh, let not me serve so, as those men serve
Whom honor's smokes at once fatten and starve;[1]
Poorly enrich'd with great men's words or looks;
Nor so write my name in thy loving books
5 As those idolatrous flatterers, which still
Their princes' styles, with many realms fulfil[2]
Whence they no tribute have, and where no sway.
Such services I offer as shall pay
Themselves: I hate dead names: Oh then let me
10 Favorite in ordinary,[3] or no favorite be.
When my soul was in her own body sheath'd,
Nor yet by oaths betroth'd, nor kisses breath'd
Into my purgatory,[4] faithless thee,
Thy heart seem'd wax, and steel thy constancy.
15 So, careless flowers strow'd on the water's face,
The curled whirlpools suck, smack, and embrace,
Yet drown them; so, the taper's beamy eye
Amorously twinkling, beckons the giddy fly,
Yet burns his wings; and such the devil is,
20 Scarce visiting them, who are entirely his.
When I behold a stream, which, from the spring
Doth with doubtful melodious murmuring,
Or in a speechless slumber, calmly ride
Her wedded channel's bosom,[5] and then chide,
25 And bend her brows, and swell, if any bough
Do but stoop down to kiss her upmost brow:
Yet, if her often gnawing kisses win
The traitorous banks to gape, and let her in,
She rusheth violently, and doth divorce
30 Her from her native and her long-kept course,
And roars, and braves it, and in gallant scorn,
In flattering eddies promising return,
She flouts the channel, who thenceforth is dry;
Then say I: That is she, and this am I.
35 Yet let not thy deep bitterness beget
Careless despair in me, for that will whet
My mind to scorn; and oh, love dull'd with pain

9. In some mss. this is titled "To His Unconstant Mistress" and "Be Not So Coy."
1. The insubstantiality of titles and other honors that only seem to enrich someone.
2. Fill up.
3. Regular officials as opposed to extraordinary ones (OED 2b).
4. She (*faithless thee*) is the poet's purgatory.
5. The riverbed.

Was ne'er so wise, nor well arm'd, as disdain.
Then with new eyes I shall survey thee,'and spy
40   Death in thy cheeks, and darkness in thine eye:
Though hope bred faith and love; thus taught, I shall
As nations do from Rome, from thy love fall.
My hate shall outgrow thine, and utterly
I will renounce thy dalliance: and when I
45   Am the recusant,[6] in that resolute state
What hurts it me to be'excommunicate?[7]

Elegy 6.[8]

Nature's lay idiot,[9] I taught thee to love,
And in that sophistry,[1] oh, thou dost prove
Too subtle: fool,[2] thou didst not understand
The mystic language of the eye nor hand:
5   Nor couldst thou judge the difference of the air
Of sighs, and say, "This lies, this sounds despair:"
Nor by th'eye's water[3] call a malady
Desperately hot, or changing feverously.
I had not taught thee then, the alphabet
10 Of flowers, how they devisefully[4] being set
And bound up, might with speechless secrecy
Deliver errands mutely, and mutually.
Remember since all thy words us'd to be
To every suitor, "Ay, if my friends agree."
15 Since household charms, thy husband's name to teach,
Were all the love tricks that thy wit could reach;[5]
And since, an hour's discourse could scarce have made
One answer in thee, and that ill array'd
In broken proverbs, and torn sentences.[6]
20 Thou art not by so many duties his
That from the'world's common having sever'd thee,
Inlaid[7] thee, neither to be seen, nor see,

6. A Roman Catholic who refused to attend Anglican services.
7. Barred from love's communion, with a pun on religious excommunication.
8. In one ms. this is titled "Upon a Woman whom the Author Taught to Love & Compliment."
9. A simpleton who is ignorant of the workings of nature.
1. Subtle argument.
2. A term for either endearment or pity (OED 1.c).
3. Tears.
4. Ingeniously.
5. Lines 15–16: Before meeting the poet, she knew only the country games that girls played to learn whom they would marry.
6. Inelegant or incoherent clichés.
7. Hidden. The OED, citing this passage, defines inlay as "To lay in, or as in, a place of concealment or preservation."

As mine: who have with amorous delicacies
Refin'd thee'into a blissful paradise.
25 Thy graces and good words my creatures be,
I planted knowledge and life's tree in thee,
Which, oh, shall strangers taste? Must I, alas
Frame and enamel plate, and drink in glass?
Chafe wax for others' seals?[8] Break a colt's force,
30 And leave him then, being made a ready horse?

Elegy 7.

Love's War.[9]

Till I have peace with thee, war[1] other men;
And when I have peace, can I leave thee then?
All other wars are scrupulous;[2] only thou
Oh fair free city, may'st thyself allow
5   To any one: In Flanders, who can tell
Whether the master press or men rebel?[3]
Only we know, that which all idiots say,
They bear most blows which come to part the fray.[4]
France in her lunatic giddiness did hate
10 Ever our men, yea and our God of late.[5]
Yet she relies upon our angels[6] well
Which ne'er return; no more than they which fell.
Sick Ireland is with a strange war possess'd[7]
Like to an'ague; now raging, now at rest;
15 Which time will cure: yet it must do her good
If she were purg'd, and her head vein let blood.
And Midas joys our Spanish journeys[8] give,
We touch all gold, but find no food to live.
And I should be in that hot parching clime
20 To dust and ashes turn'd before my time.

8. Soften the wax for others to put their seal upon. Donne also uses this sexual innuendo in "Elegy: To His Mistress Going to Bed," line 32.
9. Though "Love's War" is the traditional title of this elegy, it is not found in any ms.
1. Wage war.
2. I.e., the wars of Mars have rules but the wars of Venus do not.
3. In the Low Countries the Protestants rebel against Spanish oppression.
4. The English suffered defeats in attempting to aid the Dutch.
5. French policy towards Protestants changed with successive kings in the 1590s, and the Huguenot Protestants were often persecuted.
6. English coins borrowed from Elizabeth I.
7. Refers to the uprising in the 1590s of Hugh O'Neill, Earl of Tyrone, using a medical conceit.
8. English privateering raids on Spanish treasure ships, such as the 1596 expedition to Cádiz in which Donne participated.

To mew[9] me in a ship, is to enthrall
Me in a prison, that were like to fall,
Or in a cloister; save that there men dwell
In a calm heaven, here in a swaggering hell.
25 Long voyages are long consumptions,
And ships are carts for executions.
Yea they are deaths: Is't not all one to fly
Into an other world, as 'tis to die?
Here let me war; in these arms let me lie;
30 Here let me parley, batter, bleed, and die.[1]
Thy arms imprison me, and mine arms thee,
Thy heart thy ransom is, take mine for me.
Other men war that they their rest may gain,
But we will rest that we may fight again.
35 Those wars th'ignorant, these th'experienc'd love;
There we are always under, here above.
There engines[2] far off breed a just true fear,
Ne'er thrusts, pikes, stabs, yea bullets hurt not here.
There lies are wrongs; here safe uprightly lie;
40 There men kill men, we'll make one by and by.
Thou nothing; I not half so much shall do
In those wars, as they may which from us two
Shall spring. Thousands we see which travel not
To wars; but stay swords, arms, and shot
45 To make at home: And shall not I do then
More glorious service, staying to make men?

Elegy 8.

To His Mistress Going to Bed.[3]

Come, madam, come, all rest my powers defy;
Until I labor, I in labor lie.[4]
The foe oft times having the foe in sight,
Is tir'd with standing though they never fight.
5 Off with that girdle like heaven's zones[5] glistering,
But a far fairer world encompassing.

9. Enclose.
1. Climax sexually; refers to the belief that sexual emission shortened the length of life; see
"Farewell to Love," line 25.
2. Long-range weapons.
3. This elegy is based on one of Ovid's love elegies describing an afternoon tryst (*Amores*
1.5), but was not published until 1669.
4. Until he gets to work (on her), he will be in the torment of anticipation.
5. This conceit compares her girdle to the Milky Way.

Unpin that spangled breastplate,[6] which you wear
That th'eyes of busy fools may be stopp'd there.
Unlace yourself, for that harmonious chime
10 Tells me from you that now 'tis your <u>bed-time</u>.—*Germain Grear – a domestic arrangement*
Off with that happy busk,[7] whom I envy,
That still can be, and still can stand so nigh.
Your gown's going off, such beauteous state reveals,
As when from flow'ry meads th'hill's shadow steals.
15 Off with your wiry coronet[8] and show
The hairy diadem which on you doth grow.
Now off with those shoes, and then safely tread
In this love's hallow'd temple, this soft bed.
In such white robes, heaven's angels us'd to be
20 Receiv'd by men: Thou, angel bring'st with thee
A heaven like Mahomet's paradise:[9] and though
Ill spirits walk in white, we easily know
By this these angels from an evil sprite:
They set our hairs, but these the flesh upright.
25 Licence my roving hands, and let them go
Behind, before, above, between, below.
O my America, my new found land, *representation of the New World – land is described as virgin body*
My kingdom, safeliest when with one man mann'd,
My mine of precious stones, my empery;[1]
30 How blest am I in this <u>discovering</u> thee! *pun*
To enter in these bonds, is to be free;
Then where my hand is set, my seal[2] shall be.
Full nakedness! All joys are due to thee;
As souls <u>unbodied</u>, <u>bodies</u> <u>uncloth'd</u> must be, *religious*
35 To taste whole joys. Gems which you women use
Are as Atlanta's balls[3] cast in men's views,
That when a fool's eye lighteth on a gem,
His earthly soul may covet theirs, not them.
Like pictures, or like books' gay coverings, made
40 For laymen, are all women thus array'd.
Themselves are mystic <u>books</u>, which only we *scripture*
(Whom their imputed[4] grace will dignify)

6. Her stomacher, or "ornamental covering for the chest (often covered with jewels) worn by women under the lacing of the bodice" (OED 3).
7. Corset.
8. A band of metal worn as part of the woman's head-dress.
9. The Qur'an makes reference to an afterlife that provide sensual pleasures.
1. "Status, dignity, or dominion of an emperor" (OED 1).
2. Device used to imprint wax to signify ownership; here with sexual innuendo; see also "Elegy 6," line 29.
3. Golden apples dropped in a footrace to distract the fleet-footed Atalanta.
4. Refers to the notion that believers must rely on the attribution of Christ's righteousness by vicarious substitution; see Romans 4:6–8.

Must see reveal'd. Then, since I may know,
As liberally as to a midwife show
45 Thy self. Cast all, yea, this white linen hence,
There is no penance, much less innocence:[5]
To teach thee I am naked first: Why then,
What need'st thou have more covering than a man?

line variant
- "due to"
innocence

Elegy 9.[6]

Although thy hand and faith, and good works too
Have seal'd thy love which nothing should undo,
Yea though thou fall back,[7] that apostasy
Confirm thy love; yet much, much I fear thee.
5   Women are like the arts, forc'd unto none,[8]
Open to all searchers, unpriz'd, if unknown.[9]
If I have caught a bird, and let him fly,
Another fowler using those means, as I,
May catch the same bird; and, as these things be,
10 Women are made for men, not him, nor me.
Foxes and goats, all beasts change when they please,
Shall women, more hot, wily, wild than these,
Be bound to one man, and did nature then
Idly make them apter to'endure than men?
15 They'are our clogs,[1] and their own: if a man be
Chain'd to a galley, yet the galley'is free.
Who hath a plowland, casts all his seed corn there,
And yet allows his ground more corn should bear;
Though Danuby into the sea must flow,
20 The sea receives the Rhine, Volga, and Po.
By nature, which gave it, this liberty
Thou lov'st, but Oh canst thou love it and me?
Likeness glues love: then if so thou do,
To make us like[2] and love, must I change too?
25 More than thy hate, I hate'it: rather let me
Allow her change, than change as oft as she,
And so not teach, but force my'opinion,

5. Lines 45–46: Neither a penitent (who would wear white vestments) nor an innocent, she
   should remove her white linen undergarment (or perhaps the sheet).
6. Titled "Change" in the print editions, this elegy is titled "Inconstancy's Encomium" and
   "In the Praise of Change in a Lover" in other mss.
7. Abandon her commitment to another by falling back upon the bed with the poet.
8. Not bound to any one.
9. With a pun on "unknown sexually."
1. A block of wood attached to the leg to impede motion or prevent escape (OED).
2. Alike.

To love not any one, nor every one.
To live in one land, is captivity,
30 To run all countries, a wild roguery.[3]
Waters stink soon, if in one place they bide,
And in the vast sea are worse putrefi'd:[4]
But when they kiss one bank, and leaving this
Never look back, but the next bank do kiss,
35 Then are they purest. Change'is the nursery
Of music, joy, life and eternity.

Elegy 10.

The Anagram.[5]

Marry, and love thy Flavia, for, she
Hath all things, whereby others beauteous be.
For, though her eyes be small, her mouth is great,
Though they[6] be ivory, yet her teeth are jet:
5 Though they[7] be dim, yet she is light enough,
And though her harsh hair fall, her skin is rough;
What though her cheeks be yellow, her hair's red,
Give her thine, and she hath a maidenhead.
These things are beauty's elements: where these
10 Meet in one, that one must, as perfect, please.
If red and white, and each good quality
Be in thy wench, ne'er ask where it doth lie.
In buying things perfum'd, we ask if there
Be musk and amber[8] in it, but not where.
15 Though all her parts be not in th'usual place,
She'hath yet an anagram of a good face.[9]
If we might put the letters but one way,
In that lean dearth of words, what could we say?
When by the gamut some musicians make
20 A perfect song, others will undertake,
By the same gamut chang'd, to equal it.
Things simply good,[1] can never be unfit;
She's fair as any, if all be like her,

3. "A knavish or rascally act" (OED 2, citing this passage).
4. Made salty.
5. In the mss. this is titled variously "Upon an Ugly Gentlewoman," "A Paradox on a Foul Woman," or "The Anagram." Judging by the number of copies, this was the favorite elegy.
6. Her lips.
7. Her eyes.
8. Ambergris, used in perfumery.
9. I.e., the parts of her face can be rearranged.
1. Good in themselves.

And if none be, then she is singular.
25 All love is wonder; if we justly do
Accompt her wonderful, why not lovely too?
Love built on beauty, soon as beauty, dies;
Choose this face, chang'd by no deformities.
Women are all like angels: the fair be
30 Like those which fell to worse; but such as she,
Like to good angels, nothing can impair:
'Tis less grief to be foul, than to'have been fair.
For one night's revels, silk and gold we choose,
But, in long journeys, cloth and leather use.
35 Beauty is barren oft; best husbands say
There is best land, where there is foulest way.[2]
Oh what a sovereign plaster[3] will she be,
If thy past sins have taught thee jealousy!
Here needs no spies, nor eunuchs; her commit
40 Safe to thy foes, yea, to a marmoset.[4]
When Belgia's cities, the round[5] countries drown,
That dirty foulness guards, and arms the town:
So doth her face guard her. And so, for thee,
Which forc'd by business, absent oft must be,
45 She, whose face, like clouds, turns the day to night,
Who, mightier than the sea, makes Moors seem white,
Who, though seven years, she in the stews[6] had laid,
A nunnery durst receive, and think a maid,
And though in childbirth's labor she did lie,
50 Midwives would swear, 'twere but a tympany,[7]
Whom, if she'accuse herself, I credit less
Than witches, which impossibles confess,
Whom dildos, bedstaves, and her velvet glass[8]
Would be as loath to touch as Joseph[9] was:
55 One like none, and lik'd of none, fittest were,
For, things in fashion every man will wear.

2. Lines 35–36: The best husbandmen say the best farmland is found where roads are mud-
diest, with sexual innuendo involving tilling or toiling in the marriage bed.
3. Supreme remedy.
4. Monkeys were popular as women's pets; hence, a contemptuous term for the man (OED
3).
5. I.e., those countries surrounding the Netherlands, which are not flat.
6. Brothels.
7. A morbid swelling of the belly.
8. Lines 53–54 were omitted from the early print editions. *Bedstaves*: "stout sticks or staves
laid (loose) across the bed-stocks in old wooden bedsteads" (OED); *velvet glass*: a hand
mirror with a velvet backing.
9. Joseph refused the advances of Potiphar's wife (Genesis 39:7–20).

Elegy 11.

On His Mistress.[1]

By our first strange and fatal interview,
By all desires which thereof did ensue,
By our long starving hopes, by that remorse[2]
Which my words' masculine persuasive force[3]
5 Begot in thee, and by the memory
Of hurts, which spies and rivals threat'ned me,
I calmly beg. But by thy parents' wrath,
By all pains, which want and divorcement hath,
I conjure thee: And all those oaths which I
10 And thou have sworn to seal joint constancy,
Here I unswear, and overswear them thus:
Thou shalt not love by means so dangerous.
Temper, O fair love, love's impetuous rage,
Be my true mistress still, not my feign'd page.[4]
15 I'll go, and, by thy kind leave, leave behind
Thee, only worthy to nurse in my mind,
Thirst to come back: Oh if thou die before,
From other lands my soul towards thee shall soar,
Thy (else almighty) beauty cannot move
20 Rage from the seas, nor thy love teach them love,
Nor tame wild Boreas'[5] harshness; thou hast read
How roughly he in pieces shivered
Fair Orithea, whom he swore he lov'd.
Fall ill or good, 'tis madness to have prov'd
25 Dangers unurg'd; feed on this flattery,
That absent lovers one in th'other be.
Dissemble nothing, not a boy, nor change
Thy body's habit, nor mind's; be not strange
To thyself only. All will spy in thy face
30 A blushing womanly discovering grace.
Richly cloth'd apes, are call'd apes, and as soon
Eclips'd as bright, we call the moon the moon.
Men of France,[6] changeable chameleons,

---

1. In the mss. some variation of the title "Elegy On His Mistress, Desiring to be Disguised and Go like a Page with Him" is used.
2. Compassion or pity.
3. This phrase, *masculine persuasive force*, has been often used to characterize Donne's style as a love poet in contrast to the idealizations of the Petrarchan tradition.
4. His mistress wishes to accompany him dressed as a boyish page.
5. The north wind who, in desperation, kidnaps a woman after she refuses his gentler wooing.
6. The French were known for fashion-mongering and for amorousness.

Spitals'of diseases,[7] shops of fashions,
35   Love's fuellers, and the rightest company
Of players, which upon the world's stage be,
Will quickly know thee, and know thee, and alas
Th'indifferent Italian,[8] as we pass
His warm land, well content to think thee page,
40   Will haunt thee with such lust, and hideous rage,
As Lot's fair guests[9] were vex'd. But none of these
Nor spongy'hydroptic[1] Dutch shall thee displease,
If thou stay here. O stay here, for, for thee
England is only'a worthy gallery,[2]
45   To walk in expectation, till from thence
Our great king[3] call thee into his presence.
When I am gone, dream me some happiness,
Nor let thy looks our long-hid love confess,
Nor praise, nor dispraise me, bless nor curse
50   Openly love's force, nor in bed fright thy nurse
With midnight's startings, crying out, "Oh, oh
Nurse, Oh my love is slain: I saw him go
O'er the white Alps alone; I saw him, I,
Assail'd, fight, taken, stabb'd, bleed, fall, and die."
55   Augur me better chance,[4] except dread Jove
Think it enough for me, to'have had thy love.

Elegy 12.

On His Picture.[5]

Here take my picture, though I bid farewell;
Thine, in my heart, where my soul dwells, shall dwell.
'Tis like me now, but I dead, 'twill be more
When we are shadows both, than 'twas before.
5   When weatherbeaten I come back:[6] my hand
Perchance with rude oars torn, or sun beams tann'd,
My face and breast of haircloth, and my head

7. Carriers of venereal diseases.
8. Italians are described as indifferently heterosexual or homosexual, in either case, endangering her.
9. Angels in disguise. Lot's guests were pursued sexually by the Sodomites (Genesis 18–19).
1. Insatiably thirsty.
2. Entrance hall where she could be seen and praised.
3. God.
4. Predict for me a better fortune (than death).
5. In the mss. some variation of the title "On His Picture which He Left with His Mistress when He Went to Travail" is often used.
6. May refer to the 1596 expedition to Cádiz in which Donne participated.

With care's rash sudden hoariness o'erspread,
My body'a sack of bones, broken within,
10   And powder's[7] blue stains scatter'd on my skin:
If rival fools tax thee to'have lov'd a man,
So foul and coarse, as, Oh I may seem then,
This shall say what I was: and thou shalt say,
"Do his hurts reach me? doth my worth decay?
15   Or do they[8] reach his judging mind, that he
Should like'and love less, what he did love to see?
That which in him was fair and delicate,
Was but the milk, which in love's childish state
Did nurse it: who now is grown strong enough
20   To feed on that, which to'disus'd[9] tastes seems tough."

Elegy 14.

Love's Progress.[1]

Whoever loves, if he do not propose
The right true end of love,[2] he's one which goes
To sea for nothing but to make him sick.
And love is a bear-whelp born;[3] if we o'er-lick
5   Our love, and force it new strange shapes to take,
We err, and of a lump a monster make.
Were not a calf a monster, that were grown
Fac'd like a man, though better than his own?
Perfection is in unity: prefer
10   One woman first, and then one thing in her.
I, when I value gold, may think upon
The ductileness,[4] the application,
The wholesomeness, the ingenuity,
From rust, from soil, from fire ever free.
15   But if I love it, 'tis because 'tis made
By our new nature, use,[5] the soul of trade.
All these[6] in women we might think upon
(If women had them) but yet love but one.

7. Gunpowder's.
8. His hurts.
9. Unaccustomed.
1. The title refers to an expedition or state journey made by a royal or noble personage (OED 2).
2. The poet's claim that sexual intercourse was the true goal is meant to shock.
3. Bears were believed to lick their unformed whelps or cubs into shape after birth.
4. Pliability.
5. Custom or habit.
6. Qualities of gold.

Can men more injure women than to say
20   They love them for that, by which they're not they?
Makes virtue woman? must I cool my blood
Till I both be, and find one wise and good?
May barren angels love so.[7] But if we
Make love to woman, virtue is not she,
25   As beauty'is not, nor wealth: He that strays thus
From her to hers[8] is more adulterous
Than if he took her maid. Search every sphere
And firmament, our Cupid is not there:
He's an infernal god, and under ground
30   With Pluto dwells, where gold and fire abound.
Men to such gods their sacrificing coals
Did not in altars lay, but pits and holes.
Although we see celestial bodies move
Above the earth, the earth we till and love:
35   So we her airs contemplate, words and heart,
And virtues; but we love the centric part.[9]
Nor is the soul more worthy, or more fit
For love, than this, as infinite as it.
But in attaining this desired place
40   How much they stray, that set out at the face.[1]
The hair a forest is of ambushes,
Of springes,[2] snares, fetters, and manacles.
The brow becalms us when 'tis smooth and plain,
And when 'tis wrinkled, shipwrecks us again;
45   Smooth, 'tis a paradise, where we would have
Immortal stay, and wrinkled 'tis our grave.
The nose, like to the first meridian,[3] runs
Not 'twixt an east and west, but 'twixt two suns;
It leaves a cheek, a rosy hemisphere,
50   On either side, and then directs us where
Upon the Islands Fortunate[4] we fall,
(Not faint Canary, but ambrosial)[5]
Her swelling lips, to which when we are come,
We anchor there, and think ourselves at home:

---

7. In "The Relic" lines 25–26, the poet opines that angels are without gender; here, he disparages them as "barren," i.e., pure spirits without bodies.
8. From her essence to her mere qualities.
9. The genitals.
1. Lines 39–72 develop a witty conceit involving the exploration of the woman's body.
2. Snares for catching birds.
3. The first circle of longitude dividing the two hemispheres.
4. The Fortunate Isles of Greek mythology were thought to be in the west and were sometimes identified as the Canary Islands, off the west coast of Africa.
5. Fragrant with ambrosia, the drink of the gods.

55   For they seem all: there Sirens' songs,[6] and there
      Wise Delphic oracles[7] do fill the ear.
      There, in a creek, where chosen pearls do swell,
      The remora, her cleaving tongue, doth dwell.
      These and the glorious promontory, her chin,
60   O'erpast; and the straight Hellespont between
      The Sestos and Abydos[8] of her breasts,
      Not of two lovers, but two loves, the nests,
      Succeeds a boundless sea; but that thine eye
      Some island moles may scatter'd there descry:
65   And sailing towards her India,[9] in that way
      Shall at her fair Atlantic navel stay.
      Though thence the current be thy pilot made,[1]
      Yet ere thou be, where thou wouldst be embay'd,
      Thou shalt upon another forest set,
70   Where some do shipwreck, and no further get.
      When thou art there, consider what this chase
      Misspent by thy beginning at the face.
      Rather set out below; practice my art;
      Some symmetry[2] the foot hath with that part
75   Which thou dost seek, and is thy map for that,
      Lovely enough to stop, but not stay at.
      Least subject to disguise, and change it is;
      Men say the devil never can change his;[3]
      It is the emblem[4] which hath figured
80   Firmness; 'tis the first part that comes to bed.
      Civility, we see, refin'd the kiss,
      Which, at the face begun, transplanted is
      Since to the hand, since to th'imperial knee,
      Now at the papal foot delights to be.[5]
85   If kings think that the nearer way, and do
      Rise from the foot, lovers may do so too.
      For as free spheres move faster far than can
      Birds, whom the air resists, so may that man

---

6. The Sirens were beautiful maidens who lured mariners to their death in the *Odyssey*.
7. An ancient oracle at Delphi, Greece.
8. Leander swam across the Hellespont from Abydos in Asia to Sestos in Europe to meet Hero.
9. India, here used as a symbol of precious spices and wealth.
1. I.e., once at her navel, the current will take you to port.
2. Correspondence or likeness.
3. The devil's cloven foot could not be disguised.
4. I.e., the foot is used to represent constancy in emblem literature.
5. Lines 82–84: Gardner (1965, p. 135) explains that a kiss on the face occurs between equals, a kiss on the hand acknowledges superiority, a kiss on the knees signifies feudal service, and a kiss on the toe indicates total subservience.

Which goes this empty and ethereal way,
90 Than if at beauty's elements he stay.
Rich Nature in woman wisely made
Two purses,[6] and their mouths aversely laid,
They then which to the lower tribute owe,
That way, which that exchequer[7] looks, must go:
95 He which doth not, his error is as great,
As who by clyster[8] gave the stomach meat.

Elegy.

Sappho to Philænis.[9]

Where is that holy fire,[1] which verse is said
    To have, is that enchanting force decay'd?
Verse that draws[2] nature's works, from nature's law,
    Thee, her best work, to her work cannot draw.
5 Have my tears quench'd my old poetic fire?
    Why quench'd they not as well that of desire?
Thoughts, my mind's creatures, often are with thee,
    But I, their maker, want their liberty;
Only thine image, in my heart, doth sit,
10   But that is wax, and fires environ it.
My fires have driven, thine have drawn it[3] hence;
    And I am rob'd of picture, heart, and sense.
Dwells with me still mine irksome memory,
    Which, both to keep, and lose grieves equally.
15 That tells me'how fair thou art: Thou art so fair,
    As gods, when gods to thee I do compare,
Are grac'd thereby; and to make blind men see,
    What things gods are, I say they'are like to thee.
For, if we justly call each silly[4] man
20   A little world,[5] what shall we call thee then?
Thou art not soft, and clear, and straight, and fair,

6. The mouth and the vulva.
7. The office charged with the receipt and custody of the moneys collected by the several departments of revenue (OED 4); here, another term for the *purse* to which tribute is owed.
8. An enema.
9. Based on Ovid's erotic letters between famous lovers (the *Heroides*), this elegy is one of the earliest female homosexual poems in English. Sappho, the Greek poet (fl. 600 B.C.E.), is writing here to a young girl (*Philænis* means "female friend").
1. Poetic inspiration; also, the power of language to charm and persuade.
2. Copies or imitates.
3. Both the image of Philænis and Sappho's heart.
4. Deserving of pity, compassion; or, unlearned, unsophisticated, simple (OED).
5. The microcosm.

As down, as stars, cedars, and lilies are,
But thy right hand, and cheek, and eye only
Are like thy other hand, and cheek, and eye.
25 Such was my Phao[6] awhile, but shall be never,
As thou, wast, art, and, oh, may'st be ever.
Here lovers swear in their idolatry,
That I am such; but grief discolors me.
And yet I grieve the less, lest grief remove
30 My beauty, and make me'unworthy of thy love.
Plays some soft boy with thee, Oh there wants[7] yet
A mutual feeling, which should sweeten it.
His chin, a thorny hairy unevenness
Doth threaten, and some daily change possess.
35 Thy body is a natural paradise,
In whose self, unmanur'd,[8] all pleasure lies,
Nor needs perfection; why should'st thou then
Admit the tillage of a harsh rough man?
Men leave behind them that which their sin shows,[9]
40 And are, as thieves trac'd, which rob when it snows.
But of our dalliance no more signs there are,
Than fishes leave in streams, or birds in air.
And between us all sweetness may be had;
All, all that nature yields, or art can add.
45 My two lips, eyes, thighs, differ from thy two,
But so, as thine from one another do:
And, oh, no more; the likeness being such,
Why should they not alike in all parts touch?
Hand to strange hand, lip to lip none denies;
50 Why should they breast to breast, or thighs to thighs?
Likeness begets such strange self flattery,
That touching my self[1] all seems done to thee.
My self I'embrace, and mine own hands I kiss,
And amorously thank my self for this.
55 Me, in my glass,[2] I call thee; but alas,
When I would kiss, tears dim mine eyes, and glass.
O cure this loving madness, and restore
Me to me; thee my half, my all, my more.
So may thy cheeks' red outwear[3] scarlet dye,
60 And their white, whiteness of the galaxy,

6. Phaon was a young ferryman Sappho loved unrequitedly.
7. Is lacking.
8. Not cultivated, untilled.
9. Children.
1. Auto-eroticism.
2. Mirror.
3. Outlive.

So may thy mighty amazing beauty move
  Envy'in all women, and in all men love,
And so be change and sickness far from thee,
  As thou by coming near, keep'st them from me.

Epithalamion Made at Lincoln's Inn.[4]

  The sunbeams in the east are spread;
Leave, leave, fair bride, your solitary bed;
No more shall you return to it alone;
It nurseth sadness, and your body's print,
5   Like to a grave, the yielding down doth dint;[5]
You and your other you meet there anon.
Put forth, put forth that warm balm-breathing thigh,
Which when next time you in these sheets will smother,
  There it must meet another,
10   Which never was, but must be oft more nigh.
Come glad from thence, go gladder than you came;
Today put on perfection[6] and a woman's name.

  Daughters of London, you which be
Our golden mines and furnish'd treasury;
15   You which are angels, yet still bring with you
Thousands of angels[7] on your marriage days,
Help with your presence and device to praise
These rites, which also unto you grow due;
Conceitedly dress her, and be assign'd,
20   By you fit place for every flower and jewel;
  Make her for love fit fuel,
As gay as Flora[8] and as rich as Ind;
So may she fair, rich, glad, in nothing lame,
Today put on perfection and a woman's name.

25   And you frolic patricians,
Sons of these senators, wealth's deep oceans;
Ye painted courtiers, barrels of others' wits;
Ye countrymen, who but your beasts love none;

---

4. This is a marriage song written perhaps for a mock wedding at Lincoln's Inn (where Donne studied law from 1592 to 1595); it may have been inspired by Spenser's "Epithalamion," published in 1595.
5. Make a dent or impression.
6. Women are imperfect without men, so they put on perfection when they marry; see "The Primrose," line 25.
7. The gold coins of their dowries.
8. Goddess of flowers and the spring.

Ye of those fellowships, whereof he's one,
30 Of study, and play, made strange hermaphrodites,[9]
Here shine: This bridegroom to the temple bring.
Lo, in yon path which store of strew'd flowers graceth,
The sober virgin paceth;
Except my sight fail, 'tis no other thing.
35 Weep not, nor blush; here is no grief nor shame,
Today put on perfection and a woman's name.

Thy two-leaved gates, fair temple, unfold,
And these two in thy sacred bosom hold,
Till, mystically join'd,[1] but one they be:
40 Then may thy lean, and hunger-starved womb
Long time expect their bodies and their tomb,
Long after their own parents fatten thee.
All elder claims, and all cold barrenness,
All yielding to new loves, be far for ever,
45 Which might these two dissever.
Always, all th'other may each one possess,
For the best bride, best worthy of prayer and fame,
Today puts on perfection and a woman's name.

Oh winter days bring much delight,
50 Not for themselves, but for they soon bring night.
Other sweets wait thee than these divers meats,
Other disports than dancing jollities,
Other love-tricks than glancing with the eyes,
But that the sun still in our half sphere sweats.
55 He flies in winter, but now he stands still.
Yet shadows turn;[2] noon point he hath attain'd;
His steeds nill be restrain'd,
But gallop lively down the western hill.
Thou shalt, when he hath run the world's half frame,
60 Tonight put on perfection and a woman's name.

The amorous evening star[3] is rose,
Why should not then our amorous star inclose
Herself in her wish'd bed? Release your strings
Musicians, and dancers take some truce

---

9. A creature combining opposite qualities; here, the propensity for study and play. Also, if
   the poem is for a mock wedding, then it may also refer to the man "playing" the role of
   the bride.
1. Ephesians 5:31: "a man . . . shall be joined unto his wife, and they two shall be one flesh."
2. After noon shadows lie in the opposite direction.
3. Venus is both the evening and morning star, because it is closer to the sun than the earth
   so never appears very far from the sun in the sky.

65 With these your pleasing labors, for great use
    As much weariness as perfection brings.
    You, and not only you, but all toil'd beasts
    Rest duly; at night all their toils are dispensed;
    But in their beds commenced
70 Are other labors and more dainty feasts.
    She goes a maid, who, lest she turn the same,
    Tonight puts on perfection and a woman's name.

        Thy virgin's girdle now untie
    And in thy nuptial bed, love's altar, lie
75 A pleasing sacrifice: Now dispossess
    Thee of these chains and robes, which were put on
    T'adorn the day, not thee; for thou alone,
    Like virtue, and truth, art best in nakedness.
    This bed is only to virginity
80 A grave, but to a better state a cradle.
    Till now thou wast but able
    To be what now thou art; then that by thee
    No more be said, "I may be," but "I am,"
    Tonight put on perfection and a woman's name.

85   Even like a faithful man content
    That this life for a better should be spent,
    So she a mother's rich style[4] doth prefer,
    And at the bridegroom's wish'd approach doth lie,
    Like an appointed lamb, when tenderly
90 The priest comes on his knees to'embowel[5] her.
    Now sleep or watch with more joy: and O light
    Of heaven, tomorrow rise thou hot and early;
    This sun will love so dearly
    Her rest, that long, long we shall want[6] her sight.
95 Wonders are wrought, for she, which had no maim,[7]
    Tonight puts on perfection and a woman's name.

---

4. Distinguishing or qualifying title (OED 18b).
5. The priest comes to disembowel the lamb; the bridegroom comes to enter her (sexually, or perhaps her affections, as the *bowels* were considered the seat of the tender emotions).
6. Lack.
7. I.e., to her virginity.

Verse Letters to Several Personages

The Storm.

To Mr. Christopher Brooke.[1]

Thou, which art I[2] ('tis nothing to be so),
Thou which art still thyself, by these[3] shalt know
Part of our passage; and a hand or eye
By Hilliard[4] drawn, is worth an history,
5 By a worse painter made; and (without pride)
When by thy judgment they are dignified,
My lines are such. 'Tis the pre-eminence
Of friendship only to'impute excellence.
England, to'whom we owe what we be, and have,
10 Sad that her sons did seek a foreign grave
(For fate's, or fortune's drifts, none can soothsay;
Honor and misery have one face and way)
From out her pregnant entrails sigh'd a wind
Which at th'air's middle marble room[5] did find
15 Such strong resistance, that itself it threw
Downward again; and so when it did view
How in the port our fleet dear time did leese,[6]
Withering like prisoners which lie but for fees,[7]
Mildly it kiss'd our sails, and fresh and sweet
20 As to a stomach starv'd, whose insides meet,

---

1. Christopher Brooke (c. 1570–1628) was one of Donne's closest friends and a fellow student at Lincoln's Inn; he later helped Donne to elope in 1601. The storm took place during the Islands Expedition to the Azores of July 1597 in search of Spanish treasure; the fleet was beset by a tremendous storm and had to return to England for refitting.
2. Because two become one through friendship.
3. The lines of this verse letter.
4. Nicholas Hilliard (1537–1619), the first English miniature painter.
5. Aristotle's *Meteorologica* held that *meteors* and other exhalations were engendered in the middle region of the air because of the intense cold by *antiperistasis*—i.e., cold driven upward by the reflected heat of the sun's rays.
6. Lose.
7. Having served time in jail, they are still detained because they cannot pay fees or debts owed their jailers.

Meat comes, it came; and swole our sails, when we
So joy'd, as Sarah'her swelling joy'd to see.[8]
But 'twas but so kind as our countrymen
Which bring friends one day's way, and leave them then.
25 Then, like two mighty kings, which dwelling far
Asunder, meet against a third to war,
The south and west winds join'd, and as they blew,
Waves like a rolling trench before them threw.
Sooner than you read this line, did the gale,
30 Like shot, not fear'd till felt, our sails assail.
And what at first was call'd a gust, the same
Hath now a storm's, anon a tempest's name.
Jonas, I pity thee, and curse those men
Who when the storm rag'd most, did wake thee then.[9]
35 Sleep is pain's easiest salve, and doth fulfil
All offices of death, except to kill.
But when I waked, I saw that I saw not.
I, and the sun, which should teach me, had forgot
East, west, day, night; and I could but say,
40 If the'world had lasted, now it had been day.
Thousands our noises were, yet we 'mongst all
Could none by his right name, but thunder call.
Lightning was all our light, and it rain'd more
Than if the sun had drunk the sea before.
45 Some coffin'd in their cabins lie, equally
Griev'd that they are not dead, and yet must die.
And as sin-burden'd souls from graves will creep
At the last day, some forth their cabins peep,
And trembling ask, "What news?" and do hear so
50 Like jealous husbands, what they would not know.
Some sitting on the hatches would seem there
With hideous gazing to fear away fear.
There note they the ship's sicknesses, the mast
Shak'd with an ague, and the hold and waist[1]
55 With a salt dropsy clogg'd, and all our tacklings
Snapping, like too high-stretch'd treble strings.
And from our tatter'd sails rags drop down so
As from one hang'd in chains a year ago.
Even our ordnance placed for our defense,
60 Strive to break loose, and 'scape away from thence.

8. Sarah, the wife of Abraham, rejoiced in her pregnancy after many years of barrenness (see
   Genesis 17–21).
9. When the storm struck, Jonah was awakened by the sailors who wanted to know who
   caused the evil (Jonah 1:5–6).
1. "The middle part of the upper deck of a ship, between the quarter-deck and the forecastle"
   (OED 3); water was slow to run off, and the *waist* was often *clogg'd*.

Pumping hath tir'd our men, and what's the gain?
Seas into seas thrown, we suck in again;
Hearing hath deaf'd our sailors, and if they
Knew how to hear, there's none knows what to say.
65 Compar'd to these storms, death is but a qualm,[2]
Hell somewhat lightsome, and the Bermudas calm.
Darkness, light's elder brother,[3] his birthright
Claims o'er this world, and to heaven hath chas'd light.
All things are one: and that one none can be,
70 Since all forms uniform deformity
Doth cover; so that we, except God say
Another *Fiat*, shall have no more day.
So violent, yet long these furies be,
That though thine absence starve me, I wish not thee.

The Calm.[4]

Our storm is past, and that storm's tyrannous rage,
A stupid calm, but nothing it, doth 'suage.
The fable is inverted, and far more
A block afflicts, now, than a stork before.[5]
5 Storms chafe, and soon wear out themselves, or us;
In calms, heaven laughs to see us languish thus.
As steady'as I can wish my thoughts were,
Smooth as thy mistress' glass, or what shines there,
The sea is now. And, as these Isles[6] which we
10 Seek, when we can move, our ships rooted be.
As water did in storms, now pitch runs out
As lead, when a fir'd church becomes one spout.[7]
And all our beauty and our trim decays,
Like courts removing, or like ended plays.
15 The fighting place, now seamen's rags supply;
And all the tackling is a frippery.[8]

---

2. "A (sudden) feeling or fit of faintness, illness, or sickness" (OED 3).
3. Since darkness existed before light at the divine *Fiat* (Let there be) at the Creation (Gen 1:2–3).
4. After refitting following the storm, the fleet was divided; the squadron in which Donne sailed was becalmed.
5. In the fable, the frogs ask Zeus for a king and are given a block of wood instead; after complaining about its immobility, they are given a stork which devours them. The ship has become a motionless block.
6. The Azores, an archipelago of Portuguese Islands in the middle of the Atlantic Ocean. "Glass" (line 8): mirror.
7. The pitch used to caulk the seams of the boat now melts from the heat like the lead roof of a church on fire.
8. "A place where cast-off clothes are sold" (OED 3); the decks and rigging are now used to launder clothing.

No use of lanthorns;[9] and in one place lay
Feathers and dust, today and yesterday.
Earth's hollownesses, which the world's lungs are,
20 Have no more wind than th'upper vault of air.
We can nor left friends[1] nor sought foes recover,
But meteor-like, save that we move not, hover.
Only the calenture[2] together draws
Dear friends, which meet dead in great fishes' jaws;
25 And on the hatches as on altars lies
Each one, his own priest, and own sacrifice.
Who live, that miracle do multiply
Where walkers in hot ovens do not die.[3]
If in despite of these we swim, that hath
30 No more refreshing than a brimstone bath;
But from the sea into the ship we turn,
Like parboil'd wretches, on the coals to burn.
Like Bajazet encag'd, the shepherds' scoff,[4]
Or like slack sinew'd Samson, his hair off,
35 Languish our ships. Now, as a myriad
Of ants durst th'emperor's loved snake invade,[5]
The crawling galleys, sea-jails,[6] finny chips,
Might brave our pinnaces,[7] now bed-rid ships.
Whether a rotten state, and hope of gain,
40 Or to disuse me from the queasy pain
Of being belov'd and loving, or the thirst
Of honor or fair death, out-push'd me first,
I lose my end: for here, as well as I,
A desperate may live, and a coward die.
45 Stag, dog, and all which from, or towards flies,
Is paid with life, or prey, or doing dies.[8]
Fate grudges us all, and doth subtly lay
A scourge, 'gainst which we all forget to pray.
He that at sea prays for more wind, as well

9. Variation of lantern (OED).
1. The others squadrons of the fleet.
2. A fever frequently suffered by sailors in the tropics, which induces the delusion that the
   sea is a green field into which they can leap (OED).
3. Three children who were thrown into a furnace by Nebuchadnezzar but miraculously
   survived (Daniel 3:20–30).
4. In Marlowe's *Tamburlaine* (4.2), the former shepherd Tamburlaine keeps the Turkish
   emperor Bajazet in a cage to be mocked.
5. The historian Suetonius relates that Tiberius's pet snake was devoured by an army of ants,
   which the emperor interpreted as a warning to avoid offending the plebeians.
6. Galleys were propelled by oars, often manned by prisoners, so they appear to crawl, but
   even these move faster than becalmed ships.
7. Light crafts used to bring provisions to other ships; here, they stay near their mother ship,
   like bed-ridden patients.
8. Lines 45–46: A *stag*, which flies from death, is paid with life; a *dog*, which flies toward its
   prey, is rewarded or meets its death.

50 Under the poles may beg cold, heat in hell.
   What are we then? How little more, alas,
   Is man now, than before he was? He was
   Nothing; for us, we are for nothing fit;
   Chance, or ourselves still disproportion it.
55 We have no power, no will, no sense. I lie.
   I should not then thus feel this misery.

To Sir Henry Wotton.[9]

Here's no more news than virtue:[1] 'I may as well
Tell you Cales, or Saint Michael's tale for news,[2] as tell
That vice doth here habitually dwell.

Yet as, to'get stomachs,[3] we walk up and down,
5 And toil to sweeten rest; so, may God frown,
If, but to loathe both, I haunt court or town.

For here no one's from th'extremity
Of vice by any other reason free,
But that the next to'him, still is worse than he.

10 In this world's warfare, they whom rugged Fate
   (God's commissary)[4] doth so thoroughly hate,
   As in'the court's squadron to marshal their state:[5]

If they stand arm'd with silly[6] honesty,
With wishing prayers, and neat integrity,
15 Like Indians 'gainst Spanish hosts they be.

Suspicious boldness to this place belongs,
And to'have as many ears as all have tongues;
Tender to know, tough to acknowledge wrongs.

9. Henry Wotton (1568–1639), a friend of Donne's from Oxford, was also at one of the Inns
   of Court; he became a secretary to Essex and was on the Cádiz and Islands expeditions.
   He was later knighted and had the sort of career to which Donne at first aspired. The
   Dolau Cothi Ms. dates this poem 20 July 1598 from Court. Earlier that month the Queen
   had struck Essex at a Council meeting who left in anger with sword half drawn.
1. I.e., there is no more new news here than there is virtue.
2. *Cales* is a form of Cádiz; the Isles of St. Michael are the Azores; both were old news to
   Wotton.
3. Appetites.
4. A delegate or deputy.
5. Line 12: As to put them among those jockeying for place at court.
6. Simple, innocent.

Believe me, Sir, in my youth's giddiest days,
20   When to be like the court was a play's praise,
Plays were not so like courts, as courts'are like plays.

Then let us at these mimic antics[7] jest,
Whose deepest projects and egregious guests
Are but dull morals of a game at chests.[8]

25   But now 'tis incongruity to smile.
Therefore I end: And bid farewell awhile;
At Court,[9] though From Court were the better style.

To Sir Henry Wotton.

Sir, more than kisses, letters mingle souls:
For thus, friends absent speak. This ease controls[1]
The tediousness of my life: But for these
I could ideate[2] nothing which could please,
5   But I should wither in one day and pass
To'a bottle[3] of hay, that am a lock of grass.
      Life is a voyage, and in our life's ways
Countries, courts, towns are rocks or remoras.[4]
They break or stop all ships, yet our state's such,
10   That though than pitch they stain worse, we must touch.
If in the furnace of the even line,[5]
Or under th'adverse[6] icy poles thou pine,
Thou know'st two temperate regions girded in
Dwell there: But, oh, what refuge canst thou win
15   Parch'd in the court, and in the country frozen?
Shall cities built of both extremes be chosen?
Can dung and garlic be'a perfume? Or can
A scorpion and torpedo[7] cure a man?
Cities are worst of all three: Of all three
20   (O knotty riddle) each is worst equally.

7. Courtiers posturing as zany eccentrics.
8. Analogies drawn from the game of chess were not uncommon.
9. He signs his letter "At Court" though he would rather be far from it.
1. Relieves.
2. Form an idea of.
3. Bundle.
4. The sucking-fish was believed capable of stopping the course of any ship by attaching itself to the rudder or keel; here, impediments.
5. Equator.
6. Opposite to each other.
7. The torpedo, or numb-fish, caused numbness to humans. The point is that two noxious things cannot be combined beneficially, like dung and garlic into a perfume.

Cities are sepulchers; they who dwell there
Are carcases, as if no such[8] there were.
And courts are theaters, where some men play
Princes; some slaves; all to'one end, and of one clay.
25 The country is a desert, where no good
Gain'd, as habits, not born, is understood.
There men become beasts, and prone to more evils;
In cities, blocks,[9] and in a lewd court, devils.
As in the first chaos, confusedly
30 Each element's qualities were in th'other three,[1]
So pride, lust, covetise,[2] being several
To these three places, yet all are in all,
And mingled thus, their issue incestuous.
Falsehood is denizen'd;[3] virtue is barbarous.
35 Let no man say there, "Virtue's flinty wall
Shall lock vice in me. I'll do none, but know all."
Men are sponges, which, to pour out, receive;
Who know false play, rather than lose, deceive.
For in best understandings sin began,
40 Angels sinn'd first, then devils, and then man.
Only perchance beasts sin not; wretched we
Are beasts in all but white integrity.
I think, if men, which in these places live,
Durst look for themselves, and themselves retrieve,
45 They would like strangers greet themselves, seeing then
Utopian youth, grown old Italian.[4]
        Be then thine own home, and in thyself dwell;
Inn anywhere; continuance[5] maketh hell.
And seeing the snail, which everywhere doth roam,
50 Carrying his own house still, still is at home,
Follow (for he is easy pac'd) this snail;
Be thine own palace, or the world's thy jail.
And in the world's sea, do not like cork sleep
Upon the water's face; nor in the deep
55 Sink like a lead without a line; but as
Fishes glide, leaving no print where they pass,
Nor making sound, so closely thy course go,
Let men dispute, whether thou breathe or no.

8. No such people.
9. Blockheads.
1. In the primordial chaos, all four elements converted continuously into each other in con-
fusion.
2. Ardent, excessive, or inordinate desire (OED); now obsolete.
3. Naturalized, or given the rights of citizenship to a place.
4. An idealistic youth grown into a degenerate adult.
5. Continuing in any one place.

Only in this one thing be no Galenist.[6] To make
60 Courts' hot ambitions wholesome, do not take
A dram of country's dullness; do not add
Correctives, but, as chemics,[7] purge the bad.
But, Sir, I advise not you; I rather do
Say o'er those lessons, which I learn'd of you.
65 Whom, free from Germany's schisms, and lightness
Of France, and fair Italy's faithlessness,
Having from these suck'd all they had of worth,
And brought home that faith which you carried forth,
I throughly[8] love. But if myself I'have won
70 To know my rules, I have, and you have
                                        Donne.

To Mr. R[owland]. W[oodward].[9]

Like one who'in her third widowhood doth profess
Herself a nun, tir'd to'a retiredness,
So affects my Muse now a chaste fallowness,[1]

Since she to few, yet to too many'hath shown,
5 How love-song weeds and satiric thorns are grown,
Where seeds of better arts[2] were early sown.

Though to use and love poetry, to me
Betroth'd to no'one art, be no'adultery;
Omissions of good, ill, as ill deeds be.[3]

10 For though to us it seem,'and be light and thin,
Yet in those faithful scales[4] where God throws in
Men's works, vanity weighs as much as sin.

6. A follower of Galen, who believed disease was a general imbalance in the body's humoral
   system that could be remedied by its contrary—e.g., an excess of the hot quality could be
   tempered with something cold.
7. A follower of Paracelsus, who believed that disease was localized in a part of the body; he
   assumed that the poison that caused a disease would also cure it if administered properly
   (as twentieth-century immunization theory upholds), usually with prepared chemicals.
   Donne advised Wotton not to try to balance the evils of court with country life, but to
   purge himself of it altogether.
8. Thoroughly.
9. Rowland Woodward (1573–1637) was a close friend of Donne's who was with him at
   Lincoln's Inn; as the scribe for the Westmoreland Ms. (prepared for his employer, the earl
   of Westmoreland), he is an authoritative source for Donne's poems. This verse letter was
   apparently written in response to a request for poems.
1. A period of unproductivity.
2. The verse letters; *love-song weeds*: his elegies and other love poems; *satiric thorns*: his
   satires.
3. Not doing good is as bad as doing bad deeds.
4. Scales of justice.

If our souls have stain'd their first white, yet we
May clothe them with faith and dear honesty,[5]
15   Which God imputes as native purity.

There is no virtue but religion.
Wise, valiant, sober, just, are names, which none
Want, which want not vice-covering discretion.[6]

Seek we then ourselves in ourselves; for as
20   Men force the sun with much more force to pass,
By gathering his beams with a crystal glass,[7]

So we, if we into ourselves will turn,
Blowing our sparks of virtue, may out-burn[8]
The straw which doth about our hearts sojourn.

25   You know physicians, when they would infuse
Into any'oil the soul of simples,[9] use
Places, where they may lie still warm, to choose.[1]

So works retiredness[2] in us. To roam
Giddily and be everywhere but at home
30   Such freedom doth a banishment become.

We are but farmers[3] of ourselves, yet may,
If we can stock ourselves, and thrive, up lay
Much, much dear treasure for the great rent day.[4]

Manure thyself then, to thyself be'approv'd;
35   And with vain outward things be no more mov'd,
But to know that I love thee'and would be lov'd.

---

5. Righteousness.
6. Lines 16–18: These cardinal virtues (prudence, fortitude, temperance, and justice) are
mere names that anyone can claim, even those who are covering up their vices discreetly.
7. Magnifying glass.
8. Burn out or burn away.
9. Herbs uncompounded or unmixed though they might be infused into an oil (as here).
1. I.e., choose places where they may be heated constantly.
2. Retirement from London or the court.
3. Cultivators.
4. The Day of Judgment.

To Mr. T[homas]. W[oodward].[5]

Haste thee harsh verse as fast as thy lame measure
Will give thee leave, to him, my pain and pleasure.
I've given thee, and yet thou art too weak,
Feet, and a reasoning soul, and tongue to speak.
5   Plead for me, and so by thine and my labor
I'm thy creator, thou my savior.
Tell him, all questions which men have defended[6]
Both of the place and pains of hell are ended;
And 'tis decreed our hell is but privation[7]
10   Of him, at least in this earth's habitation:
And 'tis where I am, where in every street
Infections[8] follow, overtake, and meet.
Live I or die, by you my love is sent,
And you'are my pawns, or else my testament.[9]

To Mr. T[homas]. W[oodward].

Pregnant again with th'old twins, hope and fear,
Oft have I asked for thee, both how and where
Thou wert, and what my hopes of letters were.

As in our streets sly beggars narrowly
5   Mark motions of the giver's hand and eye,
And evermore conceive some hope thereby.

And now thine alms is given, thy letter's read,
The body risen again, the which was dead,[1]
And thy poor starveling bountifully fed.

10   After this banquet my soul doth say grace,
And praise thee for't, and zealously embrace
Thy love, though I think thy love in this case
    To be as gluttons, which say 'midst their meat,[2]
    They love that best of which they most do eat.

---

5. Thomas Woodward (b. 1576), younger brother of Rowland.
6. Debated.
7. Privation of the presence of God is hell.
8. The plague was rampant in 1592–93.
9. His verses are the pledges of love, if he survives the plague, or else his last will.
1. Dead because the poet has not heard from T. W.
2. Meal.

To Mr. E[verard]. G[uilpin].[3]

Even as lame things thirst[4] their perfection, so
The slimy rhymes[5] bred in our vale below,
Bearing with them much of my love and heart,
Fly unto that Parnassus[6] where thou art.
5   There thou o'erseest London: Here I have been,
By staying in London, too much overseen.
Now pleasure's dearth our city doth possess;
Our theaters are fill'd with emptiness.[7]
As lank and thin is every street and way
10 As a woman deliver'd yesterday.
Nothing whereat to laugh my spleen[8] espies
But bearbaitings or law exercise.
Therefore I'll leave it, and in the country strive
Pleasure, now fled from London, to retrieve.
15 Do thou so too; and fill not like a bee
Thy thighs with honey, but as plenteously
As Russian merchants thyself's whole vessel load,
And then at winter retail it here abroad.
Bless us with Suffolk's sweets; and as that is
Thy garden, make thy hive and warehouse this.[9]

To Mr. S. B.[1]

O thou which to search out the secret parts
    Of th'India, or rather Paradise
    Of knowledge, hast with courage and advice
Lately launch'd into the vast sea of arts;[2]
5   Disdain not in thy constant travailing
    To do as other voyagers, and make

3. Usually identified as Everard Guilpin (b. 1572), poet and satirist, author of *Skialethia* (1598).
4. Long for.
5. Plays on the notion, advanced by Pliny, that small creatures were generated spontaneously by the sun in the mud of the Nile.
6. The mountain on which the muses roamed; Guilpin lived at Highgate, a hill north of London.
7. Refers to the closing of the theaters due to the plague, 1592–1593.
8. The spleen was believed to be the seat of both melancholy and laughter.
9. London.
1. Younger brother of Donne's close friend Christopher (see "The Storm"), Samuel Brooke (1575–1631) later married Donne and Anne More. Donne may have sent this verse letter to him shortly after his matriculation at Cambridge in 1593. This sonnet may also reveal the poet's nostalgia for Cambridge.
2. Brooke's study at Cambridge.

Some turns'into less creeks, and wisely take
Fresh water at th'Heliconian spring.[3]
I sing not Siren-like[4] to tempt, for I
10   Am harsh, nor as those schismatics[5] with you
Which draw all wits of good hope to their crew.
But seeing in you bright sparks of poetry,
I, though I brought no fuel, had desire
With these articulate blasts to blow the fire.

To Mr. B. B.[6]

Is not thy sacred hunger of science
Yet satisfied? Is not they brain's rich hive
Fulfill'd[7] with honey which thou dost derive
From the arts' spirits and their quintessence?[8]
5   Then wean thyself at last, and thee withdraw
From Cambridge, thy old nurse, and as the rest,
Here[9] toughly chew and sturdily digest
Th'immense, vast volumes of our common law;
And begin soon, lest my grief grieve thee too,
10   Which is, that that which I should have begun
In my youth's morning, now late must be done.
And I, as giddy travelers, must do
Which stray or sleep all day, and having lost
Light and strength, dark and tir'd must then ride post.

15   If thou unto thy Muse be married,
Embrace her ever, ever multiply.
Be far from me that strange adultery
To tempt thee and procure her widowhead.[1]
My Muse (for I had one) because I'm cold,
20   Divorc'd herself: the cause being in me,
That I can take no new in bigamy,
Not my will only, but power doth withhold.

---

3. The spring on Mount Helicon, the haunt of the muses.
4. The Sirens were beautiful maidens who lured mariners to their death in the *Odyssey*.
5. Alludes to the controversy between Gabriel Harvey and Thomas Nashe over the work of Robert Greene in the early 1590s.
6. Probably Beaupré Bell, whose *hunger of science* kept him at Cambridge for a second degree (M.A.) after receiving his B.A. in 1591, before joining Donne at Lincoln's Inn in May 1594. Some regard the two stanzas as separate sonnets.
7. Filled full.
8. "The most essential part of any substance, extracted by natural or artificial processes" (OED).
9. Lincoln's Inn.
1. Widowhood.

Hence comes it, that these rhymes, which never had
   Mother, want matter, and they only have
25   A little form, the which their father gave.
They are profane, imperfect, oh, too bad
   To be counted children of poetry,
     Except confirm'd and bishoped[2] by thee.

To Sir Henry Wotton at His Going Ambassador to Venice.[3]

After those reverend papers,[4] whose soul is
   Our good and great king's loved hand and fear'd name,
By which to you he derives[5] much of his,
   And (how he may) makes you almost the same,

5 A taper of his torch, a copy writ
   From his original, and a fair beam
Of the same warm and dazzling sun, though it
   Must in another sphere his virtue stream.

After those learned papers which your hand
10   Hath stor'd with notes of use and pleasure too,
From which rich treasury you may command
   Fit matter, whether you will write or do:

After those loving papers where friends send,
   With glad grief to your seaward steps, farewell,
15 Which thicken on you now, as prayers ascend
   To heaven in troops, at'a good man's passing-bell:

Admit this honest paper,[6] and allow
   It such an audience as yourself would ask;
What you must say at Venice this means now,
20   And hath for nature, what you have for task.

To swear much love, not to be chang'd before
   Honor alone will to your fortune fit;
Nor shall I then honor your fortune, more
   Than I have done your honor wanting it.

2. Confirmed by a bishop.
3. Wotton was knighted by King James on 8 July 1604 and sailed for Venice a week later.
4. Wotton's commission as ambassador.
5. Conveys, imparts.
6. This verse letter.

25   But 'tis an easier load (though both oppress),
       To want, than govern greatness, for we are
     In that, our own and only business,
       In this, we must for others' vices care.

     'Tis therefore well your spirits now are plac'd
30   In their last furnace, in activity;
     Which fits them (schools and courts and wars o'erpast)
       To touch and test in any best degree.[7]

     For me (if there be such a thing as I)
       Fortune (if there be such a thing as she)
35   Spies that I bear so well her tyranny,
       That she thinks nothing else so fit for me.[8]

     But, though she part us, to hear my oft prayers
       For your increase, God is as near me here;
     And to send you what I shall beg,[9] his stairs
       In length and ease are alike everywhere.

                  To the Countess of Bedford.[1]

     Madam:
     Reason is our soul's left hand, faith her right;[2]
       By these we reach divinity, that's you.
     Their loves,[3] who have the blessing of your sight,
       Grew from their reason; mine from fair faith grew.

5   But as, although a squint left-handedness[4]
       Be'ungracious, yet we cannot want[5] that hand;

---

7. Lines 29–32: Wotton's good qualities will be refined by the heat of active trial (through his diplomatic service) and will become an alchemical elixir that can test the character of others.
8. Lines 33–36: Donne has become accustomed to the lack of advancement due to his clandestine marriage.
9. God's blessing.
1. Lucy Harrington Russell (1581–1627) was married to the third earl of Bedford in 1594 and resided at Twickenham Park. She became a favorite of Anne of Denmark (wife of James I) and thus one of the most influential personalities in the Jacobean court. Well educated by her parents (fluent in Italian, French, and Spanish), she associated with many leading writers and was Donne's patron from 1607 until 1615.
2. As the right hand is the more dominant, so ought faith to be.
3. Other suitors.
4. Awkwardness.
5. Lack.

So would I, not to increase, but to express
   My faith, as I believe, so understand.

Therefore I study you first in your saints,
10   Those friends whom your election glorifies;
Then in your deeds, accesses and restraints,
   And what you read, and what yourself devise.

But soon, the reasons why you're loved by all,
   Grow infinite, and so pass reason's reach;
15 Then back again t'implicit faith I fall,
   And rest on what the catholic[6] voice doth teach:

That you are good: and not one heretic
   Denies it: if he did, yet you are so.
For rocks, which high top'd and deep-rooted stick,
20   Waves wash, not undermine, nor overthrow.

In everything there naturally grows
   A balsamum[7] to keep it fresh and new,
If'twere not injur'd by extrinsic blows;
   Your birth and beauty are this balm in you.

25 But you of learning and religion,
   And virtue,'nd such ingredients, have made
A mithridate,[8] whose operation
   Keeps off or cures what can be done or said.

Yet this is not your physic,[9] but your food,
30   A diet fit for you; for you are here
The first good angel, since the world's frame stood,
   That ever did in woman's shape appear.

Since you are then God's masterpiece, and so
   His factor[1] for our loves, do as you do;
35 Make your return home gracious; and bestow
   This life on that; so make one life of two.
     For so God help me,'I would not miss you there,
     For all the good which you can do me here.

6. Universal.
7. A balm that heals and preserves the body; considered a panacea.
8. A supposed universal antidote to poison, or a panacea, or universal remedy (OED).
9. Medical treatment.
1. One who acts for another, agent.

To the Countess of Bedford.[2]

Madam,
You have refin'd me,[3] and to worthiest things
(Virtue, art, beauty, fortune) now I see
Rareness, or use, not nature value brings;
And such, as they are circumstanc'd, they be.[4]
5   Two ills can ne're perplex us, sin t'excuse;[5]
But of two good things we may leave and choose.

Therefore at court, which is not virtue's clime
(Where a transcendent height—as lowness me—
Makes her not be, or not show),[6] all my rime
10 Your virtues challenge,[7] which there rarest be;
     For, as dark texts need notes, there some must be
     To usher virtue, and say, "This is she."

So in the country'is beauty.[8] To this place
You are the season, Madam, you the day.
15 'Tis but a grave of spices, till your face
Exhale them, and a thick close bud display.[9]
     Widow'd and reclus'd else, her sweets she'enshrines
     As China, when the sun at Brasil dines.

Out from your chariot, morning breaks at night,
20 And falsifies both computations so;[1]
Since a new world doth rise here from your light,
We your new creatures by new reck'nings go.
     This shows that you from nature loathly stray,
     That suffer not an artificial day.

25 In this you've made the court th'antipodes,[2]
And will'd your delegate, the vulgar sun,

---

2. This verse letter, evidently written after a visit to the estate at Twickenham that the countess had bought from Sir Francis Bacon in 1608, imagines the effect she has had on the poet at Twickenham.
3. An alchemical metaphor suggesting her ability to transmute the poet.
4. Lines 1–4: Value is not intrinsic but depends on circumstances such as rarity or utility.
5. We are never obliged to chose between two evils and so have an excuse to sin.
6. Lines 7–9: The countess's virtue is so transcendent it is not perceived at court, while the poet's status is too low to be perceived.
7. An inversion: your virtues challenge all my powers as a poet.
8. As her virtue transcends the court, so does her beauty the country around Twickenham.
9. She is the sun that makes the flowers bud.
1. Lines 19–20: When she arrives at night, she brings both springtime and daylight.
2. Those living on the opposite side of the globe (OED); here, she inverts the seasons while in residence at Twickenham. The court has an autumnal sun while the country enjoys spring.

To do profane autumnal offices,
Whilst here to you, we sacrificers run;
    And whether priests, or organs, you we'obey,
30   We sound your influence, and your dictates say.

Yet to that deity which dwells in you,
Your virtuous soul, I now not sacrifice;
These are petitions, and not hymns; they sue
But that I may survey the edifice.[3]
35   In all religions, as much care hath been
    Of temples frames, and beauty, 'as rites within.

As all which go to Rome, do not thereby
Esteem religions, and hold fast the best,
But serve discourse and curiosity,
40 With that which doth religion but invest,
    And shun th'entangling labyrinths of schools,[4]
    And make it wit, to think the wiser fools:

So in this pilgrimage I would behold
You as you are virtue's temple, not as she,
45 What walls of tender crystal her enfold,
What eyes, hands, bosoms, her pure altars be,
    And after this survey, oppose to all
    Babblers of chapels, you th'Escorial.[5]

Yet not as consecrate, but merely'as faire;
50 On these I cast a lay and country eye.[6]
Of past and future stories, which are rare,
I find you all record, all prophecy.
    Purge but the book of fate, that it admit
    No sad nor guilty legends, you are it.

55 If good and lovely were not one, of both
You were the transcript and original,
The elements, the parent, and the growth,
And every piece of you, is both their all,
    So'entire are all your deeds, and you, that you
60   Must do the same things still: you cannot two.

---

3. Visit the countess.
4. Contentious schools of thought.
5. A magnificent monastery, palace, and mausoleum to Philip II, the Escorial was built near
   Madrid in the sixteenth century. Compared to it, all other churches are mere chapels.
6. He looks at her beauty with the eye of a layman.

But these[7] (as nice thin school divinity
Serves heresy to further, or repress)
Taste of poetic rage, or flattery,
And need not, where all hearts one truth profess;
65   Oft from new proofs and new phrase, new doubts grow,
As strange attire aliens the men we know.

Leaving then busy praise, and all appeal,
To higher courts, senses[8] decree is true:
The mine, the magazine, the commonweal,
70 The story of beauty, in Twicknam is, and you.
    Who hath seen one, would both;[9] as who had been
In paradise, would seek the cherubin.

7. The lines of this verse letter.
8. May be *senses'* or *sense's*. Though the first print editions have *sense*, most mss. and modern editors have the plural form; some moderns have a possessive (singular or plural).
9. Who had seen either Twickenham or the countess would want to see the other, just as one would seek out an angel in paradise.

Songs and Sonnets

The Message.

Send home my long stray'd eyes to me,
Which Oh too long have dwelt on thee;
Yet since there they have learn'd such ill,
    Such forc'd fashions,
5   And false passions,
    That they be
    Made by thee
Fit for no good[1] sight, keep them still.

Send home my harmless heart again,
10 Which no unworthy thought could stain;
Which if it be taught by thine
    To make jestings
    Of protestings,
    And cross[2] both
15   Word and oath,
Keep it, for then 'tis none of mine.

Yet send me back my heart and eyes,
That I may know and see thy lies,
And may laugh and joy, when thou
20   Art in anguish
    And dost languish
    For some one
    That will none,[3]
Or prove as false as thou art now.

1. Good or virtuous.
2. Cancel.
3. Will have none of you.

The Bait.[4]

Come live with me, and be my love,
And we will some new pleasures prove
Of golden sands and crystal brooks,
With silken lines and silver hooks.

5   There will the river whisp'ring run,
Warm'd by thy eyes, more than the sun;
And there th'enamour'd fish will stay,
Begging themselves they may betray.[5]

When thou wilt swim in that live bath,
10   Each fish, which every channel hath,
Will amorously to thee swim,
Gladder to catch thee, than thou him.

If thou, to be so seen, be'st loath,
By sun, or moon, thou dark'nest both,
15   And if myself have leave to see,
I need not their light, having thee.

Let others freeze with angling reeds,[6]
And cut their legs with shells and weeds,
Or treacherously poor fish beset
20   With strangling snare or windowy net.

Let coarse bold hands from slimy nest
The bedded fish in banks outwrest;[7]
Or curious traitors, sleave-silk[8] flies,
Bewitch poor fishes' wand'ring eyes.

25   For thee, thou need'st no such deceit,
For thou thyself art thine own bait:
That fish, that is not catch'd thereby,
Alas, is wiser far than I.

4. A reply to Christopher Marlowe's "The Passionate Shepherd to his Love" that was also set
   to music.
5. I.e., begging to be caught.
6. Fishing rods made from reeds.
7. To draw out or extract as with a forcible twist (OED).
8. Silk thread unraveled (or "sleaved") into smaller filaments to make flies.

The Apparition.

When by thy scorn, O murd'ress, I am dead,[9]
  And that thou think'st thee free
From all solicitation from me,
  Then shall my ghost come to thy bed,
5 And thee, feign'd vestal,[1] in worse arms shall see.
Then thy sick taper will begin to wink,[2]
And he, whose thou art then, being tir'd before,
Will, if thou stir, or pinch to wake him, think
    Thou call'st for more,
10 And in false sleep will from thee shrink,
And then, poor aspen[3] wretch, neglected thou
Bath'd in a cold, quicksilver sweat[4] wilt lie,
    A verier ghost than I.
What I will say, I will not tell thee now,
15 Lest that preserve thee, 'and since my love is spent,
I'd rather thou shouldst painfully repent,
Than by my threat'nings rest still innocent.

The Broken Heart.

He is stark mad, whoever says,
  That he hath been in love an hour,
Yet not that love so soon decays,
  But that it can ten in less space devour;
5 Who will believe me, if I swear
That I have had the plague a year?
    Who would not laugh at me, if I should say
    I saw a flask of powder burn a day?

Ah, what a trifle is a heart,
10 If once into Love's hands it come!
All other griefs allow a part
  To other griefs, and ask themselves but some;
They come to us, but us Love draws;
He swallows us and never chaws;[5]

---

9. I.e., her refusal to yield has "killed" the poet.
1. Virgins who tended the sacred hearth fires of Vesta in Rome.
2. Flicker in the presence of his ghost.
3. Quivering, as aspens move in the wind.
4. I.e., her cold sweat will be as thick as mercury (which was used to treat syphilis).
5. Chews.

15   By him, as by chain'd shot,[6] whole ranks do die;
        He is the tyrant pike, our hearts the fry.[7]

        If 'twere not so, what did become
            Of my heart when I first saw thee?
        I brought a heart into the room,
20   But from the room I carried none with me.
        If it had gone to thee, I know
        Mine would have taught thine heart to show
            More pity unto me: but Love, alas,
            At one first blow, did shiver it as glass.

25   Yet nothing can to nothing fall,
            Nor any place be empty quite;
        Therefore I think my breast hath all
            Those pieces still, though they be not unite;
        And now as broken glasses show
30   A hundred lesser faces,[8] so
            My rags of heart can like, wish, and adore,
            But after one such love, can love no more.

        X   A Lecture upon the Shadow.

        Stand still and I will read to thee
        A lecture, love, in love's philosophy.
            These three hours that we have spent,
            Walking here, two shadows went
5   Along with us, which we ourselves produc'd.
        But, now the sun is just above our head,
            We do those shadows tread.[9]
            And to brave[1] clearness all things are reduc'd.
        So whilst our infant loves did grow,
10   Disguises did, and shadows flow
        From us and our cares; but now 'tis not so.
        That love hath not attain'd the high'st degree,
        Which is still diligent lest others see.

        Except our loves at this noon stay,
15   We shall new shadows make the other way.

6. A kind of shot formed of two balls, or half-balls, connected by a chain, chiefly used in
   naval warfare to destroy masts, rigging (OED).
7. Small fish.
8. I.e., a broken mirror creates many reflected images.
9. The shadows are under their feet at noon.
1. Courageous.

As the first were made to blind
Others, these which come behind
Will work upon ourselves, and blind our eyes.[2]
If our loves faint, and westwardly decline,
20   To me thou, falsely, thine,[3]
And I to thee mine actions shall disguise.
The morning shadows wear away,
But these grow longer all the day;
But, oh, love's day is short, if love decay.
25 Love is a growing, or full constant light,
And his first minute, after noon, is night.[4]

A Valediction Forbidding Mourning.[5]

As virtuous men pass mildly away,
    And whisper to their souls to go,
And some of their sad friends do say,
    "The breath goes now," and some say, "No."

how are they related? So let us melt, and make no noise,
    No tear-floods, nor sigh-tempests[6] move;
    'Twere profanation of our joys,
    To tell the laity our love.

Moving of th'earth brings harms and fears;
10   Men reckon what it did and meant;
But trepidation of the spheres,[7]
    Though greater far, is innocent.

Dull sublunary[8] lovers' love
    (Whose soul is sense) cannot admit
15 Absence, because it doth remove
    Those things which elemented it.

---

2. Lines 14–18: The morning shadows (in love's infancy) concealed them from discovery; unless they remain at *noon*—i.e., open or honest with each other—the shadows will blind them to love's decay.
3. Line 20: Thou shalt falsely disguise thine actions to me.
4. Lines 25–26: Once love begins to decline, it is finished.
5. Walton believed Donne wrote this for his wife when he journeyed to the continent in 1611, though modern biographers dispute this claim.
6. *Tear-floods* and *sigh-tempests* were stock Petrarchan conceits and exaggerations.
7. The movement of the eighth (or ninth) sphere that was needed to account for certain phenomena, especially the precession of the equinoxes. In lines 9–12 the poet contrasts earthquakes that were taken as portents with the far greater power of the heavenly spheres that were imperceptible and thus harmless or *innocent*.
8. Beneath the lowest orbit of the immutable heavenly realm; hence, subject to change and decay.

But we by a love so much refin'd,
   That ourselves know not what it is,
Inter-assured of the mind,
20   Care less, eyes, lips and hands to miss.

Our two souls, therefore, which are one,
   Though I must go, endure not yet
A breach, but an expansion,
   Like gold to aery thinness beat.⁹

25 If they be two, they are two so
     As stiff twin compasses¹ are two;
Thy soul, the fix'd foot, makes no show
   To move, but doth, if th'other do.

And though it in the center sit,
30 Yet, when the other far doth roam,
It leans, and hearkens after it,
   And grows erect, as it comes home.

Such wilt thou be to me, who must,
   Like th'other foot, obliquely² run;
35 Thy firmness makes my circle just,
   And makes me end where I begun.

The Good Morrow.

I wonder, by my troth, what thou and I
   Did, till we lov'd? Were we not wean'd till then?
But suck'd on country³ pleasures sillily?
   Or slumber'd we in the Seven Sleepers'⁴ den?
'Twas so; but this, all pleasures fancies be;
   If ever any beauty I did see,
Which I desired, and got, 'twas but a dream of thee.

And now good morrow to our waking souls,
   Which watch not one another out of fear;

[Handwritten margin notes: "Pointing to temporal limitations"; "had only physical exchanges"; "Introducing this new exchange"]

9. In *Biathanatos* (1644, p. 155) Donne wrote that "Gold, by reason of a faithfull tenacity and ductilenesse, will be brought to cover 10000 times as much of any other Mettall."
1. I.e., the legs of a drawing compass, joined at the top.
2. Moving with deviation from the straight line or direct course (OED).
3. Rustic and unsophisticated with a possible sexual innuendo, as in *Hamlet* (3.2.105).
4. Seven Christian youths who reputedly took refuge in a cave to avoid persecution and slept for nearly two centuries. The poet likens the youths' awakening to discover a changed world to the lovers' awakening into a newly changed world.

Their love for one another controls the other loves in their lives — shows mutual ownership

10 For love all love of other sights controls,
And makes one little room[5] an everywhere.
  Let sea-discoverers to new worlds have gone;
  Let maps to others, worlds on worlds have shown;[6]
Let us possess our world: each hath one, and is one.[7]

Physical exchange

15 My face in thine eye, thine in mine appears, *They are face to face*
emotional And true plain hearts do in the faces rest. *can see eachothers*
exchange Where can we find two better hemispheres *reflection in their*
Without sharp north, without declining west? *eyes, as well as*
plain hearts. We
  Whatever dies, was not mix'd equally; *a two hemispheres*
20 If our two loves be one, or thou and I *perfect for one*
Love so alike that none do slacken, none can die.[8] *another*

our loves are so perfectly balanced that they cannot die

even though he is claiming this exchange will save them from death, there is still a temporal limit before the knew one another

SONG.

    Go and catch a falling star,
        Get with child a mandrake root,[9]
    Tell me where all past years are,
        Or who cleft the devil's foot,[1]
5   Teach me to hear mermaids singing,
    Or to keep off envy's stinging,
            And find
            What wind
    Serves t'advance an honest mind.

10 If thou be'st born to strange sights,
        Things invisible to see,
    Ride ten thousand days and nights,
        Till age snow white hairs on thee,
    Thou, when thou return'st, wilt tell me,
15 All strange wonders that befell thee,
            And swear,
            No where
    Lives a woman true and fair.

5. The bedroom where they bid each other good morrow.
6. Let others search out new worlds with maps of the heavens.
7. Each is a world to the other.
8. Lines 20–21: If our loves are composed of the same substance, they will not suffer alter-
   ation or decay.
9. The mandragora's forked root was thought to resemble a human body and have human
   qualities, though transforming it into a child was an impossibility. Donne believed the
   fruits of the mandrake could promote fertility in women while the leaves could prevent
   conception ("Progress of the Soul," line 150).
1. An abiding mystery, though the association with goats and the damned can be found in
   Matthew 25:31–46.

If thou find'st one, let me know,
20   Such a pilgrimage were sweet.
Yet do not, I would not go,
    Though at next door we might meet,
Though she were true, when you met her,
And last, till you write your letter,
25   Yet she
       Will be
False, ere I come, to two, or three.

Woman's Constancy.

Physical exchange [handwritten]

Now thou hast lov'd me one whole day,
Tomorrow when thou leav'st, what wilt thou say?
Wilt thou then antedate some new-made vow?
    Or say that now
5 We are not just those persons which we were?
Or, that oaths made in reverential fear
Of Love, and his wrath, any may forswear?
Or, as true deaths true marriages untie,
So lovers' contracts, images of those,
10 Bind but till sleep, death's image, them unloose?[2]
    Or, your own end to justify,
For having purpos'd change and falsehood, you
Can have no way but falsehood to be true?
Vain lunatic,[3] against these 'scapes I could
15   Dispute, and conquer, if I would,
      Which I abstain to do,
For by tomorrow I may think so too.

spatial limitation [handwritten, left margin]

no man/men arguing that the exchange was nothing more that physical [handwritten, left margin]

Pointing to total independence [handwritten, left margin]

The Sun Rising.

Busy old fool, unruly Sun,
    Why dost thou thus,
Through windows, and through curtains, call on us?
Must to thy motions lovers' seasons run?
5   Saucy pedantic wretch, go chide
    Late schoolboys and sour 'prentices,

---

2. Lines 8–10: Just as death unties the bonds of marriage, so a night's sleep, which is death's image, unties lovers' contracts.
3. An inconstant or mad person under the sway of the moon.

Go tell court-huntsmen[4] that the king will ride,
Call country ants to harvest offices;[5]
Love, all alike, no season knows nor clime,
10 Nor hours, days, months, which are the rags of time.

Thy beams, so reverend and strong
Why shouldst thou think?
I could eclipse and cloud them with a wink,
But that I would not lose her sight so long.
15   If her eyes have not blinded thine,
Look, and tomorrow late tell me,
Whether both th'Indias[6] of spice and mine
Be where thou left'st them, or lie here with me.
Ask for those kings whom thou saw'st yesterday,
20 And thou shalt hear, "All here in one bed lay."

She's all states, and all princes I;[7]
Nothing else is:
Princes do but play us; compar'd to this,
All honor's mimic, all wealth alchemy.[8]
25   Thou, Sun, art half as happy as we,
In that the world's contracted thus.
Thine age asks ease,[9] and since thy duties be
To warm the world, that's done in warming us.
Shine here to us, and thou art everywhere;
30 This bed thy center[1] is, these walls thy sphere.

The Indifferent.[2]

I can love both fair and brown,[3]
Her whom abundance melts, and her whom want betrays,[4]
Her who loves loneness best, and her who masks and plays,
Her whom the country form'd, and whom the town,
5 Her who believes, and her who tries,[5]

---

4. Courtiers who rode early to hunt with the king to curry favor with him. This poem was
   likely written after the accession of James I in 1603.
5. Duties.
6. The East Indies (spice) and the West Indies (gold mines).
7. I am the sole ruler and she is my entire world.
8. The pursuit of honor or wealth is as fraudulent as alchemy in comparison to our love.
9. Because the sun has been toiling daily for over five thousand years.
1. Their bed is the center of the universe around which the sun must orbit.
2. Based on Ovid's Amores 2.4.
3. Blondes and brunettes.
4. She who sells herself for money.
5. Line 5: She who believes her lover, and she who tests him.

Her who still weeps with spongy eyes,
And her who is dry cork and never cries;
I can love her, and her, and you, and you,
I can love any, so she be not true.

10 Will no other vice[6] content you?
Will it not serve your turn to do as did your mothers?
Have you all old vices spent, and now would find out others?
Or doth a fear that men are true torment you?
Oh we are not, be not you so.
15 Let me, and do you, twenty know.[7]
Rob me,[8] but bind me not, and let me go.
Must I, who came to travail[9] thorough you,
Grow your fix'd subject, because you are true?

Venus heard me sigh this song,
20 And by love's sweetest part, variety, she swore,
She heard not this till now; and that it should be so no more.
She went, examin'd, and return'd ere long,
And said, "Alas, some two or three
Poor heretics in love there be,
25 Which think to 'stablish dangerous constancy.
But I have told them, 'Since you will be true,
You shall be true to them who're false to you.' "

Love's Usury.[1]

For every hour that thou wilt spare me now,
     I will allow,
Usurious god of love, twenty to thee,
When with my brown, my gray hairs equal be.
5 Till then, Love, let my body reign, and let
Me travail, sojourn, snatch, plot, have, forget,
Resume my last year's relict:[2] think that yet
     We'd never met.

6. The vice of being faithful.
7. *Know* in a sexual sense (as with *turn* and *do* in line 11).
8. Refers to the belief that sexual emission shortened the length of life; see "Farewell to Love," line 25.
9. To weary or exert onself (OED 1.b.) but with a frequent sense of "to travel"; here the poet intends to seduce and leave her, but she hopes to make him *fixed* on her.
1. Though he accuses the god of love of usury (charging excessive interest for money on loan), for sexual freedom now the poet offers to pledge his later years to Cupid at a twenty-fold rate of interest.
2. Take up with last year's loved one as if we had never met.

Let me think any rival's letter mine,
10   And at next nine[3]
Keep midnight's promise; mistake by the way
The maid, and tell the lady of that delay;
Only let me love none, no, not the sport.
From country grass, to comfitures of court,
15   Or city's *quelque-choses*, let report
      My mind transport.[4]

This bargain's good; if, when I'm old, I be
      Inflam'd by thee,
If thine own honor, or my shame or pain,
20   Thou covet, most at that age thou shalt gain.
Do thy will then; then subject and degree
And fruit of love, Love, I submit to thee.
Spare me till then; I'll bear it, though she be
      One that loves me.

The Canonization.

For God's sake hold your tongue, and let me love.
      Or chide my palsy, or my gout;
My five gray hairs, or ruin'd fortune flout;
      With wealth your state, your mind with arts improve;
5   Take you a course, get you a place,[5]
      Observe his honor, or his grace;
And the king's real, or his stamped[6] face
      Contemplate; what you will, approve,
      So you will let me love.

10   Alas, alas, who's injur'd by my love?
      What merchant's ships have my sighs drown'd?
Who says my tears have overflow'd his ground?
      When did my colds a forward spring remove?[7]
      When did the heats which my veins fill
15   Add one more to the plaguy bill?[8]

3. I.e., show up at nine o'clock to take the place of his rival's midnight assignation.
4. Lines 13–16: The poet wants to be carefree in his pursuits without being a slave to lust or love: he wants to be as delighted with tales of country girls, the refined ladies of the court, or some fantastical person from the city (*quelque-choses* or "kickshaw" OED 2, 3).
5. Line 5: Take a course of action that leads to your obtaining a position.
6. The king's likeness on a coin.
7. Line 13: When did my bodily distemperature hinder the coming of spring?
8. Weekly lists of those who died of the plague.

Soldiers find wars, and lawyers find out still
    Litigious men, which quarrels move,
    Though she and I do love.

    Call us what you will, we are made such by love;
20   Call her one, me another fly,
    We're tapers too, and at our own cost die,[9]
      And we in us find th'eagle and the dove.[1]
      The phoenix[2] riddle hath more wit
      By us; we two being one are it;
25 So, to one neutral thing both sexes fit.
    We die and rise the same, and prove
    Mysterious by this love.[3]

We can die by it, if not live by love,
    And if unfit for tombs or hearse
30 Our legend be, it will be fit for verse;
    And if no piece of chronicle we prove,
      We'll build in sonnets pretty rooms;
      As well a well-wrought urn becomes
The greatest ashes, as half-acre tombs,
35   And by these hymns, all shall approve
      Us canonized for love;

great lovers are immortalized in poetry

And thus invoke us, "You, whom reverend love
    Made one another's hermitage;
You, to whom love was peace, that now is rage,
40   Who did the whole world's soul extract, and drove
      Into the glasses of your eyes[4]
      (So made such mirrors, and such spies,
That they did all to you epitomize)
    Countries, towns, courts: beg from above
45 A pattern of your love."[5]

the lover is one person yet everything real—

---

9. Line 21: Just as candles diminish themselves by burning, lovers shorten their lives by sexual emission; see "Farewell to Love," line 25.
1. Emblems of predatory strength and gentleness.
2. A fabled bird that regenerated itself by rising out of its own ashes after self-immolation on a pyre of aromatic twigs.
3. Lines 25–27: Through our sexual union we *die*, yet our desire does not diminish. Compare Shakespeare's description of Cleopatra (*A&C* 2.2:241–43): "Other women cloy / The appetites they feed, but she makes hungry / Where most she satisfies."
4. Lines 40–41: Whose whole world was seen in each other's eyes since only love mattered to them.
5. Lines 44–45: Ask the newly canonized saints for a pattern of their love to imitate.

The Triple Fool.

I am two fools, I know,
For loving, and for saying so
    In whining poetry;
But where's that wise man, that would not be I,
5   If she would not deny?
Then as th'earth's inward, narrow, crooked lanes
Do purge sea water's fretful salt away,[6]
    I thought, if I could draw my pains
Through rhyme's vexation, I should them allay.
10 Grief brought to numbers[7] cannot be so fierce,
For, he tames it, that fetters it in verse.

    But when I have done so,
    Some man, his art and voice to show,
        Doth set[8] and sing my pain,
15 And, by delighting many, frees again
        Grief, which verse did restrain.
    To love and grief tribute of verse belongs,
    But not of such as pleases when 'tis read.
        Both are increased by such songs:
20 For both their triumphs so are published,
    And I, which was two fools, do so grow three.
    Who are a little wise, the best fools be.

Lovers' Infiniteness.

If yet I have not all thy love,
Dear, I shall never have it all;
I cannot breathe one other sigh, to move,
Nor can entreat one other tear to fall.
5 And all my treasure, which should purchase thee,
Sighs, tears, and oaths, and letters I have spent;
Yet no more can be due to me,
Than at the bargain made was meant.
If then thy gift of love were partial,
10 That some to me, some should to others fall,
    Dear, I shall never have thee all.

---

6. Lines 6–7: The salinity of sea water was believed to be filtered as it passed through veins within the earth.
7. Verses.
8. Set to music.

Or if then thou gavest me all,
All was but all, which thou hadst then;
But if in thy heart, since,[9] there be or shall
15 New love created be, by other men,
Which have their stocks entire, and can in tears,
In sighs, in oaths, and letters outbid me,
This new love may beget new fears,
For this love was not vow'd by thee.
20 And yet it was, thy gift being general,
The ground, thy heart, is mine; what ever shall
     Grow there, dear, I should have it all.

Yet I would not have all yet.
He that hath all can have no more;
25 And since my love doth every day admit
New growth, thou shouldst have new rewards in store.
Thou canst not every day give me thy heart.
If thou canst give it, then thou never gavest it:
Love's riddles are, that though thy heart depart,
30 It stays at home, and thou with losing savest it:
But we will have a way more liberal,
Than changing hearts, to join them; so we shall
     Be one, and one another's all.

Song.

Sweetest love, I do not go,
     For weariness of thee,
Nor in hope the world can show
     A fitter love for me;
5   But since that I
Must die at last, 'tis best,
To use myself in jest
     Thus by feign'd deaths to die.[1]

Yesternight the sun went hence,
10   And yet is here today;
He hath no desire nor sense,
     Nor half so short a way:

9. Since that time.
1. Lines 6–8: To accustom myself to total separation (death) by playing at it through absence (feigned death).

Then fear not me,
But believe that I shall make
15 Speedier journeys, since I take
   More wings and spurs than he.

Oh how feeble is man's power,
   That if good fortune fall,
Cannot add another hour,
20   Nor a lost hour recall.
      But come bad chance,
And we join to'it our strength,
And we teach it art and length,
   Itself o'er us to'advance.

25 When thou sigh'st, thou sigh'st not wind,
      But sigh'st my soul away;
When thou weep'st, unkindly kind,[2]
      My life's blood doth decay.[3]
         It cannot be
30 That thou lov'st me, as thou say'st,
If in thine my life thou waste,
   Thou art the best of me.

Let not thy divining heart
   Forethink me any ill;
35 Destiny may take thy part,
   And may thy fears fulfil.
      But think that we
Are but turn'd aside to sleep:
They who one another keep
40   Alive, ne'er parted be.

The Legacy.

When I died last, and, dear, I die
   As often as from thee I go,
   Though it be but an hour ago
(And lovers' hours be full eternity),
5 I can remember yet, that I
   Something did say, and something did bestow;

2. A kind person whose weeping is unkind.
3. Sighs and tears were thought to shorten a lover's life.

Though I be dead, which sent me, I should be
Mine own executor and legacy.[4]

    I heard me say, "Tell her anon,
10   That myself, (that is you, not I)[5]
    Did kill me," and when I felt me die,
    I bid me send my heart, when I was gone;
    But I, alas, could there find none;
      When I had ripp'd me'and search'd where hearts should lie.
15 It kill'd me again, that I who still was true
    In life, in my last will should cozen[6] you.

    Yet I found something like a heart,
      But colors it, and corners had;[7]
    It was not good, it was not bad,
20 It was entire to none, and few had part;
    As good as could be made by art
      It seem'd, and therefore for our losses sad.
    I meant to send that heart instead of mine,
    But oh, no man could hold it, for 'twas thine.

A Fever.

    Oh do not die, for I shall hate
      All women so, when thou art gone,
    That thee I shall not celebrate,
      When I remember thou wast one.

5   But yet thou canst not die, I know,
      To leave this world behind, is death;
    But when thou from this world wilt go,
      The whole world vapors with thy breath.

    Or if, when thou, the world's soul, go'st,
10   It stay, 'tis but thy carcase then;
    The fairest woman, but thy ghost,
      But corrupt worms, the worthiest men.[8]

4. Lines 7–8: Though he has died by deciding to leave, he will act as the executor and his
   own legacy (i.e., something left to her).
5. My self is she (she controls him).
6. Cheat, deceive (OED).
7. I.e., the "painted" or hypocritical heart of his mistress.
8. Lines 9–12: When you, the world's soul depart, the fairest of women will be merely shad-
   ows of you, just as the worthiest of men will be as worms.

Oh wrangling schools,[9] that search what fire
    Shall burn this world, had none the wit
15 Unto this knowledge to aspire,
    That this her fever might be it!

And yet she cannot waste by this,
    Nor long bear this torturing wrong,
For much corruption needful is,
20   To fuel such a fever long.

These burning fits but meteors[1] be,
    Whose matter in thee is soon spent.
Thy beauty,'and all parts, which are thee,
    Are unchangeable firmament.

25 Yet 'twas of my mind, seizing thee,
    Though it in thee cannot persever.
For I had rather owner be
    Of thee one hour, than all else ever.

Air and Angels. ☆

Twice or thrice had I lov'd thee,
Before I knew thy face or name;
So in a voice, so in a shapeless flame,
Angels affect us oft, and worship'd be.
5   Still when to where thou wert I came,
Some lovely glorious nothing[2] I did see.
    But since my soul, whose child love is,
Takes limbs of flesh, and else could nothing do,
    More subtle than the parent is
10 Love must not be, but take a body too.
    And therefore what thou wert, and who,
        I bid Love ask, and now
That it assume thy body, I allow,
And fix itself in thy lip, eye, and brow.

15 Whilst thus to ballast[3] love, I thought,
    And so more steadily to have gone,

9. Various schools of thought on what kind of fire would destroy the world.
1. Atmospheric bodies whose heat is soon dissipated.
2. With an ethereal body of air, she is a glorious nothing.
3. Stabilize or weigh down.

With wares which would sink admiration,
  I saw I had love's pinnace[4] overfraught;
    Ev'ry thy hair for love to work upon
20 Is much too much; some fitter must be sought;
  For, nor in nothing, nor in things
Extreme and scatt'ring bright, can love inhere;
    Then as an angel, face and wings
Of air, not pure as it, yet pure doth wear,
25   So thy love may be my love's sphere.[5]
      Just such disparity
As is 'twixt air and angels' purity,
'Twixt women's love, and men's will ever be.

Break of Day.[6]

'Tis true, 'tis day; what though it be?
Oh wilt thou therefore rise from me?
  Why should we rise because 'tis light?
  Did we lie down because 'twas night?
5 Love, which in despite of darkness brought us hither,
Should in despite of light keep us together.

Light hath no tongue, but is all eye;
If it could speak as well as spy,
  This were the worst that it could say,
10   That being well I fain would stay,
And that I lov'd my heart and honor so
That I would not from him, that had them, go.

Must business thee from hence remove?
Oh that's the worst disease of love,
15   The poor, the foul, the false, love can
    Admit, but not the busied man.
He which hath business, and makes love, doth do
Such wrong, as when a married man doth woo.[7]

---

4. A light craft used to bring provisions to other ships with a possible *double entendre*.
5. Lines 23–25: Then, as an angel wears a body of air, which is not quite as pure as the angel, so thy love, which is not quite as pure as my love, will be the body for it. Without bodies of air angels are otherwise immaterial. (Each sphere was believed to have an intelligence that regulated its motion.)
6. The speaker is a woman with a conventional complaint about lovers having to depart at dawn.
7. Lines 17–18: A busy man makes love with an eye toward a quick exit, just like a married man woos his wife mechanically or without passion.

The Prohibition.

Take heed of loving me;
At least remember, I forbade it thee;
Not that I shall repair my'unthrifty waste
Of breath and blood, upon thy sighs and tears:
5 By being to thee then what[8] to me thou wast;
But, so great joy, our life at once outwears.
Then, lest thy love by my death frustrate be,
If thou love me, take heed of loving me.

Take heed of hating me,
10 Or too much triumph in the victory.
Not that I shall be mine own officer,[9]
And hate with hate again retaliate;
But thou wilt lose the style[1] of conqueror,
If I, thy conquest, perish by thy hate.
15 Then, lest my being nothing lessen thee,
If thou hate me, take heed of hating me.

Yet, love and hate me too;
So these extremes shall neither's office do;
Love me, that I may die the gentler way;
20 Hate me, because thy love's too great for me;
Or let these two, themselves, not me, decay;
So shall I live thy stage, not triumph be.[2]
Then lest thou thy love, hate, and me thou undo,
O let me live, yet love and hate me too.

The Anniversary.

All kings, and all their favorites,
All glory of honors, beauties, wits,
The sun itself, which makes times, as they[3] pass,
Is elder by a year now than it was
5 When thou and I first one another saw.
All other things to their destruction draw,

8. I.e., by being cold. *Upon* (line 4): by drawing upon.
9. Officer of the law.
1. Title.
2. Line 22: Alive I shall be the stage for your continual victory celebrations rather than a single triumphal parade.
3. Refers to the days or years (*times*) rather than to *kings*.

Only our love hath no decay:
This, no tomorrow hath, nor yesterday;
Running it never runs from us away,
10   But truly keeps his first, last, everlasting day.

Two graves must hide thine and my corse;[4]
If one might, death were no divorce.
Alas, as well as other princes, we
(Who prince enough in one another be)
15   Must leave at last in death these eyes and ears,
Oft fed with true oaths and with sweet salt tears;
But souls where nothing dwells but love
(All other thoughts being inmates)[5] then shall prove
This, or a love increased there above,
20   When bodies to their graves, souls from their graves remove.

And then we shall be throughly blest,
But we no more than all the rest.
Here upon earth we're kings, and none but we
Can be such kings, nor of such subjects be.
25   Who is so safe as we, where none can do
Treason to us, except one of us two?
True and false fears let us refrain,
Let us love nobly, and live, and add again
Years and years unto years, till we attain
To write threescore. This is the second[6] of our reign.

A Valediction of My Name in the Window.[7]

My name engrav'd herein
Doth contribute my firmness to this glass,
Which ever since that charm hath been
As hard, as that which grav'd it, was.
5   Thine eyes will give it price enough to mock
The diamonds of either rock.[8]

'Tis much that glass should be
As all-confessing and through-shine[9] as I;

4. Corpse.
5. Merely lodgers.
6. Second year of our reign.
7. In the mss. the stanzas are numbered 1–11.
8. Diamonds were classified as from either old rock or new.
9. Transparent.

'Tis more that it shows thee to thee,
10   And clear reflects thee to thine eye.
But all such rules, love's magic can undo:
    Here you see me, and I am you.[1]

    As no one point, nor dash,
Which are but accessories to this name,
15   The showers and tempests can outwash,
    So shall all times find me the same;
You this entireness better may fulfill,
    Who have the pattern[2] with you still.

    Or if too hard and deep
20   This learning be, for a scratch'd name to teach,
    It, as a given death's head[3] keep,
    Lovers' mortality to preach,
Or think this ragged bony name to be
    My ruinous anatomy.[4]

25   Then, as all my souls[5] be
Emparadis'd in you (in whom alone
    I understand, and grow, and see),
    The rafters of my body, bone,[6]
Being still with you, the muscle, sinew, and vein
30   Which tile this house will come again.

    Till my return, repair
And recompact my scatter'd body so.
    As all the virtuous powers which are
    Fix'd in the stars are said to flow
35   Into such characters as graved be
    When those stars have supremacy.[7]

    So since this name was cut,
When love and grief their exaltation had,
    No door 'gainst this name's influence shut;
40   As much more loving, as more sad,

---

1. I.e., she sees his name and herself reflected in it.
2. Lines 17–18 are obscure; perhaps she fulfills the pattern with his image in her heart or with his picture.
3. As a *memento mori* or representation of death.
4. My body which shows the ravages of time.
5. I.e., the vegetative, sensitive, and intellectual souls posited by Scholastic philosophy.
6. His skeleton, i.e., his name in the window.
7. Lines 33–36: Astrologers believed astral influences flowed into magic characters made when certain stars were ascendant.

'Twill make thee, and thou shouldst, till I return,
    Since I die daily, daily mourn.

        When thy inconsiderate hand
    Flings ope this casement, with my trembling name,
45   To look on one, whose wit or land
        New batt'ry to thy heart may frame,
    Then think this name alive, and that thou thus
        In it offend'st my genius.[8]

        And when thy melted maid,
50 Corrupted by thy lover's gold and page,
        His letter at thy pillow'hath laid,
        Disputed it, and tam'd thy rage,
    And thou begin'st to thaw towards him, for this,
        May my name step in and hide his.[9]

55   And if this treason go
    T'an overt act,[1] and that thou write again;
        In superscribing, this name flow
        Into thy fancy from the pane,
    So, in forgetting thou rememb'rest right,
60   And unaware to me shalt write.

        But glass and lines must be
    No means our firm, substantial love to keep;
        Near death inflicts this lethargy,
        And this I murmur in my sleep;
65 Impute this idle talk, to that I go,
        For dying men talk often so.[2]

Twicknam Garden.[3]

    Blasted with sighs, and surrounded with tears,
        Hither I come to seek the spring,
        And at mine eyes, and at mine ears,
    Receive such balm as else cures every thing.

8. Protective spirit.
9. Line 54: Viewing his name may prevent her from succumbing to a rival.
1. The law distinguishes between treasonable intentions and actions, such as her replying to the rival.
2. Lines 63–66: The poet attributes his idle talk (i.e., his fantastic musings on his name) to his illness.
3. The home of Lucy, countess of Bedford; spelled Twickenham today, but spelled and pronounced "Twicknam" in the mss.

5   But oh, self-traitor, I do bring
       The spider Love, which transubstantiates[4] all,
         And can convert manna to gall;[5]
       And that this place may thoroughly be thought
       True Paradise, I have the serpent brought.

10   'Twere wholesomer for me that winter did
         Benight the glory of this place,
         And that a grave frost did forbid
       These trees to laugh and mock me to my face;
         But that I may not this disgrace
15   Endure, nor leave this garden, Love let me
         Some senseless piece of this place be;
       Make me a mandrake,[6] so I may grow here,
       Or a stone fountain weeping out my year.

       Hither with crystal vials, lovers come,
20   And take my tears, which are love's wine,   *Tears*
       And try your mistress' tears at home,
       For all are false, that taste not just like mine.
         Alas, hearts do not in eyes shine,
       Nor can you more judge women's thoughts by tears,
25   Than by her shadow what she wears.
       O perverse sex, where none is true but she,
       Who's therefore true, because her truth kills me.[7]

benighted: overtaken by darkness / night OR intellectually / morally ignoran[t]

A Valediction
of the Book.

I'll tell thee now (dear love) what thou shalt do
  To anger destiny, as she doth us;
  How I shall stay, though she eloign[8] me thus,
And how posterity shall know it too;
5   How thine may out-endure
       Sibyl's[9] glory, and obscure

---

4. Changes everything to another substance; *spider love*: spiders were thought to be poison-
   ous.
5. Line 7: Can convert what is sweet to what is bitter; here, perhaps his affection for the
   countess.
6. The mandragora's forked root resembled a human body and supposedly shrieked when
   uprooted.
7. Line 26: Her faithfulness to another kills me.
8. Takes me away (French).
9. All these women helped a man achieve something great: the Sibyl at Cumae aided Aeneas
   in his descent to the underworld; Corinna taught Pindar how to write and bested him in

Her who from Pindar could allure,
And her, through whose help Lucan is not lame,
And her, whose book (they say) Homer did find and name.

10   Study our manuscripts, those myriads
      Of letters, which have past 'twixt thee and me;
      Thence write our annals, and in them will be
  To all whom love's subliming[1] fire invades,
        Rule and example found;
15   There, the faith of any ground[2]
        No schismatic will dare to wound,
      That sees, how Love this grace to us affords,
  To make, to keep, to use, to be these his records.

  This book, as long-liv'd as the elements,
20   Or as the world's form, this all-graved tome
      In cypher writ, or new made idiom,
  We for Love's clergy only'are instruments;
        When this book is made thus,
        Should again the ravenous
25   Vandals and Goths inundate us,
      Learning were safe; in this our universe,
  Schools might learn sciences, spheres music,[3] angels verse.

  Here Love's divines (since all divinity
      Is love or wonder) may find all they seek,
30   Whether abstract spiritual love they like,
  Their souls exhal'd[4] with what they do not see,
        Or, loath so to amuse
        Faith's infirmity, they choose
        Something which they may see and use;
35   For, though mind be the heaven where love doth sit,
  Beauty a convenient type may be to figure it.

  Here more than in their books may lawyers find,
      Both by what titles mistresses are ours,
      And how prerogative these states devours,
40   Transferr'd from Love himself, to womankind;
        Who, though from heart and eyes,

---

poetic contests; Lucan's wife, Polla Argentaria, helped him revise his *Pharsalia*; and Phantasia of Memphis reputedly wrote an epic on Troy that inspired Homer.
1. Purifying.
2. Fundamental belief.
3. The movement of the heavenly spheres was thought to produce irresistibly beautiful tones.
4. Drawn out of their bodies.

They exact great subsidies,
 Forsake him who on them relies,
 And for the cause, honor, or conscience give,
45 Chimeras, vain as they, or their prerogative.

Here statesmen (or of them, they which can read)
 May of their occupation find the grounds:
 Love, and their art, alike it deadly wounds,
If to consider what 'tis, one proceed.
50 In both they do excel
  Who the present govern well,
  Whose weakness none doth, or dares tell.
In this thy book, such will their nothing see,
As in the Bible some can find out alchemy.[5]

55 Thus vent thy thoughts; abroad I'll study thee,
 As he removes far off, that great heights takes;
 How great love is, presence best trial makes,
But absence tries how long this love will be;
  To take a latitude
60 Sun, or stars, are fitliest view'd
  At their brightest, but to conclude
Of longitudes, what other way have we,
But to mark when and where the dark eclipses be?[6]

Community.

Good we must love, and must hate ill,
For ill is *ill*, and good, good still;
 But there are things indifferent,
 Which we may neither hate nor love,
5 But one, and then another prove,[7]
 As we shall find our fancy bent.

If then at first wise nature had
Made women either good or bad,
 Then some we might hate, and some choose;
10 But since she did them so create,

5. Lines 53–54: In this book, which deals with true love, some will see their own emptiness.
6. Lines 55–63: Since he will be *abroad*, they can plot each other's love by determining latitude through the brightness of stars (metaphorically, "How great love is"); longitude, through dark eclipses or *absence*.
7. Try or experience.

That we may neither love nor hate,
  Only this rests: *all*, all may use.

If they were good, it would be seen;
  Good is as visible as green,
15   And to all eyes itself betrays.
  If they were bad, they could not last;
  Bad doth itself, and others waste;
    So they deserve nor blame nor praise.

But they are ours as fruits are ours;
20 He that but tastes, he that devours,
    And he which leaves all, doth as well;
  Chang'd loves are but chang'd sorts of meat;
  And when he hath the kernel eat,
    Who doth not fling away the shell?

Love's Growth.

I scarce believe my love to be so pure
  As I had thought it was,
  Because it doth endure
Vicissitude and season, as the grass.
5 Methinks I lied all winter, when I swore
My love was infinite, if spring make'it more.
But if this medicine, love, which cures all sorrow
With more, not only be no quintessence,[8]
But mix'd of all stuffs, paining soul, or sense,
10 And of the sun his working vigor borrow,
  Love's not so pure, and abstract, as they use
  To say, which have no mistress but their Muse;
  But as all else, being elemented[9] too,
  Love sometimes would contemplate, sometimes do.

15 And yet no greater, but more eminent,
    Love by the spring is grown;
    As in the firmament
  Stars by the sun are not enlarg'd, but shown,[1]
  Gentle love deeds, as blossoms on a bough,
20 From love's awakened root do bud out now.

8. "The most essential part of any substance, extracted by natural or artificial processes"
(OED).
9. Composed.
1. Lines 17–18: As the sun rises, the sky grows lighter and the stars seem larger.

If, as in water stirr'd more circles be
Produced by one, love such additions take,
Those like to many spheres, but one heaven make,
For they are all concentric unto thee;[2]
25   And though each spring do add to love new heat,
As princes do in times of action get
New taxes, and remit them not in peace,
No winter shall abate the spring's increase.

Love's Exchange.

Love, any devil else but you
Would for a given soul give something too.
At court your fellows every day
Give th'art of rhyming, huntsmanship, and play,[3]
5   For them who were their own before;
Only I have nothing, which gave more,[4]
But am, alas, by being lowly, lower.

I ask no dispensation now,
To falsify a tear, or sigh, or vow;
10   I do not sue from thee to draw
A *non obstante*[5] on nature's law;
These are prerogatives; they inhere
In thee and thine; none should forswear
Except that he Love's minion[6] were.

15   Give me thy weakness, make me blind,
Both ways, as thou and thine, in eyes and mind;
Love, let me never know that this
Is love, or, that love childish is.
Let me not know that others know
20   That she knows my pain, lest that so
A tender shame make me mine own new woe.

If thou give nothing, yet thou'art just,
Because I would not thy first motions[7] trust;

2. Since you are the center.
3. Gambling.
4. I alone received nothing, though I gave more of myself.
5. An edict hereby a law is suspended for someone.
6. Dependent or follower. The sense of lines 8–14 is that the poet can now falsify tears, sighs, or vows with impunity since he is an avowed follower of Cupid. He needs no special dispensation.
7. Emotions or impulses.

Small towns which stand stiff, till great shot
25 Enforce them, by war's law, condition[8] not;
Such in love's warfare is my case;
I may not article[9] for grace,
Having put Love at last to show this face.

This face, by which he could command
30 And change th'idolatry of any land,
This face, which, wheresoe'er it comes,
Can call vow'd[1] men from cloisters, dead from tombs,
And melt both poles at once, and store
Deserts with cities, and make more
35 Mines in the earth, than quarries were before.

For this[2] Love is enrag'd with me,
Yet kills not; if I must example be
To future rebels, if th'unborn
Must learn by my being cut up and torn,
40 Kill, and dissect me, Love; for this
Torture against thine own end is:
Rack'd carcasses make ill anatomies.[3]

Confined Love.

Some man unworthy to be possessor
Of old or new love, himself being false or weak,
Thought his pain and shame would be lesser,
If on womankind he might his anger wreak.
5   And thence a law did grow,
One should but one man know.
But are other creatures so?

Are sun, moon, or stars by law forbidden
To smile where they list, or lend away their light?
10 Are birds divorced, or are they chidden
If they leave their mate, or lie abroad a night?[4]
Beasts do no jointures[5] lose

---

8. Demand conditions.
9. Negotiate.
1. Those who have made vows of chastity.
2. For holding out so long against love.
3. Ravaged bodies make poor cadavers for dissection.
4. At night, or perhaps, for a night.
5. Property held for the joint use of a husband and wife, which could be forfeited in divorce (OED).

Though they new lovers choose;
But we are made worse than those.

15   Who e'er rigg'd fair ships to lie in harbors,
     And not to seek new lands, or not to deal with all?
     Or built fair houses, set trees, and arbors,
     Only to lock up, or else to let them fall?
             Good is not good, unless
20   A thousand it possess,
         But doth waste with greediness.

The Dream.

Dear love, for nothing less than thee
Would I have broke this happy dream.
        It was a theme
For reason, much too strong for fantasy.
5   Therefore thou wak'dst me wisely; yet
My dream thou brok'st not, but continuedst it.
Thou art so truth that thoughts of thee suffice
To make dreams truths, and fables histories.
Enter these arms, for since thou thought'st it best,
10 Not to dream all my dream, let's act the rest.

As lightning or a taper's light,
Thine eyes, and not thy noise wak'd me.
        Yet I thought thee
(For thou lov'st truth) an angel at first sight;
15 But when I saw thou saw'st my heart,
And knew'st my thoughts beyond an angel's art,[6]
When thou knew'st what I dreamt, when thou knew'st when
Excess of joy would wake me, and cam'st then,
I do confess, it could not choose but be
20 Profane to think thee any thing but thee.

Coming and staying show'd thee, thee,
But rising makes me doubt[7] that now
        Thou art not thou.
That love is weak where fear's as strong as he.
25 'Tis not all spirit, pure and brave,
If mixture it of fear, shame, honor have.

---

6. While an angel could not see into his heart, the poet believes she can.
7. Fear.

Perchance as torches, which must ready be,
Men light and put out, so thou deal'st with me:
Thou cam'st to kindle, go'st to come; then I
30   Will dream that hope again, but else would die.[8]

96, 97, 100, 102, 107, 115

❧ A Valediction of Weeping.

Let me pour forth
My tears before thy face, whilst I stay here,
For thy face coins them, and thy stamp they bear;[9]
And by this mintage they are something worth,
5   For thus they be
          Pregnant of thee;
Fruits of much grief they are, emblems of more:[1]
When a tear falls, that thou falls which it bore;
So thou and I are nothing then, when on a divers shore.[2]

10   On a round ball
A workman, that hath copies by, can lay
An Europe, Afric, and an Asia,
And quickly make that, which was nothing, *All.*[3]
          So doth each tear,
15   Which thee doth wear,
A globe, yea world, by that impression grow,
Till thy tears mix'd with mine do overflow
This world, by waters sent from thee, my heaven dissolved so.[4]

          O more than moon,[5]
20   Draw not up seas to drown me in thy sphere;
Weep me not dead, in thine arms, but forbear
To teach the sea, what it may do too soon;
          Let not the wind
          Example find
25   To do me more harm than it purposeth:

---

8. Lines 27–30: As new torches are prepared by being lit then put aside until needed, so you
kindled my passions in the dream I and must await your coming when I can at last *die*
(with the usual *double entendre*).
9. Line 3: Thy face causes my tears and bears thy reflected image (or stamp).
1. Signs of the future grief of being absent from you (with a possible pun on Anne More).
2. In different countries.
3. Lines 10–13: Artisans can create globes by pasting copies of maps onto round balls.
4. Lines 17–18: Her tears on his cheeks will flood the worlds they have created in the tear-
drops.
5. Line 19: You are brighter or more glorious than the moon.

Since thou and I sigh one another's breath,
Whoe'er sighs most is cruellest and hastes the other's death.[6]

☉ Love's Alchemy.

Some that have deeper digg'd love's mine than I,
Say where his centric happiness[7] doth lie.
    I have lov'd, and got, and told,
But should I love, get, tell, till I were old,
5 I should not find that hidden mystery.
      Oh, 'tis imposture all.
And as no chemic yet th'elixir got,
    But glorifies his pregnant pot,
    If by the way to him befall
10 Some odoriferous thing, or med'cinal,[8]
    So, lovers dream a rich and long delight,
    But get a winter-seeming summer's night.[9]

Our ease, our thrift, our honor, and our day,
Shall we for this vain bubble's shadow pay?
15   Ends love in this? That my man[1]
Can be as happy'as I can, if he can
Endure the short scorn of a bridegroom's play?[2]
    That loving wretch that swears,
  'Tis not the bodies marry, but the minds,
20   Which he in her angelic finds,
    Would swear as justly, that he hears,
In that day's rude hoarse minstrelsy, the spheres.[3]
  Hope not for mind in women. At their best,
Sweetness and wit, they're, but mummy possess'd.[4]

---

6. Sighing was thought to shorten life.
7. The center of love's happiness for a man is a woman's genitals (*love's mine*). Donne uses this crude pun in the elegy "Love's Progress," line 36.
8. Lines 7–10. No alchemist has found the elixir to transmute base metals to gold, yet falsely hails each chance occurrence in the crucible as progress.
9. Cold and short night.
1. Servant.
2. Endure the brief mockery of the wedding ceremony (which speaks of love in exalted terms).
3. Takes the raucous music of the servant's wedding for the ineffable music of the heavenly spheres.
4. Lines 23–24 were punctuated variously in the mss., thus creating various possible meanings: Women, at their best are but mummies animated by a demonic spirit. Or, women before marriage are at their best, but after are possessed. Or, when possessed by men, women are bodies without minds. *Mummia* was a substance prepared from mummified human flesh, supposed to be a panacea (OED 1.a).

The Flea.[5]

Mark but this flea, and mark in this,
How little that which thou deny'st[6] me is;
It suck'd me first, and now sucks thee,
And in this flea our two bloods mingled be.
5   Thou know'st this cannot be said
A sin, or shame, or loss of maidenhead,
      Yet this enjoys before it woo,
      And pamper'd swells with one blood made of two;[7]
      And this, alas, is more than we would do.

10 Oh stay, three lives in one flea spare,
Where we almost, nay more than, married are.[8]
This flea is you and I, and this
Our marriage bed and marriage temple is.
Though parents grudge, and you, we're met,
15 And cloister'd in these living walls of jet.[9]
      Though use[1] make you apt to kill me,
      Let not, to that, self-murder added be,
      And sacrilege, three sins in killing three.[2]

Cruel and sudden, hast thou since
20 Purpled thy nail in blood of innocence?
Wherein could this flea guilty be?
Except in that drop which it suck'd from thee?
Yet thou triumph'st, and say'st that thou
Find'st not thyself nor me the weaker now.
25   'Tis true; then learn how false fears be:
      Just so much honor, when thou yield'st to me,
      Will waste, as this flea's death took life from thee.

---

5. Poems on the flea, which could take liberties with the mistress's body denied the poet, were popular in the early Renaissance, e.g., *La Puce de Madame des Roches* (1582). Donne's originality lay in creating a witty, dramatic scene in which the flea has bitten both him and the woman, thus mingling their bloods and providing him with a new line of attack.
6. She has rejected his advances.
7. In Aristotelean physiology, intercourse was thought to involve a mingling of bloods (as was conception since semen was thought to be a form of blood).
8. Line 11: Because their bloods are mingled sexually, and they are united matrimonially.
9. The black walls of the flea's thorax or abdomen.
1. Habit.
2. Line 18: Murder in killing him; suicide in killing herself, and sacrilege in killing the sacramentally consecrated flea.

The Curse.

Whoever guesses, thinks, or dreams he knows
Who is my mistress, wither by this curse:
    His only, and only his purse
    May some dull heart to love dispose,[3]
5 And she yield then to all that are his foes;
    May he be scorn'd by one whom all else scorn,
    Forswear to others, what to her he'hath sworn,
    With fear of missing, shame of getting torn.[4]

Madness his sorrow, gout his cramps, may he
10 Make, by but thinking who hath made him such;
    And may he feel no touch
    Of conscience, but of fame,[5] and be
Anguish'd, not that 'twas sin, but that 'twas she.
    In early and long scarceness may he rot,
15   For land which had been his, if he had not
    Himself incestuously an heir begot.

May he dream treason and believe that he
Meant to perform it, and confess, and die,
    And no record tell why;
20   His sons, which none of his may be,
Inherit nothing but his infamy;
    Or may he so long parasites have fed,
    That he would fain be theirs, whom he hath bred,
    And at the last be circumcis'd for bread.[6]

25 The venom of all stepdames, gamesters' gall,
What tyrants and their subjects interwish,
    What plants, mines, beasts, fowl, fish,
    Can contribute, all ill, which all
Prophets or poets spake; and all which shall
30   Be annex'd in schedules[7] unto this by me,
    Fall on that man. For if it be a she,
    Nature beforehand hath out-cursed me.

---

3. Lines 2–4: May only his money induce some dull woman to favor him, who will then yield to all his rivals freely.
4. Line 8: Torn between fear of not winning her and shame of actually doing so.
5. Notoriety, reputation.
6. Line 24: Become a Jew to receive their charity, or curry favor with Jewish money-lenders.
7. Codicils to documents.

The Ecstasy.[8]

[handwritten: dramatic context — two lovers on riverbank with Violets]

Where, like a pillow on a bed,
    A pregnant bank swell'd up to rest

[handwritten: symbol of true love + fidelity]

The violet's reclining head,
    Sat we two, one another's best.

5   Our hands were firmly cemented
    With a fast balm,[9] which thence did spring;

[handwritten: hand to hand]

Our eye-beams[1] twisted, and did thread
    Our eyes upon one double string.

So t'intergraft our hands, as yet
10   Was all the means to make us one, *[handwritten: — hands linked]*
And pictures on our eyes to get[2]
    Was all our propagation.

As 'twixt two equal armies fate *[handwritten: army/opponent as sexual metaphor - see Elegy 8 p.34]*
    Suspends uncertain victory,
15   Our souls, which to advance their state
    Were gone out, hung 'twixt her and me. *[handwritten: — souls out of bodies]*

And whilst our souls negotiate there,
    We like sepulchral statues lay;
All day, the same our postures were,
20   And we said nothing, all the day.

If any, so by love refin'd, *[handwritten: if someone who]*
    That he soul's language understood, *[handwritten: has become]*
And by good love were grown all mind, *[handwritten: spiritualized]*
    Within convenient distance stood, *[handwritten: were nearby]*

25   He (though he knew not which soul spake, *[handwritten: — souls speak with one voice]*
    Because both meant, both spake the same)
Might thence a new concoction[3] take,
    And part far purer than he came.

---

8. Literally, the state of being "beside oneself." Ecstasy was used by mystics to describe the rapture in which the body was supposed to become incapable of sensation, while the soul was engaged in the contemplation of divine things (OED 3.a.).
9. Perspiration from the hands.
1. According to Renaissance theories of optics, the eyes emitted invisible beams that reflected the object's image to the spectator. These lovers are thus united by their eye-beams.
2. Beget.
3. Refinement or purification by heat.

[handwritten: → eyebeam went out, captured image, puts in brain Renaissance theory of optics]

This ecstasy doth unperplex
30   (We said) and tell us what we love;   *it wasn't sex,*
We see by this, it was not sex;   *even though we*
   We see, we saw not, what did move:[4]   *thought it was*

But as all several souls contain
   Mixture of things they know not what,
35 Love, these mix'd souls, doth mix again,
   And makes both one, each this, and that.

A single violet transplant,[5]
   The strength, the color, and the size,
All which before was poor and scant,
40   Redoubles still, and multiplies.

When love, with one another so   *one soul issues from*
   Interinanimates two souls,   *the two souls in*
That abler soul, which thence doth flow,   *their communion*
   Defects of loneliness controls.

45 We then, who are this new soul, know,
   Of what we are composed, and made:
For th'atomies[6] of which we grow
   Are souls, whom no change can invade.

materialist moment
But oh, alas, so long, so far,
50   Our bodies why do we forbear?   *difference between*
They're ours, though they're not we; we are   *body/mind*
   Th'intelligences, they the sphere.[7]

We owe them thanks, because they thus
   Did us, to us, at first convey,   *Plato's Symposium —*
55 Yielded their forces, sense, to us,   *ascent toward philosophy*
   Nor are dross to us, but allay.[8]   *begins with viewing a*
                      beautiful boy

On man heaven's influence works not so,
   But that it first imprints the air;[9]

4. Line 32: We now understand that we did not understand before what moved our affections.
5. Line 37: Transplant a single violet to a pregnant bank, and then. . . . The violet was emblematic of faithful love and truth.
6. Atoms or components.
7. Lines 51–52: Just as each of the Ptolemaic spheres was thought to have an angel or *intelligence* regulating it, so bodies were regulated by souls.
8. Alloy, a mixture of base and noble powers.
9. Lines 57–58: Astrologers postulated that the stars influenced the microcosm by first working through the air.

So soul into the soul may flow,
60   Though it to body first repair.

As our blood labors to beget
    Spirits,[1] as like souls as it can,
Because such fingers need to knit
    That subtle knot, which makes us man:

[handwritten: without the body's affections/ senses, the mind is like an imprisoned prince]

65   So must pure lovers' souls descend
    T'affections, and to faculties,
Which sense may reach and apprehend,
    Else a great prince in prison lies.

T'our bodies turn we then, that so   *[handwritten: body = visible]*
70   Weak men on love reveal'd may look;   *[handwritten: to weak men]*
Love's mysteries in souls do grow,
    But yet the body is his book.   *[handwritten: body as text/ scripture ∴ divine inscription]*

And if some lover, such as we,
    Have heard this dialogue of one,
75   Let him still mark us, he shall see
    Small change when we're to bodies gone.

[handwritten: conceit - reversible? the book is love's body book - where author and reader commune]

The Undertaking.[2]

[handwritten: I have only ever done one thing braver than the great men of history 'we've]
I have done one braver thing
    Than all the Worthies[3] did,
And yet a braver thence doth spring,
    Which is, to keep that hid.   *[handwritten: It would be madness to seek a skill no longer used.]*
[handwritten: Yet after I did this I did one thing braver, which was not to tell anyone]
5   It were but madness now t'impart
    The skill of specular stone,[4]   *[handwritten: because, after learning]*
When he, which can have learn'd the art   *[handwritten: the art of]*
    To cut it, can find none.   *[handwritten: cutting the stone, can then find no stone to cut,]*
[handwritten: so now if I were to reveal this, the brave thing I've done]
    So, if I now should utter this,
10   Others (because no more

1. The body produced three kinds of spirits from the blood to form intermediaries for the
    three faculties of the soul (growth, sensation, and cognition).
2. Also called "Platonic Love" in some mss.
3. The Nine Worthies were Hector, Alexander the Great, and Julius Caesar from antiquity;
    Joshua, David, and Judas Maccabaeus from the Bible; and Arthur, Charlemagne, and
    Godfrey of Bouillon from Christendom.
4. The method for cutting selenite, a stone used in antiquity for glazing but no longer avail-
    able.

Others, because I have nothing more to work with would be unchanged, loving the same.

      Such stuff to work upon, there is)
        Would love, but as before: *but he who is lovely within has discoved*

But he who loveliness within *that he hates the*
      Hath found, all outward loathes, *man who loves*
15 For he who color loves, and skin, *color & skin,*
      Loves but their oldest clothes.[5]

'because he loves only their bodies

      If, as I have, you also do
        Virtue'attir'd in woman see,
      And dare love that, and say so too,
20   And forget the He and She;

      And if this love, though placed so,
        From profane men you hide,
      Which will no faith on this bestow,
        Or, if they do, deride:

25 Then you have done a braver thing
        Than all the Worthies did,
      And a braver thence will spring,
        Which is, to keep that hid.

Love's Deity.

I long to talk with some old lover's ghost,
    Who died before the god of love was born.
I cannot think that he, who then lov'd most,
    Sunk so low as to love one which did scorn.
5 But since this god produc'd a destiny,
And that vice-nature, custom,[6] lets it be,
    I must love her that loves not me.

Sure, they which made him god, meant not so much,
    Nor he in his young godhead practic'd it.
10 But when an even flame two hearts did touch,
    His office was indulgently to fit
Actives to passives.[7] Correspondency
Only his subject was: it cannot be
    Love, till I love her that loves me.

5. The external attributes of female bodies.
6. Custom that takes the place of nature.
7. Male to corresponding female lovers.

15　But every modern god will now extend
　　　His vast prerogative as far as Jove.
　　To rage, to lust, to write to, to commend,
　　　All is the purlieu[8] of the god of love.
　　Oh, were we waken'd by this tyranny
20　T'ungod this child again, it could not be
　　That I should love, who loves not me.

　　Rebel and atheist[9] too, why murmur I,
　　　As though I felt the worst that love could do?
　　Love might make me leave loving, or might try
25　　A deeper plague, to make her love me too;
　　Which, since she loves before,[1] I'm loath to see.
　　Falsehood is worse than hate; and that must be,
　　　If she whom I love, should love me.

Love's Diet.

　　To what a cumbersome unwieldiness
　　And burdenous corpulence my love had grown,
　　　But that I did, to make it less,
　　　And keep it in proportion,
5　Give it a diet, made it feed upon
　　That which love worst endures, *discretion*.[2]

　　Above one sigh a day I'allow'd him not,
　　Of which my fortune and my faults had part;
　　　And if sometimes by stealth he got
10　　A she sigh from my mistress' heart,
　　And thought to feast on that, I let him see
　　'Twas neither very sound, nor meant to me.[3]

　　If he wrung from me'a tear, I brin'd[4] it so
　　With scorn and shame, that him it nourish'd not;
15　　If he suck'd hers, I let him know
　　　'Twas not a tear which he had got.
　　His drink was counterfeit, as was his meat;[5]
　　For eyes which roll towards all, weep not, but sweat.

8. Domain.
9. He disbelieves in the god of love.
1. She already has a lover.
2. I.e., he has reduced his love by being discreet.
3. Neither genuine nor intended for me.
4. Salted.
5. Her tears and sighs were false.

Whatever he would dictate, I writ that,
20 But burnt my letters. When she writ to me,
   And that, that favor made him fat,
   I said, "If any title be
Convey'd by this, ah, what doth it avail,
To be the fortieth name in an entail?"[6]

25 Thus I reclaim'd my buzzard[7] love to fly
At what, and when, and how, and where I choose.
   Now negligent of sport I lie,
   And now, as other falc'ners use,
I spring[8] a mistress, swear, write, sigh, and weep:
30 And the game kill'd, or lost, go talk and sleep.

The Will.[9]

Before I sigh my last gasp, let me breathe,
Great Love, some legacies: I here bequeath
Mine eyes to Argus,[1] if mine eyes can see;
If they be blind, then, Love, I give them thee;
5 My tongue to Fame;[2] t'ambassadors mine ears;
   To women, or the sea, my tears;
Thou, Love, hast taught me heretofore,
By making me serve her who'had twenty more,
That I should give to none, but such as had too much before.

10 My constancy I to the planets give;
My truth to them who at the court do live;
   My ingenuity and openness,
   To Jesuits;[3] to buffoons my pensiveness;
My silence t'any, who abroad hath been;
15   My money to a Capuchin.[4]
Thou, Love, taught'st me, by appointing me

6. As the fortieth person in line named to succeed to an estate, he could not reasonably hope for the title to her.
7. A rapacious species of hawk now reduced to tameness.
8. Start or flush.
9. The bequests are all ironic: some duplicate traits of the heirs (lines 3–6), some criticize the absence of those traits (10–15, 19–24), some restore what he has already received (28–33), and some give what is no longer needed (37–42).
1. A monster in Greek mythology with a hundred eyes, famed as a guard.
2. Rumor or ill repute.
3. The Jesuit order operated clandestinely in England as the pope's secret army.
4. A religious order of mendicant friars who took vows of poverty and were dependent on alms.

To love there, where no love receiv'd can be,
Only to give to such as have an incapacity.

My faith I give to Roman Catholics;
20   All my good works unto the Schismatics
Of Amsterdam;[5] my best civility
And courtship to an university;
My modesty I give to soldiers bare;
    My patience let gamesters share.
25   Thou, Love, taught'st me, by making me
Love her that holds my love disparity,[6]
Only to give to those that count my gifts indignity.

I give my reputation to those
Which were my friends; mine industry to foes;
30   To Schoolmen[7] I bequeath my doubtfulness;
My sickness to physicians, or excess;
To Nature all that I in rhyme have writ;
    And to my company my wit.
Thou, Love, by making me adore
35   Her, who begot this love in me before,
Taught'st me to make, as though I gave, when I did but restore.

To him for whom the passing-bell next tolls,
I give my physic[8] books; my written rolls
Of moral counsels I to Bedlam[9] give;
40   My brazen medals unto them which live
In want of bread; to them which pass among
    All foreigners, mine English tongue.
Thou, Love, by making me love one
Who thinks her friendship a fit portion
45   For younger lovers, dost my gifts thus disproportion.

Therefore I'll give no more, but I'll undo
The world by dying, because love dies too.
Then all your beauties will be no more worth
Than gold in mines, where none doth draw it forth;
50   And all your graces no more use shall have,
    Than a sundial in a grave.
Thou, Love, taught'st me by making me

5. Extreme Calvinists who believed in justification by faith alone, not through good works.
6. Beneath her.
7. Medieval philosophers who tried to integrate orthodox Christian teaching with Aristotle
   and Plato.
8. Medical books.
9. Bethlehem Hospital for the insane.

Love her who doth neglect both me and thee,
T'invent, and practice this one way, t'annihilate all three.

✿ The Funeral.

Whoever comes to shroud[1] me, do not harm
    Nor question much
That subtle wreath of hair, which crowns mine arm;
The mystery, the sign, you must not touch,
5   For 'tis my outward soul,
Viceroy[2] to that, which then to heav'n being gone,
    Will leave this to control
And keep these limbs, her provinces, from dissolution.

For if the sinewy thread[3] my brain lets fall
10   Through every part
Can tie those parts, and make me one of all,
These hairs which upward grew, and strength and art
    Have from a better brain,
Can better do't; except she meant that I
15   By this should know my pain,
As prisoners then are manacled, when they're condemn'd to die.

Whate'er she meant by't, bury it with me,
    For since I am
Love's martyr,[4] it might breed idolatry,
20 If into other hands these relics came.
    As 'twas humility
To afford to it all which a soul can do,
    So, 'tis some bravery,[5]
That since you would save none of me, I bury some of you.

✿ The Blossom. ★

Little think'st thou, poor flower,
Whom I've watch'd six or seven days,
And seen thy birth, and seen what every hour
Gave to thy growth, thee to this height to raise,

1. Prepare his body for burial.
2. The ruler of his body in place of his soul, which is now in heaven.
3. His spinal chord.
4. Reference to the Roman Catholic reverence for the relics of saints and martyrs.
5. Show of bravado.

5 And now dost laugh and triumph on this bough;
       Little think'st thou
That it will freeze anon, and that I shall
Tomorrow find thee fall'n, or not at all.

      Little think'st thou, poor heart,
10   That labor'st yet to nestle thee,
And think'st by hovering here to get a part
In a forbidden or forbidding[6] tree,
And hop'st her stiffness by long siege to bow;
      Little think'st thou
15 That thou tomorrow, ere that sun[7] doth wake,
Must with the sun and me a journey take.

     But thou,[8] which lov'st to be
      Subtle to plague thyself, wilt say,
"Alas, if you must go, what's that to me?
20 Here lies my business, and here I will stay.
You go to friends, whose love and means present
      Various content[9]
To your eyes, ears, and tongue, and every part.
If then your body go, what need you'a heart?"

25   Well then, stay here; but know,
      When thou hast stay'd and done thy most,
A naked thinking heart, that makes no show,
Is to a woman but a kind of ghost.
How shall she know my heart; or having none,
30   Know thee for one?
Practice may make her know some other part,
But take my word, she doth not know a heart.

     Meet me in London, then,
      Twenty days hence, and thou shalt see
35 Me fresher and more fat, by being with men,
Than if I had stay'd still with her and thee.
For God's sake, if you can, be you so too;
      I would give you
There to another friend, whom we shall find
40 As glad to have my body as my mind.

6. *Forbidden* suggests the relationship is illicit; *forbidding* suggests the woman is refusing the poet's advances.
7. The woman.
8. The poet's heart, who proposes to stay while the poet returns to London.
9. Satisfaction.

The Primrose.

Upon this Primrose Hill,[1]
Where, if heav'n would distil
A shower of rain, each several drop might go
To his own primrose, and grow manna so;
5   And where their form, and their infinity
Make a terrestrial galaxy,
As the small stars do in the sky,[2]
I walk to find a true love; and I see
That 'tis not a mere woman, that is she,
10 But must, or more, or less than woman be.

Yet know I not, which flower
I wish: a six, or four;[3]
For should my true love less than woman be,
She were scarce anything; and then, should she
15 Be more than woman, she would get above
All thought of sex, and think to move
My heart to study her, not to love.
Both these were monsters; since there must reside
Falsehood in woman, I could more abide,
20 She were by art, than nature falsifi'd.

Live, primrose, then, and thrive
With thy true number five;[4]
And women, whom this flower doth represent,
With this mysterious number[5] be content.
25 Ten is the farthest number; if half ten
Belong unto each woman, then
Each woman may take half us men;
Or, if this will not serve their turn, since all
Numbers are odd, or even, and they fall
30 First into this five,[6] women may take us all.

1. Printed editions from 1635 onward identified Primrose Hill in a subtitle as a hill at Montgomery Castle, the seat of the Herbert family. "The Blossom" and "The Primrose" were frequently identified with Magdalen Herbert. There is also a Primrose Hill near London.
2. Topical reference to the new telescopic evidence (first asserted by Galileo in *Siderius Nuncius* in 1610) that the Milky Way contained many smaller stars.
3. A six-petaled or four-petaled primrose; even numbered ones were considered symbols of faithful love.
4. The usual number of petals was five,
5. Ten is the mystical number of perfection, which the poet assigns to the male; to females, the number five. Donne takes for granted the superiority of male to female (as in "Air and Angels" or the refrain in the "Epithalamion Made at Lincoln's Inn").
6. Five is the first number that consists of an odd and an even number (taking one as a unity, neither odd nor even). In mystical numerology, five sometimes symbolized male and female united (two and three).

The Relic. *

When my grave is broke up again   *grave*
Some second guest to entertain,[7]

promiscuity   (For graves have learn'd that woman-head,[8]
To be to more than one a bed)
5   And he that digs it, spies
A bracelet of bright hair about the bone,
Will he not let'us alone,
And think that there a loving couple lies,
Who thought that this device might be some way
10 To make their souls at the last busy day[9]
Meet at this grave, and make a little stay?

refers to the   If (this) fall in a time or land,   *what is mis-devotion?*
object, but also   Where mis-devotion doth command,
the poem   Then he that digs us up will bring
15   Us to the bishop and the king,
To make us relics; then   *human agency makes*
Thou shalt be'a Mary Magdalen, and I   *the object a*
A something else[1] thereby.   *relic*
All women shall adore us, and some men.
20 And, since at such times miracles are sought,
I would have that age by this paper[2] taught   *wants the sacred*
What miracles we harmless lovers wrought.   *nature of their*
                                               relationship to be
                                               understood
"The   First, we lov'd well, and faithfully,
Ecstasy "   Yet knew not what we lov'd, nor why;
25   Difference of sex no more we knew,
Than our guardian angels do;
Coming and going, we
Perchance might kiss,[3] but not between those meals;[4]
Our hands ne'er touch'd the seals,
30 Which nature, injur'd by late law,[5] sets free.
These miracles we did; but now, alas,
            time / tense shift

7. Reusing hallowed burial ground was common.
8. Womanhood, but with a bawdy analogue to maidenhead.
9. At the Resurrection.
1. Some other relic, or perhaps a bone of Christ, who some believe was linked to Mary
   Magdalen.
2. The poem.
3. Lines 27–28: Kiss in salutation or in parting.
4. These kisses are the food of the soul.
5. Lines 29–30: We never had physical relations, which Nature allows to all other species,
   but which mankind has made illicit. In this context, *seals* may refer to the maidenhead.

beyond language

All measure and all language I should pass,
Should I tell what a miracle she was.

*conditional/
subjunctive mood*

The Damp. ✗

When I am dead, and doctors know not why,
        And my friends' curiosity
Will have me cut up to survey each part,
When they shall find your picture in my heart,
5   You think a sudden damp[6] of love
        Will through all their senses move,
And work on them as me, and so prefer[7]
Your murder to the name of massacre.

        Poor victories. But if you dare be brave,
10   And pleasure in your conquest have,
First kill th'enormous giant, your *Disdain*;
And let th'enchantress *Honor*, next be slain;
        And like a Goth and Vandal[8] rise,
        Deface records and histories
15 Of your own arts and triumphs over men,
And without such advantage kill me then.

        For I could muster up, as well as you,
        My giants, and my witches too,
Which are vast *Constancy* and *Secretness*;
20 But these I neither look for nor profess;
        Kill me as woman! Let me die[9]
        As a mere man; do you but try
Your passive valor, and you shall find then,
Naked, you've odds enough of any man.

The Dissolution.

She's dead; and all which die
To their first elements resolve;
And we were mutual elements to us,

---

6. Noxious exhalation.
7. Promote (i.e., by elevating the number).
8. Barbarians who sacked Rome.
9. Climax sexually; refers to the belief that sexual emission shortened the length of life.

And made of one another.
5   My body then doth hers involve,
And those things whereof I consist, hereby
In me abundant grow, and burdenous,
        And nourish not, but smother.[1]
My fire of passion, sighs of air,
10   Water of tears, and earthly sad despair,
        Which my materials[2] be,
But near worn out by love's security,
She, to my loss, doth by her death repair.[3]
And I might live long wretched so,
15   But that my fire doth with my fuel grow.
        Now as those active kings
    Whose foreign conquest treasure brings,
Receive more, and spend more, and soonest break,
This (which I am amaz'd that I can speak)
20   This death, hath with my store
        My use increas'd.
And so my soul, more earnestly releas'd,
Will outstrip[4] hers; as bullets flown before
A latter bullet may o'ertake, the powder being more.[5]

A Jet Ring Sent.

Thou art not so black[6] as my heart,
Nor half so brittle, as her heart, thou art;
What wouldst thou say? Shall both our properties by thee be spoke:
Nothing more endless, nothing sooner broke?

5   Marriage rings are not of this stuff,[7]
Oh, why should ought less precious, or less tough
Figure our loves? Except in thy name thou have bid it say,
    "I'm cheap and nought but fashion; fling me away."

    Yet stay with me since thou art come;
10   Circle this finger's top, which didst her thumb.

1. In Galenic medicine, the healthy body was characterized by a balance of the four humors; an excess of one created a dis-temperature.
2. Elements: fire, air, water, and earth (lines 9–10).
3. Replenish.
4. Overtake.
5. When the explosive charge is greater.
6. A symbol of constancy (since there were no shades of black); *thou*: the poet addresses a fragile jet ring that a woman has sent him as a love token.
7. I.e., they are of gold.

Be justly proud and gladly safe that thou dost dwell with me.
  She that, oh, broke her faith, would soon break thee.

Negative Love.[8]

    I never stoop'd so low, as they[9]
    Which on an eye, cheek, lip, can prey;
      Seldom to them[1] which soar no higher
      Than virtue, or the mind t'admire.
5   For sense and understanding may
      Know what gives fuel to their fire.
    My love, though silly,[2] is more brave;
    For may I miss, whene'er I crave,
    If I know yet what I would have.

10   If that be simply perfectest,
    Which can by no way be express'd
      But *negatives*,[3] my love is so.
      To all, which all love, I say no.[4]
    If any who deciphers best,
15   What we know not, ourselves, can know,
    Let him teach me that nothing. This
    As yet my ease and comfort is:
    Though I speed not, I cannot miss.[5]

The Computation.[6]

For my first twenty years, since yesterday,
  I scarce believ'd thou couldst be gone away;
For forty more I fed on favors past,
  And forty'on hopes that thou wouldst they might last;
5 Tears drown'd one hundred, and sighs blew out two;
    A thousand, I did neither think nor do,
    Or not divide, all being one thought of you;

---

8. In some mss. the title of this poem is "The Nothing."
9. Those who love physically.
1. Seldom stooped to Platonic lovers.
2. Unlearned, unsophisticated (OED).
3. Refers to the notion that the divine, as a perfect essence, could only be expressed by negative terms.
4. Line 13: I decline all those positive attributes that others love.
5. Line 18: Though I make no progress, I cannot fail (since I want nothing).
6. The computation of the years mentioned in the poem is 2400, thus implying that each hour away from her feels like a hundred years.

Or in a thousand more, forgot that too.
Yet call not this long life; but think that I
10   Am, by being dead, immortal. Can ghosts[7] die?

The Expiration.[8]

So, so, break off this last lamenting kiss,
    Which sucks two souls, and vapors[9] both away;
Turn, thou ghost, that way, and let me turn this,
    And let ourselves benight our happiest day.
5 We ask'd none leave to love; nor will we owe
    Any, so cheap a death, as saying, "Go."

"Go." And if that word have not quite kill'd thee,
    Ease me with death, by bidding me go too.
Oh, if it have, let my word work on me,
10   And a just office on a murderer do.
Except it be too late, to kill me so,
    Being double dead, going, and bidding, "Go."

The Paradox.[1]

No lover saith, "I love," nor any other
    Can judge a perfect lover;
He thinks that else none can nor will agree,
    That any loves but he:
5 I cannot say "I lov'd," for who can say
    He was kill'd yesterday.
Love with excess of heat, more young than old,
    Death kills with too much cold;[2]
We die[3] but once, and who lov'd last did die.
10   He that saith twice, doth lie;
For though he seem to move, and stir a while,
    It doth the sense beguile.

7. Since he died at the moment of parting.
8. In some mss. this poem is titled "Valediction."
9. Causes both to be exhaled away as a vapor; the soul was thought to be related to the breath.
1. The paradox is that love cannot be known. No one can claim to love anyone in the present tense or the past tense (lines 1–6). He can only say that he loved once, then died and became his own epitaph (lines 17–18).
2. Lines 7–8: Love kills more youth with excessive heat than death kills the aged with excessive cold.
3. With a *double entendre* on climaxing sexually.

Such life is like the light which bideth yet
    When the life's light[4] is set,
15 Or like the heat which fire in solid matter
    Leaves behind two hours after.
Once I lov'd and died; and am now become
    Mine epitaph and tomb.
Here dead men speak their last, and so do I:
20   "Love-slain, lo, here I die."

A Nocturnal Upon St. Lucy's Day, Being the Shortest Day.

middle of night, middle of darkest part of year

'Tis the year's midnight, and it is the day's,
    —Lucy's,[5] who scarce seven hours herself unmasks.
    The sun is spent, and now his flasks[6]
        Send forth light squibs,[7] no constant rays;
5   The world's whole sap[8] is sunk:
    The general balm th'hydroptic[9] earth hath drunk,
    Whither, as to the bed's feet, life is shrunk,
    Dead and interr'd; yet all these seem to laugh,
    Compared with me, who am their epitaph.

darkness is upon everyone

10 Study me then, you who shall lovers be
    At the next world, that is, at the next spring: *— resurrection, the afterlife; speaker is dead, lovers reading the poem*
        For I am every dead thing,
        In whom love wrought new alchemy.
            For his art did express
15   [A quintessence even from nothingness,[1]]
        From dull privations, and lean emptiness: *love made ruin of the speaker,*
        He ruin'd me, and I am re-begot
        Of absence, darkness, death: things which are not. *transmuted into ultimate nothingness*

    All others, from all things, draw all that's good,
20 Life, soul, form, spirit, whence they being have;
        I, by love's limbeck,[2] am the grave *by the distillation of love, I am the grave of all things nothing*
            Of all, that's nothing. Oft a flood

---

4. The sun.
5. St. Lucy's Day is December 13, the winter solstice under the Julian Calendar (still in use until 1752); thus, the shortest day of the year. A virgin martyr, Lucy plucked her own eyes to send them to a suitor who had admired them, wishing to be left in peace.
6. The stars were thought to store light from the sun in flasks (see *Paradise Lost* 7, 354–69).
7. Small firecrackers, here meaning the stars give little light.
8. As it is winter, the sap that brings life to plants is still dormant.
9. Thirsty.
1. He is a distillation of the nothingness out of which the universe was created.
2. The apparatus in which alchemical distillations were conducted.

Have we two wept, and so
Drown'd the whole world, us two; oft did we grow,
25   To be two chaoses, when we did show
Care to aught else; and often absences
Withdrew our souls and made us carcasses.

But I am by her death (which word wrongs her)
Of the first nothing[3] the elixir grown;
30   Were I a man, that I were one
I needs must know; I should prefer,
If I were any beast,
Some ends, some means; yea plants, yea stones detest,
And love; all, all some properties invest.
35   If I an ordinary nothing were,
As shadow,'a light, and body must be here.[4]

But I am none; nor will my sun renew.
You lovers, for whose sake the lesser sun
At this time to the Goat[5] is run
40   To fetch new lust, and give it you,
Enjoy your summer all.
Since she enjoys her long night's festival,
Let me prepare towards her, and let me call
This hour her vigil, and her eve, since this
45   Both the year's and the day's deep midnight is.

[Handwritten marginalia:]
if I were a beast, would have nutrition (∴ ends + means)
I am the first nothing into which God creates
the literal sun
youth
prepare for own death – suicide?
last word in a poem about absence is word of being
poem first + last line form a circle, but not a perfect circle – obsessive revolving of grief?

Witchcraft by a Picture.

I fix mine eye on thine, and there
Pity my picture burning in thine eye;[6]
My picture drown'd in a transparent tear,
When I look lower I espy.
5   Hadst thou the wicked skill
By pictures made and marr'd, to kill,[7]
How many ways mightst thou perform thy will?

But now I've drunk thy sweet salt tears,
And though thou pour more, I'll depart;

3. The primordial nothing that existed before the Creation.
4. Lines 35–36: Since he is the quintessence of the primordial nothing (and not an "ordinary nothing"), he is less substantial than a shadow or light.
5. The sun entered the sign of Capricorn at the solstice; goats were reputed to be lustful.
6. He is viewing his picture in her eyes or tears, as in "A Valediction of Weeping."
7. Some witches were reputed to be able to kill someone by making and then destroying a picture of that person.

10 My picture vanish'd, vanish all fears
        That I can be endamag'd by that art:
            Though thou retain of me
        One picture more, yet that will be,
        Being in thine own heart, from all malice free.

Farewell to Love.†

        Whilst yet to prove,[8]
    I thought there was some deity in love,
            So did I reverence, and gave
        Worship as atheists at their dying hour
5   Call, what they cannot name, an unknown power,
            As ignorantly did I crave:
                Thus when
        Things not yet known are coveted by men,
            Our desires give them fashion; and so
10 As they wax lesser, fall, as they rise, grow.[9]

            But from last fair,
        His highness sitting in a golden chair[1]
            Is not less cared for after three days
        By children, than the thing[2] which lovers so
15 Blindly admire, and with such worship woo;
            Being had, enjoying, it decays;
                And thence,
        What before pleas'd them all, takes but one sense,[3]
            And that so lamely, as it leaves behind
20 A kind of sorrowing dulness to the mind.

            Oh, cannot we
        As well as cocks and lions jocund be
            After such pleasures: unless wise
        Nature decree'd (since each such act, they say,
25 Diminishes the length of life a day)[4]
            This: as she would man should despise
                The sport,

† I am much indebted to Gary A. Stringer, "The Text of 'Farewell to Love,'" *John Donne Journal* 18 (1999): 201–13, for the textual history of this poem.
8. Still inexperienced or unproven in love.
9. Lines 7–10: When we wish for things as yet unknown to us, our desires give them form; then as our knowledge of things increases, our desires fall.
1. A painted throne at a fair.
2. The sexual act.
3. Line 18: What pleased all the senses before, pleases only one after.
4. A popular belief since sexual emission was thought to entail the loss of the life force itself.

Because that other curse, of being short
    And only for a minute made to be
30 Eager, desires to raise posterity.[5]

        Since so: my mind
Shall not desire what no man else can find;
    I'll no more dote, and run
To pursue things, which had, endamage me;
35 And when I come where moving beauties be,
    As men do when the summer's sun
        Grows great,
Though I admire their greatness, shun their heat.
    Each place can afford shadows; if all fail,
40 'Tis but applying worm-seed[6] to the tail.

Self-Love.[7]

    He that cannot choose but love,
      And strives against it still,
    Never shall my fancy move,
5   For he loves 'gainst his will;

    Nor he which is all his own,[8]
      And can at pleasure choose;
    When I am caught he can be gone,
      And when he list[9] refuse.

10 Nor he that loves none but fair,
      For such by all are sought;
    Nor he that can for foulness care,
      For his judgment is naught;

    Nor he that hath wit, for he
15   Will make me his jest or slave;
    Nor a fool for whom[1]
      He can neither want nor crave;

5. Creates desire in order to procreate.
6. A name for various plants believed to diminish sexual appetite, applied here to the penis.
7. This poem was titled "Elegy" in the mss. but does not have the metrical pattern of the other elegies; it has been called "Self-Love" since the nineteenth century. The speaker is a woman who rejects various types of lovers.
8. Completely self-possessed.
9. Please.
1. A defective line with a word (or phrase) of three syllables missing.

Nor he that still his mistress pays,
  For she is thrall'd therefore;
20 Nor he that pays not, for he says,
  Within,[2] "She's worth no more."

Is there then no kind of men
Whom I may freely prove?[3]
I will vent that humor then
In mine own self-love.

Image of Her Whom I Love.

Image of her whom I love, more than she,
Whose fair impression in my faithful heart
Makes me her medal, and makes her love me,
As kings do coins, to which their stamps impart
5 The value: go, and take my heart from hence,
Which now is grown too great and good for me.
Honors oppress weak spirits, and our sense
Strong objects dull; the more,[4] the less we see.

When you are gone, and reason gone with you,
10 Then fantasy[5] is queen, and soul, and all;
She can present joys meaner[6] than you do,
Convenient, and more proportional.
So, if I dream I have you, I have you:
For all our joys are but fantastical.
15 And so I 'scape the pain, for pain is true;
And sleep, which locks up sense, doth lock out all.

After such a fruition[7] I shall wake,
And, but the waking, nothing shall repent;
And shall to love more thankful sonnets make,
20 Than if more honor, tears, and pains were spent.
But, dearest heart and dearer image, stay;
Alas, true joys at best are dream enough;

2. To himself.
3. Try and/or approve.
4. The greater an object, the less clearly we can perceive objects near it (in this case, the mental image of her overpowers all else).
5. Imagination.
6. More common.
7. Enjoyment.

Though you stay here, you pass too fast away,
For even at first life's taper is a snuff.[8]

25 Fill'd with her love, may I be rather grown
Mad with much heart, than idiot with none.

The First Anniversary:
An Anatomy of the World.
Wherein, by Occasion of the untimely death of
Mistress Elizabeth Drury
the frailty and the decay of this whole World is
represented.[9]

When that rich soul which to her heaven is gone,   *The entry into*
Whom all do celebrate, who know they have one   *the work.*
(For who is sure he hath a soul, unless
It see, and judge, and follow worthiness,
5 And by deeds praise it? He who doth not this,
May lodge an inmate[1] soul, but 'tis not his.)
When that queen ended here her progress[2] time,
And, as t'her standing house,[3] to heaven did climb,
Where, loath to make the saints attend her long,
10 She's now a part both of the quire, and song,
This world, in that great earthquake languished;
For in a common bath of tears it bled,
Which drew the strongest vital spirits[4] out:
But succor'd then with a perplexed doubt,
10 Whether the world did lose or gain in this,
(Because since now no other way there is,
But goodness, to see her, whom all would see,

8. Our life's candle has a partially consumed wick even at its outset, so brief is life (and pleasure).
9. The first edition (1611) titled this poem *An Anatomy of the World* but subsequent editions titled it *The First Anniversary* to distinguish it from a second poem on the early death of Elizabeth Drury (d. 1610), the daughter of Sir Robert Drury, a patron of Donne. Although her death was the occasion for this poem, Donne told the poet Ben Jonson "that he described the Idea of a Woman and not as she was." Even though others, such as Jonson, derided it [see p. 179], *The First Anniversary* was important enough to Donne that he allowed four different editions of it to be published (in 1611, 1612, 1621, 1625). The notes in the margin are Donne's. *Anatomy* here means a systemic analysis of a topic.
1. As a temporary lodger.
2. A monarch's state visit to an area.
3. Permanent dwelling.
4. The body produced three kinds of spirits from the blood to form intermediaries for the soul; the vital spirits were thought to be produced in the heart to heat the body.

All must endeavor to bee good as she.)
This great consumption to a fever turn'd,
20   And so the world had fits; it joy'd, it mourn'd,
And, as men think, that agues physic are,
And th'ague being spent, give over care,
So thou, sick world, mistak'st thy self to be
Well, when alas, thou'rt in a lethargy.
25   Her death did wound and tame thee then, and then
Thou mightst have better spar'd the sum, or man.
That wound was deep, but 'tis more misery,
That thou hast lost thy sense and memory.
T'was heavy then to hear thy voice of moan,
30   But this is worse, that thou art speechless grown.
Thou hast forgot thy name, thou hadst; thou wast
Nothing but she, and her thou hast o'repast.
For as a child kept from the font,[5] until
A prince, expected long, come to fulfill
35   The ceremonies, thou unnam'd hadst laid,
Had not her coming, thee her palace made:
Her name defin'd thee, gave thee form and frame,
And thou forget'st to celebrate thy name.
Some months she hath been dead (but being dead,
40   Measures of times are all determined)[6]
But long shee'ath been away, long, long, yet none
Offers to tell us who it is that's gone.
But as in states doubtful of future heirs,
When sickness without remedy impairs
45   The present prince, they're loath it should be said,
The prince doth languish, or the prince is dead:
So mankind feeling now a general thaw,
A strong example gone equal to law.
The cement which did faithfully compact
50   And glue all virtues, now resolv'd,[7] and slack'd,
Thought it was some blasphemy to say sh'was dead;
Or that our weakness was discovered
In that confession; therefore spoke no more
Than tongues, the soul being gone, the loss deplore.
55   But though it be too late to succor thee,
Sick world, yea dead, yea putrefied, since she
Thy'ntrinsic balm,[8] and thy preservative,
Can never be renew'd, thou never live,

5. Baptismal font.
6. Terminated.
7. Dissolved.
8. An analogue to the *vital spirits* of the body which kept the earth itself alive.

I (since no man can make thee live) will try,
60   What we may gain by thy anatomy.[9]
Her death hath taught us dearly, that thou art
Corrupt and mortal in thy purest part.
Let no man say, the world it self being dead,
'Tis labor lost to have discovered.
65   The world's infirmities, since there is none
Alive to study this dissection;
For there's a kind of world remaining still,   *What life*
Though she which did inanimate and fill   *the world*
The world, be gone, yet in this last long night,   *hath still.*
70   Her Ghost doth walk, that is, a glimmering light,
A faint, weak love of virtue and of good
Reflects from her, on them which understood
Her worth; and though she have shut in all day,[1]
The twilight of her memory doth stay;
75   Which, from the carkass of the old world, free,
Creates a new world; and new creatures be
Produc'd: The matter and the stuff of this,
Her virtue, and the form our practice is.
And though to be thus elemented, arm
80   These creatures, from home borne, intrinsic harm,
(For all assumed unto[2] this dignity,
So many weedless paradises be,
Which of themselves produce no venomous sin,
Except some foreign serpent[3] bring it in)
85   Yet, because outward storms the strongest break,
And strength it self by confidence grows weak,
This new world may be safer, being told
The dangers and diseases of the old: *The sickness of the world.*
For with due temper men do then forgo,
90   Or covet things, when they their true worth know.
There is no health; physicians say that we   *Impossibility of health.*
At best, enjoy, but a neutrality.
And can there be worse sicknes, than to know
That we are never well, nor can be so?
95   We are born ruinous:[4] poore mothers cry,
That children come not right, nor orderly,
Except they headlong come and fall upon
An ominous precipitation.

9. By dissecting the dead body of the world.
1. Enclosed all light.
2. Taken up.
3. Satan in Eden.
4. Ruined by original sin, the state into which mankind was born as a consequence of the
fall.

How witty's ruin? how importunate
00 Upon mankind? It labor'd to frustrate
Even God's purpose; and made woman, sent
For man's relief, cause of his languishment.
They were to good ends, and they are so still,
But accessory, and principal in ill.
05 For that first marriage was our funeral:
One woman at one blow, then kill'd us all,
And singly, one by one, they kill us now.
We do delightfully our selves allow
To that consumption; and profusely blind,
10 We kill ourselves, to propagate our kind.[5]
And yet we do not that; we are not men:
There is not now that mankind, which was then
When as the sun, and man, did seeme to strive,
(Joint tenants of the world) who should survive.   *Shortness of life.*
15 When stag, and raven, and the long liv'd tree,
Compar'd with man, died in minority.[6]
When, if a slow-pac'd star had stol'n away
From the observer's marking, he might stay
Two or three hundred years to see't again,
20 And then make up his observation plain;
When, as the age was long, the size was great:
Man's growth confess'd, and recompenc'd the meat:
So spacious and large, that every soul
Did a fair kingdom, and large realm control:
25 And when the very stature thus erect,
Did that soul a good way towards heaven direct.
Where is this mankind now? who lives to age,
Fit to be made *Methusalem*[7] his page?
Alas, we scarce live long enough to try
30 Whether a new made clock run right, or lie.
Old grandsires talk of yesterday with sorrow,
And for our children we reserve tomorrow.
So short is life, that every peasant strives,
In a torn house, or field, to have three lives,[8]
35 And as in lasting, so in length is man.
Contracted to an inch, who was a span,[9]   *Smallness of stature.*
For had a man at first, in forests stray'd,
Or shipwrack'd in the sea, one would have laid

5. Refers to the belief that sexual emission shortened the length of life; see "Farewell to
   Love," line 25.
6. Species with substantially longer lives than humans who die in relative youth or *minority*.
7. A patriarch who lived 969 years (Genesis 5:27).
8. A leasehold of three generations.
9. Nine inches.

A wager that an elephant, or whale
140 That met him, would not hastily assail
A thing so equal to him: now alas,
The fairies, and the pygmies well may pass
As credible; mankind decays so soon,
We're scarce our fathers' shadows cast at noon.[1]
145 Only death adds t'our length:[2] nor are we grown
In stature to be men, till we are none.
But this were light, did our less volumes hold
All the old text; or had we chang'd to gold[3]
Their silver, or dispos'd into less glass,
150 Spirits of virtue, which then scattered was.
But 'tis not so: w'are not retir'd, but dampt,
And as our bodies, so our minds are crampt:
'Tis shrinking, not close weaving that hath thus,
In mind and body both bedwarfed us.
155 We seem ambitious, God's whole work t'undo;
Of nothing he made us, and we strive too,
To bring our selves to nothing back; and we
Do what we can, to do't so soon as he.
With new diseases on our selves we war,
160 And with new physic,[4] a worse engine far.
Thus man, this worlds' vice-emperor,[5] in whom
All faculties, all graces are at home;
And if in other creatures they appear,
They're but man's ministers, and legates there,
165 To work on their rebellions, and reduce
Them to civility, and to man's use.
This man, whom God did woo, and loath t'attend
Till man came up, did down to man descend,
This man, so great, that all that is, is his,
170 O what a trifle, and poor thing he is!
If man were any thing, he's nothing now:
Help, or at least some time to waste, allow
This other wants, yet when he did depart
With her whom we lament, he lost his heart.
175 She, of whom th'ancients seem'd to prophesy,
When they call'd virtues by the name of she,
She in whom virtue was so much refin'd,

1. When there are no shadows.
2. Since bodies are stretched out at death.
3. Refers to the ages of man: gold, silver, etc.
4. The new chemical medicines of Paracelsus.
5. As God's deputy on earth.

That for allay unto so pure a mind
She took the weaker sex, she that could drive
80 The poisonous tincture,[6] and the stain of Eve,
Out of her thoughts, and deeds; and purify
All, by a true religious alchemy;
She, she is dead; she's dead: when thou know'st this,
Thou knowst how poor a trifling thing man is.
85 And learn'st thus much by our anatomy,
The heart being perish'd, no part can be free.
And that except thou feed (not banquet) on
The supernatural food, religion.
Thy better growth grows withered, and scant;
90 Be more than man, or thou'rt less then an ant.
Then, as mankind, so is the world's whole frame
Quite out of joint, almost created lame:
For, before God had made up all the rest,
Corruption enter'd, and deprav'd the best:
95 It seiz'd the angels, and then first of all
The world did in her cradle take a fall,
And turn'd her brains, and took a general maim
Wronging each joint of th'universal frame.
The noblest part, man, felt it first; and then
00 Both beasts and plants, curst in the curse of man.
So did the world from the first hour decay,   *Decay of Nature in*
That evening was beginning of the day,   *other parts.*
And now the springs and summers which we see,
Like sons of women after fifty be.
05 And new philosophy[7] calls all in doubt,
The element of fire[8] is quite put out;
The sun is lost, and th'earth, and no man's wit
Can well direct him where to look for it.
And freely men confess, that this world's spent,
10 When in the planets, and the firmament
They seek so many new; they see that this[9]
Is crumbled out again to his atomies.
'Tis all in pieces, all coherence gone;
All just supply, and all relation:
15 Prince, subject, father, son, are things forgot,

---

6. In alchemy, "a supposed spiritual principle or immaterial substance whose character or
   quality may be infused into material things" (OED 6). Here it is *poisonous*.
7. The new science, especially astronomy.
8. The idea of an elemental region of fire was under attack, as were such ideas as the geo-
   centric or Ptolemaic universe, the circular orbits of the planets, and the immutability and
   perfection of the celestial realms.
9. This world is disintegrating into its constituent parts.

For every man alone thinks he hath got
To be a phoenix,[1] and that there can be
None of that kind, of which he is, but he.
This is the world's condition now, and now
220 She that should all parts to reunion bow,[2]
She that had all magnetic force alone,
To draw, and fasten sund'red parts in one;
She whom wise nature had invented then
When she observ'd that every sort of men
225 Did in their voyage in this world's sea stray,
And needed a new compass for their way;
She that was best, and first original
Of all fair copies; and the general
Steward[3] to Fate; she whose rich eyes, and breast,
230 Gilt the West Indies, and perfum'd the East;[4]
Whose having breath'd in this world, did bestow
Spice on those Isles, and bade them still smell so,
And that rich Indie which doth gold inter,
Is but as single money, coin'd from her:
235 She to whom this world must it self refer,
As suburbs, or the microcosm of her,
She, she is dead; she's dead: when thou know'st this,
Thou know'st how lame a cripple this world is.
And learn'st thus much by our anatomy,
240 That this world's general sickness doth not lie
In any humor, or one certain part;
But, as thou sawest it rotten at the heart,
Thou see'st a hectic[5] fever hath got hold
Of the whole substance, not to be controll'd.
245 And that thou hast but one way, not t'admit
The world's infection, to be none of it.
For the world's subtil'st immaterial parts
Feel this consuming wound, and age's darts.
For the world's beauty is decay'd, or gone,   *Disformity of parts.*
250 Beauty, that's color, and proportion.
We think the heavens enjoy their spherical
Their round proportion embracing all.
But yet their various and perplexed course,
Observ'd in diverse ages doth enforce
255 Men to find out so many eccentric parts,

1. The unique bird that could regenerate itself out of its own ashes.
2. Bring into harmony.
3. As a faithful steward to God.
4. I.e., she gives the West Indies their precious metals and the East their aromatics.
5. "That kind of fever which accompanies consumption or other wasting diseases" (OED).

Such diverse down-right lines, such overthwarts,[6]
As disproportion that pure form. It tears
The firmament in eight and forty shares,[7]
And in those constellations then arise
260 New stars,[8] and old do vanish from our eyes:
As though heav'n suffered earthquakes, peace or war,
When new towers rise, and old demolish'd are.
They have empal'd within a zodiac
The free-born sun, and keep twelve signs[9] awake
265 To watch his steps; the goat and crab control,
And fright him back, who else to either pole,
(Did not these Tropics[1] fetter him) might run:
For his course is not round; nor can the sun
Perfect a circle, or maintain his way
270 One inch direct; but where he rose today
He comes no more, but with a cozening[2] line,
Steals by that point, and so is serpentine:
And seeming weary with his reeling thus,
He means to sleep, being now fall'n nearer us.
275 So, of the stars which boast that they do run.
In circle still, none ends where he begun.
All their proportion's lame, it sinks, it swells.
For of meridians, and parallels,[3]
Man hath weaved out a net, and this net thrown
280 Upon the heavens, and now they are his own.
Loath to go up the hill, or labor thus
To go to heaven, we make heaven come to us.
We spur, we rein the stars, and in their race
They're diversely content t'obey our pace.
285 But keeps the earth her round proportion still?
Doth not a Tenerife,[4] or higher hill
Rise so high like a rock, that one might think
The floating moon would shipwreck there, and sink?
Seas are so deep, that whales being struck today,
290 Perchance tomorrow, scarce at middle way
Of their wish'd journey's end, the bottom, die.
And men, to sound depths, so much line untie,
As one might justly think, that there would rise

6. Transverse lines; *down-right lines*: Vertical lines.
7. Ptolemy divided the stars into forty-eight constellations.
8. New stars were identified by Johannes Kepler in 1600 and Galileo in 1610.
9. The twelve signs of the zodiac.
1. The tropics of Capricorn and Cancer run parallel to the equator to the north and south.
2. Deceiving.
3. Lines of celestial longitude and latitude.
4. A volcanic peak of some 12,000 feet in the Canary Islands.

At end thereof, one of th'Antipodes:[5]
295   If under all, a vault infernal[6] be,
(Which sure is spacious, except that we
Invent another torment, that there must
Millions into a strait hot room be thrust)
Then solidness, and roundness have no place.
300   Are these but warts, and pock-holes in the face
Of th'earth? Think so: But yet confess, in this
The world's proportion disfigured is,
That those two legs whereon it doth rely,
Reward and punishment are bent awry.
305   And, oh, it can no more be questioned,
That beauty's best, proportion, is dead,
Since even grief it self, which now alone
Is left us, is without proportion.
She by whose lines proportion should be
310   Examin'd, measure of all symmetry,
Whom had that ancient seen,[7] who thought souls made
Of harmony, he would at next have said
That harmony was she, and thence infer.
That souls were but resultances[8] from her,
315   And did from her into our bodies go,
As to our eyes, the forms from objects flow:
She, who if those great doctors[9] truly said
That th'ark to man's proportion was made,
Had been a type for that, as that might be
320   A type of her in this, that contrary
Both elements and passions liv'd at peace
In her, who caus'd all civil war to cease.
She, after whom, what form soe're we see,
Is discord, and rude incongruity,
325   She, she is dead, she's dead; when thou know'st this,
Thou know'st how ugly a monster this world is:
And learn'st thus much by our anatomy,
That here is nothing to enamor thee:
And that, not only faults in inward parts,
330   Corruptions in our brains, or in our hearts,
Poisoning the fountains, whence our actions spring,
Endanger us: but that if every thing

5. Those living on the opposite side of the globe (OED).
6. If hell is at the center of the earth.
7. Perhaps Pythagoras, who believed in a mystical, mathematical harmonics, or Galen, who believed the soul was a harmony of bodily humors.
8. "Something which issues, proceeds, or emanates from another thing" (OED 3a).
9. St. Augustine, one of the four "doctors" of the Church, described the ark as a type of the Church made in proportion to the human body; see also 1 Peter 3:20–21.

    Be not done fitly'nd in proportion,
    To satisfy wise, and good lookers on,
335 (Since most men be such as most think they be)
    They're loathsome too, by this deformity.
    For good, and well, must in our actions meet:
    Wicked is not much worse then indiscreet.
    But beauty's other second element,
340 Color, and luster now, is as near spent.
    And had the world his just proportion,
    Were it a ring still, yet the stone is gone.
    As a compassionate turquoise[1] which doth tell
    By looking pale, the wearer is not well,
345 As gold falls sick being stung with mercury,
    All the world's parts of such complexion be.
    When nature was most busy, the first week,
    Swaddling the new born earth, God seem'd to like,
    That she should sport herself sometimes, and play,
350 To mingle, and vary colors every day.
    And then, as though she could not make enow,[2]
    Himself his various rainbow did allow.
    Sight is the noblest sense of any one,
    Yet sight hath only color to feed on,
355 And color is decay'd: summer's robe grows
    Dusky, and like an oft dyed garment shows.
    Our blushing red, which us'd in cheeks to spread,
    Is inward sunk and only our souls are red.[3]
    Perchance the world might have recovered,
360 If she whom we lament had not been dead:
    But she, in whom all white, and red, and blue[4]
    (Beauty's ingredients) voluntary grew,
    As in an unvex'd paradise; from whom
    Did all things verdure, and their luster come,
365 Whose composition was miraculous,
    Being all color, all diaphanous,
    (For air, and fire but thick gross bodies were,
    And liveliest stones but drowsy, and pale to her)
    She, she, is dead; she's dead: when thou know'st this,
370 Thou know'st how wan a ghost this our world is:
    And learn'st thus much by our anatomy,
    That it should more affright, than pleasure thee.

1. The turquoise was believed to reflect the health of its wearer.
2. The plural of enough (OED).
3. The color of sin, as in "Holy Sonnet 2," line 12.
4. Theological virtues may be associated with these colors, but also her white skin, red cheeks, and blue eyes.

And that, since all fair color then did sink,
'Tis now but wicked vanity to think,
375   To color vicious deeds with good pretense,   *Weakenesse in the want*
Or with bought colors to illude[5] men's sense.   *of correspondence of*
Nor in ought more this world's decay appears,   *heaven & earth.*
Then that her influence the heav'n forbears,
Or that the elements do not feel this,
380   The father, or the mother barren is.
The clouds conceive not rain, or do not pour
In the due birth time, down the balmy shower.
Th'air doth not motherly sit on the earth,
To hatch her seasons, and give all things birth.
385   Spring times were common cradles, but are tombs;
And false conceptions fill the general wombs.
Th'air shows such meteors,[6] as none can see,
Not only what they mean, but what they be.
Earth such new worms, as would have troubled much,
390   Th'Egyptian Mages[7] to have made more such.
What artist[8] now dares boast that he can bring
Heaven hither, or constellate any thing,
So as the influence of those stars may be
Imprisoned in an herb, or charm, or tree,
395   And do by touch, all which those stars could do?
The art is lost, and correspondence[9] too.
For heaven gives little, and the earth takes less,
And man least knows their trade and purposes.
If this commerce 'twixt heaven and earth were not
400   Embarr'd, and all this trafic quite forgot,
She, for whose loss we have lamented thus,
Would work more fully'and pow'rfully on us.
Since herbs and roots by dying, lose not all,
But they, yea ashes too, are medicinal,
405   Death could not quench her virtue so, but that
It would be (if not follow'd) wond'red at:
And all the world would be one dying swan,[1]
To sing her funeral praise, and vanish then.
But as some serpents' poison hurteth not,
410   Except it be from the live serpent shot,[2]

5. Deceive.
6. Any atmospheric phenomenon; considered a bad omen or portent.
7. The magicians who changed rods into serpents; see Exodus 7:10–12.
8. Astrologer.
9. The ordered relationships between entities that knit the universe together in the Great
    Chain of Being.
1. The swan was reputed to sing only just before its death.
2. Some poisons were believed potent only while the serpent was alive.

So doth her virtue need her here, to fit
That unto us; she working more then it.
But she, in whom, to such maturity,
Virtue was grown, past growth, that it must die,
415 She from whose influence all impressions came,
But by receivers' impotencies, lame,
Who, though she could not transubstantiate
All states to gold, yet gilded every state,
So that some princes have some temperance;
420 Some counselors some purpose to advance
The common profit; and some people have
Some stay, no more then kings should give, to crave;
Some women have some taciturnity,
Some nunneries,[3] some grains of chastity.
425 She that did thus much, and much more could do,
But that our age was iron,[4] and rusty too,
She, she is dead; she's dead: when thou know'st this,
Thou know'st how dry a cinder this world is.
And learn'st thus much by our anatomy,
430 That 'tis in vain to dew, or mollify
It with thy tears, or sweat, or blood: nothing
Is worth our travail, grief, or perishing,
But those rich joys, which did possess her heart,
Of which she's now partaker, and a part.
435 But as in cutting up a man that's dead,   *Conclusion.*
The body will not last out to have read
On every part, and therefore men direct
Their speech to parts, that are of most effect;
So the world's carcass would not last, if I
440 Were punctual in this anatomy.
Nor smells it well to hearers, if one tell
Them their disease, who fain would think they're well.
Here therefore be the end: And, blessed maid,
Of whom is meant what ever hath been said,
445 Or shall be spoken well by any tongue,
Whose name refines coarse lines, and makes prose song,
Accept this tribute, and his first year's rent,[5]
Who till his dark short tapers end be spent,
As oft as thy feast[6] sees this widow'd earth,
450 Will yearly celebrate thy second birth,
That is, thy death. For though the soul of man

---

3. Either a brothel or convent, as in *Hamlet* (3.1.122, 137).
4. In contrast to the ages of gold and silver.
5. Payment for Drury's patronage.
6. The feast day of a saint.

Be got when man is made, 'tis borne but then
When man doth die. Our body's as the womb,
And as a midwife death directs it home.
455 And you her creatures, whom she works upon
And have your last, and best concoction
From her example, and her virtue, if you
In reverence to her, do think it due,
That no one should her praises thus rehearse,
460 As matter fit for chronicle, not verse,
Vouchsafe to call to mind, that God did make
A last, and lasting'st piece, a song. He spake
To Moses, to deliver unto all,
That song:[7] because he knew they would let fall,
465 The law, the prophets, and the history,
But keep the song still in their memory.
Such an opinion (in due measure) made
Me this great office boldly to invade.
Nor could incomprehensibleness deter
470 Me, from thus trying to imprison her.
Which when I saw that a strict grave could do,
I saw not why verse might not do so too.
Verse hath a middle nature: heaven keeps souls,
The grave keeps bodies, verse the fame enrolls.

7. The Song of Moses (Deuteronomy 32).

Divine Poems

LA CORONA.[1]

1.

Deign[2] *at my hands this crown of prayer and praise,*
Weav'd in my low, devout melancholy,
Thou which of good hast, yea, art treasury,
All changing unchang'd Ancient of Days.[3]
5   But do not, with a vile crown of frail bays,[4]
Reward my muse's white sincerity,
But what thy thorny crown gain'd, that give me,
A crown of glory, which doth flower always.
The ends crown our works, but thou crown'st our ends,
10   So at our end begins our endless rest.
This first last end, now zealously possess'd,
With a strong sober thirst, my soul attends.
'Tis time that voice and heart be lifted high,
Salvation to all that will is nigh.

2. Annunciation.[5]

Salvation to all that will is nigh:
That All, which always is all everywhere,
Which cannot sin, and yet all sins must bear,
Which cannot die, yet cannot choose but die,
5   Lo, faithful Virgin, yields himself to lie
In prison, in thy womb; and though he there
Can take no sin, nor thou give, yet he'll wear,
Taken from thence, flesh, which death's force may try.[6]
Ere by the spheres time was created, thou
10   Wast in his mind, who is thy son and brother;

---

1. As the title indicates, these seven sonnets form a sequence in which the last line of each poem is repeated as the first line of the next, thus forming a crown or *corona*.
2. Think it worthy to accept (OED).
3. A name emphasizing God's eternal being, from Daniel 7:9.
4. The poet's laurel crown.
5. Gabriel's announcement to Mary that she would bear a child.
6. Attempt to conquer.

133

Whom thou conceiv'st, conceiv'd; yea thou art now
Thy Maker's maker, and thy Father's mother,
Thou'hast light in dark, and shutt'st in little room,
Immensity,[7] *cloister'd in thy dear womb.*

3. *Nativity.*

Immensity, cloister'd in thy dear womb,
Now leaves his well-belov'd imprisonment.
There he hath made himself to his intent
Weak enough, now into our world to come.
5   But oh, for thee, for him, hath th'inn no room?
Yet lay him in this stall, and from th'Orient,
Stars and wise men will travel to prevent[8]
Th'effect of Herod's jealous, general doom.[9]
Seest thou, my soul, with thy faith's eyes, how he
10   Which fills all place, yet none holds him, doth lie?
Was not his pity towards thee wondrous high,
That would have need to be pitied by thee?
Kiss him, and with him into Egypt go,
With his kind mother, who partakes thy woe.

4. *Temple.*[1]

With his kind mother, who partakes thy woe,
Joseph, turn back; see where your child doth sit,
Blowing, yea blowing out those sparks of wit,
Which himself on those doctors did bestow.
5   The Word[2] but lately could not speak, and lo,
It suddenly speaks wonders: Whence comes it,
That all which was, and all which should be writ,
A shallow seeming child should deeply know?
His Godhead was not soul to his manhood,[3]
10   Nor had time mellow'd him to this ripeness;
But as to'one which hath long tasks, thinks good
With the sun to begin his business,
He in his age's morning thus began,
By miracles exceeding power of man.

7. Infinite being.
8. Come before, anticipate.
9. Herod's slaughter of the innocents (Matthew 2:16).
1. At the age of twelve Jesus stayed behind (after Mary and Joseph left) to answer questions
   posed by the doctors at the Temple (Luke 2:27–49).
2. Logos, identified with Jesus in John 1:14.
3. Christ was fully God and fully man with a human soul in a human body.

5. Crucifying.

By miracles exceeding power of man,
He faith in some, envy in some begat,
For, what meek spirits admire, ambitious hate:[4]
In both affections many to him ran.
5   But oh, the worst are most, they will and can,
Alas, and do, unto th'immaculate,
Whose creature fate is, now prescribe a fate,
Measuring self-life's infinity t'a span,[5]
Nay to an inch. Lo, where condemned he
10 Bears his own cross, with pain, yet by and by
When it bears him, he must bear more and die.
Now thou art lifted up, draw me to thee,
And at thy death, giving such liberal dole,[6]
Moist, with one drop of thy blood, my dry soul.

6. Resurrection.

Moist with one drop of thy blood, my dry soul
Shall (though she now be in extreme degree
Too stony hard, and yet too fleshly)[7] be
Freed by that drop, from being starv'd, hard or foul,
5   And life, by thy death abled, shall control
Death, whom thy death slew; nor shall to me
Fear of first or last death bring misery,
If in thy life-book my name thou enroll.
Flesh in that last long sleep is not putrefi'd,
10 But made that there, of which, and for which 'twas;[8]
Nor can by other means be glorified.
May then sin's sleep, and death's, soon from me pass,
That wak'd from both, I again risen may
Salute the last, and everlasting day.

7. Ascension.

Salute the last and everlasting day,
Joy at th'uprising of this sun, and son,

7-12

---

4. I.e., the *ambitious hate* what the *meek admire.*
5. The length of a human life; a *span* was the distance from the tip of the thumb to the tip of the little finger (OED).
6. An allotted portion.
7. The heart of stone that must be turned to flesh is a common trope; see Ezekiel 11:19: "And I will give them one heart, and I will put a new spirit within you; and I will take the stony heart out of their flesh, and will give them an heart of flesh."
8. Genesis 3:19: "Dust thou art, and unto dust shalt thou return."

Ye whose true tears, or tribulation
Hath purely wash'd, or burnt your drossy clay.
5 Behold, the highest, parting hence away,
Lightens the dark clouds, which he treads upon;
Nor doth he by ascending show alone,
But first he, and he first, enters the way.
O strong ram,[9] which hast batter'd heaven for me,
10 Mild lamb, which with thy blood hast mark'd the path,
Bright torch, which shin'st, that I the way may see,
Oh, with thine own blood quench thine own just wrath;
And if thy Holy Spirit my muse did raise,
Deign at my hands this crown of prayer and praise.

HOLY SONNETS[1]

1.

As due by many titles[2] I resign
  Myself to thee, O God: First I was made
  By thee, and for thee, and when I was decay'd
Thy blood bought[3] that, the which before was thine.
5 I am thy son, made with thyself to shine,
  Thy servant, whose pains thou hast still repaid,
  Thy sheep, thine image; and (till I betray'd
Myself) a temple of thy spirit divine.[4]
Why doth the devil then usurp[5] in me?
10 Why doth he steal, nay ravish, that's thy right?
Except thou rise, and for thine own work fight,
  Oh I shall soon despair, when I do see
That thou lov'st mankind well, yet wilt not choose me,
And Satan hates me, yet is loath to lose me.

2.

O my black soul, now thou art summoned
  By sickness, death's herald and champion;

9. Christ is typologically associated with the ram in the thicket, sacrificed by Abraham in place of Isaac (Genesis 22:13).
1. The editors of the Donne Variorum argue that there are three distinct sequences of these Holy Sonnets that Donne fashioned over the years (DV 7.1, i–xv). I have adopted the twelve-poem sequence that was also used in the 1633 *Poems* and that the Donne Variorum editors believe to be Donne's final arrangement (which they term the "revised sequence"), to which I have added the other seven sonnets found in the Westmoreland ms.
2. Legal rights.
3. Redeemed.
4. 1 Corinthians 3:16: "Know ye not that ye are the temple of God, and that the Spirit of God dwelleth in you?"
5. Intrude forcibly, illegally.

Thou'rt like a pilgrim, which abroad had done
Treason, and dar'st not turn to whence he's fled;
5   Or as a thief, which till death's doom be read,
    Wisheth himself deliver'd from prison,
    But damn'd and haled[6] to execution,
Wisheth that still he might be'imprisoned.
Yet grace, if thou repent, thou canst not lack.
10   But who shall give thee that grace to begin?[7]
Oh make thyself with holy mourning black,
    And red with blushing as thou art with sin.
Or wash thee in Christ's blood, which hath this might,
That being red, it dyes red souls to white.

3.

This is my play's last scene; here heavens appoint
    My pilgrimage's last mile; and my race,
    Idly, yet quickly run, hath this last pace;
My span's[8] last inch; my minute's last point.
5   And gluttonous death will instantly unjoint
    My body and soul, and I shall sleep a space;
    Or presently, I know not, see that face[9]
Whose fear[1] already shakes my every joint.
Then, as my soul, to' heaven her first seat takes flight,
10   And earth-born body in the earth shall dwell,
So fall my sins, that all may have their right,
    To where they're bred, and would press me, to hell.
Impute me righteous,[2] thus purg'd of evil,
For thus I leave the world, the flesh, and devil.

4.

At the round earth's imagin'd corners[3] blow
    Your trumpets, angels, and arise, arise
    From death you numberless infinities
Of souls and to your scatter'd bodies go;
5   All whom the Flood did, and fire shall o'erthrow,[4]

6. Hauled.
7. This paradox dramatizes the debate between Calvinism and Arminianism over free will and prevenient grace.
8. Life span.
9. The reading of some Group II mss.—*But my ever-waking part shall see that face*—may be an authorial improvement over this line. *That face* is God's at the Last Judgment.
1. The fear of whom.
2. Luther emphasized that Christians must rely on the attribution of Christ's righteousness by vicarious substitution; see Romans 4:6–8.
3. Revelation 7:1: "After this I saw four angels standing at the four corners of the earth."
4. The Flood and the fire that will consume the world (2 Peter 3:10).

All whom war, dearth, age, agues, tyrannies,
   Despair, law, chance hath slain, and you whose eyes
Shall behold God, and never taste death's woe.[5]
But let them sleep, Lord, and me mourn a space;
10   For if above all these my sins abound,
'Tis late to ask abundance of thy grace
   When we are there: Here on this lowly ground,
Teach me how to repent, for that's as good
As if thou had'st seal'd my pardon with thy blood.

[handwritten: Relaying the consequences he personally feels as a result of Adams]

5.

If poisonous minerals, and if that tree[6]
   Whose fruit threw death on else immortal us,
   If lecherous goats, if serpents envious
Cannot be damn'd, alas why should I be?
5 Why should intent, or reason, born in me,
   Make sins else equal,[7] in me more heinous?
   And mercy being easy and glorious
To God, in his stern wrath why threatens he?
But who am I that dare dispute with thee
10   O God? Oh, of thine only worthy blood
   And my tears make a heavenly Lethean[8] flood
And drown in it my sins' black memory.
   That thou remember them, some claim as debt;
I think it mercy if thou wilt forget.

[handwritten margin notes: why blame the snake, for being inhabited by satan? it isn't its fault.]

6.

Death, be not proud, though some have called thee
   Mighty and dreadful, for thou art not so.
   For those whom thou think'st thou dost overthrow
Die not, poor Death, nor yet canst thou kill me.
5 From rest and sleep which but thy pictures be,
   Much pleasure; then, from thee, much more must flow,
   And soonest our best men with thee do go,[9]
Rest of their bones, and soul's delivery.[1]
Thou'rt slave to fate, chance, kings, and desperate men,
10   And dost with poison, war, and sickness dwell.

5. Matthew 16:27–29: "There be some standing here, which shall not taste of death, till they
   see the Son of man coming in his kingdom."
6. Tree of the Knowledge of Good and Evil (Genesis 2:17).
7. Otherwise the same as the sins of lust or envy.
8. Refers to the river of forgetfulness in the classical underworld. He wants heaven to forget
   his sins.
9. That the good die young is an ancient proverb.
1. Death is the *soul's delivery* into new life.

And poppy or charms can make us sleep as well,
And easier than thy stroke. Why swell'st[2] thou then?
   One short sleep past, we live eternally,
   And Death shall be no more. Death, thou shalt die.[3]

7.

Spit in my face, ye Jews, and pierce my side,
   Buffet, and scoff, scourge, and crucify me:
For I have sinn'd, and sinn'd: and only he
   Who could do no iniquity hath died.
5 But by my death cannot be satisfi'd[4]
   My sins, which pass the Jews' impiety:
They kill'd once an inglorious man, but I
   Crucify him daily,[5] being now glorified.
Oh let me then his strange love still admire:
10 Kings pardon, but he bore our punishment.
And Jacob came cloth'd in vile harsh attire
   But to supplant and with gainful intent:[6]
God cloth'd himself in vile man's flesh, that so
He might be weak enough to suffer woe.

8.

Why are we by all creatures waited on?
   Why do the prodigal elements supply
   Life and food to me, being more pure than I,
Simple, and farther from corruption?[7]
5 Why brook'st thou, ignorant horse, subjection?
   Why dost thou, bull and boar, so sillily[8]
   Dissemble weakness, and by one man's stroke die,
Whose whole kind you might swallow and feed upon?
Weaker I am, woe is me, and worse than you;
10 You have not sinn'd, nor need be timorous.
   But wonder at a greater wonder; for to us
Created Nature doth these things subdue;

2. Puffed up with pride.
3. 1 Corinthians 15:54–55: "So when this corruptible shall have put on incorruption, and this mortal shall have put on immortality, then shall be brought to pass the saying that is written, Death is swallowed up in victory. O death, where is thy sting? O grave, where is thy victory?"
4. Atoned for.
5. Hebrews 6:6: "Seeing they crucify to themselves the Son of God afresh, and put him to an open shame."
6. Jacob deceived his father Isaac by covering himself with skins to receive the blessing meant for his elder brother; see Genesis 27:1–30.
7. Each of the four elements is simple, but the human body, compounded of the four elements in varying degrees, is more corruptible.
8. Foolishly, meekly.

But their Creator, whom sin nor nature tied,[9]
For us, his creatures and his foes, hath died.

9.

What if this present were the world's last night?
   Mark in my heart, O soul, where thou dost dwell,
   The picture of Christ crucified, and tell
Whether that countenance can thee affright.
5 Tears in his eyes quench the amazing light;
   Blood fills his frowns, which from his pierc'd head fell.
   And can that tongue adjudge thee unto hell,
Which pray'd forgiveness[1] for his foes' fierce spite?
No, no; but as in mine idolatry
10 I said to all my profane mistresses,
   Beauty of pity, foulness only is
A sign of rigor;[2] so I say to thee,
   To wicked sprites[3] are horrid shapes assign'd;
   This beauteous form[4] assures a piteous mind.

10.

Batter my heart, three-person'd God,[5] for you
   As yet but knock, breathe, shine, and seek to mend;
   That I may rise, and stand, o'erthrow me; and bend
Your force to break, blow, burn, and make me new.
5 I like an usurp'd town[6] t'another due,
   Labor t'admit you, but oh, to no end.
   Reason, your viceroy in me, me should defend,[7]
But is captiv'd and proves weak or untrue.
Yet dearly I love you, and would be loved fain:[8]
10 But am betroth'd unto your enemy:
Divorce me, untie or break that knot again,
Take me to you, imprison me, for I,
Except you enthrall me, never shall be free,
Nor ever chaste except you ravish me.

9. Whom neither sin nor nature restricted or constrained.
1. See Luke 23:34.
2. Beauty is a sign of pity; foulness is only a sign of rigor.
3. Spirits.
4. *The picture of Christ crucified* (line 3).
5. The Trinity: Father, Son, and Holy Spirit.
6. Occupied; the metaphor is that of the fortress of the heart, occupied by Satan, which must be battered open by God.
7. Reason should defend me against Satan, the usurper.
8. Eagerly wishes to be loved.

11.

Wilt thou love God, as he, thee? then digest,
  My soul, this wholesome meditation:
  How God the Spirit, by angels waited on
In heaven, doth make his temple in thy breast.[9]
5 The father having begot a son most blest,
    And still begetting (for he ne'er begun)
    Hath deign'd to choose thee by adoption,
Co-heir to his glory and Sabbath's endless rest.
And as a robb'd man, which by search doth find[1]
10   His stol'n stuff sold, must lose or buy'it again,
    The son of glory came down and was slain,
Us whom he'd made, and Satan stole,[2] to'unbind.
  'Twas much that man was made like God before,
  But, that God should be made like man, much more.

12.

Father, part of his double interest[3]
  Unto thy kingdom thy son gives to me;
  His jointure[4] in the knotty Trinity
He keeps, and gives me his death's conquest.
5 This lamb, whose death with life the world hath blest,
  Was from the world's beginning slain,[5] and he
  Hath made two wills,[6] which with the legacy
Of his and thy kingdom, doth thy sons invest.
Yet such are thy laws, that men argue yet
10   Whether a man those statutes can fulfil.
None doth; but all-healing grace and spirit
  Revive and quicken what law and letter kill.[7]
Thy law's abridgement, and thy last command[8]
Is all but love. Oh let that last will stand.

13.

Thou hast made me, and shall thy work decay?
  Repair me now, for now mine end doth haste.

---

9. 1 Corinthians 3:16: "Know ye not that ye are the temple of God, and that the Spirit of God dwelleth in you?"
1. By rule of law the owner of stolen property had to buy back his own property.
2. And whom Satan stole.
3. As God and man.
4. Property held for the joint use of two or more people.
5. Revelation 13:8: "the Lamb slain from the foundation of the world."
6. I.e., the Old and New Testaments.
7. 2 Corinthians 3:6: "for the letter killeth, but the spirit giveth life."
8. John 13:34: "A new commandment I give unto you, That ye love one another; as I have loved you."

I run to death, and death meets me as fast,
And all my pleasures are like yesterday.
5 I dare not move my dim eyes any way;
    Despair behind, and death before doth cast
    Such terror, and my feebled flesh doth waste
By sin in it, which towards hell doth weigh.[9]
Only thou art above, and when towards thee
10   By thy leave I can look, I rise again.
But our old subtle foe so tempteth me,
    That not one hour I can myself sustain.
Thy grace may wing me, to prevent[1] his art,
And thou like adamant,[2] draw mine iron heart.

14.

Oh might those sighs and tears[3] return again
    Into my breast and eyes, which I have spent,
    That I might in this holy discontent
Mourn with some fruit, as I have mourn'd in vain.
5 In my idolatry[4] what showers of rain
    Mine eyes did waste? what griefs my heart did rent?
    That sufferance was my sin, now I repent;
Because I did suffer, I must suffer pain.[5]
Th'hydroptic[6] drunkard, and night-scouting thief,
10   The itchy[7] lecher, and self-tickling proud
Have the remembrance of past joys for relief
    Of coming ills. To poor me is allow'd
No ease; for long yet vehement grief hath been
    The effect and cause, the punishment and sin.

15.

I am a little world[8] made cunningly
    Of elements and an angelic sprite;
    But black sin hath betray'd to endless night
My world's both parts, and Oh both parts must die.
5 You, which beyond that heaven, which was most high

9. My feeble flesh weighs me down towards hell.
1. Forestall, frustrate.
2. The loadstone was magnetic.
3. The sighs and tears of the Petrarchan lover.
4. I.e., the profane worship of the Petrarchan mistress.
5. Lines 7–8: He contrasts his suffering for his past sins with his past suffering as a lover
6. Insatiably thirsty.
7. The lecher is itchy because he is always unsatisfied or restless.
8. The poet compares the fate of his own little body (the microcosm) to that of the macrocosm through a conceit that transforms Petrarchan and biblical language.

Have found new spheres, and of new lands can write,[9]
  Pour new seas in mine eyes, that so I might
Drown my world with my weeping earnestly,
Or wash it: if it must be drown'd no more.[1]
But oh, it must be burnt;[2] alas the fire
Of lust and envy have burnt it heretofore
  And made it fouler; let those flames retire,
And burn me, O God, with a fiery zeal
Of thee and thy house, which doth in eating heal.[3]

16.

If faithful souls be alike glorified
  As angels, then my father's soul doth see,
  And adds this even to full felicity,
That valiantly I hell's wide mouth o'erstride.
But if our minds to these souls be descried
  By circumstances, and by signs that be
  Apparent in us, not immediately,
How shall my mind's white truth to them be tried?[4]
They see idolatrous lovers weep and mourn,
  And vile blasphemous conjurers to call
  On Jesus' name, and Pharisaical[5]
Dissemblers feign devotion: then turn,
  O pensive soul, to God, for he knows best
Thy true grief, for he put it in my breast.

17.

Since she[6] whom I loved hath paid her last debt
  To nature, and to hers, and my good is dead,[7]
  And her soul early into heaven ravished,
Wholly in heavenly things my mind is set.

[handwritten: to now focus on (meeting her in) the afterlife]

9. Lines 5–6: Astronomers who added new spheres to the Ptolemaic universe to account for newly observed sidereal motions or explorers who had made new discoveries.
1. Line 9: God makes a covenant with Noah not to destroy the earth again with a flood (Genesis 9:11–17).
2. The fire that will consume the world (2 Peter 3:10).
3. Psalm 69:9: "For the zeal of thine house hath eaten me up."
4. This sonnet rests on the difference in the mode of apprehension of angels and souls after death. Angels were thought to apprehend immediately by intuition, whereas humans reason inferentially by circumstances and signs.
5. Self-righteous hypocrites.
6. Anne More Donne died August 15, 1617, at the age of thirty-three, shortly after giving birth to her twelfth child.
7. Lines 1–2: She has paid her *debt* to her *nature* as a human being by dying. The punctuation in the mss. of line 2 is ambiguous so that *and to hers* can be taken with the words that precede it or follow it. The simplest reading is that, having died early is to her own good (since she is in heaven) and to the poet's, as the rest of the poem clarifies.

[handwritten: oh, no. ??]

5   Here the admiring her my mind did whet
      To seek thee God; so streams do show the head;[8]
      But though I have found thee and thou my thirst hast fed,
   A holy thirsty dropsy melts me yet.
   But why should I beg more love, when as thou
10   Dost woo my soul, for hers off'ring all thine:[1]
   And dost not only fear lest I allow
      My love to saints and angels, things divine,
   But in thy tender jealousy dost doubt[2]
   Lest the world, flesh, yea, devil put thee out.

18.

Show me, dear Christ, thy spouse,[3] so bright and clear.
     What is it she, which on the other shore
     Goes richly painted?[4] Or which, robb'd and tore,
Laments and mourns in Germany and here?[5]
5   Sleeps she a thousand, then peeps up one year?
     Is she self-truth and errs? now new, now outwore?
     Doth she and did she, and shall she evermore
On one, on seven, or on no hill appear?[6]
   Dwells she with us, or like adventuring knights
10   First travail[7] we to seek and then make love?
Betray, kind husband, thy spouse to our sights,
     And let mine amorous soul court thy mild dove,
   Who is most true, and pleasing to thee, then
   When she's embraced and open to most men.

19.

Oh, to vex me, contraries meet in one:
     Inconstancy unnaturally hath begot
     A constant habit; that when I would not
   I change in vows, and in devotion.
5   As humorous[8] is my contrition
     As my profane love, and as soon forgot:

---

8. Reveal their source or headwaters.
9. An unquenchable thirst.
1. Line 10: God woos the poet's soul, offering divine love for her love.
2. Fear.
3. The Church as the bride of Christ was a common trope (Matthew 25:1–13).
4. The Roman Catholic Church was frequently depicted by Protestants as a painted harlot.
5. The Protestant churches in Germany or England.
6. Either on Mt. Moriah in Jerusalem where the Temple stood; on the seven hills of Rome;
   or in Geneva, which is on a lake.
7. Labor, travel.
8. Changeable or subject to whim.

As riddlingly distempered,[9] cold and hot,
As praying, as mute; as infinite, as none.
I durst not view heaven yesterday; and today
10   In prayers and flattering speeches I court God:
Tomorrow I quake with true fear of his rod.
So my devout fits come and go away
    Like a fantastic ague:[1] save that here
    Those are my best days, when I shake with fear.

The Cross.

Since Christ embrac'd the cross itself,[2] dare I
His image, th'image[3] of his cross, deny?
Would I have profit by the sacrifice,
And dare the chosen altar to despise?
5 It bore all other sins, but is it fit
That it should bear the sin of scorning it?
Who from the picture would avert his eye,
How would he fly his pains, who there did die?
From me, no pulpit, nor misgrounded law,
10 Nor scandal taken, shall this cross withdraw.[4]
It shall not, for it cannot; for the loss
Of this cross were to me another cross.
Better were worse, for no affliction,
No cross is so extreme, as to have none.
15 Who can blot out the cross, which th'instrument
Of God dew'd[5] on me in the sacrament?
Who can deny me power, and liberty
To stretch mine arms, and mine own cross to be?
Swim, and at every stroke thou art thy cross.
20 The mast and yard[6] make one, where seas do toss.
Look down, thou spiest out crosses in small things;
Look up, thou seest birds rais'd on crossed wings;
All the globe's frame, and spheres, is nothing else
But the meridians crossing parallels.

9. Disproportioned (this word picks up the association with humor in line 5 to suggest the imbalance in his state).
1. A fever with alternating hot and cold spells.
2. Literally, through the crucifixion; figuratively, through his acceptance of his ministry.
3. The crucifix, regarded by some as a Roman Catholic icon, or making the sign of the cross.
4. Puritans denounced the crucifix from the pulpit and sought laws to suppress it.
5. Moistened with dew, thus emphasizing the source of the sacrament in the wound from Christ's side, a traditional iconographic representation.
6. The yardarm and the mast form a cross.

25 Material crosses, then, good physic be,
  And yet spiritual have chief dignity.
  These for extracted chemic med'cine[7] serve,
  And cure much better, and as well preserve.
  Then are you your own physic, or need none,
30 When still'd[8] or purg'd by tribulation;
  For when that cross ungrudg'd unto you sticks,
  Then are you to yourself a crucifix.
  As perchance, carvers[9] do not faces make,
  But that away, which hid them there, do take:
35 Let crosses, so, take what hid Christ in thee,
  And be his image, or not his, but he.
  But as oft alchemists do coiners[1] prove,
  So may a self-despising get self-love;
  And then, as worst surfeits of best meats be,
40 So is pride, issu'd from humility,
  For 'tis no child, but monster. Therefore cross
  Your joy in crosses, else, 'tis double loss.
  And cross thy senses, else, both they and thou
  Must perish soon, and to destruction bow.
45 For if th'eye seek good objects, and will take
  No cross from bad, we cannot 'scape a snake.
  So with harsh, hard, sour, stinking, cross the rest;
  Make them indifferent; call nothing best.
  But most the eye needs crossing, that can roam
50 And move: To th'others th'objects must come home.[2]
  And cross thy heart: for that in man alone
  Points downwards, and hath palpitation.
  Cross those dejections, when it downward tends,
  And when it to forbidden heights pretends.
55 And as thy brain through bony walls doth vent
  By sutures, which a cross's form present,
  So when thy brain works, ere thou utter it,
  Cross and correct concupiscence of wit.[3]
  Be covetous of crosses; let none fall.
60 Cross no man else, but cross thyself in all.
  Then doth the cross of Christ work fruitfully
  Within our hearts, when we love harmlessly

---

7. Paracelsian physicians extracted the "virtues"or "spiritual seed" of metals and herbs.
8. Distilled.
9. Sculptors who remove stone to reveal what was there potentially.
1. Forgers of coins.
2. To the other senses, which cannot move and can only receive objects brought to them, unlike the eye which can "cross" objects by moving them into perspective.
3. Desire to show one's cleverness.

That cross's pictures much, and with more care
That cross's children, which our crosses are.

Resurrection, imperfect.[4]

Sleep, sleep, old sun, thou canst not have repass'd,[5]
As yet, the wound thou took'st on Friday last;[6]
Sleep then, and rest; the world may bear thy stay;
A better sun rose before thee today,
5   Who, not content t'enlighten all that dwell
On th'earth's face, as thou, enlighten'd hell,[7]
And made the dark fires languish in that vale,
As at thy presence here, our fire grows pale,
Whose body, having walk'd on earth, and now
10   Hasting to heaven, would (that he might allow
Himself unto all stations and fill all)
For these three days become a mineral.
He was all gold when he lay down, but rose
All tincture,[8] and doth not alone dispose
15   Leaden and iron wills to good, but is
Of power to make even sinful flesh like his.
Had one of those whose credulous piety
Thought that a soul one might discern and see
Go from a body,'at this sepulcher been,
20   And issuing from the sheet, this body seen,
He would have justly thought this body a soul,
If not of any man, yet of the whole.
         Desunt cætera.[9]

---

4. *Imperfect* implies that the poem is incomplete. Of the eight known copies of this poem, only the Dolau Cothi ms. records the final phrase (*Desunt cætera*) which all subsequent editors print.
5. Recovered from.
6. The *wound* is the eclipse of the sun during the Crucifixion (Matthew 27:41). The poem takes place metaphorically before sunrise on Easter.
7. Refers to Christ's triumphant descent into Hell to take the faithful to Heaven; also known as the Harrowing of Hell.
8. The poem embodies an alchemical conceit: at the Resurrection, the Son, who was *gold* before, becomes a *tincture* able to transform and resurrect even sinful flesh.
9. The rest is lacking (Latin).

Upon the Annunciation and Passion Falling Upon One Day.[1]

Tamely[2] frail body, abstain today; today
My soul eats twice, Christ hither and away.
She sees him man, so like God made in this,
That of them both a circle emblem is,
5 Whose first and last concur:[3] This doubtful day
Of feast or fast, Christ came, and went away.
She sees him nothing, twice at once, who's all;
She sees a cedar[4] plant itself, and fall,
Her maker put to making, and the head
10 Of life, at once, not yet alive, and dead;
She sees at once the Virgin Mother stay
Reclus'd at home, public at Golgotha.[5]
Sad and rejoic'd she's seen at once, and seen
At almost fifty, and at scarce fifteen.
15 At once a son is promised her, and gone;
Gabriell gives Christ to her, he her to John;[6]
Not fully a mother, she's in orbity;[7]
At once receiver and the legacy.
All this, and all between, this day hath shown,
20 Th'abridgement of Christ's story, which makes one,
(As in plain maps, the farthest west is east)
Of th'angels *Ave* and *Consummatum est*.[8]
How well the Church, God's Court of Faculties,
Deals, in sometimes, and seldom joining these.
25 As by the self-fix'd pole we never do
Direct our course, but the next star[9] thereto,
Which shows where th'other is, and which, we say
(Because it strays not far) doth never stray:
So God by his Church, nearest to him, we know,
30 And stand firm, if we by her motion go.
His Spirit, as his fiery pillar,[1] doth
Lead, and his Church, as cloud; to one end both:

1. Lady Day, March 25, the first day of the old calendar that celebrated the day when the angel told Mary she would bear a child, and Good Friday fell on the same day in 1608.
2. Submissively.
3. Jesus's life ends on the same day it began, thus completing the circle.
4. Sometimes the cedar was likened to the flesh of Christ since neither suffered decay.
5. The scene of the Crucifixion.
6. See John 19:26–27.
7. Bereavement, especially the loss of a child (OED).
8. "Hail" was the greeting used by Gabriel at the Annunciation (Luke 1:28); "It is finished" are the final words of Christ (John 19:30).
9. The North Star is not actually fixed at the pole but is the best guide to its location.
1. Like the pillar of fire that led the Israelites at night through the desert (Exodus 13:21).

This Church, by letting these days join, hath shown
Death and conception in mankind is one.
35 Or 'twas in him the same humility,
That he would be a man, and leave to be:
Or as creation he had made, as God,
With the last judgment, but one period,
His imitating spouse² would join in one
40 Manhood's extremes: He shall come, he is gone.
Or as though one blood drop, which thence did fall,
Accepted, would have serv'd, he yet shed all,
So though the least of his pains, deeds, or words,
Would busy'a life, she all this day affords.
45 This treasure then, in gross, my soul, uplay,³
And in my life retail it every day.

Good-Friday, 1613. Riding Westward.⁴

Let man's soul be a sphere, and then, in this,
The intelligence that moves, devotion is;⁵
And as the other spheres, by being grown
Subject to foreign motions,⁶ lose their own,
5 And being by others hurried every day,
Scarce in a year their natural form obey:
Pleasure or business so, our souls admit
For their first mover,⁷ and are whirl'd by it.
Hence is't that I am carried towards the west,
10 This day, when my soul's form bends towards the east.
There I should see a sun by rising set,
And by that setting endless day beget.⁸
But that Christ on this cross did rise and fall,
Sin had eternally benighted all.
15 Yet dare I'almost be glad, I do not see
That spectacle of too much weight for me.
Who sees God's face, that is self life, must die;⁹
What a death were it then to see God die?

2. The Church.
3. To store up, lay up.
4. Donne stayed with Sir Henry Goodyer in the spring of 1613, then traveled west to visit Sir Edward Herbert, composing this poem along the way.
5. Just as each of the Ptolemaic spheres was thought to have an angel or *intelligence* regulating it, so *devotion* ought to guide the soul.
6. The motions of the other spheres that accounted for newly observed sidereal motions.
7. In the Ptolemaic system, the *primum mobile* imparted motion to the other spheres.
8. One of the traditional antiphons of Advent hailed Christ as the dayspring, "O Oriens, splendor lucis aeternae," i.e., the rising sun.
9. Exodus 33:20: "Thou canst not see my face: for there shall no man see me, and live."

It made his own lieutenant Nature shrink,
20 It made his footstool crack, and the sun wink.[1]
Could I behold those hands, which span the poles
And tune all spheres at once, pierc'd with those holes?[2]
Could I behold that endless height, which is
Zenith to us, and our antipodes,[3]
25 Humbled below us? or that blood which is
The seat of all our souls, if not of his,
Make dirt of dust, or that flesh which was worn,
By God, for his apparel, ragg'd and torn?
If on these things I durst not look, durst I
30 Upon his miserable mother cast mine eye,
Who was God's partner here, and furnish'd thus
Half of that sacrifice which ransom'd us?
Though these things, as I ride, be from mine eye,
They're present yet unto my memory,
35 For that looks towards them; and thou look'st towards me,
O Savior, as thou hang'st upon the tree.
I turn my back to thee but to receive
Corrections, till thy mercies bid thee leave.[4]
Oh think me worth thine anger, punish me,
40 Burn off my rusts, and my deformity;
Restore thine image, so much by thy grace,
That thou may'st know me, and I'll turn my face.

Upon The Translation of the Psalms by Sir Philip Sidney, and the Countess of Pembroke, His Sister.[5]

Eternal God (for whom whoever dare
Seek new expressions, do the circle square,[6]
And thrust into straight corners of poor wit
Thee, who art cornerless and infinite),
5 I would but bless thy name, not name thee now
(And thy gifts are as infinite as thou).

1. The earthquake and eclipse at the moment of Christ's death.
2. The image is of the cosmic Christ tuning the spheres by holding the axis of the Ptolemaic universe in the holes in his palms.
3. Line 24: He is at the highest point above the poet and, at the same time, above those in the hemisphere below the poet.
4. Cease.
5. Like Donne's poems, these translations by Sidney (1554–1586) and his sister Mary (1561–1621), circulated in manuscript. Though we now attribute the translations to Mary alone, Donne accorded them equal responsibility.
6. Squaring the circle was impossible, as was seeking new expressions for God.

Fix we our praises therefore on this one,
That, as thy blessed Spirit fell upon
These *Psalms'* first author in a cloven tongue[7]
10 (For 'twas a double power by which he sung
The highest matter in the noblest form),
So thou hast cleft that Spirit, to perform
That work again, and shed it, here, upon
Two, by their bloods, and by thy Spirit one.
15 A brother and a sister, made by thee
The organ, where thou art the harmony.
Two that make one John Baptist's holy voice,[8]
And who that psalm, "Now let the Isles rejoice,"[9]
Have both translated, and appli'd it too,
20 Both told us what, and taught us how to do.
They show us islanders our joy, our king;
They tell us *why* and teach us *how* to sing.
Make all this all, three choirs, heaven, earth, and spheres:
The first, Heaven, hath a song, but no man hears;
25 The spheres have music, but they have no tongue,
Their harmony is rather danc'd than sung;
But our third choir, to which the first gives ear
(For angels learn by what the Church does hear),
This choir hath all. The organist is he
30 Who hath tun'd God and man,[1] the organ we:
The songs are these, which heaven's high holy muse
Whisper'd to David, David to the Jews;
And David's successors in holy zeal,
In forms of joy and art do re-reveal
35 To us so sweetly and sincerely too,
That I must not rejoice as I would do,
When I behold that these *Psalms* are become
So well attir'd abroad, so ill at home,
So well in chambers, in the Church so ill,[2]
40 As I can scarce call that reform'd, until
This be reform'd. Would a whole state present
A lesser gift than some one man hath sent?
And shall our Church unto our spouse and king
More hoarse, more harsh, than any other, sing?

---

7. David sang with a *double power*: with his own voice and God's.
8. I.e., "the voice of one crying in the wilderness" (Matthew 3:3).
9. Psalm 97:1: "The LORD reigneth; let the earth rejoice; let the multitude of isles be glad thereof."
1. Christ has reconciled humankind to God through the atonement.
2. These psalms are sung privately (*abroad* and *in chambers*) in this translation so well, but in inferior translations *at home* and *in the Church.*

45   For *that* we pray, we praise thy name for *this*,
     Which, by this Moses and this Miriam,[3] is
     Already done. And as those *Psalms* we call,
     (Though some have other authors) David's all,
     So though some have, some may some psalms translate,
50   We thy Sidneian *Psalms* shall celebrate,
     And, till we come th'extemporal[4] song to sing
     (Learn'd the first hour that we see the king,
     Who hath translated[5] those translators), may
     These their sweet learned labors all the way
55   Be as our tuning, that when hence we part,
     We may fall in with them, and sing our part.

To Mr. Tilman After He Had Taken Orders.[6]

     Thou, whose diviner soul hath caus'd thee now
     To put thy hand unto the holy plough,[7]
     Making lay scornings[8] of the ministry,
     Not an impediment, but victory;
5   What bring'st thou home with thee? how is thy mind
     Affected in the vintage?[9] Dost thou find
     New thoughts and stirring in thee? and, as steel
     Touch'd with a loadstone,[1] dost new motions feel?
     Or, as a ship after much pain and care
10   For iron and cloth brings home rich Indian ware,
     Hast thou thus traffick'd, but with far more gain
     Of noble goods, and with less time and pain?
     Art thou the same materials, as before,
     Only the stamp is changed, but no more?
15   And as new crowned kings alter the face,
     But not the money's substance, so hath grace
     Chang'd only God's old image by creation,
     To Christ's new stamp, at this thy coronation?
     Or, as we paint angels with wings, because
20   They bear God's message and proclaim his laws,

<hr>

3. See Exodus 15:1–21 for Moses's song and Miriam's response to her brother's song.
4. Spontaneous, unpremeditated, as in the songs that will be sung eternally in the New Jerusalem, beyond time.
5. This line implies the poem was written after the countess's death in 1621.
6. Edward Tilman was ordained a deacon in December 1618 and a priest in 1620.
7. Luke 9:62: "No man, having put his hand to the plough, and looking back, is fit for the kingdom of God."
8. The scorn of the laity for the ministry.
9. In arriving at maturity (i.e., your acceptance of your vocation).
1. Magnet.

Since thou must do the like and so must move,
Art thou new feather'd with celestial love?
Dear, tell me where thy purchase[2] lies, and show
What thy advantage is above, below.[3]
25 But if thy gaining do surmount expression,
Why doth the foolish world scorn that profession,
Whose joys pass speech? Why do they think't unfit
That gentry should join families with it?
Would they think it well if the day were spent
30 In dressing, mistressing and compliment?
Alas, poor joys, but poorer men, whose trust
Seems richly placed in refined dust,
(For such are clothes and beauties, which though gay,
Are, at the best, but as sublimed clay).
35 Let then the world thy calling disrespect,
But go thou on, and pity their neglect.
What function is so noble, as to be
Ambassador to God and destiny?
To open life, to give kingdoms to more
40 Than kings give dignities, to keep heaven's door?
Mary's prerogative was to bear Christ, so
'Tis preachers' to convey him, for they do,
As angels out of clouds, from pulpits speak;
And bless the poor beneath, the lame, the weak.
45 If then th'astronomers, whereas they spy
A new-found star, their optics[4] magnify,
How brave are those, who with their engines,[5] can
Bring man to heaven, and heaven again to man!
These are thy titles and pre-eminences,
50 In whom must meet God's graces, men's offences;
And so the heavens, which beget all things here,
And th'earth, our mother, which doth those things bear,
Both these in thee, are in thy calling knit
And make thee now a blest hermaphrodite.[6]

2. Pursuit, livelihood (OED 4b).
3. In understanding heavenly or earthly matters.
4. Telescopes.
5. Devices.
6. Used figuratively here for a "person or thing in which any two opposite attributes or qualities are combined" (OED 4); i.e., his calling combines *God's graces* and *men's offences.*

both

A Hymn to Christ, at the Author's Last Going into Germany.[7]

In what torn ship soever I embark,
That ship shall be my emblem of thy ark;[8]
What sea soever swallow me, that flood
Shall be to me an emblem of thy blood.
5 Though thou with clouds of anger do disguise
Thy face, yet through that mask I know those eyes,
    Which, though they turn away sometimes,
    They never will despise.

I sacrifice this island unto thee,[9]
10 And all whom I lov'd there, and who lov'd me;
When I have put our seas 'twixt them and me,
Put thou thy sea[1] betwixt my sins and thee.
As the tree's sap doth seek the root below
In winter, in my winter now I go,
15   Where none but thee, th'eternal root
    Of true love, I may know.

Nor thou, nor thy religion, dost control,[2]
The amorousness of an harmonious soul,
But thou wouldst have that love thyself: As thou
20 Art jealous, Lord, so I am jealous now.
Thou lov'st not, till from loving more, thou free
My soul: Whoever gives, takes liberty:[3]
    Oh, if thou car'st not whom I love,
    Alas, thou lov'st not me.

— God (has) is like a jealous God

We are the same. Is he afraid God is not being faithful to him?

25 Seal then this bill of my divorce to all,
On whom those fainter beams of love did fall;
Marry[4] those loves, which in youth scatter'd be
On fame, wit, hopes (false mistresses) to thee.
Churches are best for prayer, that have least light:
30 To see God only, I go out of sight:

---

7. Donne accompanied Lord Doncaster on a diplomatic mission to Germany from May to December 1619. *1620*
8. A symbol of God's deliverance of his people at the Flood and through baptism (1 Peter 3: 20–21): "wherein few, that is, eight souls were saved by water. The like figure whereunto even baptism doth also now save us."
9. ~~England:~~ *Britain (is the island → England, is in it).*
1. Christ's blood.
2. Censure or restrain (OED 3b).
3. Donne uses the conceit of Christ as a jealous lover, who gives him the liberty to love only himself, in the sonnet on his wife's death.
4. Unite, join.

And to 'scape stormy days, I choose
An everlasting night.

Hymn to God, My God, in My Sickness.[5]

Since I am coming to that holy room,
 Where, with thy choir of saints for evermore,
I shall be made thy music, as I come
 I tune the instrument here at the door,
5 And what I must do then, think now before.   *anticipation*

Whilst my physicians by their love are grown
 Cosmographers, and I their map,[6] who lie
Flat on this bed, that by them may be shown
 That this is my southwest discovery,[7]
10 *Per fretum febris*,[8] by these straits to die,

I joy, that in these straits, I see my West;
 For, though their currents yield return to none,
What shall my West hurt me? As West and East
 In all flat maps[9] (and I am one) are one,
15 So death doth touch the resurrection.

Is the Pacific Sea my home? Or are
 The eastern riches? Is Jerusalem?
Anyan,[1] and Magellan, and Gibraltar,
 All straits, and none but straits, are ways to them,
20 Whether where Japhet dwelt, or Cham, or Shem.[2]

We think that Paradise and Calvary,
 Christ's cross and Adam's tree, stood in one place.[3]

---

5. Either the sickness of December 1623 that led to *Devotions Upon Emergent Occasions*, or his final illness of March 1631.
6. His body is a map since he is a little world or microcosm.
7. The torrid zone was considered to be in the south, while the west was associated with the setting sun and with death; thus his final voyage will be a *southwest discovery*.
8. Through the straits of fever (since fever will bring about his death). *Fretum* comes from a root meaning "to be in uneasy motion, to boil" and is the usual word for a "strait" (as the water boils up in a narrow channel); figuratively, *fretum* could also refer to the raging heat of the fever.
9. As a flat map could be pasted onto a round ball to make a globe.
1. Anyan was thought to separate America from eastern Asia, which may have been part of the fabled Northwest Passage in Donne's imagination.
2. In older maps, the world was configured with Jerusalem at the center and the three continents arranged around it (in a T-shape). The three sons of Noah each inherited a continent: Japhet, Europe; Ham, Africa; and Shem, Asia.
3. Donne may be conflating two legends: that Seth placed a seed in Adam's mouth when he died, from which the wood for the cross was taken; and that Adam was buried on Calvary.

antitype

Look, Lord, and find both Adams met in me;
  As the first Adam's sweat surrounds my face,
25 May the last Adam's blood my soul embrace. — *he is praying*

or

So in his purple[4] wrapp'd, receive me, Lord,
  By these his thorns give me his other crown;
And as to other souls I preach'd thy word,
  Be this my text, my sermon to mine own: *let the words of bible become his own*
30 Therefore that he may raise, the Lord throws down.

To Christ.[5]

Wilt thou forgive that sin[6] where I begun,
Which is my sin, though it was done before?
Wilt thou forgive those sins through which I run,
And do them still, though still I do deplore?
5 When thou hast done, I have not done,[7]
    For I have more.

Wilt thou forgive that sin by which I won
Others to sin, and made my sin their door?
Wilt thou forgive that sin which I did shun
10 A year or two, but wallow'd in a score?
When thou hast done, thou hast not done,
    For I have more.

I have a sin of fear, that when I've spun
My last thread,[8] I shall perish on the shore.
15 Swear by thyself, that at my death thy Sun
Shall shine as it shines now and heretofore;
And having done that, thou hast done.
    I have no more.

Donne alludes to the typological relationship between Adam and Christ—1 Corinthians 15:45: "The first man Adam was made a living soul; the last Adam was made a quickening spirit." The feverish sweat that surrounds the poet's face is a conflation of his bitter inheritance from Adam (earning bread by the sweat of his face, Genesis 3:19) and his pending mortality with his new life made possible by the bloody sweat of Christ.

4. Christ's blood, but also the mock royal garments placed on Christ at the Crucifixion (Mark 15:17).

5. According to Walton, this poem was written during Donne's illness in December 1623. There are two distinct versions. "To Christ" is as it appears in the mss. and "A Hymn to God the Father" as it was printed.

6. Original sin, the state into which mankind was born as a consequence of the fall.

7. Donne puns on his own name throughout.

8. The three Fates spun out the thread of each human life.

A Hymn to God the Father.

Wilt thou forgive that sin where I begun,
    Which was my sin, though it were done before?
Wilt thou forgive that sin, through which I run,
    And do run still: though still I do deplore?
5   When thou hast done, thou hast not done,
        For, I have more.

Wilt thou forgive that sin which I have won
    Others to sin? and, made my sin their door?
Wilt thou forgive that sin which I did shun
10   A year or two: but wallowed in a score?
       When thou hast done, thou hast not done,
        For I have more.

I have a sin of fear, that when I have spun
    My last thread, I shall perish on the shore;
15 But swear by thyself, that at my death thy son
    Shall shine as he shines now, and heretofore;
       And, having done that, thou hast done;
        I fear no more.

A Note on the Texts of
Donne's Poems

Though we now know that *Poems, by J. D. with Elegies on the Authors Death* was set from printers' copies of varying degrees of authority, this printed text was still used as the copy text (i.e., the base text believed most reliable) by many subsequent editors. A comparison of the 1633 edition to the likely manuscripts source (i.e., the Cambridge Balam ms.) reveals that the printer had "modernized" spelling and punctuation, or regularized it with a style favored by that print shop. Furthermore, this first printed edition was substantially revised in 1635, with twenty-eight new poems being added, some texts changed, and the whole arranged by genre. These extensive revisions indicate that someone had developed serious reservations about the reliability of the manuscripts used in setting the prior edition.[1] Though five subsequent seventeenth-century editions (in 1639, 1649, 1650, 1654, and 1669) added another 30 poems from other printed or manuscript sources, the editions of 1633 and 1635 essentially determined what was accepted as Donne's text and canon up to the twentieth century; and other surviving manuscript strands, no matter how authoritative their texts might be, were largely ignored until the twentieth century, when a number of editors produced scholarly editions based on a partial census of the 240 manuscripts that contained Donne's poetry.[2]

In preparing the Oxford edition that launched Donne's recovery in the early twentieth century, Sir Herbert Grierson grouped the manuscripts according to broad categories, which still remain useful for purposes of discussion. The first group include manuscripts that aspire to be complete collections of Donne's poetry, which were made by professional copyists between the years 1620–1633 and which share certain characteristics: all the poems included are canonical; no poems from after Donne's ordination are included (i.e.,

---

1. The data on Donne's mss. was derived from Ted-Larry Pebworth, "Manuscript Transmission and the Selection of Copy-Text in Renaissance Coterie Poetry" *Text* 7 (1994): 246–47 and Gary Stringer, "An Introduction to the Donne Variorum and the John Donne Society," *Anglistik* 10 (1999): 85–95.
2. See *Index of English Literary Manuscripts*, ed. Peter Beal. Vol. 1.1 (London: Mansell, 1980), 243–61.

all were written before 1615); the poems are ordered in roughly the same way; and, most importantly, their texts were similar. Grierson suggested that the Group I manuscript used in typesetting the 1633 *Poems* was an "old book" that Donne sought to obtain from his friend Henry Goodyer in 1614, while Helen Gardner similarly believed that the prototype of the Group I manuscript used to set the 1633 *Poems* was a copy of "Donne's own collection" that he had assembled for possible publication in 1614 before he took Holy Orders.[3] Likewise comprised of nearly complete collections of the poems, the manuscripts in the second group are so similar that they appear to be copies of the same source.[4] Since Group II manuscripts contain genuine Donne poems not found in the earlier Group I collections— e.g., the poem commemorating James Hamilton, "An Hymn to the Saints and to the Marquess Hamilton," who died in 1625—the source for this group seems to have been closely connected with Donne or at least had access to his papers. Both of the Oxford editors place great emphasis on the manuscripts of these first two groups, which Grierson also believed were "derived from some authoritative source, from manuscripts in the possession of members of Donne's circle."[5] Grierson and Gardner both placed great faith in the reliability of the first printed edition, especially that part that derived from a Group I source. And they were followed in this conviction by most of their twentieth-century successors.

The editors of the Donne Variorum have shown, on the other hand, that the large manuscript collections of Donne's poetry, which have been accepted unquestioningly since Grierson and therefore accorded the same relative authority, in fact, "are composite artifacts containing texts of individual poems drawn from multiple sources."[6] That is, some scribes compiled their manuscripts from several sources. And as Ted-Larry Pebworth further explains, the "smaller collections of poems within each larger compilation were of varying textual authority."[7] Grierson's postulation of a single authoritative source for these two groups is thus belied by the textual histories that the Donne Variorum has established. Using only Groups I and II to trace the variant forms of a work back to a single ancestor, the poet's lost original, in hopes of reconstructing Donne's *Ur*-text will not produce an authoritative text. Given the unreliability of any of the early editions or of any of these piecemeal groups, the Donne

3. Herbert J. C. Grierson, *The Poems of John Donne*, 2 vols. (London: Oxford UP, 1912), II xci; and Helen Gardner, *The Divine Poems of John Donne* (Oxford: Clarendon, 1952), lxiv.

4. Some have speculated that the source was a ms. Donne gave to Sir Robert Carr before going abroad in 1619; see Beal, *Index of English Literary Manuscripts*, 249.

5. Grierson, II cxi.

6. *The Variorum Edition of The Poetry of John Donne: The Elegies*, gen. ed. Gary Stringer (Bloomington, Indiana UP, 2000), lii.

7. Pebworth, 259.

Variorum is proceeding on a poem-by-poem basis, using manuscripts as copy text when they seem closer to the author's original. My edition will follow this practice in a modified way.

The efforts of the Donne Variorum, however, have provided us with further evidence about the authority of one manuscript witness, which has helped me narrow the field of choices as copy text for this edition. The Westmoreland manuscript derives from an authoritative source within Donne's circle, his close friend Rowland Woodward who prepared the manuscript for his employer, the earl of Westmoreland. Woodward presumably had access to Donne's own papers. Though Woodward's hand is not as polished as a professional scribe's, he produced a finely written manuscript for Westmoreland some time before 1603, judging from the poems addressed to "*Mr* Henry Wotton," that is, before he was knighted and would have been addressed as *Sir* Henry Wotton. It provides unique copies of some poems as well as a numbered sequence to the elegies and the sonnets that will become standard. (Unfortunately, only one of the Songs and Sonnets is contained within its folios.) Though other editors have used this manuscript, the Donne Variorum editors, through their meticulous collations in preparing texts for the Elegies and Holy Sonnets volumes, have only enhanced the stature of this artifact, taking it as copy text for most poems in those volumes. In my edition I have likewise used the Westmoreland manuscript as my copy text where possible, though I have collated it with other texts since it too contains some errors and since Donne revised some of his poetry after Woodward copied them. In one notable case, that of "Satire 3," I have used a later version of the poem from a Group II manuscript because of the significant revisions Donne made to this poem (see the essay by Gary Stringer in the Criticism section below). While the Westmoreland does not reflect changes made by Donne after 1603, it still offers an authoritative source of many poems as he once wrote them. In principle I have relied on a single manuscript for my copy text for each poem, not wishing to mix the texts from various families of manuscripts to produce a composite or hypothetical text.

Nevertheless I collated a number of manuscripts and early print versions of the poems. Because it was not practical for me to collate every artifact from these groups of manuscripts, I selected what I consider the best exemplars for collation. From Group I, Cambridge Balam (or C2, as it is abbreviated) was chosen and the Trinity College Dublin manuscript (or DT1) from Group II. The Balam manuscript, which was first discovered after Grierson's edition, may have been the copy text for the 1633 *Poems*. Written in a clear, elegant hand, the Dublin Trinity manuscript is the most authoritative of the Group II manuscripts and contains some readings that the others omit.[8] A third group of manuscripts may also be discerned that is more amorphous than Groups I and II. These manuscripts vary greatly in terms of the numbers of poems included and also attribute poems to Donne that are known to be spurious (thus they seem less closely connected to the author or his papers than those in Groups I and II), but one is especially important since it was used to make corrections and additions to the more complete second edition of Donne's poems. They also illustrate the process by which his poems were collected by his friends and admirers shortly after his death. The O'Flahertie manuscript, dated 12 October 1632, with its table of contents page, headed "The Poems of D[r]. J. Donne not yet imprinted," and logical arrangement by genre, was clearly intended for publication. It also shows evidence of having been carefully edited, with some readings supplied from the 1633 *Poems*. Passages about which there was some doubt were left blank, the missing space underscored and marked with a marginal notation, then filled in later from the first edition.

Thus, by collating these four manuscripts, the Cambridge Balam, the Dublin Trinity, the O'Flahertie, and the Westmoreland (usually my copy text), I have surveyed the most important strands of the Donne manuscripts. Such a collation reveals the frequent agreement among the texts, occasional authorial revisions, but also the scribal errors that are vagaries of manuscript transmission. For certain poems I have used other manuscripts as indicated in the textual notes. All of these manuscript readings are then collated with the seventeenth-century printed editions of the poems and with the major twentieth-century editions. The textual variants recorded in the notes below are the product of these collations and are intended to support the choices I have made. Since I regard Donne as a manuscript poet, I have seldom accepted a printed text over a manuscript as copy text, as was the general practice of my predecessors.

Furthermore, I have modernized spelling and, to a certain extent, punctuation. I believe that editions are not meant to be facsimiles and that editors should not hope to reproduce the scribal culture of an earlier age by reproducing every brevigraph, abbreviation or quaint spelling in the manuscript. We know that seventeenth-century typesetters regularly imposed a house-style on any work that passed through their hands, and, as Joseph Moxon in his *Mechanick Exercises on the Whole Art of Printing* (1683–84) makes clear, compositors were expected to amend texts "to render the Sence of the Author more intelligent to the Reader."[9] While such changes are clearly acts of interpretation, they usually produce a more intelligible

8. Grierson, II xciii.
9. Qtd. by Michael Hunter, "How to Edit a Seventeenth-Century Manuscript: Principles and Practice," *The Seventeenth Century* 10 (1995): 277–310.

text for twenty-first-century students. Since scribes tended to punctuate poetic texts lightly (e.g., the end of a line is frequently left without any mark of punctuation), reproducing such scribal practices will leave many questions unanswered. Here we are helped by the printers of 1633 *Poems* and subsequent seventeenth-century editions who punctuated the poems to make Donne's intricate syntax easier for the general public to read (and closer to the way Donne himself pointed his only surviving holograph manuscript). It seems reasonable to follow the lead of these seventeenth-century editors when trying to do the same for contemporary readers. I have therefore been guided by the punctuation of the 1633 *Poems* and subsequent editions in making the text intelligible, so long as it does not clash with the meaning as it is laid down in the manuscripts, which otherwise have priority.

One distinctive feature of my edition involves the spelling of elided words. Donne's verse is more regular metrically when his use of elision (i.e., the omission of an unstressed vowel or syllable to make scansion regular) is marked or otherwise recognized. In the first edition of his poems, care was taken to differentiate between contracted and uncontracted forms with an apostrophe used as a mark of elision, an editorial practice that I have attempted to preserve. Similarly, in my edition the distinction between final-*ed* (uncontracted) and-*'d* (contracted) is retained to make readers aware of Donne's meter. Likewise elisions such as *th'elite* for *the elite* will be retained.

The textual notes that follow make transparent what editorial choices I have made, and are reproduced in what is hoped will be a useful form for students seeking to unravel some of the textual conundra involving Donne's poems. The notes record all substantive variants, though not variants in punctuation except in special cases (e.g., line 24 of "Love's Alchemy") in the manuscripts consulted and the print sources, both the early editions as well as the significant editions of the twentieth century. Since spelling has been modernized in this edition, spelling has been regularized in the textual notes. That is, as far as possible, I have been concerned only with the word used and not how a scribe spelled it.[1] Also included in the textual notes are the titles of the poems as they appear in the manuscripts collated. Thus the title to the poem commonly called "A Hymn to Christ, at the Author's Last Going into Germany," the title used in various printed traditions beginning with 1633, is also noted as "Dr. Donne's Going into Bohemia. Hymn to Christ" in Cambridge Balam,

---

1. I am well aware that spelling and punctuation are rich with textual significance, but are beyond the scope of this edition.

"A Hymn to Christ" in Dublin Trinity, and "At the Seaside Going
over with the Lord Doncaster. 1619" in O'Flahertie.

The following, now standardized abbreviations adopted by the
Donne Variorum project, have been used:

Seventeenth-Century Manuscripts

B7   Denbigh Ms. British Library MS, Add. 18647
B46   Stowe Ms. British Library MS, Stowe 961
B47   Stowe Ms. British Library MS, Stowe 962
C2   Balam Ms. Cambridge University Library: Add. MS 5778(c)
C9   Luttrell Ms. Cambridge University Library: Add. MS 8468
DT1   Trinity College Library, Dublin: ms. 877
H4   Norton Ms. Harvard University Library: ms. Eng. 966.3
H5   Dobell Ms. Harvard University Library: ms. Eng. 966.4
H6   O'Flahertie Ms. Harvard University Library: ms. Eng. 966.5
NY1   John Cave Ms. New York Public Library, Arents Collection,
NY3   Westmoreland Ms. New York Public Library, Berg Collection
TT1   Dalhousie Ms. Texas Tech University Library: ms. PR 1171 D14
VA2   Nedham Ms. Victoria and Albert Museum, Dyce Collection, Cat. No.
        18, ms. 25.F.17

Seventeenth-Century Editions

a   1611 *An Anatomy of the World* (STC 7022)
b   1612 *The First Anniuersarie* and *The Second Anniuersarie*
        (STC 7023)
c   1621 *The First Anniuersarie* and *The Second Anniuersarie*
        (STC 7024)
d   1625 *The First Anniuersarie* and *The Second Anniuersarie*
        (STC 7025)
A   1633 *Poems, by J. D. with Elegies on the Authors Death* (STC 7045)
B   1635 *Poems.* Second edition (STC 7046)
C   1639 *Poems.* Third edition (STC 7047)
D   1649 *Poems.* Fourth edition (STC D1868)
E   1650 *Poems.* Fifth edition (STC D1869)
F   1654 *Poems.* Sixth edition (STC D1870)
G   1669 *Poems.* Seventh edition (STC D1871)
Walton 1640 *Life and Death of Dr. John Donne* (STC 7038)

Selected Modern Editions

Q   1912 *The Poems of John Donne*, H. J. C. Grierson, ed.
T   1942 *The Complete Poems of John Donne*, Roger Bennett, ed.
U   1952 *The Divine Poems*, Helen Gardner, ed.
V   1956 *The Songs and Sonets of John Donne*, Theodore Redpath, ed.
W   1963 *The Anniversaries*, Frank Manley, ed.

X   1965 *The Elegies and Songs and Sonnets*, Helen Gardner, ed.
Y   1967 *The Satires, Epigrams and Verse Letters*, Wesley Milgate, ed.
Z   1967 *The Complete Poetry of John Donne*, John T. Shawcross, ed.
BB   1978 *The Epithalamions, Anniversaries and Epicedes*, Wesley Milgate, ed.
DV2   2000 *Variorum Edition of The Elegies*, Gary Stringer, gen. ed. Volume 2 of the *Donne Variorum*.
DV6   1995 *Variorum Edition of the Anniversaries and the Epicedes and Obsequies*, Gary Stringer, gen. ed. Volume 6 of the *Donne Variorum*.
DV7   2006 *Variorum Edition of The Holy Sonnets*, Gary Stringer, gen. ed. Volume 7.1 of the *Donne Variorum*.
DV8   1995 *Variorum Edition of the Epigrams, Epithalamions and Miscellaneous Poems*, Gary Stringer, gen. ed. Volume 8 of the *Donne Variorum*.

Other Symbols and Abbreviations

<word>   word in angled brackets is omitted
Σ   all other collated sources
~   base word or phrase

Textual Notes

Satire 1 [~ C2, NY3; "Satire" in DT1; "Satire 2" H6]. Copy text: NY3. Collation: C2, DT1, H6, NY3 with A–G, Q, T, Y, Z. 1 *changling*] DT1 (as addition), H6, NY3 & B–G, T; *fondling* C2, DT1 & A, Q, Y, Z. 7 *jolly*] Σ; *wily* H6 & B–G. 13 *swear*] Σ; *swear here* H6. *love*] Σ; *love here* B–G. 16 *dost*] Σ; *do* NY3. 19 *Nor*] DT1, H6, NY3 & T, Y; *Not* Σ. 20 *courtesy*] Σ; *courtesies* H6. 23 *Wilt*] Σ; *Shalt* H6, NY3 & T. 25 *First or*] Σ; *and* NY3. 32 *raise*] Σ; *vail* H6, NY3 & T. 33 *consort*] Σ; *consort with* H6. *have*] Σ; *hast* H6. 37 *dost not only*] Σ; *not only dost* H6. 42 *birth . . . death*] Σ; *births . . . deaths* H6. 46 *yet*] Σ; *<yet>* H6 & B–G. 47 *I now*] Σ; *now I* H6, NY3 & T. 53 *that*] C2, DT1, NY3 & T, Y; *who* Σ. 55 *colored*] NY3 & C–G; *color* Σ. 60 *scheme*] Σ; *scenes* C2, DT1 & A. 62 *supple*] H6, NY3 & T; *subtle* Σ. 63 *hence*] H6, NY3 & T; *me* Σ. *canst*] Σ; *can* C2 & A–G. 70 *his*] Σ; *high* A. 71 *skip forth now*] Σ; *now step forth* H6. 72 *silken painted*] Σ; *painted silken* H6. 78 *stoops*] Σ; *stoop'd* C2, DT1 & A. *nighest the*] Σ; *the nighest* C2. Lines 81–82 omitted in A. 84 *Oh*] Σ; *yea* NY3; *or* DT1. 90 *Maybe*] H6, NY3 & T; *'T may be* Σ. 94 *on*] Σ; *in* NY3. 95 *all*] Σ; *s'all* C2 & A. 97 *cut, print*] H6, NY3 & T; *print, cut* Σ. *or*] H6, NY3 & T; *and* Σ. 98 *court*] Σ; *town* H6. 100 *hath*] Σ; *had* DT1. 102 *Which*] Σ; *Who* H6. 108 *lechery*] Σ; *liberty* A.

Satire 2 [~ C2, NY3; "Satire" in DT1, H6]. Copy text: NY3. Collation: C2, DT1, H6, NY3, TT1 with A–G, Q, T, Y, Z. 4 *toward*] NY3 & A–F, Q, Z; *towards* Σ. *towards*] Σ; *toward* TT1 & B–G; *to* H6. 6 *dearths*] Σ; *dearth* H6 & A–G. 7 *or*] H6, NY3 & T; *and* Σ. 8 *It riddlingly*] H6, NY3 & T; *Riddlingly it* Σ. 10 *not*] Σ; *nor* DT1. 11, 12 *which*] Σ; *that* H6. 12 *could not*] H6, NY3 & T; *cannot* Σ. 15 *above*] Σ; *about* DT1. 17 *rhymes*] H6, NY3, TT1 & T, Y; *rhythms* Σ. *witchcraft's*] Σ; *witchcraft* H6. 22 *boys singing*] H6, NY3 & T; *singers* Σ. 31 *these . . . which*] Σ; *those . . . that* H6; *those . . . which* TT1. 32 *swive*] H6, NY3 & T; *do* Σ. *dildos*] Σ; *<dildos>* A with a dash to indicate missing word. 33 *to*] Σ; *<to>* DT1, NY3. *Litany*] Σ; *<Litany>* A–G omitted or with dashes. 34 *all*] Σ; *of all* C2, TT1 & A. 36 *tenements*] Σ; *torments* H6 (corrected). 40 *great*] H6, NY3 & T; *just*] Σ & A. 43 *was*] Σ; *<was>* H6 & B–G. 44 *a scarce*] Σ; *scarce a* C2, H6 & A–G. *this*] Σ; *his* H6. Line 46 omitted in NY3. 54 *return'd*] Σ; *return* C2, DT1, TT1 & A. *next*] Σ; *this* NY3. 57 *words*] Σ; *world* DT1. 63 *meer*] Σ; *more* C2. 67 *which*] Σ; *who* H6. Lines 69–70, 74–75 omitted in A with dashes. 70 *yea*] Σ; *or* B–G. 75 *and*] Σ; *or* C2, TT1. 77 *our*] Σ; *the* A–G. 84 *Relic-like*] Σ; *Relicly* C2 & A–G. 86 *men*] Σ; *maids* G. 87 *parchments*] NY3 & Q, T, Y, Z; *parchment* Σ. 91 *nor*] Σ; *or* DT1. 98 *writings*] Σ; *writing* DT1, H6, TT1. 99 *slyly*] Σ; *sly* H6. 104 *These*] DT1, NY3 & T; *Those* Σ. 105 *Where*] Σ; *Where's* C2, TT1 & A, Q, Y, Z. *In*] Σ; *<In>* C2, DT1 & A. *great*] Σ; *<great>* H6, TT1 & B–G. 107 *bless*] Σ; *blessed* B–G. 108 *no*] Σ; *not* H6. 111 *none draws*] Σ; *ne'er draw* H6. 112 *laws*] Σ; *law* H6.

Satire 3 [~ C2, H6, NY3; "Satire 2" in DT1; "Satire" in TT1]. Copy text: DT1. Collation: C2, DT1, H6, NY3, TT1 with A–G, Q, T, Y, Z. 1 *chokes*] Σ; *checks* B–G. 2 *Those*] Σ; *These* NY3 & T. 3 *not*] Σ; *nor* NY3. *sins*] Σ; *sin* NY3. 4 *Can*] Σ; *May* H6, NY3 & T. 7 *in*] C2, DT1 & A; *to* Σ. *blinded*] Σ; *blind* NY3. 14 *so easy ways*] Σ; *ways easy* NY3; *ways so easy* H6. 17 *and*] Σ; *<and>* H6, NY3. 29 *coward*] Σ; *cowards* H6. 31 *Sentinel*] Σ; *Soldier* H6, NY3 & T. *his*] Σ; *this* H6 & G. 32 *forbidden*] Σ; *forbid* H6, NY3 & A–G, T. 33 *foe*] C2, DT1 & A; *foes* Σ. *whom*] Σ; *he's, whom* C2 & A, Z; *his whom* DT1; *he, whom* H6 & B–G; *is whom* TT1. 35 *quit*] Σ; *rid* H6, NY3. 39 *wither'd*] Σ; *weathered* C2. 44 *here*] Σ; *her* A. 47 *He*] Σ; *And* H6 & B–F. *the*] C2, DT1, TT1 & A–G; *her* Σ. 51 *sullen*] Σ; *solemn* H6. 53 *that*] Σ; *which* H6, NY3 & T. 57 *bid*] Σ; *bids* C2, TT1 & A–G. 64 *women*] Σ; *women's* C2. 75 *that*] Σ; *which* NY3, TT1 & T. 79 *huge*] Σ; *high* H6, NY3 & T. 80 *Cragged*] Σ; *Ragged* H6, NY3 & T. *stands*] Σ; *dwells* H6, NY3 & T. 81 *her*] Σ; *it* NY3 & T. *about*] C2, DT1, H6, NY3, TT1; *about must* Σ; *about it* G. 83 *that*] Σ; *as* H6. 84 *soul*] Σ; *mind* H6, NY3 & T. 90 *here*] H6, NY3, DT1, TT1 & Q, T, Y; *<here>* Σ. 93 *soul*] Σ; *self* H6. 94 *man's*] Σ; *men's* NY3 & T. *she*] Σ; *he* DT1, H6. *not*] Σ; *<not>* B–F. 95 *Will*] C2, DT1, TT1 & A, Y; *Oh, will* NY3 & Q, T, Z; *Or will* H6 & B–G. *boot*] Σ; *serve* H6, NY3 & T. 97 *thee*] Σ; *me* NY3 & G, T. 103 *blest*] Σ; *best* C2. *that*] Σ *which* NY3. 104 *do*] Σ; *prove* H6, NY3 & T, Y. 107; *mills, and*

165

rocks, and woods] Σ; *mills, rocks, and woods* NY3 & B–G; *mills, woods, rocks, and at the last* H6. 109 *men's*] Σ; *man's* H6.

Satire 4 [~ C2, H6, NY3; "Satire" in DT1]. Copy text: NY3. Collation: C2, DT1, H6, NY3, TT1 with A–G, Q, T, Y, Z, 2 *but*] Σ; *but yet* H6 & B–G. 5 *neither*] Σ; *nor* NY3 & T; *neithers* C2; *not* H6. 7 *new*] Σ; *yet* H6. 8 *Glare*] Σ; *Glaze* C2 & A, Q, Y, Z, 9 *a*] Σ; *<a>* C2, H6 & A–G. 10 *is*] Σ;*was* DT1. 12 *Second of*] Σ; *in* H6 & B–F. 14 *lustful*] Σ; *as lustful* C2, DT1 & A, Q, Y, Z. 16 *at*] Σ; *in* C2 & A–G. 18 *slime*] Σ; *slimes*H6. 33 *Become tuftaffeta*] Σ; *Tuftaffeta become* H6. 35 *This*] Σ; *The* H6 & A–G. 36 *knows*] H6, NY3 & T; *knoweth* Σ. 38 *one*] Σ; *no* Q, Z; *strange* TT1. 42 *enough preparatives*] Σ; *preparatives enough* H6. 47 *and*] H6, NY3 & T; *or* Σ. 56 *two*] Σ; *two most* H6. 57 *There*] Σ; *Here* B–G. 59 *was*] H6, NY3, TT1; *was;* Σ. 60 *Yet*] Σ *But* H6. 62 *wonders*] Σ; *words* C2, DT1, TT1 & A, Z, 65 *that*] NY3 & T; *the* Σ. 69 *last*] Σ *taste* TT1 & B–F, Y. 73 *to'a*] Σ; *a to* NY3 & T. *squeak'd*] Σ; *squeaks* H6. 79 *kings*] Σ; *king* H6, NY3. 83 *Mine*] Σ; *Fine* A; *in me* DT1. 84 *Frenchman*] Σ; *Sir* H6 & B–G. 86 *your*] Σ; *this* H6, NY3 & T; *the* TT1. 92 *dress*] Σ *address* C2, DT1 & A, Q, T, Y, Z. 97 *and . . . and*] NY3; *or . . . or* Σ. 99 *smil'd or frown'd*] NY3 & T; *frown'd or smil'd* Σ. 101 *loves*] Σ; *~;* A–F, Q, Y, Z; *~,* G. 102 *Hastes*] Σ; *Haste* C2. 104 *shoes, boots*] H6, NY3 & T; *boots, shoes* Σ. *or*] H6, NY3 & T; *and* Σ. 106 *blow-point or span-counter*] H6, NY3 & T; *span-counter or blow-point* Σ. *they*] Σ; *shall* TT1 & A–G. 109 *tries*] Σ; *cloys* H6 & A–G. 111 *thrusts*] Σ; *trusts* C2. *on*] Σ; *<on>* NY3 & T; *me* C2, DT1, TT1. 113 *Speaks*] Σ; *Speak* DT1. *which*] H6, NY3 & T; *that* Σ. *have*] Σ; *hath* C2, DT1 & A. 116 *sigh*] Σ; *belch* NY3. 117 *his*] DT1, H6, NY3, TT1 & T; *this* Σ. 122 *says*] H6, NY3 & T; *saith* Σ. 123 *Second that*] Σ; *<that>* B–F. 128 *loves*] Σ; *loveth* H6. 133 *in*] H6, NY3 & T; *~;* A, G, Q, Y, Z; *~,* C2 & B–F; *~.* TT1. *him.*] Σ; *~,* C–G, Q, Y, Z; *~* TT1. 134 *venom'd*] Σ; *venom* B–F, Q, Z; *venomous* G. Lines 134–35 omitted in A. 136 *he*] Σ; *be* DT1. *freed*] Σ; *freed* C2, DT1. Lines 137b–139a omitted in DT1. 147 *more jig*] Σ; *jig more* DT1, TT1. 153 *Ran*] Σ; *Run* NY3 & T. 154 *make*] NY3, TT1 & Q, T, Y, Z; *makes* H6; *haste* C2, DT1 & A–G. 156 *piteous*] Σ; *precious* C2, DT1, TT1 & A, Q, Y, Z. 159 *o're*] Σ; *on* DT1, TT1 & A, Q, Y, Z. 164 *th'*] Σ; *<th'>* C2, DT1 & A–F. 166 *whole*] Σ; *<whole>* DT1. 169 *Think*] Σ; *Thinks* C2. *yon*] H6, NY3 & T;*your* C2, DT1, TT1 & A–G, Q, Y, Z. 170 *transplanted*] H6, NY3 & T; *transported* Σ. 171 *court here*] NY3 & T; *courtiers* H6 & B–G; *presence* C2, DT1, TT1 & A, Q, Y, Z. 174 *are, their*] Σ; *are there*; NY3. 180 *th'*] NY3 & T; *their* Σ. 182 *cry*] Σ; *cries* C2, DT1, NY3, TT1 & G, T. *his*] H6, NY3 & B–F, T; *the* Σ. 183 *to*] Σ;*unto* C2, DT1. 184 *seems*] Σ; *thinks* H6. 188 *do*] Σ; *did* H6, NY3 & T. 190 *praise*] Σ; *pray so* C2. 193 *These*] Σ; *Those* H6. 194 *scarlet*] H6, NY3, TT1 & T; *scarlets* Σ. 199 *As*] H6, NY3 & T; *As'if* Σ; *At* TT1. 203 *and*] Σ; *or* NY3 & T. *with which*] H6, NY3 & T; *wherewith* Σ. 204 *surveys*] NY3 & T; *survey* Σ. 205 *tries*] Σ; *try* Q, Z. 211 *straight*] H6, NY3 & T; *he* Σ. 215 *whisper'd*] Σ; *whispers* H6 & B–G. 216 *him*] Σ; *him quite* H6. 222 *whom*] Σ; *or whom* H6 & B–G. 223 *not.*] Σ; *not he.* H6 & B–G. 224 *rusheth*] Σ; *rushes* C–G. 225 *came*] H6, NY3 & T; *meant* Σ. 226 *theirs*] Σ; *those* H6. *which*] Σ; *who* DT1. *still*] Σ; *yet still* C2, DT1, TT1 & A, Y. 230 *which*] Σ; *<which>* A–G. 234 *which*] H6, NY3 & T; *that* Σ. 238 *wit*] Σ; *wits* C2 & A–F, Z. *arts*] Σ; *art* H6. 240 *Which*] Σ; *Who* H6. *but*] Σ; *<but>* H6, NY3. *scant*] H6, NY3 & B–G; *scarce* Σ. 241 *the*] Σ; *their* H6, NY3 & T; *these* DT1; *those* TT1. 242 *known*] Σ; *<known>* NY3, TT1 & T. 243 *men* DT1, H6, NY3 & D–G, T; *man* Σ.

Satire 5 ["Satire 5" in C2, H6, NY3; "Satire" in DT1; "A Satire 3" in TT1]. Copy text: NY3. Collation: C2, DT1, H6, NY3, TT1 with A–G, Q, T, Y, Z. 12 *implies*] Σ; *employs* C2, TT1 & A. 14 *ravishing*] Σ; *ravenous* H6; *devouring* TT1. Lines 15–18 missing in TT1. 19 *excrement*] H6, NY3 & T; *excrements* Σ. 20 *who*] Σ; *that* H6. 22 *do*] Σ *<do>* H6. 23 *yet*] Σ; *and yet* H6. 26 *their*] Σ; *the* H6, TT1 & B–G. 27 *th'*] Σ; *and th'* DT1. 30 *arms drown*] Σ; *arm drowns* H6. 37 *that was*] Σ; *<that was>* H6. 38 *far*] Σ; *<far>* H6 & B–F. *Allow*] Σ; *Did allow* H6 & B–F. 39 *claim'd*] H6, NY3 & B–G, T; *demands* C2, TT1 & A, Q, Y, Z. 40 *swear and sweat*] H6, NY3 & T; *sweat and swear* Σ. 41 *other*] Σ; *others'* H6, TT1. 42 *'Scape, like Angelica*] Σ; *Like Angelica, 'scape* NY3 & T. 46 *Flow*] Σ; *Flows* H6. *main*] Σ; *mean* C2. *these*] Σ; *those* H6. 47 *to*] Σ; *into* H6, TT1. 51 *those* H6, NY3 & T; *these* Σ. 52 *thy*] H6, NY3, TT1 & B–G, T; *the* Σ. 56 *like*] Σ; *likes* NY3, TT1 & T. 58 *men*] Σ; *that men* C2 & A–F, Q, Y, Z. 59 *supplications*] Σ; *supplication* B–F. 61 *courts*] Σ; *court* C2, DT1 & A. 68 *ask*] Σ; *lack* C2 & A–F. 72 *but*] Σ; *<but>* C2, DT1, TT1 & A–G. *us*] Σ; *<us>* C2, TT1 & A–G. 73 *chairs*] NY3; *chains* Σ. 75 *In*] Σ; *As in* H6. 76 *th'*] Σ; *<th'>* A–G. 80 *erst*] Σ; *<erst>* C2, DT1 & A. 86 *much more shalt*] Σ; *shalt much more* H6. 87 *if*] H6, NY3 & B–F, T; *when* Σ. 90 *that*] H6, NY3 & T; *the* Σ. 91 *And*] Σ; *Which* H6 & B–G. *div'dst*] C2, NY3; *div'st* Σ; *div'd* H6.

Elegy 1 [~ C2, NY3, TT1; "Elegy" in DT1; "Elegy. To a Lady Whose Chain Was Lost. The Bracelet. Armilla" in H6; "Elegy XII. Upon the losse of his Mistresses Chaine, for which he made satisfaction" in B]. Copy text: NY3. Collation: C2, DT1, H6, NY3, TT1 with B–G, Q, T, X, Z, DV2. 3 *thy*] Σ; *this* C2, DT1. 6 *those*] C2, DT1, H6, NY3, TT1 & X, DV2; *these* Σ. *are*] Σ; *were* TT1 & B–G. *tied*] Σ; *knit* B–G, Q. 7 *thy*] Σ; *this* C2. 8 *luck's sake*] H6, NY3 & T, DV2; *luck-sake* G; *luck sake* Σ *bitter*] Σ; *bigger* TT1. 11 *taint*] H6, NY3 & T,

DV2; *fault* C2, DT1, TT1 & X, Z; *way* B–G, Q. 26 *lean, so pale*] C2, DT1, NY3 & X, Z, DV2; *pale, so lean* Σ. 38 *run*] Σ; *runs* C2, TT1. 40 *ragged, ruin'd*] NY3 & T, DV2; *ruin'd, ragged* Σ. 54 *me*] Σ; *<me>* C2. 60 *schemes*] Σ; *scenes* DT1. *fulfills*] Σ; *fills full* TT1 & B–G, Q, Z. 61 *hath*] Σ; *have* DT1. 62 *his*] Σ; *her* DT1, H6. 67 *the doom from him*] Σ; *from him the doom* C2, DT1, TT1 & X; *from him that doom* Q, Z. 71 *those*] H6, NY3; *the* Σ. 79 *thy*] Σ; *they* DT1. 88 *your*] Σ; *you* NY3. 90 *few fellows*] Σ; *fellows* DT1, TT1. *longer with me*] Σ; *with me longer* DT1, TT1. 92 *So much, as I*] C2, NY3, DV2; *So much that I* DT1, TT1; *So, that I almost* Σ. Lines 95–114 missing in H6. 96 *to*] Σ; *in* C2. 104 *Itchy*] Σ; *Itching* B–G, Q, Z. 105 *hurt which ever gold*] Σ; *hurt that ever gold* DT1, TT1; *evils that gold ever* B–G, Q, Z. 111 *then*] Σ; *thou* C2, DT1, TT1 & X; *thee* Q, Z. 113 *Or*] Σ; *But* B–G, Q.

Elegy 2 [~ NY3, TT1; "Elegy" in DT1, H6; "Elegy VIII. The Comparison" in B]. Copy text: NY3. Collation: DT1, H6, NY3, TT1 with A–G, Q, T, X, Z, DV2. 2 *musk cat's* (or *muskats* or *musk-cat's*)] Σ; *muskets* G. 6 *carcanets*] NY3 & T, X, Z, DV2; *coronets* DT1, H6, TT1 & A–G, Q. 9 *lawless*] Σ; *needless* DT1. 20 *yet scarce*] Σ; *scarcely* H6. 26 *dirt*] Σ; *dust* A–G, Q, Z. 31 *on*] Σ; *at* H6. 37 *dirt*] Σ; *part* DT1 & T. 43 *kisses*] Σ; *kissings* NY3 & DV2. 46 *fear'd*] Σ; *fears* A–G, Q, Z.

Elegy 3 [~ NY3, TT1; "Elegy 2" in H6; "Elegy 6" in C2; "Elegy" in DT1; "Elegy IV. The Perfume" in B]. Copy text: NY3. Collation: DT1, H6, NY3, TT1 with A–G, Q, T, X, Z, DV2. 2 *escapes*] Σ; *scapes* H6 & G. Lines 7–8 omitted in C2 & A. 9 *hath*] Σ *have* NY3, TT1 & T, X, DV2. 15 *Take*] DT1, H6, NY3, TT1 & T, X, DV2; *Takes* Σ. 21 *And*] Σ; *<And>* C2 & A, Q, Z. 22 *blushings*] Σ; *blushing* A–F, Q, Z. 29 *ingled*] Σ; *dandled* H6 & G. 37 *for*] Σ; *to* A–G, Q, Z. 40 *mine*] Σ; *my* C2. 41 *my*] Σ; *mine* DT1, TT1 & T. 42 *we were*] NY3, DT1, TT1 & Q, T, X, DV2; *were we* Σ. 43 *When . . . that*] Σ; *The . . . which* H6. 44 *pale*] Σ; *<pale>* DT1. 52 *speechless*] Σ; *senseless* H6. 54 *Next me*] Σ; *Next to my heart* H6. 63 *you*] Σ; *thou* DT1, TT1, H6. 64 *There*] Σ; *These* C2. 65 *ye*] Σ; *you* C2, H6. 67 *taken simply*] Σ; *taken simple* TT1 & T; *simply taken* H6; *single taken* C2.

Elegy 4 [~ NY3; "Elegy 3" in C2, H6; "Elegy" in DT1; "Elegy I. Jealousy" in B]. Copy text: NY3. Collation: C2, DT1, H6, NY3 with A–G, Q, T, X, Z, DV2. 1 *which*] Σ; *that* DT1. 9 *poor*] Σ; *pure* C2, NY3. *howling*] Σ; *<howling>* DT1. 10 *few*] Σ; *some few* DT1. 20 *nor*] Σ; *or* H6. 25 *that*] Σ; *it* A–G. 30 alternate line: *We into some third place retired were* H6. 31 *There*] Σ; *Then* C2.

Elegy 5 [~ NY3; "Elegy 9 in C2; "Elegy" in DT1, TT1; "Elegy 4" in H6; "Elegy VI" in B]. Copy text: NY3. Collation: C2, DT1, H6, NY3, TT1 with A–G, Q, T, X, Z, DV2. 1 *not me*] DT1, NY3, TT1 & DV2; *me not*] Σ. 3 *or*] Σ; *and* DT1, TT1. 12 *Nor*] Σ; *Not* DT1, H6, TT1. 15 *strow'd*] Σ; *straw'd* NY3 & DV2; *strew'd* DT1 & T. 26 *to*] Σ; *or* C2 & A, Q. 33 *the*] Σ; *her* DT1, H6, TT1 & B–G. 38 *well*] Σ; *so well* DT1, TT1. 43 *My*] Σ; *Mine* DT1, TT1.

Elegy 6 [~ NY3; "Elegy 12" in C2; "Elegy 5 in H6; "Elegy" in DT1]. Copy text: NY3. Collation: C2, DT1, H6, NY3 with A–G, Q, T, X, Z, DV2. 4 *nor*] Σ; *or* H6. 7 *call*] Σ; *know* H6 & B–G. 23 *which*] Σ; *who* C2 & A–G, Q, Z. 21 *world's*] Σ; *world* C2. 23 *which*] DT1, NY3 & T, X, DV2; *who*] Σ. 25 *words*] Σ; *works* C2 & G. 30 *then*] Σ; *<then>* DT1.

Elegy 7 [~ NY3; "Elegy 10" in C2; "Elegy 6" in H6; "Elegy 5" in TT1; "Elegy" in DT1]. Copy text: NY3. Collation: C2, DT1, H6, NY3, TT1 with Q, T, X, Z, DV2. 1 *Till*] Σ; *Tell* NY3; *When* TT1. 5 *can*] Σ; *tan* NY3. 8 *which*] Σ; *that* DT1, H6, TT1. 11 *angels*] Σ; *angel* TT1. 12 *which*] Σ; *that* H6. 18 *food*] Σ; *means* H6. 19 *should*] Σ; *shall* C2. *that*] Σ *the* C2, DT1. 29 *me*] Σ *we* DT1. 31 *Thy*] C2, NY3 & Z, DV2; *Thine* Σ. 32 *for*] Σ *from* H6, TT1. 36 *There*] Σ *That* TT1. 42 *those*] NY3, TT1 & T, DV2; *these* Σ. 44 *To*] Σ; *Unto* H6. *wars*] Σ; *war* DT1, TT1.

Elegy 8 [~ NY3; "Elegy 2" in C2; "Elegy 7" in H6; "Elegy 6" in TT1; "Elegy" in DT1; "To His Mistress Going to Bed" in G]. Copy text: NY3. Collation: C2, DT1, H6, NY3, TT1 with G, Q, T, X, Z, DV2. 4 *they*] Σ; *he* G, Q, Z. 5 *zones*] DT1, NY3, TT1 & T, DV2; *zone* Σ. *glistering*] Σ; *glittering* C2, DT1 & G, Q, Z. 10 *'tis your*] Σ; *it is* G, Q, Z. 11 *whom*] Σ; *which* H6 & G, Q, Z. 13 *gown's*] Σ; *gown* H6 & G, Q, Z. 14 *When*] Σ; *Where* DT1; *As when* TT1. *from*] Σ; *through* G. *hill's* (or *hills*)] Σ; *hill* TT1. 15 *your*] Σ; *that* G, Q, Z. 17 *Now*] Σ; *<Now>* C2, DT1, H6 & T, X. *then*] Σ; *<then>* H6. *safely*] Σ; *softly* C2, TT1 & G, Z. 20 *Receiv'd by*] Σ; *Reveal'd to* G. 22 *Ill*] Σ; *All* H6. 24 *They*] Σ; *Those* H6 & G, Q, Z. *the*] Σ; *our* H6 & G, Q, T, Z. 26] The order of these prepositions varies in many manuscripts; see DV2 185. *blest am I*] Σ; *am I blest* G. 31 *in*] Σ; *into* C2, DT1, H6. *these*] Σ; *those* C2, TT1. 32 *Then*] Σ; *There* C2. 36 *as*] Σ; *like* H6 & G, Q, Z. 38 *may covet theirs*] Σ; *might covet that* H6; *may court that* G. 43 *see*] Σ; *be* C2, DT1, TT1. *since*] Σ; *since that* G, Q, Z. 46 *There*] Σ; *Here* TT1 & T, X. *much less*] Σ; *due to* H6 & G, Q, Z. 47 *teach*] Σ; *show* H6.

Elegy 9 [~ NY3; "Elegy 5" in C2; "Elegy 8" in H6; "Elegy 4" in TT1; "Elegy" in DT1; "Elegy III. Change" in G]. Copy text: NY3. Collation: C2, DT1, H6, NY3, TT1 with A–G, Q, T, X, Z, DV2. 4 *confirm*] Σ; *confirms* TT1. 8 *those*] DT1, NY3, TT1 & G, DV2; *these* Σ; *the* H6. 9 *these* Σ; *those* TT1. 10 *men*] Σ; *man* DT1, TT1. 15 *and*] C2, NY3 & X, DV2; *not* Σ. 17 *plowland*] Σ; *plowed land* DT1, TT1. 20 *the*] Σ; *<the>* DT1, TT1. 23 *then if so thou do*] Σ; *and if that thou so do* A–G, Q. 24 *like*] Σ; *alike* H6. 32 *worse*] Σ; *more* A–F, Q.

Elegy 10 [~ NY3; "Elegy 4" in C2; "Elegy 11" in H6; "Elegy" in DT1; "Elegy II. The Anagram" in B]. Copy text: NY3. Collation: C2, DT1, H6, NY3, TT1 with A–G, Q, T, X, Z, DV2. 4 *are*] H6, NY3 & X, DV2; *be* Σ. 6 *rough*] Σ; *tough* H6 & B–F. 12 *thy*] Σ; *the* TT1. 18 *that*] Σ; *the* C2, H6 & A, Q, T, X, Z. *words*] Σ; *letters* C2, NY3. 23 *She's*] Σ; *She is as* C2. 24 *she is*] Σ; *is she* H6, TT1. 26 *Accompt*] C2, DT1, H6, NY3, TT1 & DV2; *Account* Σ. 29 *all like*] Σ; *like* TT1. 30 *which*] Σ; *that* H6. 36 *there*] Σ; *the* TT1. 41 *round*] Σ; *foul* H6. *countries drown*] Σ; *country is drown'd* G. 44 *Which* Σ; *Who* H6. 49 *childbirth's*] DT1, H6 (added as correction), NY3, TT1 & G, X, DV2; *childbed's* Σ. 53 *and*] Σ; *or* H6 & G. Lines 53–54 omitted in A–F.

Elegy 11 [~ NY3; "Elegy 11" in C2; "Elegy 9" in H6; "Elegy" in DT1; "Elegy On His Mistress" in B]. Copy text: NY3. Collation: C2, DT1, H6, NY3 with B–G, Q, T, X, Z, DV2. 3 *starving*] Σ; *starvling* DT1; *striving* G. 7 *parents'*] Σ; *father's* H6 & B–G, Q, Z. 9 *those*] Σ; *the* H6 & B–G, Q, Z. 11 *overswear*] Σ; *ever swear* DT1. 12 *means*] Σ; *ways* H6 & B–F, Q, Z. 18 *From other lands my soul towards*] Σ; *My soul from other lands* to H6 & B–G, Q, Z. 23 *Fair*] Σ; *The fair* G. 24 *Fall*] Σ; *Full* C2. 35 *Love's*] Σ; *Live's* C2, NY3. 37 *and know thee, and alas*] DT1, NY3 & T, X, DV2; *and alas* C2; *and no less, alas* Σ. 39 *well*] Σ; *will* C2. 40 *haunt*] Σ; *hunt* H6 & B–G, Q, Z. 46 *great*] Σ; *greatest* H6 & B–G, Q, Z. *call*] Σ; *do call* DT1. *into*] NY3 & T, X, DV2; *to* Σ. 49 *nor bless*] C2, DT1, NY3 & T, X, DV2; *nor bless* Σ. 51 *midnight's*] Σ; *midnight* C2. *startings*] Σ; *starting* DT1.

Elegy 12 [~ NY3; "Elegy 7" in C2; "Elegy 10" in H6; "Elegy" in DT1; "Elegy V. His Picture" in B]. Copy text: NY3. Collation: C2, DT1, H6, NY3 with A–G, Q, T, X, Z, DV2. 6 *Perchance*] NY3 & T, X, DV2; *Perhaps* Σ. 8 *rash*] Σ; *harsh* H6 & B–G. *hoariness*] Σ; *storms* C2, *storms being* DT1 & A, Q, Z. 16 *like'and love*] C2, NY3 & T, X, DV2; *now love* DT1, H6 & A–G, Q, Z. 17 *and*] Σ; *or* NY3. 19 *nurse*] Σ; *nourish* DT1. 20 *disus'd*] Σ; *diffus'd* DT1; *weak* D–G.

Elegy 14. Love's Progress [~ in DT1; "Elegy 13" in C2; "Elegy 13. Love's Progress" in H6]. Copy text: DT1. Collation: C2, DT1, H6, TT2 with G, Q, T, X, Z, DV2. 2 *which*] Σ; *that* H6 & G, Q, T, Z. 2 *And love*] Σ; *Love* G, Q, Z. 14 *ever*] Σ; *forever* H6 & T. 18 *First but*] Σ; *and* G, Q, Z. 25 *not*] Σ; *no* G. 27 *if he*] Σ; *if he that* H6; *he that* T. 32 *in*] Σ; *on* H6 & G, T. 38 *it*] Σ; *yet* C2. 40 *stray*] Σ; *err* G, Q, Z. 50 *directs*] Σ; *direct* DT1, TT2. 53 *Her*] Σ; *Unto her . . .* <to> G. 55 *there*] Σ; *their* C2. 59 *These*] Σ; *That* H6. 62 *but two*] Σ; *but of two* DT1. *the*] Σ; *that* TT2. 63 *that*] Σ; *yet* Q, Z. 66 *Shall*] Σ; *Shalt* H6. 66 *fair*] Σ; *<fair>* C2. 67 *thy*] Σ; *the* G. 68 *would'st*] Σ; *should'st* G. 70 *some do*] C2, DT1, TT2 & X; *many* Σ. 79 *which*] C2, TT2 & DV2; *that* Σ. 82 *begun*] C2, DT1 & X; *began* Σ. 90 *elements*] Σ; *enemies* G. 91 *woman*] Σ; *women* H6 & Q, T, Z. 95 *He which doth not*] Σ; *Who doth not so* H6. 96 *clyster gave*] Σ; *clysters gives* H6.

Elegy. Sappho to Philænis ["Sapho to Philænis" in DT1, H6]. Copy text: DT1. Collation: DT1, H6 with A–G, Q, T, X, Z, DV2. 3 *works*] Σ; *work* H6 & D–G. 22 *down*] Σ; *downs* H6. *cedars*] Σ; *as cedars* DT1 & A–G. 26 *wast*] Σ; *wert* H6. *may'st*] Σ; *may'st thou* B–G, X. 32 *which*] Σ; *that* H6. 37 *needs*] Σ; *need* DT1. 48 *Why*] Σ; *Which* DT1. 50 *they*] Σ; *thy* DT1, H6 (as correction). 53 *mine*] Σ; *my* H6. 56 *mine eyes*] Σ; *my sight* H6. 58 *thee*] Σ; *shee* A.

Epithalamion Made at Lincoln's Inn [~ in DT1; "Epithalamion on a Citizen" in H6; "Epithalamion" in NY3]. Copy text: NY3. Collation: DT1, H6, NY3 with A–G, Q, T, Z, BB, DV8. 8 *these*] Σ; *those* H6. 10 *must be oft*] Σ; *oft must be* H6 & Z. 23 *fair, rich, glad*] Σ; *fair and rich* H6 & A–G, Z. 26 *these*] Σ; *those* H6 & B–G, T. 32 *Lo*] Σ; *So* H6. 42 *thee*] Σ; *there* DT1. 45 *Which*] Σ; *Never* DT1. 47 *prayer*] DT1, NY3 & DV8; *praise* Σ. 49 *Oh*] Σ; *<Oh>* DT1 & A–G. 51 *these*] Σ; *those* H6. 54 *that*] Σ; *if* H6 (corrected from *that*). 55 *now he*] DT1, H6, NY3 & BB, DV8; *he now* Σ. 57 *nill*] Σ; *will* H6, A–G, Z. 58 *western*] Σ; *eastern* H6. 59 *run*] Σ; *come* DT1 & A. *world's*] Σ; *heaven's* H6 & B–G. 62 *should not then*] Σ; *then should not* A, Q, T. 63 *your*] Σ; *the* H6. 73 *Thy*] Σ; *The* H6. 83 *may*] Σ; *should* DT1. 95 *maim*] Σ; *name* DT1 & B–G.

The Storm. To Mr Christopher Brooke [~ C2, DT1; "To Mr. Christopher Brooke, from the Island Voyage with the Earl of Essex: The Storm" in H6; "To Mr. C. B." in NY3; "A Storm" in TT1]. Copy text: NY3. Collation: C2, DT1, H6, NY3, TT1 with A–G, Q, T, Y, Z. 3 *passage*] Σ; *passages* C2. 4 *an*] Σ; *a* C2, H6, NY3. 12 *and way*] Σ; *one way* H6 & B–F. 39 *but*] Σ; *only* A–G, Q, Z. 50 *Like*] Σ; *As* H6 & B–G. 53 *There*] Σ; *Then* A–F, Q, T, Z. 54 *an*] Σ; *this* C2, TT1. 67 *elder*] Σ; *eldest* C2 & A–G, Z. 68 *o'er*] Σ; *on* C2. *this*] Σ; *the* H6 & B–G.

The Calm [~ C2, DT1, H6; "A Calm" in TT1]. Copy text: C2. Collation: C2, DT1, H6, TT1 with A–G, Q, T, Y, Z. 4 *afflicts*] Σ; *afflicts us* DT1. 6 *heaven laughs*] Σ; *heavens laugh* H6. 7 *can*] Σ; *could* H6 & B–G. 9 *the*] Σ; *those* H6, DT1, TT1. 21 *left*] C2, DT1, TT1 & Y; *lost* Σ. 24 *jaws*] Σ; *maws* H6 & B–G. 34 *Or*] Σ; *And* DT1. 37 *sea-jails* (spelled *sea-gaoles* or *jayles*)] Σ; *sea-gulls* H6 & B–F. 38 *pinnaces*] H6 & B–F, Q, Z; *Venices* C2, TT1 & A, G, T, Y. 47 *subtly*] Σ; *so* DT1. 55 *no power, no will*] Σ; *no will, no power* DT1, TT1.

To Sir Henry Wotton ("Here's no more news") [~ C2, DT1, H6; "To Mr. H. W. July. 1598. At Court" in NY3]. Copy text: NY3. Collation: C2, DT1, H6, NY3, TT1 with A–G, Q, T,

Y, Z. 2 Cales] Σ; Calis A–G, Z. tale for news] Σ; tales <for news> H6 & B–G. 9 still is] Σ; is still DT1, H6, TT1. 14 wishing] Σ; wishes H6 & B–F. 20 play's] Σ; player's C–G. 21 are] Σ; omitted H6 & B–G.

To Sir Henry Wotton ("Sir, more than kisses") [~ C2, DT1, H6; "To Mr. H. W." in NY3]. Copy text: NY3. Collation: C2, DT1, H6, NY3 with A–G, Q, T, Y, Z. 1 more than kisses, letters] Σ; letters, more than kisses C2. 10 pitch they stain worse] Σ; stain worse than pitch H6. 11 even] Σ; raging A–F. 12 poles] Σ; pole DT1, TT1 & A–G. 17 and] Σ; or H6 & B–G. 18 and] Σ; or C2, H6 & A–G. 20 each is] Σ; all are H6. 21 who] Σ; which H6. 22 no] Σ; none H6 & B–G. there] Σ; they A; then DT1. 24 and] Σ; <and> H6 & B–G. clay] Σ; day D–G. 25 no] Σ; the H6 & B–F. 26 as habits, not] Σ; <as> inhabits not, H6 & B–F. 27 more] Σ; mere DT1; all H6 & A–G. 32 all are] Σ; are all H6. 33 issue] Σ; issue is H6 & B–G. 35 there] Σ; then C2. 44 for] Σ; in A–G; into H6. 47 then] Σ; thou C2 & A, Z. 50 his] Σ; her H6. 57 course] Σ; do DT1. 59 one thing] Σ; <one thing> H6 & B–G. 69 have] Σ; had DT1.

To Mr. Rowland Woodward ("Like one who in her third widowhood") [~ C2; "A Letter to Rowland Woodward" in H6; "To Mᵣ R. W." in NY3]. Copy text: NY3. Collation: C2, DT1, H6, NY3, TT1 with A–G, Q, T, Y, Z. 2 tir'd to a] NY3, DT1, TT1 & T; tied to <a> Σ. 4 shown] Σ; flown H6 (with shown in margin) & B–F. 5 love-song] Σ; long loves H6 & B–F. 10 be] Σ; but H6 & B–G. 23 our] Σ; the DT1. 26 soul] Σ; souls A–G, Q. 27 lie still] Σ; still lie H6. 31 farmers] Σ; termers A. 36 lov'd] Σ; beloved DT1, TT1.

To Mr. T[homas]. W[oodward] ("Haste thee harsh verse") [~ DT1, H6, NY3]. Copy text: NY3. Collation: DT1, H6, NY3 with A–G, Q, T, Y, Z. 2 pleasure.] Σ; pleasure<.> A–G. Lines 2b, 5–6, 8–10 are struck through in NY3. Lines 5–6 omitted in DT1 & A–G. 9 decreed] Σ; agreed DT1. 14 And] Σ; <And> NY3 & B–G.

To Mr. T[homas]. W[oodward] ("Pregnant again") [~ DT1, H6, NY3]. Copy text: NY3. Collation: DT1, H6, NY3 with A–G, Q, T, Y, Z. 5 mark] NY3 & T; watch] Σ. and] Σ; or] A–G. 7 thine] DT1, H6, NY3 & T, Y; thy] Σ.

To Mr. E[verard]. G[ilpin]. ("Even as lame things") [~ NY3]. Copy text: NY3. Collation: NY3 with Q, T, Y, Z.

To Mr. S. B. ("O thou which to search") [~ DT1, H6, NY3]. Copy text: NY3. Collation: DT1, H6, NY3 with A–G, Q, T, Y, Z. 12 seeing] Σ; seen H6, NY3. 13 though] Σ; thought C–F.

To Mr. B. B. [~ DT1, H6, NY3]. Copy text: NY3. Collation: DT1, H6, NY3 with A–G, Q, T, Y, Z. 18 widowhead] Σ; widowhood DT1 & A–G. 19 Muse] Σ; nurse A–G.

To Sir Henry Wotton at His Going Ambassador to Venice [~ DT1, H6]. Copy text: H6. Collation: DT1, H6 with A–G, Q, T, Y, Z. 10 pleasure] Σ; pleasures DT1 & A, T, Z. 13 where] Σ; which H6 & B–G. 24 honor wanting it] Σ; noble wanting it DT1; noble-wanting-wit H6 & B–G.

To the Countess of Bedford ("Madam, Reason is our soul's left hand") [~ C2, DT1, H6]. Copy text: C2. Collation: C2, DT1, H6 with A–G, Q, T, Y, Z. 3 Their] Σ; Those DT1. blessing] Σ; blessings A, Q, T, Z. sight] C2, DT1, H6 & T, Y; light Σ. 4 fair] Σ; far C2 & Y. 19 top'd and] DT1 & A, Q, Y, Z; to sense H6 & B–F, T; do seem G; to some C2. 33 then] Σ; thus H6. 36 This] Σ; Thy A.

To the Countess of Bedford ("Madam, You have refin'd me") [~ in C2, DT1; "~, Twicknam" in H6]. Copy text: DT1. Collation: C2, DT1, H6 with A–G, Q, T, Y, Z. 1 Madam] Σ; <Madam> DT1. 4 circumstance'd] Σ; circumstand DT1. 6 and] Σ; or G. 11 need] Σ; needs C2. there some] Σ; some there H6 & G. 16 Exhale] Σ; Awake DT1. 21 light] Σ; sight C2, H6. 25 the] Σ; your DT1. 45 enfold] Σ; unfold DT1. 50 these] Σ; those C2. 52 Second all] C2, DT1, H6 & T, Y; and Σ. 55 lovely] Σ; learned H6. 56 and] Σ; you th' H6. 58 both] Σ; worth H6 & B–G. 60 thing] Σ; things C2 & A–G. 66 As] Σ; A H6. aliens] Σ; alters H6 & B–F. 68 senses] Σ; sense A–G, Z. 71 had] Σ; hath C–G.

The Message ["Song" in C2, H6, DT1]. Copy text: DT1. Collation: C2, DT1, H6 with A–G, Q, T, V, X, Z. 3 Yet since] Σ; But if G. 4 forc'd] Σ; forg'd H6. 11 Which] C2, DT1 & A, X, Z; But H6 & B–G, Q, T, V. 14 cross] C2, DT1, H6 & Q, T, V, X, Z; break A–G. 18 know and see] Σ; see and know H6. 19 laugh and joy] Σ; joy and laugh H6; laugh when that C2. 24 art] Σ; dost G.

The Bait [no title in C2, DT1; "Song" in H6]. Copy text: DT1. Collation: C2, DT1, H6 with A–G, Q, T, V, X, Z. 2 will] Σ; shall DT1. 5 There] Σ; Then DT1. 6 thy] Σ; thine DT1, H6 & T, X. 7 there] Σ; then H6. 9 When] Σ; If H6. 11 to] Σ; unto H6. 14 dark'nest] Σ; darkness C2. 15 myself] Σ; my heart DT1. 19 fish] Σ; fishes C2. 23 sleave-silk] Σ; sleave-sick A. 25 thou] Σ; there C2. 27 catch'd] Σ; caught DT1.

The Apparition [~ in C2, "An Apparition" in DT1, H6]. Copy text: DT1. Collation: C2, DT1, H6 with A–G, Q, T, V, X, Z. 3 solicitation] Σ; solicitations H6. from] Σ; by H6. 5 feign'd vestal] Σ; fond virgin H6 (feign'd vestal in margin). 8 to] Σ; or DT1. 10 in] Σ; in a DT1, H6 and G. 11 And then] Σ; Thou C2, DT1. thou] Σ; then C2, DT1. 12 lie] Σ; be DT1. 17 rest still] Σ; keep thee H6.

The Broken Heart ["Song" in C2, "Elegy" in TT1]. Copy text: DT1. Collation: C2, DT1, H6, TT1 with A–G, Q, T, V, X, Z. 8 *flask*] H6, & A, Q, T, X, Z; *flash* C2, DT1, TT1 & B–G. 2 *an*] Σ; *one* TT1. 15 *chain'd*] Σ; *chain* DT1, H6 & X. 17 *did*] Σ; *could* DT1, H6, TT1. 20 *But*] Σ; *And* TT1. 21 *thee*] Σ; *thine* DT1, H6, TT1. 22 *thine*] Σ; *thy* C2, DT1, TT1. 24 *first*] Σ; *fierce* DT1. 30 *hundred*] Σ; *thousand* DT1, TT1.

A Lecture upon the Shadow [~ in DT1; no title in C2, TT1; "The Shadow" in H6]. Copy text: B. Collation: C2, DT1, H6, TT1 with B–G, Q, T, V, X, Z. 3 *These*] Σ; *Those* C2. *that*] Σ; *which* C2, H6. 4 *Walking*] Σ; *In walking* C2. 9 *loves*] Σ; *love* C2, H6 & G, V. 11 *cares*] Σ; *care* C2 & X, Z. *but*] Σ; *<but>* H6. 12 *high'st*] Σ; *least* H6; *last* C2. 13 *is still diligent*] Σ; *still is vigilant* H6. 14 *loves*] Σ; *love* C2, H6 & V. 17 *Others*] Σ; *Other* H6. *these*] Σ; *those* C2. 19 *If our loves*] Σ; *If our love* H6 & V; *If once love* C2. 21 *mine*] Σ; *my* H6. 23 *these*] Σ; *those* C2. 26 *first*] Σ; *short* B–G.

A Valediction Forbidding Mourning [~ in DT1; "A Valediction" in C2; "Upon the parting from his Mistress: Valediction. 1" in H6; "Elegy" in TT1]. Copy text: DT1. Collation: C2, DT1, H6, TT1 with A–G, Q, T, V, X, Z. 3 *And*] C2, DT1, TT1; *Whilst* Σ. 4 *The breath goes now*] Σ; *Now his breath goes* G. *say*] Σ; *says* TT1. 8 *our*] Σ; *of our* DT1, H6, TT1. 9 *Moving*] Σ; *Movings* H6. *brings*] Σ; *cause* H6. 15 *Absence, because*] Σ; *Of absence, 'cause* G. 16 *Those things*] Σ; *The thing* G. 17 *a*] Σ; *<a>* H6. *much*] Σ; *far* G. 20 *Care less*] Σ; *Careless* C2, DT1, TT1 & C–F. 21 *therefore*] Σ; *then* H6. 22 *go*] Σ; *part* H6. 24 *Like*] Σ; *As* H6. 27 *makes*] Σ; *maketh* TT1. 30 *roam*] Σ; *come* TT1. 32 *erect*] Σ; *direct* TT1. *it*] C2, DT1, TT1 & X; *that* Σ. 35 *circle*] Σ; *circles* C–F.

The Good Morrow [~ in DT1; no title in C2, H6, TT1]. Copy text: DT1. Collation: C2, DT1, H6, TT1 with A–G, Q, T, V, X, Z. 3 *on*] Σ; *our* TT1. *country*] Σ; *childish* C2 (corrected from *country*), DT1. *sillily*] C2 (corrected from *childishly*), DT1, H6, TT1 & G; *childishly* A–F, Q, T, V, X, Z. 4 *slumber'd*] C2 (corrected from *snorted*), DT1, TT1 & G; *snorted* Σ. 5 *this*] Σ; *as* TT1 & G. 10 *For*] Σ; *But* DT1, TT1. *sights*] Σ; *sight* C2. 11 *one*] Σ; *a* DT1, TT1. 13 *others*] DT1, H6 & V, X, Z; *other* Σ. *on*] Σ; *one* TT1; *our* G. *shown*] Σ; *<shown>* TT1. 14 *our*] DT1, H6, TT1 & X; *one* Σ. 16 *true plain*] Σ; *plain true* DT1, TT1. 17 *better*] Σ; *fitter* DT1, H6, TT1 & B–G. 18 *north*] Σ; *frost* C2. 19 *was*] Σ; *is* TT1 & G. 20 *or*] Σ; *both* H6 & B–G. 21 *Love so alike that none do slacken, none can die* C2 & A, Q, T, V, X, Z; *Love just alike in all, none of these loves can die*] DT1, H6, TT1 & B–G, V.

Song: "Go and catch a falling star" ["Song" in C2, DT1; "A Song" in TT1]. Copy text: DT1. Collation: C2, DT1, H6, TT1 with A–G, Q, T, V, X, Z. 3 *past years*] Σ; *times past* G; *pass years* DT1. 11 *to*] Σ; *go* G; *<to>* C2, DT1 (*to* erased), TT1. 14 *Thou*] Σ; *Then* DT1, TT1. *when thou return'st*] Σ; *at thy return* H6. 15 *wonders that*] Σ; *things that e're* H6. 20 *were*] Σ; *is* DT1. 21 *I*] Σ; *for I* H6. 24 *last, till*] Σ; *last so till* H6. 27 *I*] Σ; *she* G.

Woman's Constancy [~ in DT1, H6]. Copy text: DT1. Collation: C2, DT1, H6, TT1 with A–G, Q, T, V, X, Z. 3 *then*] Σ; *<then>* DT1, TT1. 8 *Or*] Σ; *For* (with lines 8–10 in parentheses) H6 & B–F. 10 *Bind*] Σ; *Last* C2 (corrected from *Bind*). *them*] Σ; *thee* DT1, TT1. 14 *Vain*] Σ; *Fond* C2 (corrected from *Vain*). *these*] Σ; *those* DT1, TT1. 16 *I*] Σ; *<I>* TT1. 17 *think*] Σ; *be* C2 (corrected from *think*).

The Sun Rising [~ in DT1; "To the Sun" in C2; "Ad solem. To the Sun. Song" in H6]. Copy text: DT1. Collation: C2, DT1, H6, TT1 with A–G, Q, T, V, X, Z. 3 *call*] Σ; *look* G. 4 *motions*] Σ; *motion* H6. 7 *will*] Σ; *doth* DT1, TT1. 11 *reverend*] Σ; *reverenc'd* TT1. 12 *Why shouldst thou*] Σ; *Dost thou not* H6, B–G. 17 *th'*] Σ; *<th'>* C2, DT1, H6, TT1. *spice*] Σ; *space* D–G. 18 *where*] Σ; *there* TT1. 19 *whom*] Σ; *which* H6. 23 *to*] Σ; *with* H6. 24 *honor's*] Σ; *honor* C2. 28 *world*] Σ; *worlds* C2.

The Indifferent [~ in DT1; "Song" in C2]. Copy text: DT1. Collation: C2, DT1, H6 with A–G, Q, T, V, X, Z. 3 *first and*] *<and>* D–F. 11 *did*] Σ; *<did>* C2. *mothers*] Σ; *mother* H6. 12 *Have*] C2, DT1, H6 & X; *Or have* Σ. *all*] Σ; *<all>* C2, H6 & X. 16 *rob*] Σ; *rack* C2. 17 *who*] Σ; *which* DT1, H6. 21 *and that*] Σ; *<and that>* B–G; *<that>* DT1, H6 & X. 23 *some*] Σ; *but* C2, DT1. 25 *'stablish*] Σ; *'establish* DT1, H6. 26 *you*] Σ; *they* C2.

Love's Usury [no title in C2, H6, TT1]. Copy text: C2. Collation: C2, H6, TT1 with A–G, Q, T, V, X, Z. 5 *reign*] TT1 & A, Q, T, V, X, Z; *range* H6 & B–G. 6 *snatch*] Σ; *match* H6, B–F. 14 *grass*] Σ; *grasses* C2. 7 *relict*] Σ; *relique* TT1. 9 *any*] Σ; *my* TT1. 15 *let*] Σ; *let not* H6 & B–F. Lines 17–18 omitted in TT1. 19 *second or*] Σ; *and* H6, TT1 & B–F. 21 *degree*] Σ; *decree* C2. 22 *fruit*] Σ; *fruits* C2, H6. 24 *loves*] Σ; *love* B, C, F.

The Canonization [~ in C2, DT1, DT2, H6]. Copy text: DT1. Collation: C2, DT1, DT2, H6 with A–G, Q, T, V, X, Z. 3 *five*] Σ; *true* B–F. 7 *And*] C2, DT1, DT2, H6; *Or*] Σ. *real*] Σ; *royal* C2. 12 *his*] Σ; *their* DT2. 14 *heats*] Σ; *heat* DT2. Line 13 omitted C2. 13 *colds*] Σ; *cold* DT1. 14 *the*] Σ; *those* DT1. 15 *more*] Σ; *man* DT1, DT2 & G, T. *plaguy*] Σ; *plague* DT2. 17 *which*] Σ; *whom* G. 18 *Though*] Σ; *While* G. 20 *me*] Σ; *and me* DT1. 24 *two*] Σ; *<two>* H6. 25 *one*] Σ; *our* DT2. 27 *Mysterious*] Σ; *Mysteriously <by>* DT2. 29 *tombs*] Σ; *tomb* DT1, H6 & G. *or*] Σ; *and* C2. 30 *legend*] Σ; *legends* C2, DT2 & A. 31 *chronicle*] Σ; *chronicles* DT2. Lines 34–45 omitted in DT1. 35 *these*] Σ; *those* H6 & B–G. 40 *extract*]

C2, DT2 & T, X, Z; *contract* H6 (corrected from *extract*) & A–G, Q, V. *drove*] Σ; *draw* C2, DT2. 45 *your*] Σ; *our* H6 & A.

The Triple Fool [~ in DT1; "A Song" in C2, H6; no title in TT1]. Copy text: DT1. Collation: C2, DT1, H6, TT1 with A–G, Q, T, V, X, Z. 5 *she*] Σ; *he* A. 6 *narrow crooked*] Σ; *crooked narrow* H6. 9 *should*] Σ; *could* C2. *them*] Σ; *then* TT1. 13 *art*] Σ; *act* DT1, TT1. *and*] Σ; *or* G. *art . . . voice*] Σ; *voice . . . art* H6. 14 *set* Σ; *sit* DT1, H6, TT1. 20 *triumphs*] Σ; *trials* H6.

Lovers' Infiniteness [no title in C2, H6]. Copy text: C2. Collation: C2, H6 with A–G, Q, T, V, X, Z. 1 *thy*] Σ; *your* C2. 5 *And*] Σ; *<And>* C2. 6 *First and*] Σ; *<and>* C2. 8 *Than*] Σ; *That* C–F. 11 *thee*] Σ; *it* H6 & B–G. 16 *Which*] Σ; *Who* H6. 20 *it*] Σ; *is* A. 21 *is* C2 & A, G, Q, T, V, X, Z; *was* H6 & B–F. 29 *Love's*] Σ; *Love* B.

Song: "Sweetest love, I do not go" ["Song" in C2, H6; no title in DT1]. Copy text: DT1. Collation: C2, DT1, H6 with A–G, Q, T, V, X, Z. 6 *Must die at last*] Σ; *At the last must part* H6 & B–G. 9 *Yesternight*] Σ; *Yesterday* H6. 19 *another*] Σ; *one other* C2. 22 *join*] Σ; *add* H6. 24 *o'er*] Σ; *on* C2. Lines 25–32 omitted in DT1. 25 *not*] Σ; *no* B–G. 28 *life's*] Σ; *life* H6. 32 *Thou* Σ; *That* H6 & B-F; *Which* G. 36 *may*] Σ; *make* C–F.

The Legacy ["Song" in C2, H6; "Elegy" in DT1, TT1]. Copy text: DT1. Collation: C2, DT1, H6, TT1 with A–G, Q, T, V, X, Z. 3 *but*] Σ; *<but>* DT1, H6 & X. Line 3 omitted in TT1. 4 *And*] Σ; *For* C2. 7 *sent*] Σ; *meant* H6 (corrected to *sent*) & B–F. *should*] Σ; *might* G. 9 *me*] Σ; *thee* C2. 10 *is*] Σ; *<is>* C2. 13 *I, alas*] Σ; *alas, I* H6. 14 *ripp'd me*] Σ; *ripp'd <me>* DT1, H6, TT1 & C, G. *hearts*] Σ; *heart* C2. *should lie*] Σ; *did lie*] C2 & A, Q, T; *should be* TT1. 22 *losses*] Σ; *loss be ye* C2; *loss be* G. 23 *meant*] Σ; *thought* DT1, H6, TT1 & B-G, X. *that*] DT1, H6, TT1 & B–G, X; *this* Σ.

A Fever [~ in C2; "Fever" in DT1; "The Fever" in H6]. Copy text: DT1. Collation: C2, DT1, H6 with A–G, Q, T, V, X, Z. 6 *this*] Σ; *the* H6. 15 *this*] Σ; *this heavenly* DT1. 18 *bear*] Σ; *endure* G. *torturing*] Σ; *tormenting* H6 (corrected from *torturing*). 19 *much*] C2, DT1 & A, F, Q, T, V; *more*] Σ. 21 *These burning fits*] Σ; *This burning fit* C2. 22 *is soon*] Σ; *soon is* H6 & G. 23 *which are*] Σ; *<which are>* H6; *which art* C2. 28 *ever*] Σ; *forever* C2.

Air and Angels [~ in C2, DT1, H6]. Copy text: DT1. Collation: C2, DT1, H6 with A–G, Q, T, V, X, Z. 5 *Still when*] Σ; *Till* C2; *So when* C. 6 *I did*] Σ; *did I* G. 13 *assume*] Σ; *assumes* C2. 14 *lip*] Σ; *lips* H6 & G. 17 *wares*] Σ; *waves* H6. 18 *saw*] Σ; *say* A. 19 *Ev'ry thy*] Σ; *Thy every* D-G. 22. *inhere*] Σ; *inherit* DT1. 24 *it*] Σ; *yet* C2. 28 *love*] Σ; *loves* H6

Break of Day [~ in DT1; no title in C2, TT1; "Sonnet" in H6]. Copy text: DT1. Collation: C2, DT1, H6, TT1 with A–G, Q, T, V, X, Z. 2 *Oh, wilt thou*] Σ; *<Oh>* DT1, TT1; *And will you* H6. *therefore*] Σ; *<therefore>* C2. 5 *which*] Σ; *that* DT1, TT1. *despite*] C2, DT1, TT1 & D–F; *spite* Σ. 6 *despite*] Σ; *spite* B–C. *keep*] Σ; *hold* DT1, TT1. 9 *were*] Σ; *is* DT1, H6, TT1 & V. *worst*] Σ; *most* C2. 11 *lov'd*] Σ; *love* H6, TT1 & V. *honor*] Σ; *lover* DT1, TT1. 12 *That*] Σ; *As* H6. *him*] Σ; *her* G. Second *that*] Σ; *which* C2, DT1, TT1. 17 *which*] Σ; *that* DT1, H6, TT1. 15 *foul*] Σ; *fool* C2, TT1. 17 *which*] Σ; *that* TT1. 18 *when*] Σ; *if* DT1, TT1. *doth*] Σ; *should* DT1, H6, TT1 & B–F, V.

The Prohibition [~ in DT1; no title in H6]. Copy text: DT1. Collation: DT1, H6, SP1 with A–G, Q, T, V, X, Z. 2 *forbade*] Σ; *forbid* H6 & T. Line 5 omitted in DT1. 5 *thee*] Σ; *me* A. *what to me*] Σ; *that which* A. 17–24 lines omitted in DT1. 18] *neither's*] Σ; *neither* H6 & T; *ne'er their* A–G. 22 *stage*] Σ; *stay* A. 23 *Then lest*] Σ; *Lest* A, G, Q, Z. *hate*] Σ; *<and> hate* A, G, T, X, V. *me thou*] Σ; *me <thou>* A, G, Q, Z. 24 *O*] Σ; *To* A, G, Q, Z. *yet*] Σ; *O* A, G, Q, Z.

The Anniversary [~ in DT1; no title in C2, H6]. Copy text: DT1. Collation: C2, DT1, H6 with A–G, Q, T, V, X, Z. 3 *they*] Σ; *these* H6 (corrected to *they* in margin) & B–F. 10 *his*] Σ; *the* C2, H6. 20 *first graves*] Σ; *grave* B, C. 22 *we*] Σ; *now* A–G. 23 *none*] Σ; *<none>* C2 & G. 24 *Can be*] Σ; *None are* C2 & H6 (corrected to *Can be*) & G. *nor*] Σ; *and* C2.

A Valediction of My Name in the Window [~ in C2; "~. My name engrav'd herein" in DT1; "Valediction 4. Of Glass. Upon the engraving of his name with a Diamond in his Mistress' Window when he was to travel" in H6]. Copy text: DT1. Collation: C2, DT1, H6 with A-G, Q, T, V, X, Z. 3 *Which*] Σ; *Who* H6. 5 *eyes*] DT1, H6 & X; *eye* Σ. 6 *diamonds*] Σ; *diamond* H6. 13 *nor*] Σ; *or* DT1, H6. 14 *accessories*] Σ; *accessory* C2, DT1. 15 *tempests*] Σ; *tempest* B–G. 19 *if*] Σ; *is* A–B. 21 *as*] Σ; *is* DT1. 23 *ragged*] Σ; *rugged* H6. 36 *those*] DT1, H6 & B–G, X; *these* Σ. 39 *'gainst*] Σ; *against* C2, H6. 44 *ope*] Σ; *out* C2, DT1 & V, X. 45 *on*] Σ; *at* H6. 47 *this*] Σ; *his* B. 50 *and*] Σ; *or* H6 & G. Line 53 Σ] *If thou to him begin'st to thaw for this* G. 55 *go*] Σ; *grow* C2, H6. 56 *that*] Σ; *<that>* DT1. 58 *pane*] Σ; *pen* H6 & B–G. 60 *unaware*] *unawares* DT1, H6. 64 *this*] Σ; *thus* H6 & B–G. *I*] Σ; *a* DT1.

Twicknam Garden [no title in C2, "Twicknam" in H6; "Twitnam" in DT1, TT1]. Copy text: DT1. Collation: C2, DT1, H6, TT1 with A–G, Q, T, V, X, Z. 2 *come*] Σ; *came* DT1, TT1. 4 *balm . . . cures*] H6 & B–G; *balms . . . cures* DT1, TT1; *balms . . . cure* Σ. 8 *may*] Σ; *might* DT1. 12 *grave*] Σ; *gray* H6. *did*] Σ; *would* DT1, TT1. 13 *to*] Σ; *in* TT1. 14 *that*] Σ; *<that>* DT1, TT1. 15 *nor leave this garden*] Σ; *<nor leave this garden>* C2 (with 14-16 shortened to 2 lines); *nor yet leave loving* A, Q. 16 *piece*] Σ; *part* DT1, TT1. 17 *grow*] Σ; *groan* DT1,

TT1 & V, Z. 19 *lovers come*] Σ; *love is come* C. 22 *that*] Σ; *which* DT1, TT1. 24 *women's*] Σ; *woman's* DT1, TT1; *women* C2

A Valediction of the Book [~ in C2, DT1, H6]. Copy text: DT1. Collation: C2, DT1, H6 with A–G, Q, T, V, X, Z. 7 *Pindar could*] Σ; *old* C2. 8 *her*] Σ; <*her*> C2. 9 *book*] Σ; *look* C2. 20 *tome*] Σ; *to me* C–F; *tomb* C2 & G. 22 *only'are*] Σ; *are only* H6. 25 *Goths*] Σ; *the Goths* A–F. *inundate*] Σ; *invade* H6 & A–G. 30 *abstract*] Σ; *abstracted* D–G. 32 *loth*] Σ; *doth* DT1. *so*] Σ; <*so*> C2. 33 *Faith's*] Σ; *Faithless* DT1. *infirmity*] Σ; *infirmities* C2 & G. 37 *in*] Σ; <*in*> C2. 39 *these*] Σ; *those* DT1, H6 & X. *states*] Σ; *rites* DT1. 40 *from*] Σ; *by* H6. 44 *or*] Σ; *and* H6. 52 *dares*] Σ; *dare* DT1, H6. 53 *their nothing*] Σ; *there something* A, G. 55 *vent*] Σ; *went* B–F. 56 *great heights*] Σ; *shadows* H6. 57 *presence*] Σ; *preference* C. 60 *fittiest*] Σ; *fittest* DT1; *fitly* H6 (corrected to *fitliest*).

Community [no title in C2, DT1, H6, TT1]. Copy text: DT1. Collation: C2, DT1, H6, TT1 with A–G, Q, T, V, X, Z. 3 *there*] Σ; *these* C2 & A. 9 *some*] Σ; *some we might* TT1. Line 9 omitted in DT1. 13 *they*] Σ; *thou* B. 14 *as*] Σ; <*as*> C2. 21 *which*] C2, DT1, H6, TT1 & X; *that* A–G, Q, T, V, Z.

Love's Growth [~ in DT1; "Spring" in C2; "The Spring" in H6]. Copy text: DT1. Collation: C2, DT1, H6 with A–G, Q, T, V, X, Z. 6 *make*] Σ; *makes* DT1. 9 *paining*] Σ; *vexing* H6 & B–G. 10 *working*] Σ; *active* H6 & B–G. Line 10 omitted in DT1. 13 *else*] Σ; *those* C2. 14 *sometimes would*] Σ; *would sometimes* H6. 15 *no*] Σ; *not* C2, DT1, H6. 19 *as*] Σ; *are* G. *bough*] Σ; *flower* C2. 20 *bud*] Σ; *but* G. *now*] Σ; *more* C2. 23 *to*] C2, DT1 H6 & X, Z; *so* Σ. 26 *times*] Σ; *time* C2, H6. 27 *remit*] Σ; *remits* C2. 28 *the*] Σ; *this* H6 & B–F; *them* G.

Love's Exchange [~ in DT1; no title in C2, H6]. Copy text: DT1. Collation: C2, DT1, H6 with A–G, Q, T, V, X, Z. 4 *and*] DT1, H6 & X, Z; *or* Σ. 5 *who*] C2, DT1, H6 & X, Z; *which* A–G, Q, T, V. 8 *no*] Σ; *not* DT1, H6 & X. 9 *or sigh*] Σ; <*or sigh*> C2, DT1; <*or*> G. 13 *thee and thine*] Σ; *thine and thee* DT1. 20 *pain*] C2, DT1, H6 & T, X, Z; *pains* Σ. Lines 19–20 combined in C2. 21 *mine*] Σ; *my* H6. 24 *which stand*] Σ; *with stand* DT1. 25 *law*] Σ; <*law*> C2; *laws* F. 37 *Yet kills*] Σ; *It skills* C2. 38 *future*] Σ; *fortune's* H6.

Confined Love [no title in C2, DT1, H6]. Copy text: DT1 Collation: C2, DT1, H6 with A–G, Q, T, V, X, Z. 3 *Thought*] Σ; *Though* DT1. 6 *should*] C2, DT1, H6 & T, X, Z; *might* Σ. 9 *or*] Σ; *and* H6. *lend*] Σ; *bend* G. 11 *mate*] Σ; *meat* F, G. 12 *do*] Σ; *did* C2, DT1. 14 *we*] Σ; <*we*> DT1. 16 *new*] Σ; <*new*> C–G. 17 *built*] Σ; *build* C2, DT1 & C–G. 18 *up*] Σ; *them up* H6.

The Dream [~ in C2, DT1, H6]. Copy text: DT1. Collation: C2, DT1, H6 with A–G, Q, T, V, X, Z. 2 *whilst*] Σ; *while* DT1. 3 *face*] Σ; *stamp* DT1. 6 *continuedst*] Σ; *continued* H6; *continuest* G. 7 *truth*] Σ; *true* H6 & B–G, X. 8 *truths*] Σ; *truth* C2, DT1. H6 (corrected to *truths*) & X. 10 *act*] Σ; *do* C2, H6 & X. 14 *For*] Σ; <*For*>] C2, DT1. *an*] Σ; *but an* C2, DT1. 19 *do*] C2, DT1, H6 & T, X, Z; *must* Σ. 20 *Profane*] Σ; *Profaneness* C2, DT1, H6 (corrected to *Profane*). 24 *That*] Σ; *Yet* H6. *where*] Σ; *when* C2. *fear's as*] Σ; *fear is* C2 (corrected to *fear's as*), DT1; *fears are* H6 & G. 28 *deal'st*] Σ; *doest* H6. 29 *then*] Σ; *thus* C2, DT1. 30 *would*] Σ; *will* C2.

A Valediction of Weeping [~ in DT1; "A Valediction" in C2; "Valediction. 2. Of Tears" in H6]. Copy text: DT1. Collation: C2, DT1, H6 with A–G, Q, T, V, X, Z. 8 *second falls*] C2, DT1 & T, V, X, Z; *fall'st* Σ. 14 *doth*] Σ; *do* B–F. 21 *thine*] Σ; *thy* DT1.

Love's Alchemy. ["Mummy" in C2, DT1, H6, TT1]. Copy text: DT1. Collation: C2, DT1, H6, TT1 with A–G, Q, T, V, X, Z. 12 *get*] Σ; *yet* DT1. *winter*] Σ; *winters* C2. 13 Second *our*] Σ; *and* DT1, TT1. 14 *bubble's shadow*] Σ; *shadow's bubble* H6 & B. 23 *women*] Σ; *woman* DT1, H6, TT1. Line 24 variously punctuated: . . . *and wit, they're but mummy possess'd*] C2, H6, TT1 & T; . . . *and wit they're but mummy possess'd* DT1; . . . *and wit they're, but, mummy*yossess'd A–F, Z; . . . *and wit, they're but mummy*yossess'd Q, V, X.

The Flea [~ in C2, H6; no title in DT1, TT1]. Copy text: C2. Collation: C2, DT1, H6, TT1 with A–G, Q, T, V, X, Z. 3 *It suck'd me*] Σ; *Me it suck'd* DT1, TT1 & G, V, X. 5 *Thou know'st that*] Σ; *Confess it* H6, DT1, TT1 & G, V, X. 6 *or . . . or*] H6, DT1, TT1 & G, V, X; *nor . . . nor* Σ. 7 *it*] Σ; *its* DT1. 11 *Where*] Σ; *When* C2. *nay*] DT1, H6, TT1 & G, V, X; *yea* C2, A–F, Q, T, Z. 14 *we're*] Σ; *yet we are* H6, TT1. 16 *you*] Σ; *thee* H6, DT1, TT1. 17 *that*] Σ; *this* H6 & X; *thy* DT1, TT1. 21 *Wherein*] Σ; *In what*] H6, DT1, TT1 & V, X.

The Curse [~ in C2, DT1, H6; "A Curse" in TT1]. Copy text: DT1. Collation: C2, DT1, H6, TT1 with A–G, Q, T, V, X, Z. 3 *His*] Σ; *Him* G. 5 *she*] Σ; *then* G. *then to*] Σ; *unto* G. 8 *With*] Σ; *For* TT1. 9 *cramps*] C2, DT1, TT1 & X; *cramp* Σ. Lines 14–16 are recorded in C2, H6 (in the margin) & A, Q, T, V, X, Z; another version: *Or may he for her virtue reverence / One that hates him only for impotence, / And equal traitors be she and his sense* DT1, H6 (in text), TT1 & B–G. 18 *Meant*] Σ; *Went* DT1. 27 *plants*] Σ; *herbs* TT1. *mines*] Σ; *mine* C2 & A–G, T. 28 First *all*] Σ; *and* TT1. 29 *Prophets and poets*] Σ; *Poets and prophets* TT1.

The Ecstasy [~ in C2, H6; "Ecstasy" in DT1]. Copy text: DT1. Collation: C2, DT1, H6 with A–G, Q, T, V, X, Z. 6 *With*] Σ; *By* H6 & B–G. 9 *intergraft*] Σ; *engraft* H6 & B–G. 10 *the*] Σ; *our* DT1, H6 & X. 11 *on* C2, DT1, H6 & T, X; *in*] Σ. 14 *uncertain*] Σ; *unequal* H6 (corrected to *uncertain*). 15 *their*] Σ; *our* H6 & B–G. 16 *hung*] Σ; *hangs* C2. 25 *knew*] Σ; *knows* C2 & A. 42 *Interinanimates*] Σ; *Interanimates* C2 & A–G. 44 *loneliness*] Σ; *loveliness* G. 51 *though they're not*]Σ; *though not* A–G. 52 *sphere*] Σ; *spheres* A–G, T, Z. 55 *their*] Σ; *these* H6. *forces, sense*] Σ; *forces, senses* C2; *senses' force* A–G. 59 *So*] Σ; *For* C2, H6 & A–G. 64 *makes*] Σ; *make* B–C. 75 *mark*] Σ; *mock* H6. 76 *gone*] Σ; *grown* H6 & B–G.

The Undertaking [no title in C2, H6; "Platonic Love" in DT1]. Copy text: DT1. Collation: C2, DT1, H6 with A–G, Q, T, V, X, Z. 3 *And yet*] Σ; *Yet* C2, DT1, H6 & X. 9 *I now*] Σ; *Now I* C2. 14 *outward*] Σ; *other* H6. 18 *attir'd*] Σ; *<attir'd>* H6 & B–G. *woman*] Σ; *women* H6. 25 *you have*] Σ; *have you* H6.

Love's Deity [~ in C2, DT1, H6, TT1]. Copy text: DT1. Collation: C2, DT1, H6, TT1 with A–G, Q, T, V, X, Z. 8 *which*] Σ; *that* H6. *made*] Σ; *make* A. 14 *till I love her that*] Σ; *if I love, who* H6 & B–F. 19 *waken'd*] Σ; *weakened* TT1. 21 *That I should love*] C2, DT1, TT1 & X, Z; *I should love her* Σ. 23 *could*] Σ; *can* TT1. 24 *first might*] Σ; *may* C2 & A–G.

Love's Diet [~ in C2, H6, TT1]. Copy text: DT1. Collation: C2, DT1, H6 with A–G, Q, T, V, X, Z. 6 *endures*] Σ; *endues* C2. 8 *fortune*] Σ; *fortunes* H6. 11 *feast*] Σ; *feed* H6 & T. 13 *so*] Σ; *too* C2, TT1. 14 *and*] Σ; *or* TT1. 16, 18 *which*] Σ; *that* H6 & T. 19 *Whatever he would dictate*] Σ; *Whatsoever he would distaste* TT1. 20 *my*] Σ; *her* B–F. 21 *first that*] Σ; *if* B–G. 24 *name*] Σ; *man* C2 & G. 25 *reclaim'd*] Σ; *redeem'd* C2 & A. 27 *sport*] Σ; *sports* A. 30 *game*] Σ; *fame* B–G. second *and*] Σ; *or* H6 & B–G.

The Will [~ in C2, H6; "Love's Legacy" in TT1]. Copy text: DT1. Collation: C2, H6, TT1 with A–G, Q, T, V, X, Z. 2. I *here*] Σ; *Here I* TT1. 8 *serve*] Σ; *love* G. 8 *her*] Σ; *<her>* TT1. 9 *That . . . as*] Σ; *Only to give to those which* H6. 16 *appointing*] Σ; *making* H6. 17 *can*] Σ; *could* TT1. 18 *such as*] Σ; *those which* H6; *such an <have>* TT1. Lines 19–27 omitted in C2, TT1. 28 *I give my reputation*] Σ; *My reputation I give* H6. 35 *who*] Σ; *that* H6. 36 *did*] Σ; *do* H6 & B–G, V. 42 *mine*] Σ; *my* H6. 45 *gifts*] Σ; *gift* C–F. 49 *doth*] Σ; *do* TT1. 53 *me and thee*] Σ; *thee and me* H6, TT1.

The Funeral [~ in C2, DT1, H6, TT1]. Copy text: DT1. Collation: C2, DT1, H6, TT1 with A–G, Q, T, V, X, Z. 3 *which crowns*] Σ; *about mine* G. *mine*] DT1, H6, TT1 & G, T, X; *my* Σ. 6 *then to*] Σ; *unto* H6. 12 *These*] Σ; *Those* C2, H6 & A–G. 12 *grew*] Σ; *grow* C2 & D–G. 17 *with*] Σ; *by* A. 20 *other*] Σ; *another's* TT1. *these*] Σ; *those* C2. 21 *As*] Σ; *And* TT1. 22 *to*] Σ; *<to>* C2, TT1. *which*] DT1, H6, TT1 & T; *that* Σ. 24 *save*] Σ; *have* C2, H6 & A–G.

The Blossom [~ in C2, DT1, H6]. Copy text: DT1. Collation: C2, DT1, H6 with A–G, Q, T, V, X, Z. 10 *labor'st*] Σ; *labors* C2 & A. 15 *that*] Σ; *the* B–G. 16 *the*] Σ; *this* C2, DT1. 21 *love*] Σ; *loves* DT1. 23 *tongue*] Σ; *taste* A–G. 24 *you'a*] Σ; *your* A–G. 33 *in*] Σ; *at* C2. 36 *had*] Σ; *<had>* C2. 38 *would*] DT1 & Q, T, V, X, Z; *will* C2, H6 (corrected from *would*) & A–G.

The Primrose [~ in C2, DT1, H6; "~. Being at Montgomery Castle Upon the Hill, on Which It Is Situate" in B–G]. Copy text: DT1. Collation: C2, DT1, H6 with A–G, Q, T, V, X, Z. 5 second *their*] Σ; *<their>* C2. 10 first *or*] Σ; *no* C2. 11 *know I*] Σ; *I know* DT1. 17 *not*] Σ; *and not* A, Q, T, V, Z. 26 *Belong*] DT1, H6 & Q, T, V, X, Z; *Belongs* Σ. 28 *their*] Σ; *the* D–G. 29 *and*] Σ; *since* B–G, T. 30 *this*] Σ; *<this>* H6 & B–G.

The Relic [~ in C2, DT1, H6]. Copy text: DT1. Collation: C2, DT1, H6 with A–G, Q, T, V, X, Z. 4 *to*] Σ; *two* DT1. 5 second *their*] Σ; *<their>* C2. 7 *he not*] Σ; *not he* H6; *<he>* not C2. 9 *thought*] Σ; *hop'd* C2, H6. *some*] Σ; *a* C2, H6. 13 *mis-devotion*] Σ; *Mass-devotion* G. 14 *Then he that digs us*] Σ; *<Then>* He that doth dig it C2, H6. 15 *and*] Σ; *or* G. 17 *Thou shalt be*] Σ; *You shall be* C2, H6. 20 *times*] DT1, H6 & X; *time* Σ. 21 *have that age*] Σ; *that age were* DT1. 24 *nor*] Σ; *and* C2. Lines 25–26 *no more we knew, / Than*] Σ; *we never knew, / No more than* H6 & B–G, V; *we never knew, / More than* C2. 28 *between*] Σ; *betwixt* C2, H6. 29 *the*] Σ; *those* DT1. 32 *measure*] Σ; *measures* DT1.

The Damp [~ in C2, DT1, H6]. Copy text: DT1. Collation: C2, DT1, H6 with A–G, Q, T, V, X, Z. 4 *my*] Σ; *mine* D–F. 13 *and*] Σ; *or* G. 15 *arts*] Σ; *acts* DT1 (corrected from *arts*) & G. 24 *Naked*] Σ; *In that* DT1 & A, Q, Z.

The Dissolution [~ in DT1, H6]. Copy text: DT1. Collation: DT1, H6 with A–G, Q, T, V, X, Z. 10 *earthly*] Σ; *earthy* H6 & B–G.

A Jet Ring Sent [~ in DT1, H6; "To a Jet Ring Sent to Me" in NY3]. Copy text: NY3. Collation: DT1, H6, NY3 with A–G, Q, T, V, X, Z. 6 *Oh*] Σ; *Or* DT1. 7 *loves*] Σ; *love* H6.

Negative Love [~ in DT1; "~; or The Nothing" in H6]. Copy text: DT1. Collation: DT1, H6 with A–G, Q, T, V, X, Z. 8 *may I*] Σ; *I may* DT1. 11 *way*] Σ; *means* H6 & G. 17 *my*] Σ; *mine* H6.

The Computation [~ in DT1]. Copy text: DT1. Collation: DT1, H6 with A–G, Q, T, V, X, Z. 1 *my*] DT1 (corrected from *the*), H6 & B–G; *the* Σ. 2 *thou*] Σ; *you* H6. 3 *For*] Σ; *And* H6 & G. 4 *thou*] Σ; *you* H6. *wouldst*] Σ; *wish* H6. 5 *drown'd . . . and . . . blew*] Σ; *have . . . drown'd . . . blown* H6. 6 *A*] Σ; *One* H6. *neither*] Σ; *nothing* H6. *nor*] Σ; *or* H6. 7 *divide*] Σ; *deem'd* H6 & B–F. Line 7 omitted in DT1. 8 *a*] Σ; *one* H6.

The Expiration [~ in DT1; "Valediction" in H6]. Copy text: DT1. Collation: DT1, H6 with A–G, Q, T, V, X, Z. 1 *break*] Σ; *leave* H6. 4 *selves*] Σ; *souls* H6. *happiest*] Σ; *happy* H6. 5 *ask'd*] Σ; *ask* A–G. 9 *Oh*] Σ; *Or* H6 & B–G, Q, V. *let*] Σ; *may* DT1. *word*] Σ; *words* DT1.

The Paradox [no title in DT1, H6]. Copy text: DT1. Collation: DT1, H6 with A–G, Q, T, V, X, Z. 3 *nor*] Σ; *or* A–G. 14 *life's light*] Σ; *light's life* Q, V, X, Z. 17 *lov'd*] Σ; *love* A–G. 20 *die*] Σ; *lie* H6 & Q, V, X, Z.

A Nocturnal Upon St. Lucy's Day, Being the Shortest Day [~ in DT1, H6]. Copy text: DT1. Collation: DT1, H6 with A–G, Q, T, V, X, Z. 4 *no*] Σ; *not* H6. 12 *every*] Σ; *a very* H6 (corrected from *every*) & B–G.

Witchcraft by a Picture [~ in DT1; "Picture" in H6]. Copy text: DT1. Collation: DT1, H6 with A–G, Q, T, V, X, Z. 8 *sweet salt*] Σ; *sweetest* H6. 10 *fears*] Σ; *all fears* H6 & B–F. 14 *all*] Σ; <*all*> H6.

Farewell to Love [~ in B46, B47, H6]. Copy text: B46. Collation: B46, B47, H6 with B–G, Q, T, V, X, Z. 10 *rise*] B46; *seize* B47; *size* Σ. 11 *last*] B46, B47; *late* Σ. 19 *so lamely*] Σ; *solemnly* B47. 21 *Oh*] B46; *Ah* Σ. 25 *Diminishes*] B46, B47; *Diminisheth* Σ. 34 *endamage*] B46 & X; *endanger* B47; *endamag'd* Σ. 36 *summer's*] Σ; *summer* D–G.

Self-Love ["Elegy" in C9, H6; no title in NY1, VA2]. Copy text: C9. Collation: C9, H6, NY1, VA2 with E–G, Q, T, V, X, Z. 4 *'gainst*] Σ; *against* E–G, V. 6 *can at*] Σ; *cannot* E–G, Z; *can all* C9, H6. 11 *foulness*] C9, H6, NY1 & X; *foul ones* Σ. 12 *is*] C9, H6; *then is* Σ. 15 *for*] Σ; <*for*> F–G. *whom* C9] *when others* Σ; *when* H6. 16 *want nor crave*] C9, H6 & T, Z; <*want nor crave*> Σ. 17 *pays*] Σ; *prays* E–G. 22 *prove*] Σ; *love* C9. 24 *In*] Σ; *E're* in C9.

Image of Her Whom I Love [no title in C2; "Elegy" in DT1, H6, TT1]. Copy Text: DT1. Collation: C2, DT1, H6, TT1 with A–G, Q, T, V, X, Z. 6 *great . . . good*] Σ; *good . . . great* H6. Line 6 omitted in TT1. 17 *such a*] C2 & G; *a such* Σ.

The First Anniversary. Copy text: a with *errata* from b. Collation: a–d, A–G, Q, T, W, Y, Z, BB, DV6. 2 *Whom*] Σ; *Who* A. *do*] Σ; *they* a. 40 *times*] Σ *time* B–G. 50 *glue*] Σ; *give* D–G. 79 *though*] Σ; *thought* c, d, A. 89 *then*] Σ; *them* D–G. 130 *new*] Σ; *true* b–G. 153 *weaving*] Σ; *weaning* a–d. 161 *Thus*] Σ; *This* B–G. 170 *is!*] Σ; *is?* b–d. 217 *there*] (*errata* from b) W, Y, Z, BB, DV6; *then* a–d, A–G, Q, T. 258 *shares*] spelled variously: *sheeres* a–d, W, Y, Z, BB, DV6; *sheires* A–B, Q; *shieres* C–G; *shires* T. 262 *towns*] (*errata* from b) Σ; *towers* a–d, A–G, Q. 273 *with*] Σ; *of* B–G. 318 *proportions*] Σ; *proportion* c–G. 415 *impressions*] Σ; *impression* b–G. 474 *fame*] (*errata* from b) Σ; *same* a–d.

La Corona [~ in C2, DT1, NY3; "The Crown" in H6]. Copy Text: NY3. Collation: C2, DT1, H6, NY3 with A–G, Q, T, U, Z. 1.2 *low*] Σ; *lone* B–G; *love* C2, H6. 1.9 First *ends*] Σ; *end* H6. *crown*] Σ; *crowns* H6. 1.10 *So*] H6, NY3; *For* Σ. *end*] Σ; *ends* B–G. 1.11 *This*] DT1, H6, NY3 & U; *The* Σ. 1.13 *voice and heart*] H6, NY3; *heart and voice* Σ. 2.10 *who*] Σ; *which* NY3. 2.11 *conceiv'st*] Σ; *conceiv'dst* NY3. 3.3 *There*] Σ; *Therefore* C2. *he hath*] Σ; *hath he* H6. 3.4 *our*] Σ; *the* H6. 3.5 *there*] Σ; *there* DT1. 3.6 *this*] Σ; *his* DT1 & G. 3.7 *shall*] H6, NY3; *will* Σ. 3.8 *effect*] Σ; *effects* A–G. *jealous*] Σ; *zealous* DT1; *dire* NY3. 3.9 *eyes*] Σ; *eye* D–G. 3.10 *Which*] Σ *Who* H6. 4.2 *your*] Σ; *thy* H6. 4.4 *those*] DT1, H6, NY3 & T, U; *the* Σ. 4.10 *had*] Σ; *hath* C2. *to*] Σ; <*to*> H6, NY3; *in* DT1. *this*] Σ; *his* DT1. 4.11 *to*] Σ; *for* A–G; *some* H6. *which*] Σ; *who* H6. *long tasks*] DT1, H6, NY3; *a long task* Σ. *thinks*] H6, NY3; *'tis* Σ. 5.3 *meek*] H6, NY3 & T; *weak* Σ. 5.8 *infinity*] Σ; *infinite* DT1 & G. *t' a span*] Σ; *to span* C2 & A–G. 6.2 *now be*] Σ; *be now* H6, DT1. 6.5 *thy*] H6, NY3; *this* Σ. *death*] Σ; <*death*> DT1. 6.6 *shall*] Σ; *shall now* DT1, H6. 6.8 *life*] Σ; *little* C2, DT1 & A, Q, U, Z. 6.9 *last long*] H6, NY3; *long* Σ; <*last long*> C2. 6.12 *death's*] DT1, NY3 & Q, U, Z; *death* Σ. 7.2 *son*] Σ; *sin* C2. 7.3 *Ye*] Σ; *Yea* C2, NY3. *true*] Σ; *just* C2, DT1 & A, Q, U, Z. 7.4 *Hath*] H6, NY3; *Have* Σ. 7.13 *thine*] DT1, H6, NY3 & U, T; *thy* Σ.

Holy Sonnet 1 [~ in H6, NY3; "1" in C2, DT1]. Copy Text: NY3. Collation: C2, DT1, H6, NY3 with A–G, Q, T, U, Z, DV7. 5 *son*] Σ; *sun* DT1. 7 *thine*] Σ; *thy* H6. 9 *then*] Σ; *thus* H6. *in*] Σ; *on* C2, A–G, Q, T. 12 *do*] Σ; *shall* H6, B–G.

Holy Sonnet 2 [~ in H6, NY3; "2" in C2, DT1]. Copy Text: NY3. Collation: C2, DT1, H6, NY3 with A–G, Q, T, U, Z, DV7. 3 *a*] Σ; <*a*> NY3. *had*] NY3, DT1 & DV7; *hath* Σ. 5 *as*] H6, NY3; *like* Σ. 13 *this*] Σ; *his* DT1.

Holy Sonnet 3 [~ in H6, NY3; "3" in C2, DT1]. Copy Text: NY3. Collation: C2, DT1, H6, NY3 with A–G, Q, T, U, Z, DV7. 2 *pilgrimage's*] Σ; *pilgrimage* C2. 4 Second *last*] C2, DT1, NY3 & U, DV7; *latest* Σ. 6 *soul*] Σ; *my soul* DT1 & A, T. *space*] Σ; *pace* C2, H6 (corrected). 7 *Or presently, I know not*] C2, H6, NY3; *But my ever-waking part* Σ. 8 *my*] Σ; *me* C2, H6. 11 *fall*] Σ; *falls* C2. 13 *thus purg'd*] Σ; *purg'd thus* H6. 14 *and*] Σ; *the* A–G, Q.

Holy Sonnet 4 [~ in H6, NY3; "4" in C2, DT1]. Copy Text: NY3. Collation: C2, DT1, H6, NY3 with A–G, Q, T, U, Z, DV7. 6 *dearth*] H6, NY3 & Q, T, U, Z; *death* Σ. 9 *a space*] Σ; *a pace* C2. 12 *lowly*] Σ; *holy* G.

Holy Sonnet 5 [~ in H6, NY3; "5" in C2, DT1]. Copy Text: NY3. Collation: C2, DT1, H6, NY3 with A–G, Q, T, U, Z, DV7. 1 *poisonous*] Σ; *poisons* C–G. *and if that*] Σ; *or if the* H6. 5 *or*] Σ; *and* H6. 9 *dare*] Σ; *dares* DT1. 10 *thine*] Σ; *thy* H6. 13 *thou*] Σ; *you* DT1. *some claim*] Σ; *no more* H6.

Holy Sonnet 6 [~ in H6, NY3; "6" in C2, DT1]. Copy Text: NY3. Collation: C2, DT1, H6, NY3 with A–G, Q, T, U, Z, DV7. 1 *have*] Σ; *hath* DT1 & DV7. 5 *pictures*] Σ; *picture* B–G.

7 *do*] Σ; *doth* C2. 10 *dost*] Σ; *doth* A. 12 *easier*] H6, NY3; *better* Σ. 13 *live*] H6, NY3 *wake* Σ.

Holy Sonnet 7 [~ in NY3; "7" in C2, DT1]. Copy Text: NY3. Collation: C2, DT1, H6, NY3 with A–G, Q, T, U, Z, DV7. 1 *ye*] DT1, H6, NY3 & U, Z, DV7; *you* Σ. 3 *only*] Σ; *humbly* NY3. 4 *Who*] Σ; *Which* NY3. *no*] Σ; *none* C2, DT1. 6 *impiety*] Σ; *iniquity* C2, DT1. 7 *man*] Σ; *<man>* NY3.

Holy Sonnet 8 [~ in NY3; "8" in C2, DT1]. Copy Text: NY3. Collation: C2, DT1, H6, NY3 with A–G, Q, T, U, Z, DV7. 1 *are we*] Σ; *am I* NY3. 4 *Simple*] Σ; *Simpler* DT1, H6 & B–G, DV7. 6 *boar*] Σ; *bear* H6. 9 *Weaker I am*] Σ; *Alas I'am weaker* NY3. 11 *greater wonder*] Σ; *great wonder* H6; *greater <wonder>* B–G.

Holy Sonnet 9 [~ in NY3; "9" in C2, DT1]. Copy Text: NY3. Collation: C2, DT1, H6, NY3 with A–G, Q, T, U, Z, DV7. 1 *Mark*] Σ; *Look* NY3. 4 *that*] Σ; *his* C2 & A–G. 7 *unto*] Σ; *to* C2. 8 *fierce*] Σ; *rank* NY3. 9 *mine*] NY3; *my* Σ. 14 *assures*] Σ; *assumes* A–G.

Holy Sonnet 10 [~ in NY3; "10" in C2, DT1]. Copy Text: NY3. Collation: C2, DT1, H6, NY3 with A–G, Q, T, U, Z, DV7. 1 *Batter*] Σ; *Better* C2. 10 *enemy*] Σ; *enemies* C2.

Holy Sonnet 11 [~ in H6, NY3; "11" in C2, DT1]. Copy Text: NY3. Collation: C2, DT1, H6, NY3 with A–G, Q, T, U, Z, DV7. 11 *son*] Σ; *sun* B–G. 13 *stole*] Σ; *stol'n* C2, H6 & A, Q, T, Z, DV7

Holy Sonnet 12 [~ in H6, NY3; "12" in C2, DT1]. Copy Text: NY3. Collation: C2, DT1, H6, NY3 with A–G, Q, T, U, Z, DV7. 4 *me*] C2, DT1, NY3 & U; *to me* Σ. 8 *doth*] Σ; *<doth>* B–G; *do* A, Q, U, Z. 9 *thy*] H6, NY3 & Q, T; *those* DT1 & U, Z, DV7; *these* C2 & A–G. 12 *and quicken*] H6, NY3 & T; *again* Σ. 14 *that*] C2, DT1, NY3 & U, Z, DV7; *this* A–G, Q; *thy* H6 & T.

Holy Sonnet 13 [~ in NY3; "Divine Meditations. 1" in H6]. Copy Text: NY3. Collation: H6, NY3 with B–G, Q, T, U, Z, DV7. 7 *feebled*] H6, NY3 & T, U, Z, DV7; *feeble* Σ. 8 *which towards*] NY3 & DV7; *which it t'wards* Σ. 12 *I can myself*] NY3 & U, Z, DV7; *myself I can* Σ.

Holy Sonnet 14 [~ in H6, NY3]. Copy Text: NY3. Collation: H6, NY3 with B–G, Q, T, U, Z, DV7. 5 *my*] NY3 & U, DV7; *mine* Σ. 7 *now I*] NY3 & Q, T, U, Z, DV7; *I now* Σ.

Holy Sonnet 15 [~ in H6, NY3]. Copy Text: NY3. Collation: H6, NY3 with B–G, Q, T, U, Z, DV7. 6 *lands*] NY3 & Q, U, Z, DV7; *land* Σ. 11 *have*] Σ; *<have>* B–G; *hath* H6 & T. 12 *those*] NY3 & DV7; *their* Σ. 13 *God*] NY3; *Lord* Σ.

Holy Sonnet 16 [~ in H6, NY3]. Copy Text: NY3. Collation: H6, NY3 with B–G, Q, T, U, Z, DV7. 8 *to*] NY3 & U, DV7; *by* Σ. 10 *vile*] Σ; *stile* B–G. 14 *true*] NY3 & Q, U, DV7; *<true>* Σ. *in*] NY3 & Q, U, DV7; *into* Σ.

Holy Sonnet 17 [~ in NY3]. Copy Text: NY3. Collation: NY3 with Q, T, U, Z, DV7. 4 *in*] Σ; *on* Q. 6 *the*] Σ; *their* Q.

Holy Sonnet 18 [~ in NY3]. Copy Text: NY3. Collation: NY3 with Q, T, U, Z, DV7.

Holy Sonnet 19 [~ in NY3]. Copy Text: NY3. Collation: NY3 with Q, T, U, Z, DV7.

The Cross [~ in C2; "On the Cross" in DT1; "Of the Cross" H6]. Copy Text: DT1. Collation: C2, DT1, H6 with A–G, Q, T, U, Z. 6 *sin*] Σ; *sins* DT1 & U. 8 *who*] Σ; *that* H6. 15 *which*] Σ; *with* DT1. 20 *make*] Σ; *makes* C2. *where*] Σ; *when* C2, H6. 23 *spheres*] Σ; *sphere* H6. 26 *And*] C2, DT1 & U, Z; *But* Σ. 36 *And*] Σ; *Or* H6. 44 *destruction*] Σ; *corruption* H6. 45 *seek*] Σ; *see* D–G. 46 *'scape a snake*] Σ; *scarce awake* H6. 47 *harsh, hard*] Σ; *hard, harsh* DT1, H6. 48 *call*] Σ; *all* H6 & A–G. 50 *others*] Σ; *other* A. Second *th'*] Σ; *<th'>* B–G, H6. 52 *Points*] DT1, H6 (*Pants* written above) & Q, U, Z; *Pants* Σ. 53 *dejections*] Σ; *detorsions* H6 & B–G. 55 *thy*] DT1, H6 & U, Z; *the* Σ. *doth*] Σ; *do* H6. 57 *brain*] Σ; *brains* H6. *works*] Σ; *work* H6. 60 *but*] Σ; *and* H6. 61 *fruitfully*] Σ; *faithfully* A–G. 63 *That*] Σ; *The* A–G.

Resurrection, imperfect [~ in DT1, H6]. Copy Text: DT1. Collation: DT1, H6 with A–G, Q, T, U, Z. 6 *enlighten'd*] Σ; *enlightened'st* DT1. 7 *fires*] Σ; *fire* DT1. 8 *fire grows*] DT1, H6; *fires grow*] Σ. 13 *lay*] Σ; *laid* DT1. 17 *one*] Σ; *any* H6. 19 *at*] Σ; *had* DT1. 23 *Desunt cætera*] omitted in DT1, H6. Of the eight known copies of this poem, only the Dolau Cothi ms. records this phrase, which all subsequent editors print.

Upon the Annunciation and Passion ["~ Falling on One Day. An. Do. 16[0]8" in H6; "The Annunciation" in C2; "Upon the Annunciation, when Good Friday Fell upon the Same Day" in DT1]. Copy Text: DT1. Collation: C2, DT1, H6 with A–G, Q, T, U, Z. 1 *body*] Σ; *flesh* H6. Second *today*] Σ; *<today>* D–G. 2 *twice, Christ*] Σ; *Christ twice* H6. 4 *them both*] Σ; *both them* DT1. 10 *and*] Σ; *yet* A, Q, T. 13 *Sad and rejoic'd*] Σ; *Rejoic'd and sad* H6. 15 *At once a son*] Σ; *A son at once* H6. 16 *gives*] Σ; *give* DT1. 19 *hath*] Σ; *is* H6. 21 *West is east*] Σ; *East is west* H6. 31 *as*] Σ; *and* B–G. 33 *these*] Σ; *those* A–G. *days*] Σ; *feasts* H6 & B–G. 34 *is*] Σ; *are* H6 & B–G. 35 *'twas*] Σ; *that* H6. *the same*] Σ; *'twas one* H6. 37 *had*] DT1, H6 & U; *hath*] Σ. 38 *the*] Σ; *his* H6. 43 *words*] Σ; *works* C2. 44 *busy*] Σ; *buy* H6. 46 *my*] Σ; *thy* H6 (corrected to *my*).

Good Friday, 1613. Riding Westward ["Good Friday, 1613. Riding towards Wales" in C2, H6, SP1; "Good Friday" in DT1]. Copy Text: DT1. Collation: C2, DT1, H6, SP1 with A–G,

Q, T, U, Z. 4 *motions*] Σ; *motion* A–G. 5 *by others hurried*] Σ; *hurried by others* C2. 9 *towards*] Σ; *toward* C2. 10 *towards*] C2, DT1, SP1; *toward*] Σ; *to* B–G. 11 *I should*] Σ; *should I* H6. 13 *this*] Σ; *his* DT1 & B–G. 22 *tune*] Σ; *turn* DT1 & Q, Z. 24 *and*] Σ; *and to* C2. Lines 22–25 omitted in C2; lines 24–25 in SP1. 27 *make*] C2, DT1, SP1 & U, Z; *made*] Σ. 30 *Upon*] Σ; *On* B–G. *miserable*] Σ; *distressed* B–G. 31 *partner*] Σ; *pattern* C2, SP1. 40 *rusts*] Σ; *rust* B–G.

Upon The Translation of the Psalms by Sir Philip Sidney, and the Countess of Pembroke, His Sister [~ in H6]. Copy Text: H6. Collation: H6 with B–G, Q, T, U, Z. 28 *hear*] *here* Σ. 46 First *this*] H6; *thy* B–G. 53 *these*] H6 & T, U, Z; *those* B–G, Q.

To Mr. Tilman After He Had Taken Orders [~ in H5, H6]. Copy Text: H6. Collation: H5, H6 with B–G, Q, T, U, Z. 4 *but*] Σ; *but a* H5. 6 *in*] H5, H6 & T, U; *since* Σ. *vintage*] Σ; *voyage* H5, T. 10 *brings*] Σ; *bringst* H5. 13 *Art thou*] H5, H6 & T, U; *Thou art* Σ. 18 *stamp*] Σ; *birth* H5. 25 *thy*] Σ; *they* H6. *gaining*] H5, H6 & T, U; *gainings* Σ. 27 *think't*] H5 & T; *think* Σ. 29 *Would . . . spent*] H5, H6 & T, U; *As if their day were only to be spent* Σ. 30 *mistressing*] Σ; *undressing* H5; *mis-dressing* H6. 32 *refin'd*] Σ; *sublimed* B–G, Q. 33 *beauties*] Σ; *beauty* B–G, Q. 34 *as*] Σ; *of* B–G, Q. 47 *engines*] Σ; *engine* B–G, Q. 48 *again*] Σ; <*again*> H5, H6. 52 *doth those things*] H5, H6 & T; *these things doth* Σ.

A Hymn to Christ, at the Author's Last Going into Germany ["Dr. Donne's Going into Bohemia. Hymn to Christ" in C2; "A Hymn to Christ" in DT1; "At the Seaside Going over with the Lord Doncaster. 1619" in H6]. Copy Text: DT1. Collation: C2, DT1, H6 with A–G, Q, T, U, Z. 2 *my*] Σ; *the* C2. 3 *swallow*] Σ; *swallows* C2, H6. *me*] Σ; *me up* H6. 5 *with*] Σ; *in* H6. *do*] Σ; *dost* C2, H6. 9 *whom*] Σ; *that* C2. *lov'd . . . lov'd*] Σ; *love . . . love* H6 & B–G; *love . . . loves* C2. *there*] Σ; *here* B–G. 10 *our*] Σ; *this* B–G; *those* H6. *seas*] Σ; *sea* C2; *flood* B–G. *'twixt*] Σ; *'tween* C2. 11 *sea*] Σ; *blood* B–G; *seas* A. 12 *root*] Σ; *sap* C2. Lines 15–28 omitted in C2. 15 *dost*] Σ; *doth* H6. 16 *an*] Σ; *a* DT1. 18 *I am*] Σ; *am I* H6. 21 *Alas*] Σ; <*Alas*> H6. 25 *fame*] Σ; *face* H6 & B–G. 26 *prayer*] Σ; *prayers* H6.

Hymn to God, My God, in My Sickness [~ in B46]. Copy Text: B46. Collation: with B46 with B–G, Walton, Q, T, U, Z. 2 *thy*] Σ; *the* C–G. 4 First *the*] Σ; *my* Walton. Second *the*] Σ; *any* Walton. 5 *now*] B46 & U; *here* Σ. 6 *Whilst*] Σ; *Since* Walton. Lines 9–25 omitted in Walton. 12 *their*] Σ; *those* B–G. 28 *other*] B46; *others'* Σ. 30 *Therefore that he may raise*] Σ; *That, he may rise; therefore* Walton.

To Christ [~ in B7, DT1, H4; "Christo Salvatori" in B46, H5, H6]. Copy Text: DT1. Collation: B7, B46, DT1, H4, H5, H6 with Q, T, U, Z. 2 *is*] Σ; *was* B46. *was*] B46, H5, H6; *were* Σ. 5 *I have*] B7, H4, H6; *thou hast* Σ. 7 *by*] Σ; <*by*> B7, H4. *won*] Σ; *have won* B7, DT1 & Q, T. 13 *a*] Σ; <*a*> B46. 14 *on*] Σ; *and* H5. 15 *thy*] Σ; *this* B7, DT1. 16 *it*] Σ; *he* H4.

A Hymn to God the Father [~ in A]. Copy Text: A. Collation: A–G, Q.

CRITICISM

CRITICISM

Donne and Metaphysical Poetry

BEN JONSON

[Conversations about Donne]†

That Donne's *Anniversary* was profane and full of blasphemies. That he told Mr. Donne, if it had been written of the Virgin Mary it had been something. To which he answered that he described the Idea of a Woman, and not as she was. That Donne, for not keeping of accent, deserved hanging. * * *

He esteemeth John Donne the first poet in the world in some things: his verses of the lost chain[1] he hath by heart; and that passage of "The Calm," *That dust and feathers do not stir, all was so quiet.* Affirmeth Donne to have written all his best pieces ere he was 25 years old.[2]* * *

That Donne said to him he wrote that epitaph on Prince Henry, *Look to me, Faith,* to match Sir Edward Herbert[3] in obscureness. * * *

The conceit of Donne's transformation or Μετεμψυχοσις[4] was that he sought the soul of that apple which Eva pulled, and thereafter made it the soul of a bitch, then of a she wolf and so of a woman. His general purpose was to have brought in all the bodies of the Heretics from the soul of Cain, and at last left it in the body of Calvin. Of this he never wrote but one sheet, and now, since he was made doctor, repenteth highly and seeketh to destroy all his poems. * * *

Donne's grandfather on the mother's side, was Heywood the Epigramatist. That Donne himself, for not being understood, would perish. * * *

† In 1619 Ben Jonson, the reigning poet laureate, traveled to Scotland and stayed with the Scottish poet, William Drummond of Hawthornden, who recorded Jonson's literary gossip. These extracts were taken from *Notes of Ben Jonson's Conversations with William Drummond of Hawthornden* (London: Shakespeare Society, 1842).
1. The elegy "The Bracelet."
2. Since Jonson knew Donne well in the 1590s when both were young men about town, his recollections are especially valuable.
3. Lord Herbert of Cherbury (1582–1648) was the elder brother of the poet George Herbert and a friend of Donne, whose "Elegy on Prince Henry" was printed in a collection in 1613.
4. Also know as "The Progress of the Soul" (not included in this Norton Critical Edition), *Metempsychosis* was to have been a satiric epic. Jonson's memory plays him false since 520 lines of the poem were written.

THOMAS CAREW

An Elegy upon the Death of the Dean of Paul's, Dr. John Donne†

Can we not force from widow'd poetry,
Now thou art dead, great Donne, one elegy,
To crown thy hearse? Why yet dare we not trust,
Though with unkneaded dough-baked¹ prose, thy dust,
5   Such as the unscissor'd² churchman from the flower
Of fading rhetoric, short-liv'd as his hour,
Dry as the sand that measures it, should lay
Upon thy ashes on the funeral day?
Have we no voice, no tune? Did'st thou dispense
10 Through all our language both the words and sense?
'Tis a sad truth. The pulpit may her plain
And sober Christian precepts still retain;
Doctrines it may, and wholesome uses, frame,
Grave homilies and lectures; but the flame
15 Of thy brave soul, that shot such heat and light,
As burnt our earth, and made our darkness bright,
Committed holy rapes³ upon our will,
Did through the eye the melting heart distil,
And the deep knowledge of dark truths so teach,
20 As sense might judge what fancy could not reach,
Must be desir'd for ever. So the fire,
That fills with spirit and heat the Delphic choir,⁴
Which, kindled first by thy Promethean⁵ breath,
Glow'd here a while, lies quench'd now in thy death.
25 The Muses' garden, with pedantic weeds
O'erspread, was purg'd by thee; the lazy seeds
Of servile imitation thrown away,
And fresh invention planted. Thou didst pay
The debts of our penurious bankrupt age;
30 Licentious thefts, that make poetic rage
A mimic fury, when our souls must be

---

† This elegy was printed in the first edition of Donne's poems (1633), from which the text
is drawn. A well-regarded Cavalier poet, Carew (1594–1640) provides us with some of the
most astute critical insights into Donne's innovative style.
1. Tasteless and flat, like unleavened bread.
2. Unshorn, as a sign of mourning.
3. A likely allusion to Donne's sonnet, "Batter my heart."
4. Apollo, god of music and poetry, was also the oracle at Delphi. The "choir" in attendance
upon him are poets such as Carew.
5. Prometheus stole fire from the heaven to give to humankind.

Possess'd, or with Anacreon's[6] ecstasy,
Or Pindar's, not their own. The subtle cheat
Of sly exchanges, and the juggling feat
35 Of two-edg'd words, or whatsoever wrong
By ours was done the Greek or Latin tongue,
Thou hast redeem'd, and open'd us a mine
Of rich and pregnant fancy, drawn a line
Of masculine expression,[7] which, had good
40 Old Orpheus[8] seen, or all the ancient brood
Our superstitious fools admire, and hold
Their lead more precious than thy burnish'd gold,
Thou hadst been their exchequer, and no more
They each in other's dust had rak'd for ore.
45 Thou shalt yield no precedence, but of time,
And the blind fate of language, whose tun'd chime[9]
More charms the outward sense. Yet thou mayst claim
From so great disadvantage greater fame,
Since to the awe of thy imperious wit
50 Our stubborn language bends, made only fit
With her tough, thick-rib'd hoops to gird about
Thy giant fancy, which had prov'd too stout
For their soft melting phrases. As in time
They had the start, so did they cull the prime
55 Buds of invention many a hundred year,
And left the rifled fields, besides the fear
To touch their harvest; yet from those bare lands,
Of what is purely thine, thy only hands
(And that thy smallest work) have gleaned more
60 Than all those times and tongues could reap before.
        But thou art gone, and thy strict laws will be
Too hard for libertines[1] in poetry.
They will repeal the goodly exil'd train
Of gods and goddesses, which in thy just reign
65 Were banish'd nobler poems; now with these,
The silenced tales o'th'*Metamorphoses*,
Shall stuff their lines, and swell the windy page,
Till verse, refin'd by thee in this last age,

6. Greek lyric poet (born ca. 550 B.C.E.). Anacreontic has come to mean a style of poem that
praises love and wine. Pindar (522–443 B.C.E.) was also a Greek lyric poet.
7. Carew's point is that lesser poets slavishly imitated these classical poets, while Donne
creatively transformed the love lyric and produced a powerful new idiom through his
complex conceits, "masculine expression."
8. A mythic poet who was said to have moved stones and trees through his verse.
9. Euphonious and metrically regular verse (in contrast to Donne's).
1. Here, poets who will resort to the cliched tales from Ovid's *Metamorphoses*. They are
apostates (line 70) who turn from Donne's poetic example to worship false, poetic *idols*
(line 69).

Turn ballad-rhyme. Or those old idols be
70   Ador'd again with new apostasy.
          Oh pardon me, that break with untun'd verse
      The reverend silence that attends thy hearse,
      Whose awful solemn murmurs were to thee,
      More than these faint lines, a loud elegy,
75   That did proclaim in a dumb eloquence
      The death of all the arts, whose influence,
      Grown feeble, in these panting numbers lies
      Gasping short-winded accents, and so dies.
      So doth the swiftly turning wheel not stand
80   In th'instant we withdraw the moving hand,
      But some small time maintain a faint weak course,
      By virtue of the first impulsive force:
      And so, whil'st I cast on thy funeral pile
      Thy crown of bays,[2] oh, let it crack a while,
85   And spit disdain, till the devouring flashes
      Suck all the moisture up, then turn to ashes.
          I will not draw the envy to engross[3]
      All thy perfections, or weep all our loss;
      Those are too numerous for an elegy,
90   And this too great, to be express'd by me.
      Though every pen should share a distinct part,
      Yet art thou theme enough to tire all art;
      Let others carve the rest; it shall suffice
      I on thy tomb this epitaph incise:

95   *Here lies a king that rul'd, as he thought fit,*
          The universal monarchy of wit;
          Here lie two flamens,[4] and both those, the best:
          Apollo's first, at last, the true God's priest.

IZAAK WALTON

From The Life of Dr. John Donne†

[*Donne Declines an Opportunity to Enter the Priesthood in 1607*]

Mr. Donne's estate was the greatest part spent in many and charge-
able travels, books, and dear-bought experience: he out of all employ-

2. Laurel wreath for poetic achievement.
3. To write in large letters, as in a legal document for emphasis (OED).
4. A Roman priest devoted to a particular deity, here the god of poetry.
† From the third edition of *The Life of Dr. John Donne* (London, 1675) by Izaak Walton,

ment that might yield a support for himself and wife, who had been curiously and plentifully educated; both their natures generous, and accustomed to confer, and not to receive courtesies: These and other considerations, but chiefly that his wife was to bear a part in his sufferings, surrounded him with many sad thoughts, and some apparent apprehensions of want.

But his sorrows were lessened and his wants prevented by the seasonable courtesy of their noble kinsman Sir Francis Wolley[1] of Pyrford in Surrey, who entreated them to a cohabitation with him; where they remained with much freedom to themselves and equal content to him for some years; and as their charge increased (she had yearly a child) so did his love and bounty.

It hath been observed by wise and considering men, that wealth hath seldom been the portion, and never the mark to discover good people; but that Almighty God, who disposeth all things wisely, hath of his abundant goodness denied it (he only knows why) to many, whose minds he hath enriched with the greater blessings of knowledge and virtue, as the fairer testimonies of his love to mankind: and this was the present condition of this man of so excellent erudition and endowments, whose necessary and daily expenses were hardly reconcilable with his uncertain and narrow estate. Which I mention, for that at this time there was a most generous offer made him for the moderating of his worldly cares, the declaration of which shall be the next employment of my pen.

God hath been so good to his Church, as to afford it in every age some such men to serve at his altar as have been piously ambitious of doing good to mankind; a disposition, that is so like to God himself, that it owes itself only to him who takes a pleasure to behold it in his creatures. These times he did bless with many such; some of which still live to the patterns of apostolical charity, and, of more than human patience. I have said this, because I have occasion to mention one of them in my following discourse; namely, Dr. Morton,[2] the most laborious and learned bishop of Durham; one that God hath blessed with perfect intellectuals and a cheerful heart at the age of 94 years (and is yet living); one that in his days of plenty had so large a heart, as to use his large revenue to the encouragement of learning and virtue, and is now (be it spoken with sorrow) reduced

---

who did not know Donne personally but interviewed many who did to produce a biography in 1640. Many of Walton's anecdotes are unverified—e.g., that Donne wrote "A Valediction Forbidding Mourning" to his wife—and so should be taken *cum grano salis*.

1. Sir Francis Wolley was a relation of Anne More and provided refuge for the young couple from 1601 to 1606.
2. Shortly before his death Thomas Morton (1564–1659) provided Walton with an account of his intercession on behalf of Donne. After the king had appointed him to the deanery at the cathedral of Gloucester on 22 June 1607 (later to the bishopric of Durham), Morton offered the *benefice*, or endowed church office, he currently held to Donne, whose reasons for rejecting it show us the high regard he held for the ministry.

to a narrow estate, which he embraces without repining; and still shows the beauty of his mind by so liberal a hand, as if this were an age in which tomorrow were to care for itself. I have taken a pleasure in giving the reader a short, but true character of this good man, my friend, from whom I received this following relation. He sent to Mr. Donne, and entreated to borrow an hour of his time for a conference the next day. After their meeting, there was not many minutes passed before he spake to Mr. Donne to this purpose:

> Mr. Donne, the occasion of sending for you, is to propose to you what I have often revolved in my own thought since I last saw you: which nevertheless, I will not declare but upon this condition, that you shall not return me a present answer, but forbear three days, and bestow some part of that time in fasting and prayer; and after a serious consideration of what I shall propose, then return to me with your answer. Deny me not, Mr. Donne; for, it is the effect of a true love, which I would gladly pay as a debt due for yours to me.

This request being granted, the Doctor expressed himself thus:

> Mr. Donne, I know your education and abilities; I know your expectation of a state-employment; and I know your fitness for it; and I know too the many delays and contingencies that attend court-promises: and let me tell you that my love, begot by our long friendship and your merits, hath prompted me to such an inquisition after your present temporal estate, as makes me no stranger to your necessities; which I know to be such as your generous spirit could not bear, if it were not supported with a pious patience. You know I have formerly persuaded you to waive your court-hopes, and enter into holy orders; which I now again persuade you to embrace, with this reason added to my former request: The King hath yesterday made me Dean of Gloucester, and I am also possessed of a benefice, the profits of which are equal to those of my deanery; I will think my deanery enough for my maintenance—who am and resolved to die, a single man—and will quit my benefice, and estate you in it— which the Patron is willing I shall do—if God shall incline your heart to embrace this motion. Remember, Mr. Donne, no man's education or parts make him too good for this employment, which is to be an ambassador for the God of glory; that God, who, by a vile death, opened the gates of life to mankind. Make me no present answer; but remember your promise, and return to me the third day with your resolution.

At the hearing of this, Mr. Donne's faint breath and perplexed countenance, gave a visible testimony of an inward conflict: but he performed his promise, and departed without returning an answer till the third day, and then his answer was to this effect:

> My most worthy and most dear friend, since I saw you, I have been faithful to my promise, and have also meditated much of your great kindness, which hath been such as would exceed even my gratitude; but that it cannot do; and more I cannot return you; and I do that with an heart full of humility and thanks, though I may not accept of your offer; but, Sir, my refusal is not for that I think myself too good for that calling, for which kings, if they think so, are not good enough: nor for that my education and learning, though not eminent, may not, being assisted with God's grace and humility, render me in some measure fit for it: but I dare make so dear a friend as you are, my confessor: some irregularities of my life have been so visible to some men, that though I have, I thank God, made my peace with him by penitential resolutions against them, and by the assistance of his grace banished them my affections; yet this, which God knows to be so, is not so visible to man, as to free me from their censures, and it may be that sacred calling from a dishonor. And besides, whereas it is determined by the best of casuists, that God's glory should be the first end, and a maintenance the second motive to embrace that calling; and though each man may propose to himself both together, yet the first may not be put last without a violation of conscience, which he that searches the heart will judge. And truly my present condition is such, that if I ask my own conscience, whether it be reconcilable to that rule, it is at this time so perplexed about it, that I can neither give myself nor you an answer. You know, Sir, who says, "Happy is that man whose conscience doth not accuse him for that thing which he does." To these I might add other reasons that dissuade me; but I crave your favor that I may forbear to express them, and thankfully decline your offer.

This was his present resolution, but the heart of man is not in his own keeping; and he was destined to this sacred service by an higher hand; a hand so powerful, as at last forced him to a compliance: of which I shall give the reader an account, before I shall give a rest to my pen. * * *

[Donne Enters Holy Orders in 1615]

About this time there grew many disputes, that concerned the Oath of Supremacy and Allegiance, in which the king had appeared, and engaged himself by his public writings now extant: And his majesty discoursing with Mr. Donne, concerning many of the reasons which are usually urged against the taking of those Oaths, apprehended such a validity and clearness in his stating the questions, and

his answers to them, that his majesty commanded him to bestow
some time in drawing the arguments into a method, and then to write
his answers to them; and, having done that, not to send, but be his
own messenger, and bring them to him. To this he presently and
diligently applied himself, and within six weeks brought them to him
under his own hand writing, as they be now printed; the book bearing
the name of *Pseudo-Martyr*, printed *anno* 1610.

When the king had read and considered that book, he persuaded
Mr. Donne to enter into the ministry; to which, at that time, he was,
and appeared, very unwilling, apprehending it (such was his mis-
taken modesty) to be too weighty for his abilities: and though his
majesty had promised him a favor, and many persons of worth medi-
ated with his majesty for some secular employment for him (to which
his education had apted him) and particularly the earl of Somerset,
when in his greatest height of favor; who being then at Theobalds
with the king, where one of the clerks of the Council died that night,
the earl posted a messenger for Mr. Donne to come to him imme-
diately, and at Mr. Donne's coming, said, "Mr. Donne, to testify the
reality of my affliction, and my purpose to prefer you, stay in this
garden till I go up to the king, and bring you word that you are clerk
of the Council: doubt not my doing this, for I know the king loves
you, and know the king will not deny me." But the king gave a positive
denial to all requests, and, having a discerning spirit, replied, "I know
Mr. Donne is a learned man, has the abilities of a learned divine,
and will prove a powerful preacher; and my desire is to prefer him
that way, and in that way I will deny you nothing for him."

After that time, as he professeth,[3] the king descended to a per-
suasion, almost to a solicitation, of him to enter into sacred orders:
which, though he then denied not, yet he deferred it for almost three
years. All which time he applied himself to an incessant study of
textual divinity, and to the attainment of a greater perfection in the
learned languages, Greek and Hebrew.

In the first and most blessed times of Christianity, when the clergy
were looked upon with reverence, and deserved it, when they over-
came their opposers by high examples of virtue, by a blessed patience
and long-suffering, those only were then judged worthy the ministry,
whose quiet and meek spirits did make them look upon that sacred
calling with an humble adoration and fear to undertake it; which
indeed requires such great degrees of humility, and labor, and care,
that none but such were then thought worthy of that celestial dignity.
And such only were then sought out, and solicited to undertake it.
This I have mentioned, because forwardness and inconsideration,
could not, in Mr. Donne, as in many others, be an argument of

---

3. Walton has a marginal note here: "In his Book of Devotions."

insufficiency or unfitness; for he had considered long, and had many strifes within himself concerning the strictness of life, and competency of learning, required in such as enter into sacred orders; and doubtless, considering his own demerits, did humbly ask God with St. Paul, "Lord who is sufficient for these things?" and with meek Moses, "Lord, who am I?" And sure, if he had consulted with flesh and blood, he had not for these reasons put his hand to that holy plough. But God, who is able to prevail, wrestled with him, as the Angel did with Jacob, and marked him, marked him for his own, marked him with a blessing, a blessing of obedience to the motions of his blessed Spirit. And then, as he had formerly asked God with Moses, "Who am I?" So now, being inspired with an apprehension of God's particular mercy to him, in the king's and others solicitations of him, he came to ask King David's thankful question, "Lord, who am I, that thou art so mindful of me?" So mindful of me, as to lead me for more than forty years through this wilderness of the many temptations and various turnings of a dangerous life: so merciful to me, as to move the learnedest of kings, to descend to move me to serve at the altar! So merciful to me, as at last to move my heart to embrace this holy motion! Thy motions I will and do embrace: and I now say with the blessed Virgin, "Be it with thy servant as seemeth best in thy sight": and so, Blessed Jesus, I do take the Cup of Salvation, and will call upon thy name, and will preach thy Gospel.

Such strifes as these St. Austin[4] had, when St. Ambrose endeavored his conversion to Christianity: with which he confesseth he acquainted his friend Alipius. Our learned author (a man fit to write after no mean copy) did the like. And declaring his intentions to his dear friend Dr. King, then bishop of London, a man famous in his generation, and no stranger to Mr. Donne's abilities (for he had been chaplain to the Lord Chancellor, at the time of Mr. Donne's being his Lordship's secretary) that reverend man did receive the news with much gladness; and, after some expressions of joy, and a persuasion to be constant in his pious purpose, he proceeded with all convenient speed to ordain him first deacon, and then priest not long after.

Now the English Church had gained a second St. Austin; for I think none was so like him before his conversion, none so like St. Ambrose after it: and if his youth had the infirmities of the one, his age had the excellencies of the other; the learning and holiness of both.

And now all his studies which had been occasionally diffused, were

4. I.e., St. Augustine, whose spiritual autobiography, *Confessions*, provides Walton with a model he makes applicable to Donne's own life—i.e., the transformation from Jack the Rake to the saintly Dr. Donne, dean of St. Paul's. Augustine saw his own conversion in the same mold as St. Paul's dramatic conversion on the road to Damascus.

all concentered in divinity. Now he had a new calling, new thoughts, and a new employment for his wit and eloquence. Now, all his earthly affections were changed into divine love; and all the faculties of his own soul were engaged in the conversion of others; in preaching the glad tidings of remission to repenting sinners, and peace to each troubled soul. To these he applied himself with all care and diligence: and now such a change was wrought in him, that he could say with David, "O how amiable are thy tabernacles, O Lord God of hosts!" Now he declared openly, "that when he required a temporal, God gave him a spiritual blessing." And that "he was now gladder to be a door-keeper in the house of God, than he could be to enjoy the noblest of all temporal employments."

Presently after he entered into his holy profession, the king sent for him, and made him his Chaplain in Ordinary, and promised to take a particular care for his preferment. * * *

[Donne's Death in 1631]

Before that month ended, he was appointed to preach upon his old constant day, the first Friday in Lent: he had notice of it, and had in his sickness so prepared for that employment, that as he had long thirsted for it, so he resolved his weakness should not hinder his journey; he came therefore to London, some few days before his appointed day of preaching.[5] At his coming thither, many of his friends (who with sorrow saw his sickness had left him but so much flesh as did only cover his bones) doubted his strength to perform that task, and did therefore dissuade him from undertaking it, assuring him however, it was like to shorten his life: but he passionately denied their requests, saying "He would not doubt that that God, who in so many weaknesses had assisted him with an unexpected strength, would now withdraw it in his last employment; professing an holy ambition to perform that sacred work." And when, to the amazement of some beholders, he appeared in the pulpit, many of them thought he presented himself not to preach mortification by a living voice, but mortality by a decayed body, and a dying face. And doubtless many did secretly ask that question in Ezekiel: "Do these bones live? or can that soul organize that tongue, to speak so long time as the sand in that glass will move towards its center, and mea- sure out an hour of this dying man's unspent life?" Doubtless it can- not; and yet, after some faint pauses in his zealous prayer, his strong desires enabled his weak body to discharge his memory of his pre- conceived meditations, which were of dying; the text being, "To God

5. Donne preached what has since been called his own funeral sermon before the king at the chapel in Whitehall on 25 February, posthumously published as *Death's Duell* (1632). He died in London on 31 March.

the Lord belong the issues from death" [Psalm 68:20]. Many that then saw his tears, and heard his faint and hollow voice, professing they thought the text prophetically chosen, and that Dr. Donne had preached his own Funeral Sermon.

Being full of joy that God had enabled him to perform this desired duty, he hastened to his house; out of which he never moved, till, like St. Stephen, he was carried by devout men to his grave.

The next day after his sermon, his strength being much wasted, and his spirits so spent as indisposed him to business or to talk, a friend that had often been a witness of his free and facetious discourse asked him, "Why are you sad?" To whom he replied, with a countenance so full of cheerful gravity, as gave testimony of an inward tranquility of mind, and of a soul willing to take a farewell of this world; and said,

> I am not sad; but most of the night past I have entertained myself with many thoughts of several friends that have left me here, and are gone to that place from which they shall not return; and that within a few days I also shall go hence, and be no more seen. And my preparation for this change is become my nightly meditation upon my bed, which my infirmities have now made restless to me. But at this present time, I was in a serious contemplation of the providence and goodness of God to me: to me who am less than the least of his mercies; and looking back upon my life past, I now plainly see it was his hand that prevented me from all temporal employment; and that it was his will I should never settle nor thrive till I entered into the ministry; in which I have now lived almost twenty years (I hope to, his glory) and by which, I most humbly thank him, I have been enabled to requite most of those friends which showed me kindness when my fortune was very low, as God knows it was: and (as it hath occasioned the expression of my gratitude) I thank God most of them have stood in need of my requital. I have lived to be useful and comfortable to my good father-in-law, Sir George More, whose patience God hath been pleased to exercise with many temporal crosses; I have maintained my own mother whom it hath pleased God, after a plentiful fortune in her younger days, to bring to great decay in her very old age. I have quieted the consciences of many, that have groaned under the burthen of a wounded spirit, whose prayers I hope are available for me. I cannot plead innocency of life, especially of my youth; but I am to be judged by a merciful God, who is not willing to see what I have done amiss. And though of myself I have nothing to present to him but sins and misery, yet I know he looks not upon me now as I am of myself, but as I am in my Savior, and hath given me, even at this present time, some testimonies by his Holy Spirit, that I am of the number of

his elect: I am therefore full of inexpressible joy, and shall die in peace.

I must here look so far back as to tell the reader that at his first return out of Essex, to preach his last sermon, his old friend and physician, Dr. Fox[6]—a man of great worth—came to him to consult his health; and that after a sight of him, and some queries concerning his distempers, he told him, "That by cordials, and drinking milk twenty days together, there was a probability of his restoration to health"; but he passionately denied to drink it. Nevertheless, Dr. Fox, who loved him most entirely, wearied him with solicitations, till he yielded to take it for ten days; at the end of which time he told Dr. Fox, he had drunk it more to satisfy him, than to recover his health; and that he would not drink it ten days longer, upon the best moral assurance of having twenty years added to his life; for he loved it not; and was so far from fearing death, which to others is the king of terrors, that he longed for the day of his dissolution.

It is observed, that a desire of glory or commendation is rooted in the very nature of man; and that those of the severest and most mortified lives, though they may become so humble as to banish self-flattery, and such weeds as naturally grow there; yet they have not been able to kill this desire of glory, but that like our radical heat, it will both live and die with us; and many think it should do so; and we want not sacred examples to justify the desire of having our memory to outlive our lives, which I mention, because Dr. Donne, by the persuasion of Dr. Fox, easily yielded at this very time to have a monument made for him but Dr. Fox undertook not to persuade him how, or what monument it should be; that was left to Dr. Donne himself.

A monument being resolved upon, Dr. Donne sent for a carver to make for him in wood the figure of an urn, giving him directions for the compass and height of it; and to bring with it a board of the just height of his body. These being got, then without delay a choice painter was got to be in readiness to draw his picture, which was taken as followeth. Several charcoal fires being first made in his large study, he brought with him into that place his winding-sheet in his hand, and having put off all his clothes, had this sheet put on him, and so tied with knots at his head and feet, and his hands so placed as dead bodies are usually fitted, to be shrouded and put into their coffin or grave. Upon this urn he thus stood, with his eyes shut, and with so much of the sheet turned aside as might show his lean, pale, and deathlike face, which was purposely turned towards the East, from whence he expected the second coming of his and our Savior Jesus. In this posture he was drawn at his just height; and when the

6. Dr. Simeon Fox attended Donne in his final illness.

picture was fully finished, he caused it to be set by his bed-side, where it continued and became his hourly object till his death, and was then given to his dearest friend and executor Dr. Henry King, then chief residentiary of St. Paul's, who caused him to be thus carved in one entire piece of white marble, as it now stands in that Church. * * *

Upon Monday, after the drawing this picture, he took his last leave of his beloved study; and, being sensible of his hourly decay, retired himself to his bed-chamber; and that week sent at several times for many of his most considerable friends, with whom he took a solemn and deliberate farewell, commending to their considerations some sentences useful for the regulation of their lives; and then dismissed them, as good Jacob did his sons, with a spiritual benediction. The Sunday following, he appointed his servants, that if there were any business yet undone, that concerned him or themselves, it should be prepared against Saturday next; for after that day he would not mix his thoughts with any thing that concerned this world; nor ever did; but, as Job, so he waited for the appointed day of his dissolution.

And now he was so happy as to have nothing to do but to die, to do which, he stood in need of no longer time; for he had studied it long, and to so happy a perfection, that in a former sickness he called God to witness, "He was that minute ready to deliver his soul into his hands, if that minute God would determine his dissolution." In that sickness he begged of God the constancy to be preserved in that estate for ever; and his patient expectation to have his immortal soul disrobed from her garment of mortality, makes me confident, that he now had a modest assurance that his prayers were then heard, and his petition granted. He lay fifteen days earnestly expecting his hourly change; and in the last hour of his last day, as his body melted away, and vapored into spirit, his soul having, I verily believe, some revelation of the beatifical vision, he said, "I were miserable if I might not die"; and after those words, closed many periods of his faint breath by saying often, "Thy kingdom come, thy will be done." His speech, which had long been his ready and faithful servant, left him not till the last minute of his life, and then forsook him, not to serve another master—for who speaks like him—but died before him; for that it was then become useless to him, that now conversed with God on earth, as angels are said to do in Heaven, only by thoughts and looks. Being speechless, and seeing Heaven by that illumination by which he saw it, he did, as St. Stephen, "look steadfastly into it, till he saw the Son of Man standing at the right hand of God his Father." And being satisfied with this blessed sight, as his soul ascended, and his last breath departed from him, he closed his own eyes, and then disposed his hands and body into such a posture, as required not the least alteration by those that came to shroud him.

Thus variable, thus virtuous was the life: thus excellent, thus exemplary was the death of this memorable man.

He was buried in that place of St. Paul's Church, which he had appointed for that use some years before his death; and by which he passed daily to pay his public devotions to Almighty God—who was then served twice a day by a public form of prayer and praises in that place. But he was not buried privately, though he desired it; for, beside an unnumbered number of others, many persons of nobility, and of eminence for learning, who did love and honor him in his life, did shew it at his death, by a voluntary and sad attendance of his body to the grave, where nothing was so remarkable as a public sorrow.

To which place of his burial some mournful friend repaired, and, as Alexander the Great did to the grave of the famous Achilles, so they strewed his with an abundance of curious and costly flowers; which course, they, who were never yet known, continued morning and evening for many days, not ceasing, till the stones, that were taken up in that Church, to give his body admission into the cold earth—now his bed of rest—were again by the Mason's art so leveled and firmed as they had been formerly, and his place of burial undistinguishable to common view.

The next day after his burial, some unknown friend, some one of the many lovers and admirers of his virtue and learning, writ this epitaph with a coal on the wall over his grave:

> Reader! I am to let thee know,
> Donne's Body only lies below;
> For, could the grave his Soul comprise,
> Earth would be richer than the Skies!

Nor was this all the honor done to his reverend ashes; for, as there be some persons that will not receive a reward for that for which God accounts himself a debtor; persons that dare trust God with their charity, and without a witness; so there was by some grateful unknown friend, that thought Dr. Donne's memory ought to be perpetuated, an hundred marks sent to his faithful friends and executors, towards the making of his monument. It was not for many years known by whom; but, after the death of Dr. Fox, it was known that it was he that sent it; and he lived to see as lively a representation of his dead friend, as marble can express: a statue indeed so like Dr. Donne, that—as his friend Sir Henry Wotton hath expressed himself—"It seems to breathe faintly, and posterity shall look upon it as a kind of artificial miracle."[7]

7. Miraculously, this marble statue, modeled from the sketch made of Donne on his death bed, was one of the few to survive the Great Fire of 1666 and can be found on the south quire aisle.

JOHN DRYDEN

[Donne Affects the Metaphysics]†

You[1] equal Donne in the variety, multiplicity, and choice of thoughts; you excel him in the manner and the words. I read you both with the same admiration, but not with the same delight. He affects the metaphysics, not only in his satires, but in his amorous verses, where nature only should reign; and perplexes the minds of the fair sex with nice speculations of philosophy, when he should engage their hearts, and entertain them with the softnesses of love.

* * *

Would not Donne's *Satires*, which abound with so much wit, appear more charming, if he had taken care of his words, and of his numbers? But he followed Horace[2] so very close, that of necessity he must fall with him; and I may safely say it of this present age, that if we are not so great wits as Donne, yet certainly we are better poets.

SAMUEL JOHNSON

[The Metaphysical Poets]†

Wit, like all other things subject by their nature to the choice of man, has its changes and fashions, and at different times takes different forms. About the beginning of the seventeenth century appeared a race of writers that may be termed the metaphysical poets; of whom, in a criticism on the works of Cowley, the last of the race, it is not improper to give some account.

The metaphysical poets were men of learning, and to show their learning was their whole endeavor; but, unluckily resolving to shew it in rhyme, instead of writing poetry, they only wrote verses, and very often such verses as stood the trial of the finger better than of

---

† From *A Discourse Concerning the Original and Progress of Satire* (1693) by John Dryden (1631–1700), an influential poet and critic.
1. A minor poet, Charles Sackville, sixth earl of Dorset (1638–1706).
2. Roman poet (65–68 B.C.E.), known for his odes, verse letters, and satires.
† In a biographical sketch of the poet Abraham Cowley (1618–1667), published in *Lives of the English Poets* (London, 1778), Samuel Johnson, the great arbiter of literary fashion of the eighteenth century, offered critical insights into what he called the "metaphysical poets," among whom he numbered Cowley. His definition of the metaphysical conceit as a *discordia concors* in which "heterogeneous ideas are yoked by violence together" has not been much improved upon.

the ear; for the modulation was so imperfect, that they were only found to be verses by counting the syllables.

If the father of criticism has rightly denominated poetry τέχνη μιμητική an *imitative art*, these writers will, without great wrong, lose their right to the name of poets for they cannot be said to have imitated any thing; they neither copied nature nor life; neither painted the forms of matter, nor represented the operations of intellect.

Those, however, who deny them to be poets, allow them to be wits. Dryden confesses of himself and his contemporaries, that they fall below Donne in wit, but maintains that they surpass him in poetry.

If Wit be well described by Pope, as being "that which has been often thought, but was never before so well expressed," they certainly never attained, nor ever sought it; for they endeavored to be singular in their thoughts, and were careless of their diction. But Pope's account of wit is undoubtedly erroneous: he depresses it below its natural dignity, and reduces it from strength of thought to happiness of language.

If by a more noble and more adequate conception that be considered as Wit, which is at once natural and new, that which, though not obvious, is, upon its first production, acknowledged to be just; if it be that, which he that never found it, wonders how he missed; to wit of this kind the metaphysical poets have seldom risen. Their thoughts are often new, but seldom natural; they are not obvious, but neither are they just; and the reader, far from wondering that he missed them, wonders more frequently by what perverseness of industry they were ever found.

But Wit, abstracted from its effects upon the hearer, may be more rigorously and philosophically considered as a kind of *discordia concors*; a combination of dissimilar images, or discovery of occult resemblances in things apparently unlike. Of wit thus defined, they have more than enough. The most heterogeneous ideas are yoked by violence together; nature and art are ransacked for illustrations, comparisons, and allusions; their learning instructs, and their subtlety surprises; but the reader commonly thinks his improvement dearly bought, and, though he sometimes admires, is seldom pleased.

From this account of their compositions it will be readily inferred, that they were not successful in representing or moving the affections. As they were wholly employed on something unexpected and surprising, they had no regard to that uniformity of sentiment which enables us to conceive and to excite the pains and the pleasure of other minds: they never inquired what, on any occasion, they should have said or done; but wrote rather as beholders than partakers of human nature; as beings looking upon good and evil, impassive and at leisure; as Epicurean deities making remarks on the actions of men, and the vicissitudes of life, without interest and without emotion. Their courtship was void of fondness, and their lamentations of sorrow. Their wish was only to say what they hoped had been never said before.

Nor was the sublime more within their reach than the pathetic; for they never attempted that comprehension and expanse of thought which at once fills the whole mind, and of which the first effect is sudden astonishment, and the second rational admiration. Sublimity is produced by aggregation, and littleness by dispersion. Great thoughts are always general, and consist in positions not limited by exceptions, and in descriptions not descending to minuteness. It is with great propriety that subtlety, which in its original import means exility of particles, is taken in its metaphorical meaning for nicety of distinction. Those writers who lay on the watch for novelty could have little hope of greatness; for great things cannot have escaped former observation. Their attempts were always analytic; they broke every image into fragments: and could no more represent; by their slender conceits and labored particularities the prospects of nature, or the scenes of life, than he, who dissects a sun-beam with a prism, can exhibit the wide effulgence of a summer noon.

What they wanted however of the sublime, they endeavored to supply by hyperbole; their amplification had no limits; they left not only reason but fancy behind them; and produced combinations of confused magnificence, that not only could not be credited, but could not be imagined.

Yet great labor, directed by great abilities, is never wholly lost: if they frequently threw away their wit upon false conceits, they likewise sometimes struck out unexpected truth: if their conceits were far-fetched, they were often worth the carriage. To write on their plan, it was at least necessary to read and think. No man could be born a metaphysical poet, nor assume the dignity of a writer, by descriptions copied from descriptions, by imitations borrowed from imitations, by traditional imagery, and hereditary similes, by readiness of rhyme, and volubility of syllables.

In perusing the works of this race of authors, the mind is exercised either by recollection or inquiry either something already learned is to be retrieved, or something new is to be examined. If their greatness seldom elevates, their acuteness often surprises; if the imagination is not always gratified, at least the powers of reflection and comparison are employed and in the mass of materials which ingenious absurdity has thrown together, genuine wit and useful knowledge may be sometimes found, buried perhaps in grossness of expression; but useful to those who know their value; and such as, when they are expanded to perspicuity, and polished to elegance, may give luster to works which have more propriety though less copiousness of sentiment.

This kind of writing, which was, I believe, borrowed from Marino[1] and his followers, had been recommended by the example of Donne, a man of very extensive and various knowledge; and by Jonson, whose manner resembled that of Donne more in the ruggedness of his lines than in the cast of his sentiments.

DENNIS FLYNN

Portrait of a Swordsman†

John Donne's earliest portrait, comparatively accessible to its primary audience, requires us to recover intimations it silently assumes are common knowledge. The original portrait was the work of Nicholas Hilliard or Isaac Oliver, artists patronized by the Elizabethan Court. Like other Tudor portrait miniatures, it was artfully contrived to express a mute but poetic and intimate message about its courtly subject—a message that, although not immediately obvious, will speak volumes when at length discerned. Image and motto complement and explicate each other. Each can be fully perceived in little space or time. And yet they remain a puzzle to be solved. The present study attempts, through recovered facts and reasonable conjectures, to shape a probable (not certain) solution to this puzzle.

Donne's first biographer, Izaak Walton, by 1675 in his distracted way already unaware of the portrait's intimations, recalls:

> I have seen one Picture of him, drawn by a curious hand at his age of eighteen; with his sword and what other adornments might then suit with the present fashions of youth, and the giddy gayeties of that age: and his Motto then was,
>
> *How much shall I be chang'd*
> *Before I am chang'd.*[1]

1. Giambattista Marino (1569–1625), an Italian poet noted for his extravagant conceits.
† From *John Donne and the Ancient Catholic Nobility* (Bloomington and Indianapolis: Indiana UP, 1995), pp. 1–11. Reprinted by permission of the publisher.
1. Walton's biography of Donne was first published in 1640 (see n. 1 below, p. 201). For this comment, see Izaak Walton, *The Lives of John Donne, Sir Henry Wotton, George Herbert, Richard Hooker, and Robert Sanderson* (London: Oxford University Press, 1956), 79. Walton seems unaware of other sixteenth-or seventeenth-century work combining the plastic and language arts (e.g., the *impresa*, discussed by Mario Praz as "nothing less than a symbolical representation of a purpose, a wish, a line of conduct . . . by means of a motto and a picture which reciprocally interpret each other"). Praz also quotes a seventeenth-century French source that defines such a work as "[U]ne Poésie, qui ne chante point, qui n'est composée que d'une Figure muette, et d'un Mot qui parle pour elle à la veue. La

Apart from William Marshall's frontispiece engraving of the lost miniature (see fig. 1), Walton's interpretation is our only eye-witness account of the original. However, Donne's appearance in the engraved portrait diverges considerably from Walton's description. For one thing, the sword does not seem to be worn merely as an adornment of gay fashion; rather as an emblem of honor, it is held up by its hilt in the foreground of the picture. Donne wears a long-breasted doublet in an Italian style that was not yet out of fashion but hardly the latest thing in England by 1591; moreover, doublets were often cut from much less plain cloth than this. Around the neck, Donne does not wear the highly fashionable ruff so often worn by the elegant subjects of miniaturists, but a plain band. And his earring, like the other features of his dress and bearing, does not fit the "giddy" fashions of the time, cast or carved as it is in the singular form of a cross. Most significantly, Walton has mistranslated Donne's Spanish motto—*Antes muerto que mudado*—which actually means "Rather dead than changed," an unwaveringly stoic asseveration far in spirit from Walton's lines of elegiac wonderment.

Donne's rigid motto is pathetic and ironical, not in Walton's sense of a contrast between youth and age, but in that its histrionic defiance suggests a rueful, cynical premonition of inconstancy. The line of verse is regendered from Montemayor's *Diana* (a romance much read at European courts in the late 1580s), where it appears as the oath of a shepherd's mistress, ironically quoted by the shepherd after her marriage to someone else.[2] So the eager swordsman holding up his sword swears an oath of steadfastness. But the viewer should remember what Donne knew: Diana was not faithful. Originally a woman's words, the motto thus suggests a self-conscious comment on the swordsman's pose, implying that it is only a pose, albeit one that Donne had held for some time and was to hold for several years after 1591.

Clearly the portrait suggests some things that Walton does not mention. Most obviously there is the martial flavor of the whole ensemble. The sword and the motto both contribute to this effect.

merveille est, que cette Poésie sans Musique fait en un moment, avec cette Figure et ce Mot, ce que l'autre Poésie ne scauroit faire qu'avec un long temps et de grands préparatifs d'harmonies, de fictions et de machines" (*Studies in Seventeenth-century Imagery* [Rome: Edizioni di Storia e Letteratura, 1975], 58 and 60). An ungainly kite, the present book will attempt to supply through historical research what *"l'autre Poésie"* might also do. On Donne's interest in sixteenth- and seventeenth-century portraiture and painting, see Ernest Gilman, " 'To adore, or scorn an image': Donne and the Iconoclastic Controversy," *John Donne Journal* 5 (1986): 62–100.

2. Judith M. Kennedy, ed., *A Critical Edition of Yong's Translation of George of Montemayor's "Diana"* (Oxford: Clarendon Press, 1968), 1–3. Donne's allusion to Montemayor in this motto was first pointed out by T. E. Terrill, "A Note on John Donne's Early Reading," *MLN* 43 (1928): 318–19.

Is Donne here dressed in a soldier's uniform? Is there a militant intensity, even an arrogance in his facial expression?[3] In any case there can be little doubt that at a time when clothes and manners were consciously chosen as ritualistic emblems, Donne meant to convey a definite message through the symbolism of his portrait. This message is certainly not the message Walton gives us—that the young Donne was a fop.

Far from giddiness or gayety, and despite Walton's inclination to misinterpret and dismiss the pose as mere vanity, the portrait makes purposeful reference to Donne's Catholic and Welsh ancestry in two features that not only add to a generally martial impression but also seem intended to symbolize Donne's descent from both his father's and his mother's families. In harmony with the warlike flavor of the whole is the coat-of-arms, precisely designating John Donne an eldest son descended on his father's side from the Welsh Dwns of Kidwelly, Carmarthenshire. From the time of King Arthur this family had borne swordsmen; its more recent generations had fought for or against English kings before the peace of Henry Tudor. While no particular evidence of Donne's descent from this noble family can be presented, his claim to the connection was consistent all his life. Moreover, the earring in the form of a cross most likely denotes the outstanding quality of Donne's mother's family, the Catholic Heywoods. By all accounts Donne was still a Catholic in 1591, and it is inconceivable that an Elizabethan Protestant would wear such a cross.[4]

Of course only a Catholic who fancied himself a swordsman would wear a cross hanging from his ear. This was an impudence evoking the cavalier style of Spanish and French *ligueur* captains, those "hard riding, loose tongued, yet devoted" adherents to "the religion of the swordsmen of Europe."[5] The earring together with the heraldic device suggests Donne's emulation of an Elizabethan type: the gentleman volunteer or captain, often Welsh or Catholic or both, who fought against Dutch Protestants for the Duke of Alva before

---

3. Edmund Gosse, *The Life and Letters of John Donne*, 2 vols. (Gloucester, MA: Peter Smith, 1959), 1: 23. The idea that Donne wears military dress was first broached by Alexander Grosart in his edition of the *Complete Poems of John Donne*, 2 vols. (London: Robson & Sons, 1873), 2:xxii. See also Baird W. Whitlock, "Donne's University Years," *English Studies* 43 (1962): 15.

4. Donne's allusions to family and lineage here can well be understood along lines drawn by M. Thomas Hester, who questions critical assumptions about the biographical basis of Donne's Satyres and suggests that the commonplace emphasis on Donne as an "innovator and initiator" of poetic style needs to be reconsidered in light of Donne's "historical and personal situation . . . *at the end*—at the end of the sixteenth century, of one phase of Christian humanism, of a movement of English literary history" (*Kinde Pitty and Brave Scorn: Donne's Satyres* [Durham, NC: Duke University Press, 1982], 4). Chapters 2 and 4 focus on Donne's Catholicism as a background to the Satyres.

5. David Mathew, *The Celtic Peoples and Renaissance Europe* (London: Sheed and Ward, 1933), 356.

FIGURE 1. John Donne, 1591. Detail of engraved frontispiece portrait by William Marshall, in *Poems by J. D. With Elegies On The Authors Death* (London: John Marriot, 1635). Courtesy of the Cushing Memorial Library and Archives, Texas A&M University.

200   DENNIS FLYNN

England and Spain were at war, fought against Spain when the
English came to the aid of the Dutch, or sometimes crossed over
and fought for England's enemy, the Prince of Parma. For such aris-
tocratic swordsmen the religious and political differences over which
the nation warred and was transformed often seemed secondary to
"honor," a dim sense of ancestral tradition, clans, and princes sym-
bolized in the forms of heraldry. These men seemed oblivious to the
fact that such vestiges of feudalism were doomed by the innovation
of the nation state.[6]

The ultimate effect Walton missed in the portrait—especially in
the sword, the motto, and the earring—is the intimation of old-
fashioned violence: a "language of the sword" used by Tudor Eng-
lishmen to express dissident political and religious commitment.
Readiness for violence expressed through such discourse was a main
way for nobility and gentry to display an independent posture on
public issues, their "language of the sword" constituting a matter of
honor. As tokens of honor, words or images could be deeds; mere
allusion to violence could be an instrument of rebellious self-
presentation, so long as such assertions were at least tacitly acknowl-
edged by an appropriate audience.[7] But what does this martial
reference to the concept of honor tell us about the pattern of
Donne's life around 1591 or, more fundamentally, about the earlier
life from which that pattern had developed? In particular, what audi-
ence was the portrait intended for?

Even as we try to construe Donne's pose and his purpose in the
portrait, a startling fact emerges from mere recognition of its idiom
and genre: Hilliard and Oliver did not paint undistinguished univer-
sity dropouts or beginning law school students. Their subjects were
courtiers who, through their portraits, were addressing other court-
iers. It is as if Donne is already, at eighteen, someone with access to
the highest levels of English society, as if he is silently presenting

6. The nature of this social type is well described by Mathew (ibid., 230–64 and 336–44).
A similarly unrealistic enthusiasm for lingering feudal forms is described in Johan Hui-
zinga, *The Waning of the Middle Ages* (London: E. Arnold, 1955), 94ff. For some inter-
esting background on sixteenth-century Celtic affinities to the *ligueur* style, see Brendan
Jennings, "Irish Swordsmen in Flanders, 1586–1610," *Studies: an Irish Journal* 36 (1947):
402–410, and 37 (1948): 189–202.
7. "The martial reference, with its framework of heroic values and chivalry, thus imparted a
flavour of violence to the 'deeds' by which honour was earned. But the man of honour did
not need to be a soldier, nor did honour necessarily require a setting of battle. In peacetime
honour could become self-assertiveness: the capture of the attention of 'the world,' and
of public esteem. For without the confirmation which the latter provided, honour remained
subjective, and so indistinguishable from vanity" (Mervyn James, *English Politics and the
Concept of Honour, 1485–1612* [London: Past & Present Society, 1978], 4). See also
Kristen Neuschel, *Word of Honor: Interpreting Noble Culture in Sixteenth-Century France*
(Ithaca, NY: Cornell University Press, 1989), 65: "Violence was not simply an instrument
to achieve a specific strategic goal; it had a broader and more elemental significance.
Violence was also an essential prerogative, an attribute of their status, a form of behavior
that delineated who they were. Consequently, noblemen did not always need to resort to
actual physical combat to defend or aggrandize themselves."

himself to an audience with whom he shares appropriate connections to the Court. While neither Walton nor subsequent biographers have noticed that Donne attended the Court as early as 1591, this is one implication of the portrait. We realize here a new truth about Donne's early life, a truth scarcely recognized during the past three hundred years.

Probably we should long ago have appreciated the testimony of Donne's Dutch friend Constantine Huygens, who, without Walton's limited outlook, wrote in 1630 that Donne had been "educated early at Court in the service of the great."[8] Though Donne's associations and even familiarity with English aristocrats have been known, his biographers have misinterpreted Huygens as referring to service begun only after Donne stopped practicing Catholicism, during his middle and late twenties. Thus it has been assumed that Donne obtained his secretarial position with the Lord Keeper, Sir Thomas Egerton, as "the son of a London ironmonger, . . . without any advantages of birth, family influence, or wealth"; and that Donne's four years in Egerton's employ not only "familiarized him with the ways of the court" but gave him grounds to "hope that by courting the favour of the great he could win a way to a life of public service."[9] In this way Donne's relations with the Court have been "problematized" if not castigated as the toadying of an outsider—an abject, "desperately ambitious" submission to the patronage system, narrowly centered in a quest for advancement in English government. But as Donne's first portrait suggests (and as Huygens seems to have known), his involvement with the Court was of longer duration and deeper significance than has been thought. In this book I propose that Donne's association with the ancient Catholic nobility began with his birth into the family of Sir Thomas More and took shape in the formative years of his adolescence. This link to the ancient Catholic nobility was a matter of honor that remained a presence throughout his life, part of his family's Catholic heritage.

Walton omitted mention of Donne's earliest portrait in the first three editions of the *Life of Donne*; the passage quoted above appears only in the final revision of 1675.[1] We know that Walton had been aware of the portrait for at least forty years, because it was he who in 1635 contributed the verses Marshall engraved under the portrait

8. Constantine Huygens to P. C. Hooft, 17 August 1630, quoted in Sir Herbert J. C. Grierson, ed., *The Poems of John Donne*, 2 vols. (Oxford: Oxford University Press, 1912), 2: lxxvii–lxxviii.
9. R. C. Bald, *John Donne: a Life* (Oxford: Oxford University Press, 1970), 94 and 125.
1. "The Life and Death of Dr. Donne" was an introductory memoir to John Donne Jr.'s edition of Donne's *LXXX Sermons* (London: Richard Royston and Richard Marriot, 1640), sigs. A5–C1. Walton subsequently published "corrected and enlarged" versions of the life of Donne in 1658, 1670, and 1675.

in his frontispiece design. These lines, in which Walton refers to Donne's early character as "Drosse" to be refined by the passing years, show that his estimate of the portrait underwent little change between 1635 and 1675. When he finally mentioned it in his last revision, he did so only to highlight by ironic contrast Donne's last portrait, for which he posed in his shroud in the macabre solemnity of those last days. Walton made no effort to integrate the meanings of these two portraits as illustrations of a single character. In his view, Donne's giddy nonage was a strange background for Dean Donne; it could reveal nothing, nor could it be related in any way to his hagiography.

Walton did not conceive of Donne's character as a development to be explained by the past, by circumstances of family life, social connection, and psychological growth; his idea was deductive, as if what Donne became late in life could suffice to suggest what his early life had been. In David Novarr's phrase, Walton "shaped the child in the image of the man." Novarr also has shown how Walton, shaping his material ever more deliberately in successive revisions after the English civil wars, was largely concerned with supporting the reestablishment of the Church of England,[2] a purpose silently approved or sometimes not perceived by following biographers.

There was no doubt a connection between this purpose and Walton's tendency not to stress Catholic associations or heritage as an active presence in Donne's life. But a biographer today needs more than abstract genealogy and the few remarks about Donne's formal schooling that satisfied Walton. What about the details of Donne's background, childhood, and adolescence, about the maturing of his personality in the context of family and social relationships? Walton provided little to satisfy our curiosity, nor did Donne say much himself. The coherent recollections we desire have long since decomposed, leaving the scattered, bare bones of institutional records and documents.

What Walton does tell us about Donne's life has always seemed somehow opaque and paradoxical. The oppressed pupil of aspiring Catholic martyrs, cast briefly into prison for his romantic elopement, languished in opprobrium for more than a decade, yet emerged to gain celebrity in middle age as one of the greatest of English preachers. This story reads, as do many of Donne's poems, like a series of riddles or like a mystery. Given Walton's view of Donne's life, he was apt to follow Donne's own lead in seeking far-fetched comparisons or ingenious theories. Thus Walton compares Donne to Augustine

---

2. David Novarr, *The Making of Walton's "Lives"* (Ithaca, NY: Cornell University Press, 1958), x, 92–94, and 485.

because after a libertine youth Donne, like Augustine, found grace in the Church.

Regarding Donne's youth, throughout the *Life* Walton seems pained at having to rehearse an account of what was for him a rather distasteful levity in Donne's early character, as though the young Donne were someone he preferred not to know much about. But this rakish image, certainly not Walton's invention, and probably not an exaggeration, nonetheless is only a partial explanation of Donne's youth. It has come to serve in Donne's biography as a concealment of other things, of traits and experiences that Walton would not or could not acknowledge sympathetically and that Donne himself sought to cast in shadow. It was Donne himself who late in life first made the simplistic distinction between mad "Jack Donne" and "Dr. Donne," the Dean of St. Paul's.[3] This bizarre contrast is at the core of what Walton wrote, in effect enabling Donne posthumously to veil his life-long involvement in the painful religious dilemma forced on him and others of his generation by the public events of their time.

Walton's treatment of Donne's Catholicism is nearly as laconic as was Donne's own. He does note that Donne was born of a Catholic mother descended from the families of More and Rastell. But he does not mention the Catholic religion of Donne's father. The boy's early tutors were instructed by his mother, says Walton, "to instil into him particular Principles of the *Roman Church*." His Catholic connections advised him not to take a degree at Oxford, in order to avoid having to swear the oath requiring graduates to acknowledge Queen Elizabeth's supremacy over the Church of England. These influences, says Walton, "had almost obliged him to their faith." Nevertheless, by the age of eighteen, Donne was somehow still his own man and had "betrothed himself to no Religion that might give him any other denomination than *a Christian*." At nineteen, resolved to choose a religion he could adhere to, he reviewed "the body of Divinity as it was then controverted betwixt the *Reformed* and the *Roman Church*." By the time he was twenty, "indeed, truth had too much light about her to be hid from so sharp an Inquirer; and, he had too much ingenuity [i.e., ingenuousness] not to acknowledge he had found her." In short, according to Walton, Donne had never really been a Catholic, and the influence of Catholicism disappeared from his life for good during his twentieth year. In relating the last thirty-nine years of Donne's life, Walton makes no further mention of what he took to be a dead issue. In Walton's view, Donne had been a

---

3. Donne to Sir Robert Ker, n.d.; John Donne, *Letters to Severall Persons of Honour* (1651), ed. M. Thomas Hester (Delmar: Scholars' Facsimiles & Reprints, 1977), 22.

Protestant from the age of twenty, though something of a libertine until a few years before his ordination. For Walton, the influence of Catholicism on Donne could be seen primarily in those of his writings that were "facetiously Compos'd," and most of these were written "before the twentieth year of his age,"[4] a theory so wildly inaccurate as to reveal less about Donne than it does about Walton himself.

Like most Englishmen born after the defeat of the Spanish Armada, Walton distrusted Catholics and Catholicism. When he was twelve, the exposure and official denunciation of the Gunpowder Plot left even Catholics doubtful of the righteousness of their own cause and demonstrated their treasonous intent in the opinion of other Englishmen. Walton and his generation never experienced anything like the spiritual dilemma that had faced three preceding generations, born into a still largely Catholic England. Walton's attitude toward their experience is reflected in his treatment of Donne's mother, whom he may have known before her death in 1631 and concerning whom Walton remarks that, "having sucked in the Religion of the *Roman Church* with her Mothers Milk, [she] spent her Estate in forraign Countreys, to enjoy a liberty in it."[5] If he does appear to appreciate the painful incongruity of religious exile, he cannot forbear expressing a pity that verges on disdain.

Although Walton compares Donne to St. Augustine more than once, he never extends the simile to mention the steadfast hope of St. Monica. He rather blames Donne's mother for her son's Catholic education, for his schooling in a woman's religion. He never even alludes to her second husband, Court physician John Syminges, important in Donne's life between the ages of four and seventeen. The way Walton speaks of Donne's coolly evaluating and choosing a religion suggests again that he was ignorant of, and insensitive to, the danger of this dilemma for a young man of Donne's time. There is something faintly condescending and almost modern about Walton's phrasing—"the body of Divinity, as it was then controverted"—expressing, perhaps, some revulsion toward so archaic and pointless a controversy. This relative insensitivity to the pain and difficulty of being Catholic is more characteristic of Walton's England than of the England of Donne's early years. To understand the experience

4. Walton, *Lives*, 24, 25, and 61. Walton's view that Donne discarded Catholicism was surely based in part on Donne's cryptic recollection that he had "used no inordinate hast, nor precipitation in binding my conscience to any locall Religion" (*Pseudo-Martyr* [London: Walter Burre, 1610], "A Preface to the Priestes, and Iesuits, and to their Disciples in this Kingdome"). As Gosse pointed out, Donne's words here, while evidencing a religious dilemma, are "scarcely in accord with Walton's view" that a conversion to Protestantism took place in Donne's twentieth year (*Gosse, Life and Letters*, I, 26).
5. Walton, *Lives*, 71. Elizabeth Heywood Donne Syminges Rainsford went into exile at Antwerp for several years beginning in 1595.

Donne endured in his formation, we need to look back at the boy
and his family through eyes other than Walton's, hardened as they
were by immediate shocks to religious life in the seventeenth cen-
tury.

Donne introduced himself to the reading public in 1610 with the
dangerous reflection that,

> I have beene ever kept awake in a meditation of Martyrdome,
> by being derived from such a stocke and race, as, I beleeve, no
> family, (which is not of farre larger extent, and greater branches,)
> hath endured and suffered more in their persons and fortunes,
> for obeying the Teachers of Romane Doctrine.[6]

This is one of only a few isolated references by Donne to the suffer-
ings of English Catholics, all understandably guarded or indirect.
Nevertheless, Donne's main point (still a delicate one at the time) is
that the persecution of his family for their religion has been the
central theme of his life. He alludes to family, and to lineage, in
terms that, for his contemporaries, had a meaning much deeper than
we would normally give them today. Often quoting this passage,
Donne's biographers have slighted it as hyperbole, not fully recog-
nizing its implications.

Among the least recognized of these has been Donne's secondary
point, his allusion to families "of farre larger extent, and greater
branches"—i.e., to families of the ancient Catholic nobility. By the
end of Queen Elizabeth's reign, such noble houses as Howard, Percy,
and Stanley had suffered enormous losses, both of lives and posses-
sions, as a consequence of the change of religions in England.[7]
Donne's awareness of this fact and its personal importance to him
have gone virtually unnoticed; but the desolation of the Catholic
peerage became part of his formative experience and deeply influ-
enced him throughout his life.

6. *Pseudo-Martyr*, "An Advertisement to the Reader." *Pseudo-Martyr* was Donne's first pub-
lication in the full sense of the word. (Though a few lines from a handful of Donne's
poems had been published by others before 1610, these were not primarily or explicitly
publications by Donne himself; see Ernest W. Sullivan, II, *The Influence of John Donne:
His Uncollected Seventeenth-Century Printed Verse* [Columbia: University of Missouri
Press, 1993], 55–58.) Anthony Raspa observes, "For writing such a book, Donne has been
described by many modern critics as ambitious. *Pseudo-Martyr*, they say, was the tactic of
a climber, of an awkward would-be courtier grovelling for James' favor. Rather, *Pseudo-
Martyr* was the first public statement of a literary figure who never knew how to meet the
world—this, in spite of the fact that he had been sufficiently well-born to meet it on its
own courtier's terms. *Pseudo-Martyr* was not motivated by courtly ambitions, but by exactly
the opposite" ("Time, History and Typology in John Donne's *Pseudo-Martyr*," *Renaissance
and Reformation* 11 [1987]: 183).
7. From the house of Howard had come, since 1067, the Earls of Arundel; from the houses
of Percy and Stanley, since 1139, the Earls of Northumberland and of Derby. These were
the three most ancient earldoms of the realm. The political destruction of these Catholic
families by the Elizabethan regime forms one panel in the broad picture drawn by
Lawrence Stone in *The Crisis of the Aristocracy, 1558–1641* (Oxford: Clarendon Press,
1979); see especially chapter 5, "Power," 199–270.

Donne's alignment of his family's experience with the experience of the ancient Catholic nobility repeats, after nearly two decades, something of the same message we saw in his 1591 portrait. Common to both expressions is his sense of sharing in a tradition of aristocratic selfhood, a tradition ultimately deriving, through the Middle Ages, from the stoic attitudes of the defeated, ancient Roman aristocracy. In this connection the motto of Donne's portrait, *Antes muerto que mudado*, can be understood as a version of the Senecan heraldic motto, *Non moveri*, and thus as part of Renaissance aristocracy's absorption of Roman stoicism in order to fortify itself against unusually dangerous and unstable times. Donne's family in particular had known danger and instability and was bound to identify it with the advent in Tudor England of "a new strain of imperial ambitiousness."[8]

One fundamental problem for biographers and critics of Donne has been to understand the politics of Donne's Catholic humanist heritage in the context of his descent from Sir Thomas More and the Elizabethan persecution of Catholics. A merely superficial approach to the problem has grown from uncritical acceptance of essentially apologetic historiographical traditions stretching back to the Reformation period. In this connection, Donne scholars stand to benefit greatly from recent revaluations of "the old religion."[9] A second, related problem centers on Donne's association with members of ancient noble families, traditionally Catholic, who were suffering progressive degradation at the hands of Tudor politicians. This important context is a key to much that has remained mysterious in Donne's life, although Donne's biographers have made almost no reference to it.

R. C. Bald, the "standard" biographer, was inspired by the plan of Donne's life Walton conceived in the seventeenth century. Bald not

8. Gordon Braden, *Renaissance Tragedy and the Senecan Tradition: Anger's Privilege* (New Haven: Yale University Press, 1985), 76 and 107. On various attitudes toward Stoicism in Donne's other writings, see John Klause, "Hope's Gambit: The Jesuitical, Protestant, Skeptical Origins of Donne's Heroic Ideal," *Studies in Philology* 91 (1994): 183.
9. E.g., by John Bossy in "The Character of Elizabethan Catholicism," *Past and Present* 21 (April 1962): 39–58, and in *The English Catholic Community, 1570–1850* (London: Darton, Longman & Todd, 1975). See also Christopher Haigh, *Reformation and Resistance in Tudor Lancashire* (Cambridge: Cambridge University Press, 1975); and Peter Holmes, *Resistance and Compromise* (Cambridge: Cambridge University Press, 1982). Also valuable, if sometimes overlooked in this connection, is the useful calculus of religion and politics in sixteenth-century England offered by Francis Edwards, *The Marvellous Chance* (London: Rupert Hart-Davis, 1968), 15–18, evincing an impartiality uncommon among historians less aware than Edwards of their own historiographical presumptions. Through such work a fertile dialectic of continuity and separation has been introduced into our understanding of the complex developments attending the Elizabethan Establishment of the Church of England, the missions of Jesuits and seminaries, and the ongoing persecution of Catholics.

only asserted his reliance on Walton's plan, he several times expressed the opinion that his own work could do little to change general views of Donne's life Walton had established. Although it is possible today "to learn more about Donne's life than Walton knew," Bald saw his own work as supplementary: "unquestionably [Walton] has traced the main outlines of Donne's life; even if the pattern has since had to be modified here and there, the essential impression remains."[1] Venturing merely to fill out a pattern, Bald nevertheless attached to Walton's *Life* so large a body of additional fact as to dwarf the original and, moreover, to strain the credibility of its main lines.

The product of Bald's work has little in common with Walton's consistent hagiography. *John Donne: a Life* eschews Walton's unifying principle, his vision of the hand of God blessing Donne with Protestantism. In place of Protestantism, Bald offers the sobering struggle for advancement as a guiding principle of Donne's life. This modification restates Walton's partial view of Donne's youth, while making his middle and later years seem but a desperate and successful groping toward affluence and security in the assured righteousness of the hierarchy of the Church of England. Whatever chain of evidence has led to this general picture of these years, it is an interpretation that does not square with the essentials of Donne's character as revealed by his life and writings to the very last. Donne simply was not a variety of place seeker, despite Bald's reluctant conclusion.[2]

---

1. Bald, *John Donne: a Life*, 1 and 13. "Bald argued that the death of Donne's brother in prison and his kinship with two Jesuit uncles were trivial facts, which deserved less attention from a biographer than Donne's signature as a witness to somebody's will" (Anthony Low, "John Carey and John Donne," *John Donne Journal* 2 [1983]: 115).
2. *John Donne: a Life* was praised by Helen Gardner (in "All the Facts," *New Statesman* 79 [1970]: 370) as "a book that will never be superseded." Gardner's assurance was only a measure of how thoroughly her own textual work and that of her fellow Oxford editors tended to rely on and corroborate both Bald's work and, more fundamentally, Walton's. Gardner continued: "It is impossible to praise too highly the industry which has searched all conceivable record sources, the skill with which the evidence is marshalled, the density of reference, the judgement with which at crucial points conflicting evidence is weighed, and the modesty of conjecture where conjecture is required" (ibid.).

    This is high encomium, largely undeserved. Bald's industry may have been praiseworthy, but it is hyperbole to speak of any historian's having "searched all conceivable record sources," or to doubt, as Gardner does, whether "it is possible that some scraps of new information may turn up" (ibid.). As for Bald's skill and judgment in handling evidence, if a picture leaves essentials out of place or inexplicable, then judgment and/or skill have been wanting. Finally, what is meant by "modesty of conjecture where conjecture is required," and can this be a virtue in a historian?

    Every interpretation of historical events must be conjecture put forward for trial to be rejected if not true. Thus in the writing of history, conjecture is required throughout, not merely in listing facts but in asserting something about their significance. A "modesty of conjecture" would presumably be one that asserted little about the significance of a body of information, or asserted only what it was not risky to assert because it seemed to have adequate explanatory power. A conjecture of this sort can be made to seem plausible by virtue of the sheer bulk of facts with which it is shown to be compatible ("density of reference"). However, this illusion can be dispelled by recognizing that enough facts to confirm a conjecture can usually be found. The crucial question about any conjecture's

Significantly, Bald's work follows Walton in leaving unexplained what has no doubt been the most pregnant of all puzzles confronting Donne's biographer: where was Donne and what happened to him between the ages of twelve and eighteen? Bald found no facts about these crucial, formative years in Donne's development, nor did he stress them as the major problem they are. Consequently, central hypotheses in Donne studies have continued to lack any solid basis in fact, resting instead on unfounded assumptions. These assumptions are only accentuated in John Carey's *John Donne: Life, Mind & Art*, where the author tries to fit what he calls "the basic biographical facts (in so far as they're known)" into his general concept that "apostasy" and "ambition" are the twisted principles informing Donne's life and writings. A telling point here is that Carey neither thinks "all the facts" are known, nor is he primarily concerned to add much new knowledge of them. Though he makes Donne's apostasy and ambition his central themes, Carey offers no new biographical evidence to substantiate these supposed obsessions or their origins in Donne's early experience. In this sense, for all his attempted departure from the traditional interpretation, as a biographer Carey takes us little beyond Bald.[3]

Our lack of information about Donne's early years has led, in biography, to a "synecdochical understanding" like the one John R. Roberts has identified in criticism of the poetry: "we have, in other words, substituted the part for the whole and then proceeded as if the part were, in fact, the whole. As a result, literary historians, critics, and teachers continue to repeat generalizations about Donne's poetry that although incomplete, partial, misleading, and sometimes incorrect, have about them almost the strength of established fact and the sacredness of a hallowed tradition."[4] For example, not truly utterances of a would-be insider, Donne's poems are misinterpreted as appeals for patronage or expressions of the desperate ambition common to a coterie of place seekers at Court. The poems' witty disdain for success at Court is explained away as if it were mere posturing.[5] But the fact remains that, despite his early Catholicism, Donne seems already to have experienced a certain familiarity with the Court by the 1590s. The value his poetry places on being "out"

---

value (e.g., about any conjecture in the present book) is not whether many facts confirm it, but whether any fact refutes it.

3. John Carey, *John Donne: Life, Mind & Art* (New York: Oxford University Press, 1981), especially chapters 1 and 3.

4. John R. Roberts, "John Donne's Poetry: An Assessment of Modern Criticism," *John Donne Journal* 1 (1982): 62–63.

5. Arthur Marotti, *John Donne, Coterie Poet* (Madison: University of Wisconsin Press, 1986) depends throughout on the biographical assumptions of Bald and Carey. Marotti marshals virtually the whole of Donne's poetry as evidence of "desperate ambition" but can give no factual explanation of how this motive came to dominate in the formation of Donne's personality.

was in this case not just envious attitudinizing. On the contrary, it had a subversive appeal specifically intended for readers delighted to share Donne's "inside" commentary on the society of the Elizabethan and Jacobean Court, as seen from the point of view of a descendant of Sir Thomas More.

*   *   *

JOHN CAREY

[Donne's Apostasy]†

The first thing to remember about Donne is that he was a Catholic; the second, that he betrayed his Faith. He was born in 1572. His father was a successful London businessman who rose to be one of the wardens of the Ironmongers' Company.[1] He died when Donne was four, and his widow remarried within six months, taking as her second husband Dr. John Syminges, a wealthy Catholic medical practitioner and President of the Royal College of Physicians.[2] Donne's mother was not only, like his father, a Catholic, but a member of one of the most celebrated Catholic families in the land. She was the youngest daughter of the poet and playwright John Heywood; and Heywood's wife—Donne's grandmother—was Joan Rastell, the niece of Sir Thomas More. So on his mother's side Donne was descended from the More circle, the foremost group of intellectuals in early sixteenth-century England, internationally famous, and devout Catholics. Donne was profoundly aware of this ancestry. When he mentions Sir Thomas More and his 'firmnesse to the integrity of the Romane faith,'[3] it is with evident pride.

The disadvantages of being a Catholic in Elizabethan England are difficult to generalize about. On the one hand, as the careers of Donne's father and stepfather suggest, it was possible, if you were sufficiently circumspect or well-connected, to prosper. On the other hand, you might end up having your intestines torn out. Developments in international politics could make your situation suddenly more dangerous, without your taking any step in the matter. You

† From *John Donne: Life, Mind, and Art* (New York: Oxford UP, 1981), pp. 15–31. Copyright © 1981 by John Carey. Reprinted by permission of Faber and Faber Ltd.
1. R. C. Bald, *John Donne: A Life* (Oxford, 1970), 26–34.
2. Baird D. Whitlock, 'The Heredity and Childhood of John Donne', *N&Q* 6 (1959), 257–62, 348–53.
3. John Donne, *Pseudo-martyr. Wherein out of certaine Propositions and Gradations, This Conclusion is evicted. That those which are of the Romane Religion in this Kingdome, may and ought to take the Oath of Allegeance* (1610), 108.

could not, if you remained faithful to your religion, hope to play any part in public life, and you were debarred from taking a university degree by the requirement that graduates should subscribe to the Thirty-nine Articles.

The financial incentives to join the Church of England were strong. By a statute of 1585, Catholics who refused to attend Anglican services were liable to a fine of £20 a month. An average parish schoolmaster's salary at the time, it's worth reminding ourselves, was £20 a year.[4] Offenders who found themselves unable to pay were to have all their goods and two-thirds of their land confiscated. This law, Catholics complained, was so strictly enforced that small farmers and husbandmen who possessed only one cow for the sustenance of themselves and their children had it taken from them, and where there was no livestock to appropriate recusant houses were stripped of bed linen, blankets, provisions and window glass. Cecil, it was rumoured, had boasted that he would reduce the Catholics to such destitution that, like swine, they'd be glad to find a husk to feed on.[5]

The anti-Catholic legislation also made it high treason for any Jesuit or seminary priest to be within the Queen's dominions, and felony for any lay person to relieve or receive him. In effect, this meant that it was felony to practise the Catholic religion, because it was necessary to receive a priest in order to hear mass or make confession. Spies, some of them renegade priests and Catholics, gave the authorities advance warning about where masses were to be celebrated. Catholic households were commonly raided, and in the search for priests' hiding places walls were knocked down, rooms ransacked and floors torn up. The householder had not only to defray the cost of this damage, but also to pay the searchers for their trouble. In their private life, Catholics were inevitably a prey to blackmail and intimidation. They could not claim redress for personal injuries, or retrieve money owed to them. If they attempted to, they found themselves threatened with exposure.

Among the victims of this persecution scares spread rapidly. A report would go round that the Queen's Council had passed a decree for the massacre of all Catholics on a certain night, whereupon terrified families would abandon their homes and pass the night in the fields. Others would hire boats and drift up and down the river. These alarms first occurred in 1585, and persisted until the defeat of the Armada, so they were a feature of Donne's early adolescence.

4. Charles Hoole, *A New Discovery of the Old Art of Teaching Schoole*, ed. E. T. Campagnac (1913), 213.
5. For my account of the persecution of Catholics as seen by Catholics, see Robert Southwell, *An Humble Supplication to her Maiestie*, ed. R. C. Bald (Cambridge, 1953); *John Gerard: The Autobiography of an Elizabethan*, trans. P. Caraman, with an Introduction by Graham Greene (2nd edn., 1956); and *William Weston: The Autobiography of an Elizabethan*, trans. P. Caraman, with a Foreword by Evelyn Waugh (1955).

At the same time, new prisons were established at Wisbech, Ely and Reading, and filled with Catholics. A separate prison for women recusants was opened at Hull. In the common prisons, Catholic prisoners were victimized. The felons incarcerated with them were encouraged to abuse them, and deprive them of their share of alms and bread. John Gerard, the English Jesuit, reports that when his manservant was captured and shut up in Bridewell he was given barely sufficient food to keep body and soul together. His cell was tiny, bedless, and crawling with vermin, so that he had to sleep perched on the window ledge. The gaolers left his excrement in the cell in an uncovered pail, and the stink was suffocating. In these conditions he waited to be called out and examined under torture. The poet and martyr Robert Southwell also testifies to the systematic starvation of Catholic prisoners: 'some for famine have licked the very moisture of the walls.'

Some of the tortures employed on Catholic suspects were so vile that Southwell cannot bring himself to speak of them, but the ones he does describe are fearful enough. Prisoners were deprived of sleep, until they lost the use of their reason; they were disjointed on the rack; they were rolled up into balls by machinery 'and soe Crushed, that the bloud sprowted out at divers parts of their bodies.' As the dislocations caused by the rack occasioned some revulsion among the public, Topcliffe, Elizabeth's chief torturer, introduced the refinement known as the manacles. These were iron gauntlets, fitted high up on a pillar. The prisoner who was to be interrogated had his wrists inserted into them, and was left hanging, sometimes for several hours. Gerard, who underwent this torture, includes an account of the procedure in his autobiography, which conveys how oddly decorous the arrangements were. 'We went to the torture room in a kind of solemn procession,' he recalls, 'the attendants walking ahead with lighted candles.' The commission of five who were to question him included Francis Bacon. When Gerard had been suspended from the pillar,

> a gripping pain came over me. It was worst in my chest and belly, my hands and arms. All the blood in my body seemed to rush up into my arms and hands and I thought that blood was oozing out from the ends of my fingers and the pores of my skin. . . . The pain was so intense that I thought I could not possibly endure it.

Gerard endured it, in fact, for five hours, during which period he fainted eight or nine times, and each time was supported until he recovered, and then left to hang again. Since he persistently refused to betray his fellow Catholics, the commissioners grew restless. 'Then hang there until you rot off the pillar,' shouted William Wade, the diplomatist, later knighted by James I. Gerard was suspended the following day also, but after that they realized he wouldn't talk, and gave up. His arms were so swollen he could not get his clothes on, and it was three weeks before he could hold a knife.

The number of Catholics actually executed was, by the standards of twentieth-century atrocities, quite small. Between the passing of the new anti-Catholic legislation in 1585 and the end of Elizabeth's reign, a hundred priests and fifty-three lay persons, including two women, were put to death. The method used to dispatch the victims amounted, however, in many cases to makeshift vivisection, so it atoned in terms of spectator interest for its relative rarity. When the Babington Plot, which had been known about and fomented almost from the first by government agents, was 'discovered' in 1586, instructions, to which the Queen was a party, were given to the hangman that 'for more terror' the young men responsible should be disembowelled alive. This operation apparently upset some of the onlookers, so the government published an official statement saying that the Queen was disgusted too, and had given orders for a more merciful slaughtering of the second batch of conspirators.[6]

It's clear, though, from eye-witness accounts, that vivisection continued to be used as a remedy against Catholics. The fate of John Rigby, killed in 1600 under the Act of Persuasions, which made it high treason to embrace the Roman religion, exemplifies this.[7] After he had been hanged, Rigby was cut down so quickly that he stood upright 'like a man a little amazed' till the executioners threw him to the ground. He was heard to pronounce distinctly, 'God forgive you. Jesus receive my soul,' whereupon a bystander put his foot on his throat to prevent him speaking any more. Other bystanders held his arms and legs while an executioner cut off his genitals and took out his bowels. When he reached up inside Rigby to extract his heart, his victim was 'yet so strong that he thrust the men from him who held his arms.'

Confronted with judicial proceedings of this kind, English Catholics felt not only pity and terror, but isolation. Their fellow countrymen were not simply indifferent, they rejoiced at the Catholics' discomfiture. 'In the midst of our calamities,' the English Jesuit William Weston recalls, writing of the Babington executions, 'the bells were rung throughout the city, sermons and festivals held, fireworks set off, bonfires lit in the public street.' The beleaguered minority could be excused for feeling that they were among not human beings but some species of jubilant demon.

6. A. G. Smith, *The Babington Plot* (1936), 212, 239–42.
7. Richard Challoner, *Memoirs of Missionary Priests*, ed. J. H. Pollen, S. J. (1924), 224–5 and *passim*.

Some readers may ask what all this has to do with Donne's poetry, but I imagine they will be few. It would be as reasonable to demand what the Nazi persecution of the Jews had to do with a young Jewish writer in Germany in the 1930s. Donne was born into a terror, and formed by it. It determined, among other things, his reading matter, which wasn't that of an Englishman but of a European intellectual. He remained aloof from the flood of patriotic English literature which was being loosed on the market in the 1590s. On the other hand, he was one of the few Englishmen of his day to know Dante in the original; he had read Rabelais; and when a correspondent asked him about Aretino—a writer of scandalous repute, scarcely whispered about in conservative English circles—Donne was able to give him an expert run-down of Aretino's works.[8] As for the English people, Donne's account of them in his earliest poems, the *Satires* and *Elegies*, quivers with disgust. They are coarse-grained, narrow-minded materialists: smug burghers with stinking feet and breath and swollen bellies, who stuff themselves with rich foodstuffs and then snore their evenings away crammed into armchairs. Donne, in the *Elegies*, defiantly cheats and cuckolds these lumbering freaks.[9] He survives on the fringes of society, a master of back stairs and side alleys, hard-up, outcast, victorious. It was a fantasy life which had magnetic appeal for a young man who could see that English society had closed its ranks against those of his Faith. Donne's fastidious withdrawal from the great mass of English people is reflected, too, in the style of his poems. Superior, difficult, designed for circulation among a few kindred spirits, they make no concessions to the barbarous clods and half-wits he had the ill luck to be living among. Most clearly of all, Donne's intractable egotism and his determination to succeed (factors which, as we shall see, mark the poems indelibly, and which some critics have censured) were a perfectly natural reaction to his early experience of injustice and victimization.

Because of his family connections, Donne was dragged into the very centre of the storm, and was forced to watch its bloody course with the closest attention. The victims were among the most gifted and intrepid of England's youth: young men like Edmund Campion, executed in 1581, who had been sent to the Catholic colleges abroad for their education, and who returned on their suicidal missions, joyfully embracing martyrdom to save their motherland from Antichrist. We know that Donne attended such executions. He records that he has seen Catholic bystanders, oblivious of their own danger,

8. E. M. Simpson, *A Study of the Prose Works of John Donne* (2nd edn., Oxford, 1948), 45, 316, 319.
9. John Donne, *The Elegies and The Songs and Sonnets*, edited with introduction and commentary by Helen Gardner (Oxford, 1965), 8–9.

praying to the priest's mangled body, in hope that the new martyr
would take their petitions to heaven with him.[1]

Possibly young Donne witnessed these sights while in the care of
the Catholic tutors whom his mother employed to educate him.
Their purpose would be to arouse in the boy a spirit of emulation,
for martyrdom was in his family and it might justifiably be hoped
that, with careful indoctrination and God's grace, he would join the
glorious company himself. Nor were their efforts vain. The martyr's
crown shone before their pupil's eyes. He dwelt tirelessly upon it,
and came to regard it almost as part of his inheritance. 'I have beene
ever kept awake,' Donne tells us,

> in a meditation of Martyrdome, by being derived from such a
> stocke and race, as, I beleeve, no family, (which is not of farre
> larger extent, and greater branches,) hath endured and suffered
> more in their persons and fortunes, for obeying the Teachers of
> Romane Doctrine, then it hath done.

Donne's account of his family's sufferings is scarcely exaggerated.
John Heywood, his grandfather, fled abroad in 1564 rather than
accept Anglicanism. Ten years later, on Palm Sunday 1574, when
Donne was two, government searchers descended upon Lady
Brown's house in Cow Lane, near the Donne home, and made a
catch: Thomas Heywood, formerly a monk of St. Osyth's and Mrs.
Donne's uncle, was arrested. On 14 June he was put to death in the
usual obscene manner.[2] Two of Donne's uncles, Ellis and Jasper
Heywood, became Jesuits.[3] For Jasper it meant throwing up a prom-
ising career. He had been a page to the then Princess Elizabeth, and
a fellow of Merton and All Souls. Like other members of his family,
he venerated the memory of Sir Thomas More. Apparently Ellis and
Jasper possessed a precious relic, one of More's teeth, which mirac-
ulously parted in two so that each of them could have half. After
taking Jesuit vows in Rome, Jasper illegally re-entered England and
became head of the Jesuit mission. It seems likely that he took refuge
in the Donne house for a while. Certainly he made contact with his
sister, Donne's mother. So the children found themselves in the mid-
dle of a real-life adventure story. It was no game. In 1583 Jasper was
hunted down. He had been trying to escape across the Channel, but
his boat ran into a storm. He was rapidly put on trail with five other
priests, found guilty of high treason, and condemned to be hanged,
drawn and quartered. While Jasper was in the Tower, Donne's
mother visited and nursed him, secretly carrying messages between
him and his fellow Jesuit, William Weston, who had come over to

1. *Pseudo-Martyr*, 222.
2. Whitlock, op. cit., 257–62.
3. On Ellis and Jasper Heywood, see Bald, 25–26 and 39–45.

carry on the fight. Eventually Weston took the immense risk of going into the Tower with her on one of her visits, so that he could consult with the prisoner. Donne, though only twelve, was selected to play a part in this escapade, and taken along too. Perhaps Mrs. Donne calculated that having a boy there would allay the warders' suspicions. The disguised Weston might even be passed off as the lad's father. Anyway, it seems clear that Donne went, because he later recalls being present at 'a Consultation of Jesuites in the Tower, in the late Queenes time,'[4] and no other plausible occasion for this is known.[5]

What must he have felt? Weston, in his autobiography, remembers his own trepidation 'as I saw the vast battlements, and was led by the warder past the gates with the iron fastenings, which were closed behind me.' To a twelve-year-old the gloomy precincts would have been even more daunting. He was entering the very lair of the great beast. No wonder the sense of perilous trespass, and the memory of a 'grim eight-foot-high iron-bound' man, striding like a colossus in front of a gate, lingered so vividly when Donne came to write his youthful love poems.[6] And was there, mingled with his fear, resentment? Did the boy grudge the hold which these stern, devoted men— his uncle and the furtive stranger—had over his mother's love and allegiance: a hold so strong that she was prepared, it seemed, to lay down her life for them? Perhaps: for he was later to let loose his rancour against the Jesuits with a pertinacity that seems to reflect a personal grudge. He could not forgive them for their intransigence. In the end he came to feel that they alone were to blame for all the slaughter and suffering. For they would not allow English Catholics to compromise. They demanded total loyalty to the Faith, and total opposition to the English crown; and so they attracted to themselves the hatred which unswerving probity always earns.

To young Donne, compromise must have seemed increasingly the most attractive course. His tutors were 'men of a suppressed and afflicted Religion, accustomed to the despite of death, and hungry of imagin'd Martyrdome;'[7] but they did not find him so hungry. He was not sent abroad to be educated at one of the Catholic colleges, but went up, instead, with his brother Henry, to Hart Hall, Oxford, a favourite resort of Catholics because it lacked a chapel, and so made avoidance of public worship easier.

Terrible stories were circulated, by priests and Jesuits, about what happened to Catholics who attended Anglican services to evade the

4. *Pseudo-Martyr*, 46.
5. See, however, Southwell, *Humble Supplication* (see n. 5 above p. 210), 70–80.
6. *Elegies*, 8.
7. John Donne, *Biathanatos. A declaration of that paradoxe, or thesis, that Self-homicide is not so Naturally Sinne, that it may never be otherwise* (1648), 17.

fines for recusancy. A certain Francis Wodehouse of Breccles in Nor-
folk, it was related, had found, as soon as he entered the polluted
sanctuary, that his stomach became a raging furnace. He drank eight
gallons of beer to put out the fire, but only when a priest was brought
to shrive him did the heat abate. He never wavered again. Donne
would certainly know of such cases, for one had occurred at his own
college shortly before he arrived there. An undergraduate called
Francis Marsh had succumbed to the temptation to enter an Angli-
can church, but immediately afterwards remorse unhinged his rea-
son. He stripped himself naked, made his way out of college, and
began to run through Oxford, heading for the market square. He was
apprehended, forcibly restrained and put to bed, and friends tried to
pacify him. But he would not be comforted, and within two days he
was dead. He 'wasted away,' a contemporary reported, 'in sheer agony
of mind.'[8] Such examples would keep before Donne the supernatural
risks incurred by backsliders.

When John and Henry Donne matriculated they gave their ages
as eleven and ten respectively. Actually they were a year older than
this, but the law required students, on reaching the age of sixteen,
to subscribe to the Thirty-nine Articles. For a Catholic, that was out
of the question, so to evade the regulations Catholics frequently
went up to university very young, or lied about their ages—or both,
as the Donne boys did.

We now come to the most obscure period of Donne's life. He matric-
ulated at Oxford in October 1584, and he was admitted to Lincoln's
Inn from Thavies Inn, where he would have had to spend at least a
year in preliminary study, in May 1592. Nothing certain can be said
about his movements between those two dates. We don't know, in
the first place, how long he stayed at Oxford. As a Catholic he was
of course debarred from proceeding to a degree, since he could not
take the required Oath of Supremacy. Walton, his first biographer,
who knew him only in later life and so may be unreliable about the
young Donne, says that he transferred from Oxford to Cambridge in
'about' his fourteenth year, and that he moved from there to London
and was admitted to Lincoln's Inn in 'about' his seventeenth. There
are no records of Donne having been at Cambridge, but that doesn't
disprove Walton's statement, since Cambridge records are incom-
plete. Walton has clearly got his dates wrong, for according to his
timetable Donne entered Lincoln's Inn in 1588 or 1589 (his sev-
enteenth year), whereas documentary evidence shows that 1592 is
the correct date. But otherwise Walton may be quite reliable: Donne

8. *Weston: Autobiography* (see n. 5 above, p. 210), 148–50, 178–84.

may have spent his teens studying at Oxford and Cambridge, and
then gone immediately to the Inns of Court.

However, Walton also says that Donne travelled for 'some years' *travels*
in his youth, first in Italy, then in Spain, studying the cultures and
learning the languages of those countries.[9] From Walton's account
it appears that Donne's travels began in 1597. That can't be so,
because in 1597 or early 1598 he started work in London. Still, he
may have travelled earlier, and there's some evidence which suggests
that he did. For one thing, he seems to have had a reputation among
his contemporaries as a traveller. For another, Walton is remarkably
circumstantial about the travels. He says that Donne originally
intended to go on from Italy to the Holy Land, to see Jerusalem and
'the Sepulchre of our Saviour,' but that he was prevented from doing
this, so went to Spain instead. In later years, Walton adds, Donne
often mentioned 'with a deploration' that he had missed seeing the
Holy Places. That sounds authentic. Another bit of evidence that
may be relevant is <u>the earliest extant portrait of Donne</u>. It survives
in an engraving by William Marshall, bears the date 1591, and gives
the sitter's age as eighteen. Donne has long curly hair, an incipient
moustache, ear-rings in the shape of a cross and a fashionably wide-
shouldered doublet. He carries a sword, the ornate hilt of which he
is rather awkwardly holding up so as to get it into the picture. The
portrait is surmounted by a Spanish motto: 'Antes muerto que
mudado' (Sooner dead than changed).

Now it's true that the authorities at Oxford and Cambridge in the
late sixteenth century were complaining that the new-style under-
graduates looked more like courtiers than scholars and were sporting
fancy hose and rapiers.[1] If Donne's portrait is that of a youth just
down from Cambridge it merely bears out their grumbles. Naturally
enough, though, <u>the Spanish motto and the picture's obtrusively
experienced air have suggested to some that it depicts a young blood
recently returned from the Continental trave</u>ls Walton speaks of.
Quite possibly Donne's stay at Cambridge was shorter than Walton
believed, and the years spent abroad were 1589–91. Whatever the
exact period, the cultures Donne chose to submerge himself in were,
of course, Catholic. He escaped from persecution and insular bigotry
to visit the home of his Faith. From this angle, the portrait's defiant
motto, the crosses Donne wears, and the militant stance may take
on a further meaning. They may be a flamboyant assertion of his
loyalty to the old religion. The very language of the motto could be

9. On Donne's travels see Bald, 50–52; John Sparrow, 'The Date of Donne's Travels', in *A
Garland for John Donne, 1631–1931*, ed. T. J. Spencer (Cambridge, Mass., 1931), 123–
51; and Baird D. Whitlock, 'Donne's University Years', *English Studies* 43 (1962), 1–20.
1. See Mark H. Curtis, *Oxford and Cambridge in Transition, 1558–1642* (Oxford, 1959),
54–55.

seen as an arrogant gesture: rather, as William Empson has remarked, as if a modern American were to display a motto in Russian.[2] For to ordinary English people Spain was still the great enemy.

If this guess about the meaning of Donne's portrait is right, he was soon given a chance to see whether he would really rather be dead than changed. The Inns of Court, to which he and his brother Henry went, were not the mere lawyer factories of modern times. Contemporaries hailed them as 'the Third Universitie of England,' though even that gives the wrong impression, for there was practically no organized tuition. Really they operated like residential clubs or hotels, accommodating well-off young men who wished to acquire some metropolitan polish. At least three-quarters of the students were from the gentry or nobility. Most of them had no intention of taking up the law as a career. They despised the poorer students who were in search of a professional qualification, and adopted aggressively cultivated and aristocratic manners to distinguish themselves from these career lawyers. They were great dabblers in poetry, and they enjoyed organizing revels and masques, which gave them the feeling that they were in touch with court life.[3] Among these bright sparks, Donne was soon an acknowledged leader. Since so many scions of the ruling class were gathered in the Inns, they were a target for Catholic missionaries. The authorities viewed them with distrust. Lincoln's Inn Fields were notorious as a haunt of priests who, it was said, would blow a special trumpet to summon the Inns of Court men to mass. The Donne boys, Walton's account makes clear, were still being educated by Catholics. Their mother appointed tutors to instruct them in mathematics and 'other Liberal Sciences,' and also to instil into them 'particular Principles of the Romish Church.' To the Catholic proselytizers the brothers must have seemed useful contacts.

It was this aspect of life at the Inns which brought Donne up against the reality of his position. In May 1593 a young man called William Harrington was arrested in Henry Donne's rooms on suspicion of being a priest.[4] Henry, of course, was taken into custody too. When charged, Harrington denied that he was a priest, but poor Henry, faced with torture, betrayed him. He admitted that Harrington had shriven him while he was staying in his rooms. Harrington had, in fact, received his calling as a boy of fifteen in his father's house in Yorkshire, where he had met and been inspired by Edmund Campion. He had been educated in the Catholic colleges at Douai

2. William Empson, 'Donne and the Rhetorical Tradition', *Kenyon Review* 11 (1949), 585.
3. See Wilfrid R. Prest, *The Inns of Court under Elizabeth I and the Early Stuarts, 1590–1640* (Totowa, NJ, 1972).
4. Bald, 58; J. Morris, 'The Martyrdom of William Harrington', *The Month* 20 (1874), 411–23.

and Rheims, and had trained to become a Jesuit in the novitiate at
Tournay. Like other Catholic martyrs, he refused to be tried by a
jury because he did not wish to implicate more men than necessary
in the guilt of his destruction. He was condemned and, on 18 Feb-
ruary 1594, taken out to die. In the cart, with the rope round his
neck, he began to address his 'loving countrymen,' only to be inter-
rupted with insults by Topcliffe. But his courage did not fail, and he
denounced Topcliffe from the scaffold as a 'tyrant and blood-sucker.'
Like the Babington conspirators, he was disembowelled alive. Stow
records that, after he had been hanged and cut down, he 'struggled'
with the executioner who was about to use the knife on him.

Henry Donne, having knowingly harboured a priest, was guilty of
felony. But he did not live long enough to come to trial. Imprisoned
at first in the Clink, he was moved to Newgate, where the plague
was raging, and died within a few days. To Donne his death brought
not only grief but peril. Because of his kinship with Henry, his own
religious activities were now likely to attract scrutiny. Plainly the
time had come for serious thought. Besides, he was now twenty-one,
and had collected his share of his father's estate—a sum large
enough to make him independent of his mother and her Catholic
advisers. The dilemma that faced him was acute. If he remained true
to his Faith, his chances of preferment and success in the world
would be curtailed. Further, the efforts of the Jesuits, with whom
his family were inextricably connected, would make it difficult to
remain neutral. Pressure would be brought on him to assist in the
mission, and if he complied how long would it be before he shared
Henry's fate?

If, on the other hand, he became an apostate, the result confi-
dently predicted by the Church was so hideous that most people
have, since Donne's day, simply refused to believe in it any more.
But for his generation eternal damnation was no myth. They were
like men walking over a furnace, separated from it by a thin crust
which might at any moment part and drop them into the flames.
There would be, as Donne later put it, 'a sodain flash of horror'[5] as
you fell in, and then unending fire. Even Satan, Donne believed,
might decline to change places with a damned soul in these circum-
stances, for its torments would be fiercer than his.[6]

Many other young Catholics had, of course, been forced to cope
with the situation now confronting Donne, and had outlined the
alternatives with dismaying clarity. Either you remained loyal to God
and his truth, or you sent your forsworn soul 'headlong to hell fire.'
This choice was that 'dreadfull moment,' wrote Robert Southwell,

5. *The Sermons of John Donne*, edited with introductions and critical apparatus by George
R. Potter and Evelyn M. Simpson, 10 vols. (Berkeley and Los Angeles, 1953–62), ii, 239.
6. *Sermons* viii, 107.

'whereupon dependeth a whole eternity.'[7] Donne had probably met
Southwell and read his *Humble Supplication* in which this statement
is made. His words, fearful in their import, seem to have stuck in
Donne's mind, and years later, trying to startle his congregation
towards the end of a sermon, he echoes them, reminding his hearers
of the endless pain of the cursed soul, and of the instant of decision
that led to it: 'upon this minute dependeth that eternity.'

Perhaps we are merely fancying that echo. But there can be no
mistake about the agony of Donne's choice. And he chose hell. That
is to say, he deserted the Catholic God, and there are still Catholics,
four centuries later, who believe that in doing so he damned himself.
He was an apostate, their spokesman declares, of a 'quite specially
shameless' kind. 'The near kinsman of martyrs, whom he reviled for
hire.' In full knowledge, he committed a mortal sin against the Faith,
and though, we are told, it may be hoped that the prayers of his
martyred relations won for him the grace of death-bed contrition, 'so
far as we know, he died an apostate and made no sign.'[8] If we are
inclined to dismiss this sort of thing as primitive superstition we shall
be far from understanding how it seemed to Donne's family and
circle, and how, in his moods of despair, it must have seemed to
Donne himself.

His apostasy was not rash or sudden. The points at issue between
the Catholic and the reformed churches had been copiously docu-
mented by rival divines, and it is typical of Donne's bookishness that
he set about reading his way through the whole controversy. Mean-
while he kept, he says, an open mind about religion, and this 'bred
some Scandall,' for acquaintances came to suspect that he had no
religion at all. Still, he persisted, searching for God among the wran-
gling theologians, and refrained from coming to any decision until
he had 'survayed and digested the whole body of Divinity, contro-
verted betweene ours and the Romane Church.' Walton records that,
among Donne's papers at his death, there were found excerpts from
1,400 authors, 'most of them abridged and analysed with his own
hand.'

The poetic evidence of this crisis is Satire III—the great, crucial
poem of Donne's early manhood.[9] For most of its length it is not a
satire at all, but a self-lacerating record of that moment which comes
in the lives of almost all thinking people, when the beliefs of youth,
unquestioningly assimilated and bound up with our closest personal
attachments, come into conflict with the scepticism of the mature

---

7. Southwell, *Humble Supplication* (see n. 5 above p. 210), 27; and *Sermons* vii, 368.
8. H. E. G. Rope, 'The Real John Donne', *Irish Monthly* 82–3 (1954), 229–34.
9. John Donne, *The Satires, Epigrams and Verse Letters*, edited with an introduction and
   commentary by W. Milgate (Oxford, 1967), 10–14.

intellect. The poem begins in a flurry of anguish and derision, fighting back tears and choking down scornful laughter at the same instant:

> Kinde pitty chokes my spleene; brave scorn forbids
> Those teares to issue which swell my eye-lids;
> I must not laugh, nor weepe. . . .

Donne seeks relief in anger, denouncing the pastimes (sex, squabbling, adventure) on which young men like himself fritter away their energies. It is a characteristic outburst: he was always, as we shall see, dismayed by what he felt to be his lack of concentration and purpose. This initial tirade over, the poem settles down to the one subject which, Donne asseverates, it is worth settling down to: 'Seeke true religion.' So far as he can see, the normal reasons for espousing Catholicism or Protestantism are pathetically inadequate. People display a senseless preference for antiquity or novelty, or they accept what their godparents tell them, or they give up trying to choose and become apathetic. Instead of thinking things out for themselves, they submit to the authority either of the Pope or, if they are Protestants, of the English monarch:

> Foole and wretch, wilt thou let thy Soule be ty'd
> To mans lawes, by which she shall not be try'd
> At the last day? Will it then boot thee
> To say a Philip, or a Gregory,
> A Harry, or a Martin taught thee this?
> Is not this excuse for mere contraries,
> Equally strong? cannot both sides say so?

   No one before Donne had written English verse in which the pressures of passionate speech could be retained with such unhindered power. What agitates the lines, and the whole poem, is terror of hell. 'The foule Devill,' Donne warns, waits to snatch your soul. Your only chance of escape is hard thinking:

> On a huge hill,
> Cragged, and steep, Truth stands, and hee that will
> Reach her, about must, and about must goe;
> And what th'hills suddennes resists, winne so;
> Yet strive so, that before age, deaths twilight,
> Thy Soule rest, for none can worke in that night.
> To will, implyes delay, therefore now doe:
> Hard deeds, the bodies paines; hard knowledge too
> The mindes indeavours reach.

These famous lines, in which Donne transposes the traditional image of the hill of Truth into his own strenuously mimetic rhythms, have rightly attained classic status. But their rather awkward relationship with what Donne says elsewhere in the poem has not been remarked on. When reprimanding youthful irresponsibility at the start, he laid the emphasis on obedience to parental example. Those who ignored it, he cautioned, might find themselves worse off than the virtuous heathen who died before Christ's coming:

> and shall thy fathers spirit
> Meete blinde Philosophers in heaven, whose merit
> Of strict life may be'imputed faith, and heare
> Thee, whom hee taught so easie wayes and neare
> To follow, damn'd?

It is true that Donne is chiefly concerned in this part of the poem with moral conduct rather than the choice of true religion. Nevertheless, the lack of consistency between the assumption that there are 'easie wayes' to salvation available from one's father, and the insistence (in the hill of Truth passage) that salvation depends on 'hard knowledge' which the individual must win for himself, is glaring. Put side by side, the excerpts reveal the conflict between adult independence and fidelity to inherited beliefs, from which all the heat and impatience of the poem evolve.

The phrase 'thy fathers spirit' has a particular resonance because we associate it with the Ghost's speech in *Hamlet* ('I am thy father's spirit'), which it's hard to keep out of our heads. Perhaps we shouldn't try to, for an early version of *Hamlet* had been acted by 1589,[1] and Donne may be echoing it. Was he also thinking of his own father (dead, like old Hamlet, and speedily replaced by a stepfather)? As he had been barely four when his father died, his memory of him must have been hazy at best. But that would not necessarily make it less poignant. Much later in life he recalled, in a letter to his mother, 'the love and care of my most dear and provident Father, whose soul, I hope, hath long since enjoyed the sight of our blessed Saviour.'[2] During the spiritual crisis which produced the 'Holy Sonnets' the thought of his father's spirit watching his struggle certainly came into his mind:

> If faithfull soules be alike glorifi'd
> As Angels, then my fathers soule doth see,
> And adds this even to full felicitie,
> That valiantly I hels wide mouth o'rstride.[3]

Reading that, it's hard to believe that in Satire III, when Donne writes about religion and fathers, he does so without any thought of

1. Peter Alexander, *Shakespeare* (Oxford, 1964), 212–20.
2. Bald, 36.
3. John Donne, *The Divine Poems*, edited with introduction and commentary by Helen Gardner (Oxford, 1952), 14.

his own father, whose religion he is about to abandon. His father
had been a Catholic, and the 'easie wayes and near' he taught were
those of Rome. Since he assumes that his father is in heaven, and
since Satire III is adamant that there is only one true religion which
leads to heaven, the argument of the poem would appear to be over
before it has begun. There is no need to start labouring up Truth's
hill; Catholicism must be right. Viewed in this way, the contrast
between the part of the poem which springs from Donne's deeper
emotional loyalties, and the part directed by his brave new investi-
gative spirit, becomes sharper. In a prose account written some fif-
teen years later, Donne was to describe in cooler terms the strife of
heart against head that he had to undergo before he could break free
of Catholicism:

> I had a longer worke to doe then many other men; for I was first
> to blot out certaine impressions of the Romane religion, and to
> wrastle both against the examples and against the reasons, by
> which some hold was taken; and some anticipations early layde
> upon my conscience, both by Persons who by nature had a
> power and superiority over my will, and others who by their
> learning and good life, seem'd to me iustly to claime an interest
> for the guiding, and rectifying of mine understanding in these
> matters.[4]

Here, time has distanced Donne's apostasy, and he is able to sound
objective. He can now talk openly about the personal bonds which
he had to sunder, and about his consciousness of disappointing peo-
ple whose lives and minds he admired. In the Satire, written during
the crisis, these aspects were too painful to mention, and had to be
suppressed. Only in the oblique and uncertain allusion to his dead
father do we get any hint of the kind of inner attachment Donne
found himself struggling against. There is no other mention of family
or friends. The poem's effort is to make out that choosing a religion
is a purely intellectual business, as unemotional as mountaineering.
Donne needed to convince himself of this, in order to allay his per-
sonal turmoil. So the Satire is not an account of a crisis but an
operative part of one. It was, for its author, a necessary poem, and
its inconsistency and misrepresentation are part of its vigorous life.

Though Donne eventually came to accept Anglicanism, he could
never believe that he had found in the Church of England the one
true church outside which salvation was impossible. To have thought
that would have meant consigning his own family to damnation.
Instead he persuaded himself that the saved would come from all
churches: 'from the Eastern Church, and from the Western Church

4. *Pseudo-Martyr*, sigs. B2v–B3r.

too, from the Greek Church, and from the Latine too, and, (by Gods grace) from them that pray not in Latine too.'⁵ This is an opinion he often repeats in his letters and sermons; but the fierce young poet of Satire III would have found it intolerably tolerant. Indeed, it is one of his chosen targets:

> Graccus loves all as one, and thinkes that so
> As women do in divers countries goe
> In divers habits, yet are still one kinde,
> So doth, so is Religion; and this blind-
> nesse too much light breeds; but unmoved thou
> Of force must one, and forc'd but one allow;
> And the right.⁶

There speaks the Catholic. For though Donne, in this Satire, is busily shuffling off his Faith, the conviction that there is one 'right' church which alone certifies salvation is part of his Catholic upbringing. No church would ever mean so much to him again, and consequently when he abandoned Catholicism he lost an irreplaceable absolute. A Catholic could not have written, as Donne was to write when he had already been three years in Anglican orders, 'Show me deare Christ, thy spouse, so bright and cleare.'⁷ The important thing about this much-disputed sonnet, in which Donne asks that he may be granted a vision of the true church, is not that it implies any 'disloy-alty' to Anglicanism but that it reveals the lasting disorientation his apostasy entailed. A Catholic would not have needed to ask; he would have known.

Although Donne, as an Anglican, consciously gave up the belief in one 'right' church, part of him, preconditioned by his Catholic childhood, still clung to it. This leads to almost comic contradictions in his sermons, in which a saintly mildness towards those of other religious persuasions coexists with diatribes against Catholics and schismatics. We should beware, he tells his congregation, of imag-ining that no opinion but our own can be true on such matters as the sacrament. Yet within a few paragraphs he is denouncing tran-substantiation as a 'heretical Riddle' and 'Satans sophistry.'⁸ The proneness of Roman Catholics to homosexuality is another subject he is fond of touching upon when incensed.⁹ And though, as we have seen, he declares that the saved may come from all churches, he can be found describing religious toleration as 'a new spiritual disease.'¹

These muddles show us two elements in Donne's personality

5. *Sermons* vi, 163.
6. *Satires*, 12–13.
7. *Divine Poems*, 15 and 121–7.
8. *Sermons* vii, 291, 294.
9. *Sermons* v, 259; viii, 102.
1. *Sermons* vii, 68

colliding. On the one side is the desire for a single, all-eclipsing viewpoint, together with the need to vilify those who dissent from it. This part of him is prominent in his satires, of course, and in some of his love poems—witness 'The Comparison,' where his own girl's perfections are contrasted with the filthy deformities of another's. But on the other side, beside family sympathies, there is an urge towards unity and assimilation which we shall often meet in Donne's imaginative world, and which inclines him to restraint. Accordingly he see-saws between the two attitudes.

When Donne renounced Catholicism isn't known, and it would be foolish to hope to pinpoint some particular day or week. Satire III shows, as we've seen, that he has been able to prise his intellect away from the old Faith, otherwise there'd be no need to set out on a search for truth. He must have been ready to pass himself off as an Anglican when he became secretary to the Lord Keeper, Egerton, in 1597. Egerton was himself an apostate, who had joined sides with the persecutors of Catholics, conducting the prosecution of several martyrs, Edmund Campion among them.[2] He would naturally sympathize with Donne's defection.

Why did Donne become an apostate? To answer that we should have to be confident that we could plumb the springs of human motivation. But three possible reasons suggest themselves: he was ambitious, he was an intellectual, and he was reacting, in a not uncommon way, against the love and admiration he had felt as a child for his elders and teachers.* * *

* * *

---

2. Bald, 94; *Gerard: Autobiography* (see n. 5 above, p. 210), 66.

Satires, Elegies, and Verse Letters

ARTHUR F. MAROTTI

Donne as an Inns-of-Court Author†

Donne seems to have composed his first poetry at the Inns of Court between 1592 and 1596. Both the institution of which he was a part and his audience within it affected his choice of literary forms and modes, the development of his characteristic style, and the subject matter of his verse—that is, all the artistic, intellectual, and social coordinates of his literary work. If there is some truth to Ben Jonson's statement that Donne wrote his best poems before he was twenty-five,[1] much of his most important poetry belongs to the Inns period. To understand it historically in its sociocultural context, it is necessary to examine the environment of the Inns of Court as well as Donne's motives for being there and for writing verse while he was in residence.

The Inns of Court as a Socioliterary Environment

In the late sixteenth century, Gray's Inn, Middle Temple, Inner Temple, and Lincoln's Inn were educational institutions for the training of young men in the common law and convenient places for the conduct of legal business. They were also "finishing schools" where gentlemen could both continue their education in a variety of subjects and acquire the civility and sophistication that would help them function successfully at Court or in other prestigious social circles. In close touch with the economic, political, and social centers of power, the Inns of Court were recognized as an avenue to opportunity and reward in the larger society. Though less distant from the heart of the society than the universities were, the Inns were

† From *John Donne, Coterie Poet* (Madison: The University of Wisconsin Press, 1986), pp. 25–27, 34–43. Reprinted by permission of the author.
1. In the "Conversations with Drummond," *Ben Jonson*, 1:135.

nevertheless a social environment distinct from the Court, the City, and the general social system. Inns members often criticized the other institutions of society at the same time as they made persistent efforts to join the Establishment—an ambivalence reflected both in their way of life and in the literature they produced.[2]

The Inns housed a larger proportion of gentlemen than the universities. These men were concerned with maintaining or improving their social and economic status, so the fashionable forms of behavior often were implicitly designed to advertise their (sometimes tenuous) gentility.[3] When Donne, for example, had his portrait painted in 1591, he made sure that his family's coat of arms was affixed: although he came from middle-class stock as the son of a member of the Ironmonger's Company, he wished to emphasize his right to be regarded as a gentleman.[4] The antagonism to the Inns gentlemen on the part of some lower-born university men and professional writers can be attributed to the socially exclusive character of Inns life. The *Parnassus* plays performed at St. John's College, Cambridge (1597–1601), for example, portray an Inns-of-Court gentleman-amorist as a villain because he uses his wealth and social position to unfair advantage.[5] Even Ben Jonson, who pointedly dedicated *Everyman Out of his Humour* to the Inns of Court and who had many close friends there, expressed his own social resentment when he characterized Ovid in *The Poetaster* as an Inns gallant punished for his degenerate way of life, a figure morally inferior to the more socially humble Horace and Virgil. Economic and social competition lay behind such expressions: after all, the main topic of the *Parnassus* plays is the sorry career prospects available in the late Elizabethan period to able, university-trained men who did not happen to be gentlemen (professional writers like Nashe and Marlowe, for

2. For a discussion of the Inns as law schools and as social environments, see Philip Finkelpearl, *John Marston of the Middle Temple: An Elizabethan Dramatist in his Social Setting* (Cambridge, Mass., 1969), pp. 3–80, and Wilfrid R. Prest, *The Inns of Court Under Elizabeth I and the Early Stuarts* (London: Longman, 1972).

3. Those who did not have the status of gentlemen, of course, could use the Inns as a means of elevating their social standing. In satirizing such social climbing, Joseph Hall wrote of the commoner's son who was sent for social polishing to the

> . . . Ins of Court of the Chancerie:
> There to learn law, and courtly carriage,
> To make amends for his meane parentage,
> Where he vnknowne and ruffling as he can,
> Goes current each-where for a Gentleman. . . .

(*Virgedemiarum*, IV.2.54–58 in *The Collected Poems of Joseph Hall*, ed. Arnold Davenport [Liverpool: Liverpool Univ. Press, 1949], p. 56).

4. See Bald, *A Life*, pp. 50–52, and Dennis Flynn, "Donne's First Portrait: Some Biographical Clues?", *Bulletin of Research in the Humanities* 82 (1979) 7–17.

5. "Amoretto" of *The Second Part of the Return from Parnassus*, in *The Three Parnassus Plays* (1598–1601), ed. with an introduction and commentary by J. B. Leishman (London: Ivor Nicholson & Watson, 1949).

example).[6] Jonson, of course, was especially sensitive to the handicap of low birth.

Within the Inns themselves the need to struggle for place and career made the atmosphere a heatedly competitive one. Whether or not they chose to prepare themselves for the legal profession (as only a relatively small minority did), Inns men were usually extremely ambitious, sharing the desire to succeed in a world in which the rewards were genuine, but the opportunities few. In his *Directions for Speech and Style*, the Inns author John Hoskins facetiously included the following examples of that species of irony considered under the term "catachresis": 1) "I am in danger of preferm[en]t"; 2) "I have hardly escaped good fortune"; and 3) "He threatens me a good turn."[7] No matter how much Inns men appeared to be wasting their time enjoying the pleasures of City and Court, they were usually eager for advancement and employment. After all, they were the trained elite of an educational system originally expanded in Tudor England to provide large numbers of competent civil servants for a centralized monarchy's growing bureaucracy. But their numbers, by the end of the sixteenth century, far exceeded the positions available. Lawrence Stone has called attention to this virtual "educational revolution" and noted that the over-production of trained gentlemen caused a competitive scramble for the few available places that were socially and economically attractive. In these circumstances, ambitious young men often had to endure the long wait for success or to scale down their expectations.[8]

* * *

Donne at Lincoln's Inn: The Early Verse Letters and the First Three Satires

John Donne entered the world of the Inns of Court in 1591 as a young man who, because of his Catholicism, had been unable to pursue his studies to a degree at Oxford or Cambridge.[9] At the Inn of Chancery, Thavies Inn, he continued his education under tutors

6. See Leishman's discussion of these plays in relation to their literary and social contexts (*Three Parnassus Plays*, pp. 24–92).
7. John Hoskins, *Directions for Speech and Style*, ed. Hoyt H. Hudson (Princeton, N.J.: Princeton Univ. Press, 1935), p. 11. Subsequent citations are to this edition, by page number.
8. See Lawrence Stone, "The Educational Revolution in England, 1560–1640," *Past and Present* 28 (1964): 41–80, and "Social Mobility in England, 1500–1700," *Past and Present* 33 (1966): 16–55. Cf. Wallace MacCaffrey, "Place and Patronage in Elizabethan Politics," in *Elizabethan Government and Society: Essays Presented to Sir John Neale*, ed. S. T. Bindoff, J. Hurstfield, and C. H. Williams (London: Athlone Press, 1961), pp. 95–126.
9. See Bald, *A Life*, pp. 45–46. John Carey emphasizes the importance of Donne's Catholicism and apostasy in his recent study (*John Donne: Life, Mind and Art* [New York: Oxford Univ. Press, 1981], especially pp. 15–59).

as he prepared himself for admission to Lincoln's Inn, which was granted in 1592.[1] Though his commitment to the law was, evidently, not a wholehearted one,[2] he fulfilled the residence requirements at Lincoln's Inn and learned enough about legal matters to serve him well in his later government employment. Donne's program of non-legal self-education was more ambitious: he read widely in many fields, including "the whole body of Divinity, controverted" (*Selected Prose*, p. 50) between Catholic and Protestant polemical writers. Though scholarly in temperament (he left, at his death, notes on some 1,400 to 1,500 authors), Donne lived the life of the fashionable gallant and wit, acquiring the urbanity and courtliness necessary for entry into sophisticated social circles. He made strong and close friendships at this time, many of which lasted the rest of his life, associating himself generally with a group of young gentlemen eager for social and political or professional advancement. Restless, ambitious, and gregarious, he thrived in the rich environment of the Inns as he familiarized himself with City and Court.

While at Lincoln's Inn and during that period before his employment with Sir Thomas Egerton, when he lived as a London gentleman and aspiring courtier, Donne tried his hand at various traditional and revived literary genres, viewing this writing as part of his social life, intending it for an audience of friends and acquaintances whose literary and sociocultural competence resembled his own. He composed epigrams, verse letters, formal satires, love elegies and libertine lyrics, and prose paradoxes—all genres fostered by the social circumstances of the Inns[3] and that male social group that developed out of this environment into those courtly and professional circles with which Donne was later connected. He imitated and wittily recreated literary forms associated with the Court, such as the love complaint, the Petrarchan complimentary lyric, and the art-song, utilizing the literary language of love sanctioned in Elizabethan England as a fit medium for certain patron-client transactions and other polite relationships in the hierarchical social system. In almost all of these works, his point of view was that of the Inns-of-Court wit who could self-critically and ironically examine the social institutions and environments with which he was involved as well as his

1. Bald writes that "At Thavies Inn in 1591 Donne was not only a Catholic, influenced and guided by Catholic tutors, but also in contact with the most active Catholic proselytizers in England" (*Life*, p. 63). For a discussion of Donne's Inns-of-Court period, see Bald, *A Life*, pp. 53–79.
2. Donne wrote his friend George Garrard in 1612 of his somewhat casual attitude toward the law: "I ever thought the study of it my best entertainment and pastime . . ." (*Letters*, p. 255).
3. Ellrodt (*L'Inspiration*, p. 23) mentions satire, epigram, the philosophical poem, the Ovidian elegy, verse epistles, lyrics in the new manner, and the prose paradox, essay, and character as forms that flourished in the Inns environment. Cf. Finkelpearl, *Marston*, pp. 19–31.

own ambivalent feelings about them. In handling different genres, Donne self-consciously reformulated their rules and conventions, sometimes mixing or conflating separate literary kinds and modes, thus questioning the social coordinates of literary forms in interesting ways;[4] he evolved a characteristic style that was both distinctively personal and, at the same time, congenial to his immediate audience of Inns gentlemen.

Although Donne regarded poetry only as an avocation, not the main business of his intellectual, moral, social, or professional life, soon after his arrival at Lincoln's Inn he wrote a number of verse letters to friends, expressing the desire to foster epistolary composition as a communal enterprise. These poems are probably not only his first literary works but also his earliest effort to define the kind of coterie audience with whom he wished to communicate. The classical and humanist models of the verse epistle determined, of course, many of the ideas he expressed in them, but he seems to have wished to relate his epistles particularly to the circumstances of his life and social relationships at the Inns of Court.[5] R. C. Bald has argued that these early verse letters, in effect, establish a "coterie of ingenious young men assiduously cultivating the Muse and warmly applauding each other's efforts" (A Life, p. 74).[6] The rhetorically familiar manner of these epistles has, in Finkelpearl's words, "the easy intimacy of someone speaking to an audience of equals."[7] Donne and most of his addressees shared a background of university education, common experiences in London and at the Inns, and a social familiarity that included visits to one another's homes or estates. Thus, Donne wrote to Samuel Brooke, the brother of his chambermate at Lincoln's Inn, advising him to write poetry while he was still at the university (To Mr. S. B.," O thou which"); in the epistle To Mr. E. G. ("Even as lame things"), he assumed his reader shared his gentleman's attitude of not taking legal study seriously, alluding to the London scene to which they were both accustomed, then changed by the plague; the letter To Mr. I. L. ("Blest are your North parts") was sent to a friend whose estate the poet's "Mistress" was visiting. In another poem to the same addressee (To Mr. I. L., "Of that short Roll of friends"), he teasingly reprimanded his friend for neglecting the "duties of Societies" (7) in being too preoccupied with a new wife.

4. For provocative discussions of the topic of the mixing of genres, see Rosalie Colie, The Resources of Kind: Genre-Theory in the Renaissance, ed. Barbara K. Lewalski (Berkeley, Los Angeles, London: Univ. of California Press, 1973), and Shakespeare's Living Art (Princeton, N.J.: Princeton Univ. Press, 1974), pp. 68–134. Cf. Corti, Literary Semiotics, pp. 115–43.
5. See D. J. Palmer, "The Verse Epistle," in Bradbury and Palmer, Metaphysical Poetry, pp. 73–99.
6. See also R. C. Bald, "Donne's Early Verse Letters," Huntington Library Quarterly 15 (1952): 283–89.
7. Finkelpearl, Marston, p. 30.

Although in another poem (*To Mr. C. B.*, "Thy friend, whom thy deserts") he expressed a more balanced attitude toward male friendship and heterosexual love—"Strong is this love which ties our hearts in one, / And strong that love pursu'd with amorous paine" (7–8)— he treated I. L.'s marriage as a threat to relationships between men (interestingly, the position of the antagonist in the later, more famous poem, "The Canonization").

These verse epistles make sense in terms of the aesthetics of poetic exchange, and Donne thought of them this way. In *To Mr. T. W.* ("All hail sweet Poet"), he acknowledged the reception of some verse from the addressee, as he did in another piece to the same man ("Pregnant again with th'old twins Hope, and Feare"). The Westmoreland Manuscript, in fact, records one of T. W.'s poems to Donne written in response to the receipt of both verse and prose epistles: "Thou sendst me prose & rimes, I send for those / Lynes, w^c beeing nether, seeme or verse or prose."[8] The writer's reference to the unpoetic character of his own verse letter matches Donne's own characterization of his epistles as "harsh verse" (*To Mr. T. W.*, "Hast thee harsh verse") that is more prosaic than poetic: " 'Twill be good prose, although the verse be evill" (*To Mr. T. W.*, "All haile sweet Poet," 27). Donne and his correspondents adopted the style of intimate plain-speaking that was both practiced in the Inns-of-Court environment and expected in the humanist verse epistle.

At the same time, Donne employed another mode in some of these poems, the language and manner of courtly Petrarchanism, using it to maintain a level of well-bred politeness proper to the style of a gentleman. In *To Mr. T. W.* ("At once, from hence"), Donne portrayed his absence from his friend as a lover's melancholy suffering. But, more typically, he used this vocabulary to refer to his relationship with a woman known to his friends as his beloved. In *To Mr. I. L.* ("Blest are your North parts"), he referred to her as "My Sun" (2), asking the addressee, who was her host, to report to her his "paine" (22)—i.e, to give her his regards. The letter *To Mr. C. B.* ("Thy friend, whom thy deserts") refers to the same woman, whom Donne had left at Brooke's house, as the "Saint of his Affection" (3), and describes his behavior as a lover in strictly conventional terms:

> . . . loves hot fires, which martyr my sad minde,
> Doe send forth scalding sighes, which have the Art
> To melt all Ice, but that which walls her heart.
> (12–14)

In *To Mr. R. W.* ("Zealously my Muse doth salute all thee"), Donne asked whether his friend had withdrawn to the country to act out

8. Printed in Milgate, *Satires, Epigrams and Verse Letters*, p. 212.

the role of the pining lover: ". . . is thy devout Muse retyr'd to sing / Upon her tender Elegiaque string?" (9–10). At this point in his career, at least, Donne thought of the love elegy in old-fashioned terms as the medium for Petrarchan complaint, a form congenial to the gentleman-amorist. (In expressing affection for a friend or a mistress, he therefore used the formulas proper to formally polite social relations, adopting a manner that clashed with his intention of plainspeaking familiarity. He had not yet successfully integrated these two rhetorical modes.[9])

Donne seems, however, to have experienced a breakthrough in the rhetorically more consistent formal satires, poems that have both generic and socioliterary affinities with his verse epistles. In these longer poems, particularly in the first two, he addressed himself with stylistic boldness to a receptive audience of peers, articulating more fully than was possible in the verse epistles some of the features of the social world in which they lived. Outside the codes of complimentary politeness, he freed his wit, his language, his critical impulses, and his feelings in the kind of verse that the Inns's atmosphere of "liberty" encouraged. In context, these poems proclaimed not only the values and attitudes poet and readers shared, but also the primary audience's personal knowledge of Donne's experience and behavior. They rested, like the verse letters, on the guarantee of intimate communication provided by their coterie circumstances. It is not surprising, then, that these poems are found in several manuscripts alongside "The Storme" and "The Calme," two ambitious epistles to Christopher Brooke, Donne's closest friend at Lincoln's Inn, the man who might also have been the addressee of *Satire 2*.[1]

Donne composed his first four satires before he entered government service, the first two clearly belonging to his early Inns period.[2] All these poems are the work of a man eager to become a part of the Establishment but angry about the forms of self-abasement necessary to succeed in a world of social, economic, and political power relationships. They were written for an audience of men similarly impatient for preferment and fond of asserting their intellectual, moral, and social autonomy. They assume common attitudes toward City and Court as well as a sophisticated knowledge of the way the social system worked. Reflecting the special interest of Inns men in such topics as religion, literature, and the social skills necessary for

9. For the preceding poems, see the notes in Milgate, *Satires, Epigrams and Verse Letters*, pp. 210–22.
1. Grierson (2:111) makes this suggestion on the basis of the note by Drummond "After C. B. Coppy," but Milgate (*Satires, Epigrams and Verse Letters*, p. 128) believes the evidence is weak.
2. Milgate (*Satires, Epigrams and Verse Letters*, pp. 117, 127) dates the first satire 1593 and the second sometime shortly after the appearance of the atrocious sonnet-sequence *Zepheria* (1594).

advancement in a competitive society, they strike a critical and self-critical stance, satirizing the various routes to success followed by Inns men, including those of the professional lawyer and the gentleman-courtier. The sins and follies that Donne attacked in these poems were part of the daily life of many Inns members. Later, in one of his sermons, he wrote: "We make Satyrs; and we looke that the world should call that wit; when God knowes, that that is in a great part, self-guiltinesse, and we doe but reprehend those things, which we ourselves have done, we cry out upon the illnesse of the times, and we make the times ill" (Sermons, 7:408). Both he and his readers knew that the stark contrasts of satire obviously distorted their world. Neither Donne nor his readers were scholar-saints, addicted as they both were to the pleasures of City and Court, to some of the very things criticized in these poems—amorous adventuring, fashionmongering, courtly ceremonies of "complement," swaggering and quarreling, and all the other vices of the Inns gentleman. One has only to look to the other satires and to the epigrammatic literature popular at the Inns in the 1590s to see how typical these targets were and how they characterized the life of the Inns residents.

The usual approach to satire by way of intellectual and literary history has obscured the social coordinates of this genre in Elizabethan England.[3] Donne and his contemporaries knew full well that satire was less a way of expressing one's devotion to moral ideals or one's condemnation of worldly vice than it was the literary form practiced by those whose ambitions were frustrated and who yearned to involve themselves more deeply in the social environments they pretended to scorn. (The satirist, as Bosola puts it in The Duchess of Malfi, "rails at those things which he wants" (I.i.25).[4] Hence, the motive of envy is habitually associated with the satiric urge.[5] Ingenioso, in the Parnassus plays, a university wit resembling Thomas Nashe, attacks the world satirically because he cannot find a satisfactory career.[6] Sir John Harington explained the composition of The Metamorphosis of Ajax as the product of his unwilling rustication and of the need to be noticed by the Court in which he sought preferment: "I was the willinger to wryte such a toye as this, because, I had layne me thought allmost buryed in the Contry these three or

3. The valuable monograph by M. Thomas Hester (Kinde Pitty and Brave Scorn: John Donne's Satyres [Durham, N.C.: Duke Univ. Press, 1982]), says little about the immediate social contexts of the poems.
4. John Webster, The Duchess of Malfi, ed. John Russell Brown (Cambridge, Mass.: Harvard Univ. Press, 1964), p. 10.
5. See O. J. Campbell, Comicall Satyre and Shakespeare's "Troilus and Cressida" (San Marino, Calif.: Huntington Library, 1938), pp. 59–61.
6. In The Second Part of The Return from Parnassus this character comes onstage reading Juvenal and expressing admiration for "truth telling Aretine" (Leishman, Parnassus Plays, pp. 225–26).

fowre yeere; and I thought this would give some occasion to have me thought of and talked of."[7] The subtext of most satiric literature, including Donne's, is the strong attraction to the very world being criticized.[8] Both the sociocultural encoding of this genre and the particular coterie context of Donne's Inns-of-Court audience confirmed this fact.

Of his five satires, the first two especially reflect the Inns-of-Court setting in which they were composed: Donne advertises in them his knowledge of the environment in which he and his audience lived. Sir Isaac Walton's description of Donne's life at Lincoln's Inn as arranged around a regimen of study from four o'clock to ten o'clock each morning, followed by less respectable activities in which he "took great liberty,"[9] seems to be reflected in the poet's splitting of himself in the first satire into the scholar-moralist and the inconstant fool addicted to the fashions of Court and City. In holding up to ridicule the pathetic gull who "Sells for a little state his libertie" (70), Donne expressed his feeling of revulsion for some of the follies in which both he and his peers indulged, particularly their imitation of some of the features of subservient courtly behavior. This antagonist figure in the first satiric poem resembles Sir John Davies' epigrammatic definition of the gull as the man who "feares a velvet gowne, / And when a wench is brave, dares not speake to her" (Kreuger/ Nemser, p. 130), a strutting gallant who is really a coward ready to endure "Knockes about the eares" (11), a fashionmonger who speaks nonsense. Donne's gull apes the manners of fashionable gallants and courtiers, bowing and scraping to "men of sort, of parts, of qualities" (105), attracted by every "many-colour'd Peacock" (92). Though he thinks he can "command" (109) at least his mistress, he competes unsuccessfully with rivals and is defeated in a duel (or "quarrel"), finally turned out of doors. His failures in the sophisticated world of social and economic power relations are an object lesson in the dangers that lie beyond the Inns's precincts. Thus, the boundary between self-satirization and satiric attack on the outside world is blurred in such a poem. Just as the satiric persona's intellectual and moral complacency is disturbed by his socially irritating association with the inconstant fool who has befriended him, so too Donne and his readers were, no doubt, morally, intellectually, and emotionally ambivalent about their own attraction to the world outside their chambers.

7. Harington, *Letters and Epigrams*, p. 66.
8. John Wilcox ("Informal Publication of Late Sixteenth-Century Verse Satire," *Huntington Library Quarterly* 13 [1950]: 191–200) has argued that writers like Donne, Harington, Davies, and Hall composed satire to draw the attention and patronage of the Court rather than simply to criticize the age for its corruption.
9. Isaac Walton, "The Life of Dr. John Donne," in John Donne, *Devotions* (Ann Arbor: Univ. of Michigan Press, 1959), p. xxxiv.

In the [second satire,] Donne expressed the Inns gentleman's snobbish hostility to professional lawyers, those "men which chuse / Law practise for meere gaine" (62–63).[1] The target of the attack is a lawyer-poet whose verse is a crass parody of true poetry, but whose real crime is his naked greed, which poses an economic threat to social superiors with whom both Donne and his readers wanted to identify. In fantasizing that this man will use his legal maneuvers to increase his real-estate holdings to the point that "Shortly . . . hee'will compasse all our land" (77), the speaker of the poem treats land as the gentleman's natural possession that should not fall into the hands of ruthless middle-class entrepreneurs—an attitude reflected in the drama of the period, especially in those private theater plays of the first decade of the seventeenth century that formulated similar class conflicts.[2] But the satirist's ethical posture and his social status are portrayed in this poem as precarious. His moral outrage is compromised by his envious resentment of the very man he criticizes. Despite the affirmation of the genteel values he shared with his readers, Donne communicated the frustration of the man whose wish to be a powerful part of the Establishment and to punish socioeconomic abuses was a futile one: ". . . my words none drawes / Within the vast reach of th'huge statute lawes" (111–12). Both this and the previous poem reflect the vulnerability of the Inns gentlemen who scorned the less-dignified kinds of legal and business careers available to them, but who felt unrewarded or rejected by the corrupt, but more socially prestigious, courtly establishment.

In this satire, Donne expressed an aversion to various forms of poetry, an attitude consistent with the harshly unpoetic stance of the formal satirist. He mocked not only hack playwrights and plagiarists, but also those who wrote complimentary verse to beg for money: ". . . they who write to Lords, rewards to get / Are they not like singers at doores for meat?" (21–22). He objected to those who slavishly followed the literary fashions of the day, including the courtly practice of composing Petrarchan lyrics. The man who "would move Love by rimes" (17) is foolish because he is not aggressive enough: "Rammes, and slings now are seely battery, / Pistolets are the best Artillerie" (19–20). Here as elsewhere, Donne rejected the polite courtly idiom of love poetry, preferring instead a less-delicate assertion of erotic desire, the form of active pursuit of sexual conquests found in those elegies and lyrics he wrote in a deliberately anti-Petrarchan and anti-courtly literary idiom.

Although it has been read primarily in the context of intellectual history,[3] [Satire 3] takes on a pointed meaning in relation to the steps

1. See Prest, *Inns of Court*, pp. 40–41.
2. See Brian Gibbons, *Jacobean City Comedy: A Study of the Satiric Plays by Jonson, Marston and Middleton* (Cambridge, Mass.: Harvard Univ. Press, 1968), pp. 32–49.
3. See the discussion in Hester, *Kinde Pitty*, pp. 54–72. See also Sister M. Geraldine, "John

Donne took to enter the world of political involvement. Given his background as a Catholic and the limitations this placed on his opportunities for advancement, this poem is, at once, both a personal and political statement.[4] In its refusal to adopt a stance of faithful Catholicism, it constitutes a necessary gesture in preparation for the pursuit of a courtly career, but, in its skeptical, even iconoclastic attitudes, it is the kind of dangerous statement whose disclosure outside his coterie Donne feared. In a letter to a friend accompanying some manuscript copies of his prose paradoxes, Donne later expressed his concern about the wider social exposure of the satires and his other verse: ". . . to my satyrs there belongs some feare and to some elegies, and these [paradoxes] perhaps, shame. . . . Therefore I am desirous to hyde them with out any over reconing of them or their maker" (*Selected Prose*, p. 111). It is not difficult to understand how Donne might have been embarrassed about the dissemination of his libertine elegies and lyrics beyond the young male audience of the Inns of Court: their ribaldry and rebelliousness belonged more to the world of the undergraduate or of the rambunctious termers than of the world of adult seriousness. But the "feare" about the satires was probably another matter, related to their socially or politically sensitive subject matter, features that led to the authorities' suppression of the form in 1599.[5]

In the *Satires*, Donne criticized harshly some of his society's central institutions—the Crown, the Court, the Church, and the legal system. This is apparent in many of the boldly irreverent similes that abound in these poems. For example, Coscus the poet-turned-lawyer in the second satire can "to'every suitor lye in every thing, / Like a Kings favorite, yea like a king" (69–70).[6] Referring to this character's vices, the speaker remarks:

> Bastardy'abounds not in Kings titles, nor
> Symonie'and Sodomy in Churchmens lives,
> As these things do in him.
>
> (74–75)

<hr>

Donne and the Mindes Indeavours," *Studies in English Literature* 5 (1965): 115–31; Thomas V. Moore, "Donne's Use of Uncertainty as a Vital Force in *Satyre III*," *Modern Philology* 67 (1969): 41–49; Camille Slights, *The Casuistical Tradition in Shakespeare, Donne, Herbert, and Milton* (Princeton, N.J.: Princeton Univ. Press, 1981), pp. 160–67; and Thomas Sloan, "The Persona as Rhetor: An Interpretation of Donne's *Satyre III*," *Quarterly Journal of Speech* 51 (1965): 14–27.

4. Milgate (*Satires, Epigrams and Verse Letters*, pp. 139–40) dates the poem sometime in 1594 or 1595, that is, at a time Donne was probably moving away from his Catholicism, but had not yet embraced the established Church. Paul Sellin's recent attempt at dating the poem in 1620 ("The Proper Dating of John Donne's 'Satyre III'," *Huntington Library Quarterly* 43 [1980]: 275–312) is not likely to win much support.

5. See the copy of the Bishops' order of 1599 printed in *Joseph Hall*, ed. Davenport, pp. 293–94.

6. Milgate notes (*Satires, Epigrams and Verse Letters*, p. 135) that these lines were omitted by the editor of the 1633 edition of Donne as politically dangerous.

The treatment of the Court in the fourth satire is merciless. But in the third satiric poem Donne came close to the treasonous and seditious. He did not merely criticize England's foreign adventurism (17–19) and satirize uncritical adherence to the established Church, but he also carefully, if indirectly, rejected the Elizabethan Oath of Allegiance, placing man's responsibility to his conscience and obedience to the laws of God above submission to a merely human law:[7]

> Foole and wretch, wilt thou let thy Soule be ty'd
> To mans lawes, by which she shall not be try'd
> At the last day? Will it then boot thee
> To say a Philip, or a Gregory,
> A Harry, or a Martin taught thee this?
>
> (93–97)

Under the guise of speaking about all kinds of legal coercion of one's conscience, whether from Catholic or Protestant sources, Donne seems to have directed his fire at the contemporary requirement that all Englishmen, including Roman Catholics, take the Oath. The issue is put finally in terms of the qualified obedience to secular power—a subject someone like Robert Southwell had tried to handle in *An Humble Supplication to Her Maiestie*:[8]

> That thou may'st rightly'obey power, her bounds know;
> Those past, her nature and name's chang'd; to be
> Then humble to her is idolatrie;
> As streames are, Power is; those blest flowers that dwell
> At the rough steames calme head, thrive and prove well,
> But having left their roots, and themselves given
> To the streames tyrannous rage, alas, are driven
> Through mills, and rockes, and woods, 'and at last, almost
> Consum'd in going, in the sea are lost:
> So perish Soules, which more chuse mens unjust
> Power from God claym'd, then God himselfe to trust.
>
> (100–110)

Donne not only stated that subscribing to the Oath of Allegiance was an act of idolatry, but that the power that demanded such compliance

7. Slights (*Casuistical Tradition*, p. 164) observes that this attitude toward human authority is a typical casuistic stance.
8. See Robert Southwell, *An Humble Supplication to her Majestie*, ed. R. C. Bald (Cambridge: Cambridge Univ. Press, 1953). Southwell's work, in the context of the anti-Catholic legislation of the 1590s (see J. E. Neale, *Elizabeth I and Her Parliaments*, 2 vols. [London: Cape, 1953–57] 2:280–97), is an impassioned plea to lessen the persecution of his coreligionists. In it, he assures Queen Elizabeth of the patriotic loyalty of her Catholic subjects, but he objects to the requirement that they attend Protestant services. He characterizes Catholic priests as missionaries facing martyrdom rather than as seditious traitors posing a danger to the state. Finally, at a time when England was still at war with Spain, Southwell claims that one of the Protestants' chief polemical adversaries, the Jesuit Robert Parsons, was responsible for the courteous treatment of the English, including English prisoners-of-war, by the Spaniards.

was "tyrannous," a dangerous term to use in this context, since it charged the (basically moderate) Elizabeth with the unjust or excessive use of power in the treatment of Catholic subjects.

Even the intellectual and religious idealism of this satire had dangerous implications. By placing Mistress Truth at the moral center of the world, Donne, in effect, ideologically displaced the idealized Queen Elizabeth, who had herself appropriated some of the features of an older Catholic Mariolatry to enhance her power.[9] Of course, by having the satiric speaker withhold his allegiance from secular authority—by refusing to endorse the Oath of Allegiance or the Queen whose power it supported—and by privileging the individual's autonomy of conscience and personal search for truth, Donne not only adopted the stance of intellectual independence favored by him and his associates but also refused to subordinate his beliefs to the demands of political expediency. As he explained in the preface to *Pseudo-Martyr*:

> . . . I used no inordinate hast, nor precipitation in binding my conscience to any locall Religion. I had a longer worke to doe than many other men; for I was first to blot out, certaine impressions of the Romane religion, and to wrastle both against the examples and against the reasons, by which some hold was taken; and some anticipations early layde upon my conscience, both by Persons who by nature had a power and superiority over my will, and others who by their learning and good life, seem'd to me justly to claime an interest for the guiding, and rectifying of mine understanding in these matters. And although I apprehended well enough, that this irresolution not onely retarded my fortune, but also bred some scandall, and endangered my spirituall reputation, by laying me open to many misinterpretations; yet all these respects did not transport me to any violent and sudden determination, till I had, to the measure of my poore wit and judgment, survayed and digested the whole body of Divinity, controverted betweene ours and the Romance Church. (*Selected Prose*, pp. 49–50)

In the third satire Donne refused to defend or reject either Catholicism or the Established Church. He dealt with religion, a subject of intense interest to Inns-of-Court gentlemen,[1] specifically highlighting the political dimension of religious commitment (Donne was all too aware of the sociopolitical dangers and handicaps resulting from his Catholicism, yet, as he explained, he would not abandon the religion of his youth until he had satisfied himself intellectually and

---

9. See John Phillips, *The Reformation of Images: Destruction of Art in England, 1535–1660* (Berkeley, Los Angeles, London: Univ. of California Press, 1973), p. 205.
1. See Prest, *Inns of Court*, p. 159 and Krueger/Nemser, *John Davies*, pp. xxx–xxxi.

morally that it was the right thing to do.) In any case, the discussion of the topic in the third satire was not meant for a general audience and Donne probably had very good reasons for fearing the transmission of such a poem beyond its restricted readership.

* * *

M. THOMAS HESTER

"Ask thy father": ReReading Donne's *Satyre III*†

interroga patrem tuum, et annuntiabit:
maiores tuos, et dicent tibi.
—Deut. 32:7

John Foxe's revisionary history of English martyrdom in the cause of "true religion" opens with the author's careful reading of the perimeters of his audience: a "Dedicatory Preface" to Queen Elizabeth is followed by a prefatory letter "To Christ," another "To the Persecutors of God's Truth, Commonly Called Papists," another "To the True and Faithful Congregation of Christ's Universal Church," and another "To All the Professed Friends and Followers of the Pope's Proceedings." Among the prefaces to John Donne's treatise on the Oath of Allegiance, *Pseudo-Martyr,* are an "Epistle Dedicatorie to King James," "An Advertisement to the Reader," and a preface "To the Priestes, and Iesuites, and to their Disciples in this Kingdom." These two representative examples confirm the *multiple audience* that English religious controversialists saw as readers of their works. It is a minor, perhaps even an obvious point, but nevertheless one not frequently taken into consideration in our own readings of their works, which too often seem to infer that their texts were intended for the "survaying and digesting" (*Pseudo-Martyr*, sig. B) of a monolithic readership.[1] Such a view is especially restrictive when the

---

† From *Ben Jonson Journal* 1 (1994): 201–18. Reprinted by permission of the *Ben Jonson Journal.*
1. I cite the 1610 edition of *Pseudo-Martyr*: Anthony Raspa's edition of the work (McGill's–Queen's University Press) had not appeared at the time of composition of this essay. All citations of the poems of Donne are to the edition of John T. Shawcross, *The Complete Poetry of John Donne* (Garden City, N.Y.: Doubleday, 1967); line numbers are indicated in parentheses. But see also Gary Stringer's study of the significant textual variants in the manuscript and seventeenth-century printed versions of *Satyre III*, in *John Donne Journal*, 10 (1991).

   Two givens about *Satyre III* not directly addressed in this essay merit attention: the focus of attention on *readers* is not intended to retract my earlier identification of its *meditative* structure, nor to deny that it can profitably be read as "a delimited case of

controversialist voices his position in the compressed equivoques of poetry and more than questionable in reading the manuscript poems of a writer as witty and paradoxical as John Donne. My major concern in the following pages is to recall those readers of Donne's earliest poem on "true religion" with whom he later said he identified at the time of its composition—those English Catholic readers of "learning and good life" who "seem'd to [him] to claime an interest for the guiding and rectifying of [his] understanding in these matters" (*Pseudo-Martyr*, sig. B)—or, at the least, to recall the lexicon and tropes of controversy, polemics, and satirical abuse of English Counter-Reformation Catholic readings of the history of "true religion" in England. To read Donne *in his time*, that is, is to read the multivalence of his wit from the perspectives of his multiple (real, imaginary, and conventional) audience, not just to evaluate his position as if only the poet, his patron(ess), or his "Prince" were the audience.

One caveat: if the following re-vision of *Satyre III* seems to make primary only those English Catholic readers who have been largely erased from Donne's audience by subsequent criticism, it is not meant to overlook the problems that the equivocal strategies of Recusant commentary present for his Protestant readers, or for those readers he later described in terms of their "curious malice"—"those men, who in this sickly decay, and declining of their cause, can spy out falsifyings in every citation: as in a jealous, and obnoxious state, a Decipherer can pick out Plots, and Reason, in any familiar letter which is intercepted" (*Pseudo-Martyr*, sig. 2). It was the presence of these precise "Decipherer[s]," in fact, that explains in part the equivocal manner of Donne's witty application of those Recusant tropes he embeds in the urbane, even Horatian, texture of his meditative address on where he "stands, . . . inquiring right" in the dangerous arena of Elizabethan religious controversy.

> History has many cunning passages.
> —T. S. Eliot, *Gerontion*

---

conscience," as recommended by Shawcross in "All Attest His Writs Canonical; The Texts, Meaning and Evaluation of Donne's Satires," in *Just So Much Honor*, ed. Peter Amadeus Fiore (University Park: Pennsylvania State Univ. Press, 1972), 268; and Camille Wells Slights, *The Casuistical Tradition* (Princeton, N.J.: Princeton Univ. Press, 1918), 160–67; and this reading accepts a time of composition in the mid-1590s for the poem. The two most recent readings of *Satyre III*—Joshua Scodel's "The Medium is the Message: Donne's 'Satire 3,' 'To Henry Wotton ('Sir, more then kisses'),' and the Ideologies of the Mean," *MP* 91 (1993); and Richard Strier's "Radical Donne' 'Satire III,' " *ELH* 60 (1993)—concur with such a proposed date of composition although they assume different doctrinal and philosophical positions on Donne's part than that I suggest here. In part, as indicated by my title, this essay proposes that the satirical thrust and the Recusant position of Donne which I emphasized in my reading of *Satyre II* and *Satyre IV* in *Kinde Pitty and Brave Scorn: John Donne's Satyres* (Durham, N.C.: Duke University Press, 1982) is of more moment in the third *Satyre* than I urged there.

At the conclusion of his epistolary verse satire on corrupt lawyers and bathetic poetasters, Donne's sardonic ironist concludes his *sermo* with this peroration:

> (Oh) we'allow
> Good workes as good, but out of fashion now,
> Like old rich wardrops; but my words none drawes
> Within the vast reach of th'huge statute lawes.
> (*Satyre II*, 109–12)

This melancholic admission is typical of Donne's equivocal wit throughout the *Satyres,* as well as in those elegies and lyrics that his contemporary readers often identified as "satires." In one sense, the play on the Protestant doctrinal erasure of Good Works, the sarcastic variation on the conventional sumptuary trope, and the saucy alliterative equation of "Good workes" and "my words" can be read as commonplaces of the sort of hectoring highjinks and moralistic claims of the genre, a version of the adolescent hyperbole familiar to Inns of Court satire. Even the reliance on a *simile* might intend impertinently to recall, in fact, the centrality of "as if" and "as" in much Protestant soteriology (by which the divine Body and Blood, for instance, are "present" only "by way of similitude" instead of "substantially"). In this sense, the satirist displays the boldness of his wit by daring to suggest his spiritual superiority to the legal abuses of language the poem attacks as well as intimating that those abuses have been "allow[ed]" through the Calvinian ethics made "fashion[able]" by the Reformation; and the mordant submission of the final clause, while admitting that poetry does not have the authority of corrupt lawyers' machinations (and, by implication, possibly those of fashionable religious Reformers—Calvin, like Donne, one might recall, was trained as a lawyer), proposes that satire is an "allow[ed]" form of criticism for which the satirist cannot be prosecuted. However impudent, conventional, or naive such a claim in the oppressive imperium of Elizabethan politics, the admission that his "Good . . . words" bring *no* malefactors before the bar would seem to substantiate his claim throughout the poem that England has as much to fear "now" from the prerogative of a national verbal fraudulence which threatens "Shortly [to] compasse all our land" as from any foreign threat or any "disarm'd" poet.

Nevertheless, in spite of the cleverness of the satirist's impressive critique—and any authority derived from its Horatian precedent in *Satyre II*.i—this impertinent taunt does disclose an incipient apprehensiveness that cannot be covered over by its hectoring sarcasm and saucy rhetorical invention. In addition to the nervous designation

of the statute laws as "huge" and "vast"—itself most likely a reference
to the Statute against Recusants (c.2 Eliz. 27) which had led to the
martyrdom of Donne's younger brother—the choice of "drawes" is
especially striking. As a reminder of the cruelty of Tudor legal
enforcement techniques, most notably the (supposedly illegal) Top-
cliffean inquisitions implemented to enforce the prolix statutes
against Roman Catholics,[2] "drawes" offers less a playful than a fear-
fully anxious perspective on the role of the religious critic and out-
sider in Donne's "jealous, and obnoxious state." The verb not only
contrasts the ineffective appeals of poetic limning to the torture of
suspected religious "Traytor[s]," but also hints at one of the central
methods of the government's secret police—the reliance on pursui-
vant spies and *agents provocateurs* to entrap anyone who, "Like [the]
old rich" ancient nobility[3] (such as the Stanleys and the Howards
and even Donne's Welsh ancestors, the DWNS of Kidwelly), still
confessed a doctrine of "Good workes" instead of allowing the new
soteriology by which the "wardrop" (wardrobe) of Christ's blood
covers the totally depraved sinner from the infinite reach of divine
Law. Even while the satirist equivocally contrasts the Catholic and
Protestant doctrines, that is, any sense of moral superiority that he
might draw from this petulant contrast is tempered by the dangerous
consequences that his peroration obliquely uncovers.

In fact, the concluding lines of *Satyre II* reiterate the comparison
of satire to a dangerous instrument of illegal religion (like English
Catholicism) that is ambiguously asserted throughout the poem. The
Catholic readers would not likely read as facetious the satirist's

2. One of the constant and continuous objections of the English Catholics to the illegal
methods of Elizabeth's court officials was to their use of torture. See especially the
exchanges between William Cecil, *The Execution of Justice in England*, and William Allen,
A True, Sincere, and Modest Defense of English Catholics (both available in the edition of
Robert M. Kingdon [Ithaca: Cornell Univ. Press, 1965]), and the later reiteration of this
condition by Robert Southwell in *An Humble Supplication to Her Maiestie*, ed. R. C. Bald
(Cambridge: Cambridge Univ. Press, 1953). Most useful appraisals of the illegality of the
ways in which the notorious Topcliffe and his colleagues such as Richard Young (who
caught Donne's younger brother in the presence of a priest in 1593) managed to "drawe"
confessions from suspected Catholics are provided by Penry Williams, *The Tudor Regime*,
(Oxford: Clarendon, 1979), and Leo Hicks, *An Elizabethan Problem* (New York: Fordham
Univ. Press, 1964); for examples of "drawe" as a synonym for *torture*, see Hicks, p. 47;
Richard Verstegan's accounts of the torture and execution of the Catholic martyrs in works
such as *Descriptions quaedam illius humanae et multiplicis persecutiones* (1584); and
Christopher Devlin's *The Life of Robert Southwell* (London: Sidgwick & Jackson, 1967),
all of which remind us that "draw" meant not only to entrap and to torture on the rack
but also to dismember and disembowel.
    Since it was a matter of piety for the Catholic faithful to witness the executions of the
martyrs, it is most likely that Donne saw (among others) the gruesome execution of Cam-
pion, Sherwin, and Briant at Tyburn in 1581 as well as that of Southwell in 1595.
3. On the importance of his ancient lineage to Donne, see R. C. Bald, *John Donne: A Life*
(Oxford: Oxford Univ. Press, 1970), esp. ch. 2; Dennis Flynn, "Donne and the Ancient
Catholic Nobility," *ELR* 19 (1989), 305–23; and Flynn's *John Donne and the Ancient
Catholic Nobility* (Bloomington: Indiana Univ. Press, 1995).

opening composition in which he quips that "Poetry indeed [is] such a sinne" that "brings . . . Spaniards in," that it is "like the Pestilence and old fashion'd love," and that its practitioners are "poore, dis-arm'd, like Papists," for they would recognize that Donne has merely appropriated the conventional Platonic/Puritan deprecations of poetry which had become commonplaces of Protestant polemics in the assault against English Catholics in the 1590s.[4] Indeed, from that perspective the comparison recalls Donne's own description of a dilemma quite familiar to the heir of a prominent Catholic tradi-tion; he "derived," he later emphasized in the first work published under his name, "from such a stocke and race, as, I beleeve, no family, (which is not of farre larger extent, and greater branches,) hath endured and suffered more in their persons and fortunes, for obeying the Teachers of Romane Doctrine, then it hath done." Even in this apologia from the *Pseudo-Martyr* it is difficult to determine just how extensive is Donne's wit—in this case whether the puns of *more* and *done* name his martyred great-grand-uncle and his family.[5] So in the earlier *Satyre,* also. Whether or not this poem engages that "meditation of Martyrdome [by which he was] ever kept awake" (*Pseudo-Martyr* lr), Donne's most provocative analogy in *Satyre II* does recall one of the central (and most recent) Establishment charges against Recusant equivocation—"*Ridlingly* it catch men." The daring and provocative challenge which concludes the poem, that is, is merely the final *equivocal*[6] appropriation of the terms of

---

4. Although no thorough treatment of the lexicon and rhetoric of the Counter-Reformation debate exists, some of the most important terms have been discussed by Elliott Rose, *Cases of Conscience: Alternatives Open to Recusants and Puritans Under Elizabeth I and James I* (Cambridge: Cambridge Univ. Press, 1975), and Thomas H. Clancy, *Papist Pamphleteers: The Allen-Persons Party and the Political Thought of the Counter-Reformation in England, 1572–1615* (Chicago: Loyola Univ. Press, 1964). Most useful for its review of the polem-ics, rhetoric, and historical accounts of the Catholic chroniclers of Elizabeth's reign is Joseph B. Code's *Queen Elizabeth and the English Catholic Historians* (Louvain: Biblio-thèque de l'Universitair, 1935), to which I am indebted for many of the details about the English Catholic critique of the Queen and her ministers. My concern in this essay is with these tropes as tropes, not with the libellous, scandalous, or personally motivated animus that generated some of them. The Fitzherbert family, for instance, had a long-running feud with Topcliffe, Code points out: some of the claims of Nicholas Rishton's continu-ation of Nicholas Sander's originary attacks on Elizabeth's parentage were "purely polem-ical writing" (Code, 24); and Stapleton's virulent attack on Elizabeth and Cecil in *Apologia* relies at times on mere gossip and hyperbole. This is not to suggest, however, that Donne knew what was "merely polemical" in these tracts or, more importantly, that the "truth" of the Protestant or the Catholic polemics was a significant issue—as he says in *Satyre III,* as far as sectarian politics are concerned "cannot both sides say so?" But the theory of the "true" church for Donne did conform to that of Catholicism; and his invoking of the tropes of the Catholic "historians" intends to focus attention on the *absence* of "our Mistresse faire Religion" in the Elizabethan "settlement."
5. See, for instance, Flynn, "Irony in Donne's *Biathanatos* and *Pseudo-Martyr,*" *Recusant History* 12 (1973): 46–49.
6. On the seminal importance of "equivocation" as treason see, among others, Christopher Devlin's *The Life of Robert Southwell* (London: Longmans, 1956), and Philip Caraman's *Henry Garnet* (New York: Farrar, Straus, 1964).

244 M. THOMAS HESTER

official Elizabethan statute and propaganda—amplified by the daring
satirist into the "odious" comparisons of his anxious confessional
apologia. At least, Donne quips, I am not a spy!

Donne returns to this same subject in his fourth *Satyre*, but not
in order to distinguish himself from the spy. After offering an even
fuller and most explicit comparison of the situations of the satirist
and the Recusant in the politics of Elizabethan religion, and after
deriding once again the spying, threats, and repressions of the Court,
in this poem he saucily confesses that he is a spy. As the devotee of
his "Mistresse Truth" (who may or may not contrast with the Queen
"worthy" of "all our Soules devotion") he risks being identified as "A
spyed Spie," a spy for the Truth who discloses the cruelty and immor-
ality of a hypocritical "Court" that would deem "Traytor" any sincere
believer who cannot accept the state religion which the "Giant Stat-
utes" were drawn to enforce. This poem evinces fully the grounds of
Donne's later admission that "to my satyrs there belongs some feare.
. . . I am desirous to hyde them wth out any over reconing of them or
there maker" (*Burley MS.,* fol. 309). However covered by the hilar-
ious caricatures and ironic portraitures which animate his juvenalian
ridicule of the divine comedy and spiritual absence of the Elizabe-
than "Presence Chamber," one cannot avoid spying a ground-tone
of "feare" when the satirist recalls how he "felte my selfe then /
Becoming Traytor, and me thought I saw / One of our Giant Statutes
ope his jaw / To sucke me in." Even though he disparages the "merit"
of his work—therein applying, as in *Satyre II,* another lexical syn-
ecdoche for Catholic soteriology—in *Satyre IV,* even in the flippant
bow to the rhetorical power of "Preachers" Donne registers his cog-
nizance of the precarious position in which his satire (and his reli-
gion) have placed him.

Recognition of the dangerous and subversive strategies that he
employs in the *Satyres,* then, would explain in part why Donne
remained a manuscript poet whose works were mostly not published
until after his death, why he guarded their circulation and strove to
limit them to a select coterie of readers, and why it yet remains
difficult to "recon" the precise spiritual and political beliefs of "there
maker."[7] Donne, whose ironic poses and careful equivocations made
him the *monarch of wit,* was also the satirical "spyed Spie" well aware
of the role of the reader as a "privileg'd spie" intent on uncovering
the illegal, ill-advised, or illegitimate "ciphers" of his religious, polit-
ical, and amatory confessions. In fact, whether framed by the meta-
phoric perspective of the verse satire, the Ovidian elegy, the love
lyric, or the Ignatian meditation, Donne's speaker is consistently

7. On Donne as a manuscript poet see Ted-Larry Pebworth, "Manuscript Poems and Print
Assumptions: Donne and His Modern Editors," *John Donne Journal* 3 (1984): 1–21.

defined by the necessity of defending, defining, or declaring his "devotion" amidst a legion of adversarial readers, voyeurs, spies, and agents—without admitting or denying his violations of their patriarchal, governmental, or ecclesiastical "Statutes."[8]

One poem which would seem an exception to this feature endemic to Donne's works is that poem poised between the daring religio-political commentaries of the second and fourth *Satyres*. As typified by such generalized descriptions of *Satyre III* as "a soliloquy," an "oration addressed to young men close to the Queen," "a dramatization of a case of conscience," or—to cite my own Graccus-like summary—a "union of private and public discourse [with] a concomitant meditative and satirical stance . . . spoken to a general Elizabethan audience, . . . both private and public,"[9] readings of this poem have been especially careful not to disturb Alexander Pope's canonization of it as "the *noblest* Work of not only This but perhaps any satiric Poet"—and therein safely *within* the "ideologically free space" of "historically undetermined poet[s],"[1] beyond the fearful anxieties and personal threats so carefully depicted in the two poems which frame it in the most reliable manuscript arrangements.[2] But where—"O where?"—Donne *stood* "inquiring right" and what "right" was to him in the 1590s (to cite his own directives in the poem)— and his hesitancy to answer these questions—are significant to the achievement of the poem. I do not want to deny, that is, that *Satyre III* shows Donne "the first poet in the world in some things"[3] (nor even to retract my own view of its meditative design in *Kinde Pitty*) but only to suggest that if the poem, to cite Coleridge, "would teach . . . scholar[s] in the highest form to read,"[4] then it would teach them to read *what cannot be said* in the poem—that is, to read the "truth" *about* this poem precisely as Donne figures Truth *in* this poem: *within* the context of the late Elizabethan political arena of religious propaganda and polemical warfare.

In this sense, without privileging either the equivocal strategies of

---

8. I trace the insistence on this view of the reader in Donne's lyrics and elegies in " 'this cannot be said': A Preface to the Reader of Donne's Lyrics," *C&L* 39 (1990): 365–85. For a somewhat different perspective on "how frequently [Donne] populates the [lyrics] with an observing third party"—as "a witness"—see William Schullenberger's suggestive essay, "Love as a Spectator Sport in John Donne's Poetry," in *Renaissance Discourses of Desire*, ed. Claude J. Summers and Ted-Larry Pebworth (Columbia: Univ. of Missouri Press, 1993), 46–62.

9. For references to these selections and a fuller list of the critical defenses of Donne's "olympian" urbanity in *Satyre III*, see ch. 3 of *Kinde Pitty and Brave Scorn*.

1. This is Lee Patterson's description of the modern critical depiction of Chaucer, *SAQ* 86 (1987): 458.

2. See John T. Shawcross, "The Arrangement and Order of John Donne's Poems," in *Poems in Their Place*, ed. Neil Fraistat (Chapel Hill: Univ. of North Carolina Press, 1986), 119–63.

3. This, of course, is Jonson's opinion of Donne's satirical poems.

4. I have taken Coleridge's words in a slightly different sense than intended, of course—but not without underscoring the validity of his view, I hope.

self-protection in the third *Satyre*—"To'adore, or scorne an image, or protest . . . May all be bad"—or the Thomistic habit of thought that shapes this meditation on religious "devotion," it is worth noting the specific advice Donne's speaker offers or considers here. The sole imperatives of his address instruct one to "feare" that he will not "be imputed" righteous, to "Know thy foes," to "allow . . . but one . . . And the right," "to stand inquiring right . . . now," to "Keepe the truth which thou has found," and, finally, to "know [and] obey Power":

> So perish Soules, which more chuse mens unjust
> Power from God claym'd, then God himselfe to trust.
>
> (ll. 109–10)

As even a brief glance at the statutes of Elizabeth's reign and even a rudimentary recollection of the instruments of political and religious conformity and censorship wielded by her secret police will show,[5] in the "last daye[s]" of the sixteenth century in England this is a stunningly provocative set of directives, imperatives that seem to flaunt their interrogation of the State Church. We need not "spy" such impudence in these lines, of course, and can follow the modern reading of a broad religious toleration in them; but such a reading reflects more the liberality of modern perspectives ("opinion,"in Donne's word) than the fear that is covered by its pose of urbane detachment. The view that in its "broadmindedness and open-mindedness" the poem is "characteristically English in spirit" might indeed suggest why *Satyre III* expresses a "modernity" that makes it "the most readable and interesting of the five" *Satyres* for some readers.[6] But such broad toleration, one might recall, was a view not readily tolerated in (Counter-) Reformation England; and Donne, as the trenchant assault on "busy" disbelievers in the lyrics and elegies reiterates, does not strike one as remarkable for any toleration of rival forms of "devotion."[7]

---

5. See Williams, *The Tudor Regime;* and Annabel Patterson, *Censorship and Interpretation* (Madison: Univ. of Wisconsin Press, 1984).
6. K. W. Gransden, *John Donne* (London: Longmans, Green 1954), 103.
7. Even in the metaphoric comparisons of the five ideologues the "Catholic" amorist comes off better than the other two major candidates—for the comparison reflects only the idol-atry bestowed on the king/"Prince" in England, not on the practice of the Catholic: the "Catholic" is compared, that is, to the idolatry of the Reformation English privileging of the secular over the spiritual which the poem attacks throughout.
    The portrait of Graius is the most severe of the five, in fact: the English Protestant "Imbraceth her, whom his Godfathers will / Tender to him, being tender, as Wards still / Take such wives as their Guardians offer, or / Pay valewes" (55–62). In the dominantly mercenary imagery—*tender, tender, offer, valewes*—wives become material objects or legal tender by which the "wills" (legal testaments and laws of Godfathers instead of God or Father) of legal substitutes (for man and God) enforce a mercenary system of oppression of the individual *will*, in line perhaps with the Calvinian total mistrust of the will (as explained by the *Institutions* of the former lawyer, John Calvin), but also in line with the

The most striking feature of *Satyre III* as a poem on "true religion," in fact, is not its urbane religious tolerance—which is actually only an equal scorn for various shapes of intellectual and spiritual laziness or stupidity—but the *absence* of "true religion" which it discovers in Elizabethan England. Just as *Satyre IV* undercuts the integrity of the "Presence Chamber" by disclosing the absence of devotion and truth in its secular "Masse in jest" in which "all are players," so in the third poem, despite the speaker's sententious and proverbial remedies for the faults he uncovers in the contemporary scene, the overall confessional health of the nation might be best described by the last lines of Donne's subsequent poem on the transmigration of spirit in his country: "The onely measure is, and judge, opinion" (*Metempsychosis* 520). What *Satyre III* exposes, that is, is the "compasse" of religious *poses* in England—what we today call "ideology." It discovers a world of "mis-devotion" and religious *adunata* in which the "sweet . . . Pilgrimage" of man's search to "find" a religion both "true, and faire" leads "No where" (*Song: "Goe and catche"*). In fact, the major thrust of the argument is that the terms of religious controversy have become rather political than confessional; for after his caricatures of the various sectarian poses, even after his submission that the issues could be relegated to interpretations of the nature and locus of Truth, the satirist concludes with a colloquy on the nature of power:

> That thou mayest rightly obey Power, her bounds know;
> Those past, her nature; and name is changed; to be
> Then humble to her is idolatrie. . . .
>
>   (100–102)

As a reiteration of the satirist's warnings about confusing the Bride of Christ and her clothing these lines certainly do not stray beyond the bounds of what one was allowed to say in Elizabethan England; but in a poem that relies throughout on the same vocabulary of Petrarchan love conventions to describe Christ's Bride that Elizabethan polemics had appropriated to "name" the Virgin Queen[8]—a vocabulary, some would have recalled, which had originally designated the adoration of earthly laurels and Lauras to be a form of

---

    Catholic recusant claim that the fines and courts—and especially the Court of Wards—of what Richard Verstegan called the "Cecilian Inquisition" (Cobb, 66) were abusive forms of mere taxation, little concerned with devotion or religion or loyalty. For more on Donne's relations to this court see my "Donne and the Court of Wards," *AN&Q* n.s. 7.3 (July 1994).

8. The seminal studies of this topic remain those of Frances Yates, *Astraea* (London: Routledge, 1975), and Roy Strong, *The Cult of Elizabeth* (London: Thames & Hudson, 1977), recently supplemented by John N. King, *Tudor Royal Iconography* (Princeton: Princeton Univ. Press, 1989).

idolatrie because of its failure "to trust" the Virgin Queen of heaven[9]—then such final sharp demarcations between local and eternal power might lead the author to be "desirous to hyde them wth out any over reconing of them or there maker." These lines recall, in fact, the precise objections of the English Catholics to the Protestant substitution of the Virgin Queen for the Virgin Mary and the political term "traitor" for the religious term "blasphemer" or "idolater." William Allen's *True . . . Defense of English Catholics*, for example, contrasted the "heretical regiment, where politiques have all the government," to the "Catholic commonwealths [where] the chief respect is and ever was . . . of the honor of God, the good of the Holy Church, [and] the salvation of the soul of their people" (117). And in his gloss of the passage that was the hallmark of Catholic verification or documentation—Mark 12:17—he said that in Protestant England

> now, and ever when the superiority temporal hath the preeminence and the spiritual is but accessory, dependent, and wholly upholden of the [political], error in faith is little accounted of, . . . [so that] all our doings, endeavours, and exercises of religion are drawn to treasons and trespasses against the Queene; themselves protestings, in all their doings, that they meddle not with us for our doctrine whatsoever; thereby insinuating that our religion is true, . . . or else that they care not for it nor what we believe, no further than toucheth their prince and temporal weal. (118–19)

In response to charges against the "idolatrie" of the Mass, the "adultery" of Mariology, and the "treason" of their recusancy, then, English Catholics responded that the true "nature" of idolatry is the substitution of the spiritual by the political: "So perish Soules." It is this specific defense that is embedded in the Thomist generalities of Donne's manuscript satire. Arguing in his usual mode of analogical

9. One of the cultural ironies of the post-Renaissance—indeed, of the Renaissance recreations of Petrarch's *Rime sparse*—is the apparent refusal of "Petrarchist" poets to accept the Italian poet's rejection of Laura and his adoration or "idolatrie" of Laura and her "name" as "mio primo giovenile errore," "Medusa l'error mio": eros is error—a view reiterated by his *Secretum*. Perhaps Donne's atypical response to the Petrarchist model derives in part from his acceptance of the premises of the Catholic poet's descriptions of the Blessed Virgin—as intimated by the reading of his *First Anniversary* by one of his first and best readers, Ben Jonson ("If it had been of the Virgin Mary"—much virtue in that *If*). This topic has been most recently explored by Maureen Sabine, *Feminine Engendered Faith: John Donne and Richard Crashaw* (London: Macmillan, 1992), especially the ways by which, "in exposing Elizabeth's false likeness to the Virgin Mother, Donne was able to draw adverse comparisons which directed attention back to Mary's original iconography" (22). Such "odious comparisons," as he terms it in "The Comparison," are central to the daring wit of the elegies as well as to the third *Satyre*, I have argued in "Donne's (Re)Annunciation of the Virgin(ia Colony) in *Elegy XIX*," *SCN* 4 (1989): 49–64, and R. V. Young has argued in " 'O my America, my new-found-land': Pornography and Imperial Politics in Donne's *Elegies*," *SCN* 4 (1989): 35–48.

conceit, riddling provocatively with the figure of Truth as the natural
daughter of Time and/or the name of the Queen (recalling Eliza-
beth's appropriation of her sister's motto), and perhaps even invoking
the primary term of the central controversy over the Eucharist—
"change," in *Satyre III* Donne's interrogation of current mis-devotion
accords in argument and terminology with recent and established
Catholic assessments.

Such "wise doubt" about the supposed detachment of Donne in
Satyre III might also lead one to question how to read the dominant
clothing motif of the poem. Does the identification of *all* English
devotion with confusions of the metaphoric, the momentary, and the
apparent comment only on *mis*-devotion in England or does it intend
to contrast Protestant doctrines of imputation with the Catholic doc-
trine of Good Works (as in *Satyre II*)? Just as Donne appropriated
the codes, strategies, and commonplaces of Protestant polemic in
the second and fourth *Satyres* in those veiled assaults on the Eliza-
bethan establishment, so the third *Satyre* rereads some of the central
charges of the Recusant polemics. If we readmit to Donne's audi-
ence, that is, those readers of his own family tradition of Catholic
"learning and good life," and if we recall at the same time his claim
to have "survayed and disgested the whole body of Divinity, contro-
verted between the [English] and the Roman Church" (*Pseudo-
Martyr*), then we might hear more than his "fathers spirit" and his
own "feare" of denying the "easie wayes and neare [of] thy fathers
spirit" in Donne's dangerous denial of a "Mistresse . . . worthy of all
our Soules devotion" in the imperial religion of Elizabeth.[1] What are
we to make, that is, of the central conceit of *Satyre III*, by which
Donne appropriates the Petrarchism that Court poets were using to
figure forth an aged virgin Queen as the "one" desirable "Mistresse
. . . worthy of . . . devotion"—especially when the poem locates her
not in the Court but "on a huge hill, / Cragged and steep," a hill that
could quite easily be the Calvary of English Catholics, Tyburn Hill?

In the same vein is the central biblical text which the poem expli-
cates—"Render unto Caesar . . ." (Matt. 22:21, Mark 12:17, Luke
20:25)—which was the nearly unanimous basis of most Recusant
protests against the state religion and its relentless system of penal
laws in Elizabeth's England.[2] And the biblical citation at the center

---

1. This is not intended to deny in any sense that these lines also evoke Donne's vision of a
   spiritual Father who *gives* the chaste Spouse to man in the very act of his "ask[ing] thy
   father," as Donne's frequent citations of Augustine's similar definitions of prevenient
   Grace in his prose letters reiterate.
2. On "penal laws" and the Catholic interpretation of them as proof that Elizabeth and Cecil
   sought to use fines of the "old rich" nobility to support the regime, see Allen's *Defense* and
   Southwell's *Supplication*, among others. For support of Allen's claim that the secular state
   "care[d] not what [the English Catholics] believed, no further than touched their prince
   and temporal wealth," (*Defense*, 119), see John Alymer's letter to Walsingham cited in
   Rose, *Cases of Conscience*, 43–44, where the institution of penal fines is recommended

of the poem evokes the same "brave" associations, for when the sat-
irist instructs the reader(s) to "aske thy father which is shee, / Let
him aske his," he refers to Deuteronomy 32:7, the passage on which
Cardinal Pole based the originary assault on English Protestantism
in his candid address to King Henry VIII in *De unitate*.[3] This passage
would remind some readers that Recusant writers such as Allen,
Persons, Stapleton, and Fitzherbert (and Sander/Rishton earlier)
never tired of urging that the "incestuous" daughter of Anne Boleyn
might have considerable difficulty in determining the identity of her
father, a difficulty she was rumored to share with her mother, whose
father might have been Henry VIII also.[4] Other details in the poem
raise similarly "odious comparisons"—the inversion of the Protestant
doctrine of imputation in the opening lines, for example, or the con-
temptuous scouring of the New World project, the identification of
the war in the Netherlands as "forbidden," the reference to the
Infanta, or the wry analogy to the Court of Wards. Even the choice
of Pope Gregory XIII as the representative of the Catholic position
in the penultimate section of the poem where religious advisors are
stripped of their earthly titles is curious, for it was Pope Pius V who
excommunicated Elizabeth; Pope Gregory XIII managed to mitigate
that papal Bull considerably.[5] And the same kind of provocative

---

on the grounds that "this manner of fininge them will procure the Queene a thousand
pundes by yeare to hir Coffers whatsoever it do more."
3. "If the will of God might be declared in the Church, where could we better understand
this than in the custom of the Church? 'Ask thy father, and he will declare it to thee'
(Deut. 32: 7)": *On the Unity of the Church* (1536), trans. Joseph G. Dwyer (Westminister:
Newman Press, 1965), 105. Cardinal Pole's originary citation of the biblical passage is
recalled too frequently to enumerate here; but see, as representative amplifications of this
directive, Sander's and Rishton's 1585 *De origine ac progresu schismatis anglicani* (trans-
lated in 1877 by David Lewis: *The Rise and Growth of the Anglican Schism* [London: Oates
and Burns]); Allen's later works, especially his defenses of William Stanley, which contain
descriptions of England's foreign wars similar to those of Donne, and his sharp attacks on
Elizabeth in his *Admonition*; the major essays of Robert Persons, especially his *Responsio*
(1581) and his defense of the succession of the Infanta in *Conference on the Succession*
(1594)—if it is his and not Verstegan's; and the most severe personal attack on Elizabeth
and Cecil, Stapleton's *Apologia* (1592). Valuable appraisals of these works are available
in Code, ch. 1.
    It might not be too inventive, moreover, to see Donne's poem in some ways as a sort of
(ironic) analogue to Pole's address to his own monarch; such a possible identification of
the Elizabethan poet with one of the original members of the More-Erasmus circle would
rest not only on their similar situations but on the long history of Donne's family's close
association with Pole. Donne's uncle, Ellis Heywood, S. J., after all, was Pole's secretary
in exile and was the author of the first book published about Donne's martyred ancestor,
Sir Thomas More—*Il Moro*—which was in fact dedicated to Pole. See Flynn, *Swordsman*,
for a thorough treatment of this crucial association.
4. Unlike the conciliatory mode of his *Defense*, in his later *Admonition* even Allen asserted
this commonplace of the controversy, calling Elizabeth "an incestous bastard, begotten
and born in sin" (cited in Code, 40n. 1), just as Sander in *De origine* had claimed in his
"report" of how Thomas Boleyn himself "confessed without hesitation [to the king himself]
that Anne Boleyn was the king's child" (I, vi), and just as Stapleton later in his *Apologia*
wrote that "Quae denique novit qua matre nota est, cum tamen de patre non inter omnes
constet" (161, cited in Code, 60n. 2).
5. Most editors and readers agree that the reference is to Gregory XIII, Pope 1572–85—the
years from Donne's birth to his accompaniment of Jasper Heywood to the Continent.

textual appropriation animates the concluding admonition, when the Elizabethan satirist endorses the central Recusant distinction between confessional and political truths by characterizing current power as "the streames tyrannous rage." This application of the precise terms of Machiavelli's figuration of Dame Fortune as *fiumi rovinosi* (*Il Principe*, ch. 25), itself a revision of Dante's *Inferno* VII.64f., would seem to endorse once again the repeated Recusant descriptions of Elizabeth and her ministers (especially Cecil) as Machiavels.[6] The concluding "Power" simile of *Satyre III* might well evoke also another complaint against illegal torture of suspected Catholics, for it describes not only the fate of those who do not "God himselfe . . . trust" but also those separated from the "Power" of the secular "head" who "are driven / Though mills, and rockes, and woods." As such it would recall Southwell's similar descriptions of "the ordinary punishments of Bridewell, now made the Common Purgatory of Priests and Catholiques, as grinding in the Mill, . . . of purpose to wring out of us some odious speeches which may serve at our Arraignments."[7]

Read in the lexical arena of the late Elizabethan sectarian wars, then, *Satyre III* might not only be remarkable for its "daring" invocation of religious toleration in an age of rigid censorship and religious suppression, but even dangerous in its inscription of the major

---

Certainly Gregory XIII's reform of the calendar alone would have made his name most recognizable (even by the English who resisted the reform for 170 years); and it is his attempts to render the (disastrous) Bull of Pius V no longer valid—or at least not a matter meriting enforcement—that are the frequent subject of the Catholic polemicists and appellants of the age. In his response to Cecil's *Execution of Justice*, for instance, Allen pointed out that Gregory XIII "never revived" the Bull of Excommunication, "but by connivance and expectation . . . suffered the sentence after a sort to die" (*A Defense*, 125). We "have sought," said Allen, "the mitigation thereof" (127). For an informative view of the problems even this mitigation created for the missionary priests, see Arnold Oskar Meyer, *England and the Catholic Church under Queen Elizabeth* (London: Routledge and Kegan Paul, 1914; rev. ed. 1967), 138–44. It should not be forgotten that the central topic of the debate about the Bull of Pius V—like the central thesis of *Satyre III*—was the "power" of spiritual and secular leaders.

6. Central to these assaults on Cecil was the complaint that because of him Elizabeth had turned her back on "the old nobility." "He hath made himself the very owner of her determinations," wrote Verstegan in *A Declaration of the True Causes of the Great Troubles* (1592); Stapleton called Cecil the true "King" of England who had gained his authority by robbing the old nobility of their lands. "A new nobility of men base and impure inflamed with infinite avarice and ambition," now ruled the country, said Allen in his *Admonition* (cited in Code, 41).

7. *Humble Supplication*, 34–35. It is pertinent to recall that in May 1593, Donne's younger brother had been apprehended by Topcliffe's colleague in the presence of William Harrington, and under "cross-examination" did reveal that Harrington "was a priest & did shriue him." Harrington was executed—hanged, drawn (dismembered and disemboweled), and quartered; but even before his death, young Henry Donne was also dead, having been transferred to Newgate, where the plague was raging, where he died. Whether the younger Donne suffered the (usual) "grinding in the Mill," the records do not reveal; but we do know that Donne's uncle, Jasper Heywood, was tortured on the rack during 1583–85 while under indictment for "treason," and that Donne himself accompanied his mother on a visit to Heywood "at a consultation of Iesuits in the *Tower*" in 1585. See John Morris, "The Martyrdom of William Harrington," *The Month* 20 (1874): 411–23; and Flynn, *Swordsman*, part 2, ch. 7.

themes, texts, allusions, and attitudes of the Recusant position.
Embedded in the "noble" satire of Donne's poem is not only an
emphatic concentration on the primacy of historicist readings—"yet
truth a little elder is"—but also a witty recollection of the (fearful)
tropes that had been used to defend the Catholicism of his "fathers
spirit." As a satirical Ignatian meditation on the primacy of Truth to
"true religion," composed in "a land, and time of misdevotion" (*The
Relic*) when the political or ideological import of "religion" was being
rendered primary by the Act of Uniformity, the Oath of Allegiance,
the Bloody Question, and the "huge" statutes which defined religious
difference as "treason"—all enforced by a system of spies and tor-
tures aimed to "drawe" one to wear the Protestant "wardrop," *Satyre
III* leaves the (re)reader with one final, typically Donnean irony: just
as he relies on multiple correspondences in *The First Anniversary* to
suggest that "all correspondence is lost" and insists after two dozen
comparisons in *The Comparison* that "comparisons are odious," so
in *Satyre III* Donne ventures a historical reading of the disease of
"true religion" in Elizabethan England in order to insist that there is
one "dazling, yet plaine" issue beyond the scope of history, ideology,
and politics—"Truth stands." And the searching inquiry after that
Truth, the poem dares to suggest, remains the goal and the "cure"
but not the "nature,'and the name," of "Mistress" Elizabeth's (and
Lord Burghley's) England. As a satire which evokes the tropes and
polemical strokes of English Catholic critiques of the state of religion
in Elizabethan England, that is, *Satyre III* seems closest to the pre-
Tridentine church of Donne's family tradition. That that Church was
lost, or that Donne himself later (or even in the 1590s) realized that
the Church of More was "gone," should not lead us to overlook or
to underestimate the essentially satirical character of this poem, or
to neglect how it would have been read by those Catholic readers for
whom it could easily have been originally intended.

ALAN ARMSTRONG

The Apprenticeship of John Donne: Ovid and the *Elegies*†

To Donne, Nashe, and the young gentleman-poets, such as Inns of
Court men, who became the principal practitioners of the genre,
Ovidian elegy presented an appealing alternative to the plaintive son-

† From ELH 44 (Autumn 1977): 419–24. Copyright © 1977 by The Johns Hopkins Uni-
versity Press. Reprinted by permission of The Johns Hopkins University Press.

nets poured forth by every would-be poet. The world of the *Amores*, with its wit, sensuality, and urban ambience, must have seemed at the same time less alien and more exotically attractive than the worlds of Petrarchan and pastoral poetry; to Donne, especially, the brilliant, irreverent wit and light-hearted cynicism of Ovid proved congenial. Such affinities between the two poets, best summed in the Ovidian phrase *musa iocosa*, served as the theme of J. B. Leishman's study of the *Elegies* in *The Monarch of Wit*, which authoritatively established the fact of Donne's debt to Ovid.[1] Recently, however, this case for an Ovidian background to the *Elegies* has been challenged, most notably by Roma Gill, who objects that such studies misrepresent Donne "as a scholar engaged in the respectable academic pursuit of imitating Ovid."[2]

Due recognition of Donne's original genius, however, need not preclude the very notion of Donne as apprentice; indeed, the *Elegies* admirably support the Renaissance belief in imitation as the friend of invention. These early poems, though devoid of "translations" or even precise verbal echoes of Ovid, nevertheless recreate Ovidian attitudes and techniques, and testify to Donne's discovery in the *Amores*, not only of a kindred spirit, but of a valuable textbook for the poet. The ensuing discussion of a few of the *Elegies* aims to show how a closer look at Donne's apprenticeship to Ovid, especially at his adoption of the rhetorical techniques which create the Ovidian self-conscious persona, can further reveal Donne's artistry, and can bring to light the origins of a poetic technique characteristically used by Donne in the *Elegies* and *Songs and Sonnets*.

Except for "The Autumnall" (distinguished from the major group of love elegies by a different manuscript tradition), Donne's *Elegies* are now believed to have been written between 1593 and 1596, during his years at Lincoln's Inn.[3] This dating places Donne in the vanguard of the poets who revived the genre for English verse, although, unlike such elegists as Campion (in Latin) and Alamanni, he made no boast of his priority. Earlier English poets had attempted quantitative elegiac verse, but none was able to carry the experiment further than Sidney's two elegies in the *Arcadia* and two elegiac epigrams in *Certain Sonnets*.[4] Finding the classical metrical conception of the genre useless in the virtual absence of quantitative English elegiacs, Elizabethan writers resorted to defining the elegy

1. J. B. Leishman, *The Monarch of Wit* (1951; rpt. London: Hutchinson and Co., 1965).
2. Roma Gill, " 'Musa Iocosa Mea': Thoughts on the *Elegies*," in *John Donne: Essays in Celebration*, ed. A. J. Smith, (London: Methuen, 1972), p. 47.
3. Helen Gardner establishes these dates in her edition of *The Elegies and Songs and Sonnets* (Oxford: Clarendon Press, 1965), pp. xxxii–xxxiii. For her discussion of "The Autumnall," see pp. 252–54 of the same edition.
4. Nos. 11 and 74 of the old *Arcadia* and nos. 13 and 14 of *Certain Sonnets* in Sidney's *Poems*, ed. William A. Ringler, Jr., (Oxford: Clarendon Press, 1962).

by its matter, rather than its meter. The prevailing Elizabethan view
of the elegy as lament had little support in classical elegy, which,
with the sole exception of Augustan erotic elegy (scarcely known to
educated Elizabethans), was remarkable instead for the diversity of
subjects accommodated,[5] a classical precedent of another kind, the
well-known *Ars Poetica* of Horace, lies behind this definition of the
genre. Ignoring the elegies of his contemporaries, and following
instead the Alexandrian grammarians (whose account of the genre
was likewise uninhibited by the example of Greek and Alexandrian
elegy), Horace regarded the elegy as a lament ("querimonia").[6] Until
the 1590's, the Horatian view prevailed in England, unchallenged by
the little-known love elegies of Tibullus, Propertius, and Ovid, and
faintly supported by the exiled Ovid's *Tristia* and *Epistulae ex Ponto*,
which served as models of elegiac meter in the schools.

Horace's brief account of the genre, however satisfactory to
authors of treatises on poetry, provided English poets no guide for
composing elegies; it did suggest, on the other hand, an impressive
classical label for poems written in other generic traditions. In the
1570's and 1580's, for instance, English writers occasionally iden-
tified the elegy with the complaint, the flourishing genre most obvi-
ously resembling the "lament" described by Horace; thus Gascoigne,
in the dedicatory letter to his *Complaynt of Philomene* (1576), calls
the poem "an Elegye or sorrowefull song."[7] When a new poetic fash-
ion prevailed in the 1590's, Horace's definition was easily stretched
to include Petrarchan love laments, so that many elegies of that
decade are merely third-rate Petrarchan poems dressed in the thin-
nest of classical guises. Beginning about 1593, the elegy became a
fashionable novelty, conspicuously advertised on the title-pages of
collections of love poetry, but such volumes almost invariably con-
tain an abundance of sonnets and only one or two elegies, which
rarely transcend the common run of amatory verse.[8] Most of the
"elegies" written before 1590, and many in the succeeding decade,
represent the resurrection only of a generic name.

5. F. W. Weitzmann, "Notes on the Elizabethan 'Elegie,' " *PMLA*, 50 (1935), 435–43, pro-
vides a useful collection of sixteenth-century references to the elegy; though Weitzmann's
arbitrary categorization of his examples obscures the fact, most of these instances reflect
the Horatian definition of elegy as lament.
6. Horace briefly notices the elegy in lines 75–78 of the *Ars Poetica*. C. O. Brink, *Horace on
Poetry* (Cambridge: Cambridge University Press, 1971), pp. 165–66, documents Horace's
use of the etymology advanced by the Alexandrian scholar Didymus.
7. French writers anticipated, and may have been responsible for, this Elizabethan generic
equation. Thomas Sebillet (*L'art poetique françois*) identified the elegy with the complaint;
Sebillet, Aneau, du Bellay, and Peletier all followed Horace in insisting on sadness as the
definitive quality of elegy.
8. Cf. Lodge's *Phillis: Honoured with Pastorall Sonnets, Elegies, and amorous delights* (1593),
Barnabe Barnes's *Parthenophil and Parthenophe: Sonnettes, Madrigals, Elegies, and Odes*
(1593), Francis Davison's *A Poetical Rapsody Containing Diverse Sonnets, Odes, Elegies,
and other Poesies* (1602), and Alexander Craig's *Amorose Songs, Sonets, and Elegies* (1606).

A genuine revival of the elegy, which contributed new models and new directions to English poetry, came when a few poets looked at last to Augustan example rather than Horatian precept. Earlier, in France and Italy, the elegies of Tibullus and Propertius ("miei primi Maestri" to Luigi Alamanni, the first vernacular elegist)[9] inspired the rebirth of the genre, but in England, the elegies of Ovid supplanted them. Marlowe's translations of the *Amores*, which established the iambic pentameter couplet as the accentual equivalent of the elegiac distich,[1] and Harington's abundant quotation from the *Ars Amatoria* and *Amores* in his popular translation of Ariosto's *Orlando Furioso*, made Ovid's erotic elegies familiar to English readers, while those of Tibullus and Propertius remained virtually unknown. Donne and Nashe quickly attempted the new genre in 1593,[2] the same year in which Barnabe Barnes, Giles Fletcher, and Thomas Lodge published the first English collections of love poetry to include elegies.

"Loves Warre," one of his earliest elegies, displays Donne in the immediate process of absorbing from Ovid the art of the self-conscious persona, as he takes up a paradoxical commonplace basic to the Augustan elegiac convention. The elegy begins with this figure of "love's wars," set in a question addressed to the lover's mistress:

> Till I have peace with thee, warre other men,
> And when I have peace, can I leave thee then?
> All other warres are scrupulous; only thou,
> O faire, free City, mayst thy selfe allow
> To any one: In Flanders who can tell
> Whether the master presse, or men rebell?
> Only wee knowe, that which all Ideots say,
> They beare most blowes which come to part the fraye.
> France in her lunatique giddinesse did hate
> Ever our men, yea and our God of late,
> Yet she relies upon our Angels well,
> Which ne'r retourne; no more than they which fell.
> Sick Ireland is with a strange warre possest,
> Like to'an Ague, now rageinge, now at rest,
> Which time will cure; yet it must do her good
> If she were purg'd, and her heade-veine let blood.

---

9. Luigi Alamani, *Opere Toscane* (Rome: Caetani, 1806), I, xvii.
1. Marlowe was anticipated by Nicholas Grimald, whose translations of two Latin elegies by Beza into rhymed pentameter couplets appeared in Tottel's *Songes and Sonettes* (nos. 129 and 130), but Grimald's solution to the elegiac distich went unnoticed.
2. R. B. McKerrow, ed., *The Works of Thomas Nashe* (Oxford: Blackwell, 1958), does not attempt to date Nashe's unpublished elegy, the "Choise of Valentines," but two contemporary allusions to the poem, if accurate, would place its first appearance between August, 1592, and September, 1593. "Papers Complaint," in *The Scourge of Folly* (1611) of John Davies of Hereford, places the poem immediately after *Piers Pennilesse*, entered in the Stationers' Register on August 8, 1592, while "The Trimming of Thomas Nashe" puts the "Choise" immediately before *Christ's Tears Over Jerusalem*, entered in the Stationers' Register on September 8, 1593.

> And Midas joyes our Spanish journeys give,
> Wee touch all gold, but find no foode to live. . . . [3]

Launched on the "love's wars" figure, the elegy suddenly veers, with the mention of Flanders, toward familiar political satire. Though the satire seems at first to desert the comparative theme, and to abandon mistress and dramatic setting altogether, we soon discover that Donne has been preparing an argument against his own service in the wars. From an initially impersonal criticism of the "Spanish journeys," he turns to a vivid account of the danger and futility which would attend his soldiership:

> And I should be in that hot parching clime
> To dust and ashes turn'd before my time.
> To mewe me in a ship is to enthrall
> Mee in a prison that were like to fall;
> Or in a cloyster, save that there men dwell
> In a calme heaven, here in a swaggering hell.
> Long voyages are longe consumptions,
> And ships are carts for executions,
> Yea they are deaths; Is't not all one to fly
> Into another world as 'tis to dye?

Only now will Donne resume his suspended metaphor of love and war. Meanwhile, he has pointedly distinguished his treatment of the commonplace from Petrarchan ones by following conventional Augustan practice instead. In Petrarchan verse, the figurative comparison of love and war had become very nearly a dead metaphor, the material for conceits which had lost sight of the literal reality of war; the Petrarchan figure was cut off from the vital conflict of private passion and public duty which informed Augustan uses of the "love's wars" commonplace. Donne, on the other hand, quickly establishes real referents for the metaphor's vehicle by introducing into the elegy contemporary wars, as Propertius had done,[4] and by involving his persona in the problem of possible duty in these wars. Donne also inclines toward his Augustan predecessors in his emphasis on the sexual aspects of the analogy, again in deliberate contrast to Petrarchan poetry. In Renaissance sonnets, "love's wars" figures usually bear on the defeats, victories, and strategies of courtship, the assault on the lady's heart, or her cruel conquest of the suitor, but Donne writes of the wars that follow upon the winning of peace and, by his double meanings, gives his elegy a distinctly un-Petrarchan tone:

3. Quotations from the *Elegies* in this essay follow the text of Helen Gardner's previously cited edition.
4. Cf. Propertius, III.iv and III.v.

Here let mee warre; in these armes let mee lye;
Here let me parlee, batter, bleede, and dye.
Thine armes emprison mee, and mine armes thee;
Thy hart thy ransome is, take mine for mee.
Other men warre that they their rest may gaine,
But we will rest that wee may fight againe.
Those warres the ignorant, these th'experienc'd love;
There wee are always under, here above.
There engines far offe breede a just true feare,
Neare thrusts, pikes, stabs, yea bullets hurt not here.
There lyes are wrongs, here safe uprightly lye. . . .

Leishman has indicated Donne's general debt in "Loves Warre" to
three of Ovid's *Amores* (I.xi, II.x, and II.xii), all of which employ the
"love's wars" figure.[5] The latter two elegies, however, are much less
closely related to "Loves Warre" than the first, since they belong to
different conventional categories; *Amores*, II.x, parodies formulaic
"Beatus ille . . ." praises of pastoral, rather than military, life, and
Amores, II.xii, is an erotic elegy of the "triumph" type, mimicking the
encomiastic poems written to celebrate martial conquests. Donne's
inspiration clearly lies in *Amores*, I.ix, an elegy given entirely to the
comparison of the lover and the soldier:

Every lover is a soldier, and Cupid has his own camp;
    Believe me, Atticus, every lover is a soldier.
The age which is fit for war is also congenial to Venus.
    An old soldier is a disgrace; an old lover, a disgrace.
The spirit that captains seek in a brave soldier,
    The pretty girl seeks in her mate.
They both stay awake all night; each rests on the ground—
    One watches over his mistress's door,
        the other over his captain's.
The soldier's duty is a long road; send the girl,
    The vigorous lover will follow without end.[6]

5. Leishmann, pp. 74–75.
6. Ovid, *Amores*, I.ix.1–10:

Militat omnis amans, et habet sua castra Cupido;
    Attice, crede mihi, militat omnis amans.
quae bello est habilis, Veneri quoque convenit aetas.
    turpe senex miles, turpe senilis amor.
quos petiere duces animos in milite forti
    hos petit in socio bella puella viro.
pervigilant ambo; terra requiescit uterque—
    ille fores dominae servat, at ille ducis.
militis officium longa est via; mitte puellam,
    strenuus exempto fine sequetur amans.

Translations of Augustan elegies in this essay are my own. The Latin text here follows
Grant Showerman, ed., *Heroides and Amores*, The Loeb Classical Library, (London: Wm.
Heinemann, 1914).

Ovid sustains this exercise for another twenty lines, exhaustively cataloguing analogies between lover and soldier. Donne, unlike many of his contemporaries, almost invariably regards such a poetic model, not as an opportunity for pedestrian borrowing, but as an example to be outdone. The form of Donne's "love's wars" argument clearly matches Ovid's orderly and thorough exploration of the general analogy, but the particular analogies are novel; moreover, Donne pushes beyond Ovid's defensive case for the likeness of lover and soldier to a more radical argument for love's superiority to war.

More compelling evidence for Donne's imitation of Ovid rests in the strikingly similar closing arguments of the two elegies. Having listed instance after instance of the lover's soldierliness, Ovid at last moves from gathering evidence to asserting his argument: "Therefore anyone who has called love slothful, / Let him desist. Love is for the man of venturesome nature."[7] But the poem does not end here, for Ovid goes on to present himself ironically as a sterling example of the soldierly discipline and vigor which love inspires in its followers:

> I myself was born for lazy and careless ease;
>> My couch and the shade had softened my spirit.
> Love for a beautiful girl drove me, idle as I was,
>> And ordered me to earn soldier's pay in a camp.
> So, you see me nimbly waging the nocturnal wars.
>> He who would not be slothful, let him love.[8]

Donne, too, closes with a tongue-in-cheek justification for his remaining a lover, rather than a soldier:

> There men kill men, we'will make one by and by.
> Thou nothing; I not halfe so much shall do
> In these warres as they may which from us two
> Shall spring. Thousands we see which travaile not
> To warres, but stay, swords, armes, and shot
> To make at home: And shall not I do then
> More glorious service, staying to make men?

Neither elegist impartially considers the merits of the analogy of lover and soldier, or love and war; instead, each puts the argument of his comparison in the mouth of a persona who is obviously com-

---

7. *Amores*, I.ix.31–32:

> Ergo desidiam quicumque vocabat amorem,
>> desinat. ingenii est experientis amor.

8. *Amores*, I.ix.41–46:

> ipse ego segnis eram discinctaque in otia natus;
>> mollierant animos lectus et umbra meos.
> inpulit ignavum formosae cura puellae
>> iussit et in castris aera merere suis.
> inde vides agilem nocturnaque bella gerentem.
>> qui nolet fieri desidiosus, amet!

mitted to love's pleasures, blatantly unwilling to endanger himself in war, and defensively aware of the public view of this posture as cowardly or indolent—but who boldly justifies himself, nevertheless, with a playful, clever argument for the superior virtue, honor, and public-spiritedness of his service in the wars of Venus. Both personae adopt the ordinary rhetorical aim of persuasion, but the conception of persona implicit in classical rhetoric, in the orator's projection of himself as a good man, is turned on its head here. The speakers in both Donne's and Ovid's elegies not only define themselves as deviants from ethical norms, but also expect their audiences to see the logical fallacies of their self-justifying arguments, as they themselves do.

*   *   *

ACHSAH GUIBBORY

"Oh, Let Mee Not Serve So": The Politics of Love
in Donne's *Elegies*†

For modern readers, accustomed to distinct separations between private and public, love and politics may seem strange bedfellows. But recent studies have made us aware of important connections between amatory poetry and patronage, between the discourse of (courtly) love and the seeking of advancement by aspiring men at Queen Elizabeth's court.[1] Arthur Marotti, especially, has analyzed the political circumstances and dimensions of Donne's amatory poetry, arguing that we should see it as "coterie" poetry written in an "encoded" language, embodying Donne's frustrated ambitions for socioeconomic, political power even when, *especially* when, he is writing about love.[2]

† From *ELH* 57 (Winter 1990): 811–33. Copyright © 1990 by The Johns Hopkins University Press. Reprinted by permission of The Johns Hopkins University Press.
1. See, e.g., Arthur F. Marotti, " 'Love is not love': Elizabethan Sonnet Sequences and the Social Order," *ELH* 49 (1982): 396–428; Louis Montrose's two essays, "Celebration and Insinuation: Sir Philip Sidney and the Motives of Elizabethan Courtship," *Renaissance Drama*, n.s., 8 (1977): 3–35, and " 'Shaping Fantasies': Figurations of Gender and Power in Elizabethan Culture," *Representations* 1 (1983): 61–94; and David Javitch, "The Impure Motives of Elizabethan Poetry," in *The Power of Forms in the English Renaissance*, ed. Stephen Greenblatt (Norman, Okla.: Pilgrim Books, 1982), 225–38. Lauro Martines has suggested similarly complex relationships between courtly love poetry and politics in a paper "The Politics of Love Poetry in Renaissance Italy," given at a conference on "Historical Criticism in an Age of Deconstruction" (University of Illinois at Urbana-Champaign, October 13–15, 1989).
2. Marotti, *John Donne, Coterie Poet* (Madison: Univ. of Wisconsin Press, 1986). Further references to this work will be cited parenthetically in the text. See also John Carey, *John Donne: Life, Mind, and Art* (New York: Oxford Univ. Press, 1981), chaps. 3–4, who similarly argues that "power is the shaping principle in Donne's verse" (117).

Marotti's discussion of the interrelations between politics and the languages of love is deservedly influential. But his argument (both in the book on Donne and in his important earlier article on Elizabethan sonnet sequences) fosters a certain distortion, for repeatedly Marotti's language implies that the *real* subject of this poetry is socioeconomic power and ambition. While he brilliantly shows the political dimensions of the languages of courtly love as used in Elizabethan poetry, the effect of his argument is to suggest not so much the *inter*relations between love and politics but the centrality of socioeconomic concerns. Love becomes merely the vehicle of the metaphor; the tenor is invariably political. In the interest of deciphering this political "meaning," amatory relations between men and women tend to all but disappear.

I want to build on Marotti's sense of the political dimension of Donne's witty love poetry, by arguing not that love is a metaphor for politics but that love itself is political—involves power transactions between men and women. By privileging neither Donne's ambitions for socioeconomic power nor his personal need for a fulfilling emotional relationship with a woman, I reevaluate the interrelationship between love and politics. I will focus on Donne's depictions of amatory relationships—his representation of the female body, sexual relations, and sexual difference—to show how he represents power relationships in love and how love repeatedly intersects public politics. In Donne's treatment of love in the *Elegies*, the public world of politics and the intimacies of the private world are often inseparable.[3]

The "direct, natural, and necessary relation of person to person is the *relation of man to woman*."[4] Though the words are Karl Marx's, the notion was well understood in the Renaissance. As Milton's portrayal of the "society" of Adam and Eve makes clear, the relationship between man and woman is thought to constitute the basic unit of society. Apparently natural but also culturally determined, that relationship offers a potential image of the organization and distribution of power in the larger society. Milton's treatment of Adam and Eve in *Paradise Lost* reveals his awareness of a political dimension to interpersonal, sexual relations. Donne, too, understood the political dimension of amatory relations, exploiting it in his *Elegies*. Donne repeatedly in these poems envisions relations between the sexes as

---

3. A. LaBranche, " 'Blanda Elegeia': The Background to Donne's 'Elegies,' " *Modern Language Review* 61 (1966): 357–68, argues that "the study of essential human relationships" is "a principal theme of the love elegy" as developed by Catullus and Ovid and later by Donne (357). LaBranche's argument should make us wary of concluding too narrowly that Donne's concern is only socioeconomic politics.
4. Karl Marx, "Private Property and Communism," in *Economic and Philosophic Manuscripts of 1844*, ed. Dirk J. Struik and tr. Martin Milligan (New York: International Publishers, 1973), 134.

a site of conflict, thereby mirroring a larger society in which there is considerable anxiety about the lines and boundaries of power.

Exploring male/female relations, Donne's *Elegies* focus insistently on the body, especially the female body. The human body commonly functions as what the anthropologist Mary Douglas has called a "natural symbol" of society—a "model" symbolically expressing the values and orders, powers and dangers, of the social body.[5] Thus it is not surprising that Donne's representations of the body, as well as of male/female sexual relations, have a sociopolitical significance.

In discussing the male/female relations in the *Elegies*, I will deal with the misogyny evident in many of these poems, but often repressed in critical readings of Donne.[6] There is in many of the *Elegies* a persistent misogyny, indeed a revulsion at the female body, which has provoked various responses. Some readers give these poems scant attention, preferring to focus on the more easily admired poems of the *Songs and Sonnets* like "The Good-morrow," "The Canonization," or "The Ecstasy," which celebrate a mutual love that attributes to the mistress special importance and value. Others see the misogyny as simply a matter of "literary convention" (which skirts the issue of why authors are attracted to some literary conventions and not to others), or as an example of Donne's desire to shock or his outrageous wit, or as one posture among many that Donne tries out in his poetry. But these critical responses effectively tame Donne's *Elegies*. Yes, Donne is being outrageously, shockingly witty, but why are women the subject of degradation in so much of the wit? Granted there is humor in these poems, but jokes often have a serious dimension and reveal much about the person. And though Donne adopts various personae and tries out a variety of postures, at some level he possesses an ability to identify (even if briefly) with these roles. It is unfair to Donne's poetry, and inconsistent, to treat the misogynous, cynical poems as rhetorical posturing or as exercises in witty manipulation of literary convention (hence, not "really"

---

5. See Mary Douglas, *Natural Symbols: Explorations in Cosmology* (London: Barrie and Jenkins, 1970), 12, and *Purity and Danger: An Analysis of Concepts of Pollution and Taboo* (New York: Frederick A. Praeger, 1966), chap. 7.
6. Marotti's otherwise excellent reading of *The Anagram*, for example, glosses over the antifeminism when he comments, "The point of the exercise is not to indulge in a virtuoso antifeminism, but to question an entire range of amorous customs and rituals" (*Coterie* [note 2 above, p. 259], 48). Other critics simply ignore those poems where the misogyny is difficult to avoid. In *The Metaphysics of Love: Studies in Renaissance Love Poetry from Dante to Milton* (Cambridge: Cambridge Univ. Press, 1985), A. J. Smith, gracefully describing Donne's celebration of mutual love and the interdependency of body and soul, lavishes attention on "The Ecstasy" but nowhere mentions the *Elegies* (chap. 3, "Body and Soul"). Recently, George Parfitt has correctly directed attention to the "reductive," "immature" view of women in the *Elegies* (*John Donne: A Literary Life* [London: Macmillan, 1989], 30–39), but the misogyny of these poems still remains to be historicized and the political implications explored.

meant) while reading the celebrations of mutual love as indicative
of Donne's "true" feelings. Though we may not like to admit the
presence of misogyny in one of the greatest love poets in the English
language, we need to come to terms with it, especially in the *Elegies*
where it appears so strongly. What I will be arguing about the *Elegies*
is not meant to be taken as the whole picture of Donne—obviously,
the canon is extensive and various, and his attitudes are quite dif-
ferent in many of the *Songs and Sonnets*—but it is one part of
Donne's works that needs to be understood and historicized rather
than repressed if we are to have a fuller understanding of the poet
and the canon.

Many if not most of Donne's *Elegies* were written in the 1590s,
when England was ruled by a female monarch who demanded faith-
ful service and devotion from aspiring men.[7] The mere presence of
a female monarch is insufficient to account for the *Elegies*, but it
does suggest an initial historical context for these poems. Elizabeth,
the "woman on top" (to use Natalie Zemon Davis's phrase) was an
anomaly in a strongly patriarchal, hierarchical culture in which
women were considered subordinate to men.[8] It is difficult to ascer-
tain the effect that rule by a female monarch had on the position of
women. Though she may have provided an encouraging example for
women, it is likely that, as the exception, she actually confirmed the
rule of patriarchy in English society.[9] But for men there were ten-
sions inherent in submission to the authority of a queen in what was

7. I have used Helen Gardner's edition of *The Elegies and Songs and Sonnets* (Oxford: Clar-
endon, 1965) for the texts of the poems, though I refer to the elegies by the numbers
assigned to them by Grierson in his 1912 Oxford edition. Specific references are cited
parenthetically in the text by line number. I accept Gardner's dating of the *Elegies* as
generally belonging to the 1590s (xxxii–xxxiii), though it is possible a few are later. *The
Autumnall* has long been assigned a later date. Annabel Patterson, reminding us to be
wary of assuming that all the elegies are early, argues that several belong to the period of
James I (see "John Donne, Kingsman?," in *The Mental World of the Jacobean Court*, ed.
Linda Levy Peck [Cambridge: Cambridge Univ. Press, 1991]).
8. Natalie Zemon Davis, "Women on Top: Symbolic Sexual Inversion and Political Disorder
in Early Modern Europe," in *The Reversible World: Symbolic Inversion in Art and Society*,
ed. Barbara Babcock (Ithaca: Cornell Univ. Press, 1978), 147–90. Davis's concern is with
the symbolism of sexual inversions, especially the image of woman on top, in popular
forms of misrule, but her discussion does not extend to Queen Elizabeth and the questions
raised by the political rule of a female monarch. This issue has recently been addressed
by Constance Jordan, "Woman's Rule in Sixteenth-Century British Thought," *Renaissance
Quarterly* 40 (1987): 421–51.
9. Davis (note 8 above, p. 261) suggests that in literature, popular festivity and ordinary life,
sexual inversions both confirmed women's subjection and offered potential for subversion
and change (see, esp. 183). But Montrose (note 1 above) observes that "because she was
always uniquely herself, Elizabeth's rule was not intended to undermine the male hegem-
ony of her culture. Indeed, the emphasis upon her *difference* from other women may have
helped to reinforce it. . . . The royal exception could prove the patriarchal rule in society
at large" ("Shaping Fantasies," 80). Jordan (note 8 above) judiciously concludes that the
actual presence of a woman on the throne in Britain did not affect social conditions for
women but did prompt debate over woman's rule and thus contribute to the general cli-
mate of rational inquiry that challenged the notion of fixed, absolute values (424).

otherwise a culture in which power and authority were invested in men. As Constance Jordan remarks, the prospect of a female ruler "could hardly have been regarded with anything but concern"; and the actual presence of a woman on the throne in England gave focus to a debate about the legitimacy of woman's rule.[1]

Tensions over submission to female rule are strikingly evident in Donne's representation of private love relationships in the *Elegies*. Many poems attack or reject female dominance in love and attempt to reassert male control. Though Marotti has well described fantasies of control in these poems, it has not been sufficiently appreciated how much the degradation and conquest of women is presented as essential to that control, nor how these efforts to control woman have a special sociopolitical meaning. "Private" relations between man and woman are closely connected to the pattern of relations in the larger social body—a point recognized by Milton in his divorce tracts, for example, when he set about to reform the institution of marriage. Though the private and public spheres became increasingly separated in England during the seventeenth century, in the world of Donne's *Elegies* they are still closely interrelated.[2] Repeatedly, the attack on female rule in amatory relations spills over into an attack on female rule in the public world. Private love and public politics become subtly intertwined as Donne's amatory elegies are inscribed in politically resonant language. Many of the poems are both explicitly amatory *and* covertly political. Hence they possess a politically subversive potential at the same time as they probe the dynamics of amatory relations.

The conventions of courtly love poetry, with its chaste, unattainable, superior woman, desired and sought by an admiring, subservient, faithful male suitor, were especially appropriate for articulating complex relationships between Queen Elizabeth and the ambitious courtiers seeking her favors.[3] That Donne rejects and mocks these

---

1. Jordan (note 8 above, p. 262), 421. Jordan examines the writings for and against gynecocracy prompted by the accessions of Mary I and Elizabeth I. Most notorious is John Knox's, *The First Blast of the Trumpet against the Monstrous Regiment of Women* (Geneva, 1558), published the year Elizabeth ascended the throne, though it was written specifically against the Catholic Mary I. Knox insisted that woman's rule is "monstrouse," "repugnant to nature," and a "subversion of good order" (see, for example, 5v, 9r, 12v, 17r, 27v, though his charges are repeated throughout). Knox's diatribe was impelled by his anti-Catholic Protestantism, but the treatise is also an exhausting argument for woman's natural inferiority to man. Knox's treatise was answered by John Aylmer's *An Harborowe for faithfull and trewe Subjectes, against the Late blowne Blaste* . . . (London, 1559), which in counselling obedience to the queen suggested Knox's position was seditious (B1r, B1v, R2v). On the tensions for men posed by obedience to a female monarch, see also Montrose, "Shaping Fantasies" (note 1, p. 259), 61, 64–65, 75.
2. Francis Barker, *The Tremulous Private Body: Essays on Subjection* (London: Methuen, 1984), argues that during the seventeenth century the "division between the public and the private [was] constructed in its modern form" (14).
3. See Javitch (note 1), and especially Marotti (notes 1 and 2 above, p. 259), "Love is not Love" and *Coterie*, chap. 1.

conventions in his poetry has not gone unnoticed. As Marotti well puts it, Donne in his *Elegies* is rejecting "the dominant social and literary modes of the Court, substituting plainspeaking directness for polite compliment, sexual realism for amorous idealization, critical argumentativeness for sentimental mystification, and aggressive masculine self-assertion for politely self-effacing subservience" (*Coterie*, 45). But it has not been sufficiently appreciated that the rejection of courtly love and the assertion of self are achieved in large part through a ritualized verbal debasement of women. It is common to speak of Donne's Ovidian "realism," but in some elegies, "realism" seems too mild a term for the debasement Donne substitutes for idealization.

Repeatedly, Donne's *Elegies* represent women, not as idealized creatures, closed and inviolable in their chastity, but as low, impure, sometimes even disgusting creatures. Donne rejects "classical" representations of the female body (finished, elevated, pure), which characterized courtly and Petrarchan love poetry, in favor of the "grotesque" female body—not so much out of an attraction toward the vitality of the grotesque body as out of an impulse to demolish the idealized image of woman, thereby making her undesirable and hence, no longer an object of worship.[4]

Elegy 2: The Anagram wittily, systematically subverts the conventions of female beauty as the speaker tells how Flavia has "all things, whereby others beautious bee" (2), but in the wrong order, proportion, places, or forms. Her small and dim eyes, large mouth, jet teeth, and red hair make her grotesque and "foule" (32). Like Shakespeare's sonnet 130 ("My mistress' eyes are nothing like the sun"), this elegy playfully mocks conventional Petrarchan descriptions of female beauty (golden hair, small mouth, pearly white teeth), but Donne's details may also glance at the physical appearance of the aging Queen Elizabeth, who in her later years had visibly rotten teeth and wore a red wig.[5] The poem itself reenacts the descent from high to

speculation

---

4. See Mikhail Bakhtin's useful distinction between the "classical" aesthetic and "grotesque realism" as two manners of representing the human body (*Rabelais and His World*, tr. Helene Iswolsky [Bloomington: Indiana Univ. Press, 1984], 18–30). But as Peter Stallybrass and Allon White well point out (*The Politics and Poetics of Transgression* [London: Methuen, 1986], 5–6), Bakhtin idealizes the grotesque when he identifies it with festivity and vitality. Donne's representation of the female body in the *Elegies* betrays a sense of revulsion that contradicts Bakhtin's sense that the bodily element is always "deeply positive" in "grotesque realism" (19).

5. The French ambassador André Hurault, Sieur de Maisse, described her in 1597 as wearing "a great reddish-coloured wig. . . . As for her face, it is and appears to be very aged. It is long and thin, and her teeth are very yellow and unequal. . . . Many of them are missing" (*De Maisse: A Journal of All That Was Accomplished . . . Anno Domini 1597*, tr. G. B. Harrison and R. A. Jones [London: Nonesuch, 1931], 25–26). On Elizabeth's appearance see also J. E. Neale, *Queen Elizabeth I: A Biography* (1934; rpt. Garden City, N.Y.: Doubleday, 1957), 356, and Paul Johnson, *Elizabeth I: A Study in Power and Intellect* (London: Weidenfeld and Nicolson, 1974), 13–14, 374–75. According to Neale, her hair originally had been reddish-gold (28).

low not only in its announced subject (the ugly mistress) but also in its movement from describing her face to describing her genitals, which are guarded by a "durty foulenesse" (42) that will keep out all rivals and ensure her chastity for the man who dares marry her. "Though seaven yeares, she in the Stews had laid, / A Nunnery durst receive [her], and thinke a maid" (48–49). Even "Dildoes" would be "loath to touch" her (53–54). The language of the poem unpleasantly links her face and her genitals—both are "foule" (32, 42). Just as the foulness of the one reflects the foulness of the other (and Donne uncovers both), so the larger implication of the poem is that this low grotesque female body mirrors, even in its distortion, the traditionally beautiful female body. She has all of "beauties elements" (9) and is thus an "anagram" of beauty. As in his *Paradoxes and Problems*, Donne delights in being outrageous, in exercising his wit in defending the indefensible. The paradox here serves to undermine the idea of female beauty (and hence desirability) and to suggest that "beauty" (and the power of beautiful forms) is humanly constructed—Donne suggests that the man can rearrange Flavia's "parts" to make her beautiful just as we arrange "letters" different ways in order to produce a variety of pleasing "words" (15–18).

If *The Anagram* presumes a continuity (not merely a contrast) between the ugly and the beautiful female body, *Elegy 8: The Comparison* makes this connection explicit.[6] The poem begins by contrasting idealized descriptions of the female body with grotesque ones:

> As the sweet sweat of Roses in a Still,
> As that which from chaf'd muskats pores doth trill,
> As the Almighty Balme of th'early East,
> Such are the sweat drops of my Mistris breast,
> And on her necke her skin such lustre sets,
> They seem no sweat drops, but pearl carcanets.
> Ranke sweaty froth thy Mistresse brow defiles,
> Like spermatique issue of ripe menstrous boils.
>
> (1–8)

The focus on excretions, however, defiles the pure, classically beautiful body. Beneath the oppositions between high and low runs the sense of what these two supposedly different women share—an open, sweating, excreting, potentially diseased body. As in so much of his writing, Donne is obsessed with decay and death, here particularly associated with the female body. The nausea which surfaces elsewhere in Donne (for example in the *Satires* and *The Second Anni-*

---

6. Marotti (note 2 above, p. 259) observes that the "satiric debasement of women" in this poem "could imply a general critique of the cult of female beauty with its prescribed forms of hyperbolic praise" (*Coterie*, 50).

versary) here is evoked by woman. Like *The Anagram, Elegy 8: The Comparison* tends to conflate face and genitals, the high and low parts of the body, metaphorically linking "menstrous boils" and "thy Mistresse brow" and moving from descriptions of the women's heads to descriptions of their breasts and finally to their genitals.

The idealized description of female beauty is progressively undermined by the grotesque one. In spite of the contrasts drawn, the differences come to seem more those of perception or description (that is, verbal and imaginative constructs) than of "objective" material reality. If the "ugly" woman is associated with death, so too is the beautiful one:

> Round as the world's her head, on every side,
> Like to the fatall Ball which fell on Ide,
> Or that whereof God had such jealousie,
> As, for the ravishing thereof we die.
>
> (15–18)

Beneath the appearance or illusion of beauty is foulness, dirt, disease, death. Though *his* mistress's breast seems "faire," the breasts of the rival's mistress are "like worme eaten trunkes, cloth'd in seals skin, / Or grave, that's durt without, and stinke within" (24–26).[7] And her breasts are an anticipation of things to come. Though *his* mistress's genitals are like a "Lymbecks warme wombe" (36),

> Thine's like the dread mouth of a fired gunne,
> Or like hot liquid metalls newly runne
> Into clay moulds, or like to that AEtna
> Where round about the grasse is burnt away.
> Are not your kisses then as filthy, 'and more,
> As a worme sucking an invenom'd sore?
>
> (39–44)

Mere touch is contaminating, defiling. The disgusting descriptions of the female body as diseased, impure, and polluting, themselves contaminate the idealized representation of woman so that by the end of the poem, the speaker's denunciation seems to include not just "comparisons" and the "ugly" mistress but woman generally: "Leave her, and I will leave comparing thus, / She, and comparisons are odious" (53–54). Perhaps the two mistresses described in the poem are not different women but rather a single woman seen in two ways. The misogynist thrust of the poem, which betrays the male speaker's desire to keep uncontaminated, may explain the discomforting comparison used to represent the speaker's sexual relations

---

7. There may be yet another glance at the appearance of the aged queen here. The French ambassador De Maisse (note 1) recorded that the queen was given to displaying publicly, and fully, her "somewhat wrinkled" breasts (25, 36).

with the beautiful mistress: "Such in searching wounds the Surgeon is / As wee, when wee embrace, or touch, or kisse" (51–52). The delicacy of mutual tenderness jars with the queasy sense of exploring tender (open? bleeding?) wounds.

The repulsion toward the female body evident in so much of the poem makes it difficult to worship or adore woman. By de-idealizing woman, Donne reconstructs male/female relationships—as embodied in the sex act—to confirm a hierarchy in which the male remains superior:

> Then like the Chymicks masculine equall fire,
> Which in the Lymbecks warme wombe doth inspire
> Into th'earths worthlesse durt a soule of gold,
> Such cherishing heat her best lov'd part doth hold.
>
> (35–38)

This passage does more than describe the temperate heat of his mistress's genitals (which contrasts with the barrenness and excessive heat of the other woman's). By drawing on the Aristotelian association of the male with fire and spirit and of the woman with earth and lower forms of matter, it also reconfirms the traditional hierarchy in which men were seen as naturally superior. As Aristotle explains in *De generatione animalium*,

> the female always provides the material, the male provides that which fashions the material into shape; this, in our view, is the specific characteristic of each of the sexes: that is what it means to be male or to be female. . . . the physical part, the body, comes from the female, and the Soul from the male.[8]

In generation, which for Donne as for Aristotle confers a purpose or end on sexual intercourse, woman is like the warm limbeck, the necessary container—and at the same time the (in itself) worthless dirt, the earth—the material that needs to be informed by a masculine soul. Merging Aristotelian sex differentiation with Paracelsian alchemy, Donne represents man as contributing the heat, the "Chymicks masculine equall [in the sense of the original Latin *aequus*, 'even'] fire," as he "inspire[s]" the "durt" with a "soule of

---

8. Aristotle, *De generatione animalium* [*Generation of Animals*], tr. A. L. Peck, Loeb Library (Cambridge, Mass.: Harvard Univ. Press, 1953), 2.4 [738 b]; cf. 1.2 [716 a]. Further references are cited in the text. Helkiah Crooke's *Microcosmographia: A Description of the Body of Man* (London, 1615), which collects anatomical information from "the best authors" from Aristotle and Galen to Casper Bauhin and André du Laurens, repeatedly cites Aristotle's description of the womb as "the fertile field of Nature" (200, 221, 270). On Aristotelian ideas of sexual difference, see Ian Maclean, *The Renaissance Notion of Woman* (Cambridge: Cambridge Univ. Press, 1980), chap. 3, and Thomas Laqueur, "Orgasm, Generation, and the Politics of Reproductive Biology," *Representations* 14 (1986): 1–41. Galenic medicine follows Aristotle's distinctions between the sexes, though Galen diverged from Aristotle in according women semen.

gold." Thus even the seemingly idealized description of woman at last reconfirms her inferiority and subordination to man.

Donne's emphasis on sex, on the body, and notably on female genitals in these poems has typically been seen as characteristic of the Ovidian influence, and of his "realism." But it is a peculiar realism that focuses so exclusively on one part of the body. The speaker in the witty, satirical *Elegy 18: Loves Progress* assumes a superior posture as he denies woman the qualities of "virtue," "wholesomeness," "ingenuity" (21, 13) and defines her essence as her genitals, the "Centrique part" that men love (36). Men should pay no attention to the face and those higher parts of the female body, which are dangerous distractions that threaten to waylay or even "shipwracke" (70) men on their journey to the harbor of love: her "hair" is "a forrest of ambushes, / Of springes, snares, fetters and manacles" (41–42), her lips give off "Syrens songs" (55), her tongue is a "Remora" (58); her "navell" (66) may be mistaken as the port; even her pubic hair is "another forrest set, / Where some doe shipwracke, and no farther gett" (69–70). Seduction becomes a journey of exploration and discovery, but also potential entrapment for the unwary male. The female body he traverses actively seeks to thwart him.

Satirizing Petrarchan idealizations of women, Donne implies that such refinements are new and monstrous perversions of nature: "Love's a beare-whelpe borne; if wee'overlicke / Our love, and force it new strange shapes to take / We erre, and of a lumpe a monster make" (4–6).

If worshipping woman from a distance and praising her virtue and beauty are modern, monstrous innovations, Donne implies he is restoring older, natural, and correct amorous relations. Mocking the platonic ladder of love (set forth first by Diotima in Plato's *Symposium* and later by Bembo in Castiglione's *The Courtier*) whereby the lover ascends from the beauty of a particular person to an admiration of beauty generally to a vision of ideal, transcendent beauty, Donne sets up a different pattern of love whereby men may "ascend" if they "set out below" and start from "the foote" (73–74).[9] The "progress" of love is thus a journey of progressive mastery, in which the goal or "right true end of love" (2) (the female genitals) is kept firmly in sight at all times. The refusal to idealize, indeed the impulse to debase that "end" of love shapes the poem's final lines, which first describe sexual intercourse as paying "tribute" to woman's "lower" "purse" and then compare the man who uses the wrong means to attain this end to a person who foolishly tries to feed the stomach by purging it with a "Clyster" (91–96).

9. *Symposium*, in *The Dialogues of Plato*, tr. B. Jowett, vol. 1 (Oxford: Clarendon Press, 1892), 580–82; Baldassare Castiglione, *The Book of the Courtier . . . done into English by Sir Thomas Hoby* [1591] (London, 1900), The Fourth Book, 357–63.

What we have here, as in so many of the *Elegies*, are strategies for reasserting male control in love. To some extent these are reminiscent of Ovid. Alan Armstrong's description of Ovid's contribution to the development of the elegy suggests both his special appeal for Donne and also a parallel in these two poets' redistribution of power in love relationships. Much as Donne would subvert Petrarchan conventions, Ovid himself undercut Latin elegiac conventions such as the enslaved lover, asserting instead that love is an art with the lover in control rather than ruled by his passions and mistress. Ovid gave the "elegiac lover a degree of rationality and self-control reflected in his urbane wit and complete self-consciousness."[1] Such a description of Ovid, with its emphasis on mastery, is more valuable in explaining the appeal and usefulness of Ovid to Donne than the commonplace label of "Ovidian realism." Ovid's concern with control may have had a political dimension (though obviously not identical to Donne's), expressing a desire for independence in a society of limited freedoms, in which one could be exiled at the pleasure of the emperor. (One thinks of the premium Cicero and Horace in their own ways placed on rationality, self-control, and self-sufficiency as means of insulation from dangerous political vicissitudes.) Ovid's love elegies continue the stance of political non-conformity evident even earlier in Catullus and Propertius. But there are differences between Ovid's and Donne's elegies, for gender assumes a special importance in Donne's efforts at mastery. The misogyny that surfaces in Donne's poems, and becomes a strategy for defining the male speaker's superiority, recalls not Ovid's elegies so much as Juvenal's *Satires*.[2]

Since the conventions of courtly love were an integral part of the ideology of Queen Elizabeth's court, appropriated and encouraged by the queen as articulating and confirming her power, Donne's sharp rejection and subversions of these love conventions might be expected to have political implications. His choice of genre itself reflects not simply his literary taste but a political stance, for he is distancing himself from the preferred discourse of the Elizabethan court. He elects in the 1590s to write not sonnets of courtly love but satires and elegies—genres marked by misogyny and insistence on the male speaker's power and control. The anti-establishment implications of his choice of genres and of the misogyny in Donne's elegies

1. Alan Armstrong, "The Apprenticeship of John Donne: Ovid and the *Elegies*," *ELH* 44 (1977): 419–42, esp. 433. Armstrong comments that Donne's elegies show "a more aggressive version of the techniques used by Ovid" (434) though the implications and significance of this aggressiveness are not the concern of his important article.
2. L. P. Wilkinson, *Ovid Recalled* (Cambridge: Cambridge Univ. Press, 1955), 44, describes Ovid's continuation of the non-conformist stance in Catullus and Propertius. For the misogynist strain in Juvenal taken up by Donne see especially Juvenal's sixth satire. Though Ovid depicts love as an art, a game, and a hunt, Wilkinson finds him "a sympathizer with women," with "an unusual inclination to see things from their point of view" (25, 86).

accord well with our knowledge that in the mid 1590s Donne was associated with the Essex circle, having embarked on two expeditions against Spain under Essex in 1596 and 1597.[3]

Throughout the 1590s Essex was engaged in a prolonged struggle for power with the queen that set him against the court establishment and that ended only in 1601 with his trial and execution for treason. His conflicts were not only with Cecil and Ralegh, his rivals for political favor, but also with the queen herself—a point evident in J. E. Neale's conclusion that "had she let a man of Essex's nature pack the royal service and the Council with his nominees, she would probably in the end have found herself a puppet-Queen, in tutelage to him." Disdaining the subservience that characterized his stepfather Leicester's relation with the queen, Essex found it difficult to subject himself to Elizabeth's will, repeatedly betraying in his actions and letters a particular and growing dislike of serving a woman.[4] A letter of advice from Francis Bacon after the Cadiz expedition warned Essex that his all too evident resistance to Elizabeth's authority was dangerous: describing Essex as "a man of a nature not to be ruled," Bacon asked "whether there can be a more dangerous image than this represented to any monarch living, much more to a lady, and of her Majesty's apprehension?" (*Lives and Letters*, 1:395).

Essex was ambitious for glory and honor. But that matters of gender were also involved is startlingly evident in the violent public argument that took place between Essex and the queen in summer 1598 over the appointment of a governor for Ireland. Angry at the queen's rejection of his candidate, Essex turned his back on her in a "gesture of contempt," which prompted the queen to strike him on the ear. Essex put his hand on his sword, swearing that "he would not put up with so great an indignity nor have taken such an affront at the hands of Henry VIII himself" (*Lives and Letters*, 1:489–90). His anger at having to take this abuse from a woman is apparent in the letter he afterwards wrote Elizabeth, complaining of "the intollerable wrong you have done both me and yourself, not only broken all laws of affection, but done against the honor of your sex" (*Lives and Letters*, 1:493). Essex's feeling that there was something perverse in her exercise of authority, in his having to submit to a female ruler and accept her humiliations, was not limited to this occasion, and it was

3. On Donne's connection with Essex, see Carey (note 2), 64–69, and especially M. Thomas Hester, "Donne's (Re)Annunciation of the Virgin(ia Colony) in *Elegy XIX*," *South Central Review* 4 (1987): 49–64. Hester argues that the opposition to the dominant court establishment that is inherent in Donne's association with Essex's circle underlies the anti-establishment implications of *Elegy 19*.

4. Neale, 350. On Essex and his relation with Elizabeth, see also Johnson (note), 369–74; J. B. Black, *The Reign of Elizabeth 1558–1603* (Oxford: Clarendon Press, 1936), 365–68, 370–73; and Walter Bourchier Devereux, *Lives and Letters of the Devereux, Earls of Essex*, 2 vols. (London: John Murray, 1853). Further references to this work will be cited parenthetically in the text.

apparently shared by others. Young men surrounding Essex were privately saying that they would not submit to another woman ruler, thus reviving the issue of gender that Elizabeth had faced at the beginning of her reign.[5] In 1597 the French ambassador Sieur de Maisse observed that, though Elizabeth's government pleased the people, "it is but little pleasing to the great men and the nobles; and if by chance she should die, it is certain that the English would never again submit to the rule of a woman."[6]

Such sentiments find an echo in Donne's privately circulated *Elegies*. The *Elegies* embody attitudes toward female rule that were also being expressed by Essex and his circle. The whole pattern of Donne's anti-Petrarchanism and revisions of gender relations betrays a discomfort with (indeed, a rejection of) the political structure headed by a female monarch. Intimate private relations between man and woman and the power structure of the body politic mirror and reinforce each other. If the private and the public are so closely related, perhaps a change in relations in the private realm will generate a corresponding change in the world of politics.

The political dimension of Donne's love elegies is particularly evident in the sense of seduction as mastery that pervades *Elegy 19: To his Mistress Going to Bed*, in which Donne moves easily between the bedroom and the political realm of empires and monarchs. In this witty, exuberant poem we are far from the degradation and disgust of *The Anagram* or *Comparison*. For the speaker joy, enthusiasm, and delight reign.[7] But even here, as the speaker commands his mistress to undress, Donne transfers power from the woman, desired and praised, to the man who hopes to possess her. She is wittily idealized and commodified through a variety of stunning conceits that aim to conquer her (his "foe" [3]) through hyperbolic praise: she is a "farre fairer world," a "beauteous state," "flowery meades," an "Angel," "my America," the repository of "whole joys" (in Donne's wicked pun) (6, 13, 14, 20, 27, 35). But the other side of compliment, admiration, and reverence is the desire to possess and thus master the colonized woman. The speaker affirms his power not only through the accumulated verbal commands of the poem but also through a crucial shift in metaphor in lines 25–32:

---

5. Neale (note 4 above, p. 270), 356.
6. De Maisse (note 4), 11–12. Montrose, who quotes this passage from De Maisse, sees the attempts of Parliament and counselors to persuade the queen to marry as in part motivated by the degradation and frustration men felt with serving a female prince, especially one not subjected to any man in marriage ("Shaping Fantasies" [note 1], 80).
7. Not all readers have stressed these qualities. Marotti (note 2 above, p. 259), for example, finds this poem "a curiously antierotic treatment of a sexual encounter" (*Coterie*, 54). Carey's emphasis on Donne's obsession with power leads him to distort the tone of this poem, which he describes as "punitive," revealing a sadistic "urge to dominate" ([note 2 above, p. 259], 106, 116, 117, 124).

> License my roving hands, and let them goe
> Before, behind, above, between, below.
> O my America, my new found lande,
> My kingdome, safeliest when with one man man'd,
> My myne of precious stones, my Empiree,
> How blest am I in this discovering thee.
> To enter in these bonds, is to be free,
> Then where my hand is set my seal shall be.

At the beginning of this passage the woman is the monarch, providing a license; but the moment she gives this license she loses her sovereignty. What was implicit from the first now is clear. The man becomes not only explorer but conquerer, and she becomes *his* land and kingdom. The repeated possessives reinforce the sense of his mastery, and by the end of this passage he has now become the monarch, setting his "seal." Self-aggrandizement, of course, characterizes much of Donne's poetry, even his divine poems, but the metaphors and images in these lines have a distinctive political resonance as they dethrone the woman and restore sovereignty to man.[8]

As soon as this politically subversive note has been sounded, Donne momentarily retreats from its implications, first praising "full nakedness" (33) then flattering the woman as both a "mystique book" and a divinity who imputes "grace" to the special few allowed to see her mysteries "reveal'd" (41–43). But once her confidence in female superiority has been reestablished, Donne gives a final twist to the argument that conclusively and wittily reasserts male supremacy by placing the man "on top": "To teach thee, I am naked first: Why than / What need'st thou have more covering than a man" (47–48). The act of sex confirms what is seen as the legitimate, rightful mastery of man—a mastery that conflicts both with the conventions of courtly love and with the political situation in England in the 1590s. Seduction fantasies, even as they represent woman as supremely desirable, complement Donne's strategy of debasement, for both aim at restoring male sovereignty.[9]

8. Cf. Essex's curious letter to Queen Elizabeth which reveals an urgent desire for mastery at the same time that he praises her as the object of all his desire: "If my horse could run as fast as my thoughts do fly, I would as often make mine eyes rich in beholding the treasure of my love as my desires do triumph when I seem to myself in a strong imagination to conquer your resisting will" (*Lives and Letters*, [note], 1: 292).
    Carey (note 2) finds Donne "profoundly excited by the thought of majesty" (113), obsessed by "royalty" (115), but he does not consider that these matters are problematic or subversive. See Hester's (note) fascinating discussion of this elegy as a subtle, radical critique of the English colonizing in Virginia, of Sir Walter Ralegh, and (by implication) of Queen Elizabeth.
9. Cf. Montrose's analysis of the seditious political implications of the seductive mastery of a queen ("Shaping Fantasies" [note 1], 62, 65). Marotti (note 2 above, p. 259) argues that Donne's seduction poems are vehicles for expressing fantasies of achievement and triumph in the social world (*Coterie*, 89–90). Both Montrose and Jordan ([note 8 above, p. 261], 450) recognize that for Elizabeth virginity was a source of power, that to yield to a man in marriage entailed a diminution of her power.

But, as readers have noticed, the mastery and control Donne's speakers strive for in the *Elegies* is often frustrated or incomplete.[1] The very metaphors describing women contain a disturbing potential for suggesting women's resistance to any individual man's control. The *Elegies* show a recurring tension between the male mastery asserted and an implicit female resistance to mastery which undermines the restoration of male sovereignty. The land, despite man's attempts to enclose and possess it, is always vulnerable to being "possessed" by other men, as the speaker of *Elegy 7* ("Natures lay Ideot . . .") only too well has learned. His mistress's husband may have "sever'd" her "from the worlds Common" (21), enclosed her as private property, and her lover may have further "Refin'd" her into a "bliss-full paradise" (24), but these acts prove inadequate attempts to civilize her. For all the speaker's position of superiority (he claims to be her teacher, even her God-like creator who has "planted knowledge" and "graces" in her [24–25]), she has thrown off his authority and is leaving him for other lovers. The poem ends with angry, impotent outbursts, in which verbal degradation reveals both the desire to control the woman through what *Elegy 16: On his Mistris* calls "masculine persuasive force" (4) and the striking inability to do so:

> Must I alas
> Frame and enamell Plate, and drinke in Glasse?
> Chafe wax for others seales? breake a colts force
> And leave him then, beeing made a ready horse?
> (27–30)

The female body's "openness" subverts all attempts at permanent masculine control, and insures that dominance will always be unstable and precarious. As the speaker in *Elegy 3: Change* puts it, "Women are like the Arts, forc'd unto none, / Open to'all searchers" (5–6). The conventional representations of woman as land/earth and as water convey a sense of her openness, her essential resistance to boundaries or limits, which Donne wittily exploits:

> Who hath a plow-land, casts all his seed corne there,
> And yet allowes his ground more corne should beare;
> Though Danuby into the sea must flow,
> The sea receives the Rhene, Volga, and Po.
> (17–20)

Embodying the Aristotelian identification of woman with the supposedly lower elements of earth and water, such representations both suggest the difficulty of mastering woman and reinforce the

---

1. Marotti, *Coterie* (note 2 above, p. 259), 52–53; also Stanley Fish's paper at the 1987 MLA, "Masculine Persuasive Force. Donne and Verbal Power," which argued that in the *Elegies* Donne and his surrogate speakers can never achieve the control they desire.

notion of her necessary inferiority to man, making male sovereignty
seem natural and imperative. Though the receptiveness of their bod-
ies shows women were not made to be faithful to one man, the
speaker argues that women are made for men in much the same
sense as nature, in the Judaeo-Christian scheme of creation, was
made for man—hence, the comparisons of women to birds, foxes,
and goats in this poem. Given such hierarchy and "natural" inequal-
ity, for a man to submissively serve a woman would be as wrong as
for animals to rule man.

Donne's discomfort with serving a woman is perhaps most obvious
in *Elegy* 6, the opening of which draws a rich, complex analogy
between love and politics:[2]

> Oh, let mee not serve so, as those men serve
> Whom honours smoakes at once fatten and sterve;
> Poorely enrich't with great mens words or lookes;
> Nor so write my name in thy loving bookes
> As those Idolatrous flatterers, which still
> Their Princes stiles, with many Realmes fulfill
> Whence they no tribute have, and where no sway.
> Such services I offer as shall pay
> Themselves, I hate dead names: Oh then let mee
> Favorite in Ordinary, or no favorite bee.
>
> (1–10)

Distinguishing himself from others, he rejects in both political and
amatory spheres a service in which the lover/suitor is submissive,
flattering, and unrewarded, and the woman falsely idealized, made
into an idol by her admirer. Instead, Donne offers a different kind
of "service," clearly sexual, which "pay[s]" the woman (compare the
"tribute" paid into the woman's "purse" in *Elegy* 18) and is in turn
rewarded. This kind of service restores male dignity, for it is not
servitude but mastery. But mastery is desire rather than accomplish-
ment, for the poem's fictive occasion is the discovery that his mistress
is unfaithful.

Recounting their relationship, he represents her as a destructive
"whirlpoole" (16) or "streame" (21), himself as the delicate "care-
lesse" (innocent) "flower" which is "drowne[d]" in the water's
"embrace" (15–17). This image of the destructive stream also
appears near the end of *Satyre III*, where the stream is explicitly
identified with royal power:

> That thou may'st rightly'obey power, her bounds know;
> Those past, her nature and name's chang'd; to be
> Then humble to her is idolatrie;

2. See Marotti, *Coterie* (note 2 above, p. 259), 56–57.

As streames are, Power is; those blest flowers that dwell
At the rough streames calme head, thrive and prove well,
But having left their roots, and themselves given
To the streames tyrannous rage, alas, are driven
Through mills, and rockes, and woods, 'and at last, almost
Consum'd in going, in the sea are lost:
 So perish Soules, which more chuse mens unjust
 Power from God claym'd, then God himselfe to trust.
          (100–110)[3]

The dating of this satire is uncertain, but the anxiety about royal power (figured as female and identified with the watery female element) would seem to place the poem in the company of those clearly written during the reign of Elizabeth.[4] These complex lines of *Satyre III* articulate both fear of and resistance to royal power, as the speaker, identifying himself with the "blessed flowers" and unjust monarchs with tyrannous streams, rejects idolatrous submission to earthly rulers and hopes to find ultimate (though not necessarily earthly) safety by dwelling at the calm head (God, the source of all power).

In *Elegy 6*, the deceptive mistress, likened to the whirlpool or stream, takes on conventionally "masculine" attributes. She is active, aggressive; he becomes the vulnerable, passive victim. Not the man but the mistress is associated with fire when like the "tapers beamie eye / Amorously twinkling, [she] beckens the giddie flie" to his destruction (17–18). He is the "wedded channels bosome" (24) which she, the "streame" (21), has deserted:

> She rusheth violently, and doth divorce
> Her from her native, and her long-kept course,
> And rores, and braves it, and in gallant scorne,
> In flattering eddies promising retorne,
> She flouts the channell, who thenceforth is drie;
> Then say I; that is shee, and this am I.
>   (29–34)

The cumulative effect of this language, transferring conventionally "masculine" terms (for example, "brave," "gallant") to the woman, is not to question traditional distinctions between male and female but to show her unnaturalness, thereby reinforcing conventional distinctions between the sexes.

These distinctions were being reexamined in medical circles, as

---

3. For the text of this satire, I have used W. Milgate's edition of *The Satires, Epigrams and Verse Letters* (Oxford: Clarendon Press, 1967).
4. Paul R. Sellin, "The Proper Dating of John Donne's 'Satyre III,'" *Huntington Library Quarterly* 43 (1980): 275–312, questions the traditional dating of this satire as belonging to the 1590s, arguing that the poem grows out of Donne's experiences in the Netherlands in 1619.

Ian Maclean has shown.[5] During the late sixteenth century a limi-
tedly revisionist medical discourse emerged as anatomists and phy-
sicians, attacking the Aristotelian idea of woman as imperfect man,
argued that women and men were equally perfect in their respective
sexes. But in contrast to medical discourses, ethical, legal, theolog-
ical, and political discourses remained conservative in their view of
woman. For all the remarkable innovation of Donne's *Elegies*, they
are conservative, even reactionary, in their representations of the
sexes. Like Aristotle, Donne presumes clear sex distinctions. Aris-
totle had justified what he saw as clear sex differentiation among the
"higher" animals according to the principle that "the superior one
should be separate from the inferior one": "wherever possible and so
far as possible the male is separate from the female, since it is some-
thing *better* and more divine" (*De generatione animalium*, 2.1
[732a]). In the *Elegies*, Donne like Aristotle is concerned to enforce
firm sex distinctions. But whereas Aristotle assumes fixed, stable cat-
egories, Donne's poems embody strong anxiety about transgressions
of hierarchical distinctions between the sexes—an anxiety under-
standable in a culture in which those categories, both physiological
and social, could no longer be assumed to be fixed or stable. Indeed,
Queen Elizabeth herself was effectively destabilizing these clear sex
distinctions by publicly cultivating an androgynous image of herself
as both a desirable maiden to be courted and a strong, martial ruler
who was master of all her subjects and noted for her "masculine"
qualities of judgment and prudence.[6]

   In Donne's *Elegy 6* the rebellious woman, imaged as both fire and
water, has transgressed the supposedly natural, proper boundaries
distinguishing the sexes (as did the promiscuous mistress in "Natures
lay Ideot," which is, I believe, why the gender changes in the last
lines, where the woman is compared to a male "colt," broken in only
to be enjoyed by another). The woman's assimilation of "masculine"
attributes has effectively "feminized" the man (he is like a flower, or
the earth that is the stream's channel). Donne's strategy is first to
expose the blurring of gender distinctions as unnatural and then to
restore those boundaries and reassert masculine dominance.[7] Once

5. On the revision of Aristotelian thought, see Maclean (note 8 above, p. 267), 43–46.
6. On the queen's androgynous image, see Montrose, "Shaping Fantasies" (note 1 above,
   p. 259), 77–78. Sieur de Maisse (note 5 above, p. 264) observes that the queen was "well
   contented . . . when anyone commends her for her judgment and prudence, and she is
   very glad to speak slightingly of her intelligence and sway of mind, so that she may give
   occasion to commend her" (37–38).
7. Douglas, *Purity and Danger* (note 5 above, p. 261), suggestively remarks that "beliefs in
   sex pollution" are likely to flourish in societies where the principle of male dominance is
   contradicted by other elements in the social life—which would suggest that misogyny and
   a reinsistence on female inferiority would flourish if the norm of male dominance in a
   patriarchal society was threatened by the rule of a female monarch. Donne's interest in
   sexual inversions, in the crossing of gender boundaries exemplifies her second category of
   "social pollution": "danger from transgressing the internal lines of the system" (122).

he has exposed her betrayal, the speaker can reassert the "proper" male authority and supremacy as he warns her:

> Yet let not thy deepe bitternesse beget
> Carelesse despaire in mee, for that will whet
> My minde to scorne; and Oh, love dull'd with paine
> Was ne'r so wise, nor well arm'd as disdaine.
> Then with new eyes I shall survay thee, 'and spie
> Death in thy cheekes, and darknesse in thine eye.
> Though hope bred faith and love; thus taught, I shall
> As nations do from Rome, from thy love fall.
> My hate shall outgrow thine, and utterly
> I will renounce thy dalliance: and when I
> Am the Recusant, in that absolute state,
> What hurts it me to be'excommunicate?
>
> (35–46)

His warning effectively gives him control as he suggests that her beauty, and thus her power and authority over him, depends on *him*. Questioning the conventions that idealize the mistress, Donne suggests that the lover empowers the mistress and thus ultimately holds the reigns of control. Perhaps this is all just wishful thinking on the speaker's part, and Donne is just wittily playing with literary conventions; but in this poem which brings together love, religion, and politics, these lines have a dangerous subversive potential. When one returns to the opening analogies between amorous and political service, this ending implies that just as the power of the mistress depends upon the good will of her lover (and the power of the Roman Church depends upon the willing consent of nations), so the power of the queen depends upon her subjects.

Elegy 6 is not the only poem to imply that monarchs can be deposed. In *Elegy 17: Variety*, the speaker rejects constancy for variety in love and invokes political language that suggests that no allegiance is permanent:

> I love her well, and would, if need were, dye
> To do her service. But followes it that I
> Must serve her onely, when I may have choice?
>
> (21–23)

Constancy in love entails a loss of man's original "liberty" (62)—it ties him to a single person and makes him subservient to a woman. Rather than being faithful to one woman (and submitting to "opinion" and "honor" [50, 45], which Donne associates with woman in the ideology of courtly love), he chooses to follow a male monarch, making a "throne" (64) for the deposed Cupid. The political implications of this poem, in which worship/admiration of a single woman

is replaced by loyalty to a king, would not have been lost on Donne's
Elizabethan readers. But the poem might well have been unsettling
even after Elizabeth's reign, for by the poem's end the attack on
woman's rule has expanded to question the sovereignty of all rulers.
Though the speaker proclaims he will now loyally serve the king of
love by pursuing a variety of women, eventually even this pursuit will
become tiresome and this new loyalty bondage.

> But time will in his course a point discry
> When I this loved service must deny,
> For our allegiance temporary is.
>   (73–75)

Paradoxically, continual variety itself will prove boring, so for a
change he will become faithful to a single mistress, if he can find one
beautiful and worthy. Then the cycle of constancy and change will
begin again. Envisioning a succession of allegiances, all of which are
provisional and temporary, the poem both explores the psychology of
desire and undermines an absolutist interpretation of monarchy.

   In their revisions of power the *Elegies* thus have a politically sub-
versive aspect which helps explain why Donne not only did not want
his poems published but also in later years apparently regretted
having written them (or at least, regretted not having destroyed
them). Five elegies (including *Loves Progress* and *To his Mistress
Going to Bed*) were refused a license to be published with his other
poems in 1633. Probably it was not simply their eroticism that
offended. Donne's elegies might have seemed dangerous not just
during Elizabeth's reign but even later in James's and Charles I's,
when Donne had finally achieved a position of prominence in the
church, for repeatedly they imply that allegiances can be withdrawn,
that monarchs can be deposed—which was precisely the fate that
awaited Charles.
   But for all their extended political resonance, I see these poems
as distinctly (though not narrowly) the product of, and a reaction to,
the historical situation of England's rule by a woman. Donne's anti-
Petrarchanism, his debasement of women, his various subversions
of women's rule, and his repeated attempts to reassert masculine
sovereignty embody both the problematics of male submission to a
female ruler and Donne's not unrelated personal sense that male
desire requires an element of conflict, a feeling of superiority (how-
ever precarious) and the promise of mastery. Participating in the
debate about women's rule as they contribute to the development of
the love elegy, Donne's elegies embody a central tension: while basi-
cally conservative, even reactionary, in their insistence on male supe-
riority and rule, they repeatedly demonstrate woman's unruliness,

her subversion of permanent male rule. Thus power (whether in private, interpersonal relations, or in public, social ones) is seen as radically unstable.

The *Elegies* suggest that Donne was deeply disturbed by the sense that the old hierarchical order was threatened by a blurring of gender and sex distinctions (he attacks effeminacy as well as voracious, rebellious, aggressive women), by conventions such as neo-Petrarchan courtly love that seemed to invert the "proper" order in male/female relations, and by rule of a female monarch which seemingly enabled these other disruptions. Clearly, many things in late sixteenth-century English culture besides the presence of the queen on the throne contributed to the unsettling of traditional orders. But even if Queen Elizabeth's reign actually reinforced the existing hierarchies, Donne's *Elegies* are striking evidence that he may have perceived in it a threat to patriarchy, with its assumption of stable, permanent hierarchies. These poems reveal a deep sense of the connectedness of private and political human relations—and a strong sense that hierarchical power relations characterize the most personal and private area of human experience.

MARGARET MAURER

John Donne's Verse Letters†

*   *   *

There are forty-three verse letters in the Donne canon;[1] and it is neither possible nor necessary to discuss all of them here. What the rest of this essay will do is discuss examples from three categories of letters to determine how Donne develops and uses the images of himself writing the poems. On this basis, we can begin to describe how the consistencies and variations of tone and argument that Donne works among these categories become elements in each poem's effect.

Three groups of Donne's verse letters can be distinguished approximately chronologically. From 1592 to 1594, Donne wrote short, sonnet-like poems to his friends and associates at the Inns of Court.[2] These early poems are characterized by the same themes and atti-

† From *Modern Language Quarterly* 37 (1976): 234–59. Copyright © 1976 by the University of Washington. All rights reserved. Reprinted by permission of the publisher.
1. Milgate's edition of the letters contains thirty-seven English poems and one Latin letter and acknowledges but does not print five poems that Helen Gardner includes in her edition of the *Divine Poems* (Oxford, 1952).
2. R. C. Bald, "Donne's Early Verse Letters," *HLQ* 15 (1952), 283–89.

tudes that dominate the satires, elegies, and early love lyrics of Donne's poetic apprenticeship: women, melancholy, satiric spleen. Later letters to the friends whom Donne cultivated in the term of his employment with Egerton through the period of his frustrated hopes of civil employment (1596–1610) suggest more studied efforts in letter-writing, imitating classical models. The recurring themes here are virtue and its cultivation in the context of friendship. Letters of the third group, written toward the end of this period (1608–1614), are to noblewomen. In these letters, discussions of virtue are shaped by the ulterior motives of the literature of patronage. By this period of his life, Donne had associated himself with prevailing religious controversies and had no doubt begun to consider the Church as his only possibility for advancement. The dominant theological cast to these letters is their most distinctive and troublesome characteristic.

Three short poems to R. W. are typical of the first group. Donne and R. W. have poetry in common. Donne's extended conceit of the Muse as the soul of the soul ("Muse not that by thy Mind," p. 63) prepares for a conventional identification of his correspondent with his Muse. Elsewhere, Donne refers to R. W.'s "mistique trinitee" of "body, mind, and Muse" ("Zealously my Muse," p. 62). Donne's Muse is barren divorced from R. W.'s, which has "retyr'd to sing / Upon her tender Elegiaque string" (9–10). In a compliment to R. W. based on the conceit of the four bodily elements ("Kindly'I envy," p. 66), Donne refers to the "Satirique fyres which urg'd me to have writt / In skorne of all" (7–8) and which are quenched by R. W.'s songs composed of all the elements. Donne's poetic temperament, compared to that of his friend, is once again the subject.

Letters to R. W. span the first two groups and allow us to witness Donne's consistency in letters to one person. Two verse letters to Rowland Woodward, both of them somewhat later than these shorter poems, discuss, with specific reference to the earlier works, the translation of his interests into more mature concerns. "To Mr Rowland Woodward" (pp. 69–70 [pp. 56–57 above]) may be tentatively dated around 1597 and was probably written in answer to a request from Woodward for copies of Donne's poems.[3] Donne explicitly recalls his former work even as he forswears it:

> Since shee [his Muse] to few, yet to too many'hath showne
> How love-song weeds, and Satyrique thornes are growne
> Where seeds of better Arts, were early sown.
>
> (4–6)

3. See Milgate's note on the date of the poem, based on the style of its beginning (p. 223). Because of the sophisticated concept of virtue Donne handles in the poem, Stapleton argues for a date as late as 1608 (p. 194). The other poem to R. W. which I treat as a later poem (1597) is so dated by Bald on the basis of the reference to Guiana ("Donne's Early Verse Letters," p. 287).

His concerns, he says, are now more sober; and retirement, the "chast fallownesse" (3) of his Muse, allows him the freedom to pursue virtue. Donne sounds a new argument that will dominate later letters:

> There is no Vertue, but Religion:
> Wise, valiant, sober, just, are names, which none
> Want, which want not Vice-covering discretion.
>
> (16–18)

It is difficult not to assume that, in explaining this turn taken by his Muse, Donne is thinking of Horace's withdrawal from the poetry of the odes, especially since he connects the change to the theme of retirement.

Another later poem to R. W., "If, as mine is, thy life a slumber be" (pp. 64–65), possibly written from abroad on the expedition to Cadiz, again relates Donne's newer concerns to the imagery invoked in earlier letters. Here is explicit discussion of the function of letter-writing:

> Never did Morpheus nor his brother weare
> Shapes soe like those Shapes, whom they would appeare,
> As this my letter is like me, for it
> Hath my name, words, hand, feet, heart, minde and wit;
> It is my deed of gift of mee to thee,
> It is my Will, my selfe the Legacie.
> So thy retyrings I love, yea envie,
> Bred in thee by a wise melancholy,
> That I rejoyce, that unto where thou art,
> Though I stay here, I can thus send my heart,
> As kindly'as any enamored Patient
> His Picture to his absent Love hath sent.
>
> (3–14)

Donne argues that this letter is his picture; to insure that it is, he includes references to his legal training, his bouts with melancholy, his love experiences. The letter continues with a description of the expedition, but a question extends the implications of his experience: "Is not Almightie Vertue'an India?" (28). The close repeats the point, recasting the arguments of earlier poems in which Woodward's song had been described as built of all the elements and his function was defined as Donne's Muse, "beeing the Soules Soule" ("Muse not that by thy Mind," 8):

> If men be worlds, there is in every one
> Some thing to'answere in some proportion
> All the worlds riches: And in good men, this,
> Vertue, our formes forme and our soules soule, is.
>
> (29–32)

The earlier verse enables us to appreciate the special propriety of this poem.

The contrast between the early and the later letters to Woodward illustrates Donne's efforts to reconcile his new arguments with the old. Likewise, his short poem "To Mr C. B." about the saint of his affection (p. 63) is certainly earlier than "The Storme" (pp. 55–57) and "The Calme" (pp. 57–59 [pp. 49–51, 51–53 above]), written as letters to Christopher Brooke, presumably while Donne was on the expedition to Cadiz in 1597. As Jonson observed, these longer poems are equal to the best of Donne's early work.[4] The structure of "The Storme" is simple: eight lines addressed to Brooke introduce a description of the tempestuous voyage. The argument that motivates this display is a more witty version of Donne's earlier letter to C. B. that accomplishes praise, complaint, and petition to his friend (and indirectly to his mistress). "To Mr C. B." describes Donne's state of mind, "Urg'd by this inexcusable occasion" (2) of leaving the two people he loves. In "The Storme" (and "The Calme," which continues the argument),[5] Donne's motive is similar. Absence from his friend moves him to describe his experience. The description is recommended by a witty endorsement: Donne insists that it is superior to anyone else's account of the voyage by virtue of the friendship he invokes to motivate it: " 'Tis the preheminence / Of friendship onely to'impute excellence" (7–8).

The ostensible subject of the poem proceeds from this. Donne intends not merely to describe a storm but to describe it in a way compelling to a friend. That is, his premise requires an emphasis on his own psychological state throughout the description with reference to the effect this will have on Brooke. The lines in "The Storme"—"Sooner then you read this line, did the gale, / Like shot, not fear'd till felt, our sailes assaile" (29–30)—and in "The Calme"— "As steady'as I can wish, that my thoughts were, / Smooth as thy mistresse glasse, or what shines there, / The sea is now" (7–9)— involve his reader in his perception of the experience and emphasize the paradox with which the first poem opens: "Thou which art I . . . / Thou which art still thy selfe" (1–2).

Yet it is certainly not accurate to describe these poems as attempts to reproduce in Brooke feelings of fear and tedium. Description is their premise, but it is not their method. It is not Donne almost drowned or becalmed that presents himself in these poems, but

---

4. See the *Conversations*, in *Ben Jonson*, I, 135.
5. The two poems address aspects of the same argument. "The Storme" has a salutation; "The Calme" begins directly, "Our storme is past." The Westmoreland MS. does not include "The Calme," a surprising exception to its otherwise complete collection of the early verse letters. Milgate, p. lxv.

Donne wittily engaged in an analysis of his experience in terms of particular interest to one who has shared activities with him in the areas to which he goes for comparison. Thus the poems are in a classical literary tradition.[6] They contain biblical references, allusions to plays, and literary echoes. At the end of "The Calme," when Donne draws the conclusion which is the point of the description, extending an account of a temporary sensation to a comment on the general condition of man, that extension is incontestably valid in terms the correspondent understands. Brooke himself has not lived through the voyage, but he has witnessed the mental process of someone he knows who has. It is crucial to the effect of his conclusion that Donne individualize that process. Hence the "preheminence of friendship" for accomplishing such a poem.

Donne's letters to his mature male friends are more sophisticated expressions of themes and attitudes in the earlier poems. A shift in tone accompanies the shift in subject. Donne's posture of inferiority as the apprentice who requires the inspiration of R. W.'s more accomplished Muse is the early version of his emphasis on reciprocal friendship. In "Muse not that by thy Mind," he pleads, "Write then, that my griefes which thyne got may bee / Cur'd by thy charming soveraigne melodee" (11–12). The tone becomes manfully self-reliant to serve the didactic function of a later address to his friend, "To Mr Rowland Woodward" [pp. 56–57 above]:

> Manure thy selfe then, to thy selfe be'approv'd,
> And with vaine outward things be no more mov'd,
> But to know, that I love thee'and would be lov'd.
>   (34–36)

The basis for both statements is the same, but the conclusion of the later poem focuses on another effect of their friendship. Consistent with a philosophy that bids "Seeke wee then our selves in our selves" ("To Mr Rowland Woodward," 19), the final lines of the later poem are a restrained expression of the same mutual affection that Donne says inspires the earlier poetry. The reciprocity of friendship explicitly motivates these didactic poems, just as it was the premise for the youthful literary games. Furthermore, these poems, like their predecessors, are demonstrations of literary talent. Donne's efforts to convey an image of himself as writer in a literary tradition are an

6. B. F. Nellist, "Donne's 'Storm' and 'Calm' and the Descriptive Tradition,' *MLR*, 59 (1964), 513: "[These poems] are concerned with the passions aroused by participation in the situation." Nellist discusses the classical tradition behind Donne's use of the sea as a metaphor for fortune. Clayton D. Lein, "Donne's 'The Storme': The Poem and the Tradition," *ELR*, 4 (1974), 137–63, documents more precisely the "rigorous classicism of Donne's poem" (p. 138).

important feature of these later verse letters. In them, he goes beyond spontaneous games to adapt literary convention to his own ends. As in the prose letters (especially to Goodere), Donne's stance is that of a letter writer concerned with ideas for which the familiar letter traditionally is the best vehicle of expression: friendship, virtue, and the cultivation of both through the process of self-examination.

The purest examples of this argument are Donne's verse letters to Sir Henry Wotton. These letters, which are the most universally admired of all Donne's verse letters, are also the ones in which critics use the word *manner* (and not *art*) to describe their effect.[7] Readers are at ease about them. Donne is neither so hyperbolic in his matter nor so contorted in his mode as to detract from his subject, and his subject is an approved one. His satiric temperament has become a stoic acceptance that the world's ills cannot be rhymed to death but are better retreated from. He would smile at them were it not an "incongruity." But for the strong lines and an occasional reference to "crooked lymbecks," the poems hardly seem typical of Donne.[8]

Yet the inadequacy of evaluating these poems simply as lucid, moral, and Horatian is evident when the letters to Wotton are isolated and considered as a group. Donne's characteristic method is plainly in evidence, and he works an ingenious variation on it. There is a consistent self-image that is an essential feature of their argument. First of all, it is striking that all these letters call attention to themselves as letters even when, as in "Sir, more then kisses" (pp. 71–73 [pp. 54–56 above]), the reflections on letter-writing seem to be merely a frame for a literary exercise.[9] Another poem, "Here's no more newes, then vertue" (pp. 73–74 [pp. 53–54 above]), apologizes for having no news to convey and closes "*At Court; though From Court, were the better stile.*" "*H. W. in Hiber. Belligeranti*" (pp. 74–75), describes the letters it expects in reply; and "To Sir Henry Wotton, at his going Ambassador to Venice" (pp. 75–76 [pp. 61–62 above]) presents itself as an "honest paper" (17) among other letters and papers on Wotton's desk.

The image of Donne as letter writer is too consistently invoked in these poems to Wotton to be without effect, and the effect is an important one. All of the verse letters to Wotton are concerned with the problem of maintaining virtue in various states of life. The extremes of that problem are described by Wotton and Donne,

---

7. See Thomson, "Donne and the Poetry of Patronage," p. 314, and J. B. Leishman, *The Monarch of Wit*, 7th ed. (London, 1965), pp. 137 ff.

8. "*H. W. in Hiber. Belligeranti*" appeared only in the Burley MS., initialed J. D. In attributing this poem to Donne in his edition, Grierson remarks of the lines containing the "crooked lymbecks" (13–15), "These lines are enough of themselves to prove Donne's authorship of the poem" (II, 152).

9. H. J. C. Grierson, "Bacon's Poem, 'The World': Its Date and Relation to Certain Other Poems," *MLR*, 6 (1911), 145–56, describes the literary debate to which this poem was a contribution. Related poems by Bacon and Wotton are extant.

assocciated with, respectively, the active and the reflective person-
ality. Donne's picture of himself, writing letters, awaiting letters to
control "The tediousnesse of my life" without which he "could ideate
nothing" ("Sir, more then kisses," 3–4), verges on complaint. Wotton
is off to Ireland with Essex (1599). Donne laments the loss of
"Respective frendship" and begs a letter, not "such as from the
brayne come, but the hart" ("*H. W. in Hiber. Belligeranti*," 3. 20).
Wotton receives an ambassadorship to Venice (1604). Donne's "To
Sir Henry Wotton, at his going Ambassador to Venice" contrasts with
the business at hand, being an "honest paper" among the "reverend,"
"learned," and "loving" ones that clutter Wotton's desk (17, 1, 9, 13).
Donne's situation in contrast to Wotton's is described in this letter:

> 'Tis therefore well your spirits now are plac'd
>   In their last Furnace, in activity;
> Which fits them (Schooles and Courts and Warres o'rpast)
>   To touch and test in any best degree.
>
> For mee, (if there be such a thing as I)
>   Fortune (if there be such a thing as shee)
> Spies that I beare so well her tyranny,
>   That she thinks nothing else so fit for mee.
>   (29–36)

The description of his own circumstance is not simply a complaint
for his misfortune; it positively gives validity to his moral observa-
tions. The "honest paper" figures the ideal conduct of an embassy:

> To sweare much love, not to be chang'd before
>   Honour alone will to your fortune fit;
> Nor shall I then honour your fortune. more
>   Then I have done your honour wanting it.
>   (21–24)

Likewise, writing to Donne from Ireland will be proof against
Wotton's mind succumbing to lethargies or crooked motives for
which the separation offers a real danger. The vice that Donne asso-
ciates with inactivity in "Here's no more newes, then vertue" is con-
trolled by the process of writing a letter that bids Wotton join him
in condemning the world of the court.[1] The letter "Sir, more then

---

1. The earliest known English prose letter-writing manual was entitled *The Enimie of Idle-
nesse* (1568). Its author, William Fulwood, tells his "weldisposed Reader": "Amongst which
I here offer unto thyne eyes this treatise, called The Enimie of Idlenesse which I have so
entitled, for that as well when urgent affaires require, as also at vacant times, when leisure
permitteth thee (for the avoiding of Idlenesse, the capital enimie to all exercise and vertue)
thou mayest occupie and practise thy selfe therein, taking pen in hand, and gratifieng thy
frende with some conceit or other: whereby thou shalt both purchase frendship, increase
in knowledge and also drive away drowsy dumps and fond fansies from thy heavy head."
The prefatory material and some examples from this handbook are printed in Paul Wolter,
The Enimie of Idlenesse, der älteste englische Briefsteller (Potsdam, 1907).

kisses" also functions as a part of a virtuous exercise. In his corre-
spondence with Wotton, Donne's presentation of himself as friend
and letter writer (letters are testimonies and seals of friendship) con-
sistently motivates the preoccupation with virtue that is their theme.

Donne's concern with the virtue of both himself and his corre-
spondent as a function of the activity in which they are mutually
engaged is likewise the theme of the verse letters to his patronesses;
but he manages the idea to different effect. In fact, the letters to
noblewomen put any theories about his epistolary methods to the
test. The most lengthy and impressive among them, chiefly those to
the Countess of Bedford, proceed from an association of the Count-
ess with a spiritual truth or moral *exemplum* that presents essential
difficulties. Most of these difficulties can be resolved to a simple
question of the intent of the association. Readers are reluctant to
limit Donne to grossly material motives—calling a benefactor God
and then bringing all the resources of his intellect to the task of
justifying the gambit when his real motives may be simply too crass
to mention. Besides projecting a sorry image of the poet, this expla-
nation reflects just as unfavorably on the person who would accept
such a compliment; she is sinfully vain and stupid to have paid for
the poem. An alternative to this explanation, mentioned above, is to
make the literal outrage the repository of higher truth: God is, in
fact, in everyone. This rescues Donne but plays his argument down.
A letter to the Countess of Bedford clearly proceeds from the
assumption that she is somehow unique. It is the uniqueness of the
association that Donne defends when he confesses his faults to
the Countess in an unfinished verse letter (p. 104) that confronts
any objections she might have to the application of these same argu-
ments to other ladies. Nor can we ignore the fact that there are six
lengthy and elaborate verse letters to Lady Bedford, not counting
other poems written to or for her that are either not complete or not
distinctly epistolary but proceed from similar associations of the
Countess with divine or perfect things. Moreover, the Countess of
Bedford was an intelligent woman; her support of the poet means
that she read the poems Donne wrote to her, possibly even answered
them. Something about them pleased.

Wesley Milgate (p. 253) dates Donne's verse letters to the Count-
ess of Bedford from 1608 to 1612, the years when his frustration at
not finding civil employment was mounting, when he began to inten-
sify his religious studies and take part in religious controversies, and
when he was first urged to entertain the idea that he seek a career
as minister of the Church.[2] We cannot be sure how much a patron

2. According to Patricia Thomson. "John Donne and the Countess of Bedford," *MLR*, 44

would have been aware of these activities and feelings; but it is significant that some of them were public statements, and it is demonstrable that Donne's relationship with the Countess of Bedford was grounded in more than conventional politeness.[3] Therefore, Donne could assume a consistent personality when writing to Lady Bedford, and this personality could reflect concerns with which he was becoming publicly associated.

The most significant problem Donne faces in his letters to Lady Bedford is also the one critics have judged he solves too recklessly. From his earliest association with her, Donne is involved in a situation that may undercut his praise of her: he is simultaneously paying court to others in similar terms. In a prose letter to Goodere, Donne describes this difficulty in terms his benefactors (then the Countesses of Huntingdon and Bedford) would have been pleased to overhear:

> For the other part of your Letter, spent in the praise of the Countesse [Huntingdon], I am always very apt to beleeve it of her, and can never beleeve it so well, and so reasonably, as now, when it is averred by you: but for the expressing it to her, in that sort as you seem to counsaile, I have these two reasons to decline it. That that knowledge which she hath of me, was in the beginning of a graver course, then of a Poet, into which (that I may also keep my dignity) I would not seem to relapse. The Spanish proverb informes me, that he is a fool which cannot make one Sonnet, and he is mad which makes two. The other stronger reason, is my integrity to the other Countesse [Bedford], of whose worthinesse though I swallowed your opinion at first upon your words, yet I have had since an explicit faith, and now a knowledge: and for her delight (since she descends to them) I had reserved not only all the verses, which I should make, but all the thoughts of womens worthinesse. But because I hope she [the Countess of Bedford] will not disdain, that I should write well of her Picture [the Countess of Huntingdon], I have obeyed you thus far, as to write: but intreat you by your friendship, that by this occasion of versifying, I be not traduced, nor esteemed light in that Tribe, and that house where I have lived. (*Letters*, pp. 103–104, no. 34)

We must regard a letter to Goodere, especially one written to him when he seems to have been an agent for two countesses, as more a public statement than a private confidence. That is, it is probably as artful as the poems it is often invoked to explain. So its argument

---

(1949), 329–40, Lady Bedford stood godmother to Donne's child in 1608. Their relationship was strained by the Countess's declining fortune, her illness (1612–13), and her more Puritan sympathies. There was no real break. Donne preached before her in 1621.
3. There is evidence that they exchanged poems (*Letters*, p. 67, no. 23).

offers yet another example of Donne's concern to project a consistent image of himself as author of his letters and to use that image to solve his artistic problems. The verse letters to the Countess of Bedford are remarkable for the way they transform the difficulties prescribed by the circumstances of their inspiration into poetry that very often achieves its praise through scrupulous attention to the integrity of its author.

The prose letter to Goodere in which Donne discusses his relationships with both the Countesses of Huntingdon and Bedford describes his attitude toward Lady Bedford in terms he uses in a verse letter to her. Donne says that he "swallowed" Goodere's opinion of her at first, and then had "an explicit faith, and now a knowledge" of her goodness. More generally, "all the thoughts of womens worthinesse" he relates to her. Lady Bedford's relationship with Donne is comparable to his later male friendships. Like his prose letters to Goodere, for example, his verse letters to Lady Bedford take up moral or theological problems. The difference is that, to Lady Bedford, Donne may apply his speculations to a specific end: explaining his affection for her or the consequences of their relationship in terms borrowed from the language of ethical or theological argument. There is a superficial resemblance here to Samuel Daniel's method of identifying the Countess of Bedford or the Countess of Cumberland with a specific virtue. If Donne's procedure were simply that, his more hyperbolic statements would be blasphemy. He effects an important difference, however, by focusing on himself as speaker of these praises. J. B. Leishman has suggested that these letters may be "a kind of elaborate game" (p. 144).[4] The observation at least acknowledges the elements of these poems that some critics would like to overlook, particularly Donne's glib use of serious matters. The crucial qualification to Leishman's remark is that *game* need not suggest trifling, and it begs the question of sincerity. Donne invites his correspondent to play his game; even when the invitation is playful, it is always complimentary in its careful avoidance of inconsistencies and truisms. When Donne addresses himself to his patroness, he presumes she knows his rules.

The reason-faith distinction that opens what is probably an early letter to Lady Bedford, "Reason is our Soules left hand" (pp. 90–91 [pp. 62–63 above]), is one that Donne must have thought about and spoken about often. It clearly became associated with him, at least after he applied it to explain his understanding of Prince Henry's death (1613) in one of the few poems published in his lifetime. He resorts to it also in the *Essays in Divinity*, parts of which he almost

---

4. Stapleton and Lewalski acknowledge the presence of this element but regard it as ancillary rather than essential to the theme of the poems.

certainly wrote in the period of his close friendship with Lady
Bedford.[5] Donne's verse letter to the Countess uses the distinction
between reason and faith to explain their relationship. Although the
argument is facetious, it has a point and is ingeniously adapted to
admit the most careful discriminations to the poem. Donne sets up
the terms of the compliment in an opening stanza where he invites
the Countess to see his position in terms of a theological argument.
He lists the correspondences:

> Reason is our Soules left hand, Faith her right,
>   By these wee reach divinity, that's you:
> Their loves, who have the blessing of your sight,
>   Grew from their reason, mine from far faith grew.
>
>   (1–4)

Donne associates the Countess with the divinity, but that associ-
ation is a premise, not the argument, of his poem. One measure of
the compliment is the straightforward tone in which he assumes that
she will take the comparison for no more or no less than it is. On
the surface, it posits an association which intimates blasphemously
high regard. All the same, it is hypothetical. Beyond that, the com-
parisons set up a mechanism which allows Donne to sidestep any
pretensions to truth or specificity. It is thus impossible for him to
resort to conventional flattery. Reason, like the "knowledge" Donne
speaks of in the prose letter to Goodere quoted above, is related to
the accomplished fact of the Countess's patronage (5–8) for which
Donne is only now making suit. Donne describes the evidence he
has for hope (9–11), but beyond that, he has no intention of making
poetry of such "reasonable" evidence. (For example, he might have
named names—Daniel, Drayton, Jonson, Goodere.) Instead, he
turns to "faith" that is, according to his terms in the first stanza, not
based on knowledge. In keeping with the terms of his opening pos-
tulates, he pursues the theological metaphor and extends it to terms
of moral perfection, proceeding from God to man. Acting on faith,
he properly speculates how divine attributes and other perfections
might be applicable to the Countess. It is only consistent with his
argument that Donne's profession of faith seems hyperbolic. The
form of his argument might disguise materialistic motives or deep
theological ones, but the motive that works and is unimpeachable is
an artistic one. Donne has assumed the posture of a student of the-
ology and ethics, and his address resorts to characteristic distinctions
and patterns of thought. Given the premise of the first stanza, his
conclusions are inevitable.

5. The elegy on the death of Prince Henry begins: "Looke to mee faith, and looke to my faith,
God: / For both my centers feele this period / Of waight one center, one of greatnesse is:
/ And Reason is that center, Faith is this" (text from Grierson's edition, I, 267). See *Essays
in Divinity*, ed. Evelyn M. Simpson (Oxford, 1952), pp. 20–21.

Stanzas 5–8 are "articles" of faith, expressed simply although always subject to some afterthought or qualification. In the last stanza, inevitably, reason intrudes. The letter returns to the demands of reason: the need for a material demonstration of the Countess's goodness. Donne's suspicion that a "squint lefthandednesse" may be considered ungracious (5–6) has been confirmed by readers who find the closing couplet too blatantly motivated. In fact, the last six lines simply state the inevitable: if the poet's faith is to be fulfilled, his reason must be satisfied. However, the poet makes his proposition not simply but in terms that relate his argument to the well-being of the Countess herself. In effect, the poet requires her to justify his faith in her, not just for his good, but for hers:

> Since you are then Gods masterpeece, and so
> His Factor for our loves; do as you doe,
> Make your returne home gracious; and bestow
> This life on that; so make one life of two.
> For so God helpe mee; I would not misse you there
> For all the good which you can do me here.
> (33–38)

The shift from flattering analogy to spiritual solicitude, a move with manifest ulterior motivation, is also consistent artistically. Each article of "faith" has contained its own qualification that applies it to the Countess, and these qualifications are implicitly concessions to "reason." Thus, no heretic can deny her goodness, but "if he did, yet you are so" (18). "Every thing" has an intrinsic *Balsamum* to keepe it fresh, and new, / If 'twere not injur'd by extrinsique blowes" (21–23). Donne slips into the description of the "methridate, whose operation / Keepes off, or cures," and then recalls himself: "Yet, this is not your physicke, but your food" (27–29). Reason, Donne's awareness that he is suing to Lady Bedford for support, has intruded all along and to a very specific effect that is the larger theme of Donne's verse correspondence with her. For motives that could be linked to Donne's spiritual and moral concerns, but that are also crucial to him as petitioner for favors, Donne is anxious that the Countess appear good (generous) in the eyes of others.[6] The world must see she is his patroness.

* * *

The interrelationship between these letters to noblewomen and some of the funeral elegies, particularly the *Anniversaries*, describes

---

6. Quotable versions of this argument appear elsewhere, in the last line of the fragment of the satiric *Metempsychosis* ("The onely measure is, and judge, opinion") and in the *First Anniversary* ("Wicked is not much worse than indiscreet," 338). The *Anniversaries* were printed in Donne's lifetime.

a different situation from one of Donne indulging in reckless, indiscriminate praise. If statements about these poems, both within them and in the prose letters referring to them, be taken for what they are meant to be, Donne's public efforts at self-consistent statements about his artistic judgments, then the question of whether he is inventing excuses for breaches of decorum no longer intrudes on an appreciation of these poems. In each statement, Donne is explaining a poem from the point of view he expects his audience to recognize that he has taken. He is requiring faith in his art, not his sincerity. In his occasional poetry, especially in the letters written to living people familiar with John Donne in his various capacities, Donne proceeds in terms that his readers are expected to recognize. Within these terms he formulates "the best praise I could give."

Donne's occasional poetry repays the same kind of attention that readers have learned to afford his lyric poetry. In his verse letters, the dramatic self-presentation that renders a love poem so compelling is, if anything, more accessible. Although the portrait of the speaker of these poems is finally shaded by the artist's hand (Donne indicates what aspects of his personality are relevant), its outlines are also consistent with what is known of his life. In fact, three of the existing portraits present a striking parallel to the epistolary pictures of himself that Donne likened to "a hand, or eye / By *Hilliard* drawne" ("The Storme," 3–4). Donne the soldier, Donne the melancholy lover, Donne the dead man are all aspects of the poet which he externalized for deliberate effect. The literary analogues to this are Donne's *Devotions*, some of his sermons, and many of his occasional poems. In these productions, he proceeds from the premise that an argument is more compelling to an audience who must perceive in its structure the lineaments of his face.

HEATHER DUBROW

Resident Alien: John Donne†

* * *

* * *In studying his relationship to Petrarchism, critics also cannot ignore chronology, for his counterdiscourses respond variously to specific moments in his culture and hence shift in important ways over time, though they never assume a simple pattern of moving from

† From *Echoes of Desire: English Petrarchism and Its Counterdiscourses* (Ithaca: Cornell UP, 1995), pp. 215–22. Copyright © 1995 by Cornell University. Reprinted by permission of the publisher, Cornell University Press.

acceptance to rejection. In particular, as I will argue, Petrarchism sparked his interest when he was a young man at the Inns, and the bitterness with which he sometimes attacks it when practicing his *acerbo stil nuovo* demonstrates again that the counterdiscourses of Petrarchism are often reactions against an earlier version of oneself. Any chronological examination of Donne's reactions against Petrarchism, however, must also be provisional, for dating his poems is more problematical than some of his critics have admitted.[1]

Petrarchan sentiments, tropes, and situations are pervasive in both Donne's major and minor poems. The *Songs and Sonets* refer repeatedly to sighs and tears, those staples of Petrarchan experience, and they focus on certain moments central to the *Rime sparse* and many of its imitators: leave-taking, the illness or death of the beloved, and the anniversary of the relationship. Whether or not the deflection of Petrarchan conceits from a woman to a young girl should make us hesitate to call the *Anniversaries* Petrarchan, as Barbara Kiefer Lewalski has asserted,[2] those poems certainly adopt the refined adulatory discourse associated with the *Rime sparse* and, of course, also focus on the death of the beloved. Similarly, the praise in the verse letters to patronesses often adapts Petrarchan tropes. Moreover, the conceits long hailed as the hallmark of Donne's poetry themselves express a debt to Petrarchism: Guss rightly reminds us of the connections between Donne's wit and certain modes of Continental Petrarchism, notably the version practiced by Serafino.[3] Such debts have editorial implications as well. The manuscript evidence for excluding "The Token" from the canon is significant though not conclusive; in light of the extent and range of Donne's Petrarchism, he could well have written an extended love sonnet, so stylistic evidence should not be adduced in support of that exclusion.[4]

Although dating most of Donne's poems is difficult, it is likely that the verse letters to male friends which identify their recipients by initials were composed in the early and mid-1590s and hence constitute some of his earliest texts.[5] These poems are far more indebted to Petrarchism than the old clichés about their author's

1. In particular, the important book by Marotti, *John Donne, Coterie Poet*, is sometimes limited by its reliance on dubious assumptions about dating, a problem occasionally acknowledged (see, e.g., pp. 83, 137) but never resolved.
2. Barbara Kiefer Lewalski, *Donne's "Anniversaries" and the Poetry of Praise: The Creation of a Symbolic Mode* (Princeton: Princeton University Press, 1973), esp. pp. 12–14. For alternative views of Petrarchan elements in these poems, see O. B. Hardison Jr., *The Enduring Monument: A Study of the Idea of Praise in Renaissance Literary Theory and Practice* (Chapel Hill: University of North Carolina Press, 1962), chap. 7; and John Donne, *The Anniversaries*, ed. Frank Manley (Baltimore: Johns Hopkins University Press, 1963), p. 10.
3. Guss, *John Donne, Petrarchist*, esp. chap. 5.
4. For the argument that it should be excluded on both grounds, see Gardner, *Elegies*, p. xlviii.
5. On the division of these poems into groups and the characteristics of these early letters, see Milgate, *Satires*, pp. xxxiii–xxxiv. On their dates, see his notes on individual poems.

anti-Petrarchism would even deem possible. Seven of the fifteen texts are fourteen lines long, an eighth consists of two fourteen-line stanzas, and a ninth has two fourteen-line stanzas plus an envoy of four lines.[6] Many of their stances, too, recall Petrarchism, with the speaker petitioning for pity in "To Mr T. W." ("All haile sweet Poet"), describing the recipient as "my pain and pleasure" in "To Mr T. W." ("Hast thee harsh verse," 2), and debasing himself in the course of showering adulation on the addressee in "To Mr R. W." ("Kindly'I envy").

Yet two particularly interesting epistles in the group also participate in and in so doing explicate the counterdiscourses of Petrarchism:

To Mr C.B.

Thy friend, whom thy deserts to thee enchaine,
    Urg'd by this inexcusable occasion,
    Thee and the Saint of his affection
Leaving behinde, doth of both wants complaine;
And let the love I beare to both sustaine
    No blott nor maime by this division,
    Strong is this love which ties our hearts in one,
And strong that love pursu'd with amorous paine;
But though besides thy selfe I leave behind
    Heavens liberall, and earths thrice-fairer Sunne,
    Going to where sterne winter aye doth wonne,
Yet, loves hot fires, which martyr my sad minde,
    Doe send forth scalding sighes, which have the Art
    To melt all Ice, but that which walls her heart.

To Mr. I.L.

Blest are your North parts, for all this long time
My Sun is with you, cold and darke'is our Clime;
Heavens Sun, which staid so long from us this yeare,
Staid in your North (I thinke) for she was there,
And hether by kinde nature drawne from thence,
Here rages, chafes, and threatens pestilence;
Yet I, as long as shee from hence doth staie,
Thinke this no South, no Sommer, nor no day.
With thee my kinde and unkinde heart is run,
There sacrifice it to that beauteous Sun:
And since thou art in Paradise and need'st crave
No joyes addition, helpe thy friend to save.
So may thy pastures with their flowery feasts,
As suddenly as Lard, fat thy leane beasts;

---

6. In arriving at the number fifteen, I include the poem to Rowland Woodward beginning "Like one who'in"; its recipient is identified by initials in some poems and by his full name in others, and the poem itself is transitional in style between the early and more mature letters to male friends. The letters to Henry Wotton are excluded.

So may thy woods oft poll'd, yet ever weare
A greene, and when thee list, a golden haire;
So may all thy sheepe bring forth Twins; and so
In chace and race may thy horse all out goe;
So may thy love and courage ne'r be cold;
Thy Sonne ne'r Ward; Thy lov'd wife ne'r seem old;
But maist thou wish great things, and them attaine,
As thou telst her, and none but her, my paine.

These lyrics, textbook instances of the Renaissance fascination with *genera mista*, boast a complex genealogy. Their debt to the Petrarchan sonnet is manifest; Donne variously writes of "amorous paine" ("To Mr C.B.," 8), evokes a saintlike woman and her icy heart, indulges in hyperbole, and focuses on the consequences of absence. The second text contains as well a proto–country house poem, complete with a version of the rhetorical staple of that tradition, the negative formula, as well as the customary allusions to the Fall.

At this point one should not be surprised to learn that both lyrics center on distance and its counterpart, loss. They comment explicitly and repeatedly on the distance from their recipients, a situation that motivates most other verse letters but often remains implicit in them. The sun, too, is distant. Various forms of negatives and privatives ("No blott nor maime" ["To Mr C.B.," 6]; "Thinke this no South, no Sommer, nor no day" ["To Mr I.L.," 8]) enact distance and loss grammatically. And the ladies in question are distanced not only geographically but also rhetorically in that the poet's sentiments are not addressed to them directly but rather filtered through messengers, the addressees of these letters. The second of these letters also includes a pattern of pairing that is rendered explicit in the wish for literal twins: it involves two forms of love, refers to two suns, and pairs words ("kinde and unkinde," 9; "chace and race," 18). And the poet who, when writing an epithalamium for the Somerset-Howard wedding nearly two decades later, was to project two versions of himself under the names "Idios" and "Allophanes,"[7] here asks his friend to speak his words and thus to become his double. These patterns of distance or privation and the pairing that in a sense is the opposite of privatives are not, I suggest, present fortuitously: they enact rhetorically the very agenda of these poems, distancing their speaker and their poet from the discourse he is practicing by pairing the Petrarchan sonnet to a mistress with the verse epistle to a male friend.

On one level that pairing serves to intensify the bond between the male friends. Both loves may be strong, as Donne insists in "To Mr

7. See my argument about those names in *A Happier Eden: The Politics of Marriage in the Stuart Epithalamium* (Ithaca: Cornell University Press, 1990), pp. 193–195.

C.B.," but it is telling that the letters are addressed to another man, not to the Petrarchan mistress. In "To Mr I.L." the role of messenger cements the bond between the men. That is, though Donne's speaker is associated with privation and the addressee with plenitude, the relationship between them does not evince the competitiveness that Donne's other poetry would lead us to expect but rather a symbiosis in which the poet depends on his friend to deliver a message and the friend depends on the poet, like his counterpart in the country house poem, for good wishes that culminate on implicit apotropaic threats. (Our expectation of rivalry is not wholly fallacious, however, for it is not so much erased as on the one hand controlled by mutual dependency and on the other displaced onto the competitive horses who appear in line eighteen of "To Mr I.L.") Hence both poems exemplify certain characteristics of homosocial desire: they assert the symmetry between the genders (in one letter mirroring it as well through the other forms of pairing which we traced) while apparently undermining that symmetry by privileging the male addressee and the relationship between him and the speaker.[8] And the erasure of the woman that often results from homosocial desire is thematized in both poems, which focus on the absence of both male friend and mistress yet reinstate the former by addressing him on the subject of the lady, as well as other topics, within the letter. Thus the Petrarchan mistress seemingly serves mainly to enable a relationship between men, a relationship that negotiates some distance from both Petrarchism and the Petrarchan lady.

The verse letters in question, then, might appear to provide a textbook example of homosocial desire. Perhaps. Certainly that model usefully directs our attention to the triangulation of the participants and the focus on the friend throughout much of both letters. Yet in making assumptions about the erasure of the woman, we need to acknowledge a countervailing factor, the radiant force she represents in these lyrics. Indeed, "To Mr C.B." concludes by contrasting the powerlessness of the poet's verse and the power of the lady's disdain: "scalding sighes, which have the Art / To melt all Ice, but that which walls her heart." Moreover, as these lines remind us, at their climactic final couplets both poems swerve from the relationship between the men to that between the poet and lady; this shift is all the more startling because it is all the more abrupt in "To Mr I.L.," where the evocation of the addressee's rural retreat has distracted us from the pains of Petrarchan love. Mr. I.L. himself enables the return to that love in that, like the poem itself, he is enjoined to bear the poet's message. And if the construction of a Petrarchan situation

8. The highly influential concept of homosocial desire was introduced by Eve Kosofsky Sedgwick in *Between Men: English Literature and Male Homosocial Desire* (New York: Columbia University Press, 1985). For a summary of some of its characteristics, see pp. 47–48.

has facilitated a link between two men, the link between those men has facilitated the Petrarchan situation inasmuch as Donne apparently feels more comfortable with Petrarchism when it is distanced by being filtered through an intermediary—or, in this case, two intermediaries, the customarily un-Petrarchan genre of the verse letter and the male friend onto whom the Petrarchan message of adulation is displaced. Thus Donne simultaneously speaks the discourse of Petrarchism and one version of a counterdiscourse as well. And in so doing he invites us to refine the paradigm of homosocial desire which has recently proved so influential. Might one find instances in other writers as well where the primacy of male bonds represents but one stage of a continuing, circular process that moves back and forth between homosocial and heterosocial relationships? In particular, should one think not simply of the erasure of the female in the service of male bonding but also of an even more unstable circular pattern in which that male bonding is then redeployed, possibly in response to homophobic anxieties, in the service of a heterosexual relationship, which may then generate further homosocial bonding, and so on?

However those questions are answered, Donne's early verse letters impel us to return to the specifics of chronology. If these poems testify to his status as resident alien in the domain of Petrarchism, his readers need to examine as precisely as possible the dates at which his visa was granted. Donne was admitted to Lincoln's Inn from Thavies Inn on May 6, 1592, paying the reduced fee for entrants who had been members of one of the Inns of Chancery associated with Lincoln's Inn for at least a year.[9] Hence he was at the Inns when Sidney's *Astrophil and Stella* appeared in 1591.

Though the consequences of this chronology are necessarily speculative, several suggestive possibilities present themselves. Sidney's sequence is in many ways not only a poet's poem but a young man's poem, and it is likely that the members of the Inns, like many other participants in London literary culture, were excited with its wit, its technical virtuosity, and its sophisticated, knowing enactment of desire. At the same time, they may well have felt some competitive unease, perhaps fearing that their own great expectations as men of letters would be hampered or at least threatened by the adulation Sidney was receiving posthumously. In any event, later in the decade many members of the Inns reacted virulently against the stylistic abuses of Petrarchism: that movement is a recurrent target in formal verse satire, and in my concluding chapter I argue that the Ovidian epyllion, another genre that proved popular at the Inns, should be read as one of the counterdiscourses of Petrarchism. If *Astrophil and*

9. See Bald, *John Donne: A Life*, pp. 54–55.

Stella engendered interest and even enthusiasm in the authors of formal verse satires early in the 1590s, that reaction may help to explain the intense repudiation within those satires of what Joseph Hall terms "patched *Sonettings*" (*Virgidemiae*, I.vii.11);[1] once again the counterdiscourses of Petrarchism disown their authors' previous interest or participation in that movement.

Ontogeny recapitulates phylogeny. We may also hypothesize with some conviction that Donne shared the excitement generated by *Astrophil and Stella* and wanted his circle at the Inns to know that he shared it: witness the extensive Petrarchism in the verse letters to young men. At the same time, for all the reasons we have traced, he probably shared as well the reservations about Petrarchism that may have been present at the Inns in the early 1590s and are indubitably manifest in some of the verse letters he composed during the 1590s. Hence the distancing devices in the poems to Christopher Brooke and "I.L." and at least some of the violence with which he mocks Petrarchism later in his career. Donne is reacting against his earlier experiments in that mode, an earlier version of his literary culture, an earlier self. Obsessed with betrayal in so many other arenas,[2] he is likely to have felt betrayed by Petrarchism—and by his own earlier attraction to it. A proverb he adduces in one of his prose letters both excuses and explicates that dual betrayal—"The Spanish proverb informes me, that he is a fool which cannot make one Sonnet, and he is mad which makes two"[3]—and his uneasy identification with the literary movement he is rejecting helps to explain why the sonneteer whom he mocks in "Satyre II" is a lawyer.

The difficulty of dating most of the *Songs and Sonets* in and of itself undermines any notion that Donne moved from youthful Petrarchism, his own *giovenile errore*, to Platonism.[4] It is more than possible that when he wrote love poetry during the final decade of the sixteenth century, Donne, like many other members of his culture, was simultaneously penning the discourses and the counterdiscourses of Petrarchism. Indeed, the *Songs and Sonets* also reminds us of the misconceptions that survive in our literary histories despite frequent disavowals of them. The notion of a neat movement from sixteenth-century lyricism to seventeenth-century realism and

---

1. Arnold Davenport, ed., *The Collected Poems of Joseph Hall* (Liverpool: Liverpool University Press, 1949).
2. Compare Carey's arguments about how apostasy affected Donne's preoccupation with betrayal (*John Donne*, esp. pp. 37–38).
3. John Donne, *Letters to Severall Persons of Honour (1651)*, ed. M. Thomas Hester (New York: Scholars' Facsimiles and Reprints, 1977), pp. 103–104.
4. The chronology of these poems is a complicated issue largely outside the scope of this chapter. For an influential but unpersuasive argument that many of them can be dated with some certainty, see Gardner, *Elegies*, pp. lvii–lxii; on the problems of dating them, see esp. J. B. Leishman, *The Monarch of Wit: An Analytical and Comparative Study of the Poetry of John Donne*, 6th ed. (New York: Harper and Row, 1966), pp. 185–187.

cynicism is as problematical as comparable mappings of Donne's career, for hardly more reason exists to define the 1590s as the decade of Petrarchan love sonnets and *The Faerie Queene* than to see it as the period of formal verse satire, the epyllion, and Donne's own amoral love poems. It is only narrative displacement that tempts us to say otherwise.

However the story of literary history is told, that tale will include the many ways Donne reacts against Petrarchism in his *Songs and Sonets*. Some poems, of course, straightforwardly satirize or rebut Petrarchism; self-consciously reversing Petrarchan assumptions and in so doing calling attention to their ideology, these lyrics announce themselves as a counterdiscourse. "The Indifferent" and "Communitie," for example, position their amoral naturalism against the idealistic assumptions of the Petrarchan discourse.[5] Similarly, the open eroticism of "The Good Morrow" stands in self-conscious contrast to the frustrations of the Petrarchan lover. As Kerrigan points out, in "Loves Diet" the figure of Love attempts to establish a Petrarchan vision that the speaker resists.[6] If, as seems likely, many of Donne's love poems were written during the 1590s, their original readers were inundated by Petrarchan sequences and hence intensely conscious of such contrasts. Thus the stance of poems like "The Indifferent" must have seemed to readers during that period—and to the poet himself—as not merely a reversal but also a rebuttal of Petrarchan idealizations.

*   *   *

GARY A. STRINGER

Some of Donne's Revisions
(And How to Recognize Them)†

At the time of his death on March 31, 1631, at the age of 59, John Donne had written about 200 poems that totaled slightly over 9,100 lines and fell broadly across the spectrum of generic types. Only a handful of these poems, however, had yet appeared in print.[1] His

---

5. On Donne's attack on Petrarchism in this poem, see, e.g., Hunt, *Donne's Poetry*, pp. 1–15.
6. Kerrigan, "What Was Donne Doing?" pp. 8–9.
† This essay appears for the first time in this Norton Critical Edition.
1. The most important of these are the Anniversaries triptych—"The First Anniuersary" (1611), "A Funerall Elegy" (1611), and "The Second Anniuersarie" (1612)—and the "Elegie on the vntimely Death of the incomparable Prince, Henry," which was included in the third edition of Josuah Sylvester's commemorative volume on the death of the

poetry was nevertheless widely known to his contemporaries, having been handed about in handwritten copies among various friends, acquaintances, patrons, potential patrons, and aficionados (of poetry or of Donne); and these initial recipients, in turn, shared them with others in an ever-expanding circle of manuscript distribution. Indeed, the section on Donne in Peter Beal's *Index of English Literary Manuscripts* (London: Mansell, 1980) lists 3997 whole or partial copies of individual Donne poems in the manuscript record (and others have since come to light), and those that survive constitute only a fraction of what must have originally existed.[2] Unfortunately, this vast body of manuscript material includes only four brief inscriptions, a Latin epitaph on his wife, and a single verse epistle—the 63-line "To the Lady Carey and Mrs. Essex Rich"—in Donne's own hand. And the copies generated by the scores of individuals whose work makes up the manuscript record, many of whom were working from exemplars many stages removed from Donne's originals, are packed with errors. Most of these, of course, are the result of simple ineptitude or carelessness, but some of them reflect the deliberate efforts of various scribes to improve Donne's poems aesthetically or to purge them of material deemed morally or politically objectionable. An additional factor complicating the interpretation of the manuscript evidence, as I will show below, is that Donne revised some of his poems over the course of time, some of them more than once, and these revised versions circulated side by side with the originals, begetting strains of authentic variation within the surrounding sea of error.

Until fairly recently, the existence of these revisions has not been much discussed, though it is possible to round up a few scattered remarks.[3] In his 1896 Muses' Library edition of Donne's poetry, E. K. Chambers admits the possibility of multiple authorial versions of some of Donne's poems, asserting that "[i]n all probability most of Donne's poems existed in several more or less revised forms" (I, xliv) within the seventeenth-century manuscript pool. And Herbert

---

Prince, *Lachrymae Lachrymarum* (1613). A full listing of printings of Donne's verse that preceded his death is given among other items in Ernest W. Sullivan, II, *The Influence of John Donne: His Uncollected Seventeenth-Century Printed Verse* (Columbia: U of Missouri P, 1993), pp. 55–96.

2. For example, sixty-two copies of Donne's elegy "The Bracelet" exist in the surviving manuscript record, yet the genealogical tree describing the textual history of this poem prior to its publication in 1635 shows that a minimum of another twenty-five copies must once have existed (see Gary A. Stringer *et al.*, *The Variorum Edition of the Poetry of John Donne* [Bloomington: Indiana U Press, 2000], 2: 45–46).

3. The following works are cited in this paragraph: E. K. Chambers, *Poems of John Donne*, 2 vols., (London and New York, 1896); Herbert J. C. Grierson, *The Poems of John Donne*, 2 vols. (Oxford: Clarendon, 1912); Simpson: "The Text of Donne's 'Divine Poems,' " *Essays and Studies*, xxvi, 1940 [1941], pp. 88–105; Helen Gardner, *John Donne: The Divine Poems* (Oxford: Clarendon, 1952; 2nd ed., 1978); Helen Gardner, *John Donne: The Elegies and the Songs and Sonnets* (Oxford: Clarendon, 1965); Wesley Milgate, *John Donne: The Satires, Epigrams, and Verse Letters* (Oxford: OUP, 1987).

Grierson, in the great Oxford edition of 1912, opines that "it is not probable, but certain, that of some poems . . . more than one distinct version was in circulation" (2: cxxi), mentioning the satires in particular, but also occasionally pointing to what he deemed variant authorial readings in poems of other genres. Another important study that touches on this subject is Evelyn Simpson's description of the Dobell ms. (DV siglum H5), published in 1941 when Harvard College Libary had recently purchased the artifact. Amongst other "preferable" (98) readings available in Dobell, Simpson notes several that she thinks preserve Donne's "first draft" (99). And Helen Gardner—though she fails to credit either Grierson or Simpson, who had successively argued this point—in her 1952 edition of the *Divine Poems* explicitly identifies "But my'everwaking part shall see that face, / Whose fear already shakes my every joynt" as Donne's revision of the earlier "Or presently, I know not, see y^t Face / Whose fear already shakes my every joint" in lines 7–8 of the Holy Sonnet "This is my play's last scene" (p. lxviii). Thirteen years later, in her edition of the *Elegies and the Songs and Sonnets* (1965), Gardner acknowledges that the Group-III manuscripts preserve a "distinct [textual] tradition" that an editor is "bound to consider" (p. lxxiii), but cannot bring herself to believe that they represent "Donne's earlier versions" (p. lxxii). Variants in these artifacts that she cannot explain away as scribal corruptions or sophistications, she thus labels merely as "genuine alternative[s]" (e.g., p. 123) and leaves it at that. The editor who most stimulated my thinking on this whole subject—and this occurred in the early 1990s, as we were beginning to see the possibility of actually getting a volume of the *Donne Variorum* into print— was Wesley Milgate, whose introduction to *John Donne: The Satires, Epigrams, and Verse Letters* (1967) called attention to "striking variant readings . . . for which it is difficult or impossible to account as due to accidents of transmission" (p. lvi). Milgate correspondingly argued that the author's revisions of the first four satires could be discerned within the corpus of manuscript copies. I subsequently came to see that Milgate was wrong in many particulars, but his remarks inspired me to carry out a complete collation of verbal variants in the manuscripts of "Satire III"; and in a symposium at the Donne Society's conference in 1992 I defended his general notion that Donne's revisionary hand could be traced through the artifactual record for that poem.

In order to test the validity of Milgate's claim, I assembled a complete list of verbal variants from the manuscripts and began to pore over them. Initially the list was quite long, but eventually those shown below and emphasized in bold type emerged as the most important:

4 **May** rayling then cure // **Can** railing then cure

7 As vertu was to the first **blind** // As Virtue was in the first **blinded**

31 who made thee, to stand / **Soldier** // (who made thee to stand / **sentinell**

33 Know thy **foes**: the foule Deuill, whom thou // Knowe thy **foe** . . .

35 his whole Realme to be **ridd** // his whole realme to bee **quitt**

47 He loues **her** raggs so // hee loues **the** raggs, soe

57 like fashions, **bidd** him thinke // like fashions, **bids** him thinke

79 On a **high** hill // on a **huge** hill

80 **Ragged** and steepe Truthe **dwells** // **cragged**, & steepe truth **stands**

84 Thy **Mind** rest // thy **soule** rest

88 Are **as** yᵉ Sun // are **like** the sun

90 In so ill case **here** // in soe ill case **[omitted]**

95 **Oh** will it then **serve** thee // **[omitted]** will it then **boote** thee

104 thrive & **proue** well // thriue & **doe** well

Taken in isolation, some of these changes would strike anyone as inconsequential, as the kind of thing a copyist might do inadvertently; others, however, are among those "striking variant readings" that Milgate found it "difficult or impossible" to explain as mere "accidents of transmission." Among these I would certainly include "Soldier" / "sentinell" in line 31, "ridd" / "quitt" in line 35, "high" / "huge" in line 79, "dwells" / "stands" in line 80, "Mind" / "soule" in line 84, "ill case here" / "ill case [*om*]" in line 90, "serve" / "boote" in line 95, and "proue" / "doe" in line 104.

Though he does not explain his thinking beyond what I have reported above, what persuaded Milgate that these variants were authorial, I suspect, was not just that the "alternatives" making up each of these pairs are "genuine"—that is, each member of each pair seems perfectly appropriate to the poetic context—but also that there are so many of them in this one poem. Considering each in isolation, one might imagine a copyist dropping the "oh" at the beginning of line 95 or the "here" in line 90—or trivializing line 104's "proue" to "doe"—but to whom other than the author would it occur to change "soldier" to "sentinell" or "ridd" to "quitt" or "high hill" to "huge hill" or "dwells" to "stand" or "mind" to "soule"? And beyond that, who other than the author would undertake to change them all? After pondering all this for a while, I concluded that Milgate was right.

Part of the thinking that led to this conclusion involved developing a kind of flow chart (or crude stemma) that traced the evolution of the poem through its early transmissional history, (see Figure 1). Analysis of the artifactual record yielded a fascinating multi-stage picture in which Donne could be seen to have revisited the poem repeatedly as he adjusted the text for esthetic, theological, and (perhaps) political reasons. This analysis showed that the earliest version of the poem is preserved in eighteen manuscripts, shown in the leftmost column of Figure 1, which represent the full complement of traditional manuscript groups. OQ1 and VA2 are small manuscript "books" that contain nothing but Donne's satires; C9, H6, and H5 are three of the traditional four Group-III manuscripts; B13 through VA2 are "associated with Group III"; NY3 is the sole Group-IV manuscript; B32, O20, and SP1 are Group Is; and the remaining four here are unclassified. The copies in all these artifacts give the first of the paired alternative readings in the first list presented above.

Moving from left to right across Figure 1, we find Donne's first revision of the poem preserved in B47 and H7, which contain all the original readings except two—they change line 33's "foes" to "foe" and line 35's "ridd" to "quit." These changes are carried over into Y3, which preserves the third version of the poem and Donne's most thoroughgoing revision, recording seven major changes to the B47-H7 text: "may" is revised to "can," "soldier" to "sentinell," "high" to "huge," "dwells" to "stands," "Mind" to "Soule," "as" to "like," and "serve" to "boot." The text as thus evolved—with the nine accumulated changes—then appears in Versions 4 (preserved in O21) and 5 (preserved in B40 and TT1), which combine to add three additional changes that carry forward in the stream of transmission. The accumulated twelve changes then descend to Version 6, which introduces two others, altering "to" to "in" in line 7 and omitting "here" in line 90. The text exhibiting these fourteen alterations is finally transmitted from this missing progenitor to four surviving manuscripts—the siblings C2 and C8 (usually members of Group I) and the parent-child pair DT1 and H4 (normally members of Group II).

In the case of authors like Donne, of whose works few holographs survive, it is hard to overestimate the importance of a reliable family tree to the work of identifying authorial variants amidst the welter of adventitious changes. The lines of connection and causation at play within a genealogical system enable a perspective on individual changes that would otherwise be unobtainable—on, for example, the "foes" to "foe" change in line 33. Considered on intrinsic merit, nei-

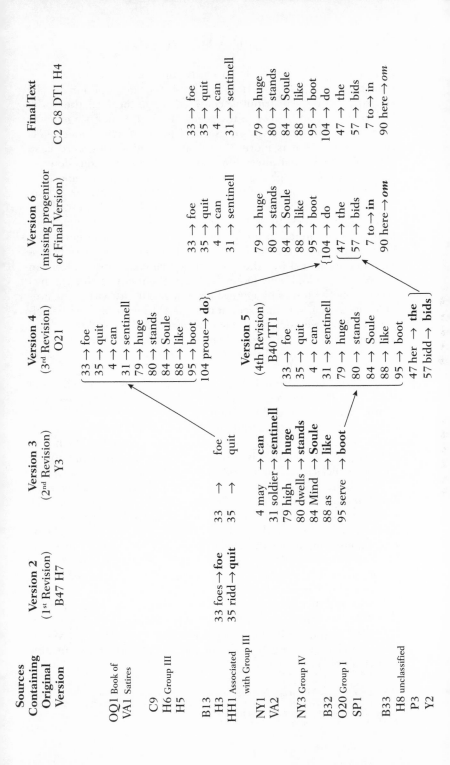

Sources Containing Original Version

Sources Containing Original Version	Version 2 (1st Revision) B47 H7	Version 3 (2nd Revision) Y3	Version 4 (3rd Revision) O21	Version 5 (4th Revision) B40 TT1	Version 6 (missing progenitor of Final Version)	Final Text C2 C8 DT1 H4

OQ1 Book of
VA1 Satires

C9
H6 Group III
H5

B13
H3
HH1 Associated with Group III

NY1
VA2

NY3 Group IV

B32
O20 Group I
SP1

B33
H8 unclassified
P3
Y2

Version 2: 33 foes → **foe** ; 35 ridd → **quit**

Version 3: 33 → foe ; 35 → quit ; 4 may → **can** ; 31 soldier → **sentinell** ; 79 high → **huge** ; 80 dwells → **stands** ; 84 Mind → **Soule** ; 88 as → **like** ; 95 serve → **boot**

Version 4: 33 → foe ; 35 → quit ; 4 → can ; 31 → sentinell ; 79 → huge ; 80 → stands ; 84 → Soule ; 88 → like ; 95 → boot ; 104 proue→ **do**

Version 5: 33 → foe ; 35 → quit ; 4 → can ; 31 → sentinell ; 79 → huge ; 80 → stands ; 84 → Soule ; 88 → like ; 95 → boot ; 47 her → **the** ; 57 bidd → **bids**

Version 6: 33 → foe ; 35 → quit ; 4 → can ; 31 → sentinell ; 79 → huge ; 80 → stands ; 84 → Soule ; 88 → like ; 95 → boot ; {104 → do} ; {47 → the ; 57 → bids} ; 7 to→ in ; 90 here→ *om*

Final Text: 33 → foe ; 35 → quit ; 4 → can ; 31 → sentinell ; 79 → huge ; 80 → stands ; 84 → Soule ; 88 → like ; 95 → boot ; 104 → do ; 47 → the ; 57 → bids ; 7 to→ in ; 90 here→ *om*

ther of these alternatives is obviously superior to the other. Even though the plural "Know thy foes" may seem more grammatically congruent with the distributive consideration of the devil, the world, and the flesh that follows in the poem, "Know thy foe," singular, as an abstract formula, gives an excellent piece of advice and works equally well. What is more, the "s" at the end of this word is so vulnerable to scribal alteration that—independently considered—the significance of a change in either direction would be impossible to assess. In the context of this genealogical chart, however, I think we can be certain that Donne himself dropped this "s." For one thing, this change of "foes" to "foe" is accompanied by the change of "ridd" to "quit"—an alteration far less likely to be scribal in origin. More importantly, both changes carry forward in the stream of transmission and are joined by others—most dramatically those in Version 3—that are undoubtedly Donne's. The authenticity of "foe" is thus certified by the forces of aggregation and continuity within the evolutionary system schematized on this chart. In light of these principles, I would even defend the legitimacy of "do" in version 4, "the" and "bids" in version 5, and "in" and the omisson of "here" in version 6. That Donne made all these changes, it seems to me, is the story that this schema tells.[4]

When this breakthrough came in the early 1990s, volume 6 of the *Variorum (The Anniversaries and the Epicedes and Obsequies)* was nearing completion; and we did not retrace our steps through that volume with an eye to identifying all instances of revision, though we did tentatively suggest that the reading "wast a Stoicks heart" might represent Donne's improvement on the more commonplace "break a stoicks heart" in line 62 of "Language thou art too narrow."[5] With volume 8, however (*The Epigrams, Epithalamions, Epitaphs, Inscriptions, and Miscellaneous Poems*), published a few months after volume 6, we were more confident, and we postulated two stages of authorial revision in both the Princess Elizabeth and Somerset epithalamions, employing the same rationale I had developed when working with Satire III: we suggested that each stage was marked by "multiple verbal alterations that cannot plausibly be explained as corruptions, sophistications, or necessary repairs of obviously defective language and that carry forward in the stream of transmission once they have entered . . ." (8:111). We also identified revision in the epigrams, noting authorial changes both in the texts of individual poems and in the organization of the three distinct manuscript sequences of these poems.

4. Figure 1 is not intended as a fully developed stemma, but merely as a model to illustrate the overall evolutionary pattern of the text of "Satire III." Volume 3 of the *Donne Variorum* includes a fully developed stemma for this poem.
5. *The Donne Variorum*, vol. 6, 1995, p. 148.

A few revisions are identified in the Elegies volume that followed in 2000. We argue that Donne altered "dandled" to "ingled" in line 29 of "The Perfume," "swolne & pamperd with high fare" to "swolne and pamperd w^t great fare" in line 21 of "Jealousy," and "Tollerable Tropique Clyme" to "habitable Tropique Clyme" in line 10 of "The Autumnal." Each of these, as is readily apparent, sharpens or adjusts an image or idea. Of greater consequence is the change of "taint" to "fault" in line 11 of "The Bracelet," where the speaker considers the likelihood that the virtue of his lost "Angels" is transitory:

ElBrac 9–12	a.	Oh shall twelve righteous Angels wch as yet
		No leauen of vile sodder did admitt;
(original version)		Nor yet by any **taint** haue stray'd or gone
		From the first State of the Creation;
	b.	Oh shall xii righteous Angells, which as yett
		Noe leauen of vile solder did admitte,
(revised version)		Nor yett by any **falt** haue strayd, or gone
		From the first state of theyre Creation;

As I have elsewhere suggested,[6] there are several reasons for regarding this alteration as an authorial revision: first, while "taint" and "fault" normally have the same number of letters and while their second and fifth letters are the same, I have never seen any seventeenth-century hand in which the two words would likely be confused; so I do not think the variant likely to have arisen from a scribal misreading. Second, this word appears buried in the middle of the eleventh line of a long poem, a place not likely to have called scribal attention to itself; anyone wanting to alter this word would have had to know it was there and to understand why it might need changing. Third, though one could elaborate a list of markedly different theological implications for each of these words, the distinction between angels that have "stray'd or gone / From the first State of their Creation" because of a "fault" as opposed to a "taint" is more subtle than any scribe, working in the relatively private sphere of manuscript transmission, would have been likely to make. And finally, although there are derivative copies in the manuscript pool that bespeak one or another scribe's anxiety over some of this poem's material, those copies tend to have entire couplets or even huge chunks hacked out. In copies at the head of the transmissional stream, "taint" / "fault" is the only notable variant in the poem. In sum, this change was made by someone who knew "taint" was there, who was capable of appreciating the fine distinction between "taint" and "fault," and who felt an owner's freedom to make the switch—i.e., it was made by

6. Gary A. Stringer, "Filiating Scribal Manuscripts: the Example of Donne's Elegies," *John Donne Journal*, 17 (1998), pp. 175–89.

Donne. An interesting last chapter to this story is that this place in
the poem apparently remained a hot spot nearly four decades after
"The Bracelet" was written, for the government licenser refused John
Marriot permission to include the elegy in the first edition of 1633;
and when Marriot sneaked it into 1635, he had altered "fault" to
"way," cleverly finessing the problem:

1635 edition: O, shall twelve righteous Angels, which as yet
                     No leaven of vile soder did admit;
(editorial change)   Nor yet by any **way** have straid or gone
                     From the first state of their Creation. . . .

A final revision amongst the elegies—interesting because it shows
us Donne in the act not just of fine-tuning an idea, but of correcting
his own misstatement—occurs in line 27 of "Love's Progress." At
this point in the poem the speaker is developing his chop-logic argu-
ment that "Perfection is in Vnity," which implies that one should
"Preferre / One woman first, and then one thing in her." By his lights,
of course, that "one thing" is not "virtue," and he contends that any-
one who confuses the essence of woman with what is merely one of
her attributes is "Adulterous":

> . . . But if wee
> Make loue to woman, Virtue is not shee,
> As Beautie'is not, nor Wealth: Hee that strayes thus
> From her to hers, is more Adulterous
> Than **if hee** tooke her maide.
>
> (23–27)

Recorded in twenty-one manuscripts and the collected edition of
1669, the above is the version of this passage we are used to reading.
An alternate line of transmission comprising fourteen manuscript
copies and three seventeenth-century printings, however, reads the
lines this way:

> . . . but if wee
> Make loue to woman, virtue is not Shee
> As beauty is not, nor wealth. He y^t strayes thus
> from her, to hers, is more adulterous
> Then **hee that** tooke her mayd.

How do we decide which version came first and who made the
change? In Volume 2 of the *Variorum*, we reckoned that the direc-
tion of change was from "hee that" to "if he" and explained our rea-
soning thus:

> What marks this change as authorial rather than scribal is not
> only that it corrects a major misstatement . . . , but also that the

error cannot be recognized as such except in retrospect, in comparison with the alternative. . . . The unexceptionable sense established by . . . [the version reading "he that took her mayd"]—that the man who strays and the adulterer are different people—would hardly draw suspicion of error on itself were it not for the clear superiority . . . [of the "if he" version], which sharpens the analogy by making the strayer and the adulterer one and the same. The likelihood that replacing "hee that" with "if hee" would have occurred to any copyist is extremely remote, and that a scribal change could have gone in the other direction seems impossible. Only the author . . . would have assumed the creative authority to effect this revision, and he, too, can only have changed "hee that" to "if hee"—not vice versa." (p. 304)

Stated very abstractly, the principles I have articulated for distinguishing Donne's revisions from scribal changes are these:

1. a variant reading must represent a "genuine alternative" in the sense discussed above;
2. a reading must not be readily explicable as a scribal misreading or slip of the pen;
3. a reading must appear authentic when viewed in the context of the poem's transmissional history.

The third of these is especially important, and I think represents the *Donne Variorum* editors' most important theoretical advance beyond the understanding of our predecessors. In practice, evaluating a variant in terms of its place on the family tree generally means that it must appear at the head of a line of transmission rather than somewhere further down the stream, which in turn means that it had better not be found in the company of other questionable or obviously erroneous readings. Given the absence from the artifactual record of many manuscripts that in their day recorded now-missing stages in the transmissional history of Donne's texts, this insistence that a variant not appear in bad company may cause us to miss the odd authorial revision here or there, but a cautious approach to this matter is surely in order. I shall briefly present a pair of initially appealing readings that principle three requires us—or at least me—not to credit to Donne.

Here, for instance, is one of the most celebrated passages in all of Donne, a couplet from the end of the elegy "Going to Bed":

ElBed 46

| | a. | . . . Cast all, yea this white lynnen hence |
| authorial | | There is no pennance, **much lesse** Innocence |

        b.   . . . cast all, yea this white linnen hence
scribal   There is no penance **due to** Innocence

Both versions have their vigorous advocates, and (of course) radically different views of the poem are entailed in this "much lesse" / "due to" crux—volume 2 of the *Variorum* gives four pages of summarized comment on this point. We have here genuine alternatives, and the variation is not likely to have arisen from misreading. In our volume, however, we had no hesitation in identifying version "b" as a scribal bowdlerization—not, as several critics and editors have argued, an authorial revision—primarily because it violated principle three. The entire thirty-seven-manuscript lineage is shot through with corruption, some exemplars much more so than others, and among the surviving artifacts we could not find an uncorrupted text from which the others could have descended. The errors that invariably accompany "due to," in other words, undermine its possible validity.

My second example comes from "Sappho to Philaenis." In volume 2 of the *Variorum*, we published the following metrically unbalanced version of lines 25–26:

    Such was my Phao a while, but shall bee neuer (11 syllables)
    As thou wast, art, and oh, maist bee ever (10 syllables)

The cognate Group-III manuscripts Luttrell (C9) and O'Flahertie (H6), however, contain a perfectly smooth rendition of the couplet, which we were initially inclined to regard as either Donne's revision or as the only rendition that had escaped corruption:

    Such was my Phao a while, but shall be neuer (11 syllables)
    as thou wert, art, & (oh) mayst thou be euer. (11 syllables)

After a good bit of dithering, which included a switch of copy-text for the poem, we eventually identified the smoother rendition as a scribal sophistication because it appeared in the company of a number of other readings that were obviously not Donne's, including regularizations of meter:

lines 19–20:
(C9-H6's scribal   For if we iustly call each silly man
"improvement")   **another** world, what shall wee call thee than?

(authorial   For if wee iustly call each syllie man
reading)   **A littell** world, what shall we call thee than?

lines 29–30:
(C9-H6's regular-   And yet I greeue ye lesse least greife remoue
ization of meter)   my beauty, & make me vnworthy loue.

(authorial   And yet I greiue the lesse, least griefe remoue
reading)   My beauty, and make mee vnworthy **of thy** loue.

My final example focuses on an interesting textual crux in the Holy
Sonnets, one showing that, no matter how systematically one seeks
to apply the guidelines, distinguishing authorial from scribal variants
can never be an exact science. The Holy Sonnets survive in three
primary manuscript sequences and exhibit a transmissional history
that resembles that of the epigrams in volume 8. Our volume prints
the three arrangements shown in Figure 2, as well as the familiar
sixteen-sonnet sequence instituted by the editor in the 1635 *Poems*.
Shown on the left is the first twelve-sonnet sequence that Donne
circulated. Never printed prior to its inclusion in the *Variorum*, it
appears in the four usual Group-III manuscripts plus the Bridge-
water (HH1), and its texts are distinguished by a number of early
authorial readings that Donne later revised. This Group-III set is
carried over directly into the Westmoreland manuscript (NY3),
which also appends—as a group of four and a group of three—seven
additional sonnets, the latter three unique to this artifact. In NY3's
recapitulation of the Group-III sequence, the texts of a number of
individual sonnets exhibit authorial revision. Finally, in the right-
hand column of the figure is listed Donne's last, revised sequence;
and it shows further authorial alteration at the level of the individual
reading. It also, as is apparent, presents a different twelve-poem
sequence, one which drops four poems from the Group-III arrange-
ment, repositions two others, and interpolates the set of four ("Spit
in my face" through "Batter my heart") that were appended as son-
nets 13 through 16 in NY3.

The general validity of this account, I trust, is demonstrated in the
Variorum volume, and I will not recap the argument here.[7] Instead,
I should like to turn to the aforementioned crux, which appears in
line 13 of "If poisonous Mineralls." Here is the text of Group III,
which—as shown on Figure 2—comprises five members for the Holy
Sonnets:

> yf poysonous Mineralls, or yf the Tree
>   whose fruite threwe death on (els immortall) vs,
>   yf letcherous Goates, yf serpents envious
> Cannott be damnd', alas, why should I be?
> 5 why should intent and reason borne in me,
>   make sinnes (els equall) in me more haynous?
>   and mercy being easy and glorious

---

7. *The Donne Variorum*, vol. 7.1, 2005. A slightly expanded version of this discussion of "If
poisonous Mineralls" is included in my "Discovering Authorial Intention in the Manuscript
Sequences of Donne's Holy Sonnets," *Renaissance Papers 2002* (Camden House, 2003),
pp. 127–44.

Figure 2

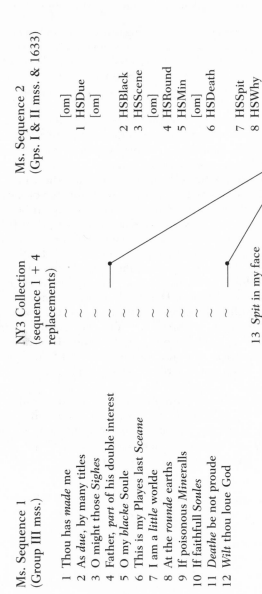

Ms. Sequence 1
(Group III mss.)

1 Thou has *made* me
2 As *due*, by many titles
3 O might those *Sighes*
4 Father, *part* of his double interest
5 O my *blacke* Soule
6 This is my Playes last *Sceane*
7 I am a *little* worlde
8 At the *rounde* earths
9 If poisonous *Mineralls*
10 If faithfull *Soules*
11 *Deathe* be not proude
12 *Wilt* thou loue God

NY3 Collection
(sequence 1 + 4
replacements)

~
~
~
~
~
~
~
~
~
~
~
~

13 *Spit* in my face
14 *Why* are we
15 *What* if this present
16 *Batter* my heart

17 HSShe
18 HSShow
19 HSVex

(unique to NY3;
not printed until
1890s)

Ms. Sequence 2
(Gps. I & II mss. & 1633)

[om]
1 HSDue
[om]

2 HSBlack
3 HSScene
[om]
4 HSRound
5 HSMin
[om]
6 HSDeath

7 HSSpit
8 HSWhy
9 HSWhat
10 HSBatter
11 HSWilt
12 HSPart

> To God, in his sterne wrath why threatens he?
> but who am I, that dare dispute with thee?
> 10   O God, o of thy only worthy bloud
> and my teares make a heav'nly Lethean floud
> and drowne in it my sinnes blacke memory
>   that thou remember them **no more** as debt,
>   I thincke it mercy, yf thou wilt forgett.

The later Westmoreland and Groups I and II, however, read the sestet this way:

> But who am I yᵗ dare dispute wᵗ thee
> 10   O God? O of thyne only worthy blood
> And my teares make a heauenly Lethean flood
> And drowne in it, my Sins blacke memoree.
>   That thou remember them, **Some clayme** as dett
>   I thinke it Mercy if thou wilt forgett.

Both the logic of the successive arrangements of the sequence and certain changes in individual texts assure us that the chronology of change is as I have described it: the "no more as debt" version precedes that reading "some clayme." The other question, though—Is this an authorial revision, or is "no more as debt" a scribal corruption that Donne had nothing to do with?—is harder. So, what happens when we apply the three rules of thumb? Thirdly—to proceed in Dogberrian fashion—"no more as debt" meets the genealogical criterion: since it appears in every member of Group III and since none of them was copied from any of the others, "no more" obviously existed in the urtext that stands at the head of this line of transmission (that is, it is not an isolated mutation that crops up somewhere far down the family tree). Secondly, no one is likely to have misread "Some clayme" as "no more"; this variant therefore satisfies criterion number two. We are thus left with the question that lurks beneath rule of thumb number one, a logico-esthetic—as opposed to a purely bibliographical—question: do these variants represent genuine alternatives?

When I first began to consider this problem, I sent a description of the whole complex matter to a number of friends and colleagues and asked whether they thought it possible that "no more as debt" could have been Donne's initial reading in line 13. The responses ranged from a terse "No way!" to a lengthy scholarly disquisition ending with a cautiously worded ". . . yes, I think Donne may have written the 'no more' version. And I just might think it's the better version to boot." Before I reveal my opinion, let me point out that, fortunately for the *Variorum*, not everything depends on this answer. Since we printed three sequences, we did not have to choose only one of these alternatives: "remember them no more as debt" is the reading of the Group-III text; "remember them, Some clayme as dett" is the reading of the others. At stake is merely how one tries to account for the difference.

With due respect to all my respondents and others who might take the other side, when all's said and done, I don't think all that's said here is Donne. I can't finally believe Donne wrote "remember them no more as debt," and I can explain in terms of the three rules. (1) That this variant passes the genealogical test is not in and of itself conclusive, for all five extant witnesses could well descend from a scribal prototype into which this error had been introduced rather than from the author's holograph, and that lost urtext need not be more than one step removed from Donne's papers (although I'm reasonably certain it was at least two). All this scenario requires is that the inscriber of that prototype should have written "no more" rather than "Some clayme." (2) And even though the replacement of "Some clayme" with "no more" cannot be explained as a scribal misreading, it can readily be explained as a scribal trivialization. Like much of Donne, "That thou remember them, Some clayme as dett" is both conceptually and syntactically difficult. By contrast, "That thou remember them no more as debt" echoes the Biblical "And their sinnes and iniquities will I remember no more" (Hebrews 10.17 and 8.12) and is as self-inscribing in Western, Christian culture as one of Donne's lovers hopes his own name will be if his mistress undertakes to address a letter to a rival. (Some might remember the iteration of this formula by the preacher who gave the benediction at George W. Bush's first inauguration.) If the scribe of the Group-III progenitor received a copy reading "some clayme as debt" and had trouble understanding the line, I can well imagine that he (or she) might have substituted a familiar phrase that seemed to make sense; and exercising such license would have been especially easy if the text he was looking at had no punctuation at the end of line 12 and if that scribe knew he was not copying Donne's holograph directly and thus felt more at liberty to change what he did not understand or could not decipher.

All this conjecture, of course, may just be my way of excusing Donne from having written what I regard as an inferior line. So, in addition to its predictability, I shall offer the brief outline of a further argument against the legitimacy of "remember them no more." Measured against the later "Some clayme," the principal effect of the "no more" reading is, of course, to shift the referent of the pronoun "them" from the "some [people]" who claim God is obligated to remember them to "sin." The resulting meaning of line 13 is "That thou remember my sins no more as debt." This redirection of the pronoun has at least the following three effects:

First, it links line 13 to line 12 in a relationship of cause and effect:

"drowne in it my sinnes blacke memory / [So] that thou remember them no more as debt." And this connection consequently detaches line 13 syntactically from line 14, leaving "I think it mercy if thou wilt forget" to stand as a single-line conclusion in a way not characteristic of Donne's usual practice. All his other sonnets, including those in "La Corona," end with a final thought that occupies at least a couplet. In structural terms, "no more as debt" thus renders this poem unique among Donne's sonnets.

Second, the syntactical realignment entailed in "no more as debt" drains the sestet of this poem of conceptual complexity and density. One of the respondents whom I polled noted that the reading runs the risk of making line 14 seem redundant, since "in a paraphrase, it might be made to say just what the preceding lines have already said." Indeed, it seems to me that line 12's "drowne . . . my Sinnes . . . memorie," line 13's "remember them no more," and line 14's "forget [them]" all do say substantially the same thing. Even though some new ideological freight is introduced by the concepts of "debt" in line 13 and "mercy" in line 14, it does not seem to me that the conclusion of the sonnet has nearly the power that we normally see in Donne and that the "some clayme" version has.

Finally, if "Some clayme as dett" were a revision of "no more as debt," it would represent a categorically different kind of change from any of those discussed above or of which I am otherwise aware. In the examples I have surveyed, Donne changes individual words (sometimes a great many of them, as in "Satire III") in order to adjust a concept or an image; or he rearranges a sequence (as with the epigrams and the Holy Sonnets), investing individual poems with different shades of meaning that arise from their altered position within the sequence. But the transformation effected by this alteration is of a different logical order: the change of a mere two little words significantly alters the poem's syntax and its particular manner of embodying the sonnet form. And it simultaneously changes the denotative content of a number of words. In the last analysis, as highly as I regard Donne's wit and as strongly as I believe that if anyone could have hit on such a miraculously transformative emendation, he could have, the likelihood that this is his revision of an originally lame passage seems less than that the lameness is the accidental by-product of a scribe's ignorant corruption of one of Donne's typically brilliant endings.[8]

8. I should like to acknowledge explicitly the immense debt that this essay obviously owes to my collaborators on the *Variorum*, particularly my co-textual editors Ted-Larry Pebworth and Ernest W. Sullivan, II.

Songs and Sonnets

DONALD L. GUSS

Donne's Petrarchism†

In the *Songs and Sonets*, Donne sometimes expresses dramatic emo-
tions through the gallant conceits of the Petrarchans. For example,
in "The Dreame"—which Mario Praz considers a variation on a
Petrarchan theme[1]—Donne says that his lady's knowledge of his
thoughts proves that she is divine. This bit of amorous theology is
an extension of the Petrarchan lady-goddess figure; it has many
Petrarchan analogues, among them Desportes' *Hippolyte* iv:

> Madame, helas! monstrez que vous estes divine,
> Lisez dedans les cœurs ainsi que font les dieux.

In the same poem, Donne compares himself to an extinguished
torch. His prosaic simile is an elaboration of the Petrarchan love-
fire metaphor; many conventional poets anticipate it, Desportes, in
Hipp. vii, quite closely:

> ainsi qu'un flambeau qu'on ne fait que d'étaindre,
> Si le feu s'en approche est aussi-tost repris:
> Dans mon cœur chaud encor un brasier s'est épris.[2]

† From the *Journal of English and Germanic Philology* 64 (1965): 17–28. Copyright © 1965
by the Board of Trustees of the University of Illinois. Reprinted by permission of the
University of Illinois Press.
1. "Donne's Relation to the Poetry of His Time," *A Garland for John Donne*, ed. Theodore
Spencer (Cambridge, Mass., 1931), pp. 51–56.
2. For several lyrics based on the comparison between poet and torch (and even between
poet and votive candle), see Joseph Vianey, *Le Pétrarquisme en France au XVIᵉ siècle*
(Montpellier, 1909), pp. 48, 55, n. 1. The lady-goddess conceit is, of course, common.
Sometimes the theology according to which it is developed is classical or Neoplatonic
rather than Christian: for example, in Son. XVIII, "O d'amor fredda, e di virtute ardente,"
Guarino compares his lady and himself to a goddess and the temple in which she is
worshipped; and in Mad. 2, "Vien dal' onde, ò dal cielo," he wittily disputes whether his
lady is the celestial or the terrestial Venus.
　　Unless otherwise noted, I use the following texts: for Jacopo da Lentini and Guido
Guinizelli, *La poesia lirica del '200*, ed. Carlo Salinari (Turin, 1951); for Francesco
Petrarca, *Le rime*, ed. G. Carducci and S. Ferrari (Florence, 1957); for the mid-fifteenth-
century Neapolitans, *Rimatori napoletani del quattrocento*, ed. Mario Mandalari (Caserta,
1885); for Chariteo, *Lirici cortigiani del '400*, ed. Alessandro Tortoreto (Milan, 1942); for
Serafino l'Aquilano's strambotti and epistles, *Opere* (Venice, 1502); for Serafino's sonnets,
Le rime, ed. Mario Menghini (Bologna, 1894), I; for Guarino, *Rime* (Venice, 1598); for

In "The Dreame" the lover's enthusiasm is evoked by a scenically conceived situation; it is expressed through Petrarchan hyperboles.

In "A Valediction: of weeping" and "Witchcraft by a picture," Donne realizes drama in Petrarchan minuteness. Serafino's Sonnet xxxvi, "Mentre che amore in me non abitava," complains that his lady, who used to enjoy seeing her picture in his eyes, has ignored him since his amorous tears began to distort her reflection. Donne uses the particularity of a similar image to reflect the intimacy and tender sorrow with which his lovers regard each other. Once more he dramatizes a Petrarchan conceit.

Such instances suggest that Petrarchism may have been important to Donne. For Donne could hardly have been unaware of English and French Petrarchism; he was acquainted with the Italian language and literature, regularly inscribing in his books a line, in Italian, from one of Petrarch's love poems; and he imitated Petrarchan ideas in "The Extasie," and a Petrarchan conceit in "A Valediction: forbidding mourning."[3] Donne must, then, have been acquainted with Petrarchism; and Petrarchism—traditionally introspective, dialectical, and conceited—offered him a clear alternative to Elizabethan neoclassicism. It is therefore significant that in two of his most characteristic poems, "The Apparition" and "The Canonization," Donne submits Petrarchan conceits to a dramatic imagination.

It is drama and Petrarchism—and not the Counter-Reformation, the metaphysical shudder, or Anglo-Saxon melancholy—that explain "The Apparition":

> When by thy scorne, O murdresse, I am dead,
>   And that thou thinkst thee free
> From all solicitation from mee,
> Then shall my ghost come to thy bed,
> And thee, fain'd vestall, in worse armes shall see;
> Then thy sicke taper will begin to winke,
> And he, whose thou art then, being tyr'd before,
> Will, if thou stirre, or pinch to wake him, thinke
>   Thou call'st for more,
> And in false sleepe will from thee shrinke,
> And then poore Aspen wretch, neglected thou

Thomas Watson, *Poems*, ed. Edward Arber (Westminster, 1895); for Philippe Desportes, *Oeuvres*, ed. Alfred Michiels (Paris, 1858); and for John Donne, *Poems*, ed. Sir Herbert J. C. Grierson (London, 1912). The translations are my own; though they are in prose, they are divided into lines to correspond roughly to their originals.

3. See Evelyn M. Simpson, "Donne's Spanish Authors," *MLR*, XLIII (1948), 185. On the compass image, see D. C. Allen, "Donne's Compass Figure," *MLN*, LXXI (1956), 256–57). On "The Extasie," see, for example, Merritt Y. Hughes, "The Lineage of the 'Extasie,' " *MLR*, XXVII (1932), 1–5, and Helen Gardner, "The Argument about 'The Extasy,' " *Elizabethan and Jacobean Studies Presented to F. P. Wilson* (Oxford, 1959), pp. 279–306. (I call the love tracts "Petrarchan" because when they treat love as a relation between two human beings they are primarily commentaries on the Petrarchan clichés.)

Bath'd in a cold quicksilver sweat wilt lye
  A veryer ghost then I;
What I will say, I will not tell thee now,
Lest that preserve thee'; and since my love is spent,
I'had rather thou shouldst painfully repent,
Then by my threatnings rest still innocent.

"The Apparition" considers the lover's afterlife in terms of his pres-
ent amorous situation. Its remote origin is the courtly-love cliché
that the poet will continue to worship his lady after death. Jacopo
da Lentini, for example, says that if his lady were not in heaven, he
would refuse to go there, but that, since she will be blessed, he will
shun damnation. This sort of amorous eschatology—which is
employed by Guido Guinizelli, among others[4]—approaches "The
Apparition" more closely in Neapolitan lyrics of the mid-fifteenth
century. These lyrics treat the lover's death for unfulfilled love as
though it were a prosaic murder, warning the lady, for example, that
she will have trouble disposing of her lover's corpse. By thus estab-
lishing the lady's guilt, they fit the theme of amorous death to the
theory that hard-hearted ladies are punished after death, saying, for
example, that when the poet has died for love, should he go to hell
he will have the consolation of seeing his lady suffer there.[5] Thus
the Neapolitans anticipate Donne in expecting that justice will be
done on the lady-murderess. In "Voi, Donna, e io per segni manifesti"
—a sonnet imitated throughout Europe, and admired by the
Marinisti—Chariteo treats the theme with magniloquence, senti-
mental refinement, and logical elaboration. He asserts that when he
and his lady are sent to hell—she for her cruelty to him, and he for
his presumption in loving her—she will suffer from the sight of him,
but he will consider himself blessed so long as he sees her. Interest-
ingly, Chariteo's sonnet has, like Donne's lyrics, been mistakenly
likened to Baudelaire.[6] In its fusion of love, death, and justice, it
develops a conventional motive, and anticipates "The Apparition."

Unlike Donne, neither Chariteo nor his predecessors threatens
that he himself will punish his lady. But in "S' io per te moro e calo
nell' inferno," Serafino adapts the conceit to a scorned lover's desire
for revenge:

4. Jacopo, Son. VI, "Io m' aggio posto in core a Dio servire." Guido—in Can. III, "Al cor
   gentil repara sempre Amore," st. 6—says that, when God reproaches him for having adored
   his lady, he will cite in his defense her angelic appearance. (Since a personal God here
   condemns human love, despite traditional criticism this stanza cannot be a defense of
   Neoplatonic love.)
5. *Rimatori*, p. 48, "Se tu me aucidi et averamie morto," and pp. 12–15, "Per certo se troppo
   dura." On the punishment of reluctant ladies, see William Allan Neilson, "The Purgatory
   of Cruel Beauties; A Note on the Sources of the 8th Novel of the 5th Day of the *Deca-
   meron, Romania*, XXIX (1900), 85–93.
6. Luigi Tonelli, *L'amore nella poesia e nel pensiero del rinascimento* (Florence, 1933),
   pp. 61–62. For imitations of the sonnet, see Tortoreto's comment, and also Vianey, p. 198.

> If I die for you and go to hell,
> All my sufferings will cry for vengeance;
> I shall compose a legal brief of accusations against you,
> And give it to the infernal furies.
>   You will be condemned to eternal fire
> And thrown down beside me;
> And should you live a while in song and holiday,
> My ghost will always stand before you.

Thus Donne's amorous eschatology is often paralleled by Petrarchan poems which do not elaborate a ghostly vengeance. The vengeance is suggested at the close of "S' io per te moro," and also in the *Aeneid*, IV, 384–87, where Dido bids Aeneas go (in C. Day Lewis' translation, Oxford, 1952):

> I'll dog you, from far, with the death-fires;
> And when cold death has parted my soul from my body, my spectre
> Will be wherever you are. You shall pay for the evil you've done me.
> The tale of your punishment will come to me down in the shades.

In *Epistola V*, "Tu sei disposto pur, crudel, lassarmi," ll. 97–112, where a Dido-figure writes to her departing lover, Serafino assimilates the Virgilian theme to the manner of Chariteo:

> But you cannot go so quickly
> As to escape my ghost, which will track you down
> And remain beside you forever, visible
>   And bleeding, exactly as I was
> When, with cruel hand, I killed myself.
> It will be next to you whether you sleep or wake,
>   Not to harm you—for I couldn't—
> But so that you may regret your errors one day,
> And understand my sufferings one day,
>   Hearing me howl wildly,
> Lamenting repeatedly on your account,
> And all my outcries reproaching you.
>   And, although my simple, foolish soul
> May be out of its weary, worn body,
> Do not hope that it will be untied from you on that account:
>   For a true love is not weakened even by death.

These lines would be very much like "The Apparition" were it not that they depart from the Petrarchan clichés by portraying a deserted lady and considering a suicide rather than an amorous wasting-away. In Strambotti 103 and 104, "E se gli é ver che l'alma tormentare" and "E se glie é 'l ver che 'l spirto vada atorno," Serafino adapts the theme of the haunting to the Petrarchan situation of an extraordinarily cruel lady and her suffering lover. He thereby very precisely anticipates "The Apparition":

And if it is true that the soul must be tormented
In the very place in which it sinned,
I hope to abide within your body,
Since through your cruelty I die damned.
And with my own hand I want to tear apart
That false heart that has been so hard to me,
Until I kill you, for my revenge:
For every sin meets its just reward at last.

And if it is true that one's ghost wanders about
When his soul is untied from his body,
Know that I will always be about you,
And never weary of warring upon you—
So much so that you will always curse the day
That you refused to content me upon earth.
And thus I hope to possess you some time,
And, alive or dead, to have you in my hand.

These analogues place "The Apparition" squarely in the Petrarchan tradition. Donne is not here more realistic, more baroque, more manly, or, indeed, more rebellious than his Petrarchan predecessors: his complaint against his lady and his conjunction of love with death are rooted in Petrarchan clichés;[7] and his picture of the afterlife follows Chariteo and Serafino. "The Apparition" is original; but its originality is the result of a dramatic imagination. Donne, more than any of his predecessors, visualizes the scene of the haunting and comprehends the feelings of the lady as, unprepared and unsupported, she suffers a horrible visitation. And, more clearly than the Petrarchans, he develops the emotional turmoil, the exacerbation and the jealous anguish, of a lover who hopes to avenge himself on his beloved after death.

For the fifteenth-century Petrarchans, the conceit of the lover's death and revenge was a means of refining the popular theme which appears in Antonio da S. Croce da Valdamo's "Venir tipossa el diavolo allo letto":

May the devil go to bed with you,
      Since I'm not welcome there,
      And may he break two ribs of your chest,
      And the other members that God made for you,
      And drag you across mountains and valleys
      And chop your head off your shoulders.

7. Donne's suspicion that his lady may prove unchaste is far from unconventional. Sexual
   jealousy, a standard Provençal theme, is common in Neapolitan court poetry (see *Rimatori*,
   pp. 38–39, 147) and in late Renaissance Petrarchism—among Tasso's clichés about love
   are the statements, that hate follows love, and that jealousy is a sign of ardent love (*Conclusioni amorose* 12 and 46).

Donne abandons the aristocratic tone, the emotional simplification, and the persuasive intent of the Petrarchans. But it is Petrarchism which separates him from such naïve statement and gross sentiments as Antonio's—which permits him his conceit and his self-awareness. And thus "The Apparition," in many ways a crucial example of Donne's style, is a dramatic elaboration of a Petrarchan conceit.

Donne's Petrarchism appears again in the third stanza of "The Canonization." In the 1633 text, this stanza reads:

> Call us what you will, wee are made such by love;
>   Call her one, mee another flye,
>   We'are Tapers too, and at our owne cost die,
>   And wee in us finde the'Eagle and the Dove,
>   The Phoenix ridle hath more wit
>   By us, we two being one, are it.
> So, to one neutrall thing both sexes fit.
>   Wee dye and rise the same, and prove
>   Mysterious by this love.

The conceits in this stanza, like many others in *The Songs and Sonets*, are related to emblem literature. The moth in the flame, the eagle, the dove, and the phoenix all appear in emblem books, as Lederer notes; and Donne uses them as the lovers' imprese, and perhaps intends them to retain some traditional emblematic significations—perhaps his eagle means virtue tired by wandering, for example, or his dove true love.[8] But, because most amorous emblems are derived from Petrarch,[9] where there is an emblematic parallel there is usually a Petrarchan parallel as well. For example, Lederer refers Donne's line 4 to an emblem in which an eagle swooping down on a caged dove signifies future ill-fortune; but this emblem—whose motto is drawn from Petrarch—is merely a pictorial representation of the conceit of Tansillo's "Come augellin, ch' umane note finge." Since, as shown by Miss Rosemary Freeman, the form of Donne's conceit is not emblematic,[1] and since the emblem itself is a manifestation of Petrarchism, it seems wisest to consider the stanza within a Petrarchan context. And in fact Petrarchism provides a clearer interpretation of line 4 than does emblem literature. For if one interprets the line emblematically it is impossible to know what the line means—the dove, for example, might be anything from

8. See Josef Lederer, "John Donne and the Emblematic Practice" *RES*, xxii (1946), 194–95, and D. Philippi Picinelli, *Mundus Symbolicus* (Cologne, 1694).
9. See Mario Praz, "Petrarca e gli emblematisti," *Ricerche anglo-italiane* (Rome, 1944), pp. 303–19. Lederer (p. 185) attributes the similarities between Donne and the Petrarchans to the Alexandrian derivation of both emblem and Petrarchan conceit. But he does not show either that Donne draws upon the emblem rather than upon Petrarchan lyrics, or that the emblem uses Greek rather than Italian sources.
1. Rosemary Freeman, *English Emblem Books* (London, 1948), pp. 148–49, *et passim*.

Christian resurrection to marital fidelity, anything from contempla-
tion to an alchemical reaction.[2] But in Petrarchan poetry the lover
is conventionally an eagle gazing at the sun of his lady's beauty,[3] and
since a beloved lady is traditionally a dove, the convention provides
a clear sense in which the lovers are noble birds, and not mere moths.

The stanza's Petrarchan background is particularly useful in elu-
cidating the lovers' death and resurrection, whose obscurity has led
to a textual difficulty. Grierson, though he maintains that the 1633
text is to be followed wherever possible, substitutes a comma for the
period after "fit" in line 7: he considers the 1633 reading to make no
sense. Later editors—Hebel and Hudson, Shaaber, Hayward, and
Bennett—follow Grierson. But Grierson's reading is itself intelligible
only if the lovers' death is sexual consummation; and if it is, Donne's
exalted confidence in his "mysterious" love seems misplaced. Thus
the editors have departed from the best text in order to get an infe-
licitous reading. And George Williamson's attempt to defend the
1633 punctuation without reinterpreting amorous death, is uncon-
vincing: for Williamson says that line 7 is a challenge to the lovers
which lines 8–9 answer; but line 7—unlike line 1, which Williamson
considers analogous—contains no syntactical indication that the
belief it expresses is not the lover's.[4] The 1633 text can be vindicated,
however, and Donne's enthusiasm explained, by a consideration of
the stanza in its Petrarchan context.

That lovers "dye and rise the same" is a conceit which, as Mario
Equicola notes, appears in classical poetry, where it expresses the
extremities of amorous desire.[5] It is a commonplace among the Pro-
vençal poets, who, with characteristic wit, assert that the lover dies

2. Besides the interpretations provided by Picinelli, see Edgar H. Duncan, "Donne's Alchem-
   ical Figures," *ELH*, ix (1942), 270–71.
3. See, for example, Pet. 19, "Sono animali al mondo di sí altera," with the note, and Serafino,
   Son. I, "L'acquila che col sguardo affisa el sole" (cf. Watson, *Hec*. 78, "What scowling
   cloudes").
      The emblem which Lederer notes is really a variation of a Provençal and Petrarchan
   conceit, the idea that the poet is the prey of the falcon love; see Francesco Flamini, *La
   lirica toscana del rinascimento (Pisa, 1891), pp. 438–40, and Watson, Hec*. 67, "When
   Cupid is content to keepe the skies." A much closer parallel is Serafino's *Epistola V*, ll,
   38–39: "My constant love would certainly have paired / The eagle and the dove as friends,"
   Donne may well have found a symbolic significance in this pun of l'Aquilano ("The Eagle-
   ite"). But the image is not unique—in "Ma petite columbelle," Ronsard says that he holds
   his lady as an eagle clasps a trembling dove.
4. Grierson, II, 15–16, and Williamson, "Textual Difficulties in the Interpretation of Donne's
   Poetry," *MP*, xxxviii (1940–41), 45–46. Though Grierson's emendation—which his 1929
   edition retains—is supported by good MSS, Williamson (pp. 37–72) and Grierson (II,
   cxiv–cxxi) agree that the 1633 text is to be followed wherever the sense permits it. Sir
   E. K. Chambers, reviewing Grierson's edition (*MLR*, IX [1914], 270), attacks Grierson's
   argument but agrees that 1633 is in fact the best text.
5. *Libro di natura d'amore* (Venice, 1536), fols. 131ᵛ–32ʳ. Interestingly, on fol. 184.ᵛ Equicola
   observes that Provençal poets often say that when their friends tell them to renounce their
   fruitless love, they refuse—a situation like that of "The Canonization." And on fol. 44ᵛ
   Equicola says that the eagle and the dove were an emblem at the marriage of Voluptu-
   ousness and Sorrow—a parallel of Donne's line 4 that has not to my knowledge been
   hitherto noted.

in his lady's radiance like a moth in a flame, and that he dies and is reborn a hundred times a day (see Equicola, fols. 183ᵛ–84ʳ, 185ʳ). Provençal poets and their imitators, with their taste for peregrine comparisons, associated this conceit with the phoenix. Giovanni d'Arezzo, for example, says in "L' uscel fenice quando ven' al morire" that, like the phoenix, he dies and is re-created in the fire of his unfulfilled love. And in "Sicomo il parpaglion, ch' a tal natura," Jacopo da Lentini says that, foolishly ignoring the dangers of his lady's radiance, he draws near her like a moth to a flame; and that, being burnt in the sweet flame, he, like a phoenix, is brought back to life by his lady's beauty.[6] In 135, "Qual piú diversa e nova," Petrarch uses the traditional conceit to describe one of the many miraculous metamorphoses which he claims to have undergone for love:

> Whatever most strange and unheard-of thing
>   Ever existed in even the most uncanny regions,
>   That thing, if one judges rightly,
>   Is most like me: to such a state have I come, Love.
>   There where the day comes forth
>   There flies a bird that, unique and without consort,
>   From a willing death
>   Is reborn, and recreated, entirely alive.
>   Similarly alone is my desire,
>   And similarly on the summit
>   Of its high thoughts it turns to the sun,
>   And similarly crumbles,
>   And similarly returns to its original condition;
>   It burns and dies, and retakes its body,
>   And then lives, a rival of the phoenix.

The love tracts, which seek truth in literature, interpret the lover's death and resurrection philosophically. Marsilio Ficino, whose influence was vast, uses it for a central statement of his belief that a lover dies in himself and is reborn in his beloved.[7] After the conceit had been used by Petrarch, explained by Ficino, and recognized by Equicola, it became, of course, a Renaissance commonplace. It is frequent in sixteenth-century French Neoplatonic poetry; in English, it is a special favorite of Thomas Watson, who uses it as a symbol of

6. These sonnets appear in Fausto Montanari, *Studi sul Canzoniere del Petrarca* (Rome, 1958), pp. 79 and 83.
7. *Commentaire sur le "Banquet" de Platon*, ed. and trans. Raymond Marcel (Paris, 1956), Sp. II, ch. 8, pp. 155–58. Ficino's Platonic casuistry here is especially suggestive of Donne's logic; and his assertion that every lover dies, that he is resurrected only by returned love, and that to refuse his love is therefore to murder him, may explain "O murdresse" in "The Apparition," and perhaps Donne's use of amorous death in general.

the torments of unfulfilled love.[8] Among the most interesting of the
lyrics which anticipate Donne's stanza is Serafino's Stram. 106, "O
morte: o la: soccorri: ecco che arrivo" (cf. Watson, *Hec.* 22):

> *Lover:* Oh Death! *Death:* Yes? *L:* Help! *D:* Lo, I am here;
> Why do you call? *L:* I burn. *D:* Who burns you? *L:* Love.
> *D:* What can I do? *L:* Take my life.
> *D:* Why, I kill you continually. *L:* Not me. *D:* Just ask
>   your heart.
> *L:* Heart! *Heart:* What is it? *L:* Are you dead? *H:*
>   Sometimes dead, sometimes alive.
> *L:* But what can you mean? *H:* Alas! *L:* Was a dead man
>   ever reborn?
> *H:* Only I. *L:* Then, Death, what can I do? Bit by bit,
> Like a phoenix I renew myself in the fire.

Perhaps the most precise analogue of Donne's stanza is an ele-
gantly sentimental bit of Neoplatonizing, Guarino's Madrigal 37,
"Una farfalla cupida, e vagante":

> My loving heart has been made
> A wandering moth, filled with desire,
> That goes, as though in play,
> Dancing around the fire
> Of two lovely eyes, and so many, many times
> Does it fly away and back, and flee and return, and circle,
> That in the beloved light
> It will at last leave both its life and its wings.
> But who sighs at that,
> Sighs wrongly. Dear, fortunate ardor [both "flame" and
>   "passion"],
> It will die a moth, and rise a phoenix.

The Petrarchan background elucidates Donne's stanza. First, the
lyrics of Jacopo and Guarino indicate that Donne's stanza is based
on the contrast between moth and phoenix. Williamson, treating the
stanza as a series of emblems, obscures this contrast. He finds in

8. See Jean Festugiére, *La philosophie de l'amour de Marsile Ficin et son influence sur la
littèrature française au XVI[c] siècle* (Paris, 1941), pp. 96–98, 110, 116, *et passim*; and Wat-
son, *Hec.* 44, 56, 57, 91, and *Tears* 40.
  Though the phoenix image is sometimes used with a sexual meaning, it is primarily the
symbol of holy mysteries, such as the union of the Virgin Mary with Jesus (see Henry
Green, *Shakespeare and the Emblem Writers* [London, 1870], pp. 383–84). Donne's own
use of the phoenix to represent the consummation of a marriage in the epithalamion "Haile
Bishop Valentine," reveals his intention of exalting both the married couple and the mir-
acle of marriage, and of considering sexual consummation as merely one element of spir-
itual union and spiritual rebirth. See also the exaltation implied by the phoenix symbol in
a similar epithalamiom. "Ecco luce amorosa," *Biblioteca di letterature popolare italiana*,
ed. Severino Ferrari (Florence, 1882) I, 184–85.

line 3 a reference to the emblem of the burning taper—which, like the moth, is an independent symbol of self-destruction. But Williamson's interpretation ignores the emphatic contrast between "Call her" (l. 2) and "We'are" (l. 3), and obfuscates the meaning of "And" in line 4—a word which clearly implies that line 3, like line 4, supports the lovers' case. In fact, lines 2–3 are both about the moth in the flame. They say that if the lover is conventionally a moth, it is his beloved who is conventionally the candle which lures him—and that therefore Donne's counsellor need not fear that the fire will be at his expense. These lines, then, mock Donne's friend's materialism—much like stanza one, which recommends that he contemplate money, and stanza two, which insinuates that he dislikes love only because he fears it may interfere with trade.[9] Then, having revealed the baseness of the world at large through his ironical use of the moth and candle, Donne proceeds to celebrate the lovers through the phoenix. And so his stanza, like its Petrarchan analogues, is primarily an opposition of phoenix to moth.

Furthermore, the Petrarchan background shows how Donne could have employed the conceit of the lover's death and resurrection with an exalted tone and a metaphysical intent; and thus it justifies the period after line 6. For Donne probably follows Ficino in arguing that the resurrection of the lovers is caused by their union (see l. 6)—he certainly uses the Neoplatonic, and therefore exalted, implications of the theory—and, since the strange immortality of lovers was generally acknowledged, it did not need the particular explanation that a comma after line 6 might afford. Donne's general intention in lines 5–9 is to prove that the lovers are the phoenix, and thereby both repudiate the accusation that they are moths in the flame, and reveal that, being "mysterious," they are superior to the counsels of reason. Donne cites three essential similarities between lovers and phoenix: their unity; the sexlessness of their joint being; and their revivification (cf. Petrarch, who cites his desire's uniqueness, exalted dwelling place, and repeated rebirth). Each of these similarities involves a paradox, and thus elevates love through the conventional theme of "loves magique" (cf. "A Valediction of my name, in the window," st. II)—much like Petrarch's claim that his transformation into the phoenix is marvellous, and Ficino's demonstration that the lovers' rebirth, being double where their death is single, is miraculous. Line 7, then, is not an explanation of lines 8–9, nor a challenge to the lovers. It is an independent and miraculous parallel between lovers and phoenix: it may echo Sperone Speroni's assertion, in the *Dialogo d'amore*, that the joint being of united lovers

9. Ficino, Sp. V, ch. 9, p. 194, says that love results in the end of lawsuits, theft, homicide, and war. In st. 2, Donne ironically reassures his adviser, comforting him with the thought that the love of a mere two people will not so upset the profitable course of worldly affairs.

is hermaphroditic,[1] and it certainly parallels Donne's own statement, in "The Extasie" (ll. 33–48), of the differences between an amorous union and the individuals who compose it. Thus the stanza is elucidated and the 1633 reading of it justified by a consideration of its Petrarchan analogues.

The third stanza of "The Canonization" is, like "The Apparition," a dramatic interpretation of a Petrarchan conceit. If Donne imitates Guarino's Mad. 37 here, he treats Guarino's langorous conjunction of two conventional sentiments as a vibrant quarrel between two uncongenial men. If not, his stanza still reveals three dramatic elements that are not found in its Petrarchan analogues. First, through a casuistic argument Donne adapts the phoenix image to a defense of mutual love—a relationship much more susceptible of dramatic development than is the introspective solitude of Petrarchism. Second, Donne brings the lover out of Arcadia and makes him aware of various non-amorous elements of ordinary life. And, third, Donne bases his mysticism on common sense. Petrarch uses the phoenix as a mystic symbol that elevates his story and distinguishes him from common men. Serafino uses it as an authoritative emblem that supports his paradoxical demonstration and his absurdly prosaic gallantry. And Guarino uses it as a catalyst to heroic and elegant folly, a Neoplatonic reminder that causes him to rededicate himself to his torment with fatuous ardor. Unlike the Petrarchans, Donne grounds the lovers' miraculousness—which the phoenix-conceit expresses—on a close and satirical observation of men as they are: he explains it as the gap between the serene lovers and base, busy worldlings. Donne thereby completes his adaptation of Petrarchan conceits to his dramatic concerns. With great originality but not unconventionality, he employs Petrarchan language to express amorous fervor and Petrarchan logic to defend love. And so "The Canonization," like "The Apparition," is a dramatic realization of a Petrarchan conceit.

1. Quoted by Tonelli, p. 287. For the interpretation of Donne's stanza, it is interesting to note that Guarino (*Il Pastor Fido e Il compendio della poesia tragicomica*, ed. G. Bragnoligo [Bari, 1914], pp. 224–25) says that lovers' bodies cannot achieve the true, hermaphroditic union of which their souls are capable.

PATRICK CRUTTWELL

The Love Poetry of John Donne: Pedantique Weedes or Fresh Invention?†

* * *

Donne's love poetry, then, is a body of verse whose effect (rather than intention; I suspect it had no intention) is to present as total a knowledge of the experience of love as one imagination could compass. If we look at it like this, the question of 'personality' and 'sincerity' becomes irrelevant; Leishman's phrase, 'the dialectical expression of personal drama', puts very well the manner in which this poetry fuses three ingredients—the analytical, the autobiographical, and the dramatic—and does so with such completeness that it is vain and foolish to try to separate them. Of this experience of love there are only two limiting conditions. It is entirely human, not divine, however much it may play with philosophical and theological concepts. And it is entirely, even aggressively, masculine and heterosexual. There is no trace of that ambi-sexual strand which is in Shakespeare's sonnets and in so much more of the poetry and art of the earlier Renaissance.

This love-experience takes place in a definite setting, which is quite clearly registered though not self-consciously described. It is a setting of cultivated, sophisticated people. It is thoroughly urban. All round the lovers is the manifold variegated life of a great city: its furtive adulteries in domestic interiors; its music-making, play-going, whoring; its church-going, funerals, marriages; its plagues; its fashions; its traders, merchants, town-criers, porters at house-doors, lawyers, alchemists, schoolboys. And nearby is the court, with its royal hunts and 'progresses', its intriguing flattering courtiers, and its ladies of easy virtue.

Beyond the city and court are hints of wider horizons. Excursions into the countryside; travel abroad by the lover, with the lady left behind; a vivid awareness of the countries and peoples of the continent, of foreign customs and foreign politics; an awareness too of war, and of that as something which the lover himself may be engaged in. And a powerful picturesque interest in the voyages of the discoverers, in the new things—spices or precious metals or jewels—they had brought back with them.

† From *Metaphysical Poetry*, eds. Malcolm Bradbury and David Palmer (Bloomington: Indiana UP, 1971), pp. 20–26. Copyright © 1970 by Edward Arnold. Reprinted by permission of Edward Arnold.

The man by whom the poems are 'spoken'—and they are virtually all composed as if 'spoken', and that by a man[1]—is well-born, highly educated, able (and very ready) to refer casually to a wide range of reading and general intellectual knowledge, including theology, law and science; well informed, indeed, about things in general, such as the characteristics of foreigners, theological squabbles, and the behaviour of courtiers, and taking towards them all an attitude of sophisticated cynicism. He thinks of himself as a thorough 'modern', living in a complex, sceptical, immoral, revolutionary age. He lives, of course, in a society in which monogamy is the sexual norm and which pronounces adultery and extra-marital copulation to be sins; but he takes it for granted that these rules are perpetually broken, for all men (and most women), he is sure, have their affairs, and all that society, in practice, demands is a modicum of concealment and a degree of theoretical deference to the concepts of feminine 'honour' or chastity. But he is very far from being a radical protester against the church-and-court society he belongs to: on the contrary, he regards protesters and outsiders (Puritans, for example, and city merchants) with great scorn. What he demands—and gets—is licence within a society to break its laws and yet stay within it.

He assumes that basically all love is one topic, whether the woman be wife, mistress, whore, or Platonic ideal 'She', and that therefore there is no need always to inform us which, at the moment, she happens to be. He assumes that the man is always the initiator, the attempter to seduce and conquer, whether successful or not, and that women may respond to his attempts either by an impregnable chastity or a wanton yielding, but that in either case they will understand the rules of the game and will play it properly: that is, if they decide to be chaste they will be so in the high Petrarchan fashion (even though they, and he, may privately know this is nonsense), and if they decide to be wanton they will be that with a full-blooded libertinism. He assumes (I consider him now as writer) that the poems he makes will be read by people largely of his own kind and, many of them, his own friends; he has no intention of getting them printed, and would regard that way of 'publishing' them as ill-bred and in the worst of taste; indeed, he professes to be somewhat annoyed if they are set to music and sung. This audience of friends and equals will understand not only the allusions and witticisms, but (what is harder) just when he is serious and when not, and just what kind of seriousness is being displayed; they will understand also where the poems are 'personal' and where not, and again just what kind of 'personality' is involved. What he writes are not exactly

1. 'Confined Love' is an exception. It is apparently spoken by a woman, who protests against the morality which enforces her sex to have only one lover. Another exception is 'Breake of Day', an aubade in which a woman pleads with her lover not to leave her.

'sugared sonnets', but they are certainly written 'among his private friends', and he would feel very sympathetic towards Mr. Shakespeare if he happened to know that the latter's sonnets had been piratically printed.

So much for the man: what of the woman? There is less to be said of her, since, as remarked above, all this poetry is composed exclusively, even domineeringly, from the viewpoint of the man. The woman is the partner in the sexual dance, and that is all she is. But because the dance is very varied, there are many alternative responses available to her, and there is at least a pretence that she has a free choice among them. The man calls the tunes, but it is up to her which of them she will elect to dance to. She may decide to strip and go to bed with him—for one occasion only, or for a long affair, or for a lifetime—or she may decide to 'kill' him with her icy 'cruelty'. Whatever she does is done in response to him—to his urging, pleading, arguing, bullying, weeping—and the typical verbal mood of these poems is the imperative: 'come, madam, come . . . ', 'enter these armes . . . ', 'stand still, and I . . . ', 'send me some token . . . ', 'send home my long strayd eyes to me', 'marke but this flea . . . ', 'oh doe not die . . . ', 'for godsake hold your tongue . . . ', 'here take my picture . . . ', 'O stay here . . . '.

Man and woman alike are members of a mature, complex, in some ways corrupt society. Therefore they don't behave in the least 'naturally'; they behave, as we all do, according to patterns characteristic of their age and situation—which means, for them, in the manner of educated English gentry during the last years of Queen Elizabeth and first years of King James. What, then, were these patterns, in the domain of sexual love?

There were three main patterns. The first was that made by Christian marriage, sacramental and monogamous. The surprising thing here—surprising, at least, to an unprepared modern reader—is its complete absence from the poetry. It never occurs, specifically. Some of the poems, such as 'The Good-morrow', the song 'Sweetest love, I doe not goe', 'Lovers Infinitenesse', or 'A Feaver', express feelings of tenderness, constancy and devotion with such power and beauty that one would 'like to think' they had something to do with Mrs. Anne Donne; and one of them, 'A Valediction forbidding Mourning', was said by Izaak Walton, Donne's first and almost contemporary biographer, to have been written for her before Donne's departure for the continent in 1611.[2] But nothing in any poem iden-

2. Miss Gardner denies this; she adduces some factual arguments which, she says, make it impossible that the poem could have been written for that occasion. Her critical attitude seems inconsistent on this matter of autobiographical content and possibility of 'identifying' the woman addressed: thus, she says that the woman of Elegie XIX ('Going to bed')

tifies the status of the woman except those few (Elegie I, 'Jealosie', Elegie XII, 'His Parting from Her') which identify her as the wife of another man.[3] This exclusion of married love, specified as such, from the domain of love poetry was of course a commonplace of the medieval-Renaissance tradition;[4] but it would be totally wrong to make any deductions from this about the poet's personal life or opinions. It was no more than a social-aesthetic convention; but it is worth remembering—since we tend to forget it—that because this major area of men's, and women's, real experience was excluded, the love poetry had almost always a certain element of fictional expression: which does *not* mean that it was untrue, still less that it was insincere, but does mean that because of this social-aesthetic convention, which was thoroughly understood by everyone, there existed this area where art and life did not meet. Life, for one thing, in that area at that time, included many things somewhat resistant to poetry—dowries, jointures, family negotiations about matters of status and money, incessant pregnancies and almost equally incessant deaths of infants and children—and Donne's own life, which included a marriage that wrecked his worldly career for years and resulted in twelve children of whom five died in childhood, taught him better than most men's the difference between the love one wrote poems about and the love one lived.

The second pattern was that of pagan libertinism. The literary ancestry of this was Roman, and its most powerful preacher was Ovid. Its basic dogma was that in some past Golden Age sexual love had been free, as it still is among the animals ('Confined Love') and still could be among us if only we lived as Nature meant ('Communitie'). But Shame and Honour (i.e., the modesty and chastity expected of Christian women) and the possessive exclusiveness which went with these idols, had destroyed that happy and natural freedom. Women had become 'cold' and 'proud', and men, therefore, were engaged in an endless war against what 'The Dampe' calls 'th' enormous Gyant, your Disdaine' and 'th' enchantresse Honor'. In

is a London prostitute, on the grounds that Donne addresses her as 'Madam' and that she is 'richly dressed'. These seem inadequate reasons for pronouncing her to be a whore. 'Madam' is surely spoken in a tone of facetious imperiousness which any man might use to a wife or mistress (and when used with brothel-associations, it doesn't usually refer to one of the girls). And I doubt if it was only the London whores who, like Regan, were 'gorgeous' in their attire.

3. When the woman is addressed, it is always in terms which do not specify her status: 'deare Love' ('Valediction of the Book', 'Dreame'); 'deare' ('Legacie', 'Lovers Infinitenesse'); 'sweetest love' ('Song'); 'love' ('Lecture upon the Shadow'); 'faire love' (Elegie XVI); 'madam' (Elegie XIX).
4. Very few poems of the seventeenth century are admittedly addressed to the writer's wife. Bishop King's 'Exequy' and Milton's sonnet to his 'late espoused saint' are perhaps the only well-known examples. Cynics might remark that in each of these poems the wife is dead.

this war they used all the weapons they could find—tears, flattery, rhetoric, casuistical arguments. And it was a war not only against the individual women whom the men desired, but also against society, which 'officially' disapproved of the men's assaults as an attack on sound morality—not to mention a frivolous waste of time. For the true lover was far too busy for 'business' ('Breake of Day') or for any sort of career ('The Canonization'); he was contemptuous of the demands of the state, and proclaimed his intention (though for reasons hardly ideological) of 'making love, not war' in the best twentieth-century manner (Elegie XX, 'Loves Warre'). In many of the poems which show this lover successful, there is a vivid sense of the pair *excluding* the rest of the world, shutting themselves away from a society conceived as hostile or simply busy with affairs which it regards as more important than love ('The Good-morrow', 'The Sunne Rising', 'The Canonization').

This lost freedom of love—however much society and morality may disapprove of it—is claimed to be what virtually all men (and quite a few women) would really like to return to. It has its mock morality, its anti-morality, whereby faithfulness and chastity and the rest are *vices*, and 'love's sweetest part' is 'variety' ('Womans Constancy', 'The Indifferent'); it proclaims too that many of the women who pretend to chastity do so only because respectability demands it: they would change sides if they dared, and after suitable treatment some of them do ('The Flea', 'The Exstasie'). Because of these crosscurrents and oppositions, 'modern love' has become immensely more difficult than love used to be; it has become complex and agonized and all-demanding, for

> . . . every moderne god will now extend
>   His vast prerogative, as far as Jove.
> To rage, to lust, to write to, to commend,
>   All is the purlewe of the God of Love . . .
>   ('Loves Deity')

And from this comes a bitter doubt if what one gains from it is worth the effort and agony, a suspicion that ' 'tis imposture all', 'a vaine Bubles shadow' ('Loves Alchimie'), which only a fool would devote his life and art to ('The Triple Foole'); and out of that doubt, again, comes a fierce contempt for the women whom all the agony is about. They are silly creatures, after all: you needn't hope for 'mind' in them ('Loves Alchimie'); their love is always less 'pure', less intellectual, than men's ('Aire and Angels'); for all their talk about Honour and sentiment, they are not really interested in a 'naked thinking heart', only in 'some other part' of a man ('The Blossome'); and they are quite capable of bedding with one man after pretending impregnable chastity to another ('The Apparition').

The third, and last, pattern of love was that formed by the Platonic-Petrarchan adoration of a woman accepted as eternally chaste, through whose cruelty the lover must die. This, of course, was the old tradition of courtly love, now in its dotage. By Donne's time, at least for someone of his intelligence and temperament, this ancient convention could no longer be taken quite straight; it had to be refreshed, either with some irony or with a new range of intellectual reference and imagery. Donne gives it both. But he is not at all inclined to abandon it. He uses it in many poems: 'The Undertaking', 'The Legacie', 'Twicknam Garden', 'The Nocturnall', 'The Funerall', 'The Relique'. . . . There are variations within the convention. In some poems the lady, though still denying, is still alive and the poet is still besieging her; in others, she is dead and the poet is left alone to grieve; in others again, both she and poet are imagined as dead. Where the presence of death is felt, these poems take on a very strong theological colouring, and one which is specifically Catholic;[5] I suspect, in fact, that the attraction of this convention for Donne was that it enabled him to make a poetry which bridged the passage between his two main subjects, sexual love and religion. These poems tend to be the most ambiguous in effect of all Donne's works, and also perhaps the most quintessentially Donne, since they include all his manners and are liable to change keys with bewildering rapidity. Take the first stanza of 'The Relique'. It begins with a down-to-earth allusion to the fact that in the crowded church-yards of Donne's London the bodies were dug up after ten years or so, the bones thrown into a common pit, and the graves used again. This leads first to a cynical joke about women's fickleness, next to that famous line ('a bracelet of bright haire about the bone') which fuses with tremendous intensity images of beauty and death, after that to a Hamlet-like evocation of a simple-minded, superstitious gravedigger, then to the image of a pair of lovers still lying together in the grave, and finally to a picture of the Day of Judgment, seen in the literal medieval manner, with all the resurrected bodies standing beside their opened graves.

* * *

5. Anglo-catholic or Roman: in this context, it makes little difference.

JOHN A. CLAIR

John Donne's "The Canonization"†

Cleanth Brooks, using "The Canonization" as a vehicle for his enlightening views on poetical paradox, sees Donne's poem as less than an organic unit: he feels that the last three stanzas are too heavy a burden for the two introductory stanzas which merely establish "a vein of irony" for the heavily weighted remainder of the poem, that is, for the Phoenix metaphor and the canonization metaphor with which the poem concludes.[1] Clay Hunt, in his excellent study of Donne's poetry, takes a similar position: that the two opening stanzas are "a debater's opening maneuver, a tactical device for disarming the opposition."[2] The functional significance of the opening stanzas pointed out by both commentators certainly is a most important aspect of Donne's colloquy, but a detailed examination of the formal Canonization *processus* as it was carried out by the Roman Catholic Church of Donne's time indicates that the poet may have intended a more complex function for the central metaphor designated in the title. The entire poem throughout the five stanzas may be said to be controlled by the Canonization metaphor as it proceeds from proof of personal sanctity, to proof of heroic virtue, proof of miracles, examination of the burial place and the saint's writings, and finally to the declaration of Sainthood and the veneration of the Saint. Thus it may be that Donne's "conceit of erotic sainthood"—as Professor Hunt calls it—derives not merely from the middle stanza but may be extended to include also the conceits of the first stanzas in which the lover offers proof of his "sanctity" and of his "heroic virtues" in precisely the order of the first steps of the *processus* governing the introductory investigation of a proposed saint. Indeed the dramatic dialogue between the lover and his antagonist on the literal level in the poem may be viewed as a remarkable ironic parallel to the antagonism between the "Devil's Advocate" and those who advance the case for the saint in the canonization procedure, for it is the position of the Devil's Advocate ever to view the prospective saint as a fraudulent seeker of canonization.

The canonization procedure of the "Romane Church" is alluded to in several of Donne's prose writings; for example, his jibe in *Ignatius His Conclave* is exceptionally bitter:

---

† From *PMLA* 80.3 (June 1965): 300–302. Reprinted by permission of the Modern Language Association of America.
1. "The Language of Paradox," *The Language of Poetry*, ed. Allen Tate (Princeton: Princeton Univ. Press, 1942).
2. *A Donne's Poetry* (New Haven: Yale Univ. Press, 1954), p. 75.

These things, as soone as *Lucifer* apprehended them, gave an end to the contention; for now hee thought he might no longer doubt nor dispute of *Ignatius* his admission, who besides his former pretences, had now gotten a new right and title to the place, by his *Canonization;* and he feared that the *Pope* would take all delay ill at his handes, because *Canonization* is now growne a kinde of *Declaration,* by which all men may take knowledge, that such a one, to whom the Church of *Rome* is much beholden, is now made partaker of the principall dignities, and places in Hell.[3]

The change in the Canonization *processus* alluded to in the passage above probably is a reference to Pope Sixtus V's strengthening of Papal control over the rites governing Canonization in 1588. From this date a complex controversy on the subject continued among ecclesiastical authorities until a formal decree by Pope Urban VIII in 1625 finally codified the regulations concerning Canonization.[4] Donne's continued interest in the problem is shown by his attack on the Church's position in a sermon preached at St. Paul's Cross on November 22, 1629:

> . . . the farmers of heaven and hell, the merchants of soules, *the Romane Church,* make this blessednesse, but an under degree, but a kinde of apprentiship; after they have beatified, declared a man to be blessed in the fruition of God in heaven, if that man, in that inferiour state doe good service to that Church, that they see much profit will rise, by the devotion, and concurrence of men, to the worship of that person, then they will proceed to a *Canonization;* and so, he that in his *Novitiat,* and years of probation was but blessed *Ignatius,* and blessed *Xavier,* is lately become Saint *Xavier,* and Saint *Ignatius.* And so they pervert the right order, and method, which is first to come to *Sanctification,* and then to *Beatification,* first to holinesse, and then to blessednesse. (ML, pp. 568–569)

Donne's reference in his sermon seems unquestionably to be to the 1625 decree of Pope Urban, which not only codified the already existing procedure for Canonization, but defined the distinction between "beatification," a decree which "permits" veneration of a Saint by certain groups within the Church, and "Canonization," a final decree which binds the Universal Church to veneration of the established Saint.[5] Donne's attitude toward what he considered to

---

3. *The Complete Poetry and Selected Prose of John Donne,* ed. Charles M. Coffin (New York: Modern Library, 1952), p. 354. Hereafter cited within text as ML.
4. Eric Waldram Kemp, "Theory and Historical Controversy from the Sixteenth Century to 1918," *Canonization and Authority in the Western Church* (London: Oxford Univ. Press, 1948), p. 145.
5. *The Catholic Encyclopedia,* ed. Charles Herbernein et al. (New York, 1907), p. 366.

be needless machinations by the Church is clear from the tone of his sermon.

But "The Canonization" clearly follows the Canonization *processus* as it existed *before* Pope Urban's decree, when the Saint was declared canonized immediately upon the termination of the inquiry and the approval of ecclesiastical authorities. The context of the poem indicates that it was written after 1588, that is, after the establishment of the extremely "litigious" nature of the *processus*, for it was only at that time that the ecclesiastical litigation which had been in effect since ancient times and which involved "the most minute and thorough enquiry" into the proposed saint's "writings, virtues and his alleged miracles"[6] was brought under the direct control of the Sacred Congregation of Rites. The inquiry, directed by the Postulator General—popularly called the "Devil's Advocate"—was submitted for approval to the Congregation; if approved, the subject was declared "Canonized."

Father Thomas F. Macken, in his book *The Canonization of Saints*, describes the meticulous juridical *processus* which is carried through several stages: an investigation into the subject's reputation and proof of personal sanctity, an inquiry into his practice of virtues in an heroic degree, an investigation of his alleged miracles, a detailed scrutiny of the subject's writings, and finally, an examination of the burial place and an identification of the remains or relics.[7] These stages of the Canonization process, followed in remarkable detail, seem certainly to have provided Donne with the dramatic pattern for his poem.[8]

At the opening of the poem the irascible lover snaps, "For Godsake hold your tongue, and let me love" at his interrogator—analogous to the Devil's Advocate—who has inquired into his reputation for personal sanctity. The irony of the next lines becomes clear when we consider that the lover answers the inquiry into his virtues with an ironic catalogue of infirmities which are, if not entirely reprehensible, at least morally questionable: "palsie," gout, baldness, and profligacy. The unmistakable reference in these lines is to diseases of age and dissolute life.[9] The next four lines addressed to the inquisitor have a twofold application: first, as Doniphan Louthan points out

6. Reverend Thomas F. Macken, *The Canonization of Saints* (Dublin, 1910), p. 35.
7. "Outline of the Procedure for Canonization."
8. It would appear that Donne's pattern for the poem follows the procedure taken for the Canonization of "Confessors"—those pious men who lead heroically virtuous lives of self-denial, that is, lives of "prolonged martyrdom"—rather than the considerably less complex *processus* involved in the Canonization of "Martyrs."
9. There is no more reason to believe, with Doniphan Louthan, *The Poetry of John Donne: A Study in Explication* (New York, 1951), p. 112, that the speaker's "five gray hairs" refers to "greying temples," than that it refers to an advanced stage of baldness, an affliction which would have shades of meaning not inconsistent with "palsie," "gout," and "ruin'd fortune" for 17th-century readers.

(p. 116), they show the renunciation of the world by the lover, that is, his virtuous self-denial for love which makes his life analogous to the saint's life. Father Macken's translation of the points of inquiry reveals how closely Donne followed the "information process"; "to enquire into the sicknesses of the servant of God, and the ordinary afflictions of life, the coldness and falling away of friends, the ridicule of the world, the opposition of even good men, the disfavour of those in authority; all his trials and sufferings are closely examined."[1] Certainly the foregoing is an apt description of the lover's complaint in the poem. But however broad the context, the opening lines describe the physical sufferings and trials of the lover which by their nature are ironically opposite to those a prospective saint might suffer. A final association is made by Donne in the stanza with his use of the word "approve." Although the lover's indifference to the investigation is marked by the words "what you will," the approbation of the virtuous reputation of the subject by the Sacred Congregation of Rites is precisely the necessary object of the first step of the ecclesiastical inquiry.

The second stanza carries the information to the next stage: the inquiry into virtues practiced in an "heroic degree." Heroic virtue is defined by Church authorities as "a habit of performing continuous acts possessing the quality of goodness in a very remarkable degree," or as "a quality arising from the repetition of acts of virtue which can ordinarily be performed only with very considerable difficulty."[2] The "heroic" character of the lover's lament expressed in Donne's satiric conceits is obvious: "sighs," "tears," "colds," and fevers sufficient to drown "ships," cause floods, change seasons, and engender plague.[3] Donne's ingenious use of the conceits of the first stanzas maintains the ironic antithesis between the lover and saint, for not only is each statement a "leading question," but the virtues are "negative" virtues, neither type of testimony being permissible by the reg-

1. Macken, p. 154.
2. Macken, p. 158.
3. A remarkable similarity exists between Donne's conceits and a description of the Phoenix legend by the fourth century Roman Christian poet, Lactantius. Lactantius' poetic description reads: "non huc exsangues Morbi, no aegra Senectus / nec Mors crudelis nec Metus asper adest / nec Scelus infandum nec opum vesana Cupido / aut Ira aut ardens caedis amore Furor; . . . non ibi tempestas nec vis furit horrida venti / nec gelido terram rore pruina tegit." "Phoenix," *Minor Latin Poets*, eds. J. Wight Duff and Arnold M. Duff (Cambridge: Harvard Univ. Press, 1934). Compare this with Donne's passage in connection with the Phoenix from his "XXII Meditation": "there is a propensenesse to *diseases* in the *body*, out of which without any other *disorder, diseases* will grow, and so wee are put to a *continuall* labour upon this *farme*, to a continuall studie of the whole *complexion* and *constitution* of our *body*. In the *distempers* and *diseases* of *soiles, sourenesse, drinesse, weeping*, any kinde of *barrennesse*, . . . and there rises a kinde of *Phoenix* out of the *ashes*, a *fruitfulnesse* out of that which was *barren* before, and *by that*, which is the barrennest of all, *ashes*" (ML, 455). Although this "Meditation" undoubtedly postdates "The Canonization," it is significant that Donne compares bodily illnesses with illnesses of the earth in general in much the same fashion as they are set down in the first two stanzas of the poem. In both works the comparisons culminate in the figure of the Phoenix.

ulations governing the investigation leading to Canonization.[4] The last lines of the second stanza, "Soldiers finde warres, and Lawyers find out still/Litigious men, which quarrels move," is at once a comparison of the lover's virtues with those unvirtuous acts of other men, and an echo of the renunciation expressed in the first stanza reminding us of the gulf that exists between the lover—or the saint—and the rest of the world. The lines are acceptable as indicating a further analogy between the "Lawyers" and "litigious men" who oppose the lover, and the Judges and Courts who prosecute and decide the case for or against the saintly subject. In the literal context, of course, the meddlesome interrogator of the dissolute lover may, quite appropriately, be a lawyer.

In the first lines of the third stanza, the lover maintains his defense against his exacting interrogator. As noted by Brooks and Hunt the interplay of imagery culminates in the metaphor of the Phoenix.[5] A close reading of the stanza will show that two "miracles" are performed by the lovers: "two being one," and dying and rising "the same." Here the "miracles" of the Phoenix's life-in-death apply, as most commentators note, to the conventional "miracle" of love by which the lovers become as one, and to the lovers' sexual resuscitation. As Brooks observes (p. 55): because the lovers' love "can outlast its consummation," they are a "minor miracle . . . love's saints." And so the third stage of the Canonization process is reached—proof of miracles.

Following the proof of miracles—which is central to the poem as well as to the Canonization *processus*—the fourth stanza parallels two well-known steps of the informative procedure: the examination of writings, and the identification of the remains of the proposed saint. The writings are "carefully examined by the Congregation to see whether they contain any errors contrary to faith or morals, or any novel doctrine opposed to the sound and pure teaching of the Church."[6] The lover, continuing to react vigorously against the examination, defends his "legend" as "fit for verse" in the event it is not acceptable to the religious legislators; if he shall not be chronicled a saint, he says, his "sonnets" will suffice as "hymns," and "all" men shall be his judge and "approve" the lovers "Canoniz'd for Love."

But the "Process on the Individual Virtues and Miracles is not complete until the body of the deceased servant of God and all relics and mementoes of the deceased are formally identified."[7] Examina-

---

4. Macken, p. 67.
5. "The Language of Paradox," p. 54. Brooks observes: "The comparison of the lovers to the phoenix is very skillfully related to the two earlier comparisons, that in which the lovers are like burning tapers, and that in which they are like the eagle and the dove. The phoenix comparison gathers up both."
6. Macken, p. 115.
7. Macken, p. 169.

tion of the tomb is then made to determine any further last cause either for or against Canonization. Here again the antithesis is evident: the unidentifiable "ashes" of the lover in the "urn" may be viewed as the ironic counterpart of the relics of the saint interred in the tomb.[8]

Finally the lovers are declared "Canoniz'd"—all that remains after the formal decree is the fulfillment of the precept that the Saint now be venerated as an intercessor to God for the Universal Church. In the final stanza Donne composes the invocation or prayer to the Lover-Saint in which the earlier elements of the poem are synthesized. Brooks summarizes this remarkable poetic coda: "The lovers in becoming hermits, find that they have not lost the world, but have gained the world in each other, now a more intense, more meaningful world. . . . They are like the saint, God's athlete: 'Who did the whole worlds soule *contract*, and *drove*/Into the glasses of your eyes' . . . The 'Countries, Townes,' and 'Courts,' which they renounced in the first stanza of the poem. The unworldly lovers thus become the most 'worldly' of all."[9]

From first to last the poem is a coherent whole; the organic unity of the poem is maintained by the imposition of the procedure of Canonization upon the literal dramatic colloquy between the lover and his detractors and upon the central metaphor of the Phoenix. As H. J. C. Grierson remarks, Donne "as usual is pedantically accurate in the details of his metaphor."[1] It is possible that Donne intends a lampoon of the taut, formal *processus* of the Church's Canonization Rites, but the complex development of the ironic, paradoxical conceit of erotic sainthood would appear to carry the significance of the work beyond such a single, restricted objective.

---

8. Although there is no doctrine of the Catholic Church expressly forbidding cremation, traditionally the practice of interment in the earth has been observed. It would be highly desirable in the Canonization rites investigation for the remains of a saint to be specifically identifiable, which, of course, ironically, they would not be, in the poem.
9. Brooks, p. 53.
1. *The Poems of John Donne* (Oxford: Clarendon Press, 1912), p. 16.

338

M. THOMAS HESTER

"this cannot be said": A Preface to the Reader of Donne's Lyrics†

* * *

Donne's sympathy with *the old religion* of his great-granduncle, Sir Thomas More, can be "spied" in the analogies he draws in his own verse *Satyres* between the dilemma of the satirist at the Elizabethan Court (as an endangered devotee to "our Mistresse faire Religion") and the precise details of the treason trial of More; and it can be "deciphered" more equivocally in his Holy Sonnets in his reliance not only on Jesuit modes of meditation but also on his martyred ancestor's treatise on The Last Things in order to interrogate the central Calvinist tenets of late Tudor Protestantism. As a young Catholic Donne attended his mother in that dangerous conference in the Tower of London in which she assisted the disguised renegade priest William Weston to consult with Donne's imprisoned Jesuit uncle, Jasper Heywood (Flynn " '*Annales* School' " 7); he probably accompanied his legendary uncle among the troop of English "traitors" gathered with Parma in 1585 (Flynn "Catholic Nobility" 7); and he was most likely as familiar as was his martyred younger brother with William Harrington, the priest who after being caught in Henry Donne's quarters suffered "the vast reach of th' huge statute lawes" (*Satrye II* 112). This is the late Elizabethan author of *Satyre III*, that Ignatian meditation on the primacy of Truth to "true religion" composed in an age and a country where the political import of religion was being rendered primary by renewed attempts to enforce the Act of Uniformity, the Oath of Allegiance, and the Bloody Question, the penal statutes which defined Catholicism as treason, by a secret police "force" created to "allow . . . but one" religion in England, even by "tyrannous rage" if necessary. This is the poet who concluded *Satyre III* with a definition of Elizabethan "Power" remarkably similar to although even more offensive than that of Southwell's *Humble Supplication*, and who concluded that "sullen" anatomy of contemporary religious politics with a warning about the "*fiumi rovinosi*" of Machiavelli's Dame Fortuna displacing the Bride of Christ in England. And this is the same poet who compared his second and fourth *Satyres* to "disarm'd Papists" being

† From *Christianity and Literature* 39; 4 (Summer 1990): 366–67, 368, 369–72, 373–74, 377–83. Reprinted by permission of *Christianity and Literature*.

threatened by spies, agents, and torture in their disputes over what could be "esteem'd Canonicall" by those "Which dwell at Court."

Nevertheless, even though few poets amplify their texts more consistently and widely with a broader range of theological discourse and religious iconography, the specific contours of Donne's own position are difficult to ascertain. *Satyre III* submits that "To'adore, or scorne an image, or protest, / May all be bad"; and even those works which (seem to) announce what Donne calls the "binding of my conscience to the locall Religion" are framed by prose paradoxes posing as prefaces to the reader which insinuate that we should "doubt wisely" the pronouncements which follow. * * * "To stand inquiring right is not to stray," he urged in *Satyre III*, but just where ("O where?") Donne does "stand" is an inquiry that his works seem most often poised to raise without answering. The most consistent answer to this central issue in Donne's texts might well be provided by excerpts from the love lyrics: "I will not tell thee now" ("The Apparition"), "this cannot be said" ("The Flea"), "All measure, and all language, I should passe, / Should I tell" ("The Relic"), "T'were profanation . . . To tell" ("A Valediction: forbidding mourning"), and it's "a braver thing . . . to keepe that hid" ("The Undertaking"). It is on this strategy of denial—or strategem of deniability—in the love lyrics that I shall focus attention in the remainder of this inquiry, in order to offer a "preface" to a reading of how and why those works tell us how and why they *will not tell*. * * * Any reading of Donne's love lyrics * * * should take into consideration this same (Counter) Reformation vocabulary. The following preface concerns how and why the precise doctrinal lexicon and rhetorical paradigms of the late Elizabethan controversy about how to read the "body" of Scripture and the "body" of Christ in the Eucharist are "survayed" and "digested" in the outrageous analogies which "measure" the "poore wit" of Donne's lyric controversies about the real presence of the body in human love.

What was current in "the whole body of Divinity" is indicated by Father Thomas Wright's 1596 *Treatise, Shewing the Possibilitie, and Convenience of the Reall Presence of our Saviour in the Blessed Sacrament*, composed while he was still under the sponsorship (and house arrest) of the Earl of Essex at York House, where Donne was in frequent attendance. "From the same Scriptures," Wright points out,

> Catholics and Heretikes draw divers lights. . . . This diversitie proceedeth not from the word of God, . . . but from the interpreters dispositions, . . . the which difference, thogh in al controversies of religion now called in question, . . . [is] yet in none so much as about the blessed Sacrament. (A2r–v)

And central to this "difference," as the many lectures on *"Hoc"* by
Cajetan might recall, is the interpretation of Christ's words of con-
secration:

> The Catholikes from these foure wordes, Hoc est corpus meum,
> deduce their dreadfull, reverent, majesticall, and deified sacri-
> fice, . . . the Heretikes their common-table Communion, their
> profane supper, their schismatticall cup, their tipicall bread,
> their unblessed breakefast. . . . [They deny that] such a great
> bodie conveied as that of Christs, with al parts and members,
> shuld be cowched or under so little an hoast. (A2r, B3r)

And from this "error," urges Wright, derives their inability to see how

> this little hoast . . . is not changed in form, but in nature . . . in
> the Sacrifice; how the body and bloud of Christ, being so little
> in comparison, [can] be resident in so many hoastes . . . in so
> many places; [and] can be really present, being really distant as
> far as heaven from earth. (4v–5r)

The Protestants differ, William Perkins responds, "only in the man-
ner of presence. For thogh we holde a real presence of Christs body
and blood in the sacrament yet do we not take it to be locall, bodily,
or substantiall but spiritual and mystical" (*Works* 1:583). As the first
English translation of Calvin's *Institutes of the Christian Religion*
phrases it, "Onely this thinge let the readers marke: . . . in wordes
verily the difference is smalle; but in the thinge it selfe, not small"
(119v).

   A useful and representative account of these "small" differences
about what English Protestants "deny" Catholic interpretation is
Henry Holland's popular 1596 *Aphorismes of Christian Religion: or,
A Verie Compendium of M. I. Calvins Institutions*, which explains
that the Scriptures teach that the Sacrament is a "marke [or] sign of
our profession"—"a Metonymy, a trope, whereby the name of the
thing signified is attributed to the signe" (135). The Holy Supper, in
Holland's translation, is "the signe, . . . a pattern, . . . by which this
mysterie of the secrete uniting of Christ with the godly [is] figured,
re-presented, & as it were set before our eyes" (134–35). Father
Wright questions at great length the logic of "a reall presence and a
corporall absence" (*Treaties* 122v), but the Protestant response is
that "Christ taught us in very plaine wordes [to distinguish between]
that broken body [and] 'This is my body' ":

> Of that bread broken, He speaketh on this wise: *This is my bodie,
> which is given, or broken for you*, that is, in asmuch as, or for
> that it is broken or given for you. For that holie bread, or as
> Paul calleth it, that bread of the Lord, is not simplie the Sac-
> rament of the Lordes body: that, was offred on the Crosse with

the sealing of Gods wrath, . . . [for] the flesh of Christ hath in
it the nature of meate, not simplie in but in a certaine respect:
that is, in asmuch as it was crucified for us. . . . Like as the body
is said to be visible, in respect of the colours thereof. (193–94)

This bread, in other words, is not *that* bread, *this* body is not *that*
body, except in the sense that "This" (*Hoc*) is "that living bread,"
"like as . . . the colours thereof." "And like as neither the water of
Baptism is chaunged, . . . so in like manner, the wine [and bread] in
the Lords Supper is not chaunged into the blood [and body] of
Christ" (135). Thus, for the Protestants, *Sacrament* remains "this
Metonymicall or Sacramentall phrase, . . . as Christ ordained and
appointed." "We deny the body of Christ to be included in the Sacra-
mentall bread, [and] it is impious and blasphemous [to] offer up
Christ as a host or sacrifice unto God . . . to be slaine" (185). "We
deny the body of Christ to be included" (167).

What interests me here is how these two treatises reiterate that
same *lexicon* of theological dispute in the Reformation battle of
books of William Whitaker and William Rainolds, William Fulke and
Gregory Martin, about the sectarian translations of the Bible earlier
in the century. This war of words about the Divine Word became
most often an encoded skirmish between "two English synonyms
which, in a neutral religious atmosphere, might be equally accept-
able as translations of a Greek or Hebrew word" (Hoff 57), such as
the Protestant defense of the Anglo-Saxon *love* and the Catholic
defense of the Latinate *charity* for the Greek *agape*. Each side saw
the other as vomiting errors that misread the spiritual food of Christ's
Word, especially what he signified by *Hoc est corpus meum* and most
especially what he meant by *Hoc*. For example, Proverbs 11, argued
Martin,

> foreshewth a type of our Lord's sacrifice, [and should be trans-
> lated as] "Wisdom hath killed her hosts, she hath mingled her
> wine into the cup, . . ." [but] the protestants, counting it an idle
> superstitutious ceremony, . . . suppress altogether this mixture
> or *mingling*, and instead thereof say, "She hath drawn her wine."
> (qtd. in Fulke 522)

"I confess," responded Fulke,

> but because that speech is not usual in the English tongue, [we]
> regarded not so much the property of the word, as the phrase
> of our tongue, [but] none did ever think that this place was to
> be interpreted of the Lords supper. (523–24)

And this wrangling over "mingles" as a figure for transubstantiation
is remarked in the ideological exegeses of *altar* and *temple, here* and

above, this and *that*. Protestants "so much do abhor the word 'altar'
as papistical," said Martin, "that in their first translation, when altars
were then in digging throughout England, they translated with no
less malice than they threw them down, putting the word 'temple'
instead of 'altar' " (516), and this attitude is also evident in their
translation of Acts 3:21 ("whom heaven must receive") as "heaven
must contain," so as to "include Christ in heaven that he cannot be
withal upon the altar" (506–07). These examples could be expanded
but would only re-mark the re-marking of the same terms. Quite
simply, in the heteroglossical dialogue about the One True Word
which Donne "survayed and digested" before 1610, Catholic exegesis
yielded a *small* but *substantial change* which mysteriously *mingles*
the *real presence* of Christ's blood and body in the *little host* of the
Sacrifice; this is not *that*, Protestants rebuked, for *this* takes place
only *spiritually* in the *re-presentation* of the *metonymical* sign or *mark*
of the *seal* of our faith in the resurrection of Christ to heaven *above*.
For the Catholic, the miracle through which Christ's death makes
meaningful his outlandish metonymy at his Last Supper changes the
meaning of the signs and substance of the Eucharist. *Hoc est corpus
meum* remains for the Protestant a sign which represents that mir-
acle and the miracle of faith which makes their re-presentation "use-
ful": the *substance* of the Supper is only a *pattern* of him who remains
above during Communion. In that war of words which Donne "sur-
vayed and digested," both lovers of "our Mistresse faire Religion"
would deny the other's interpretation of the significance of the Body
("Hoc") to their worship.

                                *   *   *

    The politics of religion, then, which had led to the martyrdom of
Sir Thomas More for "treason" also confronted his great-grand-
nephews. It led to the death of Henry Donne in prison in 1593; as
for John, in his own words, it "not onely retarded my fortune, but
also bred some scandall, and endangered my spiritual reputation"
(*Pseudo-Martyr* B3). My concern now is to suggest some ways in
which it also "bred" some of his lyrics, especially the ways in which
they appropriate the lexicon of the current doctrinal war in order to
say what "cannot be said" about his continuity with his heroic ances-
tor. Quite simply, Donne's dramatic dialogues about human sexuality
often frame a speaker who uses the terms and argument of the cur-
rent Recusant position concerning the hermeneutics of the Sacra-
ments and a protesting, scornful auditor who is given those of the
current Protestant position. In some cases, moreover, this analogy is
extended beyond the terms of the theological discourse to a reflec-
tion of/on the current terms and argument of the dispute about the
politics of the spirit(ual). The embedded allusions to the Eucharist

in Donne's analogies of sexual and divine intercourse, that is, exploit an article of faith which both churches agreed was finally "mysterious"; but the doctrinal vocabulary used to present his outrageous metonymies transfers the terms identified with the warring parties in the controversy about the Sacrament and the government's statutory responses in that war to the speaker's defense of and the auditor's response to his (libertine) amatory creed of sexual incarnation. The "lesson" of love which Donne's outrageous lover reads and explicates is not just Spenser's Easter defense by which we love *like as we ought* (*Amoretti* 68), but it is blasphemously analogous to the canon of the Catholic Mass by which "For Gods sake" we engage in the "reverend," "substantiall," "daily" descent of the real body's "dying"—the "small change" of sexual exchange that "parents grudge," authorities "deny," and no one but the lovers would "impute" to be more than the adulterous idolatry of the body. The centrality and persistence of this absurd metonymy in Donne's poems force the readers within and without the poem to determine how and why which parts of it—the metonymy—are "idle" (or merely frivolous, wittily blasphemous, and outrageously facetious) and which parts are the sort of "idol" talk of which the Protestant Establishment accused Catholics. This basic pattern is not reserved for the lyrics, of course. The lover of "our Mistresse faire Religion" who is threatened with "Becomming Traytor" in the *Satyres* and the idolizer of sexuality who is perused, interrogated, and mentally tortured by the agents of the family in the *Elegies* evince the same sectual politics as the anti-Petrarchist, anti-Neoplatonic outlaw lover of the lyrics. And all three of these rhetors for "devotion" are compared to or associated with traditional Roman Catholic "truths." Even the moral disputant of the Holy Sonnets, in fact, interrogates the creeds and lexicon of the legal Church of England so severely as to challenge their "truths" about the "mysteries" of divine Grace/Love and the "markes" of human love.

* * *

The most outrageous, the wittiest, and the most thorough application of the terms of the "currant" debate in which Catholics asserted that the "mysteries" of divine love were to be read not only in the "booke" of Scripture but also in the "body" of the Eucharist is provided by Donne's ingenious exegesis of the "honor" of sexual intercourse in "The Flea." The (Counter)Reformation debate, as we have seen, centered on the enduring significance of the metonymy that Christ spoke at the Last Supper, *"Hoc est corpus meum"*—that misnaming or substitution of names (bread for body, wine for blood) to which his death and resurrection gave meaning. "The Flea" frames "an impious and blasphemous" analogue (to borrow the Reformers' view of the Catholics' emphasis on the body) of the bloody debate, signalled by the reiteration of "this" (six times in the first nine lines) as a "Marke" whose significance can only be read in the physical incarnation. Christ's originary metonymy is petulantly and ingeniously replicated by an equally far-fetched double *misnomer* in which the significances or properties of sexual intercourse and his metonymy are transferred to the "Marke" or "suck" of the flea. And in this debate about the substance of "this" and "that" Donne once again appropriates the precise lexicon and paradigms of the current theological debate to frame a *dialogue d'amour* between a "Catholic" exegete and his "Protesting" lady about the significances of the last supper and death of a metonymical flea to the "honor[able]" incarnation of their love (which she "denyst"). As a seduction poem "The Flea" traces its own failure—unless, of course, she is to be seduced by the rigor of an erect wit that can invent a metonymy which dares to be compared in ingenuity to *that* of Christ's *"Hoc est corpus meum."* But even if read as a facetious send-up of Catholic *hocus-pocus*, the poem's bantering play with the exegesis of "this . . . this flea . . . this . . . blood of innocence" raises some provocative comparisons between Reformation hermeneutics and Donne's own witty strategies of denial.

The exegesis of the outrageous metonymy by which the "suck" of the "flea" justifies sexual intercourse begins by applying the term familiar to both parties in the "currant" doctrinal debate—"Marke"—which meant only a "signe of our profession" in Protestant sacramental theology but a "sign" of Christ's presence in the Catholic view, and then proceeds to read "this . . . marke" of the flea as a prevenient form of sexual intercourse—somewhat like Death's gracious and innocent arrival with the Knowledge of death before the demise of Everyman in the Catholic morality play. Or, to recall the Latin origins of *sacrament* as "a pledge, oath, or promise," the flea's "marke" becomes in the hyperbole of the speaker a sort of sacramental coitus that pledges and consecrates the *real* presence of their union later—just as Christ's pledge at the Last Supper, through the death on the cross, and in the Catholic Mass is a pledge of the Beatific Vision. The mark of the flea, however, never becomes like the *seal* of assurance, as the Communion of Calvin asserts in its celebration of "the penetration of the hearts of the elect" by the Spirit. But before looking at how "the last clause" of "The Flea" offers a pledge instead of seal, it is significant to see how the poem moves through a series of befuddling grammatical and figurative twists on the indefinite pronouns "this" and "that"—in serio-ridiculous affectation of the controversialists' lexical and grammatical disputations about the syntax, grammar, typology, and Greek and Hebrew sources for the (Counter) Reformation debate about the referends for

Christ's *"Hoc."* Rather than a dispute grounded in the original mean-
ings of Greek and Hebrew works, however, Donne's erotic exegete
quite appropriately offers a translation of a *French* word as his sub-
text, building multiple metonymies on the verbal associations of
puce/pucelle/Pucelle: a flea/a maiden/the Virgin.[1] In the unfolding
scholastic analogies embedded in the polyvalent puns of the poem,
the associations of the flea's bite are transferred to connotations of
being both married (no longer a maiden) and "more than maryed,"
or like and unlike the Virgin Mother who "cloistered" Christ in the
"temple" of her *pucelle.* And then the connotations of the outrageous
"blood" metonymy are transferred to the suckling Child who shed
his blood for the spiritual life of mankind. Each stanza, in fact, works
a *small change* on the *host* metonymy: in the first the flea is "one . . .
made of two" and a Virgin Conception at the same time; but in the
second the thing contained is substituted for the thing containing
(Quintilian's definition of *metonymy*) when the Virgin is the flea; and
the third transfers the name of the flea to the blood of Christ and
martyrs, or even to the children slain by Herod. But Donne's trans-
lation of the verbal play of the French pun goes beyond representing
the spirited play of the libertine French models to the literal *inscrip-
tion* of his metonymy in the orthography of his text. For if we follow
the visual pun on *f* in the Elizabethan long *s* by which the action of
the flea—it "sucks"—inscribes the English sign for sexual inter-
course in the body of the text, then it is possible to see the other part
of his metonymy when we see the *f* in "flea" as an *s* and thereby an
orthographic "mingling" of *seal*, or sacrament, in the literal amphi-
bology of the poem's mysteriously encoded *marks.* As with the her-
meneutics of the Eucharist, how we read these signs or marks
replicates how and why we interpret the significance(s) of Christ's
"Hoc"—and the poem's host of *this*es—as either a *seal* or a *presence*
of love.

The strategy of this "little" *change* by which the *marks* of the poem
inscribe or incarnate the literal truth of the speaker's metonymy is
reiterated by its *triple-entendres*, most famously in the play on the
death of the flea, lovers, and Christ in the last stanza. Every mark in
the poem seems chosen, in fact, to exploit the doctrine of the Trinity
in its three stanzas of nine lines of three rhymes each (see Madison),
each of which remarks the triplicate planes of correspondence of the
central metonymy. "Cloister," for example, is the body of the flea,
the nunnery of Venus, and the womb of the Virgin; "living walls of
Jet" signals the flea, sexual intercourse, and Christ's body and is not
"sinne, nor shame, nor losse of maidenhead," "murder . . . , selfe

---

1. Wilson discusses the *puce/pucelle* pun in his reading of the poem but does not discuss
the *Pucelle* pun.

murder . . . , or sacrilege." But these formal properties of the poet's wit have been well marked by readings of the poem. What has not been marked is the speaker's transfer of the Recusant terms and rhetoric to the properties of this flea's last supper and this lover's feast of sexual love.

His designation of the triple analogy or "this" of the poem as a "marke" that is not "that"—not a sinful, shameful, or treasonous threat to the maiden Head of England (that is "more then [they] would doe")—but an analogue for martyrdom by which innocents are killed for what they practice; his claim that "this" is "that little which thou deny'st" him, that this "mingling" of *blood* is a rite more sacred than the Protestant's non-sacramental marriage, a mingling in the "temple," within the "living walls" of Christ that Mary carried within her "living walls," this so-called "guilty" celebration of and participation in the presence of the body—all *this* replicates the English Recusants' defense and definition of their Sacrament. And even the concluding outrageous claim of the speaker that the belief in such an incarnation of Love is *honorable* derives from the same current defense.

The most telling "Catholic" strategy in the poem is the speaker's response to the virginal Venus's killing of the cupidinous flea. In many ways *this* is the ugliest feature of the poem, for it invites us to see her "Purpled . . . nail" not just as the instrument of the flea's and Christ's and her son's death, but as a sort of digital dildo that has violated her maidenhead and aborted the poetic conception of the speaker. As a rebuttal of his argument for sexual intercourse, however, her gesture is most successful: she will not "yeeld" to the *false* metonymies of his exegesis. But, ironically, her response to the death of the flea does support the Eucharist analogy on which the speaker has relied. In Father Wright's words, the "real participation" by which "the sacred Eucharist joyneth our soles and bodies really with Christ" (*Treatise* 122r) does not "take life" from me, nor him, nor "thee."

Obviously, the *hocus-pocus* of the speaker's witty consecration fails to transform this irresistible figure of cupidinous grace into a prefigurative seal that assures their sexual union; for when she "triumphant[ly]" raises the host of his metonymy (in a sort of *ridicula imitatio* of the priest's elevation of the Host in the Mass to celebrate Christ's triumph over death), her gesture *marks* only the "death" of the speaker's carnal hopes. He attempts to name "this" as a pledge (or sacrament) of future beatific intercourse—"so much. . . . *Will* wast"—but her bloodly gesture shows only the absence of mystery or miracle in his sexual metonymy; she simply "deny'st" the real sacrifice that would prove its irrational typology spiritually but not literally true. The "blood" of the flea, that is, proves that the flea/sex metonymy is only metonymy: a dead *puce* is not a real *pucelle*. But, at the same time, this shows the other metonymy to be true: just as Christ's blood verifies (analogically) the metonymy of the Last Supper, so the blood of the flea proves the requirement of the real blood of the moral Sacrifice. The flea/sex metonymy is "true" only "spiritually" or metaphorically—it remains a "true" *metonymy*, like the celebration of the absent blood in the Protestant Communion; but the death of the flea offers, by analogy, the truth of the Catholic celebration—the "death" of Christ, the "blood" of Christ in the Supper, does not kill "mee [and] thee."

That she will respond either carnally or spiritually to his arguments about sexual intercourse and about the Eucharist seems unlikely. For if it is only the spiritual argument that has been verified by the exegesis of the poem, it is significant that she has been characterized throughout as responsive only to the argument of "use." (Its usefulness, we might recall, was Calvin's major support for the celebration of Communion as a "table of friendship.") It is merely "use" and "parents grudge" that frames her denial—like the Protestant Graius in *Satyre III*—just as it was merely "locall" politics, customs, and laws that the Protestant imperial state, according to the Recusants, cited to deny the consciences of the Recusants, to imprison them in the cloisters of Bridewell, to call their martyrdom "selfe murder," to shed their "blood of innocence." And, by analogy, it is unlikely that she, or the "maidenhead" she mirrors, or any Graius who follows her will deny the "Cruel and sodaine" uses of the state's fearful and deadly assault, regardless of the humble supplications of this or any other defense of loyal Catholic "honor" which pledges not to "wast" (from *vasto*: "to empty, ravage, deprive of inhabitants") the country in its celebration of the Real Presence—as the case of Robert Southwell, or Henry Donne, showed.

But she should serve as a cautionary model when *we* "triumph" and say we now know where Donne stands in the "currant" debate. His texts, he once warned, "are quiet enough if we resist them" (Simpson 298), for even after we have "spied" the Recusant analogy in "The Flea" we should remember that vehicles are still vehicles, that "this" is not "that," that all metonymies except Christ's are *misnomers*, and that we readers remain in the seam/seme/seem which always denies the exchange of vehicle and tenor—especially in the case of poems as equivocal as those of Donne. But, then, the "art of Equivocation" (*Ignatius* 33) was continuous to Donne's "learned" family tradition as a traditional Catholic vehicle by which to "tell" what the law denied could be said against the "grudge" of public decency and private practice.

Lyrics such as "The Flea," that is, can be read as instrumental to the fearful Catholic subtext of Donne's *poetic* wit in which his

Ovidian exegeses of the real presence of the body in human love rewrite the Establishment poets' political Neoplatonisms and Virgilian *urbanitas* which had reformed Roman Mariologies to support an imperial Protestant Petrarchism. As Father Wright contended in 1596, "He which once is thoroughly grounded in the Catholique religion . . . may varie his affection, but his judgment [and] his conceit . . . hardly will he change or never" (*Treatise* A4v). If the lyrics, to cite Donne's own words in a letter describing his poems, *hide* this source of "fear" under a seal of "shame" (Simpson 298), then we might best preface any reading of Donne with the final words of Father Southwell just before he was sentenced to be hanged, drawn, and quartered for treasonous equivocation, when, in response to Topcliffe's cruel taunt that he had shown a lack of bravery by hiding when the torturer came to get him, the outlaw priest remarked, "It was time to hide when Mr. Topcliffe came" (Devlin 315).

But *this cannot be said,* for Donne was not Southwell. He may have had his "first breeding and conversation with men . . . accustomed to the despite of death, and hungry of an imagin'd Martyrdome" (*Biathanatos* 29) and "have beene ever kept awake in a meditation of Martyrdome" (*Pseudo-Martyr* 11r), but as a poetic *"pseudo-martyr"* he could use the "art of Equivocation" to "hide" a Recusant reading of the "currant" religious war in the equivoques of his witty texts without becoming a casualty himself. But this reminder of the aggressive interrogations by Topcliffe of anyone who might dare to evoke "sympathy with the old religion"—and his presence along with Baines and Poley and Cecil as potential readers of his lyrics—might just explain in part why Donne remained a manuscript poet whose works were not published until after his death, why he guarded their circulation and strove to limit them to a select coterie of readers, and why, even after we uncover the striking theological lexicon embedded in the hyperbolic conceits of his poems, it remains difficult to "decipher" the precise spiritual (and political) beliefs of their inventor. But, then, by raising such "wonder" Donne manages to do what great poetry always does: to say what cannot be said.[2]

WORKS CITED

Allen, William. *An Apologie and True Declaration of the Institution and Endevours of the Two English Colleges.* [Rhemes], 1581.
———. *A True, Sincere, and Modest Defense of English Catholics.* Ed. Robert M. Kingdon. Ithaca: Cornell UP, 1965.
Bald, R. C. *John Donne: A Life.* Oxford: Oxford UP, 1970.
Calvin, John. *Institutes of the Christian Religion.* Trans. T. Norton. London, 1561.

2. An earlier version of this paper was presented as a plenary address at the CCL Western Regional Meeting on 20 April 1990.

Cecil, William. *The Execution of Justice in England*. Ed. Robert M. Kingdon. Ithaca: Cornell UP, 1965.

Clair, John A. "John Donne's 'The Canonization.' " PMLA 80 (1965): 300–02.

Devlin, Christopher. *The Life of Robert Southwell: Poet and Martyr*. London: Sidgwick and Jackson, 1956.

Donne, John. *Biathanatos*. Ed. Ernest W. Sullivan, II. Newark: U of Delaware P, 1984.

———. *The Complete Poetry of John Donne*. Ed. John T. Shawcross. Garden City: Doubleday, 1967.

———. *Ignatius his Conclave*. Ed. T. S. Healy. Oxford: Clarendon, 1969.

———. *Poems*. London, 1633.

———. *Pseudo-Martyr*. London, 1610.

———. *Sermons*. Ed. Evelyn M. Simpson and George R. Potter. 10 vols. Berkeley: U of California P, 1953–62.

Dugmore, Clifford W. *Eucharistic Doctrine in England from Hooker to Waterland*. New York: Macmillan, 1942.

Flynn, Dennis. "The '*Annales* School' and the Catholicism of Donne's Family." *John Donne Journal* 2 (1983): 1–10.

———. "Irony in Donne's *Biathanatos* and *Pseudo-Martyr*." *Recusant History* 12 (1973–74): 49–69.

———. "John Donne and the Ancient Catholic Nobility." Forthcoming.

Foxe, John. *Acts and Monuments* Ed. S. R. Cattley. 8 vols. London: Seeley and Burnside, 1837–41.

Fulke, William. *A Defence of the Sincere and True Translations of the Holy Scriptures into the English Tongue*. Ed. C. H. Hartshorne. Cambridge: Cambridge UP, 1843.

Hester, M. Thomas. "Donne's (Re)Annunciation of the Virgin(ia Colony) in *Elegy XIX*," *South Central Review* 4.2 (1987): 49–64.

———, and R. V. Young, eds. *John Donne: Selected Prose*. Columbia: U of Missouri P, forthcoming.

Hoff, Linda Kay. *Hamlet's Choice*. Lewiston, NY: Edwin Mellen, 1988.

Holland, Henry. *Aphorismes of Christian Religion: or, A Verie Compendium of M. I. Calvins Institutions*. London, 1596.

Hughes, Paul M., and James F. Larkin. *Tudor Royal Proclamations*. 3 vols. New Haven: Yale UP, 1964–69.

Jonson, Benjamin. *Ben Jonson*. Ed. C. H. Herford and Percy Simpson. Oxford: Clarendon, 1925–52.

Madison, Arthur. "Explication of John Donne's 'The Flea.' " *Notes and Queries* ns 10 (1963): 60–61.

Martin, Gregory. *A Discoverie of the Manifold Corruptions of the Holy Scriptures by the Heretikes of our Daies*. Rhemes, 1582.

Patterson, Annabel. "John Donne, Kingsman?" Forthcoming.

Perkins, William. *Works*. 3 vols. London, 1608.

Selden, Raman. Review essay. *Modern Language Review* 82 (1987): 165–66.

Simpson, Evelyn M. *A Study of the Prose Works of John Donne*. Oxford: Clarendon, 1924.

Southwell, Robert. *An Humble Supplication to Her Maiestie*. Ed. R. C. Bald. Cambridge: Cambridge UP, 1953.

Spenser, Edmund. *Amoretti and Epithalamion*. London, 1595.

Williams, Penry. *The Tudor Regime*. Oxford: Clarendon, 1979.

Wilson, David B. "*La Puce de Madame Desroches* and John Donne's 'The Flea.' " *Neuphilologische Mitteilungen* 72 (1971): 297–301.

Wright, Thomas. *The Disposition or Garnishmente of the Soule to Receive Worthily the Blessed Sacrament*. [London], 1596.

———. *A Treatise, Shewing the Possibilitie, and Convenience of the Reall Presence of our Saviour in the Blessed Sacrament*. [London], 1596.

Young, R. V. " 'Oh My America, My New-Found-Land': Pornography and Imperial Politics in Donne's *Elegies*." *South Central Review* 4.2 (1987): 35–48.

Youngs, Frederick A., Jr. "Definitions of Treason in an Elizabethan Proclamation." *The Historical Journal* 4 (1971): 675–91.

350

THERESA M. DiPASQUALE

Receiving a Sexual Sacrament: "The Flea" as Profane Eucharist†

In a funeral elegy printed in the 1633 edition of Donne's *Poems*, Jasper Mayne urges would-be lovers to take Donne's erotic poetry as their model:

> From this Muse learne to Court, whose power could move
> A Cloystred coldnesse, or a Vestall love,
> And would convey such errands to their eare,
> That Ladies knew no oddes to grant and heare.
>
> (45–48)

Mayne praises Donne's "masculine perswasive force" ("Elegy: On his Mistris" 4) by drawing images from the master's own seduction poetry. The image of "Cloystred coldnesse," for example, reminds us of "The Flea," in which the speaker argues that he and his lady are "cloysterd in these living walls of Jet" (15).[1] The allusion fails, however, to capture the wit with which Donne applies his religious imagination to the business of seduction. In "The Flea," the cloister image is of the seducer's own making, and he puts it to his own erotic uses; it is a weapon in his arsenal, not—as in Mayne's allusion—a metaphor for the female chastity he has under siege. According to Mayne's rather conventional conceit, Donne's rhetoric is powerful enough to burst through the convent wall and melt the snowy virtue of a nun. Donne's speaker, however, addresses not a Carmelite in full habit, but an English girl who lives at home with her "grudg[ing]" parents; and his wit is too finely honed, too specific, to describe the chastity of an Anglican virgin as "Cloystred coldnesse."

Indeed, as M. Thomas Hester argues in a recent article, the denominational affiliations of the speaker and the lady help to determine the shape of the courtship drama. Using Reformation and Counter-Reformation treatises on the controversy over the Eucharist, Hester argues that the speaker in "The Flea" "appropriates the precise lexicon and paradigms of the current theological debate" in which Catholics and Protestants sought to define the word "This"

† From *John Donne's Religious Imagination: Essays in Honor of John T. Shawcross*, ed. Raymond-Jean Frontain and Frances M. Malpezzi (Conway: UCA Press, 1995), pp. 81–91. Reprinted by permission.

1. Mayne's elegy, which includes a number of verbal echoes of Donne's work, begins by asking, "Who shall presume to mourn thee, Donne, unlesse / He could his teares *in thy expressions* dresse[?]" (1–2; emphasis mine). It seems likely, then, that the cloister image is a conscious allusion.

(*Hoc*) as it functions in the all-important assertion, *"Hoc est corpus meum."* The speaker signals the analogy between his argument and the Eucharist debate "by the reiteration of 'this' (six times in the first line nines)"; and as the argument unfolds, the " 'Catholic' exegete" elevates before "his 'Protesting' lady" a quasi-eucharistic sign, telling her that, in essence, *Hoc est corpus nostrum* (Hester 377 [p. 344 above]). For Hester, however, the lady's triumphant gesture upon killing the flea *"marks* . . . the death of the speaker's carnal hopes," for her purpled nail shows "the absence of mystery or miracle in his sexual metonymy," and she is thus able simply to deny "the real sacrifice" of her virginity (Hester 381). According to Hester's reading, then, the poem "traces its own failure" as sexual persuasion, "unless . . . she is to be seduced by the rigor of an erect wit" (377). This phallic image puts a Donnean edge on the Christian concept of redeemed reason (compare Sidney's reference to "erected wit" in the *Defence of Poesy* [217]); and the argument of "The Flea" does depend upon the keenness of that edge.

But Hester's metaphor remains insufficient, for the seductiveness of the speaker's theological wit is a function not of its rigor, but of its delightful flexibility. The poem, I would argue, functions simultaneously on each of several mutually contradictory levels; for, by inscribing the speaker's argument in eucharistically charged language, Donne has insured that his signs and verbal gestures will be as polyvalent and as open to debate as the signs and gestures of the sacrament. The Lord's Supper is for one Christian an efficacious sacrifice, for another a merely symbolic action, and for yet another a dynamic event that takes place in the heart of the individual receiver; in the same way, "The Flea" may be read as a Petrarchan tribute, a libertine entrapment, or a true lover's persuasion. The poet assigns a given set of responses to the lady in the white spaces between the stanzas and—in so doing—sets up the shifting strategies the speaker makes in response to "her." But it is the reader of the poem who decides the lady's final answer in the white space following the third stanza and—in so doing—defines the effectiveness and significance of the speaker's argument as a whole. In short, the outcome of the seduction is—as any undergraduate will tell you—"left up to the reader."

Interpretations of the Eucharist are, nevertheless, always guided by theologians' readings of authoritative scriptural and patristic texts; indeed, they often allude to the importance of discovering Christ's authorial intention in the words of institution.[2] The options open

---

2. See Calvin's acknowledgment that "before that we goe any further, we must entreate of the selfe institution of Christe: specially because this is the most glorious obiection that our adversaries have, that we departe from the woordes of Christe. Therefore that we may

to the reader of "The Flea" are similarly delimited by what John Shawcross calls the "author's text" (*Intentionality* 3–4). In the poem, Donne directs reader response not only by using the language of theological debate, but also through his choice of the flea-poem sub-genre and his reworking of that lyric type as seduction-poem (in which the speaker addresses a lady) rather than as envious apostrophe (in which the flea itself is addressed).[3]

In the analysis that follows, I explore two different ways of reading the seduction as successful; each depends upon a different reading of the images and arguments presented to the lady who is the "reader" within the text. The first is an anti-Petrarchan, libertine reading, based upon the principles of radical iconoclasm; the second is a response rooted in an Anglican semiotic, which finds in the speaker's signs and gestures an invitation to genuine erotic communion. I argue, moreover, that this second way of reading the poem helps to explain some intriguing parallels between the woman in the lyric and Ann More Donne as her witty husband constructs her in a letter.

However one approaches the text, the lover's strategy suggests from the start that he wishes to anticipate "reader response," for he tailors his approach to suit his lady's wit and temperament. Clearly, she is a resourceful and practical-minded opponent, not to be impressed by helpless longing or ingenious postures of despair. Thus, the speaker's opening gambit employs neither elaborate Petrarchan compliments—which many of Donne's speakers decry as inherently self-defeating[4]—nor the despairingly lascivious alternative of the conventional flea poem, in which an unrequited lover fantasizes about being the flea in his mistress' cleavage (see Wilson, Brumble). Instead, Donne's speaker addresses the lady directly and attempts to dispense with at least one of her reasons for resisting his advances:

---

be discharged . . . our fittest beginnyng shall be at the exposition of the woordes" (*Institutes* IV.xvii.20).

3. A lyric, as Shawcross explains, is "a briefer poem in which the author intends to produce a successful literary creation by specific chosen techniques, devices, form, language, strategy, and the like in an ultimately competitive spirit for evaluation by the readers. It implies a fictive voice that may appear to be an authorial one, and that may owe its substance to an authorial voice; it is a fictive voice speaking to an auditor, implied or also fictive, who always also is the reader" (*Intentionality* 86). "The Flea" clearly provides ample opportunity for the reader to identify with the lady who is the fictive auditor; and there is no doubt that the battle-ready speaker bears a strong resemblance to Donne himself as he enters the flea-poem arena in a "competitive" attempt to rework and outdo previous lyrics of that type. In order to judge the poet's attempt "successful" while insisting that the seduction attempt fails, a reader will thus find it necessary to cling very closely to a condemnation of the intentional fallacy.

4. See "To the Countesse of Huntingdon" ("That unripe side of earth . . ."), in which the speaker claims that he "Who first look'd sad, griev'd, pin'd, and shew'd his paine, / Was he that first taught women, to disdaine" (35–36) or "The Triple Foole," in which the folly of unrequited love is doubled through the composition of "whining Poëtry" that expresses the emotion.

the fear of pregnancy. As Hester (379 [p. 345 above]) points out, the lover jokingly alludes both to the Annunciation miracle and to Renaissance theories of conception when he points to the flea as the virgin womb in which "two bloods" are "mingled" without "sinne," or "shame," or "losse of maidenhead." Though *it* "swells with one blood made of two," she needn't fear that her own womb will, for "this, alas, is more then wee would doe" (9).[5]

The lady could, if she had a mind to, play along with this mock-Christian miracle of virginal conception; but she is not impressed. The flea and the argument are both pests; and in the white space between the first and second stanzas, she moves to crush them. The speaker intervenes quickly; but the way in which he does so seems to make matters worse. Leaving behind the argumentative stance and demonstrative terminology of the polemical theologian, the speaker adopts the pleading, prayerful accents of a worshiper:

> Oh stay, three lives in one flea spare,
> Where wee almost, yea more then maryed are.
> This flea is you and I, and this
> Our mariage bed, and mariage temple is;
> Though parents grudge, and you, w'are met,
> And cloysterd in these living walls of Jet.
>   Though use make you apt to kill mee,
>   Let not to that, selfe murder added bee,
>   And sacrilege, three sinnes in killing three.
> (10–18)

The speaker here indulges in the Petrarchan hyperbole which he so carefully avoided in the first stanza; he claims to be slain by the lady's cruelty and defines his desire as a holy devotion.[6] At the same time, his phrasing and his choice of imagery lends that devotion a distinctly Catholic character. Indeed, the second stanza puts the erotic theology of the first into full-blown liturgical practice; the speaker consecrates and elevates the flea: "This flea *is*"—hoc est—"you and I"! The literalism of his hocus-pocus cannot but exacerbate the lady's irritation.[7] And as for the "living walls of Jet": what self-respecting Protestant lady would submit to being "cloysterd" anywhere? In Tudor England, the speaker's insistence that the flea is a monastery

5. The sighing note of the interpolated "alas," somewhat out of keeping with the matter-of-fact tone he has maintained up until this point, anticipates the more emotional argument of the second stanza. In implying, subtly, that he would actually prefer it if they *could* have a child together; he cunningly evokes an attitude of commitment without avowing it. Only a Donnean speaker could manage to say, "Don't worry, you won't get pregnant" and sound, at the same time, as if he were singing, "Would you marry me anyway? Would you have my baby?"
6. See Brumble (150) on Donne's adaptation of Petrarchan convention in stanza two.
7. Brumble (150) notes the movement from mere analogy in stanza one to more literal claims in the second stanza.

practically ensures that its walls will be razed, even as his pleading
tone, his exaggerated reverence, and his tribute to her "killing" pow-
ers virtually solicit the "cruel" response that is *de rigeur* for ladies
addressed in the Petrarchan mode.

But the speaker's shift in tone serves a purpose: he began by
eschewing the self-defeating language of Petrarchan courtship
which "destroyes it selfe with its owne shade" (as Donne puts it in a
verse epistle "To the Countesse of Huntingdon" [34]); but if his
insectile signifier is to die, he wants it to die as the embodiment of
such definitively frustrated and frustrating discourse. Thus, speaking
in the persecuted tones of what Donne elsewhere dubs "whining
Poëtry" ("The triple Foole" 3), the speaker reifies and venerates the
sign, insisting that violence done to it will be a "sacrilege" (18). The
lady responds to his papistical-sounding nonsense with an icono-
clast's righteous violence and acts upon the implicit dare; by the start
of the third stanza, she has demolished the jet walls of the idolatrous
"temple."[8]

In response to her action, he at first assumes a stance of shocked
indignation: "Wherein could this flea guilty bee," he asks, "Except
in that drop which it suckt from thee?" (21–22) His question evokes
a logic reminiscent of Hooker's conservative response to iconoclastic
zeal. Arguing against the destruction of medieval cathedrals and
churches, Hooker concedes that things previously put to idolatrous
uses may have to be abolished or extinguished, but he stresses that
such action cannot be considered a punishment of the thing
destroyed (*Laws* V.xvii.3).

But the lady's action and attitudes clearly render such distinctions
moot. She is flush with the excitement of iconoclastic zeal. In his
study of Renaissance iconoclasm, Gilman recounts the story of a
Lancashire boy who, when urged by a radical Protestant schoolmas-
ter "to mock the images in the chapel, . . . seized a sword from the
image of St. George and broke it over the saint's head, shouting, 'Let
me see now how thou canst fight again!' " (8). The thrill of exposing
an idol's impotence exhilarates the lady of the poem in much the
same way, and the speaker can hear the ringing defiance and mock-
ery in her voice: "thou triumph'st and saist that thou / Find'st not
thy selfe, nor mee the weaker now" (23–24).

At the very moment when she is sure that she has defeated him,
however, he once again shifts ground. Though he previously iden-
tified the signifier with the signified, claiming that it would be "selfe
murder" for her to kill the symbol which represented her, he now
admits—with Protestant care—that the reality is a thing separate

---

8. See also Gilman on Donne's ambivalence toward images and the frequent recurrence in
his poetry of what the speaker of "Witchcraft by a Picture" calls "pictures made and mard."
Gilman does not discuss "The Flea."

from the sign; her violence destroyed only the signifier, not the thing it represented. If she wants to be an iconoclast, he goes on to stress, she must be consistent; for she too has been treating a sign as though it were the very thing it signified:

> thou
> Find'st not thy selfe, nor mee the weaker now;
> Tis true, then learne how false, feares bee;
> Just so much honor, when thou yeeld'st to mee,
> Will wast, as this flea's death tooke life from thee.
>
> (23–27)

A woman's honor, his analogy implies, is the reality for which sexual abstinence—physical chastity—is but a tangible sign. An intact "maidenhead" is not the "honor" with which tradition equates it; and because there is such a gap between signifier and signified, the destruction of the sign will not affect the underlying truth. The devil can quote scripture, and a lover Augustine: the sacrament is one thing, its virtue is another.[9]

Read this way, "The Flea" is a voluptuous worldling's "Theatre for Fastidious Mistresses"; its emblems exhort a virgin to break her own most precious icon. The lady (or the reader of the poem, deciding for her) may leave it at that. She may sleep with her suitor on the understanding that tangible seals mean nothing; agreeing that the flea's death is an empty occurrence, she need attribute no significance to the "death" of her virginity. As we have seen in Mayne's verse tribute to Donne, a seventeenth-century reader was clearly capable of eliding the poet's success with the speaker's triumph. And for a significant number of twentieth-century readers, too, the seduction seems a *fait accompli*. Critics who choose to eschew the role of resisting reader, who enjoy the sheer pleasure of surrendering to Donne's wit, afford the lady at least as much latitude and argue that she will indeed yield to the speaker's "irresistible conclusion that the loss of maidenhood is nothing more than a flea bite."[1]

Other readers, however, see in the speaker's argument something

---

9. Augustine makes this assertion—"[A]liud est Sacramentum, aliud virtus Sacramenti"—in his "Tractates on the Gospel of John" (XXVI.11).

1. The quotation is from James Winny (126), who is one of seven twentieth-century critics noted by Laurence Perrine in an "annotated list of critics who believe that the seduction-attempt in 'The Flea' is successful" (16); the list also includes Helen Gardner and Patricia Meyer Spacks. Perrine blasts their readings as unfounded, insisting that the evidence provided "in the poem . . . favors the inference that this attempt on the young lady's virginity is as unsuccessful as those that have preceded it" (6). For Perrine, the poem dramatizes a witty game—as sexually fruitless as any Petrarchan ritual—played "for the 'fun' of the thing" by a perennially unrequited lover and his definitively coy mistress (7); but recent criticism of the poem—Perrine's list extends only through 1970—has persisted in taking the speaker's rhetoric considerably more seriously. See, for example, Baumlin's argument as discussed below, and Docherty's observation that "Prediction is tantamount to the generation of factuality in this poem" (59).

beyond the desire for meaningless fun. As Arthur Marotti notes, Donne's lyric differs from most erotic persuasions in mentioning marriage at all (93). And its theological imagery, gamesome though it is, does more than teach a lesson in iconoclasm. Rather, the speaker's blasphemous analogies preach a sexual-salvation-history with a Protestant flavor. The flea is set up as the incarnate union of the lover and his lady even as Jesus is the incarnate union of God and Man. And if the speaker offers it to be a sign of their oneness, the covenant between them can be fully accomplished—as in the case of Christ's Atonement—only through the *shedding* of the "one blood made of two." The killing of Jesus was the consummate sin, yet it was the only means to reconcile God and man. Similarly, it is "sacrilege" for the lady to "[Purple her] naile in blood of innocence," yet that nail of crucifixion proves instrumental in the lover's plan to make her his own.

It is here that a distinctly Protestant appeal comes into play: the Reformers rejected the Catholic conception of the Mass as a sacrifice offered by the priest because they held that Jesus' death on Calvary was the only sacrifice and could not be repeated or continued in the eucharist.[2] Similarly, the flea has served as Paschal-erotic Victim, and its spilt "blood of innocence" cancels all guilt: "[This is] the effect of his bloodshed, that sinne be not imputed unto us" (Calvin II.xvii.4). Thus, the lady's yielding will be no holocaust and no sin, but an erotic *communion*.

The analogy between sexual yielding and Protestant eucharist is set up by the poem's movement: it starts with static gazing upon an elevated sign and shifts to the un"waste"ed use of that sign; this sequence recalls the Protestant response to visual adoration of the eucharist, which for many Catholics had replaced the taking of communion.[3] The Elizabethan "Homilie of the worthy receiving and reverend esteeming of the Sacrament" urges believers not to hold back from participation in the meal "although it seeme of small vertue to some" but rather to seek the "fruition and union" of the eucharistic banquet in which they may "sucke the sweetnesse of everlasting salvation" (*Certaine Sermons* 197, 199, 200):

> To this, his commandement forceth us. . . . To this, his promise entiseth . . . So then of necessity we must be our selves partakers . . . and not beholders. (198)

2. See, for example Luther's "A Treatise on the New Testament" (*Works* 35: 94–101) and "The Babylonian Captivity of the Church" (*Works* 36: 51–55).
3. See, for example, Calvin: "They consecrate an host, as they call it, which they may carie about in pompe, which they may shew foorth in a common gazing to be loked upon, worshipped, and called upon" (*Institutes* IV. xvii. 37). For a concise explanation of medieval Catholic "communion through the eyes," see the section entitled "The Gaze that Saves" in Emminghaus's second chapter.

The speaker of the poem also feels "enticed" to do more than just look. Though Neoplatonic lovers may vilify sexual "partaking" as an act of "small vertue," he presses forward to "sucke the sweetnesse" of a "fruition and union" which can save him from the death of frustration conventionally suffered by Petrarchan lovers. He wishes to avoid the folly of stupefied gazing—so mockingly repudiated in "Elegy XIX"—and become one of those who "taste whole joys," as the speaker of the elegy puts it.

The lady moves things in the right direction by handling the sign (none too gently) rather than merely "Marke[ing]" it as the speaker first asked her. But physical violence done to outward signs does *not*, he hopes to convince her, destroy what they represent. Renaissance Protestants stressed that Christ's body is not chewed up, swallowed, and digested along with the bread; the homily on the Sacrament explains that it is "a ghostly substance" which believers "receive . . . with the hand of [the] heart" (*Certaine Sermons* 200–201). The speaker of "The Flea" wants the lady to think in the same way of her "honor"—that "ghostly" or intangible signified which she has so closely identified with the tangible signifier called "maidenhead." Though he never directly promises to receive her honor into his keeping, he hopes to convince her that its substance will not be lost and "wast"ed when her hymen breaks. Thus, the ambiguous syntax of the penultimate line gives the impression that "yeeld'st" is a transitive verb with "honor" as its direct object: "Just so much honor, when thou yeeld'st to mee," he says, and we expect to hear next what will happen after she has yielded "just so much honor" to him. Of course, "honor" turns out to be the subject of the completed sentence, "yeeld'st" intransitive, and the "when . . ." clause parenthetical, but even after we hear the speaker's statement in full, the impression remains: her honor will not be *wasted on him* because it will not be wasted *by* him when she yields.[4] He may want to consume her virginity, but as a semiotic sophisticate, he knows the difference between sign and signified, between defloration and dishonor, between giving over and giving in.

Thus, if the lady of the poem wishes to be married in fact as well as in flea, she may grant her lover's request on conditions his own imagery suggests. She may insist that he receive her eucharistic virginity—and the honor it signifies—with the reverence and faithfulness of a devout communicant who receives "with the hand of the heart." If she does so, she will be committing herself to him. For in conveying himself through the eucharist, Christ confirms that he will

4. See also Donne's insistence that we must "apply [Christ's] bloud . . . shed for us, by those meanes which God in his Church presents to us," since not to do so would be a "wastfull wantonnesse" (*Sermons* 3:162–163).

never abandon the faithful believer; as Calvin puts it, he "doth . . .
so communicate his body to us, that he is made throughly one with
us" (IV.xvii.38). In the same way, the lady who conveys her honor as
she yields her body assures the lover to whom she entrusts them that
she will never absent herself from him. The female speaker of
another Donne poem makes the point eloquently: "I faine would
stay," says the woman in "Breake of day," for "I [love] my heart and
honor so, / That I would not from him, that had them, goe" (10,11–
12; emphasis mine).

But it is a very worried lady who speaks those lines, and her
"aubade" reminds us of the dangers involved in yielding. Having sur-
rendered body, heart, and honor to her lover, the Renaissance mis-
tress must fear that he will abandon her and take everything *but* her
body with him. Will the lady of "The Flea" risk such danger? Clearly,
she still has the option of refusing altogether; she can point out that
what the speaker says about his spurious private symbol has no bear-
ing on the socially determined relation between the sign of virginity
and the substance of honor.[5] Will she allow her lover to consume
that sign? Will she convey to him that substance?

If she is anything like the woman Donne married, she may. The
lady's scruples and anxieties do not necessarily imply that the
speaker's love is unrequited. "Though parents grudge, and you, w'are
met," he says; and as Marotti points out, "the progression from 'par-
ents' to 'you' to 'we' . . . places the woman rhetorically, emotionally,
and morally between the disapproving parents and the importunate
suitor" (94).[6] This is precisely the situation in which Ann More,
Donne's own beloved, found herself; and as Edward LeComte
argues, Ann may have escaped the impasse by consummating her
relationship with Jack before the clandestine ceremony in which they
took their vows. LeComte consults two key documents: a letter
Donne wrote to his father-in-law on 2 February 1602 [New Style],
in which he claims that their wedding took place "about three weeks
before Christmas" 1601, and a record of the court's decision on the
secret marriage's validity, dated 27 April 1602. Noting the vagueness
and inconsistency of the dates cited in these documents, and con-
sidering seventeenth-century attitudes toward clandestine marriage,
LeComte speculates on the actual "sequence of events":

> Ann and John, after a separation of many months, found each
> other irresistible when at last they met again several times in

5. See also Rajan's argument (809) that the *Songs and Sonets* invite resistance, that they
evoke a response much like the one Donne solicited for the *Paradoxes and Problems* when
he described them as "swaggerers" and "alarums to truth."
6. Marotti concludes that the poem pits "a shame morality that views loss of virginity before
marriage as a woman's greatest dishonor . . . against a personalist morality that regards
the intention of commitment (and marriage) as largely legitimizing the premarital inter-
course of mutual lovers" (94).

the fall of 1601. They had made solemn promises to each other, and looked forward to marrying. Physical union was not an evasion of, but a way into, marriage: it strengthened their legal claims on each other. So, with the dissolution of Parliament on 19 December, Ann was taken back by her father to Loseley, neither a virgin nor a bride. In January, it probably was, the girl sent word to her lover in London that she had reason to believe she was pregnant. Thereupon, . . . she escaped from her father long enough for a secret ceremony. [Donne], when at last he had to inform Sir George More, predated the marriage so that the couple's first child, Constance, would be born nine months afterwards, not seven or eight. (20)[7]

   The marriage did not stay secret for long—a pregnancy would help explain that fact—and Donne found himself in a very delicate situation. Hoping to placate his father-in-law, he composed the aforementioned letter. In it, he confesses that he and Ann married in December, but claims that they had committed themselves to one another even before the ceremony; his spurious argument recalls the one advanced in "The Flea." Comparing the lovers' precontract to a building with a strong foundation, Donne argues in the letter that their private engagement was—like the flea as "marriage temple"— too holy to be torn down: "So long since as her being at York House this had *foundacion*, and so much then of promise and contract *built* upon yt, as withowt violence to conscience might not be shaken" (*Selected Prose* 113; emphases mine). He then intercedes for Ann as the poem's speaker does for the flea, begging "that she may not to her danger feele the terror of your *sodaine* anger"; Donne fears that his father-in-law will, like the lady of the poem, react with "cruell and sodaine" violence. But he can't leave it at that; with the same saucy impudence displayed by the speaker of the poem, he goes on to stress that, "Though parents grudge, . . . [they] *are* met":

> I know no passion can alter your reason and wisdome, to which I adventure to commend these particulers; that yt is irremediably donne; that if yow incense my Lord [Egerton, Donne's employer] yow destroy her and me; [and] that yt is easye to give us happines . . . (113)

"[I]t is irremediably donne"; the marriage is consummated, and Ann More is now, quite irreversibly, Ann Donne. Like the speaker of the poem, the bridegroom argues that the union he defends is a *fait accompli* and points out "How little" it would take for the addressee to make him happy. But he does so, like the speaker of the poem, partly to keep the potential benefactor from "killing three": himself, his spouse, and—if LeComte is right—their unborn child.

7. As LeComte notes, the exact dates of Constance's birth and baptism are not known.

Surely Janet Halley is right to caution readers against the hope that they can know the "real" Ann More Donne through the textual constructions of her husband.[8] But the parallels between these two texts—one a dramatic lyric and the other a petitionary letter—can lead us to a clearer appreciation for the lady who speaks in eloquent silence between the stanzas of "The Flea," and for the poet's intentions in devising her. The intention of Donne's letter to George More is clear: he wants his father-in-law's blessing (and with it his financial assistance); he wishes to defuse More's anger, to persuade him to endorse the union. He thus describes and defends Ann as a young woman who has, heroically, risked everything for the sake of mutual commitment: "We both knew the obligacions that lay upon us, and we adventured equally" (113). In the poem, Donne invites the reader to view the exchange between the speaker and the lady in a similar light, to see that, if the young lady of "The Flea" chooses to take seriously the quasi-eucharistic signs which her lover offers, she, too, will "adventure equally" and convert "what we would *doe*" to an act "irremediably *donne*." She will embrace her lover's sacramental imagery and insist that the gift of her virginity be considered no less binding than a precontract.

As critics of the poem, we can insist on no one reading, no one way of taking the sacrament; readers will continue to decide for themselves.[9] But we cannot avoid envisioning a range of specific outcomes from chaste denial to playful submission or reasoned acquiescence, and the speaker does seem set on excluding the possibility of outright refusal. As Baumlin notes, "the poem erects logically and morally specious arguments that the skeptical reader, taking the addressee's part, must seek to refute" (242), but it "cannot be fully defeated, for its arguments resist a reader's resistance, refusing to deconstruct" (244).

Calvin explains the effectiveness of sacramental grace in terms that may explain such stubborn persistence: a sacrament is like a rhetorical persuasion, he asserts, and the operation of the Holy Spirit ensures that its rhetoric cannot fail. It guarantees that the signs presented to the faithful *will* take effect, for it prepares their hearts to

---

8. Because Donne's *Songs and Sonets* cannot be dated with any certainty, the parallels between the poem and the letter cannot be applied to a biographical account of the poet, either; but as Shawcross stresses, such applications tend, at any rate, to limit rather than enrich our understanding of Donne's lyrics (see "Poetry, Personal and Impersonal"). What I am exploring in this reading, then, is not "The Flea" as biographical document, but rather the parallel between the rhetorical project Donne undertook in the letter and the lyric project he undertook in "The Flea."

9. The letter to George More, for its part, did not persuade its addressee; far from convincing Ann's father to bless the match, Donne's rhetoric seems, understandably, to have incensed him further—just as the speaker's argument provokes the lady to extreme measures in the first two stanzas of "The Flea." When Donne wrote to Sir George again on 11 February, it was from the Fleet Prison, where he was held for a brief period after having been dismissed from Egerton's service.

receive them (*Institutes* IV.xiv.9–10). In the sacramental persuasions of erotic love, a successful seduction presupposes the influence of another inward flame: the spirit of mutual desire. If that is present, it will—to borrow Calvin's wording—"truely bring to passe that the hearer . . . will obey the selfe same counsels which otherwise he wold have laughed to scorne" (*Institutes* IV.xiv.10). Such predestinate wooing, such preaching to the converted, is—Donne argues in one of his verse epistles—the only kind a man should attempt: "Man's better part consists of purer fire, / And findes it selfe allow'd, ere it desire," he says ("That unripe side of earth" 59–60). Perhaps it is this logic which underlies "The Flea," with its confident allusion to a future "When"—not "if"—the lady yields.

WORKS CITED

Augustine. "Tractates on the Gospel of John." *Patrologia cursus completus* 35. Ed. J. P. Migne. Paris: 1878–1890.

Baumlin, James S. *John Donne and the Rhetorics of Renaissance Discourse*. Columbia: U of Missouri P, 1991.

Brumble, H. David, III. "John Donne's 'The Flea': Some Implications of the Encyclopedic and Poetic Flea Traditions." *Critical Q* 15 (1973): 147–154.

Calvin, John. *The Institution of the Christian Religion*. Trans. Thomas Norton. London: Thomas Vautrollier for Humfrey Toy, 1578.

Certaine Sermons or Homilies Appointed to be Read in Churches In the Time of Queen Elizabeth I (1547–1571). A Facsimile Reproduction of the Edition of 1623. Intr. by Mary Ellen Rickey and Thomas B. Stroup. Gainesville, FL: Scholars' Facsimiles and Reprints, 1968.

Docherty, Thomas. *John Donne Undone*. London: Methuen, 1986.

Donne, John. *Selected Prose*. Chosen by Evelyn Simpson. Ed. Helen Gardner and Timothy Healy. Oxford: Clarendon P, 1967.

Emminghaus, Johannes H. *The Eucharist: Essence, Form, Celebration*. Trans. Matthew J. O'Connell. Collegeville, MN: Liturgical P, 1978.

Gardner, Helen, ed. "General Introduction." *John Donne: The Elegies and The Songs and Sonnets*. Oxford: Clarendon P, 1965. xvii–lxii.

Gilman, Ernest B. *Iconoclasm and Poetry in the English Reformation: Down Went Dagon*. Chicago: U of Chicago P, 1986.

Halley, Janet E. "Textual Intercourse: Anne Donne, John Donne, and the Sexual Poetics of Textual Exchange." *Seeking the Woman in Late Medieval and Renaissance Writings: Essays in Feminist Contextual Criticism*. Ed. Sheila Fisher and Janet E. Halley. Knoxville: U of Tennessee P, 1989. 187–206.

Hester, M. Thomas. " 'this cannot be said': A Preface to the Reader of Donne's Lyrics." *Christianity and Literature* 39 (1990): 365–385.

Hooker, Richard. *The Works of that Learned and Judicious Divine Mr. Richard Hooker*. Ed. John Keble. 7th. ed. Rev. by R. W. Church and F. Paget. 3 vols. Oxford: Clarendon P, 1888.

LeComte, Edward. "Jack Donne: From Rake to Husband." *Just So Much Honor: Essays Commemorating the Four-Hundredth Anniversary of the Birth of John Donne*. Ed. Peter Amadeus Fiore. University Park: Pennsylvania State UP, 1972. 9–32.

Luther, Martin. "The Babylonian Captivity of the Church." Trans. A. T. W. Steinhauser and Rev. by Frederick C. Ahrens and Abel Ross Wentz. *Works*. 36. Ed. Abel Ross Wentz. Philadelphia: Muhlenberg P, 1959.

———. "A Treatise on the New Testament, that is, the Holy Mass." Trans. Jeremiah J. Schindel. Rev. by E. Theodore Bachmann. *Works*. 35. Ed. Theodore Bachmann. Philadelphia: Muhlenberg P, 1960.

Marotti, Arthur. *John Donne, Coterie Poet*. Madison: U of Wisconsin P, 1986.

Mayne, Jasper. "On Dr. Donnes death: By Mr. Mayne of Christ-Church in Oxford." *Poems, By J.D. with Elegies on the Authors Death*. London: Printed by M.F. for John Marriot, 1633. Facs. ed. Menston, England: Scolar P, 1970. 393–396.

Perrine, Laurence. "Explicating Donne: 'The Apparition' and 'The Flea'." *College Literature* 17 (1990): 1–20.

Rajan, Tilottama. " 'Nothing Sooner Broke': Donne's *Songs and Sonets* as Self-Consuming
    Artifact." *ELH* 49 (1982): 805–828.
Shawcross, John T. *Intentionality and the New Traditionalism: Some Liminal Means to Lit-
    erary Revisionism*. University Park: Pennsylvania State UP, 1991.
———. "Poetry, Personal and Impersonal: The Case of Donne." *The Eagle and the Dove:
    Reassessing John Donne*. Ed. Claude J. Summers and Ted-Larry Pebworth. Columbia: U
    of Missouri P, 1986. 53–66.
Sidney, Philip. *Sir Philip Sidney*. Ed. Katherine Duncan-Jones. Oxford: Oxford UP, 1989.
Spacks, Patricia Meyer. "In Search of Sincerity." *College English* 29 (1968): 591–602. Wil-
    son, David B. "*La Puce de Madame Desroches* and John Donne's 'The Flea.' " *Neuphilol-
    ogische Mitteilungen* 72 (1971): 297–301.
Winny, James. *A Preface to Donne*. New York: Scribners, 1970.

CAMILLE WELLS SLIGHTS

A Pattern of Love: Representations of Anne Donne†

The Anne Donne of critical discourse is the absent presence in
poems of mutual love such as "A Valediction forbidding mourning"
and the present absence in the sonnet of grief and loss beginning
"Since she whome I lovd, hath payd her last debt." She is the pas-
sionate lover whom J. B. Leishman posited as the inspiration for
"The Sunne Rising,"[1] the intelligent, educated woman Dennis Flynn
has suggested as audience of "Womans Constancy,"[2] and the bur-
densome wife in John Carey's account of John Donne's life.[3] The
extent to which any of these Annes can be identified with the his-
torical Anne More who married John Donne in 1601 and died in
1617 shortly after giving birth to her twelfth child is unclear. John
Carey agrees with most critics that "Since she whome I lovd, hath
payd her last debt" refers to Anne's death but believes that the
"ardour of the love poems . . . does not correspond to the realities of
Donne's married life."[4] In his view, if the passionately loved woman
of poems like "The Sunne Rising" corresponds to reality at all, it is
as a defiantly imagined compensation for the embittering conse-
quences of Donne's marriage. Carey finds a more direct account of
the marriage in a letter from Donne to his friend Sir Henry Goodyer:
"I write from the fire side in my Parler, and in the noise of three
gamesome children; and by the side of her, whom because I have
transplanted into a wretched fortune, I must labour to disguise that

† From *John Donne's "desire of more": The Subject of Anne More Donne in His Poetry*, ed.
   M. Thomas Hester (Newark: U of Delaware P, 1996), pp. 66–67, 77–87. Reprinted by
   permission of the publisher.
1. J. B. Leishman, *The Monarch of Wit* (1951; reprint, New York: Harper & Row, 1965),
   188.
2. Dennis Flynn, "Donne and a *Female* Coterie," *Literature, Interpretation, Theory* 1 (1989):
   127–36.
3. John Carey, *John Donne: Life, Mind and Art* (London: Faber and Faber, 1981).
4. Carey, 58, 75.

from her by all such honest devices, as giving her my company, and discourse."[5] From this, Carey concludes that "[a]ctually staying in the same room as his wife was . . . scarcely more than a benign duty" for Donne.[6] Arthur Marotti believes more firmly than Carey does that some of the poems refer directly to Donne's relationship with his wife, arguing that encoded clues refer knowing readers to the actual circumstances of his marriage. But Marotti agrees with Carey that Donne's strongest feelings focused on his career prospects and on friendships with an elite group of sophisticated, intelligent men and that poetic claims of self-sufficient love compensate for bitter disappointment and powerlessness. Such witty hyperboles as "She'is all States, and all Princes, I" are emotionally authenticating for Anne, "the putative addressee or primary reader," but for Donne's coterie of male readers they "signaled his frustrated needs."[7] Even then for scholars who reject the notion of autonomous verbal structures and who investigate the relations between texts and their historical and biographical moments, Anne Donne is an elusive figure obscured by the opacities of language and the intricacies of human motive.

Written texts are cultural events that mediate relations among the world, the author, and the reader, but they cannot provide transparent access to historical reality. Interpretations differ as unavoidably as readers' experiences and expectations do, and texts transform the reality they represent. These unstable interrelations operate whether the text represents the wife from whom Donne must try to disguise the wretchedness of their common fortune in the letter to Goodyer or the beloved whose eyes outshine the sun or the dead woman who whetted her lover's mind to seek God. In each case, the text points toward, without making present, a woman existing beyond the written representation, and in each case the text foregrounds the author's self-representation. Whether we hear "benign duty" or tender solicitude in the letter, masculine egotism or sensitive responsiveness in "The Sunne Rising," and anguished grief or "disturbing fear and guilt"[8] in the sonnet, our readings are contingent on interpretations of complex verbal evidence from within different and conflicting theoretical frameworks, and inevitably they diverge. But they all focus on the perceiving speaker rather than on the woman perceived.

5. John Donne, *Letters to Severall Persons of Honour* (1651), introd. M. Thomas Hester (New York: Scholars' Facsimiles & Reprints, 1977), 137. I quote Donne's letters from this edition, giving page numbers parenthetically in my text. I quote the poetry from *The Complete Poetry of John Donne*, ed. John T. Shawcross (New York: New York University Press, 1968), citing line numbers parenthetically.
6. Carey, 74.
7. Arthur F. Marotti, *John Donne, Coterie Poet* (Madison: University of Wisconsin Press, 1986), 139, 156.
8. Marotti, 138.

When we try to recover the historical Anne Donne from the written records of her life, we find only isolated facts about her marriage and children and a few references to her exemplary behavior as wife and mother.[9] The great majority of the traces left by Anne Donne are to be found in the writings of her husband, and when we follow them, we reach John, not Anne Donne. Donne's writings give us not the actual woman but a man's representations of her or, more precisely, a man's representations of himself perceiving her. As Janet E. Halley observes, "a search for Anne Donne's historical presence in the writing of her husband . . . displaces the historical woman with masculine desire."[1]

*   *   *

As social transactions, Donne's poems, like his letters, are attempts to shape his readers' perceptions and ideals as well as to forge alliances between men. While we can never know whether or to what extent the poems of mutual love correspond to the historical reality of the relationship of Anne More and John Donne during their courtship and marriage, such knowledge is unnecessary for our acceptance of the crucial role Anne Donne plays in them. An historical entity is never identical with its poetic representation. As Wolfgang Iser observes, "its very fictionality shows that what is represented is merely an 'image,' is put in parentheses and thus accorded the status of 'as if'." Still, the obverse is also true, as Iser acknowledges: "Fiction always contains a representation of something."[2] Reading and interpreting are a process of discovering connections between representations and the world—"discovering" both in the sense of creating new perspectives on our own lives and in the sense of finding what is already there in the text that relates to the historical realities that produced it. Marotti has demonstrated that references to the circumstances of Donne's life, including puns on Anne More's name, encouraged contemporaries to read certain poems as representations of the relationship of John and Anne Donne. Subsequent readers from Isaac Walton through Janet Halley have interpreted the loved woman in the poems of mutual love as representations of Anne Donne. If the meanings of literary works are, as Iser argues, the products of interaction between text and

---

9. R. C. Bald, *John Donne: A Life* (New York: Oxford University Press, 1970), 326.
1. Janet E. Halley, "Textual Intercourse: Anne Donne, John Donne, and the Sexual Poetics of Textual Exchange," in *Seeking the Woman in Late Medieval and Renaissance Writings: Essays in Feminist Contextual Criticism*, ed. Sheila Fisher and Janet E. Halley (Knoxville, Tenn.: University of Tennessee Press, 1989), 188. I cite this essay parenthetically within my text.
2. Wolfgang Iser, "The Current Situation of Literary Theory: Key Concepts and the Imaginary," *New Literary History* 11 (1979): 18.

reader, then the power of these poems as imitable models of hetero-
sexual love relies on her.

As a fictional representation of a loved woman, Anne Donne is a
powerful and empowering presence, and Donne's male friends are
marginalized as fictive and actual spectators and readers. A distinc-
tive feature of Donne's poems of mutual love is the opposition
between the humiliating dependency demanded by the external
world ("Goe tell Court-huntsmen, that the King will ride") and the
power the lovers enjoy ("She'is all States, and all Princes, I"). Even
representations of the loved woman's absence testify to her power:
("Thy firmnes makes my circle just, / And makes me end, where I
begunne"). Unlike the early *Elegies*, where women are objects to be
conquered and possessed, these poems move to obliterate the sub-
ject/object distinction in an evocation of mutual desire. Compare,
for example, the imagery of new-world exploration in "Elegie: Going
to Bed":

> O my America! my new-found-land,
> My kingdome, safeliest when with one man man'd,
> My Myne of precious stones: My Emperie,
> How blest am I in this discovering thee!
>
> (27–30)

with its use in "The good-morrow":

> Let sea-discoverers to new worlds have gone,
> Let Maps to others, worlds on worlds have showne,
> Let us possesse one world, each hath one, and is one.
>
> (12–14)

Even "The Sunne Rising," which reinscribes the culture's gender
hierarchy, simultaneously uses geopolitical images to undermine it.
The woman is first "both the'India's of spice and Myne" (17); next,
"She'is all States, and all Princes, I" (21); and then: "Princes doe but
play us" (23). Figuring the woman in sequence as exploitable riches,
the universal body politic, and (along with the speaker) the only gen-
uine ruler, the poem progressively empowers her. Finally, as third-
and first-person singular pronouns give way to first-person plural,
the topic becomes not the lovers but their relationship, their present
happiness: "compar'd to this, / All honor's mimique; All wealth
alchimie" (23–24). Considerations of relative power are never very
far from Donne's texts and do not disappear when he turns from
witty libertine elegies and lyrics to celebrations of reciprocal love.
But by deliberately foregrounding and undercutting gender hierar-
chies, these poems effectively, if temporarily, neutralize them.

They not only dislocate the social and political structures of male dominance, they also undermine the Petrarchan fantasy of female dominance. By such strategies as mocking the clichés of "tearefloods" and "sigh-tempests" ("A Valediction forbidding mourning," 6), placing the lovers in bed ("The Sunne Rising"), and wittily exploiting such sexual puns as "Wee dye and rise the same" ("The Canonization," 26), the poems conspicuously reject the literary tradition of representing the male as an impotently suffering lover and the female as unmoved mover. Donne's poems also avoid the poetic *blazon* of women's beauty through which, as Nancy Vickers has shown, many Renaissance love poets defended themselves against female power by figuratively objectifying and fragmenting the female body.[3] Instead of dissecting the female body into eyes, lips, and hands, Donne famously presents images of wholeness and mutuality: "Love . . . makes both one, each this and that" ("The Extasie," 35–36); "Let us possesse one world, each hath one, and is one" ("The goodmorrow," 14); "The Phoenix ridle hath more wit / By us, we two being one, are it" ("The Canonization," 23–24).

Donne's poems do not display woman's fragmented body to the voyeuristic gaze of male readers, but they do illustrate one of the primary strategies of control Vickers analyzes: they silence the woman's voice. Although an occasional poem like "Breake of day" or "Sapho to Philænis" ventriloquizes a woman's voice and "The Flea" reports a woman's speech in indirect discourse, in general Donne's poems do not provide even the limited feminine speech of Sidney's Stella or Spenser's Elizabeth. Nevertheless, the poems of mutual love ascribe subjectivity, independent ideas and desires, and effective agency to a woman who is not a passive object either of sexual desire or of adoration. For example, the argument presented in "A Valediction forbidding mourning" implicitly assumes that the woman addressed requires persuading.[4] But our access to her interiority is filtered through her lover's perceptions, and her power is limited to eliciting his response. As noted earlier, the representations of Anne Donne in John Donne's prose letters are twice removed from the actual woman. She does not represent herself in any extant text— we have only her husband's representation, and he represents not her directly but himself responding to her. Similarly, in the most impassioned love poems the beloved's identity is wholly dependent on her lover's perception of her.

But the corollary of that observation is that his is dependent on her. The speaking subject in the poems of reciprocal, consummated

3. Nancy Vickers, "Diana Described: Scattered Women and Scattered Rhyme," *Critical Inquiry* 8 (1981): 265–79.
4. See Ilona Bell's suggestive argument that most of Donne's lyrics are shaped by the speaker's accommodations to the point of view of the woman addressed. "The Role of the Lady in Donne's *Songs and Sonets*," *Studies in English Literature* 23 (1983): 113–29.

love constitutes itself through perceptions of the beloved's responses. Often, he defines both their lives in terms of their perceptions of each other. In "The Anniversarie" he recalls "When thou and I first one another saw" (5) and then describes a present and plans a future contingent on that mutual recognition. "The good-morrow" contrasts his earlier unitary perceptions, "If ever any beauty I did see" (6), with their present all-controlling mutuality:

> And now good morrow to our waking soules,
>   Which watch not one another out of feare;
> For love, all love of other sights controules,
>   And makes one little roome, an every where.
>   (8–11)

Even in "The Sunne Rising" with its arrogant self-assertion ("I could eclipse and cloud them with a winke"), his independent power is controlled by his perception of her: "But that I would not lose her sight so long" (13–14). By enacting the interdependence of the lovers' perceptions of themselves and their world, these poems escape from the subject/object model and construct an identity that views another person not as wholly external but as helping to constitute the self.

These explorations of interdependent wholeness contrast radically with the fear of losing integrity and autonomy through participation in society that runs through Donne's writings. A verse letter to Sir Henry Wotton, roughly contemporary with the satires, laments our necessary involvement in social relations: countries, courts, towns are equally evil, but "though then pitch they staine worse, wee must touch" ("Sir, more then kisses," 10). "Men are spunges" (37), Donne complains; similarly in his role as satirist listening to scurrilous court gossip, he "felt [him] selfe then / Beccomming Traytor" ("Satyre IV," 130–31). In a letter to Goodyer discussed above, Donne deplores fragmentation rather than contamination, decrying life at court as "a line discontinued, and a number of small wretched points, uselesse, because they concurre not" (61–62). Some of Donne's love poetry too expresses this fear of losing personal wholeness, the other side of the bullying assertion of control in the *Elegies* and some of the *Songs and Sonets*. In "Loves exchange," for example, the lover gives his soul but receives nothing in return but the torture of "being cut up, and torne . . . and dissect[ed]" (39–40). In "The broken heart" love is figured as permanent loss of physical wholeness: "I brought a heart into the roome, / But from the roome, I carried none with mee" (19–20):

> . . . I thinke my breast hath all
>   Those peeces still, though they be not unite;
> And now as broken glasses show

A hundred lesser faces, so
  My ragges of heart can like, wish, and adore,
  But after one such love, can love no more.
                    (27–32)

And in Donne's variation on the exchange of hearts conceit in "The Legacie," love entails not merely self-loss but invasion by an alien entity entirely without integrity. Ripping himself open, the speaker found:

  . . . something like a heart,
    But colours it, and corners had,
    It was not good, it was not bad,
  It was intire to none, and few had part.
                    (17–20)

In the early verse letters to male friends the solution proposed to the dangers of an unstable self is withdrawal into the self. A verse letter to Rowland Woodward recommends that we seek "our selves in our selves," advising that, just as a lens can concentrate the sun's rays, so we can ignite our virtues to burn away impurities "If wee into our selves will turne" ("Like one who'in her third widdowhood," 19, 22). Similarly, the answer to the problem of being a sponge in the verse letter to Sir Henry Wotton is "in thy selfe dwell" (47). Though the poem addressed to Woodward uneasily recommends "retirednesse" (28) as a way to the self, this poem to Wotton unequivocally argues for psychological not physical detachment. Learn from the "white integritie" (42) of beasts, Donne advises. Imitate the snail, which "Carrying his owne house still, still is at home," and "Bee thine owne Palace" (50, 52) wherever you are. Imitate fish:

  Fishes glide, leaving no print where they passe,
  Nor making sound; so, closely thy course goe;
  Let men dispute, whether thou breathe, or no.
                    (56–58)

The poems of mutual love in the *Songs and Sonets*, then, are notable not in their acknowledgment of threats to personal autonomy but in their claims for unified wholeness through, rather than in spite of, relationships with other people. In "Loves infinitenesse," for example, the exchange of heart conceit undergoes yet another transformation, representing what I, drawing on the object-relations theory expounded by Nancy Chodorow and Carol Gilligan, will call a relational self:

  Loves riddles are, that though thy heart depart,
  It stayes at home, and thou with losing savest it:
  But wee will have a way more liberall,

> Then changing hearts, to joyne them, so wee shall
> Be one, and one anothers All.
>
> (29–33)

According to Chodorow, object-relations theory conceives of a self that is "intrinsically social, and, because it is constructed in a relational matrix and includes aspects of the other, it can better recognize the other as a self and, ultimately, attain the intersubjectivity that creates society." This model of the self with a "relationally based capacity both to be alone and to participate in the transitional space between self and other self that creates play, intimacy, and culture" correlates closely with the reconceptualization of public and private selves in the letters written after Donne's marriage and with the concept of the self in Donne's poems of mutual love.[5]

Probably his most famous image for a loving relationship that acknowledges interdependence while respecting individual difference is the compass analogy in "A Valediction forbidding mourning." This image is presented as an insight that emerges through the interaction between the inseparably separable lovers. Through the process of trying to persuade his beloved not to mourn, the speaker comes to understand his relational identity, gradually complementing and correcting partial insights. His response to her creates his voice, but the fact that he gives her no voice is a necessary manifestation of her otherness. His language can subsume them both in "our love" (8), but it cannot absorb her into his subjective interpretation of that experience. Through adherence to the interpretive power of individual consciousness developed in dialogue with another, Donne's poetic celebrations of mutual love control life's potentially destructive contingencies: "none can doe / Treason to us, except one of us two" ("The Anniversarie," 25–26); "houres, dayes, moneths" are seen as "the rags of time" ("The Sunne Rising," 10); and "one little roome" becomes "an every where" ("The good-morrow," 11). In contrast to the verse letter to Wotton where "Cities are Sepulchers," "Courts are Theaters," the "Country is a desert" ("Sir, more then kisses," 21, 23, 25), and participating in any of them puts the self at

---

5. Nancy Julia Chodorow, "Toward a Relational Individualism: The Mediation of Self Through Psychoanalysis," in *Reconstructing Individualism: Autonomy, Individuality, and the Self in Western Thought*, ed. Thomas C. Heller, Morton Sosna, and David E. Wellbery (Stanford: Stanford University Press, 1986), 204, 203. Also see in the same volume Carol Gilligan, "Remapping the Moral Domain: New Images of the Self in Relationship," 237–52. By using a term from object-relations theory, I do not intend to imply that Donne's concept of self transcends temporality. As Jane Roland Martin warns, the fear of ahistoricity can deprive us of useful concepts. Instead of avoiding Chodorow's and Gilligan's concepts as ahistorical, we can more productively historicize them (Jane Roland Martin, "Methodological Essentialism, False Difference, and Other Dangerous Traps," *Signs* 19 [1994]: 630–57). My argument that Donne constructs a self resembling the relational self is not intended as a critique of the hypothesis that today the relational self speaks in a female voice. Rather, I hope to contribute to the project of exposing to view changing concepts of the self.

risk, in these poems relations with others become a site of achieved identity.

This assertion of stability and wholeness in the face of the destructiveness of physical nature and of coercive political structures is often interpreted as an escape into an entirely self-contained private world transcending the contingencies of real life. For example, David Aers and Gunther Kress refer to "the socially alienated lovers" of "A nocturnall upon S. Lucies day . . ." and to Donne's claim for the lovers of "The Canonization" of "an utter self-sufficiency which seals them off from the social environment."[6] Anthony Low agrees, arguing that "Donne was among the earliest and most powerful proponents of love as a shelter and defense against the world" and finding in his private poems "the invention of an inner space, a magic circle of subjective immunity from outward political threat and from culturally induced anxiety."[7] I think that the boundary between the lovers and the outside world is far more permeable than these critics contend. Certainly love is a transforming experience in these poems, but the lovers are not detached from the rest of the world. The speaking subject constitutes himself in dialogue with the world as well as with his lover. Although Donne consistently thinks of interiority in terms of self-reflexivity,[8] his poetic speakers do not reflect in solitary meditation: for Donne, self-reflection is a dialogic process. Often, as in "A Valediction forbidding mourning," the lover incorporates awareness of social relations and structures into the lovers' realm through metaphor, analogy, and contrast. Sometimes he addresses a representative from the outside world, a representative either present, as in "The Canonization," or imagined, as in "The Sunne Rising." Whether internalized as the lover's contempt for "Dull sublunary lovers" and "Court-huntsmen" or externalized as an officious friend proffering worldly advice, the voice of the world beyond the lovers' relationship is always present, its assumptions and values making up part of the lover's consciousness and helping to shape his relational identity.

Typically, in the poems of reciprocal love, the lover defines himself and the lovers' private world in opposition to the public world,

6. Aers and Kress, 56, 60.
7. Low, 473, 474. Low suggests the term "communal" for Donne's private world that involves being in the company of another, but his emphasis is on the lovers' separateness from ordinary society.
8. See, for example, *Letters*, 12: "for as the greatest advantage which mans soul is thought to have beyond others, is that which they call *Actum reflexum*, and *iteratum*, . . . so of those which they call *Actum reflexum* the noblest is that which reflects upon the soul itself, and considers and meditates it." Cf. "18 Meditation": "They see the *soule* is nothing else in other *Creatures*, and they affect an *impious humilitie*, to think *as low of Man*. But if my *soule* were no more than the soule of a *beast*, I could not thinke so; that *soule* that can *reflect* upon it selfe, *consider* it selfe, is *more* than so": *Devotions Upon Emergent Occasions*, ed. Anthony Raspa (New York: Oxford University Press, 1987), 91.

celebrating the permanence and mutuality of their love in contrast to the mutability and dependency that vitiate and debase the lives of other people. Then, having set up a contrast between the private and public, he collapses the opposition by including the public world within the private one. The first stanza of "The Sunne Rising" dismisses the sun and the power of time as relevant to the outside worlds of city, court, and country but irrelevant to love. But by the last stanza the sun is welcomed to the lovers' bed that now contains the entire world, including its political and economic structures as well as its geographical expanse. Similarly, "The Canonization" first impatiently rejects all forms of social ambition that are not love and justifies love on the grounds of its self-containment. The lover claims that his love has no effect on the rest of the world:

> Alas, alas, who's injur'd by my love?
>   What merchants ships have my sighs drown'd?
> Who saies my teares have overflow'd his ground?
>   (10–12)

And the world has no effect on the lovers: "Call us what you will, wee'are made such by love" (19). But in the last stanza the lovers have taken possession of that excluded world: their "eyes" have been.

> . . . made such mirrors, and such spies,
>   That they did all to you epitomize,
> Countries, Townes, Courts . . .
>   (42–44)

Some readers interpret this intrusion of the public into the private as an artistic flaw caused by Donne's frustrated ambition showing through the cracks of his projected image of moral superiority to worldly success. According to Arthur Marotti, the "mention of the larger environment that surrounds the loving couple contaminates the context of religious, amorous, and aesthetic idealization with a pointed reference to the society in which the poet's career has been 'ruin'd' (3)," and the lover's exaggerated claims "reveal the breakdown of the strategy of idealizing rather than the transcendence of the context in which the conflicts between love and ambition are painfully experienced."[9] While I have no quarrel with Marotti's hypothesis that Donne's need for a job influenced the writing of such poems as "The Canonization," I want to argue that his rhetorical strategy is not to idealize the private as transcendent self-containment but to undermine the dichotomy of public and private by showing the interaction of the personal and the political, the private and the public. The satisfactions of love afford Donne's lovers the distance to be

9. Marotti, 165.

critically aware of the contentiousness and humiliations of most social and political relations and to choose to form a relationship of trust and mutuality rather than of competition and domination, one in which both are "Kings" and both "subjects" and "none can doe / Treason to us, except one of us two" ("The Anniversarie," 23, 24, 25–26). Awareness of the political helps to form the personal, and the security of the personal provides not a refuge but a basis from which to evaluate and instruct the public.

This active interchange between the lovers and the world also characterizes the representation of the physical. While the subjective experience of union enables the lover of "A Valediction forbidding mourning" to claim that physical separation is not "A breach, but an expansion" (23), physical limitations provoke him to a more complex understanding of an emotional bond between two people. In letters, fear of death leads Donne to articulate a sense of relational identity. Writing to Goodyer during "the saddest . . . nights passage that I ever had" while he feared for Anne's life, Donne claims, "I should hardly have abstained from recompensing for her company in this world, with accompanying her out of it" (*Letters*, 147). Several years later when sickness threatens his family, Donne again registers his sense of interdependent lives: Anne has "fallen into an indisposition, which would afflict her much, but that the sicknesse of her children stupefies her: of one of which, in good faith, I have not much hope. . . . I flatter myself in this, that I am dying too: nor can I truly dye faster, by any waste, then by losse of children" (*Letters*, 152–53). In poems too the precariousness of life triggers perception of the union of selves through love. In "A Feaver," "The Dissolution," and "A nocturnall . . ." the loved woman is dead or dying, and physical vulnerability overwhelms private emotional space. "The Anniversarie," which claims that "All other things, to their destruction draw, / Only our love hath no decay" (6–7), admits that "Two graves must hide thine and my coarse" (11), and this awareness motivates the choice of commitment and constancy. Because the lover is aware of the sun's inexorable movement in "Lecture upon the Shadow," he realizes the need to avoid self-deception and understands that "Love is a growing, or full constant light / And his first minute, after noone, is night" (25–26).

The world of Donne's lovers, then, is not hermetically sealed, divorced from contingency and process. Nor are the lovers "such mirrors, and such spies" that they quietly reflect and assess the folly of other mortals as unobserved observers. They are not a pair of snails moving slowly in tandem or two cold fish going so "closely" that "men dispute, whether [they] breathe, or no" ("Sir, more then kisses," 57, 58). Admittedly, "The undertaking" attributes virtue to the concealment of a nonsexual love; the unrequited lover in "The triple Foole" and "Loves exchange" sees merit in keeping love hidden; and the lover working his way to understanding love in "A Valediction forbidding mourning" sees imperceptibility as positive. But a far more characteristic feature of Donne's self-representation as a loved lover is a propensity for publishing his love to the world. This impulse is clearly evident in "The Canonization," where he rejects the genre designed for recording public events as unsuitable for the lovers' story in favor of a personal literary form ("And if no peece of Chronicle wee prove, / We'll build in sonnets pretty roomes" [31–32]), only to replace the private sonnet with a communal hymn by which "all . . . approve" the lovers and acknowledge needing a "patterne of [their] love" (35, 45). Although this strategy of offering the lover's perceptions as an imitable model is most fully worked out in "The Canonization," it recurs in various forms. "The Sunne Rising" moves from withdrawal from the world to an exhibitionistic welcoming of the world's gaze, and the idea of kingship transforms from contemptuously dismissed other: "Goe tell Court-huntsmen, that the King will ride" (7); through metaphor: "She'is all States, and all Princes, I" (21); to a figure in which the lovers are the pattern imitated: "Princes doe but play us" (23). In "A nocturnall" the speaker invites other lovers to "Study me" (10). In "Valediction of the booke" he urges his "deare Love" to "write our Annals" (1, 12) for the benefit not just of lovers but of all posterity, including scholars, clergy, lawyers, and statesmen.

These poems calling the world's attention to the lovers as a pattern, often in the form of a written text, enact within the poem's fiction its function as a speech act. While they probably helped Donne to relieve his frustrations and to maintain relations with coterie readers, as Marotti argues, they also enabled him to construct a self-representation that reconciles the desire for wholeness and integrity with the duty to participate as a member of "the body of the world." In many of the works apparently written before his marriage, Donne represented himself either as exerting control over others or as suffering fragmentation of self through vulnerability to others' power. In the poems of reciprocal love, he created images of human relationships that accept the permeability and dependency of identity as constructive rather than destructive. By representing his relationship with Anne as an imitable model of mutual respect and vulnerability, he replaced the dilemma of choosing between isolation and contamination with the image of a private world contributing actively to "the sustentation of the whole." We cannot know certainly whether Donne developed his concept of "confident and mutuall communicating" (*Letters*, 121) by corresponding with his male friends or by living with his wife, but we can acknowledge that he gave it fullest verbal expression in poems that invite us to read them as representations of his marriage.[1] Possibly Donne in his own life achieved the mark of engaging actively *with* the world while not being *of* the world more fully as preacher than as lover and husband, but in the poems of mutual love John and Anne Donne have provided us with a pattern for reconciling duty and desire that, although it does not dismantle gender and political hierarchies, exhilaratingly disrupts hierarchical modes of perception.

I am not arguing that Donne completely transcended his masculinist culture: assumptions of male superiority are reinscribed in the poetry as well as the sermons and likely influenced relations with his wife. And I am not arguing that John Donne's representations give us access to the reality of Anne Donne's life or that she (or any other woman) enjoyed full participation in the social world by nourishing her husband's creativity. But a broader conception of authorship allows us to consider these representations as results of Anne Donne's active agency as well as of her husband's poetic skill. Doing so enables us to recognize the exercise of female power in a past society that offered women few options, and, as Munich advises, "in order to imagine a different future we cannot exclude any portion of our past."[2] So in opposition to Halley's argument that these textualizations exclude and silence Anne Donne and that studying them has only "acrid rewards" (203), I am urging that they give voice to ideas of mutuality despite hierarchy and social interaction without submersion in society's dominant values that may well be useful for us as we imagine and negotiate ways of living within our own deeply hierarchical societies.

1. I am suggesting that the circumstances of coterie poetry encourage us to find Anne Donne's presence behind some of Donne's poetic representations of love, but I am not arguing for a single causal connection between Donne's relationship with her and changes in his concepts of self and others. Among other circumstances shaping Donne's work was the replacement of a woman by a man on England's throne. See Achsah Guibbory's persuasive argument that the anxiety about control and mastery of women in the *Elegies* was in part a reaction to a female monarch. " 'Oh, Let Mee Not Serve So': The Politics of Love in Donne's *Elegies*," *ELH* 57 (1990): 811–33.
2. Adrienne Munich, "Notorious Signs, Feminist Criticism and Literary Tradition," in *Making a Difference: Feminist Literary Criticism*, ed. Gayle Greene and Coppélla Kahn (London: Methuen, 1985), 244.

Holy Sonnets / Divine Poems

R. V. YOUNG

Donne's Holy Sonnets and The Theology of Grace†

The flowering of the English devotional lyric, long treated as an Anglican phenomenon with Catholic overtones distinct from Puritanism,[1] is now widely regarded as unambiguously Protestant, with negligible debts to Continental Catholicism. With increasing frequency in recent years, a distinctively Protestant poetics has been designated the source of the English tradition of devotional poetry.[2] The Holy Sonnets of John Donne have furnished especially fertile ground for theological speculation. Once seen as examples of the influence of Ignatian meditation on Anglican poetry, the Holy Sonnets are now more often interpreted as an expression of the final crisis in the poet's conversion from Catholic recusancy to a Calvinist orientation consistent with Anglican orthodoxy. Despite the broad acceptance it now enjoys, this view of the Holy Sonnets is flawed in several ways. First, it is based on a simplistic and inaccurate view of the theological issues of Donne's era. Second, it attempts to establish the existence of an exclusively Protestant mode of poetry without determining whether the same features of theme and style are available in contemporaneous Catholic poetry. Finally, it forces the Holy

† From "Bright Shootes of Everlastingnesse": The Seventeenth-Century Religious Lyric, ed. Claude J. Summers and Ted-Larry Pebworth (Columbia: U of Missouri P, 1987), pp. 20–39. Copyright © 1987 by the Curators of the University of Missouri. Reprinted by permission of the publisher.
1. See especially Helen C. White, The Metaphysical Poets (1936; rpt. New York: Collier, 1962); Helen Gardner, ed., John Donne: The Divine Poems, 2d ed. (Oxford: Clarendon, 1978); Louis L. Martz, The Poetry of Meditation, 2d ed. (New Haven: Yale University Press, 1962); and Anthony Low, Love's Architecture: Devotional Modes in Seventeenth-Century English Poetry (New York: New York University Press, 1978).
2. See especially William Halewood, The Poetry of Grace:Reformation Themes and Structures in English Seventeenth-Century Poetry (New Haven: Yale University Press, 1970); Barbara K. Lewalski, Donne's Anniversaries and the Poetry of Praise (Princeton: Princeton University Press, 1973); Andrew Weiner, Sir Philip Sidney and the Poetics of Protestantism: A Study of Contexts (Minneapolis: University of Minnesota Press, 1978); and Lewalski, Protestant Poetics and the Seventeenth-Century Religious Lyric (Princeton: Princeton University Press, 1979). "Protestant Poetics" was the topic of a special session at the 1983 MLA convention in New York.

Sonnets into a doctrinal frame that often overlooks the equivocal
resonance and play of wit in Donne's poetry.

Scholars who espouse the notion of Protestant poetics are fond of
observing that the Reformation maintained that man's justification
begins with what is called *prevenient grace*. William Halewood
quotes one of Donne's sermons on this point: "He is as precise as
Taylor in his use of the nomenclature of Reformation theology," Hal-
ewood writes. "The grace which provokes the faith which leads to
justification is *preventing* or *prevenient*: 'no man can prepare that
worke, no man can begin it, no man can proceed in it of himselfe.
The desire and the actual beginning is from the preventing grace of
God' (*Sermons*, 2:305)."[3] Barbara Lewalski is even more emphatic:

> Because man's natural state is so desperate, there can be no
> question (as in some Roman Catholic formulations) of man's
> preparing himself through moral virtue for the reception of
> grace, or of performing works good and meritorious in them-
> selves; everything that he does himself is necessarily evil and
> corrupt. As the tenth of the Thirty-nine Articles of the estab-
> lished church put it, "The condition of man, after the fall of
> Adam is such that he cannot turne, and prepare himselfe by his
> owne naturall strength, and good workes, to faith, and calling
> upon God, wherefore we have no power to doe good workes
> pleasant, and acceptable to God, without the grace of God pre-
> venting us, that we may have a good will, and working with us
> when we have that good will."[4]

Now this is all very puzzling. "Prevenient grace" hardly seems to
qualify as a decisive example of "the nomenclature of Reformation
theology" since the term is used in the Council of Trent's *Decree on
Justification* (1547), which states quite explicitly that the work of
salvation begins not with man's efforts, but with the unmerited grace
of God:

> [The Council] declares further that the beginning of this same
> justification in adults must be received from the prevenient
> grace of God through Christ Jesus; that is, from his call, by
> which they are called for no existing merit of their own, in order
> that those who have by sins turned away from God, might be
> disposed through his awakening and help to turn to their own
> justification, by freely assenting to and cooperating with that
> grace. Thus as God touches the human heart with the light of
> the Holy Spirit, the man himself is not wholly inactive, inas-
> much as he might cast it aside. Nonetheless, without God's
> grace he cannot move himself toward justice in God's sight by

3. *The Poetry of Grace*, pp. 62–63.
4. *Protestant Poetics*, pp. 15–16.

his own free will. Hence when it is said in Sacred Scripture, "Turn toward me and I shall turn toward you" (Zach. 1: 3), we are reminded of our freedom; and when we respond "Convert us, Lord, to you and we shall be converted" (Lam. 5:21), we confess that we are anticipated by God's grace.[5]

This is not a Tridentine novelty. St. Thomas Aquinas makes it clear that the "preparation for grace" attributed by Lewalski to "some Roman Catholic formulations" can only come after and as a result of God's prior gift of grace: "But if we speak of grace as it signifies a help from God moving us to good, no preparation is required on man's part anticipating, as it were, the divine help but rather, every preparation in man must be by the help of God moving the soul to good."[6] Or as the mystic, St. John of the Cross, succinctly puts it, "without his grace one is unable to merit his grace."[7]

There are, to be sure, significant differences between Protestant and Catholic versions of justification; the insistence of the Council of Trent on the cooperation of man's free will with God's grace is an example, and will presently receive further consideration. But there is no basis for suggesting that the concept of prevenient grace was a discovery, even a rediscovery, of the Reformation. At times it appears that the proponents of Protestant poetics have derived their concept of Catholic theology wholly from Reformation polemics. In any case, many commentators of recent years have read Donne's devotional poems, along with those of his English contemporaries, as expositions of an exclusively Protestant, indeed a Calvinist, view of election and grace. According to one critic, Donne's Holy Sonnets "yield more fully to an analysis of their biblical motifs, their anguished Pauline speaker, their presentation of states of soul attendant upon the

5. Quoted from *Enchiridion Symbolorum, Definitionum et Declarationum de rebus fidei et Morum,* ed. Henr. Denzinger and Clem. Bannwart, S.J., 17th ed. (Fribourg: Herder, 1927), 797: "Declarat praeterea, ipsius iustificationis exordium in adultis a Dei per Christum Iesum praeveniente gratia sumendum esse, hoc est, ab eius vocatione, qua nullis eorum exsistentibus meritis vocantur, ut qui per peccata a Deo aversi erant, per eius excitantem atque adiuvantem gratiam ad convertendum se ad suam ipsorum iustificationem, eidem gratiae libere assentiendo et cooperando, disponantur, ita ut tangente Deo cor hominis per Spiritus Sancti illuminationem neque homo ipse nihil omnino agat, inspirationem illam recipiens, quippe qui illam et abicere potest, neque tamen sine gratia Dei movere se ad iustitiam coram illo libera sua voluntate possit. Unde in sacris litteris cum dicitur: 'Convertimini ad me, et ego convertar ad vos' (Zach 1, 3), libertatis nostrae admonemur; cum respondemus: 'Converte nos, Domine, ad te, et convertemur' (Thr 5, 21), Dei nos gratia praeveniri confitemur."
6. *Summa Theologica,* 1–2.112.2: "Sed si loquamur de gratia secundum quod significat auxilium Dei moventis ad bonum, sic nulla praeparatio requiritur ex parte hominis quasi praeveniens divinum auxilium; sed potius quaecumque praeparatio in homine esse potest, est ex auxilio Dei moventis animam ad bonum." The Latin text is from the Blackfriars edition of St. Thomas Aquinas, *Summa Theologica,* vol. 30, *The Gospel of Grace,* ed. and trans. Cornelius Ernst, O.P. (London: Eyre & Spottiswoode, 1972), p. 148.
7. *Cántico espiritual,* 32.5: "sin su gracia no se puede merecer su gracia." *Vida y obras completas de San Juan de la Cruz,* ed. Crisógono de Jesús, O.C.D., Matías del Niño Jesús, O.C.D., and Lucinio del SS. Sacramento, O.C.D., 5th ed. Madrid: BAC, 1964), p. 718.

Protestant drama of regeneration, than they do to any other medi-
tative scheme," and the first of these sonnets, "As due by many titles,"
has been called a treatment of "the problem of election."[8]

Here and there in the Holy Sonnets there are explicitly Calvinist
terms, as well as passages that suggest a Calvinist theology of grace—
the phrase "Impute me righteous" in Sonnet 3, for instance, or the
famous paradox that closes "Batter my heart," Sonnet 10. But neither
the first sonnet, "As due by many titles," nor the Holy Sonnets gen-
erally can be read as a specifically Calvinist, nor even Protestant,
exposition of grace. In fact, the persona of the Holy Sonnets seems
almost to be "trying out" different versions of grace in order to arrive
at a theologically moderate position. We know from his letters that
Donne inclined this way. Writing to Henry Goodyere within a year
of the time he is believed to have composed most of the Holy Son-
nets, he praises his own verse litany, "That neither the Roman
Church need call it defective, because it abhors not the particular
mention of the blessed Triumphers in heaven; nor the Reformed can
discreetly accuse it, of attributing more then a rectified devotion
ought to doe"; and in another letter to Goodyere, written about the
same time, he says of Catholic and Protestant churches, "The chan-
nels of Gods mercies run through both fields; and they are sister
teats of his graces, yet both diseased and infected, but not both
alike."[9] This is hardly the attitude of militant Calvinism.

Donne's "ecumenical" inclination is further developed in his
Essays in Divinity, probably composed during the three or four years
before his ordination. As Evelyn Simpson observes this work would
hardly have commended Donne to Anglican orthodoxy, as repre-
sented by the Calvinist archbishop of Canterbury, George Abbot,
since "Abbot was a narrow-minded man bitterly hostile to the
Church of Rome."[1] In the *Essays* Donne maintains, however, that
despite sharp differences between the Anglican and Roman com-
munions, they share the same foundation: "yet though we branch
out *East* and *West,* that Church concurs with us in the root, and
sucks her vegetation from one and the same ground, *Christ Jesus.*"
Donne continues, "so Synagogue and Church is the same thing, and
of the Church, *Roman* and *Reformed,* and all other distinctions of
place, Discipline, or Person, but one Church, journying to one

8. Lewalski, *Protestant Poetics,* pp. 265–66. Unlike Lewalski, I follow the order of the first
twelve sonnets in the Gardner edition of the *Divine Poems,* which seems to have been
vindicated by Patrick F. O'Connell, "The Successive Arrangements of Donne's 'Holy Son-
nets,' " *Philological Quarterly* 60 (1981): 323–42, esp. p. 334.
9. *Letters to Severall Persons of Honour* (1651), introd. M. Thomas Hester (fac. rpt.; New
York: Delmar, 1977), pp. 34, 102. Hester gives as the dates of these letters 1608 and 1609
respectively, in the Schedule, pp. xviii–xxii.
1. See the Introduction to her edition of Donne's *Essays in Divinity* (Oxford: Clarendon,
1952), p. xi.

Hierusalem, and directed by one guide, Christ Jesus." Most remarkably, Donne even goes so far as to prefer a unity based on the form of *any* of the principal churches—Roman, Genevan, or Anglican—to the disunity prevailing in his day:

> And though to all my thanksgivings to God, I ever humbly acknowledg, as one of his greatest Mercies to me, that he gave me my Pasture in this Park, and my milk from the brests of this Church, yet out of a fervent, and (I hope) not inordinate affection, even to such an Unity, I do zealously wish, that the whole catholick Church, were reduced to such Unity and agreement, in the form and profession Established, in any one of these Churches (though ours were principally to be wished) which have not by any additions destroyed the foundation and possibility of salvation in Christ Jesus; That then the Church, discharged of disputations, and misapprehensions, and this defensive warr, might contemplate Christ clearly and uniformely.[2]

Again, this is not the tone of Calvinist rigor, and the emphasis on the corporate unity of the Church seems incompatible with the stress on individual election urged by Calvin and his more vociferous English followers.

Hence when Donne plainly repudiates Calvin on the specific matter of grace in a subsequent passage of the *Essays in Divinity,* his theology is perfectly consistent. Although in his reply to Cardinal Sadoleto, Calvin names "justification by faith, the first and keenest subject of controversy between us,"[3] his own *Antidote to the Council of Trent* clearly establishes that the central theological issue of the Protestant Reformation was freedom of the will. Calvin says "amen" to the Council's first three canons on justification, which stipulate, respectively, that man cannot be justified by his own human works or the law without the grace of Christ; that this grace does not merely make salvation easier, but is absolutely necessary; and that prevenient grace is requisite to dispose man even to desire salvation. Calvin only begins to take exception with the fourth canon, which says, "If anyone say that the free will of man, moved and excited by God, in no way cooperates by assenting to God's stimulus and call, by which it disposes and prepares itself for receiving the grace of justification, and that it is unable to resist, if it would, but that as a thing inanimate it is able to do nothing and is held merely passive, let him be anathema."[4] Calvin's rejoinder: "the efficacy of divine grace is such, that

---

2. *Essays in Divinity,* pp. 50, 51, 51–52.
3. *John Calvin: Selections from His Writings,* ed. John Dillenberger (New York: Doubleday, 1971), p. 95.
4. *Enchiridion Symbolorum,* ed. Denzinger and Bannwart, 814: "Si quis dixerit, liberum hominis arbitrium a Deo motum et excitatum nihil cooperari assentiendo Deo excitanti atque

all opposition is beaten down, and we who were unwilling are made obedient, it is not we who assent, but the Lord by the Prophet, when he promises that he will make us to walk in his precepts."[5] Calvin raises similar objections to canons 5 through 7, which assert that Adam's sin did not obliterate free will; that man does evil only on his own with God's permissive will and not his proper consenting; and that man is not utterly incapable of doing good before justification.

When Donne meditates on God's mercy in the *Essays in Divinity,* his discussion of grace and nature is Thomistic, his view of the human will far more Tridentine than Calvinist:

> in our repentances and reconciliations, though the first grace proceed only from God, yet we concurr so, as there is an union of two Hypostases, *Grace* and *Nature.* Which, (as the incarnation of our Blessed Saviour himself was) is conceived in us of the Holy Ghost, without father; but fed and produced by us; that is, by our will first enabled and illumined. For neither God nor man determine mans will; (for that must either imply a necessiting therof from God, or else *Pelagianisme*) but they condetermine it.

Above all Donne denies Calvin's notion of irresistible grace by which "all opposition is beaten down": "And yet we may not say, but that God begins many things which we frustrate; and calls when we come not."[6] The issue would not go away for Donne, even after his ordination. Of course, in his very public sermons far more discretion was required than in his letters or *Essays,* which remained unpublished during his lifetime. Still, Donne clung consistently to an un-Calvinist belief in freedom of the will. In a sermon of 1626, for example, he affirms what seems to be predestination: "Christ doth not now begin to make that man his, but now declares to us, that he hath been his from all eternity. . . ." But a few pages further, immediately after referring to "the Eternal Decree of my Election," he attacks what— for Calvin—seems the necessary corollary, the doctrine of irresistible grace (which Donne attributes to "the later School"): "He came not to force and compel them, who would not be brought into the way: Christ saves no man against his will."[7] Like the fathers of the Council of Trent, Donne seeks to formulate the delicate balance between grace and nature, predestination and free will. If his conclusions differ from theirs, they likewise differ from Calvin's.

vocanti, quo ad obtinendam iustificationis gratiam se disponat ac praeparet, neque posse dissentire, si velit, sed velut manime quoddam nihil omnino agere mereque passive se habere: anathema sit."
5. *Calvin: Selections,* ed. Dillenberger, p. 194.
6. *Essays in Divinity,* pp. 80, 81.
7. "A Sermon Preached to the Household at White-hall, April 30, 1626," in *The Sermons of John Donne,* ed. George R. Potter and Evelyn M. Simpson, 10 vols. (Berkeley: University of California Press, 1953–1962), 7:153, 156.

It is not surprising, therefore, to find many of the theological features of the Holy Sonnets paralleled in the devotional poems of Donne's Catholic contemporaries, who exhibit an equal concern over the problem of election and grace. A good example is furnished by the *Heráclito cristiano* (*Christian Heraclitus*, 1613) by Francisco de Quevedo (1580–1645). Like Donne's Holy Sonnets, it is a collection of penitential lyrics that focus on the spiritual condition of the poetic persona. The parallels begin to emerge with the first poem of each set. The octave of Donne's "As due by many titles" establishes the misery of man's natural condition by seeing his situation as that of an unreliable debtor who tries to cancel his debts by inviting God to foreclose on his hopelessly overmortgaged self:

> As due by many titles I resigne
> My selfe to thee, O God, first I was made
> By thee, and for thee, and when I was decay'd
> Thy blood bought that, the which before was thine,
> I am thy sonne, made with thy selfe to shine,
> Thy servant, whose paines thou hast still repaid,
> Thy sheepe, thine Image, and till I betray'd
> My selfe, a temple of thy Spirit divine. . . . [8]

The proliferation of metaphors, suggesting various relationships with God, is an indication of the speaker's uncertainty and the feebleness of his position. Hence it is not surprising that the sestet dwells queasily on the prospect that the proffered self may not be worth the cost of refurbishing, that only the devil is still interested:

> Why doth the devill then usurpe in mee?
> Why doth he steale, nay ravish that's thy right?
> Except thou rise and for thine owne worke fight,
> Oh I shall soone despaire, when I doe see
> That thou lov'st mankind well, yet wilt'not chuse mee,
> And Satan hates mee, yet is loth to lose mee.

Like this first of the Holy Sonnets, the first poem of Quevedo's *Heráclito* is an intense reflection of the poet's fearful sense of his utter dependence on divine grace:

> A new heart, a new man, Lord,
> Are what my soul has need of;
> Strip me of myself, for it could be
> That in your pity you might pay what I owe.
>   I take doubtful steps in the blind night,
> For already I have come to hate the day,
> And I fear that I shall find cold death

8. The Holy Sonnets are quoted from Gardner's second edition of the the the *Divine Poems*.

Wrapped in a deadly bait (although sweet).
   I am of your making; your image, Father, I have been,
And, if you have no concern for me, I believe
That nothing else will take my part.[9]

Donne describes himself as "due by many titles" to God; Quevedo
mentions the debt that he "owes" to God, and describes himself as
of God's "making" and formerly His "image" until corrupted by sin.
Donne says that he is God's "owne worke" and his "image." Both
emphasize that God must take their part and "fight for" or "defend"
the sinner, who is helpless without such assistance. Indeed, the fun-
damental theme of both poems is the utter hopelessness of the sin-
ner's situation without divine intervention. Donne closes on the
brink of despair, awaiting some sign that God will "chuse" him;
Quevedo calls upon God to take decisive action on behalf of a sinner
who turns away from spiritual health: "Do what is demanded by the
way I seem, / Not what I demand; for, like a profligate, / I hide my
salvation from my desire."

There are Catholic poets of grace besides Quevedo, and not all
are confined to Spain. The Frenchman Jean de la Ceppède (1550–
1622), for example, closes one of his *Théorèmes Spirituels* (1613–
1621) with the plea of a hapless sinner for divine help: "But it is for
you, Lord, to make me capable / Of sharing in your riches: for my
guilty soul / Does not know how, without your aid, to return to you."[1]
The close of another of La Ceppède's sonnets recalls a figure fre-
quently associated with Luther's view of justification: "Oh Christ, oh
holy Lamb, deign to hide / All my scarlet sins, the kindling twigs of
the abyss, / Within the bloody folds of the cloak of your flesh."[2] These
lines suggest that a Catholic poet can use the metaphor of having
his sins covered by the righteous blood of Christ without invoking
the Reformation doctrine of imputed, rather than infused, grace.
Hence there is little reason to find anything specifically Protestant

---

9. Quevedo is quoted from Francisco de Quevedo, *Obras completas,* ed. José Manuel Blecua
   (Barcelona: Editorial Planeta, 1963), 1:20: "Un nuevo corazón, un hombre nuevo / ha
   menester, Señor, la ánima mía; / desnúdame de mí, que ser podría / que tu piedad pagase
   lo que debo. / Dudosos pies por ciego noche llevo, / que ya he llegado a aborrecer el día,
   / y temo que hallaré la muerte fría / envuelta en (bien que dulce) mortal cebo. / Tu hacienda
   soy; tu imagen, Padre, he sido, / y, si no es tu interés en mí, no creo / que otra cosa
   defiende mi partido. / Haz lo que pide verme cual me veo, / no lo que pido yo: pues, de
   perdido, / recato mi salud de mi deseo."
1. Quoted from *European Metaphysical Poetry,* ed. Frank Warnke (New Haven: Yale Uni-
   versity Press, 1961), p. 104: "Mais c'est à vous, Seigneur, de me rendre capable / D'avoir
   part en vos biens: car mon ame coulpable / Ne scauroit sans votre aide, / à vous s'en
   revoler."
2. Quoted from *The Baroque Poem,* ed. Harold B. Segel (New York: Dutton, 1974), p. 172:
   "O Christ, ô saint Agneau, daigne-toi de cacher / Tous mes rouges péchés, brindelles des
   abîmes, / Dans les sanglants replis du manteau de ta chair." See Luther's *Commentary on
   Galatians,* in *Martin Luther: Selections from His Writings,* ed. John Dillenberger (New
   York: Doubleday, 1961), p. 129: "So we shroud ourselves under the covering of Christ's
   flesh, . . . lest God should see our sin."

in the closing lines of Donne's "Hymne to God my God, in my sick-nesse":[3]

> Looke Lord, and finde both *Adams* met in me;
>   As the first *Adams* sweat surrounds my face,
>   May the last *Adams* blood my soule embrace.
> So, in his purple wrapp'd receive mee Lord,
>   By these his thornes give me his other Crowne.
>
> (ll. 23–27)

Obviously here, as in the Holy Sonnets, Donne is concerned with the problem of grace, conceived in terms of Pauline typology; how-ever, this is hardly a theme unique to the Protestant Reformation. As the examples of Quevedo and La Ceppède indicate, Continental Catholic poets were equally sensitive to man's hopeless sinfulness before God and radical dependence on his grace. In all of these poems the expression of Christian experience seems more important than the articulation of theological distinctions.

Even in those Holy Sonnets that seem to display most explicitly the severities of Calvinism, it is difficult to find in Donne an uncrit-ical propounder of Reformation theology. At first glance the famous conclusion to Sonnet 10, "Batter my heart," suggests nothing so much as the effects of Calvinist "irresistible" grace: "Take mee to you, imprison mee, for I / Except you'enthrall mee, never shall be free, / Nor ever chast, except you ravish mee." But even the critic who has recently been most resolute in turning up Calvinism in the Holy Sonnets finds it hedged in by important reservations. John Stachniewski writes that "the essential subject matter" of Sonnet 10 is "the conflict between [Donne's] personal integrity and the demands of a theology which brutalized self-esteem." Stachniewski concludes that Donne's Calvinism in the Holy Sonnets is a tempo-rary phase in his transition from Catholic to High Anglican, arising from his sense of worldly disappointment at the time of the poems' composition: "Donne felt his dependence on God to resemble his dependence on secular patronage with its attendant frustration, humiliation, and despair."[4]

3. Cf. Lewalski, *Protestant Poetics*, pp. 16–17; and Richard Strier, *Love Known: Theology and Experience in George Herbert's Poetry* (Chicago: University of Chicago Press, 1983), p. 130. On La Ceppède's relation to the Counter-Reformation, see P. A. Chilton, *The Poetry of Jean de la Ceppède: A Study in Text and Context* (Oxford: Oxford University Press, 1977), pp. 24, 50–52. Terence Cave, *Devotional Poetry in France, c. 1570–1613* (Cambridge: Cambridge University Press, 1969), pp. 22–23, observes that the differences between Catholic and Protestant poetry in France are largely negative; i.e., some subjects available to Catholics are not available to Protestants.
4. "John Donne: The Despair of the 'Holy Sonnets,'" *ELH* 48 (1981): 690, 702–3. See also Wilbur Sanders, *John Donne's Poetry* (Cambridge: Cambridge University Press, 1971), pp. 120–31; Lewalski, *Protestant Poetics*, pp. 120–31; John Carey, *John Donne: Life, Mind, and Art* (New York: Oxford University Press, 1981), pp. 51–59. There is a similar

R. V. Young

It is not necessary, however, to turn the Holy Sonnets into a sub-
limated manifestation of the poet's socioeconomic frustration to
question whether a few scattered suggestions of Calvinism make the
poems a Calvinist work. "Batter my heart" is precisely a prayer to
God for grace, which, if the Calvinist notion of the irresistibility of
grace be true, is essentially pointless. However inappropriate the use
of quasi-mystical imagery at the end of Donne's sonnet may be, Hugh
Richmond has pointed out a striking parallel in a similar sonnet by
the French Catholic poet Ronsard.[5] In any case, Donne pleads that
God stop tinkering with him ("for, you / As yet but knocke, breathe,
shine, and seeke to mend") and instead reforge him altogether: "That
I may rise, and stand, o'erthrow mee,' and bend / Your force, to
breake, blowe, burn and make me new" (ll. 1–4). Now this may quite
plausibly be read as a plea for infused sanctifying grace (*gratia gra-
tum faciens*) which, as Barbara Lewalski insists, is an idea contrary
to the Protestant Reformation: "The Reformers were adamant in
their insistence that this justification is only imputed to the sinner,
not infused into him as the Roman Catholics held, so as actually to
restore God's image in him; however, the imputed righteousness is
really his because he is joined to Christ as body to head."[6] Of course,
there is no denying that Donne's sonnet expresses a sense of pro-
found depravity and fear of damnation—not without Calvinist rever-
berations—for the very reason that the poet has abandoned Catholic
sources of consolation without yet discovering or devising acceptable
alternatives. This is a matter of rather delicate discriminations, how-
ever, and it is questionable whether the close of "Batter my heart"
yields a clear theological resolution.

The trouble with theological categorizing of the Holy Sonnets is
that it is likely to flatten out the wit and daring that are characteristic
of Donne's poetry. The equivocal implication of the third of these
sonnets, "This is my playes last scene," with its explicit reference to
imputed righteousness, furnishes a good example. The octave pres-
ents a traditional meditative theme, the deathbed:

> This is my playes last scene, here heavens appoint
> My pilgrimages last mile; and my race
> Idly, yet quickly runne, hath this last pace,
> My spans last inch, my minutes last point,
> And gluttonous death will instantly unjoynt
> My body,'and soule, and I shall sleepe a space,

politicizing of Donne's *Songs and Sonets* and his *Devotions* in Jonathan Goldberg, *James I
and the Politics of Literature* (Baltimore: Johns Hopkins University Press, 1983), pp. 66–
67, 80–83, 107–12, 211–19.

5. *Divine Poems*, ed. Gardner, pp. 152–53.

6. *Protestant Poetics*, p. 17.

> But my'ever-waking part shal see that face,
> Whose fear already shakes my every joynt.

Clearly this poem is based on the standard Ignatian meditative topos of the Four Last Things.[7] Even as the octave evokes death and judgment, so the sestet adds heaven and hell:

> Then, as my soule, to'heaven her first seate, takes flight,
> And earth-borne body, in the earth shall dwell,
> So, fall my sinnes, that all may have their right,
> To where they'are bred, and would presse me, to hell.
> Impute me righteous, thus purg'd of evill,
> For thus I leave the world, the flesh, and devill.

This closing couplet could be seen as turning the Ignatian meditation into something emphatically Calvinist. Yet this almost magical invocation of the Calvinist dogma has troubled more than one critic. Wilbur Sanders calls these lines "blatant theological sophistry" and adds that "the spiritual malady so obviously won't give way to the patent medicine applied to it, that it seems almost to be a part of the poetic strategy to make us aware of this fact."[8] There is perhaps more to what Sanders says than he realizes: it is quite as likely that Donne is playing with a theological concept in a dramatic and witty fashion as it is that he is writing bad verse theology.

With this approach in mind, it is instructive to consider two other references to "imputation" in the Donne canon. The first comes from Satyre III, "Of Religion":

> and shall thy fathers spirit
> Meete blinde philosophers in heaven, whose merit
> Of strict life may be imputed faith, and heare
> Thee, whom hee taught so easie wayes and neare
> To follow, damn'd?
>
> (ll. 11–15)[9]

In raising the theme of the virtuous heathen—a lively topic in the Middle Ages and among Renaissance humanists—Donne simply stands Calvinism on its head: instead of Christ's righteousness

---

7. *The Spiritual Exercises*, 1st week, 5th exercise, in *Obras completas de San Ignacio de Loyola*, ed. Ignacio Iparraguirre, S.J. (Madrid: BAC, 1963), pp. 214–16. Lewalski, *Protestant Poetics*, p. 268, argues that the use of the pilgrimage and race tropes in the opening lines of this sonnet make it Protestant in mood. But the notion of life as a pilgrimage is too familiar an idea in the Middle Ages to require illustration. St. Thomas More combines the theme of life as a pilgrimage with the contemplation of death in a Latin epigram, *Vita Ipsa cursus ad mortem est*, in Fred Nichols, ed., *An Anthology of Neo-Latin Poetry* (New Haven: Yale University Press, 1979), p. 462.

8. *John Donne's Poetry*, p. 128.

9. Quoted from *The Complete Poetry of John Donne*, ed. John T. Shawcross (Garden City, N.Y.: Doubleday / Anchor, 1967), p. 23.

imputed to a man on the basis of his faith, Donne speculates that virtuous pagans might have faith imputed to them on the basis of righteousness. This passage comes in a poem that questions Catholicism, Calvinism, Anglicanism, and indifferentism alike on behalf of the sincere individual believer, who is exhorted to "doubt wisely" (l. 77). Thus the severe Calvinist version of grace is subverted by a witty turn growing out of a moderate Erasmian attitude amidst the horrors of sixteenth-century religious strife.[1]

The Calvinist concept of imputed righteousness is subjected to an especially extravagant outburst of Donne's wit in Elegy 19, the notorious "Going to Bed," in which the poetic persona is occupied with getting his mistress undressed and into bed as quickly as possible:

> Like pictures, or like bookes gay coverings made
> For laymen, are all women thus arraid;
> Themselves are mystique bookes, which only wee
> Whom their imputed grace will dignify
> Must see reveal'd.
>
> (ll. 39–43)[2]

Like his principal classical model, Ovid, Donne uses the erotic elegy as a vehicle for ridiculing the most revered ideals and institutions of respectable society. Amatory figures become quick thrusts in a perilous antiestablishment poetic game. Here, beneath the surface of outrageous wit and blasphemous sensuality, Donne indulges in a momentary gesture of theological satire. In a context of "imputed grace" and the removal of clothing, it is difficult not to recall how Luther explains God's imputation of righteousness to the sinner, in his *Commentary* on *Galatians,* by comparing it to *covering* his sin by grace and not *seeing* it.[3] For Donne's speaker the woman's "imputed grace" permits him to *uncover* (or *discover*) and *see*. The implication of the conceit emerges when it is reversed: the justification of the elect, an inscrutable act of divine power according to the Calvinist formulation, makes God's work of salvation as arbitrary and fickle as a woman's choice of the lover admitted to her bed. Hence this risqué poem by a young law student and flamboyant dandy is also a sly send-up of the dominant theology of the Reformation.

To be sure, the Satyres and Elegies, if Dame Helen Gardner's dating is reliable, were written more than ten years before the Holy Sonnets; and when the latter were composed Donne had already undertaken the labor of an Anglican polemicist, and the idea of

1. Donne could well have absorbed a pre-Tridentine Erasmian Catholicity from his Jesuit uncle, Jasper Heywood. See Dennis Flynn, "The 'Annales School' and the Catholicism of Donne's Family," *John Donne Journal* 2 (1983): 1–9.
2. Quoted from *John Donne: The Elegies and the Songs and Sonnets,* ed. Helen Gardner (Oxford: Clarendon, 1965), p. 16.
3. *Luther: Selections,* ed. Dillenberger, p. 129.

entering Anglican orders had at least been broached to him. But the Holy Sonnets, like almost all Donne's poetry, are private exercises, circulated for the most part among his friends. There are undeniable marks of the poet's Catholic upbringing in their themes and structures, and the specifically Calvinist elements are handled tentatively, even with an air of provisionality. Sonnet 3, "This is my playes last scene," with its reference to imputed righteousness, a doctrine ridiculed by Donne in other poems, seems to ask, "Does this work? Will my sins simply drop away into hell as I am 'purg'd of evill' by imputation?" There is an air of nervousness here—a result, perhaps, of Donne's embarrassed or even guilty recollection of earlier flippant treatments of matters of eternal life and death. Still, a negative answer is implied in the nine remaining sonnets of the set, which keep seeking different approaches to the problem of justification and grace.

This is not to say that the doctrines of the Reformation, especially Calvin's view of justification, had no bearing on the Holy Sonnets, but that the impact of Calvinism was oblique rather than direct. In fact, there is often a Calvinist subtext, like a magnetic field, exerting a subtle but continuous force over the most unlikely of the Holy Sonnets. For instance, the ninth sonnet, "What if this present were the worlds last night?," discloses under scrutiny the spiritual strains generated by the terrifying yet fascinating concept of irresistible grace.

At first glance the octave of the poem seems an extravagant sacred parody of a Petrarchan love sonnet, done in Continental style. Donne's anguished meditator, recalling the counsel of Astrophil's muse, attempts to convince himself that he need only "looke in [his] heart and write."[4] What he sees there is a graphic, Spanish baroque crucifix:

> What if this present were the worlds last night?
> Marke in my heart, O Soule, where thou dost dwell,
> The picture of Christ crucified, and tell
> Whether that countenance can thee affright,
> Teares in his eyes quench the amasing light,
> Blood fills his frownes, which from his pierc'd head fell,
> And can that tongue adjudge thee unto hell,
> Which pray'd forgivenesse for his foes fierce spight?

Even as Astrophil assures "sleepe" that no better image of Stella is available than what is in his mind (*Astrophil and Stella*, sonnet 39), so Donne's speaker assures himself by means of the image of Christ in his mind. Yet the octave ends, literally, with a question mark; and,

---

4. *Astrophil and Stella*, sonnet 1, cited here and below from *The Poems of Sir Philip Sidney*, ed. William A. Ringler, Jr. (Oxford: Clarendon, 1962).

though Christ "pray'd forgivenesse for his foes fierce spight," when
he returns as Judge of the world, some at least will indeed be
adjudged "unto hell."

The sestet undertakes a strengthening of the persona's assurance
of salvation by encouragement of an emotional and aesthetic
response to the interior image of Christ that he has evoked. Again
the conventions of Petrarchan/Neoplatonic love poetry are parodied:

> No, no; but as in my idolatrie
> I said to all my profane mistresses,
> Beauty, of pitty, foulness onely is
> A signe of rigour: so I say to thee,
> To wicked spirits are horrid shapes assign'd,
> This beauteous forme assures a pitious minde.

The very slyness of these lines is troubling. In a poem resonant with
echoes of Sidney, one can hardly forget that "two Negatives affirme"
according to the "Grammer rules" of *Astrophil and Stella*, sonnet 63.
Can Donne's "No, no," like Stella's, be construed as an implicit *yes?*
The speaker of "What if this present" must fear a certain poetic
justice, since as a youthful seducer he seems, like Astrophil, to have
distorted the conventions. In his Neoplatonic discourse in the *Book
of the Courtier,* Pietro Bembo tells us that a "beauteous forme" is a
"signe" not of "a pitious minde" but of a virtuous soul.[5] Samuel
Daniel's Delia, after all, was "faire, and *thus* vnkinde."[6] In view of
the evident duplicity of the persona's addresses to his "profane mis-
tresses" in the past, his present analogous address to his own soul—
patently intended to be overheard by the divine lover—is at best
questionable, and a dubious means of assuring oneself of salvation.

In a Calvinist perspective this is a crucial issue, for the interpre-
tation of the "picture" in the persona's heart—is it a "marke" of elec-
tion or condemnation?—is contingent upon the speaker's emotional
response to Christ's countenance. To find this tearful, bloody visage
beautiful is not a natural response; it requires grace, grace that in
Calvin's view is irresistible. The picture of the suffering Christ within
will be an image of beauty to the man who has faith, when faith
means the subjective, unpremeditated realization that one is in fact
saved. "A right definition of faith," Calvin says in *The Institutes*
(3.2.7), is "a firm and certain knowledge of God's benevolence
toward us, founded upon the truth of the freely given promise in

---

5. Baldasarre Castiglione, *The Courtier,* book 4, trans. Sir Thomas Hoby, in *Three Renais-
   sance Classics,* ed. Burton A. Milligan (New York: Scribner's, 1953), p. 599: "Whereupon
   doth very seldom an ill soule dwell in a beautifull bodie. And therefore is the outwards
   beautie a true signe of the inwarde goodnesse. . . ."
6. *Delia,* sonnet 6, in *Poems and a Defence of Ryme,* ed. Arthur Colby Sprague (1930; rpt.
   Chicago: University of Chicago Press, 1965): "O had she not been faire, and thus vnkinde,
   / My Muse had slept, and none had knowne my minde."

Christ, both revealed to our minds and sealed upon our hearts through the Holy Spirit." Seeking a "signe" of "pitty" instead of "rigour," seeking, that is, the "marke" of his faith and election, a man has nothing to consult but his feelings; for as Calvin adds, in the next section of *The Institutes* (3.2.8), "that very assent itself . . . is more of the heart than of the brain, and more of the disposition than of the understanding."[7] Donne's persona seems to be trying to stimulate in himself the appropriate feelings toward the crucified Christ—a passionate attraction at least as intense as what he once felt for his "profane mistresses." The manipulative insincerity of the erotic analogy, however, infects his expression of desire for Christ.

The air of tentativeness, if not downright factitiousness, in Donne's sonnet becomes apparent when it is set beside an anonymous Spanish sonnet of the same era, "To Christ Crucified":

> No me mueve, mi Dios, para quererte
> el cielo que me tienes prometido;
> ni me mueve el infierno tan temido
> para dejar por eso ofenderte.
>
> Tú me mueves, Señor; muéveme el verte
> clavado en una cruz y escarnecido;
> muéveme ver tu cuerpo tan herido;
> muévenme tus afrentas y tu muerte.
>
> Muéveme, en fin, tu amor, y en tal manera,
> que aunque no hubiera cielo, yo te amara,
> y aunque no hubiera infierno, te temiera.
>
> No tienes que me dar porque te quiera;
> pues aunque cuanto espero no esperara,
> lo mismo que te quiero te quisiera.[8]

(I am not moved, my God, to love you / by the heaven you have promised me; / nor am I moved by fear of hell / to leave off offending you for this. / / You move me, Lord; I am moved to see you / nailed to a cross and ridiculed; / I am moved to see your body so wounded; / I am moved by your mistreatment and your death. / / Your love, at last, moves me and in a way / that though there were no heaven, I would love you, / and though there were no hell, I would fear you. / / You need give me nothing for me to love you; / for though I might not hope as I do hope, / I would love you the same as I do love you.)

Everything about this poem bespeaks a guileless simplicity, a spontaneous and passionate longing for the crucified Christ. The contrast

7. *Calvin: Selections,* ed. Dillenberger, pp. 380, 381.
8. *An Anthology of Spanish Poetry, 1500–1700,* ed. Arthur Terry (Oxford: Pergamon, 1968), 2:96–97. The poem was first published in 1628, but, as Terry points out, it could have been written any time after the middle of the sixteenth century.

with Donne's sonnet is striking. Although the Donne poem is in
many ways compatible with baroque Catholicism and seems, at first,
to be on the same theme, Donne introduces an element of uneasy
self-consciousness. The Spanish poem addresses Christ on the cross;
the speaker of the Donne sonnet addresses his "Soule" with Christ
as an inferential overhearer. The speaker of the Spanish poem simply
dismisses any consideration of salvation as irrelevant to his exalted
love of Christ, while Donne's persona is obsessed with finding suf-
ficient love for Christ in his heart to be assured of salvation. Calvinist
notions of grace pervade the Holy Sonnets in this fashion: not as
principal theological inspiration, but as a lingering fear of faithless-
ness haunting the background of poems that in most of their features
resemble the Catholic devotional poetry of the Continent. It is not
surprising that Donne should handle such traditional forms with a
certain diffidence and trepidation: he was, as he composed the Holy
Sonnets, neither still Catholic nor yet Protestant in a settled way
that gave his conscience peace; and, as it is phrased in one of his
letters, "to be no part of any body, is to be nothing."[9]

But though Donne's persona is hag-ridden by doubts of his own
sincerity, and hence by doubts of the validity of his sense of grace,
the Calvinist dynamic does not finally dominate the Holy Sonnets.
The last sonnet, "Father, part of thy double interest," closes with the
law of love—not faith—as the ultimate Christian obligation:

> Yet such are those laws, that men argue yet
> Whether a man those statutes can fulfill;
> None doth, but all-healing grace and Spirit,
> Revive againe what law and letter kill.
> Thy lawes abridgement, and thy last command
> Is all but love; Oh let that last Will stand!

These lines are not notably Catholic or Protestant. Donne is not here
taking a position on the theology of justification and grace; he is
praying for grace and exhorting himself to love. Herein he is typical
of the English devotional poets of the seventeenth century, who,
though generally Protestant, are not, *in their poetry,* so much militant
proponents of the Reformation as Christians confronting God.

These poets bring to their poetic encounter with God varied expe-
riences and draw upon a number of Christian resources—Catholic
and Protestant, Medieval and Renaissance. What is conspicuously
missing is a definitely Protestant theology of grace embodied in
poems decisively incompatible with Catholic theology. Calvin's pres-
ence, like that of other divines of the era, remains marginal when it

9. *Letters to Severall Persons of Honour,* p. 51.

is not equivocal. Instead of versified theological expositions, marks of the strains exerted by competing versions of grace and salvation ought to be the quarry of the critic. For it is the poets' sensitivity to the theological tensions of the era that generates the urgency peculiar to their poems.

LOUIS L. MARTZ

[Donne's Holy Sonnets and "Good Friday, 1613"]†

> Our Meditation must *proceed* in due order, not troubledly, not preposterously: It begins in the understanding, endeth in the affection; It begins in the braine, descends to the heart; Begins on earth, ascends to Heaven; Not suddenly, but by certaine staires and degrees, till we come to the highest.
>
> JOSEPH HALL, *The Arte of Divine Meditation*, 1606

During the latter half of the sixteenth century and the first half of the seventeenth, all the important treatises on meditation show a remarkable similarity in fundamental procedure. A large part of this similarity is directly due to the widespread influence of the *Spiritual Exercises* of St. Ignatius Loyola, disseminated throughout Europe by religious counselors and by dozens of Jesuit treatises. The *Exercises* mark the beginning of a new epoch; as Brou says, from the time of their composition (1521–41) "the methods, the treatises of prayer, the collections of meditations, the retreats began to multiply, above all in the seventeenth century."[1] At the same time it is important to remember that the *Exercises* do not stand alone in their kind, but represent a summary and synthesis of efforts since the twelfth century to reach a precise and widely accepted method of meditation. The older methods and treatises which underlie the *Exercises* continued to exert strong influence in their own right. In explaining the methods of meditation followed during our period I shall therefore take the Jesuit manual as a base or skeleton, but shall constantly cite other writers of every affiliation, in an effort to show both the central pattern and the delicate refinements it received at various hands. The entire course of these spiritual exercises constitutes what the

---

† From *The Poetry of Meditation: A Study in English Religious Literature of the Seventeenth Century* (New Haven: Yale UP, 1954), pp. 25–32, 43–56. Reprinted by permission of Yale University Press. [Martz uses Grierson's edition of *Donne's Poetical Works*, 2 vols. (Oxford: OUP, 1912) throughout.]

1. Alexandre Brou, *Les Exercices Spirituels de Saint Ignace de Loyola. Histoire et Psychologie* (2d ed., Paris, P. Téqui, 1922), p. 217. See also James Brodrick, *The Origin of the Jesuits*, London, Longmans, Green, 1940; and *The Progress of the Jesuits (1556–79)*, London, Longmans, Green, 1947.

seventeenth century came, consistently, to call "mental prayer"—the term which has come down to the present day. In this process of mental prayer, meditation proper formed the major component: the rest of the process consisted either of preparation for the meditation or of "affections" flowing from it. Consequently the phrases "method of meditation" and "method of mental prayer" are used synonymously during our period. For convenience, I shall simply use the term "meditation."

The *Exercises* of St. Ignatius were designed to be performed during approximately a month set apart for extraordinary devotional intensity. He divided his materials into four "weeks." The first is purgative, being devoted to meditations on sin and hell; the second is given over to meditations (St. Ignatius calls them "contemplations") on the life of Christ from the Incarnation to Palm Sunday; the third deals with the events of Passion Week; and the fourth deals with events from the Resurrection to the Ascension. During this month these exercises were normally performed five times daily, for periods of about one hour apiece; a great part of the remainder of the day was given over to preparing for, and examining the results of, these devotions.

As the *Exercises* grew in popularity, their methods were adapted for use during an hour or two of daily meditation. The adaptation was based on the old medieval practice of setting apart a period for meditation every morning and every evening, a practice popularized during the sixteenth century by such writers as Fray Luis de Granada, San Pedro de Alcántara, Gaspar Loarte, and Juan de Avila. The usual procedure was to set forth two sequences of seven meditations each: one, normally followed in the evening, was devoted chiefly to self-knowledge and the fear of God. Thus in Fray Luis de Granada we have the following typical sequence: (1) the knowledge of ourselves and of our sins; (2) the miseries of this life; (3) the hour of death; (4) the Day of Judgement; (5) the pains of Hell; (6) the glory and felicity of the Kingdom of Heaven; (7) the benefits of God. Such a sequence obviously accorded very well with the nightly practice of examining the conscience. The seven morning meditations then dealt with the life of Christ from the washing of the apostles' feet to the Resurrection.

Thus all the central aspects of the Christian faith were set forth for meditation in regular rotation and, more important, with a method for each period that developed a regular sequence of beginning, middle, and end: preparatory steps; meditation proper, divided into "points"; followed by "colloquies," in which the soul speaks intimately with God and expresses its affections, resolutions, thanksgivings, and petitions. St. Ignatius for his first exercise advises "a preparatory prayer and two preludes, three principal points and a colloquy,"² and elsewhere expands the procedure to include three preludes, five points and three colloquies.

The preparatory prayer is a simple, short request for grace in the proper performance of the exercise. But the first prelude is the famous "composition of place, seeing the spot"—a practice of enormous importance for religious poetry. For here, says St. Ignatius, "in contemplation or meditation on visible matters, such as the contemplation of Christ our Lord, Who is visible, the composition will be to see with the eyes of the imagination the corporeal place where the thing I wish to contemplate is found" (p. 20). And this, as his followers make clear, is to be done with elaborate, exact detail. We must see, says the English Jesuit Gibbons,

> the places where the thinges we meditate on were wrought, by imagining our selves to be really present at those places; which we must endeavour to represent so lively, as though we saw them indeed, with our corporall eyes; which to performe well, it will help us much to behould before-hande some Image wherin that mistery is well represented, and to have read or heard what good Authors write of those places, and to have noted well the distance from one place to another, the height of the hills, and the situation of the townes and villages. And the diligence we employ heerin is not lost; for on the well making of this *Preludium* depends both the understanding of the mystery, and attention in our meditation. (§ 2, ¶ 10)

Even more important for the poet, St. Ignatius directs that one must also use the image-forming faculty to provide a concrete and vivid setting for a meditation on invisible things; for example, in meditation upon sins, he says, "the composition will be to see with the eyes of the imagination and to consider that my soul is imprisoned in this corruptible body, and my whole self in this vale of misery, as it were in exile among brute beasts" (pp. 20–1). We must attempt, says the Jesuit Puente,

> to procure with the imagination to forme within our selves some figure, or image of the things wee intende to meditate with the greatest vivacity, and propriety that wee are able. If I am to thinke upon hell, I will imagine some place like an obscure, straight, and horrible dungeon full of fier, and the soules therin burning in the middest of those flames. And if I am to meditate [on] the birth of Christ, I will forme the figure of some open place without shelter, and a childe wrapped in swadling cloutes, layed in a manger: and so in the rest. (*I*, 23)

2. *The Text of the Spiritual Exercises of Saint Ignatius, Translated from, the Original Spanish,* with preface by John Morris (4th ed., Westminster, Md., Newman Bookshop, 1943), p. 20.

Or, Gibbons adds, if we are meditating on Heaven, we may visualize

> the spatious plesantnes of that celestiall Countrie, the glorious
> companie of Angels and Saintes. Yf on Gods iudgment which
> must passe upon us, our Saviour sitting on his Iudgment Seate,
> and we before him expecting the finall Sentence: if on death,
> our selves laied on our bed, forsaken of the Physitians, com-
> passed about with our weeping friends, and expecting our last
> agony.

Whatever the subject, he insists, we must find "some similitude,
answerable to the matter" (§ 2, ¶ 11).

The way in which a Jesuit would develop these "similitudes" in
actual practice is shown in a passage from the Latin exercises of
Robert Southwell, printed from a manuscript in which he appears
to have recorded meditations pursued while he was undergoing prep-
aration to enter the order, somewhere around the year 1580. The
following passage appears to offer three alternative "compositions"
for the meditation on sin advised for the first exercise of the First
Week:

> Consider first how thou wert the captive and slave of the devil,
> bound hand and foot by the chains of sin and at the very gates
> of hell. Thy King, hearing of this, laid aside His royal majesty,
> His power, His attendants, and His state, clothed Himself in
> coarse and torn garments and came into this vale of tears. For
> thirty-three years He sought thee, wandering about hidden and
> unknown and suffering many injuries and misfortunes. As He
> was praying for thee, with many tears and with sweat of blood,
> thy sins rushed in upon Him, tortured and scourged Him, and
> put Him to a shameful death, whilst thou didst go free.
> Next regard thyself as a son who has left his Father and wan-
> dering far has at length fallen in with the army of His enemies.
> They have made thee a miserable captive, and cast thee into the
> filthy dungeon of thy sins. Thy Father, hearing of thy fate, has
> sent thy brethren to seek thee, but they have all been captured
> and put to death by thy enemies. Then thy Father Himself,
> moved with pity for thee, has left His household, put on the
> garb of a slave and willingly become an exile and a wanderer in
> search of thee. At length he too has fallen in with the army of
> thy enemies, and after most painful tortures has been put to
> death. But by His death thou hast been freed.
> Or again think of Him as the Good Shepherd who has left
> His sheep upon the mountains and sought thee far and wide in
> the desert. He has been torn by thorns and has been without
> protection from the rains and storms, but at length He has

found thee amongst the wolves. He has freed thee, but the wolves have attacked Him and He has been slain.[3]

The modern practice of capitalization has, in the translation, somewhat disturbed the effect of graceful familiarity given by the Latin original; but what is most important here is the easy colloquial style into which the composition falls: the practice of dramatizing theological points, after the manner of Gospel parables, has become almost second nature to the meditator. It is this habit of feeling theological issues as a part of a concrete, dramatic scene that the meditative writers of our period stress as all important for the beginning of a meditation.

Fray Luis de Granada and St. François de Sales strongly advise this method in meditations on the life of Christ, death, hell, judgment, Paradise, and similar matters where the dramatic setting can be easily visualized, "that by meanes of such a representation of these thinges, the consideration and feelinge of them maie be the more lively in us." St. François de Sales notes that "we may use some similitude or comparison, to help our consideration" in dealing with "invisible mysteries," but he fears that this may weary the mind with "searching out curious inventions," and he prefers, with Fray Luis, that we begin with "a simple proposing" of any "wholly spirituall" matter.[4]

It is clear from the various practices mentioned by these writers that there were three different ways of performing this imaginary "composition." The first is to imagine oneself present in the very spot where the event occurred: "to see the arrangements in the holy sepulchre, and the place or house of our Lady, beholding all the parts of it in particular, and likewise her chamber and oratory." The second is to imagine the events as occurring before your eyes "in the very same place where thou art." And the third is performed when persons "imagin that everie one of these thinges whereupon they meditate passeth within their owne harte"—a method strongly recommended by Fray Luis, although St. François de Sales warns that this method is "to subtil and hard for young beginners." Whatever the method, the result is that "By the meanes of this imagination, we lock up our spirit as it were within the closet of the mysterie which we meane to meditate." The effect is an intense, deliberate focusing of the "mind and thought . . . within the bounds, and limits of the subiect . . . either by imaginarie representation, if the matter may be subiect to

3. *Spiritual Exercises and Devotions of Blessed Robert Southwell, S.J. Edited for the first time from the Manuscripts,* with intro. by J.-M. de Buck and translation by P. E. Hallett (London, Sheed and Ward, 1931), pp. 47–8.
4. Luis de Granada, pp. 303–4; St. François de Sales, *Introduction,* pp. 126–7, 129; unless otherwise identified, all subsequent references to St. François allude to his *Introduction.*

the sences; or by a simple proposing and conceit of it, if it be a matter above sence," or, for those following St. Ignatius, some concrete similitude dramatizing even spiritual matters.[5]

The point toward which I am working is perhaps already evident: that such practices of "composition" or "proposing" lie behind the vividly dramatized, firmly established, graphically imaged openings that are characteristic of the poets we are considering. We recall those grand and passionate openings of Donne's "Holy Sonnets," where the moment of death, or the Passion of Christ, or the Day of Doom is there, now, before the eyes of the writer, brought home to the soul by vivid "similitudes":

> Oh my blacke Soule! now thou art summoned
> By sicknesse, deaths herald, and champion;
> Thou art like a pilgrim, which abroad hath done
> Treason, and durst not turne to whence hee is fled,
> Or like a thiefe. . . .

> This is my playes last scene, here heavens appoint
> My pilgrimages last mile; and my race
> Idly, yet quickly runne, hath this last pace,
> My spans last inch, my minutes latest point. . . .

> Spit in my face you Jewes, and pierce my side,
> Buffet, and scoffe, scourge, and crucifie mee. . . .

> What if this present were the worlds last night?

> At the round earths imagin'd corners, blow
> Your trumpets, Angells. . . .

Hutchinson has noted how, "after the example of Donne," Herbert also "often begins with an abrupt question or other provocative phrase, so that the problem gets stated at the outset: 'What is this strange and uncouth thing?,' 'Who says that fictions onely and false hair Become a verse?,' 'Kill me not ev'ry day,' 'The harbingers are come. See, see their mark.' "[6] We may wonder whether all this is due to Donne's example. Is it not rather that Herbert is himself an adept in meditative practices, adept in proposing the subject, adept in the composition of introductory similitudes?

---

5. St. Ignatius, p. 71; St. François de Sales, pp. 126–9; Luis de Granada, p. 304. Cf. Gaspar Loarte, *The Exercise of a Christian Life,* [trans. Stephen Brinkley], ([Rheims?], 1584), p. 67, where he explains that the points of meditation "are in suche wise to be meditated, as though they happed even in that instant before thine eyes, in the selfe same place where thou art, or within thy soule: or otherwise imagining thou wert in the very places where suche thinges happed. . . ."

6. F. E. Hutchinson, "George Herbert," in *Seventeenth Century Studies Presented to Sir Herbert Grierson* (Oxford, Clarendon Press, 1938), p. 157.

What doth this noise of thoughts within my heart?

The shepherds sing; and shall I silent be?

Lord, how can man preach thy eternall word?
    He is a brittle crazie glasse. . . .

      I have consider'd it, and finde
There is no dealing with thy mightie passion. . . .

O blessed bodie! Whither art thou thrown?
No lodging for thee, but a cold hard stone?

      O day most calm, most bright,
The fruit of this, the next worlds bud,
Th' indorsement of supreme delight,
Writ by a friend, and with his bloud. . . .

Or best of all, the opening of "The Collar," with its dramatic sacrilege against the Communion table, "God's board":

      I struck the board, and cry'd, No more.
      I will abroad.

And we can go beyond Donne and Herbert to find, perhaps, these habits of composition in the visualization, the colloquial ease, and the similitude of:

      I saw Eternity the other night
      Like a great *Ring* of pure and endless light. . . .

But these are matters which here will be suggestive only: we must return to them after considering the structure of the whole meditative process.

           ✢   ✢   ✢

✢ ✢ ✢What I should like to stress at this point is the way in which the total movement of these poems resembles, in its rudiments, the "intellectual, argumentative evolution" of Donne's or Herbert's poetry: the "strain of passionate, paradoxical reasoning which knits the first line to the last," and performs this knitting through close analysis and elaboration of concrete imagery. Southwell seems to be struggling toward the qualities that Hutchinson has thus accurately described as the dominant characteristic of Herbert: "Almost any poem of his has its object well defined; its leading idea is followed through with economy and brought to an effective conclusion, the imagery which runs through it commonly helping to knit it together." Southwell's poems give that impression of a "predetermined plan" which Palmer has noted as a characteristic of many of Herbert's poems,[7] and which is also, I think, a strong characteristic of Donne's. May it not be that all three poets are working, to some extent, under the influence of methods of meditation that led toward the deliberate evolution of a threefold structure of composition (memory), analysis (understanding), and colloquy (affections, will)?

The "Holy Sonnets" seem to bear out this conjecture. Holy Sonnet 12 bears a very close resemblance to the conclusion of St. Ignatius Loyola's second exercise for the First Week, a "meditation upon sins," where the fifth and last point is:

> an exclamation of wonder, with intense affection, running through all creatures in my mind, how they have suffered me to live, and have preserved me in life; how the angels, who are the sword of the Divine Justice, have borne with me, and have guarded and prayed for me; how the saints have been interceding and praying for me; and the heavens, the sun, the moon, the stars, and the elements, the fruits of the earth, the birds, the fishes, and the animals; and the earth, how it is it has not opened to swallow me up. . . .
> The whole to conclude with a colloquy of mercy, reasoning and giving thanks to God our Lord, for having given me life till now, and proposing through His grace to amend henceforward. (pp. 24–5)

In Sonnet 12 this problem, simply and firmly proposed in the opening line, is elaborated with a single, scientific instance in the first quatrain:

> Why are wee by all creatures waited on?
> Why doe the prodigall elements supply
> Life and food to mee, being more pure then I,
> Simple, and further from corruption?

The problem is then examined in greater detail through a shift to direct questioning of the animals, which runs through the next six lines:

> Why brook'st thou, ignorant horse, subjection?
> Why dost thou bull, and bore so seelily
> Dissemble weaknesse, and by'one mans stroke die,
> Whose whole kinde, you might swallow and feed upon?
> Weaker I am, woe is mee, and worse then you,
> You have not sinn'd, nor need be timorous.

---

7. *Works of Herbert,* ed. Hutchinson, p. xlix; *Works of Herbert,* ed. Palmer, *I,* 142.

The "colloquy of mercy" then appears to follow, as the speaker addresses himself, the representative of all mankind, "reasoning," developing the sense of "wonder," and implicitly "giving thanks":

> But wonder at a greater wonder, for to us
> Created nature doth these things subdue,
> But their Creator, whom sin, nor nature tyed,
> For us, his Creatures, and his foes, hath dyed.

Puente's development of this Ignatian topic will provide, perhaps, a more convincing proof of our argument for Jesuit influence here:

> The fourth pointe, shall bee, to breake out with these consid-
> erations into an exclamation, with an affection vehement, and
> full of amazement; As, that the creatures have suffered me, I
> having so grievously offended their Creator, and benefactor. . . .
> That the elements, the birdes of the aire, the fishes of the sea,
> the beastes, and plantes of the earthe have helped to sustaine
> mee. I confesse that I deserve not the breade I eate, nor the
> water I drinke, nor the aire I breathe in: neither am I worthy to
> lift up myne eyes to heaven. . . . (l, 70–1)

At the same time, it seems that Holy Sonnet 15 bears some general relation to St. Ignatius' "Contemplation for obtaining love," a special meditation, annexed to the Fourth Week, which aims at achieving "an interior knowledge of the many and great benefits I have received, that, thoroughly grateful, I may in all things love and serve His Divine Majesty." The meditation opens by calling to mind

> the benefits received, of my creation, redemption, and particular
> gifts, dwelling with great affection on how much God our Lord
> has done for me, and how much He has given me of that which
> He has; and consequently, how much He desires to give me
> Himself in so far as He can according to His Divine ordinance;
> and then to reflect in myself what I, on my side, with great
> reason and justice, ought to offer and give to His Divine Maj-
> esty. (pp. 74–5)

This seems to be exactly what the speaker is so deliberately telling himself to do in Sonnet 15:

> Wilt thou love God, as he thee! then digest,
> My Soule, this wholsome meditation,
> How God the Spirit, by Angels waited on
> In heaven, doth make his Temple in thy brest.
> The Father having begot a Sonne most blest,
> And still begetting, (for he ne'r begonne)
> Hath deign d to chuse thee by adoption,
> Coheire to'his glory, 'and Sabbaths endlesse rest.

And as a robb'd man, which by search doth finde
His stolne stuffe sold, must lose or buy'it againe:
The Sonne of glory came downe, and was slaine,
Us whom he'had made, and Satan stolne, to unbinde.
'Twas much, that man was made like God before,
But, that God should be made like man, much more.

In lines 3 and 4 there may be a reminiscence of a part of the "second point" of this exercise, where one is advised to "consider how God dwells in creatures . . . and so in me, giving me being, life, feeling, and causing me to understand: making likewise of me a temple. . . ." But the resemblances are only general, and of course the sonnet does not trace the progress of a complete exercise: it is analysis only, understanding; part of a complete exercise.

This, I believe, is what we should expect to find in most of the "Holy Sonnets" (and in most of the other religious poems of the time related to the art of meditation): a portion of an exercise which has been set down in explicit poetry; especially the colloquy, in which the "three powers" fuse, become incandescent, as Fray Luis de Granada says: "When we talke unto almightie God, then the understanding mounteth up on highe, and after it followeth also the will, and then hath a man commonly on his parte greater devotion, and attention, and greater feare, and reverence of the majestie of almightie God, with whom he speaketh . . ." (p. 309). The complete exercise was long—an hour or more in duration—and its deliberate, predominantly intellectual method would not, for most of its course, provide material for poetry. Now and then a poet might recapitulate an exercise in miniature, or compose a poem that developed under the impulse of his frequent practice of the stages in a full sequence; but more often we should expect the poetry to reflect chiefly the final stages of the sequence. Furthermore, the formal procedure for a full exercise was not by any means necessarily followed on every occasion. All the meditative treatises explain that this full framework is provided as an aid for beginners or as a method to fall back upon in times of spiritual dryness. Even the Jesuit exercises, which might appear to prescribe the most rigorous of all plans, are actually very flexible, for St. Ignatius expects them to be performed under the direction of a priest who will adapt them to the needs and capacities of each individual. Adepts in meditation are encouraged, both by the Jesuits and by other writers, to follow the lead of their affections. Thus we find Tomás de Villacastín warning that "the infinite goodnes and liberality of God is not tyed to these rules" (p. 55); Fray Luis de Granada explaining that he has set down "diverse and sundrie poyntes, to the intent, that emonge so great varietie of considerations, everie one might make his choise of such thinges, as might best serve his devotion" (p. 49); and St. François de Sales urging the reader to "take this for a generall rule, never to restraine, or with-hold thy affections once inflamed with any devout motion, but let them have their free course" (p. 138).

In accordance with this freedom of procedure we find that colloquies may be made not only at the end of the set sequence but at any time during an exercise: indeed, the Jesuit Gibbons says "it will be best, and almost needfull so to do" (§ 2, ¶ 25); and Puente proves the point by scattering colloquies frequently throughout the course of his meditations. In these colloquies of Puente we find something very close to the tone and manner of Donne's religious poetry: subtle theological analysis, punctuated with passionate questions and exclamations:

> O my soule, heare what this our Lord saieth: Which of you can dwell with devouring fier? O who shallbee able to dwell in these perpetuall ardours? If thou darest not touche the light fier of this life, why doest thou not tremble at the terrible fier of the other? Contemplate this fier with attention, that the feare thereof may consume the fier of thy insatiable desire, if thorough thy want of fervent zeale, the fier of God's love bee not sufficient to consume them. (l, 144)

> O God of vengeance, how is it that thou hast not revenged thy selfe on a man so wicked as I? How hast thou suffred mee so long a time? Who hath withhelde the rigour of thy justice, that it should not punish him, that hath deserve[d] so terrible punishment? O my Soule, how is it, that thou doest not feare, and tremble, considering the dreadefull judgement of God against his Angells? If with so great severitye hee punished creatures so noble, why should not so vile, and miserable a creature as thou, feare the like punishment? O most powerfull creator, seeing thou hast shewed thy selfe to mee not a God of vengeance, but a father of mercye, continue towardes mee this thy mercye, pardonning my sinnes, and delivering mee from hell, which most justly for them I have deserved. (l, 55)

More specific similarities are found in the passage where Puente urges that in addressing colloquies to God, or Christ, or the Trinity we should offer "titles and reasons, that may move them to graunt us what wee demaund." In Christ, he says, we may claim such titles as his sufferings and his love,

> Sometimes speaking to the eternall Father, beseeching him to heare mee for the Love of his Sonne; for the Services hee did him; and the Paines that for his love hee endured. Other times speaking to the Sonne of God: alledging unto him the love that hee bare us, the Office that hee holdeth of our Redeemer, and Advocate; and the greate Price that wee cost him. . . .

Other Titles there are on the part of our Necessitye, and Mis-
erye, alledging before our Lord, like *David,* that wee were con-
ceived in Sinne, that wee have disordered passions, strong
enemies . . . and that without him wee are able to doe nothing.
That we are his Creatures made according to his owne Image,
and Likenesse, and that for this cause the devill persecuteth us
to destroye us, and that therefore it appertayneth to him to pro-
tect us. (*l,* 4–5)

Donne's Sonnet 2 certainly looks like a colloquy stemming from such
advice as this:

As due by many titles I resigne
My selfe to thee, O God, first I was made
By thee, and for thee, and when I was decay'd
Thy blood bought that, the which before was thine;
I am thy sonne, made with thy selfe to shine,
Thy servant, whose paines thou hast still repaid,
Thy sheepe, thine Image, and, till I betray'd
My selfe, a temple of thy Spirit divine;
Why doth the devill then usurpe on mee?
Why doth he steale, nay ravish that's thy right?
Except thou rise and for thine owne worke fight,
Oh I shall soone despaire, when I doe see
That thou lov'st mankind well, yet wilt'not chuse me,
And Satan hates mee, yet is loth to lose mee.

Such general or fragmentary parallels between Donne's poetry and
Jesuit methods of meditation are strongly supported by the fact that
at least four of the "Holy Sonnets" appear to display, in their total
movement, the method of a total exercise: they suggest the "pre-
meditation" or the recapitulation, in miniature, of such an exercise;
or, at least, a poetical structure modeled on the stages of a complete
exercise. Such a threefold structure, of course, easily accords with
the traditional 4-4-6 division of the Petrarchan sonnet, and thus
provides a particularly interesting illustration of the way in which
poetical tradition may be fertilized and developed by the meditative
tradition. Perhaps the clearest example is found in Holy Sonnet 11,
which suggests the traditional meditative procedure briefly described
by Antonio de Molina: "Thus when we see our Saviour taken pris-
oner, and used so ill, whipped and nayled on the Crosse; we must
consider that we be there present amongst those villaines, and that
our sinnes be they who so abuse him, and take away his life";[8] and
developed with dramatic detail by Puente:

8. Antonio de Molina, *A Treatise of Mental Prayer,* [trans. J. Sweetman], ([St. Omer], 1617),
   pp. 60–1. The original appeared in 1615.

Then I am to set before mine eyes Christ Jesus crucified, beholding his heade crowned with thornes; his face spit upon; his eyes obscured; his armes disioincted; his tongue distasted with gall, and vineger; his handes, and feete peerced with nailes; his backe, and shoulders torne with whippes; and his side opened with a launce: and then pondering that hee suffereth all this for my sinnes, I will drawe sundrye affections from the inwardest parte of my heart, sometimes trembling at the rigour of God's iustice . . . sometimes bewailing my sinnes which were the cause of these dolours: and sometimes animating myselfe to suffer somewhat in satisfaction of myne offences, seeing Christ our Lord suffered so much to redeeme them. And finally I will beg pardon of him for them, alledging to him for a reason, all his troubles, and afflictions, saying unto him in amorous colloquie.

O my most sweete Redeemer, which descendest from heaven, and ascendest this Crosse to redeeme men, paying their sinnes with thy dolours, I present myselfe before thy Majestie, grieved that my grievous sinnes have been the cause of thy terrible paines. Upon mee, O Lord, these chastizements had been iustlie imployed, for I am hee that sinned, and not upon thee that never sinnedst. Let that love that moved thee to put thyselfe upon the Crosse for mee, move thee to pardon mee what I have committed against thee. (*l*, 59–60)

Similarly, in Donne's sonnet, the speaker has made himself vividly present at the scene, so dramatically conscious of his sins that he cries out to Christ's persecutors in lines that throw a colloquial emphasis on the words "my," "mee," and "I":

> Spit in my face you Jewes, and pierce my side,
> Buffet, and scoffe, scourge, and crucifie mee,
> For I have sinn'd, and sinn'd, and onely hee,
> Who could do no iniquitie hath dyed:

but after this passionate outcry the tone of the next quatrain shifts to one of tense, muted, intellectual brooding, as the understanding explores the theological significance of the scene:

> But by my death can not be satisfied
> My sinnes, which passe the Jewes impiety:
> They kill'd once an inglorious man, but I
> Crucifie him daily, being now glorified.

And then, with another marked shift in tone, the speaker turns to draw forth in himself the appropriate "affections," suffusing intellectual analysis with the emotions of love and wonder:

> Oh let me then, his strange love still admire:
> Kings pardon, but he bore our punishment.

> And *Iacob* came cloth'd in vile harsh attire
> But to supplant, and with gainfull intent:
> God cloth'd himselfe in vile mans flesh, that so
> Hee might be weake enough to suffer woe.

Likewise, in the first quatrain of Sonnet 7 we may see the dramatic operations of both imagination and memory, for here the speaker remembers the description of Doomsday in the book of Revelation, especially the opening of the seventh chapter: "I saw four angels standing on the four corners of the earth"; and he cries out, seeing them there in a vivid composition of place:

> At the round earths imagin'd corners, blow
> Your trumpets, Angells, and arise, arise
> From death, you numberlesse infinities
> Of soules, and to your scattred bodies goe. . . .

With the "matter" of the meditation thus "composed" and defined, the understanding then performs its analysis in the second quatrain, "discoursing" upon the causes of death throughout human history: a summary of sin and a reminder of its consequences:

> All whom the flood did, and fire shall o'erthrow,
> All whom warre, dearth, age, agues, tyrannies,
> Despaire, law, chance, hath slaine, and you whose eyes,
> Shall behold God, and never tast deaths woe.

Finally, in the sestet, the will expresses its "affections" and "petitions" in colloquy with God, "as one friend speaks to another, or as a servant to his master":

> But let them sleepe, Lord, and mee mourne a space,
> For, if above all these, my sinnes abound,
> 'Tis late to aske abundance of thy grace,
> When wee are there; here on this lowly ground,
> Teach mee how to repent; for that's as good
> As if thou'hadst seal'd my pardon, with thy blood.

"When wee are there"—those words which so puzzled I. A. Richards' students[9] may be explained if we realize that this is part of a traditional colloquy with God after a visualization of the Day of Doom.

---

9. I. A. Richards, *Practical Criticism* (New York, Harcourt, Brace, 1935), pp. 44–5. Miss Gardner would interpret this sonnet as developing in accordance with the two preludes of the Ignatian method, the octave giving the "composition" and the sestet the petition "according to the subject-matter." This seems to me a valid interpretation: since the whole progress of the exercise would have been "premeditated" and foreseen, the action of the "three powers" would be anticipated in the preludes. See her excellent analysis of this and other "Holy Sonnets" in John Donne, *The Divine Poems,* ed. Helen Gardner (Oxford, Clarendon Press, 1952), pp. l–liv.

"Wee," though no doubt including all sinners, suggests primarily God and the individual speaker's soul; "there" refers to the throne of Judgment in the heavens, as presented in the book of Revelation; "there" is thus in sharp contrast with the "lowly ground" where the soul now prays for grace, with theological overtones relating to the Catholic sacrament of Penance.

Somewhat the same procedure appears also to be operating in Holy Sonnet 9, where an example of Donne's besetting sin of intellectual pride is "proposed" in an audacious, blasphemous evasion of responsibility:

> If poysonous mineralls, and if that tree,
> Whose fruit threw death on else immortall us,
> If lecherous goats, if serpents envious
> Cannot be damn'd; Alas; why should I bee?

The problem thus set forth concretely is then pursued abstractly in the second quatrain, which reveals the speaker's knowledge of the proper theological answer to his question, but he continues the evasion and increases the blasphemy by first an implied ("borne in mee"), and then a direct, attack on God's justice:

> Why should intent or reason, borne in mee,
> Make sinnes, else equall, in mee more heinous?
> And mercy being easie, and glorious
> To God; in his sterne wrath, why threatens hee?

But at last, and very suddenly, the thin wall of this uneasy argument collapses and the poem concludes with one of Donne's most vehement colloquies, giving the answer that has been implicit and premeditated throughout:

> But who am I, that dare dispute with thee
> O God? Oh! of thine onely worthy blood,
> And my teares, make a heavenly Lethean flood,
> And drowne in it my sinnes blacke memorie;
> That thou remember them, some claime as debt,
> I thinke it mercy, if thou wilt forget.

And fourthly, with a slightly different division of lines, I believe that we can follow the same movement in Sonnet 5, which presents in its first four lines a "composition by similitude" defining precisely the "invisible" problem to be considered:

> I am a little world made cunningly
> Of Elements, and an Angelike spright,
> But black sinne hath betraid to endlesse night
> My worlds both parts, and (oh) both parts must die.

The next five lines form a unit overflowing the usual Petrarchan division; and appropriately, since the intellect is here using a mode of violent hyperbole:

> You which beyond that heaven which was most high
> Have found new sphears, and of new lands can write,
> Powre new seas in mine eyes, that so I might
> Drowne my world with my weeping earnestly,
> Or wash it, if it must be drown'd no more:

and then, inevitably, the last five lines, another firm unit, show the passionate outburst of the affections thus aroused, ending with a petition in colloquy with God:

> But oh it must be burnt! alas the fire
> Of lust and envie have burnt it heretofore,
> And made it fouler; Let their flames retire,
> And burne me ô Lord, with a fiery zeale
> Of thee and thy house, which doth in eating heale.[1]

We can see then why, as Grierson records, three manuscripts of the "Holy Sonnets" entitle them "Devine Meditations."[2] They are, in the most specific sense of the term, meditations, Ignatian meditations: providing strong evidence for the profound impact of early Jesuit training upon the later career of John Donne.

Finally, let us turn to examine the adumbrations of this method of meditation in one of Donne's longest, greatest religious poems, one for which, unlike the "Holy Sonnets," we can give the precise date and occasion: "Goodfriday, 1613. Riding Westward." The manuscript headings recorded by Grierson fill out our information: "Riding to Sr Edward Harbert in Wales"; "Mr J. Dun goeing from Sir H. G. on good friday sent him back this meditation on the way."[3] The first ten lines of this meditation form an elaborate, deliberately evolved "composition by similitude":

> Let mans Soule be a Spheare, and then, in this,
> The intelligence that moves, devotion is,
> And as the other Spheares, by being growne
> Subject to forraigne motions, lose their owne,
> And being by others hurried every day,
> Scarce in a yeare their naturall forme obey:

---

1. Cf. Puente, *l,* 88: "O most just judge, and most mercifull Father, I confesse that I am thorough my sinnes a blacke, and filthy cole, and halfe burnt with the fier of my passions, washe mee, o Lord, and whiten mee with the living water of thy grace, and therwith quench this fier that burneth mee. . . ." Also Puente, *l,* 274: "in steede of drowning the worlde againe with another deluge; or burning it with fier like Sodom; hee [God] would drowne it with abundance of mercies, and burne it with the fier of his love. . . ."
2. *The Poems of John Donne,* ed. Herbert J. C. Grierson (2 vols., Oxford, Clarendon Press, 1912), *l,* 322.
3. *Idem, l,* 336.

> Pleasure or businesse, so, our Soules admit
> For their first mover, and are whirld by it.
> Hence is't, that I am carryed towards the West
> This day, when my Soules forme bends toward the East.

The composition has thus precisely set the problem: profane motives carry the soul away from God, while the soul's essence ("forme"), *devotion,* longs for another, greater object. The speaker then proceeds, by intellectual analysis, to develop (lines 11–32) this paradox of human perversity, by playing upon the idea that the speaker, in going West on human "pleasure or businesse," is turning his back upon the Cross. He is thus refusing to perform the devotion proper to the day; he is refusing, that is, to *see* the place and participate in its agony as if he were "really present":

> There I should see a Sunne, by rising set,
> And by that setting endlesse day beget;
> But that Christ on this Crosse, did rise and fall,
> Sinne had eternally benighted all.
> Yet dare I'almost be glad, I do not see
> That spectacle of too much weight for mee.
> Who sees Gods face, that is selfe life, must dye;
> What a death were it then to see God dye?

Nevertheless, in the very act of saying that he does not see these things, he develops the traditional paradoxes of the scene in lines that echo the meditative treatises:

> Could I behold those hands which span the Poles,
> And turne all spheares at once, peirc'd with those holes?
> Could I behold that endlesse height which is
> Zenith to us, and our Antipodes,
> Humbled below us? or that blood which is
> The seat of all our Soules, if not of his,
> Made durt of dust, or that flesh which was worne
> By God, for his apparell, rag'd, and torne?[4]

And next, as we should expect of one reared in the Catholic meditative tradition, he considers the sorrows of the Virgin:

---

4. Cf. Luis de Granada, pp. 288–9: "Lift up thyne eies unto that holie roode, and consider all the woundes, and paines, that the Lorde of maiestie suffereth there for thy sake.... Beholde that divine face (which the Angels are desirous to beholde) how disfigured it is, and overflowed with streames of bloude.....

"That goodly cleare forhead, and those eies more bewtifull than the Sunne, are now dimned and darkened with the bloude and presence of deathe. Those eares that are wonte to heare the songes of heaven, doe now heare the horrible blasphemies of synners. Those armes so well fashioned and so large that they embrace all the power of the worlde, are now disjoynted, and stretched out upon the crosse. Those handes that created the heavens, and were never injurious to anie man, are now nayled and clenched fast with harde and sharpe nayles."

If on these things I durst not looke, durst I
Upon his miserable mother cast mine eye,
Who was Gods partner here, and furnish'd thus
Halfe of that Sacrifice, which ransom'd us?

And now, with the analysis completed, the speaker ends his medi-
tation, with perfect symmetry, in a ten-line colloquy which accords
with the directions of St. Ignatius Loyola:

Imagining Christ our Lord before us and placed on the Cross,
to make a colloquy with Him . . . Again, to look at myself, asking
what I have done for Christ, what I am doing for Christ, what
I ought to do for Christ; and then seeing Him that which He is,
and thus fixed to the Cross, to give expression to what shall
present itself to my mind. (p. 23)

Though these things, as I ride, be from mine eye,
They'are present yet unto my memory,
For that looks towards them; and thou look'st towards mee,
O Saviour, as thou hang'st upon the tree;
I turne my backe to thee, but to receive
Corrections, till thy mercies bid thee leave.
O thinke mee worth thine anger, punish mee,
Burne off my rusts, and my deformity,
Restore thine Image, so much, by thy grace,
That thou may'st know mee, and I'll turne my face.

Thus similitude, visualization, theological analysis and the eloquent
motions of the will have all fused into one perfectly executed
design—a meditation expressing the state of devotion which results
from the integration of the threefold Image of God: memory, under-
standing, will. And thus once again the process of meditation appears
to have made possible a poem which displays this "articulated struc-
ture," this "peculiar blend of passion and thought":[5] the perfect equi-
poise of a carefully regulated, arduously cultivated skill.

*   *   *

5. *Works of Herbert*, ed. Palmer, *l*, 140; *Metaphysical Lyrics and Poems*, ed. Grierson, p. xvi.

DAVID M. SULLIVAN

Riders to the West: "Goodfriday, 1613"†

East and west are the most important compass points in Donne's symbolic and poetic landscape. Images of maps appear frequently in his work, mostly in his *Divine Poems* and in his sermons. East is consistently associated with Christ and the Resurrection, west with death. These ideas are not unique to him. A. B. Chambers shows in some detail that a long line of Christian geographical symbolism, beginning with Zachariah and extending through the imaginative literature of the Church Fathers into the Renaissance, preceded him in making these same associations.[1]

In the tradition and in Donne's poetry the map metaphor works like this: we are born in the east, and like the sun we are delivered into our grave in the west; but death means resurrection from death, the circle is completed by a kind of fiat, and west automatically becomes its opposite, the east, this time as the eternal joy of heaven. We can watch this symbolism working in one of Donne's finest religious lyrics, the "Hymne to God my God, in my sicknesse":

> Whilst my Physitians by their love are growne
>   Cosmographers, and I their Mapp, who lie
> Flat on this bed, that by them may be showne
>   That this is my South-west discoverie
>   *Per fretum febris,* by these streights to die,
>
> I joy, that in these straits, I see my West;
>   For, though theire currants yeeld returne to none,
> What shall my West hurt me? As West and East
>   In all flatt Maps (and I am one) are one,
>   So death doth touch the Resurrection.[2]

The "South-west discoverie," Clay Hunt says, "refers to the discovery of the navigational passage which the merchant explorers had sought for generations, an ocean passage to the Orient."[3] He means the Straits of Magellan, the stormy passage the navigator discovered on his way west to the Pacific and the Philippines, where he died. In a similar way, the speaker knows, he must pass "through the strait of

† From *John Donne Journal* 6.1 (1987): 1–7. Reprinted by permission of the publisher.

1. A. B. Chambers, " 'Goodfriday, 1613. Riding Westward': The Poem and the Tradition," *ELH* 28 (1961), 31–53.
2. *John Donne: The Divine Poems,* ed. Helen Gardner (Oxford: Clarendon, 1952), p. 50. References to poetry are from this edition.
3. Clay Hunt, *Donne's Poetry: Essays in Literary Analysis* (New Haven: Yale Univ. Press, 1954), p. 101.

fever," as the Latin phrase has it, on his journey west and to death, whose "currants yeeld returne to none." But he joys to see his west because touching death he touches its opposite. "Take a flat Map," says Donne, "a Globe *in plano,* and here is East, and there is West, as far asunder as two points can be put: but reduce this flat Map to roundnesse, which is the true form, and then East and West touch one another, and are all one. . . ."[4] As Hunt puts it nicely,

> He does not regret that the currents will allow him no return from his passage, and he is not afraid to face the hardship and danger which he may expect as he goes farther into the West that now opens before him. . . . He thinks of the West (death) simply as the region that he must pass through to arrive at the East (resurrection and the joy of eternal life in heaven), the goal which all men have dreamed of and which truly adventurous men have actually sought.[5]

It is in this general sense that the symbolism of "Goodfriday, 1613. Riding Westward" has traditionally, and rightly, been understood. So far so good. But "Riding Westward" was a colloquialism of Donne's time that meant literally "going to Tyburn"—going to hang on the Middlesex gallows, sometimes called Tyburn tree, located in the west end of London on the west bank of the Tyburn tributary.[6] The speaker of this poem is a man condemned to die, and riding out, in no uncertain terms, to be executed. To appreciate the drama of this poem we must read it as it was understood by Donne's contemporaries, who would have recognized in it the elaborate conceit so highly dated that it has become lost since, and with it part of the poem's coherence and wit.

The *OED* does not record the phrase "riding westward" as ever having had a usage other than as the subtitle of Donne's poem. It does give "to westward," however, as having had the particular connotation I mention, citing the following example from H. Parrot's *Cures for the Itch* (1626): " 'If anything happen. . . . , it must accrew from the next Sessions, provided there be some to travel westward.' "

I have discovered several other witty allusions to this sense of the phrase which the subtitle of Donne's poem seems to echo. Robert Greene concludes his tale of "howe an honest substantiall Citizen was made a Connie," in his *Third Part of Conny-catching* (1592), with an observation that the masters of those houses that fence

4. "Preached to the Lords upon Easter-day, at the Communion, The King being then dangerously sick at New-Market." Sermon No. 9 in *The Sermons of John Donne,* ed. G. R. Potter and E. M. Simpson (Berkeley: Univ. of California Press, 1962), II, 199.
5. Hunt, p. 102.
6. "Tyburn," in *The Encyclopaedia Britannica,* 11th ed. (Cambridge: Cambridge Univ. Press, 1911), XXVII, 493–94; and *Encyclopaedia Britannica: Micropaedia,* 15th ed. (London: Helen Hemingway Benton, 1974), X, 215.

stolen goods may "beare countenance of honest substantiall men, but all their living is gotten in this order, the end of such (though they scape awhile) will be sayling westward in a Cart to Tiborn."[7]

There is a passage in Thomas Dekker's *Belman of London* (1608) describing London's society of cut-purses and pickpockets within which "The Treasurers office is very truly (though he be an arrant theefe) to render an account of such moneies as are put into his hands uppon trust: for of every purse (that is cleanly conveied and hath good store of *Shelles* in it) a ratable proportion is deliverd . . . to the Treasurer, to the intent that when any of them is taken and cast into prison, a *Flag* of truce may presently be hung out, and composition offered to the wronged party, thereby to save a brother of the society from riding *Westward*."[8]

Finally, as a transition from the allusion to the poem itself, I wish to cite this passage from the sermon, quoted previously, that Donne preached upon Easter Day 1619, on this text from Psalms 89:48: "What man is he that liveth, and shall not see death?"

> Wee are all conceived in close Prison; in our Mothers wombes, we are close Prisoners all; when we are borne, we are borne but to the liberty of the house; Prisoners still, though within larger walls; and then all our life is but a going out to the place of Execution, to death. Now was there ever any man seen to sleep in the Cart, between New-gate, and Tyborne? between the Prison, and the place of Execution, does any man sleep? And we sleep all the way; from the womb to the grave we are never throughly awake; but passe on with such dreames, and imaginations as these, I may live as well, as another, and why should I dye, rather then another? but awake, and tell me, sayes this Text, *Quis homo?* who is that other that thou talkest of? *What man is he that liveth,* and shall not see death?[9]

It pleased Donne to think of death as an execution. This idea is not necessarily a conceit: insofar as to be a Christian means to imitate Christ, it has an historical justification in the Crucifixion; and some correspondence, actual or symbolic, in the manner of dying, was, for Donne, both inevitable and good. Such a view of death, I am arguing, is the controlling metaphor of "Goodfriday, 1613. Riding Westward" and a key to understanding it.

"Goodfriday" falls into two parts, and in each the meaning of death is different. It is first of all a dramatic poem: it records a change of mind, as the Holy Sonnets do frequently. The first part, which

7. Robert Greene, *The Third and Last Part of Conny-catching,* ed. G. B. Harrison, Elizabethan and Jacobean Quartos (Edinburgh: Edinburgh Univ. Press, 1966), p. 20.
8. Thomas Dekker, "The Belman of London," in *The Guls Hornbook and the Belman of London* (London: J. M. Dent, 1928), pp. 150–51.
9. Sermon No. 9, ed. Potter and Simpson, II 197–98.

constitutes the bulk of the poem, ends with a series of rhetorical questions. While they are being asked, a change of heart occurs and the rider resolves to embrace the kind of death, literally or symbolically, that his religion and faith require.

As the poem opens, the rider betrays that he is dying a kind of spiritual death. Pleasure and business have taken over from devotion and the proper rule of his soul and are whirling him away from the risen Christ of the east, on whom the rider's attention is fixed, and toward the west, distancing him, as he perceives it, from his true faith.

> Let mans Soule be a Spheare, and then, in this,
> The intelligence that moves, devotion is,
> And as the other Spheares, by being growne
> Subject to forraigne motions, lose their owne,
> And being by others hurried every day,
> Scarce in a year their naturall forme obey:
> Pleasure or businesse, so, our Soules admit
> For their first mover, and are whirld by it.
> Hence is't, that I am carryed towards the West
> This day, when my Soules forme bends toward the East.

Chambers shows that Donne has reversed his cosmology. The primum mobile, in a tradition stretching far back into antiquity, was always westward in motion. Its influence on the spheres, whose motions were naturally recalcitrant and desired to turn eastward, forced them to whirl westward with it. It was the same with the soul. The rational faculties of the soul were also, like the primum mobile, naturally "westward" in motion. They compelled the irrational faculties of the soul to whirl with them against the inclinations of their own baser nature.[1] Whereas, in the traditional cosmology, it was natural for the rider to be carried toward the west, here Donne makes the motion of the first mover naturally eastward in direction in order to emphasize that death is the consequence of the rider's betrayal. Behind and above him in the east, the risen Christ hangs bloody, ragged, and torn. The speaker's predicament is that he cannot, or will not, turn his face to the east: he is afraid to die.

> Yet dare I'almost be glad, I do not see
> That spectacle of too much weight for mee.
> Who sees Gods face, that is selfe life, must dye;
> What a death were it then to see God dye?
> It made his owne Lieutenant Nature shrinke,
> It made his footstoole crack, and the Sunne winke.

Though my interpretation of this poem, emphasizing the nature of punishment and expiation, is fundamentally different from that of

1. Chambers, pp. 31–41.

Chambers, who analyzes it in terms of the nature of the soul, I agree
fully with his observation that at this point the "westward journey
... becomes not a rational movement but a departure from the
Christian path, a turning from light to enter the ways of darkness."[2]
I agree, too, that the rider, at once both Donne and Everyman, "must
be pierced, must assume the 'rag'd and torn' apparel of God, and
must then be scourged of the deformity thus put on."[3]

    The journey westward is both right and wrong. I am assuming that ✗
for Donne it is right because, as a follower of Christ, he is naturally,
ineluctably, pursuing the path which Christ took as a mortal man—
westward to death and execution. Of the inevitability of his end the
rider is painfully aware. The journey is wrong, on the other hand,
because he is at this moment afraid to meet his fate. Again, we must
interpret the essential ambiguity of the poem in terms of Crucifixion.
For the rider, the Crucifixion—his Tyburn, if you will—means both
the agony of his physical death and his death to the pleasure and
business of the world which have usurped the operation of his soul.
For Donne and the poets of his time, the word "sun" could hardly
pass from pen to paper without a thought that the reader would
immediately check for a play on the well-worn tradition that asso-
ciated sun with Son, by an effective cosmological analogy, as the two
rulers of the heavens. When meditating on the agony of the Cruci-
fixion, the speaker acknowledging that it made "the Sunne winke,"
he is only too conscious of the physical and spiritual pain he himself
must undergo in order to die fully into his faith. Being able to behold
the east means being able to make this leap, and he finds the thought
of it excruciating:

>   Could I behold those hands which span the Poles,
>   And tune all spheares at once, peirc'd with those holes?
>   Could I behold that endlesse height which is
>   Zenith to us, and to'our Antipodes,
>   Humbled below us? or that blood which is
>   The seat of all our Soules, if not of his,
>   Made durt of dust, or that flesh which was worne
>   By God, for his apparell, rag'd, and torne?
>   If on these things I durst not looke, durst I
>   Upon his miserable mother cast mine eye,
>   Who was Gods partner here, and furnish'd thus
>   Halfe of that Sacrifice, which ransom'd us?

In posing these questions, however, he becomes able to answer
them. He finds that he can meet his religion on its own terms, for
we find that in the next few lines, the second and concluding part

2. Chambers, p. 48.
3. Chambers, p. 52.

414 DAVID M. SULLIVAN

of the poem, the speaker is anticipating his punishment with reso-
lution and even eagerness:

> Though these things, as I ride, be from mine eye,
> They'are present yet unto my memory,
> For that looks towards them; and thou look'st towards mee,
> O Saviour, as thou hang'st upon the tree;
> I turne my backe to thee, but to receive
> Corrections, till thy mercies bid thee leave.
> O thinke mee worth thine anger, punish mee,
> Burne off my rusts, and my deformity,
> Restore thine Image, so much, by thy grace,
> That thou may'st know mee, and I'll turne my face.

When the speaker recognizes that his westward journey is good—"I
turne my backe to thee, but to receive / Corrections"—he accepts
the destiny of Christ as man; and in this acceptance and awareness
of it he becomes, as it were, fully awake: "was there ever any man
seen to sleep in the Cart, between New-gate, and Tyborne? between
the Prison, and the place of Execution, does any man sleep? And we
sleep all the way; from the womb to the grave we are never throughly
awake. . . ." The rider is now "conscious." He now sees his death,
physical and spiritual, as a punishment which redeems.

Christ is a military figure in this poem, at least inasmuch as Nature
is "his owne Lieutenant." And Christ himself, of course, was the
victim of a state execution, crucifixion being the punishment com-
monly reserved for traitors and slaves. He was a traitor by Roman
law and paid with his life for the crime. In this sense, the rider is
like Christ: for he also is, or was, a traitor, by virtue of his weakness
to pleasure and business which he admitted at the outset. Hence his
desire for punishment: to be redeemed from fire by fire. By a kind
of irony it is Christ, however, who will become his executioner. The
moment of his freedom becomes the moment of his ultimate captiv-
ity. The speaker resolves the dilemma of his western movement like
this: he accepts the consequences of proceeding westward as nec-
essary, even though they mean spiritual and eventually physical
death. He accepts them because the punishment which is conse-
quent upon his spiritual death will reform him, just as the fact of his
physical death will mean eventually his resurrection. I believe that,
for Donne, to turn one's face to the east is possible only after death;
for it is presumably only on Resurrection Day that Christ will reap-
pear to the eyes. In making his plea for dissolution, the speaker finds
some solace in what Chambers calls his "devotional memory."[4] By
this means, as a guide to repentance, the Christian can contemplate

4. Chambers, p. 51.

the spectacle of the Crucifixion by such imperfect means as are available to him.

When Donne rode westward on the day he composed this poem, as seems fairly certain, he was meditating on several important matters. He was about to enter holy orders—a step he had delayed until he could be sure his mind was set wholly on heavenly things. He was about to die, he must have felt, to a whole way of life. Perhaps it struck him as a strange coincidence, even as a kind of fate, that the eve of his conversion was Good Friday. The speaker of this poem, whether Donne or not, is a man sentenced to die. "That [Christ] was crucified with his face towards the West," says Sir Thomas Browne, "we will not contend with tradition and probable account. . . ."[5] This is the significance of the subtitle and such phrases as "carryed towards the West," "as I ride," and "punish mee." I do not believe that the poem dramatizes the meditations of a man actually being carted off to Tyburn, only symbolically, insofar as he is Everyman, and inasmuch as he is, in a minor key, by imitation, Christ himself, as I have tried to show. This poem records a crucial moment in the man's moral life when he becomes fully conscious of his dying, yet manages to meet it with humility and acceptance, though not without fear and trembling. He accepts that to ride westward is not only inevitable but finally more good than bad, since that was the path Christ himself took, who suffered a real death, both before and during the execution, and who yet knew, paradoxically, that in his case, as in the case of all those who, like the rider, imitate Christ, death means life.

DONALD R. DICKSON

The Complexities of Biblical Typology in the Seventeenth Century†

The last decade has seen a resurgence of interest in biblical typology among scholars of seventeenth-century literature. Early studies by William Madsen, Murray Roston, and Barbara Lewalski paved the way for the broader application offered by Earl Miner's collection of essays, *Literary Uses of Typology*, and Lewalski's *Protestant Poetics*.[1]

5. Sir Thomas Browne, "Hydriotaphia," in *Sir Thomas Browne: Selected Writings*, ed. Geoffrey Keynes (London: Faber & Faber, 1968), p. 139.
† From *Renaissance and Reformation/Renaissance et Réforme* 23 (1987): 253–72. Reprinted by permission of the publisher.
1. William G. Madsen, *From Shadowy Types to Truth: Studies in Milton's Symbolism* (New Haven and London: Yale Univ. Press, 1968); Murray Roston, *Biblical Drama in England from the Middle Ages to the Present Day* (Evanston: Northwestern Univ. Press, 1968);

This renewed interest in typology, however, has led some critics to a reductive paradigm to account for the use of figurative language in the seventeenth-century devotional literature: since one image prefigured another more perfect manifestation of that image, all one had to do was simply match types with their corresponding antitypes. By recognizing that much of this figurative language was governed by a simple paradigm of promise and fulfillment, scholars were hoping to respect the religious sensibilities of those Renaissance poets and theologians who had rejected the medieval fourfold allegory that had turned the literal text of Scripture into a hidden veil pointing to a meaning beyond itself. Though seventeenth-century Protestants valued the literal text above all, their actual practices show that they regarded the Bible as a complex text, the full significance of which could only be recovered by means of a sophisticated reading act. By examining some of the many Protestant guides to godliness and other "helps" designed to open Scripture up to its readers, we shall see that Protestants continued to read the Bible—and especially to identify biblical types—using a methodology and a vocabulary not so unlike the approach they had sought to replace. Thus, there is more continuity with medieval hermeneutics than has generally been acknowledged by those who advocate a distinctly "Protestant poetics"; accordingly, the typological wit of Protestant devotional poets may be more complex than has been recognized.

Perhaps the greatest advance offered by the work of Lewalski has been to establish a methodology familiar to modern readers for interpreting devotional poetry. Her approach is to view the Bible as a unified poetic text requiring close reading to recover its full meaning (and in this, her work in indebted to Northrup Frye's). Since seventeenth-century readers saw Scripture "as a complex literary work whose full literal meaning is revealed only by careful attention to its poetic texture and to its pervasive symbolic mode—typology," the Bible also provided its own hermeneutic key through the collation of one text with another to recover its meaning.[2] Biblical typology is being increasingly regarded as a method of decoding, or more properly as a set of reading practices, which determined largely the way many seventeenth-century readers perceived the organizing structures (both narrative and metaphoric) of the Bible. Though much has been written of late on typology in the Renaissance,[3] little atten-

Barbara K. Lewalski, "*Samson Agonistes* and the Tragedy of the Apocalypse," *PMLA*, 85 (1970), 1050–61; Earl Miner, ed., *Literary Uses of Typology from the Late Middle Ages to the Present* (Princeton: Princeton Univ. Press, 1977); and Barbara K. Lewalski, *Protestant Poetics and the Seventeenth-Century Religious Lyric* (Princeton: Princeton Univ. Press, 1979).

2. Lewalski, *Protestant Poetics*, p. 117.
3. The locus classicus on typology in the context of English Protestantism is Lewalski's *Prot-*

tion has been given to the rather systematic rules that seventeenth-century Protestants were offered. By examining typology as a formal method of decoding a text, we shall see that, as it became increasingly recognized as the fundamental symbolic mode of the Bible, the reformers began to use biblical typology in a more complex way than simply matching Old Testament types with New Testament antitypes. The typological explications commonly available in the seventeenth century linked the history and drama of Christ's life (as foreshadowed and then fulfilled in the two testaments) with the salvation drama of each believer and with the whole span of sacred history. The Bible was seen as telling one essential story, Christ's; but, through his story, the history of the creation, fall, redemption, and glorification of both man and the universe was told typologically. It is necessary to recognize, therefore, in addition to the familiar *Christological* types (which do depend on a simple type and antitype relationship), *sacramental* types—through which the individual's salvation history is told in imitation of Christ—and *eschatological* types—through which the ultimate glorification of Christ, man, and the universe is foreshadowed and fulfilled. The implications of this complex view of typology are especially significant for students of the devotional poetry of the early seventeenth century, since so much of this literature was influenced by and dependent on the way the Bible was read and understood.

* * *

In addition to the traditional Christological types and the sacramental types explained above, one other kind of type was implicitly recognized by seventeenth-century typologists. Their handbooks made frequent reference to what can be called the typology of the *eschaton* to describe the ultimate perfection of the events prefigured by both Christological and sacramental types that would occur in the

estant Poetics. The work of Jean Danielou remains helpful on patristic typology, especially *The Bible and the Liturgy*, no trans. given (Notre Dame, IN: Notre Dame Univ. Press, 1956) and *From Shadows to Reality: Studies in the Biblical Typology of the Fathers*, Wulstan Hibberd, trans. (London: Burns & Oates, 1960). On the literary application of typology, see Paul J. Korshin, *Typologies in England, 1650–1820* (Princeton: Princeton Univ. Press, 1982); Ira Clark, *Christ Revealed: The History of the Neotypological Lyric in the English Renaissance*, Univ. of Florida Monographs, Humanities No. 51 (Gainesville, FL: Univ. Presses of Florida, 1982); Mason I. Lowance, Jr., *The Language of Canaan* (Cambridge, MA: Harvard Univ. Press, 1980); Miner's *Literary Uses of Typology*; and Joseph A. Galdon, *Typology and Seventeenth-Century Literature* (The Hague: Mouton, 1975). General studies on typology include Erich Auerbach, "Figura," in *Scenes from the Drama of European Literature*, Ralph Manheim, trans. (New York: Meridian, 1959), pp. 11–76; Victor Harris, "Allegory to Analogy in the Interpretation of Scriptures During the Middle Ages and the Renaissance," *PQ*, 45 (1966), 1–23; and John R. Mulder, *The Temple of the Mind* (New York: Pegasus, 1969), pp. 130–50. For a general bibliography on typology, see Sacvan Bercovitch, ed., *Typology and Early American Literature* (Amherst: Univ. of Massachusetts Press, 1972), pp. 245–337.

418 DONALD R. DICKSON

fullness of time. If the type was but a shadow compared to the anti-
type, that light is weak compared to the blaze of glory with which
the truth shall be illumined in the kingdom of glory:

> Even now, in this marvellous light of the Gospell, we have our
> divine ceremonies and sacraments, see him afarre off, know but
> in part, darkly as in a glasse, and receive our best contentment
> by the acts of faith, while the Word and Spirit make us know
> the things freely given us of God in Christ Jesus. But time shall
> bee when (to say nothing of the estate of the Church after the
> ruine of Antichrist, and calling of the Jewes) we shall in heaven
> see him whom we beleeved, face to face, clearly, perfectly,
> immediately, without Sacraments or Types, in the fullest vision,
> nearest union, and absolutest fruition.[4]

Eschatological typology is a term that describes the ultimate fulfill-
ment of God's promise in the New Jerusalem—to which even New
Testament antitypes were merely shadows. This eschatological per-
fection would also be a recapitulation of Christ's perfection: "Christ's
glorious transfiguration, was a forerunner of that glory that wee shall
have in heaven: *wee shall be made conformable to his glorious body,
1 Joh. 3.2.*"[5] Milton, in a well-known passage in *De Doctrina Chris-
tiana,* described the "incomplete glorification" that believers attain
in this life and the "complete glorification" that would be attained
in eternity. And Isaac Ambrose in his sermons on regeneration and
the last things, *Prima & Ultima* (1640), wrote:

> everie part and power of body and soule must have its part of
> sanctification, though no part his full perfection, before the dis-
> solution of our earthly tabernacles: Hence (say Divines) there
> is a regeneration, or sanctification (it is all one) *inchoata* and
> *consummata*; *inchoata,* begun in this life, *consummata,* per-
> fected in that other.[6]

Though other scholars describe the "application" of types differ-
ently—notably Lewalski who prefers to describe them as "correla-
tive" or recapitulative types—the terms Christological, sacramental,
and eschatological correspond better with Glass's division of types
(according to past, present, and future time) and to the complexities

4. William Jemmat, "Epistle Dedicatory" to Taylor's *Christ Revealed,* sig, A2v. See also, Guild,
   p. 76, and Lukin, p. 117.
5. John Weemes, *The Portraiture of the Image of God in Man in His Three Estates, of Creation.
   Restauration. Glorification,* 2nd ed. (London, 1632), pp. 38–39.
6. John Milton, *Christian Doctrine,* John Carey, trans., Maurice Kelley, ed., vol. VI of *The
   Complete Prose Works of John Milton* (New Haven: Yale Univ. Press, 1973), pp. 502, 614.
   Isaac Ambrose, *Prima & ultima: The First & Last Thinges; or, Regeneration and Meditation
   Sermons* (London, 1640), pp. 10–11.

of the actual typological commentary, especially its eschatology.[7] These terms also correspond to Luther's schema for the multiple exegesis of texts, which he based on the three advents of Christ—in the flesh, in the soul, and in the *eschaton*.[8] We can easily make these distinctions consonant with Auerbach's terminology: if the type is the *forma inferior* and the antitype is the *forma perfectior*, in the *eschaton* the believers can look forward to the *forma perfectissima*.

The seventeenth-century practice of relying on three kinds of types in sermons and the like does bear some similarity to the medieval fourfold exegesis that discovered four distinct senses hidden in a text. Dante, for example, in his well-known letter to Can Grande della Scala explained that Psalm 114:1–2 described the departure of the children of Israel from Egypt (the literal sense), the redemption wrought by Christ (the allegorical sense), the conversion of the soul from grief (the moral sense), and the deliverance of the faithful to the New Jerusalem (the anagogical sense).[9] While the reformers would have accepted Dante's explication of the text, they would have done so only because their commentary on the typology of the Exodus could be confirmed by other textual evidence from the Bible. In theory, the reformers continued to reject the notion that Scripture has more than one sense. Generally they argued that the allegorical, tropological, and anagogical "are not properly divers senses but divers applications of one sense."[1] By insisting that any additional level of meaning must be recovered as a dimension of the literal level of the text, the reformers were trying to avoid the mistakes of medieval exegetes, who had, they believed, erred in removing the sign from its literal, historical context. Once the text was freed from the interpretive constraints of its context, there seemed to be no way of governing how the texts could signify; and they attributed the excesses of patristic allegory to just such privatistic readings. In practice, however, the typologists of the seventeenth century were as capable of producing readings as imaginative as their patristic forebears (as the commentary on the tree of life, discussed below, illustrates). The complexities of the three kinds of types recognized implicitly by Protestant commentators ought to be a reminder of the continuity between medieval and Renaissance, even between Roman and reformed, spiritual practices. While the terms Christological,

7. See Lewalski's *PMLA* article on "*Samson Agonistes* and the 'Tragedy' of the Apocalypse." Danielou, *The Bible and the Liturgy*, pp. 5–6, and *Shadows*, p. 277, also distinguishes among Christological, sacramental, and eschatological types to explain the complex traditions behind the liturgy (though he does not use them systematically as I attempt to do).

8. See James Samuel Preus, *From Shadow to Promise: Old Testament Interpretation from Augustine to the Young Luther* (Cambridge, MA: Belknap, 1969), pp. 192–99.

9. Charles S. Singleton, *Dante's Commedia: Elements of Structure*, Dante Studies, No. 1 (Baltimore and London: The John Hopkins Univ. Press, 1954), pp. 84–90.

1. John Weemes, *Christian Synagogue*, 4th ed. (London, 1633) p. 234.

sacramental, and eschatological do not exactly correspond to the
terminology of fourfold allegory and while the reformers' method-
ology was more firmly grounded in the literal text itself, the similar-
ities reveal the common difficulties of recovering the riches of an
intricate, demanding text.

Recognizing that such distinctions among kinds of types exist is
necessary nonetheless, especially for students of literature, since it
provides us with a vocabulary for describing the complexities of typo-
logical symbolism in the seventeenth century. For example, in the
"Hymne to God my God, in my sicknesse," an occasional meditation
on Donne's own death-watch, the speaker perceives his personal
drama in terms of the typological drama staged in Scripture. The
complex typological symbolism of the fifth stanza is the figurative
centre of the poem.

> We think that *Paradise* and *Calvarie,*
>   *Christs* Crosse, and *Adams* tree, stood in one place;
> Looke Lord, and find both *Adams* met in me;
>   As the first *Adams* sweat surrounds my face,
>   May the last *Adams* blood my soule embrace.[2]

One level of signification in this stanza obviously depends on the
Christological typology that the biblical allusions pointedly establish:
just as Adam is the *forma futuri,* "the figure of him that was to come"
(Rom. 5:14), Christ is identified as the "last Adam" (I Cor. 15:45)
who is the fulfillment of the Adamic type. And in the symmetrical
minds of medieval commentators (and in Donne's own), the cross
was erected on the spot where Adam was buried to highlight this
typological correspondence. Christ as the fulfillment or antitype of
Adam is patently a dimension of the poem's meaning. However,
other typological dimensions exist that critics have difficulty dis-
cussing. For the speaker announces that he too plays a role in this
same drama, as he finds "both *Adams* met in me." The typological
symbolism suggests the speaker's own recapitulation of the mysteries
of the fall, atonement, and salvation. He knows too well that the
sweat of the first Adam lines his face—literally, the feverish sweat
of his sickness, but figuratively the postlapsarian "sweat of thy face"
(Gen. 3:19), the birthright of man and the speaker's true sickness.
He prays that he too will be embraced by Christ, mystically com-
mingling his sweat with the blood and sweat of Christ's own brow.
The Christological fulfillment, that is, has made possible a sacra-
mental recapitulation whereby the speaker can hope to be trans-
formed into a Christ-like, second Adam himself. The image of the

---

2. *The Complete Poetry of John Donne,* John T. Shawcross, ed. (Garden City, NY: Anchor,
1967), p. 391. Lewalski also recognizes the typological foundation of these lines, *Protestant
Poetics,* pp. 280–82.

blood and sweat is also probably meant to suggest the blood and water flowing from the wound in Christ's side, the source of the sacraments and the "effectual sign" of grace.

Yet another level of signification is involved through the allusion to *Adam's tree*. Though medieval legend identified the wood of the cross as either from the tree of life, from the tree of knowledge of good and evil, or from the tree of mercy (seedlings of which were planted at Adam's grave), no one has ascertained which tradition Donne is following. As Stanley Stewart shows, iconographic traditions linked the tree of life, the tree of knowledge, the apple tree of the Canticles, and the tree of Jesse; he calls them all types of a single, fruit-bearing tree, the Christ-Tree.[3] The fact that Donne designates it ambiguously as "Adams tree" probably ought to shift our attention away from any precise identification and toward the typological connection (which all the Christ-Trees would have shared): the tree which brought man death is fulfilled by the tree/cross which brings man life through death. This typological relationship may also be pointing ahead to the eschatological fulfillment of this type, the tree of life in the New Jerusalem that gives eternal life to the faithful (Rev. 22:2), especially in a poem whose speaker is contemplating his own death and looking ahead to his hoped-for glorification. Just such an understanding of the promise foreshadowed by the tree of life (in the flesh, in the soul, and eschatologically) can be found in popular handbooks on typology. William Guild began *Moses Unvailed* with the tree of life, and his three observations established that the tree of paradise has a Christological, a sacramental (through the church), and an eschatological antitype:

1. As it was called the Tree of life.	*So Christ is that true Tree of Life, giving the fruit & juice both of grace and glory, Joh.15.1.*
2. It was in the midst of the Garden.	*So Christ is to be found in the midst of his church, Mat.18.20.*
3. It was in the earthly Paradise planted.	*So Christ is in the heavenly placed, Mar.16.19.*[4]

3. Stanley Stewart, *The Enclosed Garden: The Tradition and the Image in Seventeenth-Century Poetry* (Madison: Univ. of Wisconsin Press, 1966), pp. 75-86. Similarly, David Pareus, *In Genesin Mosis commentarius* (Geneva, 1614), cols. 321–22, called the tree of life a *sacrament* which symbolized the admonishments man had accepted of God; it also symbolized man's heavenly reward; finally it symbolized Christ in whom Adam and all men are recuperated. See also, D. C. Allen, "John Donne's 'Paradise and Calvarie,' " *MLN*, 60 (1945), 398–400; John Donne, *The Divine Poems*, Helen Gardner, ed., 2nd ed. (Oxford: Clarendon, 1978), pp. 135–37; and Donald K. Anderson, Jr., "Donne's 'Hymne to God my God, in my sicknesse' and the T-in-O Maps," *SAQ*, 71 (1972), 465–72.
4. William Guild, *Moses Unvailed*, 2nd. ed. (London, 1623), p. 1.

Thus typology was used to link distinct but intersecting moments of time in the history and drama of Christ to foreshadow the typological drama of the believer and the whole span of sacred history; each of these moments, furthermore, was preparing for and moving toward one end. Put another way, there is one Christian faith—Christ mysteriously dead and risen—but this mystery is manifested in different ways: it is prefigured in the Old Testament and realized historically in the New; it is reenacted mysteriously through the sacraments; and it will be consummated eschatologically in the fulness of time. Donne himself offers clear evidence of this view of history in his *Holy Sonnet* "I am a little world made cunningly," which features the eschatological relationship between the flood and the apocalypse. In the new covenant made after the flood, God had promised never again to reduce the world to a watery, chaotic state; so, as a prefiguration of baptism, the flood had its eschatological fulfillment in the final regeneration by fire at the apocalypse. Since "black sin hath betrayed to endless night" the body and soul of Donne's speaker (1. 3), he entreats astronomers and explorers to discover new sources of purifying water,

> that so I might
> Drowne my world with my weeping earnestly.
> Or wash it if it must be drown'd no more.
> (ll. 7–9)

But his own contrition is both insufficient and, finally, inadequate.

> But oh it must be burnt; alas the fire
> Of lust and envie have burnt it heretofore,
> And made it fouler; Let their flames retire,
> And burne me, o Lord, with a fiery zeale
> Of thee and thy house, which doth in eating heale.
> (ll. 10–14)

These lines connect the promise to regenerate the macrocosm by fire with the speaker's sacramental participation in the double baptism of fire and water. The typology of this sonnet thus links personal and sacred history together, revealing how one essential salvation drama is being played through the archetypal patterns of the Christian *mythos*. Readers of the Bible in the seventeenth century recovered these multiple levels of signification by collating text with text, image with image. To respect the complexity of the figuralism in seventeenth-century devotional poetry, we must therefore recognize the complex typological wit of such poets as Donne, Herbert, Vaughan, and Traherne.

John Donne: A Chronology

1572   Born in Bread Street, London, to Elizabeth, the daughter of the poet John Heywood and a relative of St. Thomas More, and John Donne, a well-to-do ironmonger and a Roman Catholic.

1576   His father dies suddenly, leaving three children to be raised by their mother.

1584   Enters Hart Hall, University of Oxford, with his brother Henry where he studies for three years, but leaves before having to subscribe to the Queen's supremacy and the Thirty-Nine Articles at age sixteen.

1587   Studies at the University of Cambridge, but leaves before having to take the Oath of Supremacy required at graduation. Probably travels on the continent in Catholic circles from 1589–91.

1591   Enters Thavies Inn for preliminary study of the law.

1592   Enters Lincoln's Inn on May 6 to continue legal studies in preparation for a diplomatic career at court. Befriends the poets Christopher Brooke and Ben Jonson, who later quips that all of Donne's best pieces were written before he was twenty-five. Manuscript copies of his *Satires* and his *Elegies* circulate among his friends during this period, as do copies of some of the *Songs and Sonnets*. Remains at Lincoln's Inn until about 1595.

1593   Donne's brother Henry dies of a fever in Newgate Prison after being arrested for giving sanctuary to a Catholic priest, who later suffers the traitor's death of being hung, disemboweled, and quartered. Receives about £700 from his father's estate.

1596   Sails with the naval expedition of the Earl of Essex against Cádiz, Spain, along with several hundred other gentlemen adventurers and several thousand soldiers.

1597   Sails with another expedition (to the Azores); writes "The Storm" and "The Calm."

1598   Begins a promising public career as private secretary to Sir Thomas Egerton, Lord Keeper of the Great Seal. Later

becomes member of Parliament for Brackely, a seat con-
trolled by Egerton.

1601   Secretly marries Lady Egerton's niece, seventeen-year-old
Anne More, daughter of Sir George More, thereby ruining
his public ambitions. Walton reports that after his dismissal
Donne quips in a letter to his wife: "John Donne, Anne
Donne, Un-done." Is imprisoned briefly, then lives at Pyr-
ford near Guildford, Surrey, through the generosity of oth-
ers.

1605   Is granted a license to travel abroad; travels to France and
probably Italy.

1606   Moves to Mitcham, near London, where he lives incom-
modiously in a little house; attempts to find employment and
cultivate patronage, especially with Lucy, Countess of Bed-
ford.

1608   Writes *Biathanatos* (first published in 1644), in which he
argues that suicide is not naturally sinful. Seeks a secretary-
ship in Ireland without success.

1609   Is reconciled with his father-in-law who finally pays his
daughter's dowry, thus relieving the couple from some of
their financial hardships. Seeks a secretaryship with the Vir-
ginia Company but is refused.

1610   Publishes an anti-Catholic polemical work, *Pseudo-Martyr*,
which argues that English Catholics should take the Oath
of Supremacy to the monarch. Publishes the following year
an anti-Jesuitical satire in Latin to assure a European audi-
ence (also published in English as *Ignatius His Conclave*).
Both works win him favor from the king. Receives an hon-
orary M.A. from Oxford.

1610   Writes "A Funeral Elegy" on the death of Sir Robert Drury's
fifteen-year-old daughter Elizabeth; lives for a time in Drury
House. Publishes two Anniversaries commemorating her
death, *An Anatomy of the World* (1611) and *Of the Progress
of the Soul* (1612).

1613   Visits Sir Henry Goodyer at Polesworth and Sir Edward Her-
bert at Montgomery Castle in April. Publishes "Elegy on
Prince Henry" in *Lachrymae Lachrymarum*.

1614   Is elected to Parliament for Taunton.

1615   Having declined to enter the priesthood in 1607, takes holy
orders on January 23 and is appointed to the profitable post
of chaplain-in-ordinary to the king. In March Donne attends
King James during a royal visit to Cambridge University
where an honorary doctorate in divinity is conferred upon
him.

1616   Is appointed reader in divinity at Lincoln's Inn, thus giving him a sophisticated audience for his sermons (over 160 survive), which are filled with the same elaborate metaphors and characterized by the same dramatic wit as his poems. Preaches at court for the first time on April 21.

1617   Anne Donne dies on August 15, aged thirty-three, after giving birth to their twelfth child (seven of whom were then alive). Donne writes "Since she whom I lov'd hath paid her last debt."

1619   Attends Viscount Doncaster in his embassy to Germany as chaplain (May–December). Writes "A Hymn to Christ, at the Author's Last Going into Germany." Preaches at Heidelberg and The Hague.

1621   Is appointed dean of Saint Paul's, where he preaches many sermons.

1623   Falls victim to a serious illness; during his convalescence, writes *Devotions upon Emergent Occasions* (published in 1624).

1631   Preaches what was called his own funeral sermon before the king on February 25, posthumously published as *Death's Duell* (1632). Dies in London on March 31.

Selected Bibliography

This bibliography will list some of the critical texts and major studies of Donne's work. Students are well advised to begin any serious inquiry by consulting John R. Roberts, *John Donne: An Annotated Bibliography of Modern Criticism, 1912–1967* (Columbia: U of Missouri P, 1973); *John Donne: An Annotated Bibliography of Modern Criticism, 1968–1978* (Columbia: U of Missouri P, 1982); and *John Donne: An Annotated Bibliography of Modern Criticism, 1979–1995* (Pittsburgh: Duquesne UP, 2004).

• indicates works included or excerpted in this Norton Critical Edition.

1. TEXTS OF DONNE'S POETRY

The best text of Donne's poetry is the *Variorum Edition of the Poetry of John Donne* under the general editorship of Gary Stringer, of which the four volumes listed have been published to date. Other texts include:

The Anniversaries. Ed. Frank Manley. Baltimore: Johns Hopkins UP, 1963.
The Complete English Poems. Ed. A. J. Smith. Harmondsworth: Penguin, 1971.
The Complete English Poems of John Donne. Ed. C. A. Patrides. London: Dent, 1985.
The Complete Poems of John Donne. Ed. Roger Bennett. Chicago: Packard, 1942.
The Complete Poetry of John Donne. Ed. John T. Shawcross. Garden City, NY: Anchor, 1967.
The Divine Poems. Ed. Helen Gardner. Oxford: Clarendon, 1952.
The Elegies and Songs and Sonnets. Ed. Helen Gardner. Oxford: Clarendon, 1965.
The Epithalamions, Anniversaries and Epicedes. Ed. Wesley Milgate. Oxford: Clarendon, 1978.
The Satires, Epigrams and Verse Letters, Ed. Wesley Milgate. Oxford: Clarendon, 1967.
The Songs and Sonets of John Donne. Ed. Theodore Redpath. London: Methuen, 1956.
Variorum Edition of the Anniversaries and the Epicedes and Obsequies. Gen. Ed. Gary Stringer. Bloomington: Indiana UP, 1995.
Variorum Edition of The Elegies. Gen. Ed. Gary Stringer. Bloomington: Indiana UP, 2000.
Variorum Edition of the Epigrams, Epithalamions and Miscellaneous Poems. Gen. Ed. Gary Stringer. Bloomington: Indiana UP, 1996.
Variorum Edition of The Holy Sonnets. Gen. Ed. Gary Stringer. Bloomington: Indiana UP, 2005.

2. TEXTS OF DONNE'S PROSE

Biathanatos. Ed. Ernest W. Sullivan, II. Newark: U of Delaware P, 1984.
Devotions upon Emergent Occasions. Ed. Anthony Raspa. Montreal: McGill-Queen's UP, 1975.
Ignatius His Conclave: An Edition of the Latin and English Texts. Ed. T. S. Healy. Oxford: Clarendon, 1969.

John Donne's 1622 Gunpowder Plot Sermon: A Parallel-Text Edition. Ed. Jeanne Shami. Pittsburgh: Duquesne UP, 1997.
Letters to Severall Persons of Honour. 1651. Ed. M. Thomas Hester. Rpt. Delmar, NY: Scholars' Facsimiles and Reprints, 1977.
Paradoxes and Problems. Ed. Helen Peters. Oxford: Clarendon, 1980.
Pseduo-Martyr. Ed. Anthony Raspa. Montreal: McGill-Queen's UP, 1995.
The Sermons of John Donne. Ed. George R. Potter, and Evelyn M. Simpson. 10 vols. Berkeley and Los Angeles: U of California P, 1953–1962.

3. BIOGRAPHICAL STUDIES

Bald, R. C. *John Donne: A Life.* Oxford: Clarendon, 1970.
• Carey, John. *John Donne: Life, Mind and Art.* London: Faber; New York: Oxford UP, 1981.
• Flynn, Dennis. *John Donne and the Ancient Catholic Nobility.* Bloomington: Indiana UP, 1995.
———. "Donne's *Ignatius His Conclave* and Other Libels on Robert Cecil." *John Donne Journal* 6 (1987): 163–83.
———. "Jasper Mayne's Translation of Donne's Latin Epigrams." *John Donne Journal* 3 (1984): 121–30.
Keynes, Sir Geoffrey L. "More Books from the Library of John Donne." *Book Collector* 26 (1977): 29–35.
Pebworth, Ted-Larry, and Claude J. Summers. "'Thus Friends Absent Speake': The Exchange of Verse Letters between John Donne and Henry Wotton." *Modern Philology* 81 (1984): 361–77.
Ray, Robert H. "Herbert's Words in Donne's Mouth: Walton's Account of Donne's Death." *Modern Philology* 85 (1987): 186–87.
Sellin, Paul R. "John Donne: The Poet as Diplomat and Divine." *Huntington Library Quarterly* 39 (1976): 267–75.
Summers, Claude, and Ted-Larry Pebworth. "Donne's Correspondence with Wotton." *John Donne Journal* 10.2 (1991): 1–36.
Shapiro, I. A. "Donne's Birthdate." *Notes and Queries* 197 (1952): 310–13.

4. TEXTUAL STUDIES

Beal, Peter. "More Donne Manuscripts." *John Donne Journal* 6 (1987): 213–18.
Kelliher, Hilton. "Donne, Jonson, Richard Andrews and the Newcastle Manuscript." *English Manuscript Studies* 4 (1993): 134–73.
• Marotti, Arthur F. *John Donne, Coterie Poet.* Madison: U of Wisconsin P, 1986.
Pebworth, Ted-Larry. "John Donne, Coterie Poetry, and the Text as Performance." *Studies in English Literature* 29 (1989): 61–75.
———. "Manuscript Poems and Print Assumptions: Donne and His Modern Editors." *John Donne Journal* 3 (1984): 1–21.
———. "The Editor, the Critic, and the Multiple Texts of Donne's 'A Hymne to God the Father.'" *South Central Review* 4 (1987): 16–34.
Pebworth, Ted-Larry, and Ernest W. Sullivan, II. "Rational Presentation of Multiple Textual Traditions." *Papers of the Bibliographical Society of America* 83 (1989): 43–60.
Shapiro, I. A. "The Text of Donne's *Letters to Several Persons.*" *Review of English Studies* 7 (1931): 291–301.
Shawcross, John T. "A Text of John Donne's Poems: Unsatisfactory Compromise." *John Donne Journal* 2 (1983): 1–19.
———. "Scholarly Editions: Composite Editorial Principles of Single Copy-Texts, Multiple Copy-Texts, Edited Copy-Texts." *Text* 4 (1988): 297–317.
———. "The Making of the Variorum Text of the *Anniversaries.*" *John Donne Journal* 3 (1984): 63–72.
Stringer, Gary A. "Evidence for an Authorial Sequence in Donne's Elegies." *Text* 2000 (13) 175–91.
———. "The Text of 'Farewell to Love.'" *John Donne Journal* 18 (1999): 201–13.
———. "Words, Artifacts, and the Editing of Donne's Elegies." In *New Ways of Looking at Old Texts.* Ed. W. Speed Hill. 3 (2004): 13–26.
Sullivan, Ernest W., II. "Bibliographical Evidence in Presentation Copies: An Example from Donne." *Analytical and Enumerative Bibliography* 6 (1982): 17–22.
———. "Donne Manuscripts: Dalhousie I." *John Donne Journal* 3 (1984): 203–20.
———. "Donne Manuscripts: Dalhousie II." *John Donne Journal* 2 (1983): 79–89.

———. "Replicar Editing of John Donne's Texts." *John Donne Journal* 2 (1983): 21–29.
Wollman, Richard B. "The 'Press and the Fire': Print and Manuscript Culture in Donne's Circle." *Studies in English Literature* 33 (1993): 85–97.

5. GENERAL STUDIES OF THE POETRY AND PROSE

Allen, Don Cameron. "Donne's Knowledge of Renaissance Medicine." *Journal of English and Germanic Philology* 42 (1943): 322–42.
Anderson, Judith H. "Life Lived and Life Written: Donne's Final Word or Last Character." *Huntington Library Quarterly* 51 (1988): 247–59.
———. "Patterns Proposed Beforehand: Donne's Second Prebend Sermon." *Prose Studies* 11 (1988): 37–48.
Arndt, Murray D. "Distance on the Look of Death." *Literature and Medicine* 9 (1990): 38–49.
Bald, R. C. "Donne's Early Verse Letters." *Huntington Library Quarterly* 15 (1952): 283–89.
Bennett, R. E. "Donne's Letters from the Continent in 1611–12." *Philological Quarterly* 19 (1940): 66–78.
———. "Donne's *Letters to Severall Persons of Honour*." *PMLA* 56 (1941): 120–40.
———. "Walton's Use of Donne's Letters." *Philological Quarterly* 16 (1937): 30–34.
Cathcart, Dwight. *Doubting Conscience: Donne and the Poetry of Moral Argument*. Ann Arbor: U of Michigan P, 1975.
Clark, Ira. " 'How witty's ruine': The Difficulties of Donne's 'Idea of a Woman' in the First of His *Anniversaries*." *South Atlantic Review* 53 (1988): 19–26.
Clark, James Andrew. "The Plot of Donne's Anniversaries." *Studies in English Literature* 30 (1990): 63–77.
Clements, Arthur L. *Poetry of Contemplation: John Donne, George Herbert, Henry Vaughan, and the Modern Period*. Albany: SUNY P, 1990.
Coffin, Charles Monroe. *John Donne and the New Philosophy*. New York: Columbia UP, 1937.
Collmer, Robert G. "The Function of Death in Certain Metaphysical Poems." *McNeese Review* 16 (1965): 25–32.
Corthell, Ronald J. "Donne's *Metempsychosis*: An 'Alarum to Truth.' " *Studies in English Literature* 21 (1981): 97–110.
Cunnar, Eugene R. "Donne's Witty Theory of Atonement in 'The Baite.' " *Studies in English Literature* 29 (1989): 77–98.
Docherty, Thomas. *John Donne, Undone*. London and New York: Methuen, 1986.
Doerksen, Daniel W. *Conforming to the Word: Herbert, Donne, and the English Church before Laud*. Lewisburg: Bucknell UP, 1997.
• Dubrow, Heather. *Echoes of Desire: English Petrarchism and Its Counterdiscourses*. Ithaca: Cornell UP, 1995.
Flynn, Dennis. "Donne and a Female Coterie." *Literature-Interpretation-Theory* 1 (1989): 127–36.
Frost, Kate. "John Donne's *Devotions*: An Early Record of Epidemic Typhus." *Journal of the History of Medicine and Allied Sciences* 31 (1976): 421–30.
———. *Holy Delight: Typology, Numerology, and Autobiography in Donne's "Devotions Upon Emergent Occasions."* Princeton: Princeton UP, 1990.
Gottlieb, Sydney. "*Elegies upon the Author*: Defining, Defending, and Surviving Donne." *John Donne Journal* 2.2 (1983): 23–38.
Gray, Dave, and Jeanne Shami. "Political Advice in Donne's *Devotions*: No Man Is an Island." *Modern Language Quarterly* 50 (1989): 337–56.
Grierson, Sir Herbert J. C. "John Donne and the 'Via Media.' " *Modern Language Review* 43 (1948): 305–14.
Hall, Michael L. "Circles and Circumvention in Donne's Sermons: Poetry as Ritual." *Journal of English and Germanic Philology* 82 (1983): 201–14.
Haskin, Dayton. "A History of Donne's 'Canonization' from Izaak Walton to Cleanth Brooks." *Journal of English and Germanic Philology* 92 (1993): 17–36.
———. "New Historical Contexts for Appraising the Donne Revival from A. B. Grosart to Charles Eliot Norton." *English Literary History* 56 (1989): 869–95.
Hester, M. Thomas. " 'This Cannot Be Said': A Preface to the Reader of Donne's Lyrics." *Christianity and Literature* 39 (1990): 365–85.
Höltgen, Karl Josef. "Donne's 'A Valediction: Forbidding Mourning' and Some *Imprese*." In *Aspects of the Emblem: Studies in the English Emblem Tradition*. Kassel: Reichenberger, 1986. 67–90.
Kermode, Frank. "Dissociation of Sensibility." *Kenyon Review* 19 (1957): 169–94.
———. *John Donne*. London: 1957.

Klawitter, George. "John Donne and Woman: Against the Middle Ages." *Allegorica* 9 (1987–1988): 270–78.

Larson, Deborah Aldrich. "Donne's Contemporary Reputation: Evidence from Some Commonplace Books and Manuscript Miscellanies." *John Donne Journal* 12 (1993): 115–30.

Leishman, J. B. *The Monarch of Wit: An Analytical and Comparative Study of the Poetry of John Donne.* 6th ed. London: Hutchinson, 1962.

Lewalski, Barbara K. *Donne's Anniversaries and the Poetry of Praise: The Creation of a Symbolic Mode.* Princeton: Princeton UP, 1973.

Low, Anthony. "Donne and the New Historicism." *John Donne Journal* 7 (1988): 125–31.

Masselink, Noralyn. "Donne's Epistemology and the Appeal to Memory." *John Donne Journal* 8 (1989): 57–88.

• Maurer, Margaret. "John Donne's Verse Letters." *Modern Language Quarterly* 37 (1976): 234–59.

McClung, William A., and Rodney Simard. "Donne's Somerset Epithalamion and the Erotics of Criticism." *Huntington Library Quarterly* 50 (1987): 95–106.

McIntosh, Mark A. "Theology and Spirituality: Notes on the Mystical Christology of John Donne." *Anglican Theological Review* 77 (1995): 281–89.

[Papazian] Arshagouni, Mary. "The Latin 'Stationes' in John Donne's *Devotions upon Emergent Occasions.*" *Modern Philology* 89 (1991 Nov): 196–210.

———. "Donne, Election, and the *Devotions upon Emergent Occasions.*" *Huntington Library Quarterly* 55 (1992): 603–19.

Parrish, Paul A. " 'A Funerall Elegie': Donne's Achievement in Traditional Form." *Concerning Poetry* 19 (1986): 55–66.

———. "Poet, Audience, and the Word: An Approach to the *Anniversaries.*" In *New Essays on Donne,* ed. Gary A. Stringer. Salzburg: Institut für Englische Sprache und Literatur, 1977. 110–39.

Raspa, Anthony. "Time, History, and Typology in John Donne's *Pseudo-Martyr.*" *Renaissance and Reformation/ Renaissance Et Réforme* 11 (1987): 175–83.

Roberts, John R. "John Donne's Poetry: An Assessment of Modern Criticism." *John Donne Journal* 1 (1982): 55–67.

Sellin, Paul R. *John Donne and "Calvinist" Views of Grace.* Amsterdam: Free UP, 1983.

Shami, Jeanne M. "Kings and Desperate Men: John Donne Preaches at Court." *John Donne Journal* 6 (1987): 9–23.

———. "Donne's Protestant Casuistry: Cases of Conscience in the Sermons." *Studies in Philology* 80 (1983): 53–66.

Sherwood, Terry G. *Fulfilling the Circle: A Study of John Donne's Thought.* Toronto: U of Toronto P, 1984.

Simpson, Evelyn M. *A Study of the Prose Works of John Donne.* 2nd ed. Oxford: Clarendon, 1948.

Slights, Camille Wells. *The Casuistical Tradition in Shakespeare, Donne, Herbert and Milton.* Princeton: Princeton UP, 1981.

• ———. "A Pattern of Love: Representations of Anne Donne." In *John Donne's "desire of more": The Subject of Anne More Donne in His Poetry.* Ed. M. Thomas Hester. Newark: U of Delaware P, 1996. 66–88.

Stanwood, Paul G., and Heather A. R. Asals, eds. *John Donne and the Theology of Language.* Columbia: U of Missouri P, 1986.

Stein, Arnold. "Handling Death: John Donne in Public Meditation." *ELH* 48 (1981): 496–515.

Stringer, Gary A. "Donne's Epigram on the Earl of Nottingham." *John Donne Journal* 10 (1991): 71–74.

Summers, Claude J. "Donne's 1609 Sequence of Grief and Comfort." *Studies in Philology* 89 (1992): 211–31.

Swiss, Margo. "Donne's Medieval Magdalene: Apostolic Authority in 'To the Lady Magdalen Herbert, of St. Mary Magdalen.' " *English Studies in Canada* 18 (1992): 143–56.

Walker, Julia M. "Donne's Words Taught in Numbers." *Studies in Philology* 84 (1987): 44–60.

Willard, Thomas. "Donne's Anatomy Lesson: Vesalian or Paracelsian?" *John Donne Journal* 3 (1984): 35–61.

6. SATIRES

Baumlin, James S. "From Recusancy to Apostasy: Donne's 'Satyre III' and 'Satyre V.' " *Explorations in Renaissance Culture* 16 (1990): 67–85.

Corthell, Ronald J. "Style and Self in Donne's Satires." *Texas Studies in Literature and Language* 24 (1982): 155–84.

- Hester, M. Thomas. " 'Ask thy father': ReReading Donne's *Satyre III*." *Ben Jonson Journal* 1 (1994): 201–18.
  ———. "Genre, Grammar, and Gender in Donne's *Satyre III*." *John Donne Journal* 10 (1991): 97–102.
  ———. *Kinde Pity and Brave Scorn: John Donne's Satyres*. Durham: Duke UP, 1982.
  Wall, John W., Jr. "Donne's 'Satyre IV' and the Feast of the Purification of Saint Mary the Virgin." *English Language Notes* 23 (1985): 23–31.

7. ELEGIES AND SONGS & SONNETS

- Armstrong, Alan. "The Apprenticeship of John Donne: Ovid and the Elegies." *ELH* 44 (1977): 419–24.
  Bauer, Matthias. "Paronomasia Celata in Donne's 'A Valediction: Forbidding Mourning.' " *English Literary Renaissance* 25 (1995): 97–111.
  Baumlin, James S. "Donne's 'Satyre IV': The Failure of Language and Genre." *Texas Studies in Literature and Language* 30 (1988): 363–87.
  Bedford, R. D. "Ovid Metamorphosed: Donne's 'Elegy XVI.' " *Essays in Criticism* 32 (1982): 219–36.
  Bell, Ilona. "The Role of the Lady in Donne's *Songs and Sonets*." *Studies in English Literature* 23 (1983): 113–29.
  Benet, Diana Treviño. "Sexual Transgression in Donne's *Elegies*." *Modern Philology* 92 (1994): 14–35.
  Blank, Paula. "Comparing Sappho to Philaenis: John Donne's 'Homopoetics.' " *PMLA* 110 (1995): 358–68.
  Brooks, Helen B. " 'Soules Language': Reading Donne's 'The Extasie.' " *John Donne Journal* 7 (1988): 47–63.
  Chambers, A. B. "Glorified Bodies and the 'Valediction: forbidding Mourning.' " *John Donne Journal* 1 (1982): 1–20.
- Clair, John A. "John Donne's 'The Canonization.' " *PMLA* 80 (1965): 300–302.
- Cruttwell, Patrick. "The Love Poetry of John Donne: Pedantique Weedes or Fresh Invention?" In *Metaphysical Poetry*. Ed. Malcolm Bradbury and David Palmer. London: Edwin Arnold, 1970. 11–39.
- DiPasquale, Theresa M. "Receiving a Sexual Sacrament: 'The Flea' as Profane Eucharist." In *John Donne's Religious Imagination: Essays in Honor of John T. Shawcross*. Ed. Raymond-Jean Frontain and Frances M. Malpezzi. Conway, AR: U of Central Arkansas P, 1995. 81–95.
  Frontain, Raymond-Jean "Moses, Dante, and the *Visio Dei* of Donne's 'Going to Bed.' " *American Notes and Queries* 6 (1993): 13–17.
  ———. "Donne's Erotic Spirituality: Ovidian Sexuality and the Language of Christian Revelation in Elegy XIX." *Ball State University Forum* 25 (1984): 41–54.
  Guibbory, Achsah. "Donne, the Idea of Woman, and the Experience of Love." *John Donne Journal* 9 (1990): 105–12.
- ———. " 'Oh, Let Mee Not Serve So': The Politics of Love in Donne's *Elegies*." *English Literary History* 57 (1990): 811–33.
  Hester, M. Thomas. "Donne's (Re)Annunciation of the Virgin(ia Colony) in Elegy XIX." *South Central Review* 4 (1987): 49–64.
- ———. " 'this cannot be said': A Preface to the Reader of Donne's Lyrics." *Christianity and Literature* 39 (1990): 365–85.
  Labriola, Albert C. " 'The Dialogue of One': Rational Argument and Affective Discourse in Donne's 'Aire and Angels.' " *John Donne Journal* 9 (1990): 77–83.
  Linden, Stanton J. "Compasses and Cartography: Donne's 'A Valediction: Forbidding Mourning.' " *John Donne Journal* 3 (1984): 23–34.
  Lockwood, Deborah H. "Donne's Idea of Woman in the *Songs and Sonets*." *Essays in Literature* 14 (1987): 37–50.
  Low, Anthony. "Donne and the Reinvention of Love." *English Literary Renaissance* 20 (1990): 465–86.
  Mann, Lindsay A. "Radical Consistency: A Reading of Donne's 'Communitie.' " *U of Toronto Quarterly* 50 (1981): 284–99.
  ———. "Sacred and Profane Love in Donne." *Dalhousie Review* 65 (1985–1986): 534–50.
  Mueller, Janel. "Women among the Metaphysicals: A Case, Mostly, of Being Donne For." *Modern Philology* 87 (1989): 142–58.
  Perrine, Laurence. "Explicating Donne: 'The Apparition' and 'The Flea.' " *College Literature* 17 (1990): 1–20.
  Revard, Stella P. "The Angelic Messenger in 'Aire and Angels.' " *John Donne Journal* 9 (1990): 15–18.

432 SELECTED BIBLIOGRAPHY

Roebuck, Graham. "Donne's Visual Imagination and Compasses." *John Donne Journal* 8 (1989): 37–56.

Shawcross, John T. "Donne's 'Aire and Angels': Text and Context." *John Donne Journal* 9 (1990): 33–42.

Spinrad, Phoebe S. " 'Aire and Angels' and Questionable Shapes." *John Donne Journal* 9 (1990): 19–22.

Stringer, Gary. "Learning 'Hard and Deepe': Biblical Allusion in Donne's 'A Valediction: Of My Name, in the Window.' " *South Central Bulletin* 33 (1973): 227–31.

———. "Donne's 'The Primrose': Manna and Numerological Dalliance." *Explorations in Renaissance Culture* 1 (1974): 23–29.

Walker, Julia M. "John Donne's 'The Extasie' as an Alchemical Process." *English Language Notes* 20 (1982): 1–8.

Young, R. V. "Angels in 'Aire and Angels.' " *John Donne Journal* 9 (1990): 1–14.

———. " 'O my America, my new-found-Land': Pornography and Imperial Politics in Donne's *Elegies*." *South Central Review* 4 (1987): 35–48.

8. DIVINE POEMS

Baumgaertner, Jill. " 'Harmony' in Donne's 'La Corona' and 'Upon the Translation of the Psalms.' " *John Donne Journal* 3 (1984): 141–56.

Benet, Diana Treviño. " 'Witness this Booke, (thy Emblem)': Donne's *Holy Sonnets* and Biography." In *Wrestling With God: Literature and Theology in the English Renaissance.* Ed. Mary Ellen Henley and W. Speed Hill. *Early Modern Literary Studies Special Issue,* 7 (2001): 1–36.

Chambers, A. B. " 'Goodfriday, 1613. Riding Westward': Looking Back." *John Donne Journal* 6 (1987): 185–201.

• Dickson, Donald R. "The Complexities of Biblical Typology in the Seventeenth Century." *Renaissance and Reformation/Renaissance et Réforme* 23 (1987): 253–72.

DiPasquale, Theresa. "Ambivalent Mourning: Sacramentality, Idolatry, and Gender in 'Since She Whome I Lovd Hath Payd Her Last Debt.' " *John Donne Journal* 10 (1991): 45–56.

———. "Cunning Elements: Water, Fire, and Sacramental Poetics in 'I Am a Little World.' " *Philological Quarterly* 73 (1994): 403–15.

Duncan, Joseph E. "Donne's 'Hymne to God my God, in my sicknesse' and Iconographic Tradition." *John Donne Journal* 3 (1984): 157–80.

Flynn, Dennis. " 'Awry and Squint': The Dating of Donne's Holy Sonnets." *John Donne Journal* 7 (1988): 35–46.

Frontain, Raymond Jean. "Donne's Biblical Figures: The Integrity of 'To Mr. George Herbert.' " *Modern Philology* 81 (1984): 285–89.

———. "Donne's Imperfect Resurrection." *Papers on Language and Literature* 26 (1990): 539–45.

———. "Redemption Typology in John Donne's 'Batter My Heart.' " *Journal of the Rocky Mountain Medieval and Renaissance Association* 8 (1987): 163–76.

• Guss, Donald L. "Donne's Petrarchism." *Journal of English and Germanic Philology* 64 (1965): 17–28.

Johnson, Jeffrey. *The Theology of John Donne.* Cambridge: Brewer, 1999.

———. "Gold in the Washes: Donne's Last Going into Germany." *Renascence* 46 (1994): 199–207.

Malpezzi, Frances M. "Adam, Christ, and Mr. Tilman: God's Blest Hermaphrodites." *American Benedictine Review* 40 (1989): 250–60.

———. " 'As I Ride': The Beast and His Burden in Donne's 'Goodfriday.' " *Religion and Literature* 24 (1992): 23–31.

• Martz, Louis L. *The Poetry of Meditation.* New Haven: Yale UP, 1954.

Maurer, Margaret. "The Circular Argument of Donne's 'La Corona.' " *Studies in English Literature* 22 (1982): 51–68.

O'Connell, Patrick F. " 'Restore Thine Image': Structure and Theme in Donne's 'Goodfriday.' " *John Donne Journal* 4 (1985): 13–28.

———. "The Successive Arrangements of Donne's 'Holy Sonnets.' " *Philological Quarterly* 60 (1981): 323–42.

Strier, Richard. "John Donne Awry and Squint: The 'Holy Sonnets,' 1608–1610." *Modern Philology* 86 (1989): 357–84.

• Sullivan, David M. "Riders to the West: 'Goodfriday, 1613.' " *John Donne Journal* 6 (1987): 1–8.

• Young, R. V. "Donne's Holy Sonnets and the Theology of Grace." In *"Bright Shootes of Everlastingnesse": The Seventeenth-Century Religious Lyric.* Ed. Claude J. Summers and Ted-Larry Pebworth. Columbia: U of Missouri P, 1987. 20–39.

Index of Titles

Index of First Lines